PORTAGE BAY
PUGET SOUND
A DESCRIPTION OF
THE SEA WATERS OF PUGET SOUND
SAN JUAN ISLANDS & VANCOUVER ISLAND
DRAWN THIS TWELFTH DAY OF JULY NINETEEN HUNDRED
AND SIXTY THREE BY C.BONNER

James R. Warren

Library of Congress Cataloging-in-Publication Data
Warren, James R.
The centennial history of the Seattle Yacht Club, 1892–1992 / by James R. Warren.
p. cm.
Includes bibliographical references and index.
ISBN 0-9631960-0-6
1. Seattle Yacht Club—History. I. Title.
GV823.S43W37 1992
797.1'24606'0797772—dc20 91-43559
CIP

Design, production coordination and publishing services provided by Laing Communications Inc., Redmond, Washington.

Contents

FOREWORD

Over the past four years, we have reconstructed the history of the Seattle Yacht Club from many sources. This time-consuming process was necessary because most club records, even official minutes for the years prior to the mid-1960s, were discarded in two unrelated happenstances.

Club records were preserved through the many moves of the Seattle Yacht Club, including the move to the present clubhouse. Old-timers told us that minutes, photographs, and clippings filled several filing cabinet drawers. Then, at some time in the 1960s, as the staff was clearing storage areas in preparation for major remodeling, a club manager relegated most of the historical materials to the dump.

The historical data that remained was later taken home by a senior member who intended to write a history of the Seattle Yacht Club. However, he died before he started the history. Several months later his widow, preparing to move from their home and believing the materials to be worthless, discarded them.

As a result, all but a few of the club's historical documents were destroyed. We were forced to rely on newspapers, periodicals, scrapbooks and reminiscences of members for SYC history prior to the 1960s. As a result, particularly in the coverage of the earlier years, the book reflects the interest of the press in races and the more competitive side of yachting, with an occasional spotlight on cruising, personalities, and yachts. Material concerning board actions, social events, fiscal matters, membership efforts, and other internal activities of the early years is scarce. A few scrapbooks and diaries of early yachtsmen were preserved in family archives. Senior members of the club, some of them descendants of pioneering yachtsmen, contributed information and reminiscences concerning the 1920s and later decades. We sought in every way possible to include events and personalities important in the history of the Seattle Yacht Club, but with the dearth of records, we undoubtedly overlooked important events and people. For that we apologize.

Finally, a brief explanation of the organization of the book. Originally, the intent was to develop chapters around movement and change in the club, a sort of progression of maturation. However, since the print medium was the major source—in some cases the only source—of information, and with many official club documents missing, we instead placed the details in simple chronological order. More than 100 "sidebars" were then added to highlight specific events, personalities, and yachts, to help interpret the era. More than 150 historic photographs were added to the text.

The Pacific Northwest Yachting fraternity is a close and friendly group, and the Seattle Yacht Club desired to recognize as many Northwest yachtsmen as possible in this book. Brief histories were solicited from all yacht clubs of the region through the Interclub Association. The response was gratifying and most yacht clubs are represented herein.

James R. Warren and
The Seattle Yacht Club History Committee

ACKNOWLEDGEMENTS

Without the assistance of dozens of Seattle Yacht Club members, this book could not have been written. A special thanks to the Editorial Board: Norm Blanchard, who carries the history of yachting in his head; Jack Austin, the organizer, who continually updated the "to do" list and who collected much hard-to-find information; Arthur Ayers, who has lived so much yachting history (he owned the *Sir Tom* for a time and his mother was the wife of Captain James Griffiths); Don Thompson, the former commodore, whose memory is long and whose patience is notable; Doug Wilson, the likable rememberer of little known historical facts; Dave Williams, who provided a powerboat and Judge Advocate's perspective; and Ann F. Bayless who spent many days collecting and filing photographs and many days researching and writing the history of the women's involvement at SYC. These people met with me each Thursday morning for months to review manuscripts, add details, identify photographs and reminisce. Other members joined us from time to time, but the above seven were there nearly every week.

The Historical Committee headed by Bill Stewart, the droll Texan, led us surely to the established goals during those crucial months leading to the Centennial Year and acted as the liaison group with the officers and the board. George A. Bayless, a member of the committee, helped develop publication specifications and contract arrangements with the publishing services firm, Laing Communications Inc. SYC members active on these committees over recent years were: Wally Ackerman, Chet Adair, Webster and Frances Anderson, Jack Austin, Arthur Ayers, Ann and George Bayless, Ben Benton, Norm and Mary Blanchard, Mike Butler, Virginia Cluck, Norm Cole, James H. Curran, Doug Egan, Charles Erickson, John Fedor, Mrs. Dan Fiorito, John and Harriet Ford, Churchill Griffiths, George Heideman, Harold Hovland, Anderson Joy, Con and Ann Knutson, Harry McGuane, Wallace Ovens, Dr. John Sauntry, Dr. John Scott, Elinor Sheafe, Bill and Betty Stewart, Don Thompson, Don and Katie Whitworth, and Douglas Wilson. The commodores, other officers, and board members provided vital support and guidance throughout the difficult months planning and preparing this book.

I want also to thank Director Carl Lind, Librarian Rick Caldwell, and Photographic Technician Howard Giske of the Museum of History and Industry for their involvement in the production of this history.

To the many others who assisted, thank you. So many helped, in fact, we surely cannot remember them all. But we tried as we prepared the list that follows.

Proofreaders:

Glenn and Margaret Botsford
Dr. Robert and Kay Camber
James Vaupell

Contributors of Information

Barrie Arnett	Sally Laura
Ellie Austin	Walt Little
Helene Becker	Phil Luther
Ben Benton	Cal McCune
Bob Berst	Harry McGuane
Mike Butler	Peter McTavish
Dick Chang	Bob Ovens
Virginia Cluck	Bob Ross
Doug Egan	Charlie Ross
Charlie Erickson	Alan Schmitz
Ellie Fiorito	Michele Shaw
Janet Footh	Dr. Bob Simpson
Ray Goad	John Soderberg
Pat Goodfellow	Jim Stirrat
Dick Griffiths	Diane Sweezey
Hortense Harley	Bob Sylvester
Anne Hovland	Jim Torrance
Elaine Kidd	Sunny Vynne
Eugene Kidd	Bob Withington
Con Knutson	Victoria Wodrich
Thurston Lane	

and many others including the families of Andy Joy and John Graham, Sr. and Jr.

Photo Assistance:

Wally Ackerman and his son Mark of Wallace Ackerman Photography provided many hours of photographic services, including duplicate photos of trophies and most commodore head shots.

Many other members supplied photos from their personal collections and the Museum of History and Industry (MOHAI), operated by the Historical Society of Seattle and King County, and the Puget Sound Maritime Historical Society (PSMHS) provided numerous photographs.

Budget Assistance:

John Fedor

I also must acknowledge the many days my daughter Gail spent researching ancient newspapers on microfilm, a head-achy task at best. And thanks to my wife Gwen who knows so much more about computers than I do and who kept me punching in the right codes as the manuscript was typed and transferred to floppy disks for the publisher.

Though I had much invaluable help on the book, any errors or omissions are, of course, my responsibility.

J.R.W.
Bellevue, Washington
July, 1991

Patrons Who Made This Book Possible

Seattle Yacht Club member-patrons made this book possible. Over a three-year period, the *Binnacle* carried notices asking for contributions to help defray the cost of preparing this *Centennial History of the Seattle Yacht Club*. Members, several of them now deceased, responded with a total of $16,410.

In addition, hundreds of members ordered the book at a pre-publication price, helping to offset production costs as they were incurred.

The SYC Centennial Committee thanks you all.

The Patrons

The Seattle Yacht Club donated $1,000 to start the Seattle Yacht Club history account at the Museum of History and Industry. The names of the donors are taken from the checks submitted unless the donor indicated otherwise.

R. D. Abendroth
Mr. Chester C. Adair
Donald J. Adams
Hiromasa Akita
Ellie and Jack Austin
Ann F. and George A. Bayless
Helene I. L. Becker (in memory of Serge J. Becker)
Charles F. Bell
Barbara and Ben Benton
Mr. and Mrs. Norman C. Blanchard
S. A. Brand
John G. Braun
Harris B. Bremer
Mrs. Jerry C. Bryant
Betty and Mike Butler
Carmen and Robert J. Cadranell
Barbara F. and Sidney D. Campbell
Joy Ann and John Carey
Virginia Cluck
Norman R. Cole
Cora and Robert Condon
Bill Conner
Frank J. Coyle
The Currans (in memory of Mr. and Mrs. Robert R. (Bob) Fox, Jr.)
Mr. and Mrs. Dan P. Danilov
Mr. Frederick Danz
Mr. and Mrs. Brewster C. Denny
Col. Josef Diamond
Dr. Jack M. Docter
Allen B. Dorsey
Gilbert L. Duffy
Ed Dunn, Sr.
Jessie J. and Robert W. Dupar
Dacia and John Emmel
Mildred and Charlie E. Erickson
Kay and John Fedor
Fred E. Fellows
Mrs. Dan N. Fiorito
Harriet and John Ford, Sr.
Louis H. Ford
Dr. and Mrs. William A. Freitag
Marian M. and Elwood Fryer
Mary Ellen Gaffner
Mr. and Mrs. J. David Gardner
Eva Mae and Louis Geisert
Bob and Lee Gibb
Pilar M. and Ralph J. Gibbons
Mark J. Gilkey
Carol and Don Glockner
Carl Graffenstatte
Guy A. B. Grafius
Robert W. Graham
Albert V. Griffiths
Mr. and Mrs. Churchill Griffiths
Richard W. Griffiths
Pamela R. and James J. Hagen
Dr. and Mrs. James W. Haviland
Charlotte W. Helmick
Elliott B. Higgins
Jane and John Holland
John E. B. Holmstrom
Mrs. Harold Hovland
Robert W. Hutton
Mr. and Mrs. J. W. Irvine
Dr. Carl D. F. Jensen
Mrs. Harry Jensen
Mr. and Mrs. Chester H. Johnson
Mr. and Mrs. Dixon W. Kelly
Jeanne and David Kelly
Ann and Conrad Knutson
Henry L. Kotkins
Thelma and Arthur Kuppler
The Laura Family
John F. Leutzinger
Mr. and Mrs. Frederick Lhamon
John P. Lidral
M. B. Lyda (in memory of Dr. Wood Lyda)
Irvin F. Matson
Jana and David Maxwell
Bruce R. McCaw
H. W. McCurdy
James J. McGinnis
Molly and Harry McGuane
Mrs. Ira O. McLemore
Darlene and Paul McTaggart
Jean and Peter McTavish
L. Ross Merrill
Tim, Tom, and Shannon Morris (in memory of Frank Morris)
Anita K. Murray (and the late Harold B. Murray)

Peg Locke Newman
William A. Noll
L. M. Norton
James W. O'Brien
Carolyn and Bruce O'Donnell
John W. Osberg
Chris Otorowski
Gerald T. Parks, Jr.
George H. Parson
Charles E. Peterson
Myrn and Richard C. Philbrick
Elmer Rasmuson
Dorothy and John Rasmussen
H. E. Richmond
Volney Richmond, Jr.
Dale Robbins (in memory of Connie Cadranell Robbins)
Beverly and David Romano
David A. Rowley
John N. Rupp
Mr. and Ms. Arthur J. Sahlberg
Audrey and G. Lawrence Salkield
Robert W. Scarff
Capt. Harry Schwartz
Eleanor and Dale Seeds
Judith F. and Steven L. Sherman
Mr. and Mrs. Jon Shirley
Mary and Don Simpson
D. E. Skinner
Bruce B. Smith
Richard J. Smith
Emmy and John A. Soderberg
Amelia J. and Vinton Sommerville
Harold E. Stack
Gwen and Arden C. Steinhart
Betty and Bill T. Stewart
Betsy and Paul Sunich
John Sylvester
Robert O. Sylvester
Dr. and Mrs. Del M. Ulrich
Elna and Russ Van Moppes
Mr. and Mrs. A. J. Van Skyhawk
Robert R. Walker
Tedrowe Watkins
Mr. and Mrs. D. K. Weaver
Dorothy R. Westlund (Mrs. Bernard John "Bud" Westlund)
Mr. and Mrs. Tom W. Wheeler, Jr.
Elmer J. White
Treva and Peter S. White
William W. Whiteley
Don C. Whitworth
Mary and David L. Williams
Nancy and Doug Wilson
Barbara and Victor M. Winquist
T. Evans Wyckoff
Dr. and Mrs. Joe T. York
Frank N. Young, Jr.
Jean and Gordon Zwiebel
Otto W. Zylstra

SEATTLE YACHT CLUB

INTRODUCTION

Mankind has long utilized the buoyancy of water. At some time in the distant past, our ancestors found ways to ride the current on floating logs. First they learned to bind timbers into rafts, then to add decking and rails. They learned to propel these craft with poles and paddles and to steer them with rudders. They hollowed logs into rough canoes, developing over time a technique that produced vessels of both utility and beauty.

During one of earth's earliest civilizations, the Pharaohs of Egypt used the River Nile as their highway. In an Egyptian tomb sealed around 1500 B.C., the model of a 100-foot pleasure craft was preserved undisturbed until modern times. We know Romans sailed the Mediterranean and Atlantic and were fond of boat racing.

Many ancient peoples, including Pacific Northwest natives, constructed craft of indigenous woods. In the Pacific Ocean, natives of the Solomon Islands and of Polynesia built boats of various sizes and shapes, including canoes as long as 70 feet. Fijians were among the first to use trustworthy catamarans. In Java *peroques* were developed and in New Guinea the *Lakatoi*; both were used as small trading vessels. In China, the junk, clumsy in appearance with mat sails that were difficult to trim, served effectively for centuries. Houseboats, ranging from tiny sampans to sumptuous royal barges, have long been used on the rivers of China, Burma, and India. Elements of all of these craft contributed to later boat designs.

During the Middle Ages, the ruling classes on the European Continent rigged pleasure craft with sails of the finest cloth. Early Anglo-Saxon chronicles speak of "*pleg scripts*" or "play ships," most likely tiny sailing craft, though their design is unknown today. During the late sixteenth century, Queen Elizabeth I is known to have enjoyed her royal barge.

SYC Clubhouse on Portage Bay in 1991. (Photo by Mark Ackerman)

Early Yachting in Europe

During the seventeenth century, the Dutch, on their many waterways, freighted produce on small sailboats which they occasionally raced. These races led the Dutch to design "*jagts*" or "*jachts*," a word stemming from "*jagten*," meaning "to speed." In 1604, Henry, Prince of Wales, was reported to have sailed on such a "yacht," the first known use of this word in English.

King Charles II is credited with introducing the sport of yachting to his English subjects. Before he became king, he had been exiled in Holland, where he learned to enjoy pleasure boating. When he assumed the throne of England in 1660, the city of Amsterdam, aware of his passion for sailing, presented him with a Dutch-built state yacht, the royally ornamented, 66-foot *Mary*. Dutch merchants soon added the smaller yacht *Bezam* to the king's fleet.

Between 1661 and 1663, Peter and Christopher Pett and Master Thomas Shish designed five additional royal yachts, patterned along the lines of British warships. In 1660 Samuel Pepys noted in his famous diary:

> Before we dined this day we had the great pleasure of seeing the trial with the King's and Duke's yachts and two Dutch ones; but Commissioner Pett's did prove much better than the two of Dutch build.

Over time, King Charles accumulated 15 different pleasure craft. As he tired of them, he passed them on to the Royal Navy.

English King William III, son of the Dutch Prince of Orange, brought with him to England the long-lived royal yacht *Princess Mary*. This vessel served three monarchs—William III (who reigned 1689–1702), Queen Anne (1702–1714), and George I (1714–1727)—and ended service as a collier. The *Princess Mary* finally sank in 1827 after 139 years of carrying kings, queens, and coal.

The Irish promulgated a major yachting flurry when, in 1720, they formed the world's first sailing organization—the Water Club of the Harbour of Cork. The 25 members donned fancy uniforms for meetings, fired their cannon, and merrily consumed victuals and drink. The Water Club flourished for 45 years. In the early 1800s, survivors of this first yachting association founded The Little Monkstown Club, later renamed the Royal Cork Yacht Club, which today is the world's oldest active yachting organization.

In 1815, the Thames Yacht Club (now the Royal Thames) was formed. Over the next half century, yachtsmen organized throughout the British empire in such diverse locations as Gibraltar (1829), Bermuda (1834), Tasmania (1838), India (1846), Canada (1852), South Africa (1858) and New Zealand (1871).

The First American Yacht

In 1816, the first American boat built exclusively for pleasure slid down the ways at Becket's shipyard in Salem, Massachusetts. It belonged to George Crowninshield of the shipping family which, during the War of 1812, accumulated great wealth from privateering forays against the British. The sale of captured enemy vessels and cargo in Boston netted the family more than $1 million, a tremendous sum in those days.

George Crowninshield, who never married, retired from the family business to devote his time to building his yacht. More than 100 feet long, with a 23-foot beam and a draft of 11 1/2 feet, this brigantine was square-rigged on the foremast, but with mizzenmasts fore-and-aft rigged. Expense was not spared in outfitting her. In all, she cost Crowninshield about $50,000. He christened her *Cleopatra's Barge*.

In 1817, Crowninshield invited 14 guests to accompany him to the Mediterranean aboard his new yacht, a journey that attracted attention on both sides of the Atlantic. Wherever the yacht moored, throngs gathered to view the magnificent floating palace. In Barcelona, 8,000 visitors crowded aboard during a single day. Crowninshield apparently enjoyed the attention, for he lived aboard and led tours of his yacht.

A life-size, gaily-painted wooden Indian of the cigar store type, ensconced on the deck of *Cleopatra's Barge*, was an enigma to some European visitors. One Frenchman insisted on saluting it. Some Italians, believing it to be the statue of an American saint, kneeled and kissed its feet.

After *Cleopatra's Barge* sailed home late in 1817, Crowninshield immediately began planning a voyage to England and the Baltic, but he died before the journey could begin. After his death the yacht, though not built to withstand heavy duty, was used for a time as a merchant vessel. King Kamehameha of the Sandwich Islands (Hawaii) rescued her from drudgery in 1820 by acquiring her to use as his royal vessel. Soon after, however, she struck a reef and sank.

During the first three decades of the nineteenth century, pioneering Americans had little time for pleasure boating. In Britain, however, yachting continued to flourish among the landed gentry. Lord Belfast, the outstanding yachtsman of those years, owned the fastest cutter afloat, the *Louisa*. He also built a square-rigger named *Waterwitch*, whose superior lines influenced later design of warships built for the Royal Navy.

Evolution of Yachting in the United States

Pleasure sailing first developed as an American sport on New York's Hudson River during the 1840s. The sandbagger design, numbered among the first and most famous of the Hudson River craft, resulted in sloop-rigged boats up to 30 feet long, wide of beam and with a centerboard. These boats took their name from the sandbag ballast, which the crew shifted to the windward side after each tack to prevent capsizing.

John Stevens, known as the father of American yachting, grew to manhood on the Hudson River. He owned the fast 51-foot schooner *Gimcrack*, aboard which the New York Yacht Club was founded in 1844.

The following year this New York group sponsored the first formal race in the United States. Stevens' *Gimcrack* finished third, a position he considered untenable, so he decided to develop a speedier craft. He and his brother Edwin commissioned the sloop *Maria*, which, with its hollow masts and booms and other unique features, soon proved to be the swiftest of all East Coast yachts.

John Stevens and George Schuyler then formed a syndicate of New York Yacht Club members to build the *America*. They sailed her to England in 1851 to challenge the British, who until then reigned supreme in yacht racing. The *America* defeated 15 British yachts and was presented a magnificent trophy, known ever since as the America's Cup.

Of all the British yachtsmen, the most persistent was Sir Thomas Lipton, developer of a grocery empire which included the tea named for him. In 1899, racing under the flag of the Royal Ulster Yacht Club, he attempted to wrest the America's Cup from the Yankee upstarts. In so doing, this genial gentleman overcame considerable ill feelings generated as long ago as the Revolutionary War.

In 1899, the Americans succeeded again, this time when the *Columbia* bested Lipton's *Shamrock*. Sir Thomas immediately began construction of *Shamrock II*, which in 1901 lost to the *Columbia* a second time. He promptly built *Shamrock III*, but lost again, this time to the new American yacht *Reliance*. Lipton took 10 years to build the *Shamrock IV*, only to have World War I postpone the America's Cup race until 1920. That year the American racer *Resolute* broke a mast, and the Lipton craft won the first race. But in the series, the *Resolute* crossed the finish line first in three of the five races. In 1931, Lipton's *Shamrock V* lost to the Yankees' *Enterprise*. The following year, Sir Thomas Lipton died. Though more than 80 years old, he was planning yet another challenger for the America's Cup.

At the time of Lipton's death, yacht racing had been a popular sport for more than a century, and the great inland sea known as Puget Sound was widely recognized for its fine sailing waters. Sir Thomas Lipton himself sailed these waters in 1913 and donated the Lipton Cup to the Seattle Yacht Club where it is now on exhibit. Until recently, Six-Meter class yachts raced for this fine trophy.

Yachting on Puget Sound

In *The Yachts and Yachtsmen of America*, a tremendous tome published in 1894, Dr. Henry A. Mott extols the canoes of the original inhabitants of the Puget Sound area and the Strait of Juan de Fuca. A sketch in his book depicts the large Northwest Indian dugout canoe, which was exhibited at the Centennial Exhibition in Philadelphia in 1876 and later at the National Museum (Smithsonian Institution) in Washington, D.C. This beautiful example of Indian craftsmanship carried as many as 100 persons and their equipment!

First Yachting Event on Puget Sound

The first true yachting event on Puget Sound may have taken place in 1792, when our "Mediterranean of America" was as yet an unknown, unnamed body of water. The event was strictly informal and was pulled off between the *Chatham*, an "armed tender" of 186 tons and the *Discovery*, a "sloop of war" under the command of Capt. George Vancouver.

This race, while not establishing any records for fast sailing, was destined to go into history, and toward the close of day the doughty captains decided to call all bets off and anchored under the lee of what is now Blake Island. Calling his three lieutenants, Zacariah Mudge, Peter Puget, Joseph Baker, and the Ship's Master Joseph Whidbey about him, Captain Vancouver proposed the health of the king and set about to find appropriate names for the wonders of this beautiful inland sea. To the north of him was a lofty snowcapped peak; to the east an unbroken mountain chain; to the south a majestic dome of perpetual snow; to the west a sawtooth range, the highest peak of which was even then named Olympus; and all around was this beautiful, liquid turquoise sea fringed by emerald forests. When it came to the momentous question of suitably naming this body of water, what a blessing it was that his choice fell upon his second lieutenant [Peter Puget] instead of upon his first lieutenant [Zacariah Mudge].

—*Post-Intelligencer*,
May 21, 1905

It had been presented to Nootkan chief Maquinna, grandson of the Maquinna mentioned in the journal of Capt. George Vancouver, the British explorer who in 1792 charted the waters of Puget Sound and named them for Peter Puget, a lieutenant on his ship *Discovery*.

Puget Sound and its tributary streams served as the highways for Native Americans and the first white explorers, traders, and settlers.

> The delightful serenity of the weather greatly aided the beautiful scenery that was now presented; the surface of the sea was perfectly smooth and the country before us exhibited everything that bounteous nature could be expected to draw into one point of view. As we had no reason to imagine that this country had ever been indebted for any of its decorations to the hand of man, I could not possibly believe that any uncultivated country had ever been discovered exhibiting so rich a picture. . . .
>
> Between us and the snowy range, the land . . . rose here in a very gentle ascent and was well covered with a variety of stately forest trees. . . .
>
> As we advanced, the country seemed gradually to improve in beauty. The cleared spots were more numerous and of larger extent, and the remote lofty mountains covered with snow reflected greater lustre on the fertile productions of the less elevated country. . . .
>
> —*Capt. George Vancouver, Log,* May 2, 1792

During the strenuous decade of the 1850s, in which Seattle, Olympia, Port Townsend, Victoria, and other Northwest towns were founded, a series of stormy events deterred development of pleasure boating on Puget Sound: The Indians were restless through most of the 1850s; unfriendly relations persisted between Britain and the United States from the War of 1812 through the San Juan dispute (Pig War) of 1859; the American Civil War was heating up and would break into battle in 1861; negligible population growth throughout the period was a problem, and the embryonic frontier economy allowed few families the income or free time for recreation.

However, as early as 1858, a Royal Navy regatta was enjoyed off Victoria, and on May 24, 1867, during the celebration of Queen Victoria's birthday, races involving canoes were part of the festivities. In 1870, at Esquimalt, the Royal Navy Squadron staged rowing and sailing races that attracted thousands of spectators, including citizens from Washington Territory who arrived on the steamer *Olympia*. Cutters, galleys, launches, and pinnaces competed, the winners in most classes being crews from ships of Her Majesty's Navy. This naval regatta, scheduled each year until 1888, helped transplant the sailing and rowing traditions of Great Britain to the Pacific Northwest on both sides of the border. ☆

DRUGS
Y.M.C.A
BOATS TO LET.
BOAT HOUSE

One

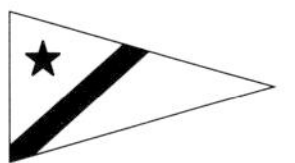

1870-1892

The first evidence of yachting on Elliott Bay is found in local newspaper reports of the 1870s. At the time, Seattle was a rustic frontier village clinging to a forested hillside. The 1870 census takers counted 1,107 residents. Though the population would triple to 3,533 residents by 1880, Seattleites still muddied their feet crossing the streets. Simple frame dwellings with accompanying outhouses, gardens, barns, and wells clustered around the waterfront and commercial structures in the heart of the town, the area known today as Pioneer Square.

Throughout the 1870s, travel to and from Seattle was slow and difficult, usually by sail or paddle. A few hardy individuals traversed the Indian paths that meandered through the dense forests. A wagon track hewn over Snoqualmie Pass in the 1860s proved impossible to maintain and soon was choked with deadfalls. This isolation stunted the town that Arthur Denny had platted in 1852. Salvation awaited in the form of a transcontinental rail line that would connect Seattle to the rest of the country.

Budlong's Boat House, built in 1880 at the foot of Columbia Street, became the first home of Seattle yachtsmen. (MOHAI)

In 1872, Northern Pacific Railroad representatives arrived on Puget Sound, seeking the most advantageous site for a terminus. Though Seattle citizens enthusiastically promoted their town, the railroad commissioners chose tiny Tacoma, where their company's real estate arm had purchased most of the waterfront. Not until 1893 would James J. Hill's Great Northern Railway tracks reach Seattle, providing the first direct transcontinental link.

Meanwhile, a fleet of small steam vessels, called the Mosquito Fleet, which used Seattle as home port, became the major means of travel about Puget Sound.

> The early Mosquito Fleet [vessels] were the miniature mail order houses which supplied the settlers with their conveniences and small luxuries. Their masters were the friends

Indian canoes were found along Seattle's waterfront and could be rented for pleasure or transportation. (MOHAI)

of the village people. They carried with them a store of pithy yarns, a large fund of the latest gossip and a good word for old and young.

—*Clarence Bagley,* History of King County, Washington

At the small local shipyards that launched these commercial craft, an occasional pleasure boat was constructed.

In this struggling but energetic society of the 1870s, what little available leisure time was left after working ten-hour days and six-day weeks was spent largely on outdoor activities, such as hunting and fishing. After the founding of the Washington Jockey Club in 1870, horses raced at a track established on the Duwamish flats near what is now Georgetown. As early as 1876, Seattle's first organized baseball nine was competing against teams from nearby towns.

1875: The First Regatta on Puget Sound

Independence Day, the major summer holiday for the pioneers, was always celebrated with gusto and patriotic fervor. Parades, picnics, orators, band music, games, and races filled much of the day. The first reports of Seattle's yachting activities were associated with these Fourth of July activities. The weekly four-page *Intelligencer* described what was apparently the first regatta on Elliott Bay:

> A Boat Race—On Saturday, July 3, 1875. There was a large crowd in attendance at all the wharves on our city front to witness the improvised regatta, as it was called, which came off on that day. The prize to be won was a silver cup offered by Colonel Larrabee to the fastest craft. Six sail entered the lists, but only four of them—the yachts *Amelia*, *Lillie Bell*, *Jolly Times*, and *Mabrey*—rounded the first stake or made any contest for the prize, which was finally won by the *Mabrey*, sailed by Capt. Willoughby, of the *Fauntleroy*. Of the remaining three, the *Lillie Bell* [of Seattle] came in second, the *Amelia* [of Seattle] came in third, and the *Jolly Times* last.
>
> —Intelligencer, *July 10, 1875*

The Centennial Race of 1876

The following year Americans celebrated the 100th anniversary of the Declaration of Independence. The *Intelligencer* reported that 15 boats were entered in this second Seattle regatta:

> Everybody and their friends assembled on the Yesler, Crawford and Harrington, and McCallister and McCarty wharves and on the shipping and steamers adjacent at 10 o'clock on Tuesday, July 4, 1876, to witness the centennial regatta.
>
> —Intelligencer, *July 6, 1876*

The race course for the large and mid-sized sloops extended from the buoy off Crawford and Harrington's wharf to a second buoy near the Eagle Harbor entrance, to Four-Mile Rock, and back to the starting point. The course for smaller boats omitted the Eagle Harbor buoy.

The first prize of $100 for large boats was won by the *H. L. Tibbals*; second prize of $30 went to the *Minnie*. Owners and/or skippers were not identified.

Even in those days, race results were sometimes contested. The unnamed *Intelligencer* reporter explained, "We have heard rumors to the effect that the boat to which the public expectation was chiefly directed was clandestinely handicapped in a peculiar fashion which prevented her from winning the race." In other words, somebody cheated.

In the second class race, *Harvest Home* placed first, with *Albatross* second. In third class, *Charles XII* outpaced the other Whitehalls (slender rowing boats rigged with sails), and *Centennial* was second.

1877

On July 4, 1877, eight boats entered the first class race, three entered second class, and the single registrant in third class was asked to compete in second class.

> In sailing on the wind from the second buoy home, the *Harvest Home* did the best sailing and won the silver tea set given by Messrs. L. P. Smith and Son as the prize for first class boats. The second boat to round the home buoy was the *Lone Star*, and was awarded the second class prize, she having entered in that class. The *Sea Eagle* won second prize for second class boats.
>
> —Intelligencer, *July 6, 1877*

Clarence Bagley in his book, *History of Seattle,* describes the regatta as a success. He also adds a bit of whimsical information about another type of contest called "The Greased Pole," which was then a popular event in each Fourth of July celebration:

> A greased pole extending out [horizontally] from the old bark *Windward* lying near the present Colman Dock, afforded much amusement; 62 attempts to walk it failed, Mr. Anderson finally winning.
>
> —*Clarence Bagley,* History of Seattle

1878

In 1878, the yacht races were proudly proclaimed "the most interesting feature" of Independence Day activities. For the first time in the local newspaper reports, boat sizes were specified for each division of the race.

First class, open to all sloops measuring 16 to 30 feet, attracted five entrants: *Caswell*, of Port Blakely; *Nip and Tuck*, of Belltown (then a Seattle suburb); *Adda*, of Port Discovery; *Nellie*, of Port Townsend and *Amelia*, of Seattle.

Registrants in the second class race, "open to all boats sloop rigged," were *Mena* and *Lone Star*, of Port Blakely; *Lillie Bell*, of Seattle; *Tom Paine* and *Iowner*, of Milton (now West Seattle); *Harvest Home*, of San Francisco and *Lena*, of Belltown. A reporter described the race in these words:

> The boats started all together from a line stretched from the ship *War Hawk* to the end of the S & W W [Seattle and Walla Walla] RR Company's wharf at exactly 10:00 A.M. at the signal of the [Race] Commodore, Captain Winsor. On they shot before the wind like skipping missiles; now one and now another appearing to gain the advantage. . . .

Among the larger boats, *Nip and Tuck* took first prize of $50; *Adda* won the second prize of $25. In second class, *Lena* won $25 for first, and *Lone Star* received a silver ice bucket donated by L. P. Smith and Son for second place.

The First Seattle Yacht Club

Local newspapers are the major sources of information about yachting in the 1870s, but the reports are somewhat erratic and usually brief. Tantalizing bits of information lie scattered on the yellowing pages: Yacht names can be found but often without mention of owners; people involved can be found but frequently only the last names are reported, making identification difficult. Nevertheless, much can be learned from these early articles.

One of the first, somewhat incomplete, reports of the Seattle Yacht Club is in the *Intelligencer* of May 15, 1879. The paper casually mentions: "The Seattle Yacht Club desires to give notice that the first sailing race of their club will come off on the Fourth of July." The officers of the new organization were listed as Commodore William Hammond, a shipbuilder and marine architect; and two board members, J. F. T. Mitchell, boat builder, and Frank Hanford, bookkeeper. No other records concerning this early club, not even a charter, can be found. Furthermore, copies of Seattle's only paper at the time, the *Intelligencer*, were apparently all destroyed for those months when that first Seattle Yacht Club organized. From all indications, it was a small, informal group.

The First Pleasure Craft on Puget Sound

In 1874, Capt. Charles E. Clancy built a small sharpie at Olympia, which he called the *Tilden*. This boat was designed entirely for pleasure, and it is considered to have marked the beginning of pleasure boating in the Northwest.

However, in all fairness, Dr. Frederick W. Sparling can be called the "father" of yachting on Puget Sound. During the 1880s the doctor built several small boats of merit, but his sloop *Sappho* is the best remembered, having held her own against all comers for several seasons. Other yachts of this period were the *Lillie Bell*, built by Capt. A. E. Hanford, and the *Seattle*, by Capt. J. F. T. Mitchell.

About this time Capt. George Budlong moved to Seattle from Olympia, bringing his boathouse, a fleet of small catboats, and his schooner *Olympia*. It was left to Captain Budlong and Capt. William Lake, of Ballard, to start a rivalry for the supremacy in boat building and these two men turned out some smart little packets for their time. Among Captain Lake's earlier successes were the sloop *Nip and Tuck*, the *Nevermind*, and the *Adventurer*. Captain Budlong's schooner *Eureka* met the *Nevermind* and the *Adventurer* in many a race for stakes ranging from $200 to $500 with varying success, for it was "give and take" between the two builders. The *Eureka* was finally converted into a steamer for light towing, a fate which also befell the *Adventurer*.

—Adapted from the
Seattle Post-Intelligencer,
May 21, 1905

Seattle in 1882, three years after the first yacht club was formed. Numbers refer to (1) Duwamish River, (2) Tide flats against Beacon Hill, (3) Jackson Street Coal Wharf, (4) Yesler's Wharf, (5) Schwabacher's Wharf, (6) David and Catherine Blaine's home, (7) Henry and Lascelle Struve's home, and (8) Arthur and Mary Denny's home. (MOHAI)

Two months prior to the race on July 4, 1879, the club predicted that 20 sloops would enter, but actually only nine were on hand to contest for the new "Corporation Challenge Cup." The 23-mile course extended southwest from Maddock's Wharf around the ship at the Coal Wharf Buoy, then around Blakely Rocks, then to the stake boat off Belltown, and finally back to the Coal Wharf.

The boats and owners in the first class race were *City of Olympia* (Budlong of Olympia), *Nip and Tuck* (Stevens of Samish in Skagit County), *Hard Times*, (T. W. Lake of Seattle), *Rob Roy* (Ross of Port Madison), and *Amelia* (Collins of Victoria). The second class entrants were *Newport* (Anderson), *No. 2* (Hall), *Lone Star* (Holt of Port Blakely), *Mena* (Antoine of Port Blakely) and *No Name* (Fowler of Port Blakely).

The first class winner, *Nip and Tuck*, completed the course in 2 hours and 20 minutes and won $50 and a refund of the entrance fee. In the second class race, *Lone Star* and *No. 2* fouled each other on the first offshore tack. The judges decided to divide the $25 prize between the two.

This race prompted the *Intelligencer* to praise a boatbuilder for the first time.

> The result of the race speaks volumes of praise for Mr. T. W. Lake. He built the *Nip and Tuck*, and she outstripped all rivals. He then built the *Hard Times*, and she was only second to the *Nip and Tuck*, and had the boats been awarded prizes as on former occasions where the measurement was taken into consideration, Commodore F. W. Sparling, M.D., informs us that she would have been entitled to the race and money. Mr. Lake intends soon to commence the construction of a yacht to outrun both of them.
>
> —Intelligencer, *July 6, 1879*

Thus, it was during the late 1870s that yacht racing became a familiar sport on the salty waters of Elliott Bay.

The 1880s

The decade of the 1880s brought a

flood of newcomers to Seattle, spurring a growth that only accelerated throughout the decade, increasing the number of Seattleites from 3,533 in 1880 to 43,000 by 1890. By 1884, Seattle had become the largest town in the territory.

1880

The Sunday, July 4, 1880, edition of the *Intelligencer* mentioned that Commodore Budlong, his two sons, and three assistants had arrived from Olympia on July 3 in their new sailboat, the *Eureka*, which they had built in Olympia. (The Budlongs would soon erect a boathouse at the foot of Columbia Street in Seattle.) Captain J. F. T. Mitchell's new sailing yacht *Seattle* was also reported in trim for the race, as was the 1879 first class race winner, *Nip and Tuck*.

The course, about 30 miles in length, began alongside the ship *Yosemite*, moored at Yesler's Wharf. It then proceeded south around the buoy off the Coal Wharf, to the buoy off Four-Mile Rock, to Blakely Rock, back to the Coal Wharf buoy and on to the finish line off the stern of the *Yosemite*. The Whitehall racers' course

A Forgotten Pioneer Seattle Yacht Club Commodore

In the 1880s, the commodore of the fledgling Seattle Yacht Club, Dr. Frederick W. Sparling, was a noted pioneer.

The original Seattle Yacht Club, apparently a struggling and informal organization, was founded in 1879. Its major role was as sponsor of the annual Fourth of July yacht races. In 1892, the organization was reconstituted, and it is from that year that the modern Seattle Yacht Club traces it lineage.

Dr. Sparling lived an exciting life in intriguing times. Born in Ireland and raised in Canada, young Sparling moved to Detroit to practice medicine. When the Civil War began, he was appointed an army surgeon and served until he was mustered out in 1865. He then enlisted in the regular army for a time and served as Surgeon General for the state of Tennessee. He also was assessor of the Fifth District of Tennessee, thanks to an appointment by President Ulysses S. Grant.

Sparling later moved to Washington, D.C., and in 1873 he traveled west under orders of the Surgeon General of the U.S. Army to serve in the Department of the Columbia, which covered the Northwest. He was post surgeon at Fort Cape Disappointment at the mouth of the Columbia River, at the American garrison on San Juan Island and at Port Townsend. In 1875, he resigned from the army and moved to Seattle to practice medicine.

In 1877 Sparling was named medical superintendent for the Hospital for the Insane at Steilacoom, but resigned when he was elected quartermaster general of Washington Territory.

In 1880 President Rutherford B. Hayes appointed Dr. Sparling to the post of supervisor of the Territorial Census (which reported 3,533 residents living in Seattle). In 1881, President James Garfield named Dr. Sparling registrar of the U.S. Land Office in Vancouver, Washington. He was reappointed to this position by President Chester A. Arthur. He resigned when President Grover Cleveland, a Democrat, was elected in 1888.

Dr. Sparling then resumed his private practice in Seattle until 1890, when he was asked to fill the position of appraiser of tidelands.

The records for SYC commodores during the 1880s are somewhat sketchy. Seattle newspapers mentioned Dr. Sparling as being elected SYC commodore in 1880, and then he is listed only twice more as a commodore: In 1886 and in 1890. Since no other names crop up as being commodores during those years, we might presume that, even though he was away for much of the time, Dr. Sparling was the only SYC commodore during the 1880s. ◇

rounded the buoy off Milton rather than sailing over to Blakely Rock, reducing the distance to about 12 miles. Judges for the race were SYC Commodore Fred W. Sparling, M.D., lawyer J. C. Haines, and shipbuilder William Hammond.

Because Independence Day fell on a Sunday, the boat races, under the auspices of the Seattle Yacht Club, were scheduled for July 5, but on that day the wind failed, delaying the races until July 6.

The *Intelligencer* reported that of the three boats racing in first class, the *City of Seattle*, owned by boatbuilders Taylor and Mitchell, won the $75 first prize, Stevens' *Nip and Tuck* and Budlong's *Eureka* of Olympia crossed the line in second and third place, respectively. In second class, *Sweepstakes* of Port Blakely claimed first, and *Lulu* of Olympia came in second.

The papers for the years 1881, 1882, and 1883 mention Independence Day activities, but there are no reports of yacht races.

1884

The Independence Day Regatta of 1884 was mentioned briefly in the *Post-Intelligencer*. Measuring the competing yachts took longer than expected, and the races were delayed until 1:00 P.M. Midway through the race, the wind died, causing "a desultory finish." The first class winner, A. A. Holt's *Lookout*, completed the course in a slow 5 hours and 7 minutes to claim the $50 prize.

1885

The 1885 race results were as follows:

> The *Meteor* [A. A. Holt] overhauled and passed the *Madcap* [Budlong] before she reached Smith's Cove. When about two hundred yards ahead of the *Madcap*, a heavy squall struck the *Meteor* and capsized her. The judges' boat rescued the crew and uprighted the boat and towed her to Yesler's Wharf.
>
> The *Lookout* [also owned by Holt] came in first and *Madcap* second, the difference in time being two minutes. The *Lotus* [Charles J. Haines and Maurice McMicken] struck a calm, which gave the other boats a chance to get away from her, otherwise her chances of winning were good. The *Lookout* took the $100 prize and the *Madcap* the second money, $25.
>
> —*Seattle* Daily Post-Intelligencer, *July 7, 1895*

An 1885 yacht race on Elliott Bay. Denny Hill, now the regrade area, can been seen to the left in the background. (MOHAI)

1886

The Seattle *Times* published its first issue on May 3, 1886. On the following July 6 it reported that the Independence Day yacht race had been becalmed. The next day, with the wind still slight, none of the boats completed the race within the allotted three hours.

> The Seattle Yacht Club have [sic] given the following notice: The race for the challenge cup and $100 added will be sailed on Tuesday, the 20th next. . . .
>
> —*Seattle* Times, *July 6, 1886*

Apparently the race was postponed yet again, for on July 27, 1886, the *Times* carried this notice:

> **Seattle, July 26, 1886**
>
> We, the undersigned, judges of the postponed race, sailed on the above date, hereby award the first prize of the challenge cup donated by Mr. Albert Hansen, and $100 donated by the Fourth of July committee, to the sloop *Madcap* owned by George Budlong; second prize, silver pitcher donated by A. A. Smith and opera glasses donated by H. C. McLaughlin to the sloop *Violet* owned by Captain Joseph Green.
>
> We also rule the sloop *Adventure* owned by Lake out of the race, in consequence of fouling the sloop *Lookout* owned by A. Holt, off Milton buoy.
>
> J. A. Hatfield
> F. W. Sparling
> J. F. T. Mitchell
> Judges
>
> —*Seattle* Times, *July 27, 1886*

According to Clarence Bagley in his book *History of Seattle*, the first motorboat seen in Seattle was an 18-foot naphtha launch, which arrived from the East in the fall of 1886. (Naphtha was an early volatile distillate of coal or petroleum commonly used to power the first engines driven by oil products.) Bagley wrote:

> So well was it liked that George Budlong built here a similar one 28 feet long and placed therein a four-horse power naphtha motor. Upon her completion in the spring of 1887, she was named *Flirt* and carried from fifteen to twenty persons, and could travel from seven to nine miles an hour. Her trial trip was made April 23, 1887, with a select party from Colman's Wharf to Smith's Cove and return, six miles in one hour.
>
> —*Clarence Bagley,* History of Seattle

1887

The Fourth of July races attracted six

The naptha launch Pet *and others like her were introduced on Northwest waters in the late 1880s and were common sights by the 1890s. (PSMHS)*

The Unhappy Fate of Andrew Holt, Yachtsman

Boatbuilder Andrew Holt appeared on Puget Sound in 1880 with his sloop *Lookout*. This fast little craft soon had a worthy rival for speed in the sloop *Chippie*, constructed by the talented hands of George Budlong. These boats were evenly matched and a single challenging word from either owner called forth an immediate response from the other, usually backed by a substantial bet. Side bets of from $200 to $500 were common, and the rivalry in the early 1880s created great interest in the sport.

The *Annie*, the last boat to be built by Andrew Holt, was not designed as a yacht, but rather as a coast trader. The *Annie* never raced, for she had no competitors. She was by all odds the fastest vessel on Puget Sound.

> Holt built her in the closest secrecy at his ranch, which was located at the present site of Pleasant Beach, and outfitted her with goods for the Alaska trade among the Indians. He sailed to the North and carried on his trade at the different settlements, but the remarkable fact that a sudden and violent epidemic of drunkenness and lawlessness followed in his wake soon had the revenue officers after him to determine if he carried on the illicit selling of liquor to the natives.
>
> —Post-Intelligencer, *May 21, 1905*

Though searched time and again, nothing could be found on the *Annie* to incriminate Holt. Finally, at Sitka, Alaska federal officials concluded that Holt must be smuggling whiskey, though none had ever been found on board. They tied *Annie* to a wharf after dismantling her sails. Holt was allowed to live aboard the boat, and he bided his time.

One day the barometer began a precipitous fall, and he thought he saw an opportunity to make his escape. He rescued his sails from the warehouse and soon had them bent on in readiness for the storm he knew was coming. The fury of that gale cast the entire fishing fleet that was in the port upon the beach, and the *Annie* disappeared. After the storm abated, a government cutter was dispatched to search the Inside Passage for some sign of Holt.

> But Holt had not taken the Inside Passage. With the daring of his kind he struck boldly out into the Pacific and not only weathered the storm, but sailed his craft into the harbor at Victoria and had the *Annie* registered under the British flag.
>
> —Post-Intelligencer, *May 21, 1905*

Soon after his escape, he came back to Puget Sound, and while lying at anchor in Salmon Bay he was boarded by a customs officer named Coblentz. What transpired on board was never fully known, but Holt was shot by Coblentz, and the *Annie* was confiscated by the government. Most confiscated boats were sold at auction, so several local yachtsmen were hoping to pick up this speedy boat at a bargain. However, customs officers at Port Townsend claimed the boat and used her to run down craft of the same kind.

> She was in this service for several years until she met with an accident which tore off some of the outside planking and rendered it necessary to put her in drydock for repairs. Then the secret was revealed. The *Annie* was double-hulled, with copper tanks between the sheathings and upon closer investigation it was revealed that there was still close to one hundred gallons of illicit whiskey on board which Holt had failed to dispose of.
>
> —Post-Intelligencer, *May 21, 1905*

—Adapted from the Seattle Post-Intelligencer, *May 21, 1905*

entries. Boatbuilder A. A. Holt's *Lookout* took the first prize, $50 in coin and the championship cup. Law clerk A. E. Hanford's *White Wings* took the second prize of $25; boatbuilders Morrison & Clark's *Nevermind* placed third to win $15.

1888

Winners in Class One (sloops 25 to 40 feet in waterline measurement) were *White Wings* (A. E. Hanford) and *Violet* (Captain Joseph Green). The entrance fee was $5.

In Class Two (boats 16- to 25-feet waterline length) winners were *Chippy* (L. W. Wilson) and *Windward* of Tacoma. The entrance fee was $2.50.

The Year of the Great Seattle Fire

On June 6, 1889, the commercial heart of downtown Seattle, including Budlong's Boat House, was consumed by the great fire. Scheduled events for the following Fourth of July celebration were canceled; everyone was too busy rebuilding the city.

In November 1889 Washington Territory, after a long struggle, achieved statehood.

The 1890s

Seattle developed rapidly during the 1890s. Population increased from about 43,000 to more than 80,000, and yachting activity increased commensurately. In fact, boating fever was on the rise everywhere in the Northwest.

1890

Apparently on March 31, 1890, the Seattle Yacht Club was founded, or at least resuscitated. According to a constitution and bylaws booklet, which Fred W. Sparling donated to the Seattle Yacht Club many years ago, 1890 SYC officers were Commodore Fred W. Sparling; Vice Commodore George E. Budlong; Secretary John W. Brauer; and Measurer R. S. Clark. The 22 members who joined the new yacht club within the first month paid an initiation fee of $2.50 and monthly dues of 50 cents. This group intended to sponsor three events each year—an Opening Day cruise, a regatta with club pennants as prizes, and a July open regatta for prizes. Like its predecessors, this organization must have faded rather rapidly for, as we shall see, two years later the club was again reorganized.

A Northwest family sailing in the late 1880s. (PSMHS)

On Independence Day, 1890, this new group apparently sponsored the July yacht races. The many new Puget Sound residents mingled with old-timers to watch the contests, but little excitement was generated by the race.

> The lack of wind made the regatta of the Seattle Yacht Club almost a drifting contest. The start was delayed two hours to await the wind, and then it was made in a little breeze from the south that hardly carried the boats over the course in the required time. In the first class race for boats over twenty-four feet in length, the *McLaren* [Phillip Savery] took first prize, a spirit compass; and the *Vitella* [Captain Hansen] of Port Blakely, second prize, a box of cigars.
>
> —Post-Intelligencer, *July 5, 1890*

The *Idler* (R. S. Clark) won the second class race for boats under 24 feet in length and the judges awarded her "a beautiful silver water set." The *Lottie* (Captain Keesling), for second place, won a silver card tray and $10 in cash. Third place was taken by the *Viking* (Capt. George Waite), which won a silver clock and $10 in cash. Judges were: H. H. Morrison, G. A. Zeiger, and H. W. Riddle.

1891

The 1891 regatta of Saturday, July 4, involved 11 sloops and four catboats. For some unexplained reason, the race was started at 10:00 A.M., three hours before the scheduled hour. As a result, spectators arrived on the waterfront at the appropriate time only to find the race nearing completion. There was considerable grousing about the situation.

> After figuring out the time allowances, the judges made the following awards: Sloop class—first prize of $125 to the *Hettie Belle*, entered by G. B. Johnson; second prize of $50 to the *Essie Tittell*, entered by Taber and Hartwig; third prize of silver cup to the *Winnie*, entered by Parker and Eckardt.
>
> Catboat class—First prize of $75 to the *Chippie*, entered by William Howe; second prize of $15 to the *Petrel*, entered by Clark and Bartlett; third prize of silver cup to the *Montie*, entered by G. B. Morrison.
>
> —Post-Intelligencer, *July 5, 1891*

1892

The year 1892 was a critical one for yachting circles on Puget Sound. The number of yachts was increasing steadily, and international yacht racing was being promoted, making better-organized clubs a necessity. As we shall see in the next chapter, the Seattle Yacht Club and other yachting organizations began to develop into more formal institutions. The Seattle Yacht Club of today marks its founding as that reorganization of 1892.

To conclude this chapter, a few general observations are helpful. Seattle, in its infancy, was even more water-oriented than it is today. Many pioneers arrived by ship and some of them brought with them the lore of the sea and the skills and experiences that made them handy at building and repairing things, including boats. Many an early yacht was built on a vacant beach lot amid stacks of lumber by men using hand tools. Most were simple 25- or 35-foot sloops, and many were put to a variety of uses, including freight and passenger hauling, fishing, and recreation. Planks in their hulls were fastened with nails or rivets; their sails were of ordinary heavy canvas, and their power came from wind or oar.

The average man had little time for recreation in those years of ten-hour work days and six-day work weeks. On the other hand, comparatively few pastimes were available to fill even those few empty hours. Since most citizens had a relative or friend connected with the sea, they were aware of the joys of sailing, one of the few means of fast and smooth travel. Residents from all walks of life gathered to watch yacht races. While sailing for fun was considered a wealthy man's sport, a few working-class men would occasionally skip a day of labor to sail as members of a crew. As time went on, and as leisure hours became more plentiful, increasing numbers of Seattleites took to the water beneath what the newspapers often referred to as "white canvas wings." ☆

MACHINE SHOP

Two

1892-1909

The Seattle Yacht Club built its first clubhouse, with tower, in West Seattle in 1892. (PSMHS)

Puget Sound's earliest yachtsmen left few clues about the success of their organizations. The first pleasure craft sailed on Puget Sound in the mid-1870s, and the first Seattle Yacht Club was formed in 1879, but the longevity of the early yachting organizations apparently was limited by the small number of pleasure craft, recurrent financial recessions, and a rivalry among clubs that diminished memberships. How many such groups were formed and then faded is not known, but it seems that there were several. Newspaper items hint that for more than 20 years, prior to its formal organization in 1892, the Seattle Yacht Club reorganized frequently in its struggle to survive.

In 1892 the time was ripe for a yacht club to succeed. The Great Northern Railroad had earlier chosen Seattle as its Pacific terminus, and in 1893 the first transcontinental trains steamed into town. Seattle, with its mid-sound location, protected deep-water harbor and thriving mercantile and service industries, experienced a tremendous population surge, eclipsing all neighboring towns as the following census figures illustrate:

City	1890	1900	1910
Seattle	42,837	80,671	237,194
Tacoma	36,006	37,714	83,743
Everett (incorporated 1893)		7,838	24,814
Bellingham	8,135	11,062	24,298
Olympia	4,698	3,863	6,996
Port Townsend	4,558	3,443	4,181
Anacortes (incorporated 1891)		1,476	4,168

Successful Seattle businessmen found their profits—and their leisure time—increasing. Those who loved water sports invested in sailboats which, during the 1890s, became common sights on both salt and fresh water.

> Of late yachting has become very popular, and many parties have been formed to enjoy a few days' sail on the sound waters. It would be hard to find a city better adapted for

The Tacoma Yacht Club

The Tacoma Yacht Club was founded in 1889 with a clubhouse at Manzanita on the southern end of Maury Island, but the financial panic of 1893 caused the organization to declare bankruptcy. The TYC commodore purchased the club property and assets for $700.

C. E. Hogberg, a boat fanatic from Chicago, moved to Tacoma shortly after the turn of the century and by 1908 had incorporated a new Tacoma Yacht Club. The Northern Pacific Railroad agreed to provide space in the heart of Tacoma Harbor. A clubhouse was built, and by 1909 some 30 sail- and powerboats floated at moorage.

During World War I, the club's lease was canceled because the property was needed in the war effort. After several months, the Tacoma Park Board agreed to lease the Point Defiance property where the club is now located. The clubhouse was barged to the new site at the end of a huge breakwater made up of slag from the nearby smelter. At the time, the breakwater hardly protected the boat basin, and winter storms swept several yachts away. Most boaters moved their craft to Gig Harbor or elsewhere until facilities could be improved. To reach the clubhouse, members scrambled down the Point Defiance bluff from their autos parked on the top. In spite of these problems, by 1919 the club membership had increased to more than 100.

During the 1920s, the former office building of the Seaborn Shipyard was purchased and barged to the Point Defiance site where it was remodeled to become the new TYC clubhouse.

By 1934 a road had been carved down to the site and enough slag had been added to the breakwater to provide increased shelter for the moorages. In 1937 the yachtsmen's wives created the shipmates' auxiliary.

In 1941 DeWitt Rowland presented the club with some property above Wollochet Bay, just an hour south by boat through the Tacoma Narrows from Point Defiance. This outstation, surrounded by giant evergreens, was equipped with a cookhouse, showers, and picnic facilities.

Membership continued to grow through the 1940s and 1950s. The 1952 club yearbook listed 436 members and 290 boats. That year the boat basin had been dredged and expanded, and the first Daffodil Weekend had been scheduled. This event, still held near the first of April each year, is sponsored by the club and includes a parade of flower-decorated boats along Ruston Way to downtown Tacoma. It is the Tacoma equivalent of Seattle's Opening Day boat parade.

By the late 1960s many members were discussing the need for a new clubhouse. A bold design was approved, bonds were sold to members, and the building was completed in the fall of 1971. Members formed work parties and replaced all wooden floats with concrete floats.

Now boats move in and out of Commencement Bay all year long. The club schedules fewer summer events (that is when the most cruising or vacationing is going on), but in September the busy season starts with the annual fishing derby. Dances, cruises, and gala winter parties follow. In February many members enter the Bremerton Heavy Weather Race, and in March the TYC hosts a crab feed.

The Tacoma club has joined with sailors from three other regional yacht clubs to form the Tacoma Area Racing Council, which coordinates a fall and winter series of races.

The Oro Bay Outstation has become an increasingly popular rendezvous for club powerboaters.

Today, at the tip of the slag breakwater by the site of the now-defunct smelter sits a large, modern clubhouse. Between the breakwater and the shore are the boathouses and yachts of the Tacoma Yacht Club, a thriving, growing organization that in 1991 counted 710 members, 233 boathouses, and 89 sailboat slips.

—Based on material provided by Billie Kreiner

yachting than Seattle. The sound on one side and Lake Washington on the other, both afford advantages which have only begun to be realized. One year ago there were comparatively few sailing yachts on Lake Washington, but at the present time it only requires a good brisk breeze to bring many small craft from their moorings. . . .

Yesterday afternoon the water was dotted thickly with the white wings, and that in the face of a poor breeze. At one time twenty or more sails were counted, while the rowboats hovered about in all directions.

Not infrequently a boat would shoot by rowed by a young lady who was evidently enjoying a row for the benefit of her health.

SYC's Forgotten Commodores of the 1890s

Commodores who led the Seattle Yacht Club in the 1890s, two decades before the SYC's amalgamation with the Elliott Bay Yacht Club, have been largely forgotten, as have those who served prior to that decade. From mentions found in old newspapers and city directories, it would appear that as early as the 1870s, Seattle yachtsmen were calling fellow members "Commodore." For example, on July 6, 1878, the *Intelligencer* mentions a "Commodore Captain Winsor" in relation to a yacht race, but further information about him has not been found. In 1879 William Hammond was named the commodore of the "new" Seattle Yacht Club. In the 1880s Frederick W. Sparling apparently served as commodore.

In the "Gay '90s," at least three different men served as commodore of the Seattle Yacht Club.

Joseph Green, who became commodore in 1891, was born in England in 1854. He came to America with his parents in 1859, and in years that followed they migrated west, settling in Oakland, California. There young Joe completed high school and business college and worked in his father's produce business.

In 1883, Joe Green moved north to Seattle, population 6,000. He founded a produce business and the next year organized the Northwest Fruit Company, which imported citrus and deciduous fruits and farm products. He expanded his market to include all of Washington State and British Columbia.

Green served in the Seattle Rifles, a local militia group that later became part of the Washington National Guard, and from 1884 through 1891 held the rank of captain in the guard. Hence, the 1891 Seattle newspapers referred to him as "Seattle Yacht Club Commodore Captain Joseph Green."

Fred E. Sander headed the SYC from 1892 to 1895. Mississippi-born, Sander arrived in Seattle in 1879 and within a decade was one of the town's most successful businessmen.

J. H. Johnson, mentioned as commodore in 1895, was a ship captain who, according to McCurdy's Marine History of the Pacific Northwest, died in 1899. He was on a run out of Nome, Alaska, when his ship ran aground in a gale. The seven people aboard escaped to shore but exhausted their provisions during the severe cold and died of exposure and starvation, except for one man who was rescued by the Eskimos and who, six months later, managed to board another ship for civilization and report the story. ◇

Far away is a cedar shell which shoots through the water like an arrow. It is owned by Magnus and A. T. Borelle, who are considered among the best oarsmen on the lake.

On the bay things were also interesting, although the yachts were evidently bound on longer trips than those seen in Lake Washington. Mr. W. C. Heilbron, accompanied by Dr. George Thompson, Mr. T. M. Reed, and Mr. Ross Eckhardt took a sail to Port Blakely in the sloop *Ludlow*. Many of the young men have come to the conclusion that it is much pleasanter to pass Sunday on the water than to stay in the city. With this view yachting parties are formed during the week, and when Saturday afternoon comes provisions and reading matter and other things necessary to a sailor's comfort are brought to the landing and stored away in the boat's cuddy. The sloop *Edna M*, one of the fastest on the sound, usually leaves the harbor Saturday evening, sailing from point to point along the Sound, and returning in time for the opening of business on Monday morning. On board are Mr. W. Barry, Mr. J. A. Jackson, Mr. Seabrandt, Mr. D. Boyd, and Mr. Frank H. Lawton. Mr. Ross Eckhart and Mr. Alex Ranke. . . . Mr. J. F. McNaught makes many trips about the sound in his steam launch *Aquila* and it is a familiar sight to see her sharp prow cleaving the water. . . .

—Post-Intelligencer, *Sept. 7, 1891*

Among the newcomers on the sound were several former residents of Atlantic seaport cities who brought with them a yen for yachting. Admiring the excellent sailing waters but dismayed at the lack of appreciation shown by most local residents, these yachtsmen voiced their enthusiasm in hopes of gaining adherents of the sport they loved.

Among these new residents was D. M. Simonson, a former member of New York sailing groups. According to the *Post-Intelligencer* staffer who interviewed him:

. . . On coming to the sound, he began agitating for a yacht club. In 1889 the club was organized, but inside of a year interest began to lag and it finally died out altogether. The Fourth of July races a year ago revived interest for a time, but it soon died out again. . . .

—Post-Intelligencer, *July 11, 1892*

Simonson, the article continued, found that Puget Sound yachting potential surpassed that of New York and Brooklyn, where a great many people had taken to the sport. He believed that unfamiliarity with yachting was a reason for the dearth of sailing craft on Puget Sound. He explained that many people considered a sailboat dangerous, but those same people did not hesitate to step into a rowboat. Yet a rowboat, he explained, is several times more dangerous than a good sailboat:

Of course it requires some little knowledge to manage a sailboat, and unless this knowledge is possessed, the chances of a sailboat capsizing are much greater than a rowboat. But nearly all sailboats built now have center-boards and are very buoyant, carrying but little ballast, and many of them have airtight cylinders placed around the sides, so that if the boat does capsize, it is buoyed right up, one-third to one-half of it remaining above water. . . .

—Post-Intelligencer, *July 11, 1892*

Simonson suggested that the yacht club accept members "ignorant of skills" in managing a boat and teach them at the expense of the club.

Pierson Haviland was quoted in the same article:

The sound and lake on both sides of our city afford two of the finest and safest yachting waters in this country, and more should be done by our citizens to further this grand sport. We have among us many good yachtsmen and probably the fastest boat on the Sound, besides many other boats which, in their classes, would make strong competitors. Throughout this country today, great attention is being laid to all health-giving sports, two of the foremost being yachting and rowing. With the advantages we have in beautiful and convenient waters, we should have a yachting and rowing club here very soon that will excite the interest and admiration of the citizens of this city.

—Post-Intelligencer, *July 11, 1892*

H. H. Meeker also voiced hope that a club would be organized to attract more young men to the sport. One reason for

Moorage at Frank Faber's Brighton Boathouse at the foot of Battery Street left yachts at the mercy of a southwest wind. (MOHAI)

the lack of success, he explained, stemmed from the fact that some Seattleites have "boats on the lake while others prefer the salt water." Therefore, "no concerted interest could be kept up, neither party being large enough to create much interest alone."

Reorganizing the Seattle Yacht Club

In 1892 the time appeared ripe for the reorganization of yachting groups in the region. D. M. Simonson had recently received an invitation for Seattleites to join a new international racing association being organized by gentlemen in Victoria, B.C., and Fairhaven (later part of Bellingham, Washington). This prompted him to speak to a newspaper reporter about the need for a new Seattle Yacht Club. He was quoted as follows: "An effort will be made in a few days to get the members of the old Seattle Yacht Club and such others as desire to take an active part in yachting together and see if the club cannot be revived." (*Post-Intelligencer*, July 11, 1892)

Another reason for reorganizing the club was that most Seattle boats were tied up at Frank Faber's Brighton Boathouse at the foot of Battery Street. The moorings were strung out to the south because no piers existed north of Pike Street. Former Commodore Ted Geary recalled in an SYC speech in the 1950s: "The lee in a southwest wind was the Great Northern Railway trestle and despite strong moorings, boats occasionally broke loose and were smashed or damaged."

On Aug. 2, 1892, Seattle yachting enthusiasts met in the Bank of Commerce building. Attendance was larger than anticipated because a recent campaign had swelled club membership to 50. At the meeting, an entrance fee of $5 was established for charter members who joined within the next 30 days. At the end of that time, permanent officers would be elected, rules of order prepared, and the amount of monthly dues established.

At a second meeting held a week later at the Young Men's Republican Club in the Bailey Block, four committees were appointed to search for permanent quarters, nominate officers, draft bylaws, and increase membership. In addition, C. P. Blanchard and E. I. Ruddy were appointed delegates to a meeting in Victoria where an international yachting association was to be formed.

During the first week in August, the cutter yacht *American* of Anacortes with a jovial crew visited Seattle. By touring the sound these young men hoped to increase interest in yachting.

> Sailing has had full swing during the last few days and all the old yachtsmen of New York Harbor, Narragansett Bay, Long Island Sound and Boston Harbor have become enthused again and are fully ripe for the organization of a successful yacht club. The anticipations of D. M. Simonson, one of the old standbys of the home club, an old Brooklyn Club member, and the Nestor in the sport, are about to be realized. Seattle is to have one of the strongest, richest, and gamiest [sic] clubs on the Sound and thus, in addition to being the commercial center, will surely become the largest center of sailing craft on the Sound, and the leader in all regattas and cruising. . . .
>
> —Post-Intelligencer, *Aug. 8, 1892*

Seattle Yacht Club members entertained the visitors from Anacortes. G. V. Johnson took them for a sail in his sloop *Hettie Bell.* Then Captain R. W. Riddle invited them to ride his smart little steamer to Madison Park. Those aboard were C. P. Blanchard, D. M. Simonson, E. I. Ruddy, Amos Brown, and A. W. Barr, all of Seattle; D. M. Tomblin, who was visiting from San Francisco; and the Anacortes crew of the *American*—W. R. Hagan, F. H. Boynton, W. V. Gilbranson, Eugene Shrewsbury, Homer Shrewsbury, and G. A. Carpenter.

That evening, the visitors invited their hosts on board for a sail. To the above Seattle group were added: O. A. Spencer, J. A. Johnson, M. Sawyer, and *Post-Intelligencer* reporter John F. Cronin. The next day the *American* sailed on to Tacoma to promote yachting there.

On Sept. 3, 1892, during a meeting at Red Men's Hall, permanent officers were chosen to lead the new Seattle Yacht Club. Fred E. Sander was elected commodore; J. H. Johnson, vice commodore; Carl Siebrand, port captain; W. W. French, secretary; and A. R. Pickney, treasurer. The members voted to incorporate the club and issue 200 shares of stock at $5 each. The first 200 to pay the $5 membership fee would be considered charter members. After the time for charter memberships elapsed, the initiation fee would jump to $25. Dues were set at $1 per month. Annual meetings were scheduled for the second Tuesday in October.

Three members—R. R. Spencer, Amos Brown, and J. H. Johnson—were given the duty of incorporating the club. Charles Lovejoy, R. T. Englebrecht, and J. R. Hayden, Jr., were appointed to assist the efforts of the ways and means committee in meeting expenses for the upcoming Northwest International Yachting Association Regatta. James Leddy and Charles Lovejoy were elected members of the legal committee. D. A. Spencer, A. Earle, and J. R. Hayden, Jr., were named to the house committee. Carl Siebrand was officially thanked for furnishing the plans for the proposed clubhouse.

The members accepted the offer of the steamer *Wasco* as a flagship to be used by the commodore and the guests at the coming regatta.

The committee assigned to find a site for a boathouse reported that the best offer came from the West Seattle Land and Improvement Company, which for $1 a year would provide a 200-foot strip of waterfront located a short distance southeast of Duwamish Head on the inside harbor.

J. A. Baillargeon and SYC Commodore Fred Sander purchased a float and boathouse from Frank Faber which they towed to the West Seattle site. The moorage area was established in 125 feet of water. A ten-cent, half-hour ferry ride from the foot of Yesler Way to the West Seattle

The Seattle Yacht Club's towered clubhouse, built in 1892, nestled against the base of Duwamish Head. This 1908 photo shows Luna Park to the right. (PSMHS)

dock placed the commuter only a short walk from the yacht club.

Former Commodore Ted Geary in the 1950s reminisced about those events of more than a half-century earlier.

> The fleet and personnel at the new club included the 60-foot schooner *Henrietta* owned by George U. Piper, publisher of the *Post-Intelligencer*; the 42-foot schooner *Drift* owned by Fred S. Stimson; the 50-foot cutter *Falcon*, designed, built, and owned by Harvey Nugent; the 48-foot cutter *Kelpie* owned by J. A. Baillargeon, Fred E. Sander, law professor Dean Condon of the University of Washington and Frank Foster, the perennial secretary of the yacht club. There were no powerboats in those days except for a few naphtha launches and the 70-foot steam yacht *Xanthus*, owned by the Seattle pioneer Coleman family which also owned the Coleman Building and the Iron Works which bore their name. These powerboats were based on Lake Washington.
>
> C. D. Stimson, then owner of the 32-foot sloop *Evelyn May* kept his smaller boat on the Seattle side, as did Dr. George E. Thompson, owner of a pointed scow sloop similar to flatties but larger and faster, being 23 feet long. Ted Hinkling, owner of a Seattle laundry, had a duplicate boat and these two were enthusiastic competitors in some hot match races.
>
> —*Ted Geary, 1950s*

The First SYC Clubhouse

For the new West Seattle site the board of trustees authorized a clubhouse which was to cost no more than $3,000. To assure funding, yearly membership dues of $12 were collected in advance. Admission fees already paid by 194 members would provide the remainder of the funding. If possible, the clubhouse was to be completed by the time of the first Northwest International Yachting Association Regatta scheduled for Seattle in the fall (it was not completed in time). The two-story structure with tower had hardly opened before many members concluded the location was inconvenient. A few years later this original club building stood vacant.

Fourth of July Races

The *Post-Intelligencer* carried a lengthy article about the July 4 events under the headline "Very Exciting Yacht Race." After the steamer *Chinook* carried the judges to the course, some time was lost. It was 11:50 A.M. before the three whistles notified the boats to get ready. Then a calm hit the sound, forcing some of the skippers to unlimber their oars, when:

> . . . suddenly the coveted breeze filled the *Chet*'s sails and she seemed to fly. . . . The *Leota* was the first to pass the line and the *Chet* was second, but the time allowance was so much in the latter's favor that she was given first prize. The *Albatross* really made the best time of all and took first prize in second class. As the boats came in every boat in the harbor set up a shrill whistle, all the spectators shouted for their favorite and the most intense excitement prevailed.
>
> —Post-Intelligencer, *July 5, 1892*

Of the sloops, the *Edna M* (belonging to J. F. Hawkins) won first prize, a fine pair of field glasses. Of the "jib and mainsail" racing boats, *Chet* (A. M. Towle) received the first prize of $35. In the catboat race, *Albatross* (George Budlong) received the $25 first prize.

The two rowing races on the 1892 regatta schedule can be considered the precursors of the Opening Day crew races through the Montlake cut that became traditional a half-century later. These 1892 races were from Schwabacher's Wharf to the city buoy. The two crews (12 oarsmen each with coxswain) in Charleston cutters were well matched. The winning boat won by scarcely two feet, and the dozen crewmen split the $50 prize. Ensign W. S. Burke acted as referee in the race, and to the losers he presented a box of cigars.

A "free-for-all" race attracted eight boats, each pulled by two oarsmen. A pair of burly longshoremen in a boat rented from Towle's Boathouse claimed the $25 prize.

First Fairhaven Regatta

On Aug. 25, 1892, the Fairhaven Yacht Club hosted its first regatta on Bellingham Bay. Of the 15 entries from Tacoma, Seattle, Port Townsend, Victoria, Anacortes, Fairhaven, and Whatcom, the winners were *Hettie Bell* of Seattle, *Ripple* of Fairhaven, *Hornet* of Whatcom, and *Wanda* of Fairhaven.

The next day, the Fairhaven club invited the fastest racers to try again. This time, before a stiffer wind, the *Hornet* sped in first, two minutes ahead of the *Hettie Bell*, with *Ripple* running a close third.

That evening the yachtsmen assembled officially to organize the Northwest International Yachting Association (NIYA). Seattle was chosen as the site for their first official regatta.

The First International Sailing Regatta

Oct. 3, 1892, became an historic day in Pacific Northwest yachting. The first regatta under the auspices of the new NIYA was hosted by the new Seattle Yacht Club, which at that time could boast more than 200 members and a clubhouse under construction in West Seattle.

The regatta was promoted widely in newspapers around the sound. Because the international racing association had not completed its organization, the event was officially raced under three commissioners from the Seattle Yacht Club—Captain J. A. Hatfield, D. M. Simonson, and Amos Brown.

Rules for the race were adopted, as follows:

- All yachts are to gather at 9:00 A.M. off the West Seattle club site for inspection, classification, and numbering.
- The course is to run from an imaginary line drawn from the bell buoy off Duwamish Head to a flag buoy anchored in a northwesterly direction therefrom; thence to and around a flag buoy anchored off West Point lighthouse, thence to and around a flag buoy anchored off Blakely Rock, thence to and across the starting line off Duwamish Head, leaving all flag buoys on the port side. The course would be reversed if the committee deemed such advisable.
- Yachts are to be segregated into three classes. First class: schooners, sloops and cutters with cabins and standing ballast. Second class: open boats over 20 feet, corrected length. Third class: open boats under 20 feet, corrected length. Mea-

surement figured under twenty feet, corrected length. Measurement figured the mean between the length on the load water line and length over all. Time allowance was three seconds per foot to the mile.

- For the cabin boats, the crew should not exceed one man for each five feet or fraction thereof in length in addition to the helmsman; and for open boats, helmsman plus one crewman for each four feet of fraction thereof in length.

—Post-Intelligencer, *Oct. 3, 1892*

Because the listings are available from old newspapers, it is possible to name the entrants of that first NIYA Regatta of Oct. 6, 1892:

First Class [all were sloops but the two cutters, *Petrel* and *American*]:
Edna M (Seattle, Carl Siebrand)
Petrel (Victoria, Commodore Foote)
Thistle (Seattle, J. Dunlap)
McLaren (Tacoma, P. Savery)
Marjory (Seattle, G. H. Heilbron)
Francel (Port Townsend, Admiral Barneson)
Constance (Tacoma, F. W. Snow)
American (Seattle, A. B. Kibbe)

Second Class [all were jib and mainsail]:
Chet (Seattle, A. M. Towle)
Hettie Bell (Seattle, Johnson and Son)
Ancel (Anacortes, R. E. Trafton)
Idlewild (Seattle, French Brothers)
Wanda (Fairhaven, M. Bierdorf)
Ripple (Fairhaven, O. H. Garland)
Hornet (Whatcom, Captain Simpson)
Essie Tittell (Seattle, Fabre and Hartung)

Third Class [both were jib and mainsail]:
Bremerton (Seattle, W. Hensel)
Petrel (Seattle, Clark and Bartlett)

—Post-Intelligencer, *Oct. 7, 1892*

On the evening of Oct. 6, 1892, the Northwest International Yachting Association met in the Grand Hotel in Seattle to continue organizing.

The following were elected officers: president, E. B. Leaming, Whatcom; vice president, C. P. Blanchard, Seattle; treasurer, H. R. Foote, Victoria; secretary, Arthur Gamwell, Fairhaven. The executive committeemen elected were John Barneson of Port Townsend, F. A. Boynton of Anacortes and C. B. Hurley of Tacoma. Delegates to the next annual meeting were C. P. Blanchard and E. I. Ruddy of Seattle; C. B. Hurley, F. W. Snow, and M. M. Smith of Tacoma; J. P. Nelson and F. H. Boynton of Anacortes; A. H. Clark and Arthur Gamwell of Fairhaven; J. L. Byron and E. B. Leaming of Whatcom. The following were elected fleet officers: admiral, John Barneson of Port Townsend; vice-admiral, W. H. Cushman of Tacoma; commodore, H. R. Foote of Victoria; vice-commodore, J. P. Nelson of Anacortes; fleet captain, W. C. Heilbron of Seattle.

Before the close of the meeting, after several amendments were considered, a constitution and bylaws were adopted.

Weather Fails the First Regatta

This first international regatta at Seattle had to be scrubbed after three days of weather problems. On the first day, because of the lack of wind, none of the boats completed the race within the maximum time allowed.

On the second day three additional Seattle boats entered the races: the schooner *Rainier*, owned by W. C. Heilbron, and the *Vernia*, owned by Ira Bronson, entered in first class, and the *Lorna Doone*, owned by J. H. Johnson, entered in second class. Again the wind failed.

After the second windless day, some of the yachtsmen became anxious about the need to return home to business. John Barneson tied his sloop *Francel* to a steamer bound for his home port of Port Townsend, but *Francel* plowed her nose under water, forcing Barneson to cast her loose and return to Seattle. On the third day, Oct. 7, 1892, a fog rolled in, and this first international yachting event was canceled.

The original plan had called for the winner of each NIYA race to receive a first-place cup and for second- and third-place winners to receive cash awards. Some yachtsmen complained that the money was a better prize than the silver cups and feared that the competitors might try for second or third rather than first. However, since the race was canceled, the problem was temporarily avoided.

The Seattle Yacht Club race, originally scheduled for the second day of the regatta, was rescheduled for Oct. 8, 1892, which dawned clear and breezy. First prizes of $50 were awarded to the *McLaren*, raced in first class by P. Savery of Tacoma, and the *Ripple*, sailed in second class by S. G. McKay of Fairhaven. Second prizes of $30 each went to the *Edna M*, captained by Carl Siebrand of Seattle, and the *Wanda,* captained by C. T. Redfield of Fairhaven. Apparently the prize money was raised by charging entrance fees.

Sailing on the Lake

In 1892, for the first time, races on Lake Washington were mentioned in the *Post-Intelligencer* (Aug. 3 and 5, 1892). On Aug. 5, the *Idlewild* (W. W. and F. F. French) defeated the *Hettie Bell* (G. V. Johnson) in a two-boat, Lake Washington contest. Both yachts had previously raced on Elliott Bay, and the *Hettie Bell* on Aug. 26 raced at Fairhaven, which raises the question of how they were transported from saltwater to the lake or vice versa. Most likely, they were towed up the Duwamish and Black rivers. (When the ship canal opened in 1917, Lake Washington was lowered by about eight feet. Until then the Black River, which flowed to the Duwamish, served as the outlet at the south end of Lake Washington.) The yachts might have been hauled from the sound to Lake Washington on railroad cars or on wagons, but this is doubtful.

Cruising in '92

One of the first articles describing pleasure cruising appeared in the Oct. 2, 1892, *Post-Intelligencer*. It explained that SYC members George D. Ruddy, David Boyd, and H. M. Burpee for 10 days enjoyed life aboard the *Edna M* with Captain Jensen. They spent the first night off Edmonds, the second at Port Townsend and then headed for Victoria in a night passage, arriving at 11:00 P.M. There they stayed several days, were royally entertained by the Victorians, and enjoyed a concert at Beacon Hill Park by the band of the French flagship *La Dubourdieu*, then undergoing repairs at Esquimalt. The Seattle sailors returned by way of the San Juan Islands, anchored off Anacortes, passed through a gale to spend another night at Port Townsend, then moved on to Mukilteo, where the crew awoke to find their anchor had dragged nearly two miles while they slept. From there they returned to Seattle, eager to share their experiences.

1893

Two successful regattas were staged in 1893. The first, at Victoria on May 21, honored Queen Victoria on her 75th birthday. A panoply of activities typical of the times provided entertainment. Baseball and cricket matches drew large crowds, and representatives from several towns contested for prizes in trapshooting, track and field events, and bicycle racing.

Twenty-four yachts entered the Victoria regatta. Fifteen of these (eight from Seattle, two from Tacoma, and five from Port Townsend) crossed the Strait of Juan de Fuca as a flotilla the day before the races.

In first class, the 41-foot sloop *Gracie Felitz*, built and owned by Captain Towle of Seattle, was the winner. The *Myth* of Whatcom won in second class.

The Northwest International Yachting Association race was sailed at Port Townsend on the Fourth of July. In those more formal days, at midnight July 3,

The Royal Victoria Yacht Club

By 1876 sailing races had become a key part of Victoria, B.C.'s annual celebration of Queen Victoria's birthday. But no one thought about forming a yacht club until 1892 when four boats from newly formed clubs in Anacortes, Bellingham, and Seattle sailed into the harbor, announced their intention to challenge the local fleet and made off with all the top prizes. Galvanized into action, local yachtsmen met on June 8, 1892, to form the Victoria Yacht Club. They had one goal in mind—to organize a fleet capable of humbling the Americans at their races on July 4. That objective proved to be beyond their grasp. However, two members of the Victoria club were on hand in August when the Northwest International Yachting Association was formed. And over the next few years, continuing rivalry with American clubs ensured that the Victoria Yacht Club would thrive and grow.

In 1895 a floating clubhouse was launched on Victoria's Inner Harbour. An elegant twin-towered little building, the clubhouse sank three times, and after its foreshore lease expired, members quite sensibly chose to acquire a waterfront lot. But while the land-based clubhouse proved to be more secure, the boats moored at its float found themselves threatened by the wash from ever-increasing harbor traffic and by the fumes from the nearby chemical works.

By 1912 the club was on the move again. Encouraged by speculators who were turning acres of farmland into a planned "garden community," the club acquired an acre of land on the waterfront at Cadboro Bay and became the centerpiece of the Uplands development. With its prestigious new location and the added eclat of the Royal Warrant granted to the club in 1911, membership in the Royal Victoria Yacht Club grew apace, and the city's elite were in attendance for the opening of the new clubhouse in 1913. Designed by architect and club member Bill Rochfort, the building continues to serve as the clubhouse to this day.

During World War I, with more than a quarter of its members on active service, the yacht club had to struggle to survive. And even after the war, with the city gripped by an economic depression, recovery was agonizingly slow. The club had only just found its feet when World War II sent it reeling, with 115 younger members volunteering for active service and with older members patrolling the waterfront in the citizens' powerboat squadron.

In the years following the war, the club experienced steady growth. As the number and size of boats increased, members came to grips with the fact that Cadboro Bay is dangerously exposed to winter gales. A breakwater, completed in 1972, now allows for year-round moorage of almost 300 boats. Eighty-five additional spaces are provided at the Tsehum Haven Outstation established 10 years earlier.

The Royal Victoria Yacht Club retains its devotion to sail (the current ratio of sail to power is 4:1). Likewise the club remains dedicated to competition—whatever the weather. Even the bleak months of January and February can find as many as 17 scheduled events.

The club has played host to many national and international events, but it is perhaps best known for hosting and organizing the Swiftsure Lightship Classic—the premier annual yachting event in the Pacific Northwest.

While it enjoys a special relationship with other "Royal" clubs around the world, the RVYC also has reciprocal privileges with over 50 American clubs in Washington, Oregon, California, and Hawaii.

The Royal Victoria Yacht Club—the oldest sailing club on Canada's Pacific coast—is delighted to share its centennial with the Seattle Yacht Club. ◇

more than 100 yachtsmen gathered at the Key City Club to hear welcoming speeches by NIYA President Libbey and NIYA Commodore Barneson. After a "bounteous repast," speeches in response were delivered by yacht club Commodores Foote of Victoria, Sander of Seattle, and Leaming of Whatcom and SYC member Theodore Haller, a noted orator.

For the first time, the newspapers listed the crews of the Seattle boats.

Xora, Captain: H. Hensel; Crew: Jacob Wall, C. F. Cawley, F. I. Pearl, W. Hensel, C. Christopher.

Marjory, Captain: George Heilbron; Crew: Bernard Pelly, W. A. Peters, D. A. Brock.

Idlewild, Captain: Stewart; Crew: Will French, J. Dunlap, J. C. Allen, Fred French, David Boyd, W. C. Harrison.

Kelpie, Captain: Commodore Sander; Crew: J. H. Hayden Jr., Albert Brawn, J. A. Hatfield, Carl Siebrand, Ed Nicholls.

Earl, Captain: Amos Goodell; Crew: T. E. Drake, George Brown, C. Green.

Comet, Captain: Joe Fellows; Crew: Ed Dow, Joe Brown, Bert Chapman.

Gracie Felitz, Captain: A. M. Towle;

Fred E. Sander

The 1893–95 Commodore of the Seattle Yacht Club

The Seattle Yacht Club commodores who served before the 1909 merger of Seattle and Elliott Bay yacht clubs are not included among the portraits in the Commodore's Room. However, those from the Elliott Bay club are included. Fred Sander has been all but forgotten even though he served as commodore of the Seattle Yacht Club some 16 years before the two clubs merged.

Fred Sander was born in Corinth, Mississippi, in 1854. After the Civil War, while in his early teens, he went to sea. In 1869 he sailed into Elliott Bay for the first time and immediately liked the small town he found nestled on the shore. He returned in 1879 and was employed as a bookkeeper at the Stetson and Post Mill.

By 1887 Sander was involved in building street railways and soon owned cable lines on Yesler Way and Jackson Street and built the Grant Street line to South Seattle. With others he invested in the James Street and Front Street (First Avenue) cable lines. He built part of the Seattle-Tacoma Interurban and the Seattle-Everett Interurban. In 1886, he erected the plant of the Washington Electric Company, which generated some of the first power for lighting purposes.

The financial panic of 1893 caused him great losses, but within a few years he had recouped his fortune thanks to wise investments in real estate. He was said to have handled more property transactions than any other Seattleite at that time.

In 1900, he formed the Fred E. Sander Corporation where he served as president; his wife Nellie was vice president, and their son Henry was secretary-treasurer. Fred Sander was a stockholder in several financial institutions and belonged to many clubs, including the Elks, Masons, Knights of Pythias, Ancient Order of United Workmen, the Lotus and Salmigundi clubs of New York, and the Seattle Golf and Country, Arctic, and Rainier clubs. His son Henry was also a longtime Seattle Yacht Club member. ◇

Crew: F. D. Ogden, Will D. Wilson, George A. Newman, John Allen.

—Post-Intelligencer, *July 4, 1893*

Gracie Felitz beat out three contestants to win in Class A. *Myth* of Fairhaven won the Class B competition over seven others, and *Hettie Bell* of Port Townsend crossed the finish line before the three other entries in the Class C race. (She had recently been sold to Port Townsend Yacht Club Commodore John Barneson by G. V. Johnson of Seattle for $300.) The *Bremerton* won over two other flatties in Class D.

A Major Recession

In 1893 a British banking house called Baring Brothers failed, causing British investors to unload American securities. The result was a gold drain that brought the New York Stock Exchange crashing downward, triggering a severe depression.

Mass unemployment and economic distress moved westward across the country. In 1894, Populist Jacob S. Coxey of Ohio called for the unemployed ("Coxey's Army") to march upon the nation's capital and demand relief and a public-works program. Hundreds of Puget Sound residents gathered at Puyallup to demand free rail transport but were rebuffed by the Northern Pacific. A few hopped freight cars and headed east, but after Coxey and two other leaders were arrested in Washington, D.C., for trespassing on the Capitol grounds, the effort was disbanded.

It was a difficult time all across the country. The amount of cash in circulation continued to diminish. Fewer yachts were seen during these difficult years. Then in 1897, the Alaska Gold Rush began, and Seattle became the supply center for thousands of miners heading north. The grip of the depression was quickly broken.

NIYA Regatta of 1894

The Northwest International Yachting Association Regatta on Bellingham Bay on July 4, 1894, was a bust. Shortly after the races started, the boats were becalmed near Point Frisco, and the event was canceled.

The next day, the NIYA race was combined with the locally sponsored Bellingham Bay Regatta. A stiff breeze sped the 19 contestants around the course. Winners were:

Class A (five entries): *Xora* of Seattle and *Josephine* of Everett.

Class B (shifting ballast, two entries): *Myth* and *Lulu*, both of Whatcom.

Class B (standing ballast, eight entries): *McLaren* of Tacoma and *Eddie McKay* of Fairhaven.

Class C (four entries): *Garland* of Fairhaven and *Daisy Bell* of Victoria. (The latter was described as a "skimming dish" with a four-inch draft.)

Seattle-area papers noted unhappily that Seattle boats won only one first prize, while Bellingham Bay boats took three.

Founding of the Elliott Bay Yacht Club

In spite of depressed times, a noteworthy event occurred in 1894 when a new yacht club was founded. Years later, Ted Geary explained how it came about.

In 1892 when the larger yachts moved to West Seattle, a number of yachtsmen, particularly the small boat owners who were not in favor of the expense and fearful of the location, elected to withdraw and stay with the old location at the foot of Battery Street. They organized the Elliott Bay Yacht Club, stayed at the moorings and rented an upstairs room in Brighton Boathouse. This gave easy access to their boats. . . . Not having paid hands, they could get to their boats in windy weather by bicycle or street car to check their mooring lines, etc. Henry Hensel, Seattle jeweler, had the largest boat remaining at Battery Street, the 45-foot *Xora*, so he was chosen the first commodore.

—Ted Geary, 1950s

As explained in the *Post-Intelligencer* the following day, this "lively group" organized on July 25, 1894.

> About 40 men who are interested in aquatic sports met at the Brighton Boathouse in North Seattle last evening and formed what is to be known as the Elliott Bay Yacht Club. The boathouse in which the meeting was held is to be the headquarters and the upper floor will be fitted to suit the conveniences of the club members. The following officers were elected: commodore, Henry Hensel; vice commodore, A. M. Towle; treasurer, Amos Brown; secretary, R. J. McClelland; house committee, S. Rothy, William Hensel, M. Lang; club measurer, Amos Goodall; trustees, Henry Hensel, A. M. Towle, D. M. Simonson, Hugh Graff, John Mungall.
>
> —Post-Intelligencer, *Aug. 26, 1894*

About 50 men and 26 yachts formed the nucleus of the new club, and they began planning immediately for a Labor Day Regatta which would become an annual event. The race was open to all Northwest boats, and the course extended from the Brighton Boathouse to Four-Mile Rock, then to the Bell Buoy off Duwamish Head, then to the ship buoy off the Oregon Improvement Company coal bunkers near the foot of Jackson Street, then back to the clubhouse. The course came to an estimated 14 nautical miles.

The 15 prizes included the *Press-Times* Challenge Cup, a spirit compass, a mariner's glass, ensigns, pennants, and anchors.

Nineteen boats entered the various races. In Class One, Henry Hensel's *Xora* won first. In Class Two, the cat sloop *Truant*, owned by Fred F. Billings, came in first. Both these boats raced under the colors of the Elliott Bay Yacht Club. Of Class Three sloops, the *Petrel* of Clark and Bartlett was swiftest, and in Class Four, the yacht sloop *Mermaid*, belonging to W. F. Farr, won. Both smaller sloops raced unaffiliated with any club.

A final noteworthy event of 1894 was mentioned in Clarence Bagley's book:

> With the appearance of gasoline engines in 1894, a new field opened to Seattle shipbuilders. Gas made small motor driven pleasure boats possible and many beautiful and serviceable vessels have since been built in the city. About this time Ballard [then a separate town] took first place among Puget Sound localities building small boats—a place she has ever since occupied.
>
> —*Clarence Bagley,* History of Seattle

1895

On July 4, the NIYA races were hosted by the Seattle Yacht Club but were held on the Elliott Bay Yacht Club course. The new Elliott Bay club had officially joined the international group at the annual meeting the night before.

A committee of J. H. Johnson and I. A. Nadeau of the Seattle Yacht Club, and Henry Hensel of the Elliott Bay Club had worked up a special event for the evening after the races—a parade of boats alight with Chinese lanterns. Fred E. Sander was appointed special commander of this illuminated fleet. All yachts, with paper lanterns swinging from stem to stern, were towed at twilight to the starting point. Fireworks costing $1,000 were distributed to the yachts, all to be fired off on signal. An estimated 5,000 persons gathered on the shore to watch. Then just as the parade began to move, a stiff breeze extinguished the candles in the lanterns. Even though the yacht owners had gone to the expense of canvassing their boats to protect them from fire, the rising breeze caused the fireworks display to be canceled also. The disappointed spectators quickly dispersed.

NIYA Regatta officials precipitated a major dispute when they barred the *Myth* from the July 4 races. The *Post-Intelligencer* explained:

> It is a foregone conclusion that it is a waste of time and expense for any boat on Puget Sound to compete with her except, possibly, in a cyclone. The matter places the clubs in a very embarrassing position, as it

A regatta off Port Townsend in the 1890s. (MOHAI)

> does not look like etiquet [sic], to say the least, to bar any yacht that comes here to race, but rumor again has it that this class of boat is not allowed to enter any of the eastern races.
>
> —Post-Intelligencer, *July 8, 1895*

The reason given by the officials was that the *Myth* was built for racing only, and that while she had a cabin, it had been added for the sake of formal compliance and was of no practical use.

New rules were adopted for the Elliott Bay club's Labor Day races, which put cruising yachts on equal terms with light draft boats commonly known as skimming dishes and racing machines. This was a clear indication that handicapping had arrived in the Pacific Northwest. The action taken was obviously aimed at the *Myth* of Whatcom and the *Hettie Bell* of Victoria. Lee Coolidge, the Elliott Bay Yacht Club measurer, explained that these new rules were in use elsewhere, the hull depth measurement in England and the sail square root measurement on the Atlantic Coast. He concluded that these rules would put full-bodied cruising boats on equal terms with light craft boats built for racing.

The Labor Day Races were sailed beneath glorious skies. Four raced in first class. The *Xora*, owned by EBYC Commodore Hensel came in first. In second class, of the six entrants, *Truant*, *McLaren*, and *White Star* placed. In third class, *Dolphin* finished first. In fourth class, the Victoria club's *Flora* won.

E. F. Sweeney's palatial steam yacht *Aggie* and other large craft followed the racers around the course.

1896

Port Townsend hosted the July 4, 1896, NIYA Regatta. Under the new measurement rules, "skimmer-type" boats were equalized with true cruisers.

Ten clubs had now joined NIYA—Seattle, Elliott Bay, Port Townsend, Tacoma, Everett, Port Angeles, Whatcom, Fairhaven, Coupeville, and Victoria.

Of the eight races over the two days, the Elliott Bay Yacht Club boats won four firsts and one second.

The *Xora* sailed off with first prizes

in both the Key City and NIYA Class A races. In Class B the *Hettie Bell* took a first and was on her way to a second win when she lost the cringle from the tack of her mainsail. She limped to a second-place finish.

The 1896 Labor Day races of the Elliott Bay club were described in the *Post-Intelligencer*:

> The most glorious yacht races ever sailed in this harbor. Every foot of the course laid out by the Elliott Bay Yacht Club was contested hotly and the sight of twenty-two yachts careening with the strong breeze will not be soon forgotten. The crews were picked men and laid down to their work like true sailors.
>
> —Post-Intelligencer, *Sept. 8, 1896*

The Class A winners were *Gracie Felitz*, owned and commanded by A. M. Towle, followed by the *Xora*, the yacht of Henry Hensel. In Class B, *Falcon*, owned by John Nelson, took first, and *White Star*, belonging to S. B. Stewart, placed second. The Class C race was rerun because the crew of the *Kaleta* stopped to rescue the crew of the *Lucinda*, which had capsized. As one *Post-Intelligencer* reporter said, "When sails are frisky, a blow is brewing." In special class, George Thompson's *Imp* beat the *Chispa* of Edward Hickling.

1897

The July 1, 1897, NIYA Regatta was curtailed by gale winds. Of the 19 entries, only five dared compete: *Falcon*, *White Star*, and *Pilgrim* in second class; only the *Kelpie* ran the course for the first class prize; and *Evelyn May*, originally built for C. W. Stimson, won in third class. No fourth class boats ventured out in the rough seas.

The Labor Day race of the Elliott Bay Yacht Club was won by *Kelpie* in first class, *Truant* in second class, *Kaleta* in third class, and *Little Champion* in fourth class.

By the end of the year, most of the Seattle Yacht Club members had returned to moorages on the east side of the bay, leaving the clubhouse and site at West Seattle all but abandoned. The Seattle and Elliott Bay clubs coexisted, occupying much the same mooring area and centering activities at Battery Street, yet they maintained separate identities.

The sloop Kelpie *won many races in the 1890s. Here she is in drydock at Port Blakely. (SYC Historical Collection)*

Again, to quote Ted Geary:

> Across the Bay SYC was having trouble. The steamer *Flyer*, a really fast Tacoma passenger boat of the day threw big swells into the mooring grounds, frequently washing the dinghies off the float. There were other troubles and by 1897 most of the fleet had trickled back to the old location and the House and site at West Seattle were abandoned.
>
> About this time, the EBYC fleet was as follows: *Kaleta*, a 21-foot sandbagger with about an 11-foot beam, 19-foot bowsprit, and a mainboom overhang to watch, which carried a crew of ten, each with two 50-pound sandbags to lug to weather on each tack; the two 23-foot racing scows *Calista* and *Lucinda*, a pair of large fast centerboarders owned by Dave Boyd and John Munga; and a 32-foot strip-built cedar clipper bow and sloop by Eugene Thurlow. This boat was still sailing at age 50.
>
> The 32-foot plumb steam sloop *Motor*

was owned by C. H. Harper and W. S. Geary [Ted's father]. About this time Dr. Thompson brought the 50-foot fast sloop *Hornet* down from Bellingham. She capsized in the first race and all hands got a good scare as she was sinking from inside ballast, but a passing purse seiner threw her net around her and saved boat and crew. Dr. Thompson put a ballasted fin keel on her and discarded inside ballast as did all large center board boats hereabout after that experience. *Lucinda* also capsized in that race and sank in Elliott Bay, but the crew, including my father, was rescued by the steamer *Flyer*.

—Ted Geary, 1950s

Another event of note in 1897: Many avid teenaged boaters moored their vessels near Brighton Boathouse—among them George H. Wayland, Lloyd B. and Dean Johnson, Ted Geary, Bert Griffiths, Frank and Charles Newman, Orlo Peterson, James and Frank Griffiths, Jesse Hall, and Ed Burdett. Their boats crowded the moorage. Neither the Seattle nor Elliott Bay club allowed memberships for those under 21. The young men held a meeting, assessed themselves $1 each and created

Anecdotes of the Times: 1897

In 1897 I was 11 and Lloyd B. Johnson was 12. He and I built a nine-foot by three-foot canoe with which we sailed and paddled all over Elliott Bay. A nice day's cruise was from Seattle to the Duwamish Head bell buoy where we would tie up, open ship's stores of a one-pound nickel can of salmon and a nickel's worth of crackers, have a feed, and paddle or sail on back.

Our first boat was soon stolen from its mooring under the dock at the foot of Madison Street. Lloyd then acquired a 16-foot sailing canoe with folding centerboard, and I crewed for him as we circumnavigated Seattle by water when the town was bounded on the north by separate towns of Ballard and Fremont, on the east by Lake Washington and on the south by the Duwamish River and the townships of Renton, Georgetown, and West Seattle.

Starting early one morning from Budlong's Boat House on Lake Union, at what is now Fairfax and Galer, we paddled to the portage about where the SYC docks are now. Many will remember when Lake Washington was ten feet above Lake Union and the drainage canal ended in a wooden flume about 200 feet south of the present SYC clubhouse. This flume was built to shoot logs from Lake Washington into a booming ground in Portage Bay and some of us used to shoot it in canoes and rowboats borrowed from Budlong's.

We carried the canoe to the head of the flume, paddled into Lake Washington and sailed fast to the south end of the lake into the Black River, which drained out of the lake in those days before the lowering. We paddled down the Black to the Duwamish and on to Elliott Bay to the foot of Battery Street, arriving at 8:00 P.M., slept on the boathouse deck, and next morning paddled out around West Point, through Salmon Bay and up the creek that is now the Lake Washington Ship Canal, portaged over the Brace and Hergert Sawmill property on the Fremont side about where the Fremont Bridge now stands and arrived back at Budlong's on Lake Union at 2:00 P.M.

—Ted Geary, 1950s

the first Queen City Yacht Club, an unincorporated volunteer organization that met at Oscar Laurence's boathouse. This organization expired a few years later when EBYC arranged for junior memberships.

1898

The results of the July 4, 1898, race were not reported, but the Labor Day race winners were as follows: Of seven boats entered in the first class race, *Kelpie* crossed the finish line first but was disqualified for sailing the wrong course, so *Daphne* was declared the winner followed by *Falcon*; in second class, *Idlewild* and *Hornet* won first and second; in third class, the winners were *Windward* of Tacoma and *Evelyn May*; fourth class honors went to *Chispa* and *Imp*.

Of all the boats the stout-hearted *Hornet* crew received special mention:

> The *Hornet*, Commodore Thompson's smart little sloop, capsized soon after turning West Point buoy. She was carrying every inch of canvas and while heeling over, her main boom dragged in the water, tipping and upsetting her. The sails kept her from turning over and allowed the crew to find a safe place on her upturned side rail. A fishing boat was close by when the *Hornet* keeled over, and with the assistance of the fishermen the crew got the sloop righted, bailed her out, and sailed into the clubhouse reefed, amid loud cheers. As the *Paloma* had not finished, the plucky crew of the *Hornet* went over the balance of the course and got second prize.
>
> —Post-Intelligencer, *Sept. 6, 1898*

1899

The annual NIYA races attracted "24 craft commanded by the most skilled skippers on the sound," according to the *Post-Intelligencer* of July 4, 1899. Four-and-a-half hours after the start of the Elliott Bay club-hosted event, all but five of the yachts were moored at the clubhouse. The final five ran out of wind and drifted home in the early dusk.

In first class, the *Jubilee* of Victoria, owned by Captain C. H. Collins (who was described as a man "who had money enough to build an international cup defender and skill to navigate it to the honor of his country") might have won the cup had it not slightly brushed the starting buoy. The judges did not notice the foul, so Collins sailed back to round the buoy a second time but lost to *Lavita*, a new 44-foot cutter that had been built by Charles Abernathy and a syndicate of

The Olympia Yacht Club

The Olympia Yacht Club, the third oldest yacht club in the Puget Sound area, was founded in 1898 as "The Olympia Boating Club." The name was changed to Olympia Yacht Club in 1904.

The main station is located at 201 North Simmons Street in Olympia, and the one outstation, known as Island Home, is located in Pickering Pass, Mason County, less than a mile south of the Hartstene Island Bridge.

In 1991 the Olympia Yacht Club counted 351 members and 271 boats. The main station has 230 moorage slips.

Regular dinner meetings are scheduled at the clubhouse on the first Wednesday of every month from September through June. The board meets on the third Wednesday of every month.

Among races sponsored by OYC are the Toliva Shoal Race (sail), and The Governor's Cup Race and the Tacoma/Olympia Challenge Race (power).

One special event, sponsored annually by OYC, the Olympia chamber of commerce, and the Olympia Salmon Club is the "Foofaraw." Members of all branches of the military are honored as guests on a cruise to Island Home for a salmon bake.

One of the most prestigious OYC-sponsored events is the Capital-to-Capital Race, a 1,000-mile contest from Olympia to Juneau. This is held every 10 years. The first such race, which attracted national attention, began on June 26, 1928, and contestants had only 10 days to complete the lengthy journey.

—Based on materials submitted by Shirley R. Kornmann, OYC Secretary

These unknown Elliott Bay Yacht Club sailors were awarded their prizes in 1899. The burgee, bottom right, was retained when EBYC and the Seattle Yacht Club merged in 1909. (SYC Dick Griffiths Collection)

Elliott Bay Yacht Club members; it was later owned by the well-known yachtsman Scott Calhoun. In second class, the *Hornet* placed first, and the *Daphne* placed second. The third class winner was *Kaleta*, followed by *Windward*. In fourth class, *Imp* sailed in a few minutes before *Nevermind*.

The Elliott Bay club's Labor Day races were hardly worth the effort with only two entries in each category. Most of the problem stemmed from the fact that 10 of the leading yachtsmen had decided to celebrate the holiday by cruising down the sound aboard some of the more noted racing craft in the area.

In 1899, after Fred Stimson had *Bonita* built, he sold his schooner *Drift* to Maurice McMicken. McMicken installed a Seattle-built four-horsepower gas engine in her, creating what was probably the Northwest's first auxiliary sailboat.

Ted Geary and Russell G. Wayland, having outgrown Geary's 16-foot catboat, built the 24-foot sloop *Empress*, which they raced successfully. Over the next four years they would capture permanent possession of the NIYA Class D trophy.

1900

As the century turned, yachting activities picked up on Puget Sound. The *Post-Intelligencer* issued a special report on Sunday, July 1, 1900, that included a full page of pictures:

> Never in the history of yachting in this section of the country has a season opened under more favorable circumstances than has the present one. The sport has had slow but steady growth on Puget Sound until now. In the opinion of many, it is destined to become the chief pastime of the people. The great sheet of water available for racing and cruising, with its natural harbors, magnificent scenery, and freedom from severe storms

makes Puget Sound an ideal locality for the yachtsman. The winds are, as a rule, steady and reliable, and that great danger to the sailor, the reef, is an unknown quantity. . . .
—Post-Intelligencer, *July 1, 1900*

The outstanding boats were listed:

The Hornet, the 35-foot flagship sloop, owned by Dr. Thompson, was considered the fastest racer in Class B and had won more races than any other yacht in the sound.

Lavita, 44 feet in length, owned by Oliver Abernathy, was launched in 1899 and had taken all Class A races since.

Olympic, a 63-foot yawl owned by C. D. Stimson, was largest on the sound. This was her first year.

Drift, a schooner owned by Maurice McMicken, was a good heavy-weather racer and a comfortable cruiser.

Halcyon, owned by Fred Stimson, was considered of the same class as the *Drift*.

Kelpie, a cutter owned by the Kelpie Club, often took friends on delightful summer cruises.

Rainier, owned by Albert Hansen, was "popular with the society people of the city."

Evelyn May, a sloop known as an up-to-date Knockabout was owned by C. W. Stimson.

In addition, the article reported that more than 20 boats of the smallest class were sailing the waters about Seattle.

The article concluded that the Elliott Bay club rented part of the boathouse at the foot of Battery Street, but that members were working on plans for a home of their own. Then the paper added, "The clubhouse of the old Seattle Yacht Club in West Seattle has been unused for years because of the inconvenience of its location."

At Port Townsend on July 2, the 1900 NIYA Regatta attracted 14 starters. Of the six in Class A, the *Lavita* won the cup. In Class B, of the four starters, *Wide Awake* of Victoria finished first, and Classes C and D attracted only two contestants each. After the festivities, several yachting families cruised the waters off nearby Hadlock and Irondale.

On July 4, the Key City Trophy was won by *Lavita*, and a sketch of this yacht was included in the July 8 *Post-Intelligencer*. She had entered seven races and won them all, including the contest held the previous May 24. *Lavita*'s helmsman was Oliver Abernathy, and her crew consisted of Chris Ernst, J. A. Spencer, Frank Neuman, Amos Goodell, Ed Duffy, A. A. Shephard, C. E. Shephard, and Ed Baker.

On Labor Day the races of the Elliott Bay Yacht Club started well. At one point the wind died, but then it livened up again at about 5:00 P.M., in time to propel the yachts speedily across the finish line. The winner in Class A was *Olympic* (C. D. Stimson), which caught the slight breezes in her club topsail and beat out the *Lavita* by 10 minutes. The Class B winners were *Evelyn May* (Charles Willard Stimson) followed by *Zephyr* (A. Heine). *Heron* (Adolph Rohlfs), followed by *Melissa* (H. Griffiths), took Class C, and the two winning flatties for Class D were *Empress* (Wayland and Henry) and *Nevermind* (G. H. Wayland).

1901

The NIYA races scheduled for Tuesday, July 2, at Port Townsend were becalmed. The association agreed to combine this contest with the Key City Trophy Race the following day, but this, too, was postponed until Thursday, July 4, for lack of wind. On that day, nine Class A yachts sailed the 21-mile course. At the finish, the Stimson brothers of Seattle were the rivals. The schooner *Bonita*, built the previous winter for Fred S. Stimson, established a time of 2 hours 57 minutes and 33 seconds. The yawl *Olympic*, owned

Boats at the Turn of the Century

In 1897 I was a grammar school classmate with Lloyd B. and Dean B. Johnson. We became interested in a pair of skipjacks moored at Oscar Lawrence's boathouse at the foot of Union Street. These were vee-bottom sloops similar to the present Snipe, but they had inboard rudders and were much larger, having three- and four-man crews. They had been built by Bert Griffiths, who lived at First and Virginia streets. Griffiths' personal boat was a Hurricane named *Coon*. Another Hurricane was owned by Frank and Charles Newman, the theater operators.

The 43-foot Lavita, *launched in 1899, was usually in front. She won every class A race over the next two years. (SYC Historical Collection)*

Dean and I, at age 12, were talked out of building a boat as large as these, so we tackled the well-known, 16-foot, shovel-nosed scow catboat *Lark*, whose plans just then appeared in *Rudder* magazine. Lloyd and George came up with the 18-foot skipjack *Nevermind*. We launched both *Lark* and *Nevermind* in 1898.

Then we found out about four other new skipjacks in Seattle, and when the fleet gathered, the moorage at the foot of Union Street was taxed. Some of the boys tried to join the Elliott Bay Yacht Club or the Seattle Yacht Club, but we were all under 21 and the big clubs had no provisions for members under that age. As a result, we held a meeting, dug up $1 each, and formed the first Queen City Yacht Club. Members' names, including those mentioned above, were Jim Griffiths, Frank Griffiths, Jesse Hall, Orla Peterson, Harold and Ed Burdett, and possibly half a dozen more.

One very windy day, Dean and another fellow took *Lark* out for an unscheduled scrub race with *Coon* and *Nevermind*. *Lark* was swamped, and in attempting to tow her with *Coon*, the mooring ring forward pulled out, and she drifted into Smith Cove and was lost. Lloyd sold his share of *Nevermind*, and we had some time for other things.

In 1899 Russell G. Wayland and I built the 24-foot *Empress*, and at Port Townsend in 1900 won the first leg on the Class D trophy, which we took for keeps after four years. This boat also raced at Victoria, Vancouver, and Bellingham and helped yacht racing grow in these cities.

Also in 1899 Oscar Lawrence passed away and his boathouse was sold to Tacoma, so our moorage was gone. Since the little Queen City Yacht Club had died out, the Elliott Bay Yacht Club arranged a membership for those of us who wished to carry on. In 1898 C. D. Stimson built the 58-foot yawl *Olympic*, and his nephew C. W. (Cully) Stimson, who did so much for Seattle Yacht Club as commodore in the tough years 1934–35, took over *Evelyn May*. That year a syndicate headed by Charles Abernathy of Elliott Bay Yacht Club built the 44-foot cutter *Lavita*. Abernathy was considered the best skipper among the amateurs and taught us younger fellows a lot. In later years *Lavita* was owned by Scott Calhoun and Elmer Todd.

In 1899 Fred S. Stimson built the 66-foot schooner *Bonita* from a design by L. H. Coolidge. M. M. McMicken took over his schooner *Drift*, installed a four-horsepower gas engine, and thereby made *Drift* the first auxiliary in the Northwest.

The brothers Stimson raced intensively with *Bonita*, usually winning in Class A regattas or match races. About 1900 H. C. Henry of the Seattle Yacht Club built *Owasco*, a 50-foot cutter, and for several years thereafter, no more large boats were turned out. All these cutters and two stickers had triple head rigs with large club topsails over gaff-headed mainsails except *Drift*, which was bald-headed with leg-of-mutton main.

—Ted Geary, 1950s

The Key City Trophy (Port Townsend) which the Lavita *won in 1900. (Wallace Ackerman Photography)*

by Charles D. Stimson, finished second five minutes later.

On July 14, the *Post-Intelligencer* carried a full page of yachting fashions:

> [The yachting girl] knows to a fraction how much of a dip she can bear and where upon the yacht the swells come easiest. She makes no mistake in this matter, the yachting girl, for to be able to stay on deck is one of the things which mark the new woman. . . .
>
> There is a yachting blue this year that may rival the navy in point of popularity. It is a little darker than Yale blue, and it comes in serges and cashmeres, in flannels and in lightweight cloth. . . .
>
> The little caps, such as seamen wear, are also seen—little peak cap and sailor caps. They are made of a material to match the gown, and will be fashioned by any hatter, if given a bit of the dress material. . . .
>
> The yachting "pedestrian" is longer than the walking skirt, and much longer than the golf skirt. It is also longer than the bicycle dress or the one that is for tennis. It touches the deck all the way around, when in repose, though it does not drag. In walking it just escapes the deck.
>
> —Post-Intelligencer, *July 14, 1901*

So much for fashion at the turn of the century.

The Labor Day races scheduled for Sept. 2, 1901, were canceled when the breeze died midway around the course, leaving some of the yachts to inch their way back to the boathouse. Many didn't arrive until after dark.

1902

The only sailing race reported for the year 1902 was the NIYA at Port Townsend where the Victoria Yacht Club won two firsts and a second. In Class A, the *Bonita* of Seattle was the winning yacht.

First Powerboat Race on Lake Washington

Until 1902, the number of motorboats in Seattle could be counted on one hand. Then interest increased suddenly after two launch owners began arguing over who owned the fastest boat.

Billy Beland's *Florence R* was touted as the boat to beat. He had spent a considerable sum on the launch, "sacrificing everything for speed." Vince Faben, however, was causing him considerable worry. Faben, after several years of studying motors, had built the *Dolphin.*

The two decided to race a straight course from Madison Park to Thorn's Boathouse at Leschi and then continue around Mercer Island.

The *Idlewild*, owned by the Thorn's Boathouse, then entered the race. Ironically it crossed the finish line first, 45 feet ahead of the *Dolphin*. The *Idlewild* then dropped from the race to allow the two

C. D. Stimson
SYC Commodore, 1901-1909

After SYC merged with the Elliott Bay Yacht Club in 1909, only the list of Elliott Bay's former commodores was carried forward. The leaders of the Seattle Yacht Club prior to the merger were forgotten.

Charles Douglas "C. D." Stimson was born in Michigan in 1857. At age six he skinned his right arm while swimming. Though the wound was so minor that he hardly noticed it, a persistent infection developed. In spite of all the doctors did to treat the infection, for three years it steadily worsened. At age nine, C. D. lost his right arm. It did not slow him down much; he learned to compensate, became a good golfer and even saved a fellow swimmer.

C. D. Stimson, commodore, Seattle Yacht Club, 1901-1909. During the time he was commodore he owned the 63-foot yawl Olympia. *(Stimson Collection)*

Stimson attended seminary and two years at Racine College. After Stimson finished school, his father put him to work in his sawmill. But Stimson thought he was being paid too little, so he asked for a raise. When he was refused, he went out on his own at age 21. He returned 18 months later after his father agreed that he could take over their planing mill and keep the profits. In 1882 Stimson married Harriet Mary Overton.

The family later operated four steamers on the Great Lakes. Realizing the forests of the Midwest would soon be logged out, Stimson and his family were sent to Puget Sound in 1888 to buy some of the big timber and build a mill. The Stimson Land Company was founded in 1889 and the Stimson Mill Company was founded in 1890. C. D. Stimson was treasurer of both and manager of the mill in Ballard. A large shingle mill was soon added.

The 1893 financial panic found Stimson with $35,000 in savings which, while land prices were depressed, he invested in properties a few blocks north of Seattle's business district. The Alaska Gold Rush of 1897 escalated property values, and Stimson quickly made a fortune of nearly $1 million from his investments.

In 1900 the Stimsons moved to a new home at Minor and Seneca streets, which today is preserved as the Stimson-Green mansion. In the late 1890s Stimson revived his interest in yachting and bought the 75-foot yawl-rigged *Olympic*. His brother F. S. Stimson built the *Bonita*. C. D. Stimson was commodore of the Seattle Yacht Club "during its first ten years" according Cornelius Hanford's *Seattle & Environs*.

Stimson brought the first gas-powered car to Seattle in 1902. He was the first president of the Highlands (an exclusive residential area in north Seattle) and a commissioner of the Alaska-Yukon-Pacific Exposition on the University of Washington campus in 1909.

During World War I, he delegated authority for his business concerns and devoted his time to Red Cross work. In the 1920s he was chairman of the committee that planned and raised funds to build the Olympic Hotel.

In 1920, Stimson bought the *Gloria*, a 65-foot powerboat, then two years later commissioned the 90-foot yacht *Wanda*.

Late in his life, Stimson served as a director of the Metropolitan Bank and as an organizer and director of the General Insurance Company of America (now SAFECO).

C. D. Stimson died on Aug. 29, 1929, at the age of 72. He was survived by his wife Harriet, son Thomas, and a daughter, Dorothy Stimson Bullitt. ◇

major contestants to roar on around the island. Faben's *Dolphin* crossed the finish line ahead of the *Florence R.*

Beland immediately challenged Faben to a second race, stating that he would back his launch with any size bet. But Faben demurred, explaining that he was in the launch business for "what fun there is in it." He refused to wager on the outcome of any race.

More would be heard from motorboat owners.

1903

For the second consecutive year Port Townsend was the site of the NIYA Regatta. On the way to these races, the skipjack *C. S.* capsized in a squall off Fort Flagler. The crew—Captain Moran, son of shipbuilder Robert Moran, and a Mr. Young—crawled over the weather rail onto the bottom as she turned over. The nearby tug *Pioneer* rescued them from all but wet feet and tried to tow the hull, but failed. The rip tide tore the *C. S.* to pieces; only her sail was saved.

As for the contests, lack of wind canceled the July 2 start, but on July 3 there was a fine breeze. In Class A, the *Bonita* beat out the *Lavita* for first place. In Class B, the *Wideawake* of Victoria outclassed *Ariadne* of Whatcom. In Class C, *Empress* of Seattle was first; *Banshee* of Port Townsend was second.

The Key City Trophy Race the following day resulted in *Bonita* and *Wide-*

The Royal Vancouver Yacht Club

When the town of Vancouver, British Columbia, was incorporated in 1886, sailing was already a popular pastime. Three pioneer boatbuilders were turning out sturdy pleasure craft.

In 1887, the Burrard Inlet Sailing Club was formed with 16 charter members. They sponsored their first regatta on July 1, 1887, in honor of the Queen's Jubilee, but the club languished and died shortly thereafter.

In 1891 the British Columbia Yacht Racing Association came into being. But a serious economic slump caused its demise three years later.

In 1897 a Vancouver Yacht Club was founded, but it didn't last long either.

By 1902 a dozen competing yachts were seeking a club for a home. Yachtsmen in Seattle were very active and looking for competitors. The Seattle *Times* took up the cause and campaigned for the reestablishment of a yacht club in Vancouver. The *Times* described realtor Walter Graveley as "the daddy of them all in the Vancouver yachting world." Graveley had sailed in the Canadian challenger for the America's Cup. With all this urging, a new Vancouver Yacht Club was organized in February 1903 with Graveley as commodore. A small dinghy house at the foot of Thurlow Street in Coal Harbour was rented from the Vancouver Rowing Club.

The first race of the new club was on English Bay for the Hodson Cup. A waterfront lot was leased at the foot of Bute Street, and there the club built a 30- x 60-foot floating clubhouse.

By 1904 the Vancouver Yacht Club was a lively place, and the first powerboats were joining its fleet. The little clubhouse on its bit of land soon proved to be inadequate. A site on the Coal Harbour shore of Stanley Park was secured from the park commission, and in 1905 the floating clubhouse was towed to the new location.

In 1906 the members were delighted to receive the royal warrant creating the Royal Vancouver Yacht Club. Walter Graveley retired after three years as RVYC commodore and was replaced by R. H. Alexander. Plans were made to build a new, larger clubhouse on the Stanley Park property. This structure burned in 1909 after two short years of

awake again sweeping the field. The Class C race was canceled because of too much wind.

The 1903 Labor Day race was the last to be sponsored by the Elliott Bay Yacht Club until they reorganized three years later. It seems they had lost their lease at the Brighton Boathouse. Though their 1903 Labor Day races were twice becalmed, the *Bonita*, skippered by George Francis Fay, finally won first place. *Linda*, with Benjamin H. Ferris at the tiller, took second.

1904: The Mackie Cup

All across America, yacht clubs located along the U.S.-Canadian border were contesting for various international cups—the Seawanaka Cup, for example, won by the Royal St. Lawrence Club of Montreal in 1896. At about the same time, Americans captured the Canada Cup in a race on Lake Ontario.

In 1903, W. W. Beaton, sports editor for the *Vancouver Ledger*, secured a trophy from Percy Jeffry Mackie, head of Mackie Brothers, distillers of White Horse Scotch whiskey. The "Mackie Cup" was elaborate: It boasted a large highland ram's head mounted on a pedestal, finished in solid silver and decorated with cairngorms, amethysts, and other precious stones and was topped by a solid silver white horse, the trademark of the donor's firm.

Beaton quickly extended a challenge

---

occupancy, but it was replaced immediately.

During World War I, 87 of the nearly 200 RVYC members served in the armed services, and 16 of them gave their lives in the effort.

In 1925 the club leased property at Jericho Beach, its present site, and the following year the RVYC built a new and larger clubhouse.

During World War II, more than a third of the 600 RVYC members served in the armed services. Others were involved in naval training and in the volunteer yacht patrol.

In the years since World War II, the Royal Vancouver Yacht Club has been thriving. Membership in 1991 stood at nearly 4,000 (in seven categories) and the club listed 927 boats in its fleet. The clubhouse on Jericho Beach at Point Grey is a busy place.

Traditions of the club are especially meaningful to members. The Opening Day Sail-Past is held the second Saturday of May. The Commodore's Reception is scheduled each January 1. An Easter service and cruise are now traditions, as is the November 11 Remembrance Service at sea and in the clubhouse. The Annual General Meeting is held in November, as is the prize-giving meeting.

There are several traditional special events, including the Seattle Yacht Club Visitation, Robert Burns Night, Big Band Night, Seattle Yacht Club Opening Day, Opening Day Dinner Dance, Commodore's Ball, Women's Committee Annual Spring Dinner, Women's Committee December Dinner, Children's Christmas Party, and New Year's Eve Dinner Dance.

The club also sponsors junior events and cruising and club parties. The Master Gunner and Gun Crew attend traditional events, there is a special children's cruise, a staff Christmas party, and special dinner dances celebrating ethnic groups.

And on top of all this, there are the many races and cruises each year.

The Royal Vancouver Yacht Club maintains six outstations—Tugboat Island among the Gulf Islands, Alexandra Island in Howe Sound, Wigwam Inn on Indian Arm, Scott Point on Salt Spring Island, Pender Harbour, and Secret Cove.

For more details about the Royal Vancouver Yacht Club, refer to their fine history book, *Annals: Royal Vancouver Yacht Club, a History of Organized Racing and Cruising in British Columbia Coastal Waters.* ◇

to Seattle sailors. The Seattle *Times* egged them on:

> A little town like Vancouver hasn't got much license to get so cocky about a trophy and it behooves the Seattle yachtsmen to pick up the gauntlet thrown down in such a sportsmanlike manner.
>
> —Seattle Times, *Sept. 6, 1903*

The first race for the cup was staged in Vancouver in 1904 at the Vancouver regatta. Beating out the gallant *Wideawake* of Vancouver, B.C., was the new *Gwendolyn* of Seattle, which was built in an old fire station on Queen Anne Hill by Lloyd and Dean Johnson, who used a design Ted Geary drew before he went to

Cruise of the *Lotus*

The proud Lotus *is an active yacht to this day. (PSMHS)*

Some notable cruises were undertaken on early Seattle yachts. One on the *Lotus* serves as an example. She was owned in the early days by Maurice McMicken and Col. J. C. Haines. These two men, accompanied by their wives, left port for a May 1905 trip to the Gulf of Georgia, a journey fraught with thrilling experiences.

One night, while at anchor in the lee of an island, a gale blew up, and after the anchor would not hold in the face of the wind, the *Lotus* headed out to the open sea for safety. The wind blew so fiercely that the commands from the wheel of Colonel Haines had to be relayed to McMicken in the bow by the women, who were crouching along the deck channels.

The time came for the return to port of the party, but no *Lotus* appeared. In view of the number of storms that had occurred during their absence, the party's friends grew apprehensive. After several days had passed with no news of the *Lotus*, tugs and revenue cutters were dispatched in search of the party. The daily papers even went so far as to prepare obituaries for print at the first confirmation of their worst fears. Happily this was not necessary, for one of the tugs found the party weather-bound near Utsalady at the north end of Camano Island and towed them home in triumph. ◇

The 22-foot power racer Mercury, *propelled by a four-cylinder, two-cycle gasoline engine, won many races in 1906. (MOHAI)*

the Massachusetts Institute of Technology to study engineering.

1905

The second race for the Mackie Cup in Seattle on July 9, 1905, resulted in the *Gwendolyn* again beating a Canadian boat, the *Madeline*, but only by 14 seconds. Near the start of the race the *Madeline* broke her gaff, which took about 10 minutes to repair. Even so, *Madeline* nearly caught *Gwendolyn* at the finish line. After the race, the crew of the winning yacht treated their gallant Canadian rivals to a festive banquet.

The *West Seattle Tribune* of July 14, carried several items about yachting families. It noted that F. S. Stimson had taken his wife and son and Mr. and Mrs. Eaton cruising on *Bonita* to Mukilteo and back. The yacht *Drift* had carried Fred Wing, E. C. Hughes and a Mr. Brainard to and from Eagle Harbor. Furthermore the paper noted that the finest yachts were still moored in West Seattle, including those of F. S. Stimson, H. C. Henry, Maurice McMicken, and several others.

1906

Powerboats monopolized the headlines all through 1906. "Two of the fastest in the world are owned in Seattle," the *Post-Intelligencer* trumpeted. Edward Roesche of Buffalo, who was spending his summer in Seattle, brought two of his speedsters with him—the *Comet* and the *Mercury*. The 33-foot *Comet* boasted a 40-horse engine and that "20 miles per hour was child's play" for her. His *Mercury* was a 22-foot racer powered by a four-cylinder, two-cycle gas engine. She had beaten *The Chip*, which had won the American Power Boat Association $1,000 Challenge Cup in the east. Roesche extended a standing $1,000 wager to the Tacomans who owned the *Tillicum*, reputedly the fastest boat on the sound, but they refused to race.

Seattleites were buying powerboats in considerable number. August Hambach had ordered a 46-foot, 24-horse launch from the Racine Boat Company outlet at 321 First Avenue South.

Orion O. Denny (son of Seattle founder Arthur Denny) had launched a handsome new pleasure motorboat, the *Tuk-wil-la* at the Eagle boathouse on Lake Washington. On her trial run, the 25-horse Union engines running at half speed pushed her the six miles to Denny's summer home on the north shore of Lake Washington (now Denny Park) in 20 minutes.

The *Tuk-wil-la* was 40 feet long and carried engines weighing 3,000 pounds. Her finish was in oak, and the cabin was fitted with plate glass windows. Denny built her to replace his naphtha launch, which could travel at only nine miles per hour. He even extended his boathouse to accommodate the longer *Tuk-wil-la*.

That summer, a new-style motorboat made news in Seattle. Owned by W. W. Sisco, it was:

> . . . shaped like a torpedo which had been cut half way through at the middle and then sliced off toward the stern post. Technically she is known as a rough water cruiser or hunting boat. Half of her twenty-seven feet of length is covered by what is known as a trunk cabin. With such a complete protection from the waves she is perfectly safe for a cruise to Alaska or anywhere along the Coast.
>
> —Post-Intelligencer, *Aug. 12, 1906*

She was complete even to "a toilet room."

Fred Lincoln built a 50-foot "motor launch" on the shore of Lake Washington in 1906. Well-known builder Captain Jacob E. Johnson was in charge of construction. All the latest ideas were incorporated inside and out. Power was from a 30-horse Buffalo engine, and the estimated cost was $4,000.

The Roche Harbor Yacht Club

The Roche Harbor Yacht Club, an unincorporated, nonprofit organization, dates its origin to about 1906, according to Ruben J. Tarte. He acquired all records of the club in 1956, along with the properties of the Tacoma and Roche Harbor Lime Company. Tarte reported in club records, "In the beginning there were two excellent club rooms, one with a maple dance floor and stage, the other a projection room and a billiard table." Those must have been interesting years at this old Hudson's Bay Company post.

The founder and guardian of the RHYC was John Stafford McMillin, general manager of the lime company (later called the Roche Harbor Lime and Cement Company). He established the town of Roche Harbor in 1886, a true "company town"; both the town and the yacht club flourished and faltered with the fortunes of the company.

In 1908, when John S. McMillin was the commodore of the RHYC, his 50-foot yacht, *The Calcite*, was the flagship of the club, which in the fall of that year undertook the first "Canadian 500" cruise.

Since Roche Harbor was very much a company town, the last known entry of the Roche Harbor Yacht Club coincided with the closure of the Hotel de Haro in 1942. By then few members remained.

The hiatus during the war years and the early 1950s was followed by the reactivation of the Roche Harbor Yacht Club in 1957 by Ruben Tarte and his family. Tarte served as club commodore during 1957 and 1958. He wrote:

> The first annual meeting of the reactivated club was held on Feb. 22, 1957, at which time about 25 people joined. During the summer and fall of 1957, about 75 more members were accepted. The club joined the Puget Sound Interclub Association, and paid its entrance fee, and contributed $75 toward the Sunday and Holiday Custom Pool, which the Interclub Association sponsors so that American and Canadian boats may enter at Roche Harbor and Friday Harbor without excessive cost during the yachting season.
>
> —*Roche Harbor Yacht Club records*

Further, RHYC Commodore Tarte noted a factor which played an important part in the club's future:

The papers from time to time reported experiences on motorboats. The *Walter H*, rented from Johnson's boathouse by a party of young people, was the focus of one item.

Soon after leaving the boathouse the launch began to leak, and later the water in the boat rose so fast that it extinguished the spark in the gasoline engine and the engine refused to work. For half an hour the young people watched the water rise. They assert that the man who ran the launch was helpless, seemingly too frightened to take any measures toward saving the boat which was tossing in the trough of the waves that by then were alarmingly high.

Soon the members of the party were standing on seats to keep above the water. . . . Then one young woman took up an empty candy box and began to bail out the boat. Another bailed, and after a while they succeeded in getting the water down low enough for the engine to be run.

Members of the party declare that the engineer was incompetent and cowardly. "It was a piece of criminal carelessness to send out that engineer," said one of the young ladies yesterday. "He was either drunk or frightened. He did not even attempt to save us and would not even help to bail out the boat."

—Post-Intelligencer, *Aug. 1, 1906*

The first motorboat regatta on Lake Washington drew crowds on July 4, 1906. Winners of the five events were *Mosquito* (W. K. Danner), *El Rio* (C. W. Coleman), *Zebra* (S. M. Milne), a George Budlong boat that was the only one entered in the fourth race, and *Madeline* (N. R. Abrams).

For Labor Day 1906 the Motor Boat Association staged another regatta on Lake Washington. The several races attracted a

Most of the members reside at great distance from Roche Harbor. It is hoped that this situation will correct itself in the near future as it places considerable burden on our few local members. The Commodore is a part-time resident. We hope, at the 1959 annual meeting, to see many new faces.

—Roche Harbor Yacht Club records

The Roche Harbor Lime and Cement Company continued to play host to the club, furnish its quarters and to lend general support. Under Commodore Heny Shelly (1962–1963) the club began to show signs of independence. It negotiated a lease with the company to pay rent, to refurbish the club rooms, and to provide floats for visiting yachts. Gradually, however, there was a shifting of activities, particularly during the off-season. Cruises and social functions became centered in Seattle, where most of the officers and members resided. While Roche Harbor remains the club's spiritual home, for all practical purposes the Roche Harbor Yacht Club has disengaged itself from its lime company origins. Despite the disadvantages of having no fixed headquarters, the club remains an active force among yacht clubs of the region and maintains a strong membership and an active fleet.

Milestones in the RHYC's history include

1957—Reactivation of the RHYC

1962—First roster published. Lease and restoration of club facilities at Roche Harbor under Commodore Heny Shelly

1970—Gro-Bond savings program instituted under Commodore James Stephens.

1974—"Canadian 500" cruises initiated under Commodore Don McClintick

1975—Kingston Outstation established under Commodore Milt Larson

1978—RHYC ladies luncheon program instituted by Dorie Swan and Associates.

The 1991 roster listed 106 active members, all of them boat owners. An outstation is maintained at Kingston. Ten of the club's past commodores are living. Administration is the responsibility of a board of trustees and two general meetings are held each year.

—Adapted from materials provided by Commodore Cecil H. Tice

big crowd to Leschi Park. Eddie Roesche's *Mercury* lived up to its name as the fastest boat on the lake, if not in the world. The big surprise was the *Meteor*, owned by C. H. Jones of the Kilbourne-Clarke Company, which won the race around Mercer Island, covering the 16-mile course in just over an hour.

So much attention was diverted to powerboats that the *Post-Intelligencer* on Sept. 2, 1906, carried an article headlined "Sport of Yachting Will Never Die." The reporter assured readers that the popularity of powerboats would not affect sailing craft other than for the fact that many owners are installing motors.

Elsewhere in sailing, at the July 4 regatta at Bellingham, the Class A race was won for the second year in a row by the *Gwendolyn* of Seattle. This outstanding 25-foot L-W-L Knockabout carried 1,000 square feet of canvas. Johnson had built his first yacht at age 11 and later had apprenticed at Moran's steel shipbuilding plant. He was the most noted of Seattle's yacht builders at the time.

In May, skippered by her builder and crewed by Dean Johnson, Henry Henke, and Norman J. Blanchard, the *Gwendolyn* sailed for seven weeks on the Inside Passage to Southwest Alaska and home again.

In June 1906 the Seattle Yacht Club annual cruise attracted nine yachts and six motorboats. SYC Commodore C. D. Stimson led the way in his *Olympic*. The *Bonita*, owned by his brother F. S. Stimson was also along, as were Maurice McMicken, C. W. Wylie, J. A. Baillargeon, H. C. Henry, Scott Calhoun, C. H. Lilly, and H. M. Field. Motorboats owned by J. C. Marmaduke, J. A. Kerr, C. R. Collins, C. F. Crane, Fred Fisher, and A. M. Brooks putted along with the sailing vessels. They arrived at Port Washington in a rain squall, stayed overnight, and returned the next day.

1907

The big news in 1907 concerned the reorganization of the Elliott Bay Yacht Club, which had been inactive after it lost its lease at the Brighton Boathouse in 1904 (this had resulted in crowded moorage conditions and lack of financial support). In 1907 a group of Elliott Bay members met to find ways to revive the club. Among these members, most of them young, were C. W. Wiley, Adolph and Oddie Rohlfs, Herbert Moss, Dr. Tom Mesdag, Harold Burdett, Ted Geary, and Quent Williams. All the club maintained was a dinghy float moorage south of the West Seattle ferry landing where it kept its sailing and power fleet moored to buoys.

> For several seasons there has been little done in the bay to the way of yacht racing, but before that time the Elliott Bay Yacht Club held several interesting regattas. With the reorganization of the old club there are excellent prospects of its securing permanent quarters at West Seattle. Every man who has a yacht, sail boat, power boat, or who has any interest in yachting is invited to the meetings.
>
> —Post-Intelligencer, *March 2, 1907*

The site of the new clubhouse and float was north of the Novelty Mill and a couple of blocks south of the ferry landing in West Seattle. In 1907 C. W. Wiley was elected commodore and Ted Geary vice commodore.

Motorboat Activities

So many new motorboats were appearing on Lake Washington by 1907 that old-timers complained they could no longer keep track of them. Among the new owners in 1907 were H. A. Chadwick, proprietor of the weekly newspaper *Argus*, and Clair and Earl Bigelow, sons of H. A. Bigelow, who, according to the *Post-Intelligencer*, "owns enough Pike Street real estate to bring him within hailing distance of the millionaire's class." The *Post-Intelligencer* of May 9,

The Old Clubhouse

Few are those of us who remember a little shanty, some 43 years ago, perched on a cedar float that rolled precariously with the waves on each hourly arrival of the ferry boat from Yesler Way. Although this modest domicile was quite remote from town—it was way over in West Seattle—and although the plumbing, furnishings, and fixtures were not exactly lush, it still harbored a gay and hardy group of mariners. From the yard arm flew a white pennant crossed with a blue stripe and spangled with a red star near the hoist. That was the sum total of the Seattle Yacht Club in 1907.

Enthusiasm and diligence of our early members brought about the need for expansion, and in 1909 Mayor Hi Gill of Seattle, Scott Calhoun, and Miller Freeman were instrumental in negotiating a long-term lease on a waterfront site about a block south of the original clubhouse, approximately at the foot of what is now Charles Street. This area was partially occupied by a lumber mill. However, their lease had expired and was granted to the yachtsmen by the city of Seattle.

Scuttlebutt was that the mill owners were in an ejecting mood, should any construction take place which might encroach on their booming grounds, so one bright and sunshiny Saturday when the mill was closed a contingent of the hardiest boarded Adolph Rohlfs' new yawl *Acquilla*, and accompanied a pile driver to the site. Equipment included the necessary piling and caps for a new clubhouse, plans for which had been drawn up by a promising young architect named John Graham, Sr., plus, for either persuasion or protection purposes, four not-so-white shotguns, which graced the railings of the committee boat. The committee, you might guess, was composed of Bill Hedley, Adolph Rohlfs, Herb Moss, Tom Mesdag, and Quent Williams.

The opposition was there in force, but not as adequately equipped, so the work went on all night and the next day, until the injunction arrived Monday morning. Later, after the courts sanctioned the construction work, the building of the clubhouse resumed under less stringent circumstances. Everything was fine except a small item of finances. Operating at the time as the Elliott Bay Yacht Club, a maneuver was made to consolidate with the Seattle Yacht Club, which netted $1,200 in the treasury and boosted the membership. The Elliott Bay Club officers and flag were retained in return for the treasury and a few promising members such as one Cully Stimson. The clubhouse was completed in the summer of 1909. . . .

World War I put a sudden stop to the many races and regattas, always viewed and arranged from the front porch veranda, and negotiations were effected which sold the entire holdings to the Navy for a small fraction of its appreciated value. . . . The club did without a site until 1920, when the present station was acquired and the clubhouse built. The old original clubhouse in West Seattle later became the Seattle Rod and Gun Club, but at present [1950] is reverted back into a boathouse, rolling precariously with the waves every time the *Kalakala* goes by.

—Quent Williams, SYC Yearbook, 1950

Commodores of the Elliott Bay Yacht Club—1898-1909

(Elliott Bay Yacht Club merged with Seattle Yacht Club in 1909)

HENRY HENSEL
1894-1898
Occupation: Manufacturing Jeweler
Boat: Xora

GEORGE E. THOMPSON
1898-1906
Occupation: Dentist
Boat: Auxiliary sloop Hornet

C. W. WILEY
1907-1908
Occupation: President, Crosby Towboat Company
Boat: Schooner Henrietta

H. W. GOCHER
1909
Occupation: Skinner and Eddy Shipbuilding
Boat: 50-foot auxiliary yawl Leba

1907, also mentioned that "Nels Lewis, one of the pioneer boating men of Lake Washington, had put his launch, *The Countess*, in the water the previous week. She was thoroughly overhauled and was one of the best-looking boats on the lake. Lewis has purchased a houseboat and would live the summer at Wolf's Cove."

The same article mentioned that the gasoline launch "to be used by the company controlling the Laurelhurst property on Union Bay, is practically completed and will soon be running between Madison Street and the company landing on Union Bay. The boat was built at Everett, towed to Seattle, and taken overland to Lake Washington."

Late in May the local papers reported that the Seattle Motor Boat Club was contemplating locating its boathouse on Foster Island in Union Bay, but the plan apparently was dropped.

In the spring of 1907, ground was broken for the Alaska-Yukon-Pacific Exposition. To celebrate the event, the Motor Boat Club scheduled an illuminated parade that attracted nearly 100 boats, including rowboats and canoes.

Late in June, the annual cruise attracted 20 motorboats that traveled from the foot of Madison Street to McMaster's Mill near the outlet of Squak Slough (now known as the Sammamish River), where everyone went ashore for a picnic.

The July 4, 1907, regatta of the Seattle Motor Boat Club was postponed until July 5 to avoid competing with the yacht club races. The *Mercury*, now owned by Seattle Motor Boat Club Commodore Clarence Jones, swept all races for 40-footers. Later in the month, the *Comet*, owned by the Washington Motor Boat Company, won the Jacob Furth Challenge Cup.

Sailing Activities

On June 9, the *Post-Intelligencer* waxed poetic.

> With their white sails flashing in the sunlight and salt water boiling into foam under the bows, the swift little boats of the Se-

attle Yacht Club sailed away from the harbor yesterday on the first cruise of the year. Nearly twenty boats were in the squadron, with Commodore C. D. Stimson in his flagship *Olympic*, directing the movements of the fleet.

—Post-Intelligencer, *June 9, 1907*

They sailed around Bainbridge Island via Agate Pass. Ted Geary, who was on the cruise, later recalled seeing SYC Commodore C. D. Stimson raise his artificial right arm and dive under the keel of three boats. This, Geary said, was the last cruise of the old Seattle Yacht Club before the amalgamation with the Elliott Bay group two years later.

At the Seattle Yacht Club Fourth of July regatta, the Alexandra's Cup was awarded for the first time. Ted Geary described the situation:

Vancouver was prospering from its real estate boom in 1906 and offered to build a boat and put up a cup and race at Seattle. We agreed and it was decided that 29 foot units of rating would produce a boat about the size of *Gwendolyn*, a 42-foot sloop built by Lloyd and Dean Johnson in 1903.

We appealed to Scott Calhoun, the sugar daddy for everything in yachting and he assured us he would raise the necessary $3,000 by popular subscription at $20 per ticket and conduct a raffle for the boat. Accordingly we designed a boat 42 feet by 26 on the waterline with 960 square feet of sail in jib and main, hired the discarded fire house on Queen Anne Hill, built the boat, trucked her with a four-horse outfit for the launching to the foot of Yesler Way. We named her *Spirit* after the going slogan of the time, "The Seattle Spirit." She became a great favorite with Seattle right from the start.

The Canadians had announced they were building a boat 48 x 28, with 1,275 square feet of sail designed by William Fife of Fairlie, Scotland, the designer of *Shamrock I* and *Shamrock III*. They announced that her name was *Alexandra* and named their new cup Alexandra's Cup. We don't know yet whether their Queen donated the cup or whether they named it for their boat in anticipation of winning it as the *America* did the America's Cup donated by Queen Victoria a half century ago. [Newspaper accounts of the time indicate the donor was Lt. Gov. James Dunsmuir of British Columbia.]

The races twice around the six-mile triangle from Duwamish Head to West Point and around the outside Eagle Harbor buoy were quite exciting with *Spirit* winning the first race handily. The second was won by *Alexandra* by five seconds. *Spirit* took the third by four seconds. This caused great excitement in Seattle and on the excursion boats where it was said much money changed hands.

—*Ted Geary, 1950s*

In August when the *Spirit* was auctioned off, Fred S. Stimson won her. The proceeds from the auction helped send young Ted Geary, designer of the *Spirit*, to the Massachusetts Institute of Technology to study naval architecture.

With many Canadian yachts on hand for the Independence Day Regatta, Seattle Yacht Club members led a fleet of 50 yachts on a quick sail to Port Orchard to view the Bremerton Navy Yard, a sight that was said to have impressed the visitors.

1908: Year of the Great White Fleet

The major story in 1908 concerned the arrival of the Great White Fleet that President Theodore Roosevelt had sent steaming around the world. Officially known as the Atlantic Battleship Fleet, it sailed north from San Francisco on May 18, passed through the Strait of Juan de Fuca on May 21, then split into four groups of several ships. The first three groups headed for Port Townsend, Bellingham and Port Angeles, and the fourth group of three ships steamed to the Bremerton Navy Yard for minor repairs. On May 23, 1908, 16 of these ships assembled in Elliott Bay. Both Seattle yacht clubs provided a flotilla of pleasure craft to greet the fleet. The sailing craft were towed to Point Monroe, 12 miles down sound, by fleet launches. As the yachts came abreast the flagship *Connecticut*, each dipped its flag in accordance with navy custom.

As the battleships approached West

The graceful Gwendolyn II, *owned by the Johnson brothers, raced from California to Hawaii in 1908. (N. C. Blanchard Collection)*

Point, all boat traffic was stopped from entering Elliott Bay. Once anchored, the huge ships were not to be approached by any craft. Lines were drawn from Duwamish Head to Skiff Point on Bainbridge Island, and from Restoration Point to Jefferson Head north of Port Madison, beyond which no excursion boats were to cross. Stake boats were stationed off the West Point lighthouse, Four-Mile Rock and Smith Cove to ensure that no smaller craft ventured too close.

After the ships were anchored, the water between the line of ships and the Seattle wharves was reserved for navy boats. This was to prevent collisions as launches ferried crew members back and forth.

The new YMCA building served as headquarters for enlisted men from the fleet. Working with the Seattle Chamber of Commerce, the YMCA set up an information bureau, check room, reading and writing tables, and general headquarters in a large tent on Pier 6. Five hundred army cots were set up for sailors wishing to spend the night ashore. The "high-class" entertainment presented on shore was transported to the ships on Saturday and Monday evenings. A religious service was presented aboard each ship on Sunday night.

Needless to say, the visit of the Great White Fleet was a memorable event in Seattle's maritime history. Those yachtsmen who met the fleet would never forget the experience.

Another historical happening of 1908 occurred when a Seattle Yacht Club boat entered the Trans-Pacific Race. *Gwendolyn II*, owned by the Johnson brothers, raced from California to Hawaii. The rules were bent to allow the 48-foot *Gwendolyn II* to compete, for she was a couple of feet under size. Her crew included Lloyd and Dean Johnson, Walter B. "Billy" Jack, Eddie "Stub" Russell, Henry Henke, Jim Redfern, and Frank Rotch.

The race began on July 4 from San Pedro, California. The *Gwendolyn II* arrived in Hawaii 14 days, 4 hours, 7 minutes, and 8.75 seconds later and earned second place behind the *Lurline*. This was an outstanding victory for the young crew. On their return they were feted in San Francisco. Though they slipped into the West Seattle moorings almost unnoticed, the Elliott Bay Yacht Club later gave them a royal welcome, and the *Post-Intelligencer* devoted the front page of their Sept. 20, 1908, magazine section to them in an illustrated article titled "How *Gwendolyn II* Won Second Place in Trans-Pacific Race."

The annual Fourth of July regatta scheduled at Vancouver, B.C., attracted hundreds of yachtsmen from the Puget Sound region. The Alexandra's Cup was in the possession of the Elliott Bay Yacht Club thanks to Ted Geary and his *Spirit*, and the upcoming contest drew considerable press space.

The *Alexandra* won the first race, and the *Spirit* won the second. The third was extremely close, but the *Alexandra*, with Captain Jimmy Deane as skipper, sailed over the finish line two minutes ahead of Ted Geary and the *Spirit*. The Vancouver Yacht Club took possession of the Alexandra's Cup for the year.

The annual regatta of the Vancouver club, which was held between Alexandra's Cup heats, resulted in only a single win for a Seattle boat, the *Lavita*, which sailed in first in the special cruiser contest.

At the outset of the Vancouver festivities, a long-distance motorboat race from West Seattle to Vancouver was won by the *Traveler*, owned by Dr. L. C. Neville and operated by Eugene Ward. It averaged 10 miles per hour over the 182-mile journey.

Powerboating remained enough of a novelty in 1908 to attract considerable interest. The Seattle Motor Boat Club, under Commodore Clarence Jones, was seeking a clubhouse where members could host guests during the 1909 exposition. They were also attempting to attract "saltwater men" as members.

By May, all along the western shore of Lake Washington, motorboat activity was picking up. From Jacob E. Johnson's at the foot of Madison Street to Budlong's at Leschi Park, boats were being readied for the season. The big launch *Greata*, owned by the Kreilsheimer brothers, was out of the water for an overhaul. Commodore Jones was readying his *Meteor*. Former commodore Vince Faben was already using his *Dolphin* to commute from his home on Mercer Island. A new speedster skimmed the lake in July—the *Red Devil*, owned by Norman Abrams. She was clocked at 25 miles per hour.

On July 5, the Northwest International Power Boat Association was launched at the Royal Vancouver Yacht Club and Seattleite R. H. Parsons was elected first commodore.

The two yacht clubs in Seattle thrived during 1908. Elliott Bay was building a new float at its West Seattle site and was asking for a moorage on the Seattle side of the bay; its membership was at 105 and growing.

At the annual meeting of the Seattle Yacht Club, C. D. Stimson was reelected commodore. F. H. Boynton was asked to chair a committee to find permanent quarters in which to entertain visiting yachtsmen during the coming Alaska-Yukon-Pacific Exposition. The club members discussed whether to retain the present anchorage and maintain space for business and social affairs in the city proper, or whether to forestall the inevitable overcrowding of the West Seattle anchorage and seek a location further removed from the city. No decisions were reached.

In 1908 neither yacht club foresaw the solution 1909 would bring: The merger into a single organization.

1909: The Year of Amalgamation

Mayor Hiram Gill, Scott Calhoun (who later served as city attorney and attorney for the Port of Seattle), and Miller Freeman were enlisted in the effort to find a new and better location for the Elliott Bay Yacht Club. They were instrumental in negotiating a long-term lease on tidelands and a waterfront site near the foot of what is now Charles Street. But there was a problem. The Erickson Mill Company, which had buildings on the shoreline at the site, contested the club's right to build there. The *Post-Intelligencer* on May 14, 1909, explained that "a pitched battle between a pile-driving crew working for the Elliott Bay Yacht Club and employees of the Erickson Mill Company . . . was narrowly averted yesterday at noon. . . ." The mill company was given a temporary injunction that halted the yacht club's building activity at that site until May 22. On that date, the paper continued, "[the yacht club] won its long fight to build a clubhouse at the foot of Georgia Street," when Judge John F. Main of the Superior Court refused to issue a permanent injunction barring the club from proceeding.

Late in 1909 the Elliott Bay Yacht Club occupied its new clubhouse; however, the Seattle Yacht Club was moribund. As Ted Geary remembered:

> The Seattle Yacht Club had not taken in new members for years, but there was $1,260 in the treasury. Scott Calhoun, fiscal agent for *Spirit II*, reminded us that she was only two-thirds paid for and it was difficult to get the balance after the way the races went. He had talked to Frank Foster, the old SYC secretary, about the remaining members joining up with us. [Geary belonged to the Elliott Bay group]. The result was EBYC took their name, members, and treasury. The new Seattle Yacht Club bought $1,200 worth of tickets. With one-third of the tickets, the new SYC won the boat, sold her to the Canadians and came out well on the deal.
>
> —*Ted Geary, 1950s*

On Oct. 26, 1909, supplemental articles filed by the Elliott Bay Club indicated it and the Seattle Yacht Club had merged. The Seattle *Post-Intelligencer* reported on the amalgamation in a lengthy article:

> Yachting interests of Seattle are united at last. After existing as separate organizations for fifteen years, the Seattle and Elliott Bay Yacht Clubs last night amalgamated and henceforth there will be one name, one flag, and one club.
>
> The name of the one club will be the Seattle Yacht Club but in nothing else will the Elliott Bay club lose its identity. Today on the yachts belonging to the Seattle club the red and blue quartered flag with its white longitudinal stripe and red star will be hauled down and the Elliott Bay club pennant, a white triangle with a blue diagonal stripe and red star will be run up instead.
>
> The officers of the Elliott Bay club will be confirmed as officers of the merged clubs with Commodore H. W. Gocher at the helm. The property of the two will hereafter simply be held in the name of the Seattle Yacht Club. The only legal formality necessary is the filing of supplementary articles of incorporation changing the name of the Elliott Bay club to the Seattle Yacht club. As a matter of fact, today the organization is formally launched.
>
> The merger meeting was held last night in the Chamber of Commerce rooms with more than a hundred active yachtsmen in attendance and Commodore Gocher of the Elliott Bay Yacht Club in the chair. The preliminaries had been taken care of by a joint committee of the two clubs and the report of this committee recommending amalgamation was read by C. R. Wood. No discussion was needed on the report and resolution, for the sentiment of the meeting was complete agreement with the plan of merging. The vote adopting the resolution and this effecting amalgamation was unanimous and when the result was apparent the yachtsmen present burst into applause. Afterward, speeches of satisfaction were made by a number of the

leaders in the movement and Harold Lee of the Seattle Yacht Club, in a short talk declared that his organization was in complete accord with the action taken.

Any jealousy between the two clubs that may have existed in the past has been forgotten and nothing but harmony and enthusiasm have marked the final steps toward making the two bodies one in fact as well as in name. It is the aim of the local yachtsmen to make the Seattle club one of the greatest and best known in the world, and with the rapid growth of yachting on Puget Sound, this aim is no idle dream.

The merging of the clubs is the result of natural conditions. The Seattle Yacht Club was organized in 1890, and in 1891 its first clubhouse was opened at West Seattle. In 1891, the Elliott Bay Yacht Club was organized by a number of the younger tars. [Actually the SYC was reorganized in 1892 and the EBYC was founded in 1894.] In 1893 interest in yachting died down greatly, due largely to the Alaskan rush. [Actually a severe depression was the cause, the Alaska gold rush began in 1897.] It was not until the spring of 1897 that the Elliott Bay club was revived. Since then it has been the more active of the two and the Seattle Yacht Club, in joining readily in the movement for a merger, is recognizing the enthusiastic spirit of the younger generation of amateur sailors.

The amalgamation will be of immediate value in the destination of the yacht *Spirit II* after the international races. About 220 shares out of the 250 constituting the capital stock of the *Spirit II* will now be held by members of the club and as the yacht will be disposed of at a drawing of shareholders, the chances in favor of the club members are strong. The Seattle Yacht Club's treasury was also in splendid condition so that the united interests start out with the brightest of prospects.

—Post-Intelligencer, *June 23, 1909*

The Alexandra's Cup Dispute

All yacht clubs on Puget Sound had planned a big regatta to help entertain visitors to the Alaska-Yukon-Pacific Exposition during the summer of 1909. Two weeks of yacht racing were scheduled. The sponsors hoped to attract entrants from nearly every American port on the Pacific. The major race would be the Alexandra's Cup.

As Ted Geary told the story:

Good old Scott Calhoun said we should have a new boat for 1909 so we designed the *Spirit II*, 48 x 28 x 1,275 feet of sail. She was built by Adolph Rohlfs and Merrill at their new plant on the East Waterway. She proved to be a witch in light to moderate going which is to be expected at Seattle in summer.

She beat *Alexandra* in the first race. One windward leg was sailed in a momentarily hard breeze and *Alexandra* almost overtook *Spirit II*. There had been some dissatisfaction with the method of measuring *Spirit II* but after waiting until a half hour before the start of the second race the Canadian fleet weighed anchor and left for home on orders of their Commodore. *Spirit II* took a "sailover" and claimed the cup, but we never saw it. This incident could probably best be left unmentioned here but it led to strained relations with our good friends across the border which lasted four years.

—Ted Geary, 1950s

Prior to that second race, Captain Jimmy Deane and Commodore C. B. MacNeill of the Royal Vancouver Yacht Club had delivered a letter to Commodore Gocher of the Seattle Yacht Club refusing to race because, they claimed, the *Spirit II* had not been measured fairly.

The problems arose over the methods of measurement:

The prevailing measurement rule on this continent was the Seawanaka Rule featuring waterline and sail area until in 1905 Nat Herreschoff of America's Cup fame evolved the Universal Rule, taking into account the shape of hull and displacement. It gave promise of being the best rating rule ever and was adopted by all saltwater clubs and associations in the United States except here in the Northwest where the Canadian clubs insisted on the International Rule as used in Europe. This [Seawanaka] rule took in also girths and freeboard and seemed to need changing every year or so. In the interests of racing, we agreed to go along and it was adopted by the Northwest International Yacht Racing Association.

—Ted Geary, 1950s

According to newspaper reporters, the defection of the Vancouver club caused a heated exchange. Ted Geary declared he would never again race for the Alexandra's Cup.

The cover and officer listings from the 1910 Elliott Bay Yacht Club yearbook issued shortly after the amalgamation with the Seattle Yacht Club. (Wallace Ackerman Photography)

Vancouver members claimed that the keel of *Spirit II* had a slot or niche that allowed her a smaller girth measurement than she should have. Secondly, they charged, "*Spirit II* had been measured with her boom and gaff up and down along the mast and her anchor hung at the bow" (*Post-Intelligencer*, July 8, 1908). The effect of this, it was alleged by the Vancouver yachtsmen, was to depress the bow and raise the stern, which would show a shorter water line. In other words, designer/skipper Ted Geary "had beaten the rules."

Geary responded that the keel of the *Spirit II* had no slot. "The lines of the lead were carried full until they came to the place of girth measurement where the sides of the keel near the bottom are swelled similarly to the extreme forward end, which is shaped not unlike the head of a fish. Aft of this the lines fared into the rudder, but the whole hump was but little larger than one's hand" (*Post-Intelligencer*, July 11, 1908).

Charges and countercharges were aired in the press. The arguments became personal between Scott Calhoun, retiring secretary of the Northwest International Yacht Racing Association, and C. B. MacNeill, commodore of the Vancouver Yacht Club. Ted Geary, the Seattle member of the Northwest International Yacht Club Committee, at the next meeting proposed a shift from English (or "International") to Universal regulations of measurement, a proposal that was accepted in 1910.

Meantime the race judges declared the *Spirit II* the winner. The Vancouver club, however, argued that the race was never completed. Since they controlled the trophy, having won it the previous year, they refused to give it up. Four years would pass before the heat dissipated sufficiently to allow international racing to resume. By then the *Spirit II* had been raffled off in Seattle by the original syndicate and won by C. P. Blanchard, Jr., who took her to Vancouver and sold her.

Meanwhile the Northwest International Yacht Racing Association languished and was not revived for a decade. Then it was reconstituted as the Pacific International Yachting Association. The international ill will generated by this tiff later prompted Sir Thomas Lipton to donate a $3,000 trophy for racing the 20-raters of the R class under Universal Rules.

Motorboat activity picked up during the summer months when the 1909 Alaska-Yukon-Pacific Exposition occupied the University of Washington campus. The major motorboat event was a race from Vancouver, B.C., to Seattle in which 23 boats participated. The first place award—the Rudder Cup—was provided by Thomas Fleming Day of *Rudder* Magazine. On race day, the boats fought heavy seas. Seattle boats placed first, second, fourth, fifth, and sixth. Third place, incidentally, was captured by a woman—Mrs. James B. Wood of Winslow in her boat *Clansman*.

The Seattle Motor Boat Club and the Algonquin Club (which represented canoeing and rowing interests) joined forces to develop a temporary clubhouse in the former Madrona Park Hotel on Lake Washington. This gave them room to entertain exposition visitors.

During the summer, motorboats raced several times on Lake Washington, including a July 1 speed test around Mercer Island. Several of these races began and ended at Union Bay, adjacent to the exposition grounds. A Portland boat, *Wolf II*, won most of these races.

Motorboat activities were heating up in other cities, too. For example, in 1909, the Bellingham Motor Boat Club opened fine new quarters on Lake Whatcom.

During the years covered in this chapter—1893 to 1909—Seattle's population was increasing at a furious rate, but the increase in the number of sailing yachts was not proportionate. Even so, some of the new sailing vessels were of trim new design and larger than those of the previous decade, and sailboats from all over the Northwest congregated for the various regattas, often towed by steamers to their destinations.

The most noteworthy developments of this period came in the powerboat field, then so new and unique that the media focused increasing attention on events involving boats with engines. Steam yachts were more common than those propelled by gasoline, because gas engines, many of which were manufactured locally, were large and bulky and not considered very safe.

Photographs of the time show yachting to have been a rather formal affair. Privileged gentlemen (and a few ladies) are shown aboard yachts attired in typical Victorian-era garments—heavy wool suits and head-to-toe dresses, hats, and ankle-high shoes.

While pioneers were seldom yachtsmen, several of the leaders of this era were second-generation Seattleites, inheritors of the wealth accumulated by their pioneering parents. O. O. Denny, for example, was the millionaire son of Seattle founders Arthur and Mary Denny. Other old families, like the Stimsons and the Henrys, were also involved in yachting.

The yacht clubs of the Northwest during this era reinforced their foundations, making them strong enough to survive over the next century. With these more formal institutions came better organized sailing events. Handicapping, for example, was introduced to make racing more of a contest. In other words, as Northwest society became more sophisticated, so did the pastimes, including yachting. ☆

THREE

1910-1919

The Seattle Yacht Club in West Seattle, c. 1912. (MOHAI)

The years between 1910 and 1920 found Seattle's population increasing from 237,194 to 315,312, but these were not financially rewarding years for most families. During this decade World War I came and went, women were emancipated, prohibition became the law of the land, and the automobile began to replace "Old Dobbin."

After a strenuous 1909, which had brought the Alaska-Yukon-Pacific Exposition and the squabble over the Alexandra's Cup, the new decade dawned comparatively calmly.

1910

In May several Seattle Yacht Club members cruised south to picnic with families of the new Olympia Motor Boat Club on the beach north of Mud Bay Spit.

The club's first motor cruiser race for the R. C. Doman Cup occurred on May 29, 1910. B. F. Jacobs of Tacoma in his *Marana* inched out Seattle's *Lady May.*

An SYC "High Jinks" cruise in June attracted 35 Puget Sound yachts to Port Madison for a feast. In its publication the committee in charge promised "an Igorotte war dance plus a meal of boiled dog meat, and other features that yachtsmen enjoy," (the Igorottes were Filipino aborigines, reportedly dog eaters, who had performed at the recent world's fair).

Victoria hosted the 1910 Northwest International Yachting Association Regatta and did such a good job that the board voted to hold the next two regattas there with other clubs sharing costs. However, when 1911 arrived and other clubs were asked to defray $1,750 in expenses (Seattle was sent a bill for $100), not one responded with dollars. The 1911 regatta was canceled, and, in essence, the NIYA ceased to operate.

The Fourth of July motorboat trials were held in Vancouver that year, and the *Seattle Spirit*, a 32-footer owned by the

SYC 1892

The SYC Burgee

SYC 1910

Our special yachting vocabulary often causes disputes over the meanings of words. People noted for engaging in these arguments are known as "sea lawyers." One of the most famous SYC disagreements involved Andy Joy's frequent and typically feisty reminders that the technical name for the SYC flag is "pennant," not "burgee." The technicality is that a "burgee" has two points on its tail rather than one. People paid attention to what Andy said because he was almost always right. Chapman, on flag etiquette in his boaters' bible, *Piloting, Seamanship and Small Boat Handling*, recognizes the semantic conflict:

The *burgee* we might regard as a swallow-tailed flag which is (1) commonly pointed, triangular (2) often truncated, as in some Navy signals (3) sometimes swallow-tailed (4) occasionally a long thin streamer.

The trouble with Andy's argument was that virtually every yacht club has a single-tailed flag which it calls a "burgee." When people hear the word "pennant," they usually think of what is waved at a football game. Perhaps single-pointed flags are popular because they are easier to make than double-pointed ones.

Boating customs and yachting etiquette have long been a tradition maintained by Puget Sound yachtsmen. For example, they want to follow the proper procedure in displaying signal flags.

The Seattle Yacht Club emblem is a vestige of the amalgamation of the Seattle and Elliott Bay yacht clubs in 1909. Our present burgee—with its red star and blue bar imposed on a field of white—was originally the pennant of EBYC.

All flying signal flags should be sized proportionally to the boat displaying them. This is true of SYC's burgee, too. On sailboats and powerboats with signal masts, the fly (length) of the burgee should be proportioned to have one half inch of length for each foot in height of the tallest truck or mast above the waterline. For powerboats on the plane, the fly should be five-eighths inch for each foot of overall length. The preferred location to fly the burgee is at the masthead of the forward spar. Alternate locations are at the bow (jack) staff or at the forward starboard spreader flag halyard. No flag may be displayed above the national ensign except the burgee when it is hoisted to the masthead location.

When constructing the SYC burgee, a swatch of pure white virgin material should be selected. The basic triangle will be cut such that the hoist (width) will be two-thirds of the proper fly length. The width of the blue bar is to be one-fifth the length of the hoist. The blue bar rests at a 45-degree angle from the lower end of the hoist such that it bisects the white field into two triangles. The red star rests in the center of the upper triangle with the fifth ray pointing in a vertical position. ◇

West Seattle Ferry Dock, with the Seattle Yacht Club and moorage beyond it to the right, c. 1910. (George A. Bayless Collection)

Brace and Hergert Mill Company (they had taken over the former David Denny Mill at the southern tip of Lake Union), covered the 30-mile course in 59 minutes and 4 seconds. This, the newspapers exclaimed, was faster than "a mile in two minutes!" But in the actual race, this speedster caught fire and, though the flames were contained, had to be towed to dock. The ever-present, Portland-owned *Wolf II* took the $500 prize.

The most publicized race of the year was the motorboat stamina test from Ketchikan to Vancouver in early August. A $500 trophy donated by Seattleite A. V. Cominga, publisher of *Pacific Motor Boat* magazine, was awarded to the *Limit*, owned by A. L. Page of Vancouver, B.C. *Limit* covered the 600 miles in 58 hours.

The 1910 Yearbook—A First!

The *1910 Club Book of the Seattle Yacht Club*, the first ever published, contained some interesting history. Originally prepared by the Elliott Bay Yacht Club, it was issued shortly after the 1909 amalgamation of the two clubs and therefore contained only the names of Elliott Bay members and their boats and the rules and bylaws of that club. The following is taken from this old yearbook.

> The Elliott Bay Yacht Club was organized March 1, 1894, with 50 members and 26 yachts enrolled. Club quarters were leased from the Brighton Boathouse at the foot of Battery Street, where they remained in active participation and encouragement of yacht racing and sailing until the lease expired in 1904, when the Club adjourned until they could secure new quarters.
>
> The fleet and members remained loyal to the Club and kept the Club colors in evidence at all cruising and racing events during the following three lax years.
>
> In the early spring of 1907, a location for a clubhouse and fleet anchorage at West Seattle being secured, the Club was called together and reorganized.
>
> The Elliott Bay Yacht Club joined the Northwestern International Yacht Racing As-

sociation in 1894 and has remained in good standing and taken part in all of its regattas and affairs to date. The association meeting races were held at Seattle under the auspices of the E.B.Y.C. in 1899.

The annual regatta of the Club held on Labor Day of each year from 1894 to 1903, open to all yacht clubs of the Northwest, was invariably the best regatta of the year in point of entries and management. First and second trophies and racing flags being awarded in each of the four classes.

On the next page this "addenda" was boldly framed in black:

Since going to press an amalgamation of the Elliott Bay Yacht Club and the Seattle Yacht Club has been effected, the new organization taking the name of the Seattle Yacht Club—which was considered to be the better and more distinctive name. The flag of The Elliott Bay Yacht Club was adopted, and the officers of that club retained their respective positions in the new club. Signed: C. Benson Wood, M.D., Secretary.

—1910 Club Book of the Seattle Yacht Club

A bit of fashion advice for yachting women was found in the *Post-Intelligencer* in the summer of 1910.

The girl who sails her own catboat looks best in a simple white waist and skirt and a plain sailor or Panama hat. A sailor blouse with a plaited or plain gored skirt is year after year the fashionable sailing costume, and there is no real alteration in this dress from summer to summer.

For yachting, heavy duck or canvas coat and skirt costume are worn with simple white bodice. The sailor blouse and plaited skirt are also worn on a yacht, and there must be provided a white flannel or serge dress and coat for the days when the ocean breezes blow cool and fresh. . . .

—Post-Intelligencer, *Aug. 1, 1910*

The 1910 yearbook described the official men's dress uniform as "a plain dress suit with white dress vest, with fouled anchor buttons in gilt on same; white tie and club ribbon worn diagonally across the bosom from right to left." "Undress" called for "double-breasted sack coat of blue serge or white flannel with vest of same material as coat. The black club button to be worn with the blue and the gilt button with the white. Trousers of same material as coat, or of white duck may be worn with the blue."

The Seattle Yacht Club was not the only busy club on the sound in 1910. Newton Greene wrote in *Pacific Motor Boat* for November 1910 that the Everett Yacht Club sponsored the Labor Day races and invited a flotilla to the eastern shore of Whidbey Island where a camping spot had been prepared, and "something less than a million clams had been gathered for a bake to be pulled off later in the day." The Lake Union Yacht Club of Seattle was thriving with 35 sailing enthusiasts as members, most of whom resided near the lake. They sponsored Sunday regattas during the summer months. Joseph E. Peterson was commodore of this club.

1911

A "rousing meeting" was held on April 20, 1911, at the Seattle Yacht Club to plan for April 29 Opening Day. "Wives and sweethearts" of members were recruited to welcome visitors. All boats were on display with flags flying, and bands performed all during the afternoon. At 11:00 A.M. the Hansen Cup Power Boat Race to Everett began. In the early afternoon a race was scheduled for larger sailing craft to compete for the Sunde and Erland Cup. Later a dinghy race for the trophy awarded by the Max Kuner Company (now the Captain's Trophy Company) was scheduled.

A special committee chaired by Robert E. Magner recommended that SYC initiation fees be reduced to $10 for the remainder of 1911 and that a recruiting drive begin. The plan worked, for within six months 43 new members had been added to the roster, many of them motorboaters. This brought the total

Commodores of the Seattle Yacht Club—1910-1919

S. A. HOYT
1910
Occupation: Master Mariner
Boat: 45-foot auxiliary schooner Reverie

H. W. STARRETT
1911
Occupation: Manager, Sunset Boat and Engine Company

DR. HARRY V. WURDEMANN
1912
Born: 1865
Education: George Washington University
Occupation: Physician
Boat: 57-foot cruiser Lady May

JOHN GRAHAM, SR.
1913
Occupation: Architect
Boat: Yawl Ortona, *40-foot auxiliary schooner* Sovereign

ROBERT E. MAGNER
1914
Occupation: Manager, Warner Instrument Company

WILLIAM G. NORRIS
1915
Occupation: Owner, Norris Safe and Lock
Boats: 55-foot cruiser Geoduck *and 75-foot schooner* La Viajera

J. E. CHILBERG
1916
Occupation: Manager, Steamship Line; Insurance Agent

NORVAL H. (NED) LATIMER
1917-1919
Born: 1863, Berwick, Ill.
Occupation: President, Dexter Horton Bank

membership to 292.

A noteworthy launching occurred in 1911. The 96-foot *Taconite*, belonging to William E. Boeing, was completed at Heath's Shipyard on the Duwamish River. (This shipyard later became the site of Boeing's first airplane factory. One of the original buildings, known today as the "Red Barn," is located at the Museum of Flight.)

As a final note on this year, a rather humorous story involving the first Elliott Bay Yacht Club commodore was found in *Pacific Motor Boat*:

It isn't often that a motor boat owner deliberately goes around looking for trouble, but a recent event in Seattle Yacht Club circles makes the friends of Henry Hensel, chairman of the house committee of that club and one of the best of all 'round sportsmen, think that he is guilty of such a failing. For Mr. Hensel was recently assessed a very interesting little fine by Uncle Sam for certain failures as to equipment, etc., etc., and thereby hangs a very funny tale.

Mr. Hensel had his motor boat thoroughly overhauled this spring and on the very first trip out thereafter he didn't take the precaution to see that every requirement of the federal statutes was lived up to in his equipment. Everything might have been all right had Mr. Hensel not decided to go over to the Pacific Net and Twine Co. for some supplies. When he got there he found what he supposed was a big tug tied up to the dock and, as he was going to stay but a few moments, he tied up to the tug and started to cross her decks to go over and get his supplies. He had hardly set foot on deck before a jaunty revenue officer approached him and with a pleasant "Good morning" informed him that, as long as he was there he guessed he would look over Mr. Hensel's boat. Mr. Hensel gazed aloft, and fluttering from the supposed tug's foremast was the barred pennant of the revenue service. It was the revenue tug *Arcata*, just in for supplies, and the Seattle yachtsman found that he had literally sought and bound himself to trouble, trouble, trouble. The fine was assessed, but there were a great many extenuating circumstances and the result was that Mr. Hensel ultimately did not have to pay it. And then to get even, Mr. Hensel, who is a wholesale manufacturing jeweler, closed a contract with the government to supply the *Arcata* with a full new equipment of silverware, so the whole affair ended as happily as marriage bells.

—Pacific Motor Boat, *(undated clipping)*

1912

The sailing year began in April when the Seattle Yacht Club staged the Protection Island Race, the first in the Tri-Island series for the Metropolitan Club's handsome challenge cup. The course extended from the Seattle Yacht Club to and around Protection Island, which guards the mouth of Port Discovery, and return to Seattle. The course totaled about 120 miles. W. D. Wiley's sloop, *Bat*, of Seattle sailed the course in the best time, which was 29 hours and 23 minutes.

The Seattle Yacht Club was also involved in July's Golden Potlatch celebration, which was a forerunner of Seafair. SYC Commodore Wurdemann was chairman of the Potlatch Marine Committee, composed entirely of SYC members. This committee was responsible for managing the marine parade, entertaining visiting yachtsmen, and for all "water features" of Potlatch. The most imposing spectacle of the event was the marine parade of July 17, 1912, which featured the "treasure ship" *Portland*, the Alaskan steamer that had carried the first gold from the Yukon on July 17, 1897. Escorted by a fleet of steamboats, torpedo vessels, revenue cutters and most of the yacht club fleet, the *Portland* paraded around the harbor and into the Grand Trunk Dock to the accompaniment of screeching whistles and booming cannon.

The Potlatch sail races pitted the Seattle yacht *Spirit II* against the Everett-owned *Genevieve*. The *Spirit II* recently had been acquired by Burt Fenn and Cal Blanchard. *Genevieve* was owned by Commodore H. B. Goldfinch of the Everett Yacht Club. *Spirit II* not only won the Potlatch trophy but also the Sunde and Erland sailing trophy.

Two large powerboats struggled through three races for the Pacific Net and Twine Company's Cup and the SYC powerboat championship. Ferdinand Schmitz' *Sans Souci II* captured the first race, and Commodore H. V. Wurdemann's *Lady May* took the second during Potlatch week. In the final race on Aug. 3, 1912, the *Sans Souci II* crossed the finish line first to win the championship.

This was also the year SYC Commodore Wurdemann prepared a comprehensive chart of cruising waters in the Pacific Northwest. This handsome litho-

"A Night on the Barbary Coast" was a melodrama presented in honor of Sir Thomas Lipton by SYC members on Jan. 18, 1913, in the West Seattle clubhouse. The cast, from the left, included Quent Williams, Jack Chisholm, Dietrich Schmitz, Mel Cushing, Chatham Burt, Philip Moore (standing in the rear), Lester Wilson, Dr. F. E. O'Connell as Sir Thomas Longlip, Dean Johnson, Harold Chutter, Dick Morris, Hulmuth Schmitz, Lloyd Johnson, Dr. Warbols, F. J. Dobson, and Wynn Jones. (Photo by Esther Anderson)

graph was mailed to boating organizations throughout the country by the Seattle Yacht Club and the Seattle Chamber of Commerce. To this day one hangs on the wall in the SYC Marine Room.

Yacht club members continued the search for new club and mooring sites. During 1912 two suggested locations—Bainbridge Island and the south end of Lake Union—were considered but dropped.

The biggest yachting news in several years was the arrival of Sir Thomas Lipton in Seattle in November 1912. The distinguished visitor, one of the most successful British grocers and tea men, sailed in from Victoria on the Canadian Pacific liner *Princess Adelaide*. He praised Seattle's growth and development over the previous two decades, during which the population had increased from about 100,000 to 240,000.

Ted Geary recalled:

> [Sir Thomas and his male secretary] seemed to enjoy talking to Seattle yachtsmen more than being hauled around by bigwigs. So we had plenty of time to tell him about our strained relations with our Canadian friends. He offered to put up a $3,000 cup for racing with 20 raters under the Universal Rule. We called up Ron Maitland and Billy MacKenzie in Vancouver. They promptly challenged. We named the Seattle syndicate boat *Sir Tom* and sent him clippings of her success down the years, which pleased the old gent no end.
>
> —*Ted Geary, 1950s*

1913

With the rebirth of yachting enthusiasm, by 1913 SYC could count 371 members and a fleet of 88 yachts. Many events were scheduled for that year, as the list of races in the SYC 1913 yearbook indicated:

March 28—Protection Island Race

April 28—Hat Island Race

May 3—Opening Day (The Sunde and Erland Cup was awarded for best time over course. The Pacific Net and Twine Cup was planned for cruising powerboats. Dinghy races were scheduled for ladies and for members.)

May 30—Sunde and Erland Cup Race (from Seattle to Tacoma Yacht Club) and the Doman Cup Race (for cruisers over 30 feet, awarded to first boat to round Bainbridge Island and complete race at Tacoma Yacht Club)

June 14—Augustine and Kyer Trophy Race from Seattle to Tacoma to Seattle for cruisers over 40 feet (the third heat is for yachts under 40 feet)

June 28—Sunde and Erland Cup Race (third heat for this cup and second heat for the Pacific Net and Twine Cup) and a catboat regatta

July 16-19—Potlatch week (special races for sail and power)

August 4-9—Victoria Water Carnival, Pacific International Power Boat Association

August 10—Naval Burial at Sea and Big Yachtsman's Power Cruise from Victoria to Prevost Harbor on Stuart Island

August 16—Olympic Brewing Cup Race (powerboats racing from SYC to Olympia)

August 30—Sailing and power races to Everett (Labor Day events were held at Everett)

An advertisement in the 1913 yearbook stated: "You can get big benefits from the Seattle Yacht Club even if you are not a boat owner. Become an associate member. Dues $5 per year. No initiation fee." (Program of Races, SYC Yearbook, 1913)

The *Post-Intelligencer* published a special March 1913 yachting section under the title "Piping Breezes on Puget Sound." The article by Rear Commodore C. P. Constantine of the Seattle Yacht Club described the excellent nearby cruising waters and concluded with information about yachting events.

> The Seattle Yacht Club promises much to its members this coming season. The regatta committee has planned a veritable carnival of outdoor sports, which began with the long-distance race around Protection Island on March 28, 1913.
>
> The club is also providing about nine or ten one-class boats designed for safety as well as speed, for the use of its members, with the hope that this will do much to encourage yachting, particularly among the younger men of Seattle, and eventually get them interested enough to invest in boats of their own and enjoy to the full the joys of yachting and cruising on Puget Sound.
>
> The Sunday Club cruises to Bainbridge Island and other points are another popular feature. During Potlatch week the club is pledged to do everything possible to help the water carnival features by arranging races for all classes of boats, and to take part in the water parade.
>
> —Post-Intelligencer, *April 6, 1913*

In the middle of the article was this little poem set off in a box:

> When the northwest wind is blowing
> hard
> And the blue and white is in the sky
> And the sharp-cut waves are streaked
> and scarred
> Where the darting squalls race by:
> When the leeward shrouds are
> whelmed in green
> And the leeward deck's afoam,
> And a dancing wake all white is seen
> Back toward the shores of home—
> Oh, that is the day my heart would
> choose
> For setting sail on a summer cruise.
>
> —*M. A. De Wolfe Howe,*
> Post-Intelligencer, *April 6, 1913*

In April, the Seattle Yacht Club presented its final preseason stag smoker at the clubhouse. The program gives an idea of what went on at those affairs in 1913. The big feature was a member-produced circus, which was described as follows:

> Every feature that goes with a regular circus will be in evidence, as well as many new and novel stunts. Special moving pictures of the champion speed boat races on the Hudson and the Mississippi rivers will be shown. The Knickerbocker quartet will furnish music during the evening and refreshments will be served with the usual generosity of sailors.
>
> —Post-Intelligencer, *April 20, 1913*

Once again the civic Potlatch celebration was a time of much activity at the yacht club. A series of speedboat races were scheduled over three days, and three races for new catboats were scheduled on Puget Sound. Of course the usual handicapped sail races were major events, as well. D. Thomas Davies, port warden, reserved space on the city floats at the foot of Pike Street for moorage of out-of-town boats. In the Potlatch contests, SYC Commodore John Graham's yawl *Ortona* and George F. Wiley's sloop *Bat* won the Potlatch cups.

In early August the Seattle Yacht Club provided transportation from Victoria to Seattle for the famous John Henry Mears, who was attempting to travel around the world in 35 days. Vince Faben, in his speedy power yacht *Maude F*, met the liner *Empress of Russia* at the British Columbia quarantine station and rushed

The *Sir Tom*

The *Sir Tom* is without doubt the most famous sailboat in Seattle Yacht Club history. She was designed to the Universal 20-rater rule by L. E. (Ted) Geary in 1913 to compete for the Sir Thomas Lipton Perpetual Challenge Trophy. Her builders were Norman J. Blanchard, Dean and Lloyd Johnson, and Joseph McKay. She was financed by a Seattle Yacht Club syndicate of Fred Fisher, W. G. Norris, John Graham, Sr., Philip Bornstein, Edgar Webster, O. O. Denny, and Ted Geary.

The Sir Tom *as she appeared in the late 1940s. (MOHAI)*

She first raced in an elimination series on Elliott Bay against two boats: *Defender*, owned by Joseph Parker, and *Spray*, owned by Quent Williams. After winning handily, *Sir Tom* took on Canadian challengers for the Lipton Cup. Over the years, she out-sped *Turenga*, *Patricia*, *Lady Pat*, *Riowna*, and *Lady Van*, holding the Pacific International Yachting Association R class championship from 1914 to 1929. She also held the Pacific Coast and U.S. R class championships, defeating all contenders in San Diego, Santa Barbara, Newport Beach, San Pedro, and San Francisco over a 14-year period.

Throughout most of her racing days, *Sir Tom* was skippered by her designer, Ted Geary. The following men served on her crew during various stages of her career: N. J. Blanchard, Dean Johnson, Lloyd Johnson, Joseph McKay, Bert Griffiths, Stanley Griffiths, Colin Radford, Forney Dobson, Walter S. Geary, George White, John Dreher, Fritz Hellenthal, Ray Anderson, Jack Chisholm, John (Jack) Graham, Jr., Douglas Egan, William MacKenzie, J. Swift Baker, Roy W. Corbett and Anderson S. Joy.

Art Ayers purchased *Sir Tom* from the syndicate and guided her to still more wins during the 10 years he owned her. He later sold *Sir Tom* to Norman J. Blanchard, Sr. Finally, in 1956, after this proud 43-year-old speedster was found to be suffering from deterioration, she was consigned to the scrap heap.

—Adapted from the SYC Yearbook, 1957

The crew of John Graham's Ortona *c. 1913 included (from left) Ted Geary, unknown, Norm J. Blanchard, Sr., John Graham, Sr., Lloyd Johnson, and Fritz Hellenthal. (N. C. Blanchard Collection)*

Mears to Seattle in time to catch the Northern Pacific "Flyer" for St. Paul. Mears was attempting to better the record time of 39 days, 19 hours, and 43 minutes, held by Andre Jaeger Schmidt, a French newspaperman.

First Outstation

In 1913 the Seattle Yacht Club purchased five acres and leased another five on Manzanita Bay on the northwest side of Bainbridge Island. There, near a settlement that in 1908 had been named Venice after the California town, they planned an "outside station." The property extended across the point to the inside bay, providing landing possibilities both outside and inside the bay. A handsome clubhouse was planned, and ranch buildings on the property were leased until the clubhouse was ready. Architect John Graham, Sr., quickly prepared plans for the structure.

A barbecue and clambake were scheduled on the new site in July. Special steamers carried visitors who could not find space on yachts. Plans called for a float on the Manzanita Bay side and a new 178-foot-long pier. Members discussed the potential for tennis courts and even a golf course on the site. This was the first outstation developed by the Seattle Yacht Club.

1914

Opening Day fell on May 16 and the program included several races, an evening dance, and card games. A month later, the race for the Sunde and Erland Cup was won by Quent Williams' sloop *Spray*.

In mid-June, the papers reported on a 1,500-mile cruise taken by Mr. and Mrs. Louis Hemrich and friends on their private yacht *Rainier*. They had explored the inlets along the coast of British Columbia while hunting and fishing. They hoped to bring home some grizzly bear skins as trophies, however:

> The shaggy denizens of the dense thickets and craggy ravines showed nothing but a

Seattle Yacht Club

GENERAL MEETING AND SMOKER

At the Club House, Tuesday Evening, Oct. 7th, 8 P. M.

Presentation of the Sir Thomas Lipton Cup to the Club by the Lipton Club Committee.

Presentation of Race Trophies to winners by the Regatta Committee.

There'll be something doing. Come.

C. L. Burt, Secretary.

Robert E. Magner, Vice Commodore.

The invitation to the trophy presentations of Oct. 7, 1913.

desire to remain in seclusion. The party saw only one, which they wounded. This big fellow was crossing an old snowslide near Gardner's Inlet and was not over 300 yards away from the boat when sighted. He was scrambling over the rocky ground at an astonishing speed and displaying an unwonted agility for so bulky a brute. Every one on board grabbed a rifle and opened fire on him, but, although he was badly wounded, as was discovered later by bloodstains on the ground, he managed to get away, and the search had to be discontinued on account of darkness.

—Post-Intelligencer, *June 15, 1914*

While in the Gardner's Bay region, the Hemrich yacht narrowly escaped being swamped as the result of a huge snowslide. Those aboard saw the slide begin high on the mountainside and watched it uproot trees and pick up huge rocks before it slammed into the bay about half a mile from the yacht, stirring up huge waves that for a time threatened to engulf the *Rainier*.

The Seattle Yacht Club development at Venice on Bainbridge Island received a page in the *Post-Intelligencer* real estate section on June 18, 1914. The article mentioned that 13 new houses had been completed and four more were under construction near the site. Among the yacht club members living there were Robert Zinkle of the Carnation Milk Company; R. E. Bates of Pacific Telephone and Telegraph Company; L. K. Cummings, manager of Pacific Motor Boat Company; and Quent Williams, rear commodore of the Seattle Yacht Club. Thousands of dollars were spent on the park and grounds under the direction of

SYC's first outstation was established at Manzanita Bay on Bainbridge Island in 1913 and disposed of at a later date. (John Graham, Sr., Collection)

Albert B. Lord, president of the Bainbridge Island Land Company.

Over the years, the West Seattle clubhouse was frequently used for social events. For example, here is an item from the *Seattle Examiner*, the West Seattle newspaper.

Reception at Yacht Club

A brilliant reception was given at the Yacht Club Wednesday afternoon by Mrs. Dana Brown and Mrs. Joseph Harris in compliment to Mrs. Howard Edward Luby, sister of Mrs. Harris. The receiving room and veranda were gay with potted plants, native greens and bright colored flowers. A large basket of Chatney roses centered the tea table at which Mrs. Clarence Wiley and Mrs. John L. Marr presided, assisted by Mrs. J. Walter Hainsworth, Mrs. Paul Richardson, Miss Mabel Luby, and Mrs. Delbert Andrews. Sweet peas were prettily arranged on the punch table where Mrs. Percy Truax and Mrs. Benjamin Easterbrook served. The hostesses were assisted in receiving by Mrs. J. B. Shorett, Mrs. W. H. Hainsworth, Mrs. Charles Armstrong, Mrs. Murray Holland and Mrs. Sergo Migliavacca. Over one hundred guests were present.

—Seattle Examiner, *July 1, 1914*

First Lipton Cup Race

In April the newspapers began touting the first Lipton Cup Race which was scheduled as part of Seattle's Potlatch celebration. Several clubs had promised to send competitors, but most dropped out prior to the July date. The Royal Victoria yachtsmen reported they could not raise the funds to build a new racer. The spreading war in Europe may have had something to do with this.

Three Seattle yachts raced elimina-

How the Lipton Cup Came to the Seattle Yacht Club

Sir Thomas Lipton, the world-famous yachtsman, stopped for three days in Seattle in mid-November 1912 on his way from London to attend an international conference of yachtsmen in San Francisco. He was amazed at the vitality of the city on Elliott Bay and predicted even greater growth.

The development of Seattle from a seashore settlement on Puget Sound to a world metropolis in less than a quarter of a century, marvelous as it is, will be as naught compared to its prodigious growth following the opening [in 1914] of the Panama Canal. . . . Apart from the abundant evidence of your Queen City's great industries and enterprises one only has to look at the map to be gripped instantly with the tremendously fine strategic position occupied by this metropolis. I don't see any port on the whole Pacific Coast to which the opening of the canal will mean more than this city. I think the future of Seattle will be a revelation to the whole world when the Panama Canal is open.

—Seattle Times, *Nov. 14, 1912*

Sir Thomas reminded local citizens that they have been unaware of Seattle's immense growth and development over the two previous decades from 40,000 in 1890 to 240,000 in 1910, figures that staggered some members of Sir Thomas' party.

While still on the *Princess Adelaide* last night, Sir Thomas on seeing the lights of the Queen City for the first time, said to the *Times*' representative: "I cannot see your city but, by George the very lighting of your streets tells all the world there is the proper sort of ginger in the citizens of Seattle."

Met by the reception committee of the Seattle Press Club and prominent yachtsmen on landing, Sir Thomas asked all to accompany him to his headquarters at the Hotel Washington, where he entertained them in an interesting chat. On the way to the hotel, the lighting on Second Avenue drew forth the admiring remark that this is the most beautifully lighted city ever he had seen.

A few minutes with Sir Thomas brings conviction that there is no secret about his tremendous world-wide popularity. From out the rollicking, jovial atmosphere of the man there exudes the underlying love of good sport and his whole conversation has a kindly tinge for the people in it.

And the British baronet makes no secret of his pride in American institutions and his affection for our people. In one breath: "By George, it's good to be under the Stars and Stripes." In another: "The best friends I have in the world are the American citizens."

—Seattle Times, *Nov. 14, 1912*

The Sir Tom *(SYC) and* Turenga *(Vancouver) in the first competition for the Lipton Cup, 1914. (N. C. Blanchard Collection)*

After private business meetings, Sir Thomas welcomed a group of University of Washington students. Later, he interrupted his drive around the boulevards long enough to address the student body at the university. According to Sir Thomas, the university was a splendid institution and turned out much good material.

> When you are going in for sport, I hope that you will not forget yachting, the healthiest, cleanest and best sport in the world. There is no place I should think in all the world better for the sport than your wonderful Puget Sound and Lake Washington.
>
> —Seattle Times, *Nov. 14, 1912*

The cup Sir Thomas Lipton gave to the Seattle Yacht Club in 1912. (Wallace Ackerman Photography)

Sir Thomas was entertained at the Press Club and at the Rainier Club, and he saw a play at the Metropolitan Theater which starred Maclyn Arbuckle, a son of one of Sir Thomas' friends.

At the conclusion of the Press Club entertainment, Sir Thomas, very aware of the bitterness resulting from the dispute over the Alexandra's Cup, announced that he would present a perpetual international challenge cup to the Seattle Yacht Club. He would order the cup from London silversmiths upon his return home and have it forwarded to the Seattle Yacht Club. The noted yachtsman expressed his hope that British Columbian and American yachtsmen on this coast would contest for the cup on Puget Sound, which he pronounced one of the finest sailing courses he had ever seen. Seattle Yacht Club Commodore H. V. Wurdemann expressed thanks on behalf of his club and of all yachtsmen on this coast.

That massive silver Lipton Cup, created more than three-quarters of a century ago, is on display in the lobby of the Seattle Yacht Club.◇

tion heats to see which would represent SYC: J. H. Parker's *Defender*, Quent Williams' *Spray*, and *Sir Tom*, sailed by Ted Geary. The new Geary boat easily outclassed the other two.

The Lipton Cup finals, which pitted the Royal Vancouver Yacht Club's *Turenga* against the *Sir Tom*, were really no contest. The *Seattle Times* reported on the second and final heat:

> By a margin of slightly less than two minutes, the Seattle sloop *Sir Tom*, Skipper Ted Geary, won over the Vancouver challenger for the Sir Thomas Lipton Cup, the *Turenga*, Skipper Ronald Maitland, in a 12-mile windward-leeward race in Seattle Harbor yesterday afternoon. The successful defense of the Lipton trophy by the *Sir Tom* means that the Seattle Yacht Club, under whose pennant the Geary boat sailed, will have the honor of placing the first plate on the great wooden base of the magnificent trophy.
>
> —Seattle Times, *July 18, 1914*

Thus began the long reign of the *Sir Tom*. Her designer and skipper Ted Geary, in 1960, just four months before his death, composed a brief history of this proud sloop to be attached to the 3/4-inch scale model on display at the yacht club. Here is part of what he wrote.

> The Canadians in Vancouver quickly challenged and named R boat *Turenga*, then being designed by E. B. Schock. The Seattle group was quick to provide defenders: *Spray*, designed, built and financed by Quent Williams, prominent member of the Seattle Yacht Club; a second boat named *Defender* was financed by Joseph T. Parker from designs by L. H. Coolidge; a third one by a Seattle Yacht Club syndicate consisting of O. O. Denny, P. J. Bernstein, F. T. Fischer, L. E. "Ted" Geary, John Graham, Sr., W. G. Norris, and Edgar Webster. The Syndicate quickly named her *Sir Tom* after the donor of the cup. *Sir Tom* was built by Johnson Brothers and Blanchard from plans by L. E. "Ted" Geary.
>
> This model was made by Edwin Monk to three-fourths-inch scale, rigged by Charles Allen and Capt. F. L. Wingo.
>
> Dimensions:
> L.O.A. 38'+
> L.W.L. 23'-0"
> Breadth 7'-10"
> Draft 5'-6"
> Displace 8,500 lbs.
> Lead Keel 4,500 lbs.
> Sail Area 400 sq. ft.
> Rating 19.99
>
> All the trial races to select the defender were won by *Sir Tom*. She met *Turenga* at Seattle in the 2nd, 3rd, and 4th of July races and won quite handily.
>
> World War I started the first of August 1914, and the British did not race again for about four years. *Sir Tom* had plenty of competition; she held the Northwest championship until 1931, a matter of 17 years, and in 1926, while most of her crew were helping win the Honolulu race with Don Lee's schooner *Invader*, John Graham, Jr., *Sir Tom*'s spinnaker man, took the helm and under his hand she kept her Northwest title intact. . . .
>
> Her active career ended about 1931 and like all good racing sailboats she was finally broken up about 1957 for the bit of lead in her keel.
>
> During her racing career she was practically rebuilt twice and the rig changed to keep up with the times. Many will remember how Seattle Yacht Club's little R boat *Sir Tom* kept on top those 20-odd years.
>
> —*Ted Geary, Jan. 27, 1960*

1915

Though the year started well with many plans for yachting events, the war in Europe curtailed much of the activity. The Royal Victoria and Vancouver yacht clubs did not participate in any international races.

On the other hand, San Francisco yachtsmen were anxious to race against the *Sir Tom*, especially at the Panama-Pacific Exposition, which was scheduled in that city over the summer. The *Sir Tom* won by such wide margins that potential competitors often junked plans to build challengers.

A number of cruises to the outstation at Venice were planned during the year. On April 24, 1915, a raft of logs was towed to yacht club properties to be used as pilings for the new pier. The Kitsap Transportation Company ferries began serving Venice a couple of weeks earlier than usual because of yachting activities.

The crew of the Sir Tom *in 1915 (from left): Fritz Hellenthal, Dean Johnson, Ted Geary, Norm J. Blanchard, Sr., Lloyd Johnson. (N. C. Blanchard Collection)*

The 21st anniversary of the SYC was celebrated on March 13, 1915, at the Butler Hotel banquet hall. The room was divided into two sections, with "windjammers on one side and powerboat men on the other. The officers and the guests sat at a cross section table between. . . ." (*Post-Intelligencer*, March 14, 1915)

During the year, W. E. Jones began writing a feature column called "With the Yachtsmen," for the *Post-Intelligencer*. He reported activities down to the smallest detail. In the first column of March 14, 1915, he described the annual SYC banquet and mentioned several yachts of note: SYC Vice Commodore C. P. Constantine had sold his *Sabrina* and purchased the *Bonita* from its Tacoma owner. Colonel H. W. Rowley of Billings was building a 50-foot cruiser at Johnson Brothers and Blanchard in Georgetown. Rowley intended to take advantage of "the finest sheet of water in the western hemisphere for yachtsmen—Puget Sound." A syndicate of Seattle yachtsmen purchased the schooner *La Viajera*, a name translated as *The Wanderer*. In 1916, this boat would be purchased by SYC Commodore William G. Norris to use as a charter vessel.

Three big stories of the year kept SYC in the headlines. The Shriners' convention in mid-July resulted in all sorts of boat races to entertain the 50,000 visitors. The contest for the Nile Cup resulted in the *Sir Tom* winning the first and third races against the speedy *Myth* of Everett, and the latter winning the second race.

The second event was a race from Seattle to San Francisco won by Captain John Barneson's sloop *Genevieve*. She traveled the 804 miles in 140 hours and 58 minutes, beating out John Graham, Sr.'s *Ortona*.

The third race of note resulted in Ted Geary sending the *Sir Tom* to San Francisco aboard an American-Hawaiian steamer. He and most of his crew then boarded Graham's *Ortona* as crew members on the race south. In the R-boat class races at the San Francisco Exposition, the *Sir Tom* was invincible. She and the *Ortona* brought back five cups.

In 1915 and 1916 the Seattle Yacht Club published the *Yachtsman*, "the official magazine" of the club. How many issues were published is not known, and apparently no copies exist today.

As a final activity for 1915, Seattle yachtsmen decided to try to revive the Northwest International Yacht Racing Association which had been defunct since the 1910 Alexandra's Cup disagreement. A committee of Daniel Pratt, Ted Geary, Scott Calhoun, Dr. Frank O'Connell, John Graham, Sr., and SYC Commodore William Norris invited other yacht clubs of the Pacific Northwest to a meeting to consider reorganizing. However, World War I, then sweeping through Europe, killed the effort.

1916

Seattle Yacht Club officers boasted that 20 new boats had joined the club fleet, making a total of more than 100 fine yachts.

In the spring of 1916 William E. Jones reported in the *Post-Intelligencer* that an effort was afoot to organize a regional Puget Sound Yacht Association. Perhaps a motivating factor was Canadian involvement in the spreading European war which prevented Canadian yachts from racing. However, as Jones explained it in his column:

> . . . in recent years there has been a lack of unity among different clubs and also between the motorboat and sailboat men. The various clubs were members of the Pacific International Power Boat Association, organized for the promotion of motor boating and from which the sailboat men derive little or no benefit. The same clubs have also belonged to the Northwest International Yacht Racing Association, whose offices are for the sailors and from whom the powerboat men derive little or no benefit. It is the purpose of the organizers of the Puget Sound Yachting Association to bring into touch yachtsmen of both kinds of craft. In the past the regattas of the two organizations have been held on different dates and the lack of support has finally resulted in several of the Puget Sound clubs practically dropping from active membership.
>
> —Post-Intelligencer, *March 12, 1916*

The Queen City Yacht Club

To pleasure boaters' delight, the completion of the Lake Washington Ship Canal and the Hiram Chittenden Locks in 1916 made Lake Washington, Lake Union and all of Puget Sound accessible.

About this time, J. W. Lough, a founder and second commodore of the Queen City Yacht Club, inserted an item in the *Fremont Colleague*, inviting motorboat owners interested in forming a club to a meeting. Fifteen showed up and joined at a fee of $1 each. They planned a club for the "average man," where his family would be in proper surroundings, and he would have the opportunity to meet other boatmen.

The first official meeting was held on May 15, 1916. A simple set of bylaws was fashioned, using the old Elliott Bay Yacht Club bylaws as a guide. The pennant committee completed a new design for the club. When choosing a name, most suggestions ended with "motorboat association," until Captain McNichols suggested "yacht club." Lough then suggested "Queen City Yacht Club," because in those days Seattle was known as the "Queen City of the Northwest."

At the third meeting, officers were elected and William Herman was named commodore. Three weeks later Herman, in his boat *Friendship*, led a fleet of 12 vessels on a cruise across the sound to LaView, near Point Monroe, for a clambake.

Growing pains made apparent the need for a permanent meeting place, so a committee was formed to submit plans to the Seattle Port Commission, asking them to build a meeting room on one of the stub piers of the Salmon Bay dock. The port commissioners approved, and the club occupied its new $1,500 home less than six months from the date of the organization's founding. Rent was $50 per quarter.

In early 1918 Seattle shipyards, struggling to keep up with World War I orders, needed more space, so the Queen City Yacht Club willingly released its location on Salmon Bay. Members decided to build a floating clubhouse with member-volunteers acting as loggers, carpenters, and bosses. By November they were firmly established in a floating structure at the end of Westlake Avenue.

Though it was rent free, this clubhouse proved to be unstable, and the location not ideal. Funds that had accumulated in the treasury were used to purchase two lots in the vicinity of the south pier of the University Bridge. But membership was increasing rapidly, and it became obvious that the 150 feet of

The 1916 yachting season opened on May 20 with a program of sail and power races on Elliott Bay and entertainment at the West Seattle clubhouse. A series of six races to Venice, the club's summer station, was announced.

Winners of Opening Day races included Class A sailboats, the yawl *Bonita* (Captain E. W. Hutchison); Class B sloops, *Defender* (Captain J. T. Pugh); powerboats, *Billikin* (Captain C. Doudd); dinghy races, men's, Herbert Moss; and boys, Vernon Latimer.

In June, five fast cruisers from SYC with important guests including Mayor Hi Gill aboard raced to La Conner to help celebrate that town's mid-summer festival.

Because of Canadian involvement in the war, three local yachts raced for the Lipton Cup on Elliott Bay: the *Defender*, owned by Joseph Parker and captained by Joseph Pugh with J. Farrow, George Wayland, W. J. Shertzer and David Brown as crew; *Spray*, with Quent Williams as captain and crewed by John Lind, John Eckles and J. Nelson; and SYC's *Sir Tom*, captained by Ted Geary with Scott Calhoun and D. A. Young as crew. The defending *Sir Tom* won the first and third races to keep the cup.

waterfront at the new location was not adequate. A partial payment was made on a site at Edgar Street and Fairview Avenue on Lake Union.

In 1926, with notes subscribed by members, the large old building owned by the Seattle Rod and Gun Club on Duwamish Head (formerly the site of the Seattle Yacht Club) was purchased. With QCYC Commodore Ernie Wolfe in charge, members cut off most of the piling, pushed a barge under the building at low tide, and when the tide came in, they floated the structure to the Fairview site.

In 1935 the mortgage on the Fairview property was paid off, but the board of directors, realizing they needed still larger quarters, had already purchased another site. This included 400 feet of Seattle's finest waterfront, acquired for $12,000, or $30 per front foot. There the present clubhouse was opened on Nov. 8, 1938. The mortgage was paid off in January 1944, just in time for yet another expansion. All piers were rebuilt by 1948, and a lower lounge, snack bar, and caretaker's quarters were added.

The largest project ever undertaken by the club was the building of covered moorage. The first stage, providing moorage for 70 boats, was completed in 1959. The second stage, completed in 1963, provided spaces for 78 additional vessels. The club also purchased a number of offshore lots from the state of Washington for $37,000, assuring entrance and egress to their property. In all, more than $300,000 was raised in an over-subscribed bond issue among members to pay for the moorage improvements and underwater lots.

In 1943 the women organized the "Tarettes" and made many gifts to the club, including drapes, dishes, furniture, and a public address system. They organize many events throughout the year, including the traditional Opening Day breakfast for visiting yachtsman.

During the QCYC's 50th anniversary in 1966, a plaque commemorating the founding of the club was placed at the entrance of the premises.

The club leased an outstation at Winslow and towed 100 feet of floats from the clubhouse across the sound to the site. Piles were driven, and wiring was installed. Under the leadership of Cliff Roberts, a clubhouse was constructed from donated materials. In 1975, with the lease cost increasing, the club reached an agreement to purchase this property from the owner.

In 1985, on Portage Bay, many of the deteriorated boathouses were replaced with modern floating covered moorages. Furthermore, the bylaws were revised to bring membership eligibility rules into conformity with contemporary attitudes.

The Queen City Yacht Club celebrated its 75th anniversary in 1991. ◇

The first semi diesel motor-ship built on the Pacific Coast was launched at the Blanchard and Johnson boat yard as the Kuscoquin *for a firm headed by John Graham, Sr. Ted Geary was the designer. The yawl* Ortona *is in the foreground, built by Norm J. Blanchard, Sr. and owned by John Graham, Sr. (MOHAI)*

Three hundred Seattle yachtsmen, concerned about the Victoria Yacht Club's loss of membership (down to 140 dues-paying members compared with 325 before the war), boarded the excursion boat *Princess Charlotte* to sail north to that city. Their intention was to cheer up the club while so many of its members were away at war.

Later, on Aug. 15, 1916, the *Post-Intelligencer* mentioned that SYC members and friends, 140 strong, sailed on the *Princess Mary* to Canadian waters for two days and then home. The sightseers enjoyed Butte and Jervis inlets and glimpsed Princess Louisa Inlet. A short stop was made at Nanaimo, where "English women sold tiny Union Jacks to benefit the boys in the trenches. . . ." (*Post-Intelligencer*, Aug. 15, 1916)

The war was coming ever closer to the United States. In April SYC Commodore Chilberg and Vice-Commodore J. S. Gibson called a meeting of all powerboat

Portage Bay prior to clubhouse construction. University and World War I naval training facility in background, 1917. (Pierson & Co.)

owners to discuss formation of a squadron, the first organized on the Pacific Coast. The main objectives of this group were to teach high skill in the handling of motorboats, to cooperate with the U.S. government in navigation matters, and to provide a qualified body of yachtsmen who could volunteer for assistance to the navy in time of war.

1917: The United States Declares War

In April, the United States entered the war. Until then the Seattle yacht clubs had not curtailed their activities.

On April 18, 1917, Richard K. Morris, SYC secretary, was accepted as a lieutenant in the U.S. Naval Coast Defense Reserve. He and George Gandy were the first Seattle yachtsmen to be so commissioned. Morris immediately began recruiting. The navy had begun to eye some of the larger yachts and qualified Prescott Oaks' *Curlew*, F. C. Miller's *Discoverer*, Robert E. Magner's *Gloria*, William G. Norris' *Geoduck*, R. W. Rowley's *Harriett H*, and 14 other vessels. Robert Moran offered his new yacht *Sanwan* and volunteered to serve even though he was well past the maximum age of 40.

1918: Seattle Sells its Clubhouse

In June, the U.S. government bought the Seattle Yacht Club's West Seattle clubhouse and moorage area for $3,000. The U.S. Shipping Board promptly converted it to a station for training officers and men for the Merchant Marine. More than $50,000 was invested in additions, site improvements, and repair of two steamers, the *Iroquois* (Captain O. E. Beaton) and the *Chippewa* (Captain F. A. Parker). These two training vessels were

moored at a large dolphin installed just east of the training station.

The veranda of the former clubhouse was rebuilt as a ship's bridge for instruction purposes. A ship's compass was used to teach the simpler principles of navigation. Davits installed on the south side of the building were utilized to teach handling of lifeboats. Spaces were set aside for knot tying, rope splicing, and seamanship training. The first floor was converted to a mess hall and general assembly room, the latter serving as officer's mess, as well. The second floor was cleared and filled with bunks. A 40-foot addition housed the paymaster, purchasing agent, and accounting department.

The adjacent J. T. Heffernan Dry Dock and Ship Equipping Plant was also utilized in training merchant mariners. A large barge given to the station by the Waterfront Employers' Association was used as a floating dormitory.

This former yacht club, according to

Lake Washington Ship Canal and Portage Bay

The opening of the Lake Washington Ship Canal in 1917 was important in the history of Northwest yachting. Construction of the canal was justified on the basis of commercial usage, but the effect on pleasure craft has been great. It not only made a large freshwater area available for racing, cruising, mooring, repair and construction facilities but, as a result, lakefront owners could now keep boats to use for both freshwater and saltwater pleasures.

The combination of protected water and excellent spectator space in the middle of a large metropolitan area makes possible what may be the largest and best known Opening Day of the yachting world. In 1991, SYC's Opening Day was seen 'round the globe on the CNN cable-television network.

After years of considering alternative canal routes (a cut through Beacon Hill, for example) and after facing opposition by such groups as the mill owners on Salmon Bay, ground was broken for lock construction in 1911. In 1915 the part of Lake Union east of the old Latona Street Bridge was renamed Portage Bay in commemoration of the traditional way of transporting boats, logs and other materials from Lake Washington to Lake Union. In October 1916 the canal was opened from Salmon Bay to Lake Union, and the following May it was open for navigation to Lake Washington.

An earlier canal had existed. According to the abstract of title for property on Portage Bay owned by the Seattle Yacht Club, in 1861 this federal property (obtained from the American Indians by treaty) was sold by the appropriate board of commissioners to raise funds to build a territorial university. Harvey Pike, the purchaser, obtained 161.83 acres at the north end of what is now the Montlake District for $242.75.

Pike tried with a pick and shovel to connect the two lakes with a small canal but found the job too big. In 1883 a group of prominent men, including David Denny, hired Chinese laborers to open a small wooden-lined flume south of where SYC's Pier 1 is now located. Logs from the shores of Lake Washington were floated through this canal to David Denny's mill at the south end of Lake Union. The end of this log flume can be seen in early pictures of the SYC site. Guillotine locks on the Lake Washington end controlled the flow of water into Lake Union, which was 8 1/2 feet lower.

The present ship canal with its Montlake cut was located 500 feet north of the old canal, avoiding a difficult turn at the east end of the cut. In 1910, before excavation began, control gates were installed at the eastern end of the cut for use in lowering Lake Washington to the level of Lake Union. A coffer dam was built on the west end and the cut then was excavated. On Aug. 26, 1916 this dam was opened and 43 million gallons of Lake Union water gushed into the cut, filling it in an hour. After the debris was

newspaper reports, became the "most completely equipped station now conducted by the Shipping Board. At no other point in the United States are the station buildings so ideally located and handy to the training ships. . . ." (*Post-Intelligencer*, Aug. 11, 1918)

Experienced instructors trained the men. W. J. Grambs, the regional director of the Sea Service Bureau, was in charge. A graduate of Annapolis, he had long been identified with Seattle shipping interests. He hired one instructor for each 10 recruits to be trained.

The first group of young men, 260 recruits from the Puget Sound region, arrived on July 18, 1918. They were paid $30 a month plus room and board and received uniforms similar to those worn in the navy. The Merchant Marine anticipated receiving about 500 trained seamen every six weeks from this Seattle station. They were badly needed to man the emergency fleet being formed to carry food,

cleared away, the gates at the eastern end of the cut were opened. It took more than a month for enough water to escape from Lake Washington to lower it to the level of Lake Union.

The official opening of the canal on July 6, 1917, was made notable by a parade of 250 craft of all sizes moving through the canal. Thus the first Opening Day parade through the Montlake cut was not sponsored by SYC.

In 1870 Pike had filed "H. L. Pike's First Addition to Union City," which was a plat of what is now the Hamlin and Shelby streets area. It was probably the most valuable part of his property since it had frontage on both lakes. Hamlin and Shelby were called "A" and "B" streets. After a complicated series of conveyances, the property came into the hands of Josepth A. Baillargeon (grandfather of long-time member J. C. "Bill" Baillargeon and of Jane Baillargeon Sylvester, wife of SYC Commodore Jack Sylvester) and others who replatted it in 1909 to today's configuration as the "Montlake Park Addition to the City of Seattle."

The subdivision was cut off on the north and south by the new and old canal rights-of-way, and the west end was deeded to the city for park purposes. The SYC area (Lot 1, Block 3) was designated as "Casino Grounds." This probably was meant to designate not a gambling center but a place where people gather, and it did become a gathering place—for yachtsmen, their families, and guests. ◇

The opening of the coffer dam on the west end of the cut allowed Lake Union waters to gush in. (MOHAI)

clothing, ammunition and other supplies required by the American Expeditionary Force in France.

For the next three years the Seattle Yacht Club existed without a clubhouse by scheduling business meetings in the board room of the Dexter Horton Bank. Membership dropped to 70 active members and the club fleet, reduced to just one-third of its previous size, was dispersed to various commercial moorings around Elliott Bay.

In November 1918 the Germans surrendered and hostilities ceased.

1919: The New Clubhouse Site

During the war years, the Lake Washington Ship Canal had been completed, connecting Lakes Union and Washington to Puget Sound. When the war ended, Seattle Yacht Club members, after considerable thought, purchased a site adjacent to the sanitary landfill on Portage Bay. They used funds received for the old site in West Seattle to pay for this new property, and a bond issue was floated to pay for a new clubhouse. After negotiations with city, state and federal authorities, permits were received to build piers adjacent to the city park property. On March 20, 1919, *Post-Intelligencer* headlines proclaimed "New Home of Yachtsmen Is Now Assured!" More than 50 prominent businessmen had pledged funds to construct the facility for the rapidly growing club. The membership limit was increased beyond the original 350, and the initiation fee was reduced from $50 to $25 to entice more yachtsmen to join.

On Sunday, May 18, 1919, newspaper readers were told that the piers and locker rooms, composing the first unit of the new yacht club, were completed. This allowed the fleet, then scattered around Elliott Bay and Lake Union, to move to permanent anchorage in the cove "opposite

An assortment of small day sailers on Lake Union, c. World War I. Sailboat on right is flying Lake Union Yacht Club burgee. (MOHAI)

The new SYC clubhouse under construction in 1919. (SYC Historical Collection)

the university in front of the club's property at Montlake Park" (*Post-Intelligencer*, May 18, 1919). The plans for the clubhouse had been completed, and construction work was to begin immediately.

Members planned the club as a center for sports activities, and it included facilities for tennis, bowling, golf, and other recreations. The University of Washington decided to lay out a golf course on the site of the wartime naval training unit just across the Montlake cut from the clubhouse. The parks department, which was to develop the lawn bowling facilities, never did so. The SYC did install tennis courts east of the clubhouse where today the western half of the upper parking lot is located.

The 1910–1920 decade had been a busy one for Seattle's yachtsmen. As technology improved, more families invested in powerboats. The design of sailing craft also improved drastically during the decade as college-trained naval architects such as Ted Geary became increasingly active. Measurement rules (handicapping or ratings) were applied to all yachts that raced together, which generated increased interest in the contests.

This was the decade when the automobile became more than a luxury to the American people. Yacht clubs became more sophisticated, developed new strengths and individuality which sometimes resulted in more friction between organizations. Bitter feelings existed for many years between Canadian and American yachtsmen. Yachting also became increasingly commercial, with cups and awards donated and named for local merchants, among them Augustine and Kyer, Sunde and Erland, and Pacific Net and Twine.

The city of Seattle matured, and skyscrapers such as the Smith Tower became part of the skyline. The Lake Washington Ship Canal improved the water access to the lakes in 1917, and members widened their interests to other sports such as tennis and golf. Expenses for operating the club increased, so membership drives became common, and initiation fees were often reduced to secure more members. ☆

FOUR

The 1920s

The new Seattle Yacht Club clubhouse and piers as they appeared in about 1924 from across Portage Bay. C. D. Stimson kept his yacht *Wanda* in the large boathouse to the right. (MOHAI)

Living in the 1920s has been described as similar to riding a roller coaster. Good times were here to stay, the politicians promised, and it seemed they were. After the financial relapse that followed World War I, business picked up, and in certain areas, the decade truly earned the sobriquet "The Roaring Twenties."

It was a strange era in many ways. National prohibition decreed all alcoholic beverages to be unlawful, but in Seattle liquor was always available, at least to those with enough money to pay for it. A former police lieutenant named Roy Olmstead became the most successful local rumrunner. He could be trusted to deliver unopened, undiluted goods imported from Canada. Within a few years he was living in a big home in Seattle and had bought a summer place or "headquarters" on Orcas Island. Olmstead also financed one of Seattle's first radio stations for his wife, a would-be actress. She read stories for children, and it was claimed that she was broadcasting secret signals to the liquor-carrying boats at the same time. The station's transmitter engineer, Nick Foster, insisted that this was not true. All this hoopla ended when Olmstead was sentenced to McNeil Island penitentiary. He later accepted religion and counseled prisoners and alcoholics.

It was the decade when both Sand Point Naval Air Station and Boeing Field were built to service the growing numbers of aircraft, and it was the decade when Seattleites elected Bertha Landes as their mayor, the first woman to head the government of any major American city. Male students at the University of Washington wore coonskin coats and coeds favored short, straight-line dresses, new short hair styles and bright lipstick. Many a mother worried about her daughter during those years of sudden and drastic social changes.

This bright world dimmed late in 1929 when the stock market crash ushered in the most severe depression of the century.

Early in the decade, the Seattle Yacht Club at its new clubhouse on Portage Bay soon established itself as the premier yacht club in the region. Though the Pacific Northwest did not provide as grand a lifestyle as did some other parts of the country, sailing and yachting, especially the R class races, received much attention. The decade also saw an increasing number of power yachts on Puget Sound.

1920

On May 1 the Seattle Yacht Club formally dedicated its new home on Portage Bay. Those Opening Day ceremonies established traditions that are still followed to this day.

> A reverberating salute boomed out over the quiet waters of Lake Union, the Stars and Stripes mounted to the yard, the club pennant to the peak and the new home of the Seattle Yacht Club had been officially put in commission. While the ceremonies that marked the dedication of the building were going on the dark expanse of the lake was splotched with the white of myriad sailing craft passing to and fro on the shoulder of the wind. The starred ensign of the club was everywhere.
>
> —Post-Intelligencer, *May 3, 1920*

On June 27 the *Post-Intelligencer* carried an article by William E. Jones that stated the objectives of the persons who formed the Seattle Yacht Club in 1892:

> . . . to hold yacht races; to encourage clean sportsmanship; develop and improve boat design and generally to have an organization of persons who loved the water and who appreciated the thousand and one points

The Portage Bay Property

In 1919 [SYC] Commodore N. H. Latimer, with the strong support of Commodore J. S. Gibson and Captain James Griffiths, commenced land purchase and building details for the new Seattle Yacht Club clubhouse at 1807 East Hamlin.

If there is one man, however, who shares the glory of the achievement as represented in the new clubhouse and grounds with Commodore Latimer more than any other, that man is Past Commodore John Graham. It was Mr. Graham who acted as the architect of the property and who not only designed and laid out the club's new home but also supervised its construction in every detail as well as contributing to its financing. Here again, the club was fortunate in having an past commodore who not only is an enthusiastic and thorough yachtsman in spirit and training but who also was in a position to combine his knowledge of the needs of the yachtsmen with a keen ability as a designer and engineer. How well he did his work may be evidenced from the fact that the new home has been unanimously pronounced in point of convenience and arrangement one of the finest yacht club buildings in the country, although there are many clubs in the East which represent an investment of many times its cost.

[Built in] "the old Colonial style, with the addition of the lighthouse tower to lend a nautical touch. . . .

—*Daniel L. Pratt,* Pacific Motor Boat *magazine, May 1920*

Pratt reported that the top floor housed a card room and reading room where members could find quiet when the bottom floors were used for social purposes. Off this room were small private quarters for the commodore. Elsewhere on this floor was a complete living apartment of several rooms for the caretaker and his wife as well as several other bedrooms for members of the clubhouse staff.

The large room on the lower floor was designed as a billiard room but was used more as a smoking and lounging room for the paid crews from the yachts.

Pratt also described the large covered shed at the rear of the building, which contained "stalls for the members' automobiles." The entire yard and floor of the shed were paved with concrete. This structure also contained storage space for spars, sails, dinghies, and other yachting paraphernalia. Beyond the auto shelter were two double tennis courts.

For many years the Portage Bay station was known simply as the "clubhouse" or the "moorage." Most frequently it was called "The Seattle Yacht Club." Actually, according to longtime judge advocate and

of scenic beauty on the sound that are accessible only to the yachtsman.

—Post-Intelligencer, *June 27, 1920*

The article mentioned that a new clubhouse had first been considered in 1913, and now, seven years later, it was a reality. The members told the reporter that their facilities were an important facet of the city's image, for they had entertained scores of guests from all over the country during the three months the clubhouse had been open. The facility also attracted new members in great numbers, increasing total membership to more than 400 in 1920.

The PIYA is Organized

With World War I now history, international racing returned in 1920. The Seattle Yacht Club sent Captain James Griffiths, Ted Geary, Quent Williams, G. E. Richardson, and Daniel L. Pratt to Victoria to meet with representatives of the Vancouver, Victoria, Everett, Tacoma, and Queen City clubs. The representatives recommended consolidation of the Pacific International Power Boating Association and the Northwest International Yacht Racing Association; on May 16, 1920, the Pacific International Yachting Association (PIYA) was officially formed with James Griffiths as the first commodore.

As the new organization was being formed, Secretary H. Y. Burton Brooks of the Royal Vancouver Club wrote to Secretary George C. Congdon of the Seattle Yacht Club stating that Vancouver sailors were challenging Seattle sailors for the Sir

The original shoreline of the SYC site on Portage Bay before 1916 and development of West Montlake Park. (MOHAI)

mudlands negotiator Dave Williams, the Seattle Yacht Club should be viewed as a social institution that would continue even if it lost its present properties. This view of the club as independent of its physical facilities is justified when one considers that many SYC functions are scheduled away from the Portage Bay clubhouse. Consider also that at the eight outstations are four other clubhouses. Today, some members who fly the SYC burgee seldom use the Portage Bay station. As a member of the 1986–87 permanent planning committee, Williams recommended that the home station be known as the "Portage Bay Club House" and "Portage Bay Moorage," and he drafted the bylaw amendments necessary to effect the changes which were adopted at the annual meeting.

The Portage Bay Clubhouse, though it has weathered nearly 75 years of history, remains relatively unchanged on the exterior. ◇

The 100-foot motor yacht Malibu *was designed by Ted Geary and built in 1925 at the Blanchard Boatyard. It is still in use today. (MOHAI)*

Thomas Lipton Cup, then on display at the Seattle club. As a result, the race was scheduled as part of the July 1–3 regatta off Victoria.

Considerable space in local newspapers highlighted the two boats—the *Sir Tom* and the *Turenga*. The latter now carried the maximum sail allowed an R class boat. Nonetheless, in two races, the first over a Cowichan Bay course and the second following the Royal Road course off Esquimalt, *Sir Tom* again was invincible.

Seattle yachts brought home seven trophies from the Victoria regatta. George Wiley's yawl *Gazeka* won two of them. The Pacific Motor Boat Cup presented by *Pacific Motor Boat* magazine was awarded to Captain Griffiths. Other trophy winners at this regatta were Ray Cooke, E. H. Hutchison, and Robert DeGroff.

On the way home from Victoria, two Seattle yachts, the *Muriel* (Commodore J. S. Gibson) and the *Katedna* (Rear Commodore Fred H. Baxter), sailed through the San Juans to the private estate of Rosario where the two club officers stopped to visit with Robert Moran, an old shipbuilder and former Seattle mayor. He welcomed them warmly, as he did all visitors.

Catboat races were scheduled throughout the 1920 season. Much to the delight of his mentors, one of whom was Ted Geary, the champion catboater was Jack Graham, the 12-year-old son of John Graham, Sr. Time and again he piloted his 15-foot standard-design catboat over the course, keeping ahead of some of the club's best sailors. At season's end, he was presented the John Graham Cup provided by his father.

Late in August the *Claribel* won the Erlich and Harrison Cup, but smoke from local forest fires obscured the race from shore watchers.

During the 1920s women began to race in earnest. In September 1920 three SYC races were scheduled for women on

History of the Portage Bay Property

In 1919 the Seattle Yacht Club purchased Lots 1, 2, 3, and 4 of Block 3 of the Montlake Park Addition to the City of Seattle. The clubhouse was built on Lot 1, and a combined storage and caretaker's apartment structure was built on Lot 2. A public alley ran between the clubhouse and the other buildings. Lots 3 and 4, which comprise part of the upper parking lot, originally were the site of SYC's tennis courts.

Current Boundaries of the Portage Bay Upland Ownership

On the west side of the SYC Portage Bay property, 96.96 feet of Lot 1 forms the boundary with West Montlake Park and the southern 23.981 feet of Lot 1 fronts on Portage Bay, providing SYC with its only owned waterfront access to Portage Bay.

On the south side of SYC property is the "Old Canal Reserve" which had been purchased under condemnation by King County and deeded to the U.S. government. The U.S. Bureau of Fisheries occupies much of this property. SYC's south parking lot and storage shed area on the south side of Lot 1 sits on the remainder of the reserve and adjacent State shorelands.

SYC purchased Lots 5, 6, and 7, which extended SYC property to the Fisheries' driveway (officially 19th Avenue East). The alley easement between Lots 1 and 2 on the south edge of Lots 2, 3, 4, 5, 6, and 7 has been vacated by city ordinance.

Early Changes to Underwater Areas

In 1919, when the Portage Bay property was purchased, the state of Washington owned all land underlying Portage Bay. West Montlake Park, when established by the Montlake Park plat, was a small steep strip of land sloping to the water from Lot 1, Block 1, south along West Park Drive and along Lot 1, Block 3. The state deeded to the city, for park purposes only, enough underwater land to increase the park to its present size. The park was then bulkheaded, filled, and graded to its present configuration. This change in the park provided a level lawn to the west of the clubhouse and a stable upland face from which to extend piers. Since the yachts of those days were long and thin, originally four piers without fingers extended from the park. The piers were connected to the clubhouse area by a wooden walkway along the seaward side of the park bulkhead. The walkway was separated from the park by a fence. There was also an L-shaped pier in approximately the present location of Pier 1. The walkway and the pier were on underwater land leased from the state. By 1950 the original piers had been eliminated and the present piers constructed.

Platting of Underwater Lands

About 1960, Pearl Wanamaker, state superintendent of public instruction, requested that state land be sold to provide money for schools. As a result, Bert Cole, commissioner of public lands, established a plat of the portion of Portage Bay shoreward of the combined U.S. Bulkhead and

Continued on the next page

Pierhead Line (State Harbor Line). This platted underwater land did not include the Pier 1 area which was reserved as a navigational area. Because the state was required by law to offer the land to the adjacent upland owners, the plat was divided into lots at the same places as the upland ownership. The Pier 2, 3, and 4 area in front of the park became Lot 1 and a strip 23.98 feet by 745.96 feet on the south, 703.37 feet on the north and 48.87 feet on a diagonal on the east in front of the clubhouse became Lot 2. This Lot 2, which was purchased by SYC, was the south 23.98 feet of the slip area of Pier 2 as it was before the 1988 remodel.

The Area South of Pier Two

Today, the Pier 1 area south of underwater Lot 2 continues to be leased from the state. The state underwater plat continues south of the open water area, which is partially covered by the Highway 520 viaduct. A large part of that area belongs to the city as part of Montlake Playfield.

Purchase of the Mudlands

As the upland owner under state law, the city had in 1962 a preferential right to purchase Lot 1 in front of the park. The city wanted to collect the rent from Piers 2, 3, and 4 and to own underwater Lot 1 as an adjunct to the park, but it wanted the state to donate the land as it had donated the previous addition to the park. An agreement was made that SYC would take title to Lot 1, at a purchase price of $77,080 (to be paid over 10 years) and deed Lot 1 to the city in the year 2002.

Use of the Park

At the time the covers were put on Piers 1, 3, and 4, Pier 2, which had attached to the wooden walkway near the clubhouse and Star dock, was modified with a diagonal dogleg connecting directly to the southwest corner of the park. The wooden walkway along the outside of the park was eliminated and Piers 2, 3, and 4 were then all connected to the clubhouse by a concrete walkway over the park. This change, together with the facts that SYC's flagpole and a large anchor were in the park and the steep grade from the park to the clubhouse had been eliminated when the new dining room replaced the south sunporch, had led some members to believe that the lawn to the west of the clubhouse was club property. In the mid 1970s, this mistake about ownership of the lawn caused friction with the parks department and the neighborhood after the SYC manager ordered installation of a low hedge of prickly bushes around the north side of the flagpole. The hedge was quickly removed, but some of the neighbors were still complaining about the incident at the time of the mudlands swap more than 10 years later.

Status of Pier 1 Area

In 1963 the south parking lot was built upon what had formerly been part of the shoreline area of Portage Pay east of Pier 1. The ownership of this parking lot is divided by the Meander Line (old shoreline) which runs from near the northwest corner of the storage shed to the southeast corner of the property. This diagonal line marks the westerly edge of the adjacent portion of the U.S. Department of Fisheries' property and the easterly edge of the state-owned Pier 1 area which SYC leases. A permit from the U.S. government to use that portion of the Fisheries Department's property for a parking lot was arranged by Judge Advocate (later Honorary Life Commodore) Chet Adair. It was Adair who coined the term "mudlands" to refer to the lands under the piers.

The Mudlands Swap

For several years prior to 1983, attempts had been made to negotiate with the city for a release of its right to receive from SYC in the year 2002 a deed to the mudlands under Piers 2, 3, and 4. This matter was complicated by a law stating that the city could not sell park land, which the mudlands in question in front of West Montlake Park were considered. However, the city could trade the mudlands for other park land. Land adjacent to the south end of Leschi Park was offered, but the parks board voted never to release its interest in the club's Portage Bay moorage. In 1983 Eric Van of SYC's permanent planning committee learned through his membership on the board of Northwest Seaports (owner of the historic sailing ship *Wawona*) that the city was interested in obtaining a small triangle of land known as the Embar property, located near the southwest corner of Lake Union, as a park.

Committee Chairman Don Thompson recommended that SYC pay the part of the purchase price of the Embar property that was equal to the city's remainder interest in the mudlands. An appraisal of the mudlands area, including Piers 2, 3, and 4, came in at $625,000, and the then current value of the city's right to ownership in the year 2002 was $245,000. That meant that the club's ownership value was $625,000, less the city's $245,000—or $380,000. Each succeeding year the city's ownership value would increase and SYC's interest would decrease until 2002, when the city would have complete ownership. At the rate of inflation experienced between the 1962 and 1983 appraisals, the value at the year 2002 could be as much as $6 million. Something had to be done and fast.

At a special meeting of the board in August 1983, Commodore Scarff was authorized to make an offer of $300,000 toward the purchase of the Embar property in exchange for the city's interest in the mudlands. He was also granted further authority to negotiate a price of up to $350,000. Then ensued a lengthy series of negotiations conducted by 1983-84 Commodore Don Simpson; former Judge Advocate Dave Williams; and the Trust for Public Lands, an organization that facilitates public purchases. In December 1983, the club and the trust each paid $25,000 as a down payment to buy the Embar property at a bargain price.

The purchase stalled when the city's appraiser valued Lot 1 of the moorage at $1,170,000, which made the new value to SYC of the reversion increase to $548,000. Since that was far higher than the appraisal obtained by the club, Simpson and Williams thought that the price was unreasonable. The problem was solved by reducing the size of the mudlands purchased and by paying half the cost of a third appraisal. Because of community and Shorelines Coalition opposition, the club agreed to deed the north 75 feet of Lot 1 to the city so that finger piers could not be added to the north side of Pier 4. That deed reduced the price of the remaining part of the mudlands by $77,000. It had appeared to the club that it would have been unlikely to obtain permission to extend Pier 4 in any event because of Shoreline Act restrictions and the restrictions in its original agreement with the city. The reduction for the 75 feet, plus the results of a review appraisal, reduced the price to $380,807. After Judge Advocate Jack Allen made several reviews of and corrections to the elaborate paperwork prepared by the Trust for Public Lands and the city attorney, the city council approved the exchange and it was concluded in December 1984 for the total purchase price of $404,000, including closing costs and interest. As a further consideration the club agreed that it would not modify the piers in any way that would further restrict the view from the park. ◇

Lake Washington. Hundreds of spectators gathered on shore between Madison and Leschi parks to witness Mrs. Stanley (Elsa) Griffiths, with Ted Geary at her elbow, guide the *Sir Tom* to victory. This appears to have been the first R class race for women.

1921

According to the SYC yearbook, honorary memberships were freely dispensed during the 1920s. Honorary members listed in 1921 included Sir Thomas J. Lipton, Bart. K.C.V.O.; J. W. Isherwood, London, England; W. P. Collings, Lloyd's Surveyor, Sunderland, England; the commandant of the Bremerton Navy Yard; U.S. supervising inspector of steam vessels for the Puget Sound District; local inspectors of steam vessels for the Puget Sound District; commandant and officers of the State Nautical School at the University of Washington; the secretary of the interior;

Seattle Yacht Club Bells

Standing silent watch throughout the Seattle Yacht Club are several bells. Each plays a significant role in the history and traditions of the club.

The Griffiths' Bell hangs at the Hamlin Street main entrance to the club. A brass plate explains that the bell once served on the *Carondelet*, built in Newcastle, Maine, in 1872. This ship was operated by the Griffiths and Stetson Steamship Company during much of the 1880s and from 1908–1910. She carried the first cargo of merchandise imported directly from England to Seattle. The *Carondelet* was lost in Alaska waters in 1910.

Captain James Griffiths donated the bell for the front door of the new Portage Bay clubhouse when it opened in 1920. At the time, no modern intercom systems existed, so when a phone call came in for a member who was working down at the moorages, Elsie Palmer, the club's assistant manager, would run from her desk to the front door, ring the bell vigorously, then shout through a megaphone in the direction of the moorages. It was an effective system. More recently, however, the club had to remove the clapper from the bell because members who had stood a long watch in the Marine Room or passing teenagers occasionally rang the bell late at night, waking the neighbors.

The Luther Bell that hangs over the south entrance of the club once rang aboard the steamship *Spokane*, which was launched in San Jose, California, in 1906. Back then it was a passenger vessel known as the *Honeymoon Ship*. When she was cruising between Seattle and Alaska a young Phil Luther served aboard her as a cadet. He recalled that many important passengers, including President Theodore Roosevelt, sailed on the *Spokane* to Alaska. After the *Spokane* was scrapped, Captain Luther discovered the bell in a junk heap, purchased it for $10, and later donated it to the club in 1980.

In the Marine Room over the fireplace is a bell inscribed with the words "Go and Win." It was awarded to Dean and Lloyd Johnson on May 17, 1908, by members of the Elliott Bay Yacht Club just prior to the Johnsons' entering their *Gwendolyn II* in the second annual Trans-Pacific Yacht Race. The 48-foot *Gwendolyn II*, the smallest yacht in the race, finished in second place after 14 days and 4 hours at sea.

One bell that still rings at SYC is mounted on a teak plank. Each week this bell calls the Thursday Men's Luncheon to order. Even more important is its function at the Seattle Yacht Club's annual meetings. At precisely eight bells on the first Friday in October this bell also sounds to call a quorum to order. Later in the meeting the bell is put to a more solemn use. As all present stand, it tolls once for each club member who has passed away during the previous year. ◇

Capt. James and Mrs. Ethel Ayers Griffiths in the pilothouse of their Sueja III, *1928. (A. Ayers Collection)*

the secretary of the navy; Mayor Hugh Caldwell; the park board of the city of Seattle; the harbor master, Port of Seattle; Professor Henry Suzzallo, president of the University of Washington; Professor Clark P. Bissett of the University of Washington; Col. E. H. Schulz, U.S. engineer; regents of the University of Washington; W. H. Searing, chief of police of the city of Seattle; and newspaper representatives. A separate list of 14 consuls of foreign nations followed.

Life members were also numerous in 1921: W. E. Boeing, Scott Calhoun, Frank E. Case, Hugh Chilberg, J. E. Chilberg, Fred T. Fischer, Miller Freeman, W. L. Gazzam, J. S. Gibson, John Graham, Sr., J. T. Heffernan, Frank T. Hunter, N. H. Latimer, A. W. Leonard, Frank McDermott, Sherman Moran, W. G. Norris, W. H. Parsons, Dietrich G. Schmitz, Eugene Schmitz, Henry Schmitz, H. W. Starrett and David Whitcomb.

Daniel Pratt, secretary of the PIYA, wrote of this organization:

> Marking the revival of yachting on the North Pacific Coast on a large scale, the clubs of Puget Sound and British Columbia joined together last year in a new alliance for the general promotion of motor boating and yachting and formed a new association known as the Pacific International Yachting Association.
>
> The purpose of the Association was to get the clubs of this district thoroughly organized so they would act as a unit in promoting the sport of yachting in these waters, and also to provide machinery through which big inter-club and international regattas could be promoted and conducted.
>
> The first meeting was held at the Royal Victoria Yacht Club's home . . . early last spring at which the organization plans were perfected.
>
> The first annual regatta of the Association was staged at Victoria and Cowichan Bay, B.C., last July and it was the biggest event of its kind ever held on the North Coast. The regatta was preceded by a long distance power boat race from Seattle to Brentwood, and on the opening day at Cowichan Bay over 150 boats . . . from all over Puget Sound and British Columbia were anchored in a fleet to view the first heat of the international race for the Lipton Cup, Class R. . . . The regatta was promoted and entirely financed through the Association, the Victoria Club standing only its proportionate share of the cost. A contribution of thirty-five cents per head from the members of the different yacht clubs was sufficient to entirely take care of the costs for the regatta.
>
> This year the Association plans the repetition of the events staged so successfully last summer, and the races will again be held at Cowichan and Victoria. . . .
>
> The program as outlined will give yachtsmen of Puget Sound a chance to spend a week's vacation in British Columbia waters in a very enjoyable manner, combining the pleasure of the cruise with the interest of witnessing some of the finest races ever held on the Pacific Coast. . . .
>
> —*SYC Scrapbook, 1921*

The year 1921 witnessed 24 SYC-sponsored races, about half of them for catboats. These small craft raced every Saturday except when regattas were scheduled. Built to be unsinkable, when turned over these little craft could usually be righted without assistance. That was all to the good, for on windy days a sensitive hand was needed at the tiller and a cool eye on the sheet to avoid a dunking.

Catboats raced at three locations: off Madison Park on Lake Washington, on Lake Union, and on Portage Bay. Often a woman or two was listed among the crews. Among the outstanding women racers of 1921 were Eva Pape and Geraldine Hillman.

Over Memorial Day, SYC powerboats raced from Shilshole to Cadboro Bay near Victoria. The first to arrive, Gilbert M. Skinner in his large and powerful *Winifred*, traveled the distance in the record time of 3 hours and 50 minutes.

One of the big improvements in motorboating noted in the papers was the detachable outboard motor. This intrigued all sorts of sportsmen, including fishermen.

The Memorial Day sailboat races were over a 30-mile triangular course from Ediz Hook across the strait to Brotchie Ledge and back. Fritz Hellenthal skippered the *Gwendolyn II* to victory. The ensuing races were canceled for lack of wind.

Seattle yachtsmen feared they might lose the Lipton Cup in the PIYA race scheduled off Victoria over July 4. The Royal Vancouver club proudly announced a new contender, the *Patricia*, to be skippered by experienced racer Ronald Maitland. But as before, the *Sir Tom*, under the sure hand of Ted Geary, eased in

SYC Entertainment During the 1920s

The "Roaring Twenties" were a shocking time for the older generation. Music "deteriorated" to the jazz idiom. Daughters' skirts rose above the knee, and lightweight undergarments replaced whalebone corsets. Women even took to wearing lipstick and smoking cigarettes. Young men started wearing raccoon coats and bragged of fast cars and fast women. Prohibition did little to dampen the spirits of those who really wanted a drink, even though it did raise the price of booze. The most reliable bootlegger, a former Seattle police lieutenant named Roy Olmstead, sold undiluted Canadian liquor brought in by his fleet of fast motorboats to hidden bays. He finally was convicted and served 35 months at McNeil Island Penitentiary before prohibition ended and he was pardoned by President Franklin D. Roosevelt.

Members really enjoyed their new Seattle Yacht Club building on Portage Bay, which had opened in 1920. Exotic dinner dances were all the rage. On March 26, 1921, for example, an ethnic dinner dance was arranged with Turkish music, dancing girls, and food. Later that year a cabaret and fashion show were held, followed by a special farm dinner featuring roast goose.

On New Year's Eve 1921, a cabaret and high jinks were the theme. The floor show featured the Hippodrome

Seattleite Samuel Hill brought his friend Queen Marie of Rumania to the Northwest in 1926 to dedicate the Peace Portal which he had built on the U.S.-Canadian border. She was invited to tea at the Seattle Yacht Club and a group assembled to receive her. (MOHAI)

first, even though the *Patricia* was wearing a lofty Marconi rigging that pushed her trim hull easily through the sea. For another year the Lipton Cup resided in the Seattle yachtsmen's new quarters.

The Isherwood Trophy

In 1920 a new trophy was presented to Northwest yachtsmen by English naval architect J. W. Isherwood. One of the finest silver cups in the world, the Isherwood was designed by Alfred Green of Joseph Mayer, Inc., manufacturing jewelers of Seattle, at a cost of more than $3,000. The 1921 Labor Day contest, the first for this new trophy, called for the cup to be awarded to the first R-boat to take three out of five consecutive-day races. Surprise! The winner was *Sir Tom*. (The Isherwood Trophy is on display at the Seattle Yacht Club. It has not been awarded for many years because R class boats no longer race.)

1922

A first for the Seattle Yacht Club, a "ladies' smoker," was scheduled early in 1922. It provided entertainment and later Review (a local show of scantily attired dancing women). A Vienna-style beer garden was open all evening (serving near beer?) and dancing continued until 3:00 A.M. The cost was $2.50 per person.

Feb. 13, 1922, brought the first Ladies' Smoker and Dinner Dance to the club. Berliner's Orchestra, said to be Seattle's best dance aggregation, provided the music. Admission was $1.50 per person.

On Feb. 28, 1922, a Mardi Gras Ball featured a Seattle Yacht Club Review and prizes for the best costume. On March 20, 1922, male members at the semi-monthly stag smoker heard Captain Frank Andrews of Tacoma lecture on the old glorious days of sailing ships.

On May 1, 1922, the members celebrated the second anniversary of the opening of the new clubhouse with a buffet dinner, featuring a speech by Captain James Gibson.

Formal dances, such as the Director's Dinner Dance on Nov. 7, 1925, were popular and frequent. On Nov. 24, 1927, the club provided an "Evening before Thanksgiving Buffet," an informal party costing 75 cents per plate.

The juniors' formal dance and "Night in Esquimoland" of October 5, 1928, had the orchestra performing under a "snowbank" and the punch served from a mock igloo.

March 6, 1929, found the members enjoying a "Gwendolyn Night." The invitation read: "The hard-boiled crew/Of the Gwendolyn Two/Will cook up a stew/And serve it to you." That year Fritz Hellenthal, owner of the *Gwendolyn II*, was chairman of the entertainment committee. After the meal a Mr. Young of Honolulu gave a talk on the Hawaiian Islands "illustrated with movie pictures."

Yacht Club memorabilia from the Roaring Twenties—an identification card, tickets, postcards and souvenirs. (Wallace Ackerman Photography)

On Dec. 10, 1929, members enjoyed an "Arctic Night" program, which featured real reindeer steak and slides on Alaska. The upper deck featured a Klondike Night with roulette, faro, and black jack.

No doubt about it, Grandpa and Grandma had fun at the Seattle Yacht Club of the 1920s! ◇

Yachts of the 1920s

Sovereign, *owned by John Graham, Sr., who later owned the yachts* Mary *and* Blue Peter. *(N. C. Blanchard Collection)*

The Samona *was built by N. J. Blanchard for W. J. Hole of Balboa, California. Norm Blanchard, age 13, in knickers and cap. (PSMHS)*

The Mary *was designed by L. E. Geary, built by Lake Washington Shipyard and owned by John Graham, Sr. in 1922. (MOHAI)*

The Silver King *was designed by Ed Monk, built in 1927 and owned by Mrs. Eskridge. (PSMHS)*

The Rudder Cup has long been awarded to SYC member predicted log racers. (Wallace Ackerman Photography)

a dance. Stag smokers were semi-monthly events at the club.

The Pacific International Yachting Association Regatta was hosted by the Seattle Yacht Club July 24–29. SYC Commodore James Griffiths secured the support of the chamber of commerce, Seattle Rotary and Kiwanis clubs, the One Hundred Percent Club and other kindred organizations to assure a memorable first Seattle hosting of the international races since the war.

In a departure from the usual program, eight-oared shells representing the University of Washington, the Portland Rowing Club and the Seattle Yacht Club raced on Saturday.

The *Sir Tom* competed with the *Patricia* of the Royal Vancouver Yacht Club for R class honors on Lake Washington. The shores were thronged with people on July 26, 1922, but the wind refused to blow. The next day was no better. Finally, on July 28 the *Sir Tom* caught the breeze and handily defeated the Canadian boat. One of the proudest members of the crew was nine-year-old Jim F. Griffiths, grandson of the commodore, decked out in full uniform as mascot.

One race that was completed on the first windless day pitted a Curtis airplane against the fastest motorboat on the coast, the *Volga Boy V* of Portland. Lee Huber piloted the aircraft to an easy victory.

In August Ted Geary took the *Sir Tom* to California where, at Newport Harbor, he won the Southern California Yachting Association Open Sailboat Regatta.

On the way home, Geary stopped at Los Angeles Harbor long enough to accept challenges from boats there. Though gale winds were blowing, Geary, good sportsman that he was, raced the *Sir Tom*, which preferred "summer sailing and calm waters." He lost all three races to the California challengers.

Fritz Hellenthal's *Gwendolyn II* kept to her winning ways by capturing the Hat Island Race and the 400-mile Waadah Island contest, as well as Opening Day honors.

Among boats commissioned in 1922,

The famed Isherwood Trophy, one of the most elaborate in the SYC collection. (Wallace Ackerman Photography)

the *Wanda*, built for C. D. Stimson, was a standout. Designed by Ted Geary and put together at the N. J. Blanchard boatworks, this 90-foot "floating palace" was used for pleasure trips up and down the coast.

Model yachts developed as a fad in 1922 and succeeding years. Built by both young men and women, these 40-inch models were a means of interesting youth in yachting. The Seattle Yacht Club scheduled several model races over ensuing years.

1923

The first regatta of the season beckoned vessels to Lake Washington on April 22. The *Gwendolyn II* won the featured

Junior Activities During the 1920s

The SYC Junior Yacht Club was started in 1921 with a membership made up primarily of the children of senior members. It was formed to acquaint the younger set with sailing and sailboats. Long-time member Art Ayers remembers:

> The juniors were always available to crew for the seniors and many sailed on such well known boats as Fritz Hellenthal's *Gwendolyn II*, Ellis Provine's *Gwendolyn I*, Stanley Griffiths' *Gazeka*, Ted Geary's *Sir Tom*, Ray Cook's *Circe*, and many others.
>
> The first boats used exclusively to teach the Juniors to sail were catboats. After them came the flatties and later the Star boats. Each of these boats was privately owned and many of the young skippers became good sailors and well known for being almost unbeatable in their classes—Jack Graham in cats, Bert Davis in flatties, Charlie Ross in Stars. Although girls were not members at the time, several had flatties and Stars, foremost among them being Mary Helen Corbett and Hortense Harley.
>
> —*Art Ayers, 1991*

Sometimes junior racing became more than exciting. In the 1929 Opening Day flattie race, 25-mile-per-hour winds ripped sails and sent Hortense Harley overboard and capsized the *Weno*, dousing Norm C. Blanchard and Ray Fletcher.

> In the 1920s members could remain juniors through age 26 and many started their business careers while still junior members. Several of these older juniors ran the junior club—Doug Stansberry, Russ Gibson, Swift Baker, Andy Joy, Jim and Bob Hodges, and Chuck Konker, to name a few.
>
> Juniors scheduled a meeting once a month but had no meeting place, so they built their own meeting place around the basement fireplace (now the Heritage Room). Fritz Hellenthal donated a pool table for which the juniors built an additional room. After the meetings the older juniors often played cards while the younger ones played pool.
>
> Besides the sailing activities, the juniors had two major parties each year which were chaperoned by senior members. One was the Junior Commodore's Ball and the other was an informal or costume party. While I was junior commander and Norm Blanchard was the entertainment committee chairman, the second party developed into what was then called "The Waterfront Brawl." It became such a well-attended affair that the seniors took it over and for several years had it as one of their annual parties.
>
> —*Art Ayers, 1991*

Fred Harley maintained a scrapbook of junior activities in the late 1920s, which is preserved in the SYC archives. It indicates that these were busy days for the younger set in the new Hamlin Street clubhouse. Several eye-catching invitations to juniors are pasted in the book. One beckoned young men to party at the "Pirates' Lair" on Whidbey Island, another in the form of a telegram invited them to a meeting in the new Juniors' Room at the club. There were invitations to a winter formal, to a farm dinner and barn dance, and to a "Comic Cabaret" at which Barney Google, the Grand Exalted Angora of the Billy Goats, was the honored guest.

Most of the juniors graduated to senior membership and became involved in sail and powerboat circles. Among the better known were Jack Graham, Swift Baker, the Seaborn brothers, Gary Horder, Art Ayers, Norm C. Blanchard, and many others. ◇

Edward H. Hutchison was owner and skipper of the Uwhilna *from 1924 to 1934. When the English-born yachtsman was transferred to Seattle to manage the local office of the Yangtze Marine Insurance Co., he joined the Seattle Yacht Club. In 1934 he retired and returned to London where he lived in the Pembridge Gardens Hotel which was damaged by bombs during World War II. Many of Hutchison's belongings were destroyed. He died shortly after World War II. (J. P. Sauntry Collection)*

The 48-foot Uwhilna, *owned by Edward H. Hutchison, was built in Hong Kong in 1909 from designs by Charles G. Mower, boasted a teak-planked hull over Philippine hardwood frames and copper fasteners. From 1924 to 1934 it was moored at SYC. (J. P. Sauntry Collection)*

sailing race and Robert Alvin was the best of the junior pilots on catboats.

On Opening Day, Junior Commodore Swift Baker in his *Crazy Cat* crossed the finish line just ahead of Captain Burns Ryan in *Dormouse* and Willard Branch in *Hellydid*.

During the 1920s, the Star began to take over as the favorite junior racer and is mentioned increasingly. For example, on May 27, 1923, the papers reported that Jack Graham piloted his new Star boat *Betelgeux* over the Portage Bay finish line just inches ahead of Colin Radford in the *All Star*. In the junior catboat races, Willard Branch, in his *Tiger Cat*, sailed in just seconds before Andy Joy in *Crazy Cat*.

In the combined Memorial Day program on May 30, the Queen City and Seattle yacht clubs hosted powerboat and sailing races. Eighteen boys from Adams school raced their model yachts as an added feature.

The 1923 PIYA races, contested on Cowichan Bay off Vancouver Island, attracted representatives of five yacht clubs—Seattle, Vancouver, Victoria, Tacoma, and Los Angeles. Again the *Sir Tom*, piloted by Ted Geary, retained both the Lipton and Isherwood trophies.

The final race of the year, on September 23, was for the Commodore's Cup and resulted in a win for Ray Cooke's yawl *Claribel*. The race course was from the West Point buoy to Eagle Harbor buoy, to the Duwamish Head bellbuoy,

Yachting Associations

Since 1892, when the Northwest International Yachting Association was formed, regional associations have helped shape and strengthen the Pacific Northwest yachting community. Today, in 1991, it seems undeniable that the center of yachting activity has moved to the west coast of the United States. The recent capture and defense of the America's Cup, emblematic of the world championship of sailing, attests to that. West Coast dominance is not an accident; yachtsmen of this area are organized in a manner that promotes competition and excellence and satisfies the needs and desires of its membership. Regional yacht clubs have formed associations to foster interclub rivalries.

The Pacific Coast Yachting Association (PCYA) is the umbrella organization that joins all yacht clubs on the west coast of North America into a solid competitive group of both power and sail. The PCYA is divided into four general regions. The Northwest Region includes both Canadian and Oregon clubs, as well as clubs on Puget Sound. The other regions are Northern California, which represents the San Francisco area associations, and two Southern California areas, representing the Los Angeles and San Diego associations.

The Northwest region is served by the Pacific International Yachting Association (PIYA) which was formed from the old Northwest International Yachting Association or NIYA (founded at Fairhaven in 1892 to sponsor regattas in Washington and British Columbia), the International Power Boat Association (IPBA) and the Northwest Sailing Foundation. The IPBA has three divisions: Two are operated in Canada, and the other is operated here in the United States to direct the major predicted log racing programs in those areas. The Northwest Sailing Foundation is a not-for-profit educational organization that promotes the arts of sailing. The PIYA governs regional interclub sailing activities in the Northwest, including British Columbia. There are 10 separate yachting associations in the California areas, representing many yacht clubs. Hawaii is also included in PCYA, but none of its associations are currently participating.

PCYA was founded on Jan. 2, 1923, at the Bohemian Club in San Francisco with an objective of coordinating the racing for the Pacific Coast championship. Al Soiland was the first commodore. The first general meeting of PCYA was also held at the Bohemian Club on Jan. 27, 1923. Attending that first meeting and representing the Northwest and PIYA were Captain James Griffiths and Daniel Pratt. Since that time, 14 Northwest yachtsmen have served as PCYA commodores—James Griffiths, Ronald M. Maitland, Harold Jones, Dr. R. Phillip Smith, Andrew Wright, Eustace (Sunny) Vynne, Jr., Howard Richmond, Tom Wheeler, Serge Becker, Garrett Horder, Ward Doland, Phil Johnson and Pat Goodfellow, the current reigning commodore. Gil Middleton is the current secretary and will be the commodore in 1995.

Each year the area of the then-sitting commodore of the PCYA stages the Harry Barusch Memorial Trophy competition, which is emblematic of the West Coast Predicted Log Championship and the Jesse L. Carr Memorial Trophy competition, which is emblematic of the West Coast Sailing Championship. The Carr Trophy is match-raced in one-design boats with skippers all over 50 years of age and crews over 40 years of age. Carr Trophy winners from the Northwest have been Sunny Vynne, Hans Otto Giese, Larry Shorett (twice), and Pat Goodfellow. Northwest winners of the Barusch Trophy race include Lester Lewis (SYC), 1971–72; Charles King (Edmonds), 1978; W. Al Smith (QCYC), 1979–80; Don Bancroft (SYC), 1979; and Ed Gulich (QCYC), 1989.

PCYA awards the Charles A. Langlais Trophy to the yachtsman who is deemed to have made the most outstanding contributions to the sport of yachting each year. Sunny Vynne and Gary Horder are the two Northwest yachtsmen to have been honored as the Langlais Trophy selections since the award was commissioned in 1974. ◇

The palatial 92-foot yacht Wanda *was commissioned in 1922 by C. D. Stimson, designed by Ted Geary, and built by the N. J. Blanchard Boat Co. (N. C. Blanchard Collection)*

then a return to the starting line, hopefully leaving all buoys to port.

1924

The *Log* was published by the juniors as the official organ of the Seattle Yacht Club in 1924. It was sprinkled with what passed as humor:

> She: Tell me, have you ever loved another?
>
> He: Why yes, of course, dear. Do you think I'd practice on a nice girl like you?

The *Log*'s advertisements were also something to behold.

> For goiter, swollen glands, rheumatism, bad nerves, give Deer Lodge National Mineral Water a faithful trial. Wonderful results accomplished for many. Bottled at the spring in gallon bottles. Deliveries made in the city limits by City Distributing Co, 1526 Westlake Avenue, MA 6531.

The yachting year opened on April 28, 1924, with an all-yachtsmen smoker at the clubhouse. Prohibition allowed no cocktails so dinner was served at 6:30 and was followed by a "sober" program honoring new members.

Opening Day, May 3, provided races for all classes on Lake Washington. Fritz Hellenthal's *Gwendolyn II* won the seven-mile race from Madison Park to Hunts Point by 10 seconds over Stanley Griffiths' *Imp*. That evening a dance was scheduled at the club with receptions on various yachts moored nearby.

Crew of the Sir Tom *in 1923 were, from the left, Colin Radford, A. V. Griffiths, L. E. Geary, S. A. Griffiths, and N. J. Blanchard. (N. C. Blanchard Collection)*

Commodores of the Seattle Yacht Club—1920s

JAMES S. GIBSON
1920
Occupation: President, Washington Stevedoring Company
Boat: Motor yacht Muriel

CAPTAIN JAMES GRIFFITHS
1921-1922
Born: 1861, Newport, Monmouthshire, England
Occupation: Owner Stevedoring and Steamship Companies
Boats: Several, the last was the 117-foot motor yacht Sueja III

HENRY SEABORN
1923-1924
Occupation: Comptroller, Skinner and Eddy
Boats: 75-foot motor yacht Charlotte S.

F. C. HELLENTHAL
1925-1926
Born: 1890, Conroe, Tx.
Education: University of Washington
Occupation: Owner, Hellenthal Plumbing and Heating
Boats: Petrel *and* Gwendolyn II

JAMES D. HOGE
1927
Born: 1871, Zanesville, Ohio
Occupation: Banker, Publisher, Real Estate
Boats: None listed

CAPTAIN JAMES GRIFFITHS
1928
(see years 1921-22)

JOHN GRAHAM, SR.
1929
Occupation: Architect
Boats: Several but best-known was 65-foot motor yacht Blue Peter

Memorial Day was again jointly celebrated by the Queen City and Seattle yacht clubs. The waters of Portage Bay and Lake Union "were strewn with flowers" in memory of those deceased, especially the servicemen who died in World War I. Yachtsmen then sailed for Champagne Point on the east shore of Lake Washington for races.

The PIYA regatta of 1924 was hosted by the Tacoma club. Because British Columbia interests had sold the only true competitor, the *Patricia*, to California sportsmen, the *Sir Tom* had no chal-

Cats, Stars, and Knockabouts

The catboat was designed by John Winslow when he lived in Vancouver, B.C. Norman J. Blanchard and Ted Geary lightened the boat, building it so that it wouldn't sink when it capsized. The original cat models were owned by SYC members, and on them many junior members learned the rudiments of sailing. Catboats were a common sight on Portage Bay and Lake Washington during the 1920s. They were the first popular local one-design boats.

When Norman C. Blanchard was eight years old, his father and Ted Geary took him sailing in a catboat race. The boat capsized but was righted and finished the race. By then young Norm was turning blue from the icy soaking, and his teeth rattled like castanets. Once across the finish line, his dad and Geary headed for John Graham, Sr.'s *Sovereign*, which had been acting as timing boat. Norm was helped aboard and seated on a desk. Graham, who had witnessed the capsizing, handed the timer's watch to the older Blanchard and told him to get the finish times for the balance of the racers.

As Norm relates the story:

> John took me into the cabin, stripped off my clothes, and wrapped me in two large Turkish towels he had warmed in the oven. Boy! were those things hot against my cold skin. He rubbed me down from head to foot, then wrapped me in a scratchy wool World War I Army blanket. Then he reached up to a fiddle shelf and brought down two old fashioned keg-shaped glasses, grabbed a fifth of White Horse Scotch whiskey and poured about two fingers in each glass, added two quick pulls from the galley pump and ordered: "You drink this right down!" I thought it was the most horrible medicine I had ever tasted. That was 70 years ago; since then I've changed my mind about Scotch.
>
> The original catboats fea-

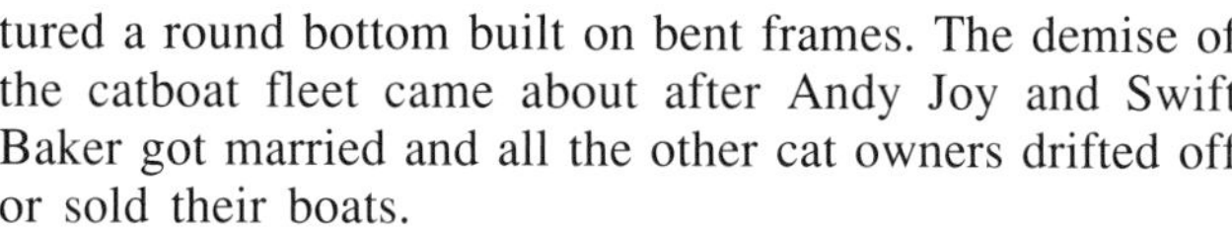

> tured a round bottom built on bent frames. The demise of the catboat fleet came about after Andy Joy and Swift Baker got married and all the other cat owners drifted off or sold their boats.
>
> —*Norman C. Blanchard, Summer 1991*

Star Boats

Jack Graham and Ted Geary influenced competitive racing on Puget Sound with introduction of the Star. The Blanchards built four Star boats in 1923. The Star became an international design and was popular on the East Coast and in Europe. The original design was by a man named Gardener.

The Star was a natural evolution from the catboat and was almost unsinkable. Nonetheless, its popularity dropped off quickly in 1925, after a tragedy on Lake Washington in which four University of Washington students drowned. These students were on their way to a fraternity party across the lake. They filled the forward flotation compartments with party supplies and removed the foredeck hatch to provide room for an ice cream freezer. Then three couples climbed aboard. This was too many even for calm water. A sudden storm blew up, and in those days before floating bridges curtailed the sweep of the wind, huge swells swamped the boat. Two of the women survived, but the loss of four young lives put a damper on Star boat sailing. The boat was marked as unsafe; this was a bad rap.

Many a Seattle yachtsman learned to sail in a Star-class boat. (MOHAI)

Originally the Star had what was called a sliding Gunter rig. Later, taller rigs became popular with a full main but with a much shorter main boom. Class rules were changed accordingly.

The Star recovered its popularity by 1931. A meeting in the late fall of 1929 attracted about 50 sailors in an effort to establish a common design for competitive racing. Some wanted high-performance catboats with hard chines because these boats were easier to build and cheaper, and others wanted a more sophisticated boat that could perform better. There were a lot of ideas for boats under 30 feet. The Star was the consensus choice of most of the sailors. Stars were popular worldwide and were raced in many championships, including the Olympics.

Senior Knockabouts became popular in the early 1930s. (Photo by Ken Ollar)

Knockabouts

The next boat to become popular was the Blanchard Knockabout, a second-generation Star boat that gained popularity about 1934. Clint Harley, Sr., Roy Corbett, and the young Norm C. Blanchard sailed some of the earliest models. This was before Bob and Charlie Ross were old enough to race in Knockabouts.

The Knockabout was designed according to the lines of the Star. The younger Norm, his father and two uncles were building four Star boats, two of them for the Lamson brothers. With the Depression of the 1930s at its deepest, they worked seven days a week. In those days, walking was a popular pastime on Sunday afternoons, and passers-by often would stop to chat and many remarked about how lovely the little Star boats were, but that it was too bad they didn't have a cabin. After hearing that several times, the elder Blanchard grabbed a batten off the floor and held it alongside one of the Star boats and said, "Let's build a cheap boat with a cabin on it!"

After the spring rush was over, young Norm went to the shop early one Sunday and found that his dad had laid out the plans for the Star. He had drawn two lines, one the profile of the bottom keel and the other the shear line. He told Norm that he wanted him to take over and finish the design. Young Blanchard had designed two powerboats (which had been built and were in service) prior to this time. His first Knockabout plan called for a 22-foot, 9-inch hull, which made the Knockabout five or six inches longer than a Star.

The Blanchards built the original mold right off the loft floor from the pencil drawings. Knockabout B-1 was sold to Joe Williams' father for $650, and young Norm helped him sail it to the Williams' holdings on Bainbridge Island. This model had the same keel as the Star boat. One of the reasons for building the Knockabout was the availability of those particular keels. The foundry was practically giving those 842-pound keels away at scrap prices. The original name was to be Star-Knockabout, but Star fleet boat owners were irritated by the inference that the Knockabout was a Star.

A few Knockabouts survive to this day.

Other one-design boats used on Puget Sound include flatties, Snipes, Dragons, Pacific Class (or PCs), Lightnings, Penguins, El Toros (which were eight-foot plywood boats), International 14s, 110s and 210s, OK Dinghies, Finns, C-Larks, Cubs, Thunderbirds, Snowflakes and Columbia River One Design (CRODs). This last was designed and built by Joe Dyer of the Astoria Ship Building Company in the early 1930s for racing on the Columbia River. The lines were taken from the Columbia River gill netters, but the CROD was not double ended like the gill netters. Theo Johnson in West Seattle sailed a CROD, as did Barbara Nettleton and Jack and Ellie Austin.

—From a taped interview with Norman C. Blanchard

lenger. Still, the regatta drew an estimated 100,000 spectators. As had happened in Seattle the year before, the wind refused to fill the sails, delaying the races. The *Volga Boy V* of Portland, which had been clocked at 62 miles per hour, won the powerboat event. Hellenthal's *Gwendolyn II* was the first yawl to cross the finish line, Jack Graham won Star class honors, and Fenton Radford's entry captured the catboat races.

Quent Williams, chairman of the SYC Sailboat Committee, returned from a visit to Detroit, his former home, exclaiming over a ride he had experienced while seated beside Gar Wood in the hydroplane *Miss Detroit*, which had skimmed the waters at 62 miles per hour. Wood had earlier won the Sweepstake Trophy and $10,000, piloting his hydroplane while outfitted in white flannels, blue coat, and an officer's cap.

The Bellingham Yacht Club

On Feb. 14, 1925, a small group of avid boaters met at Garland's Boathouse and created the Bellingham Yacht Club. First officers were Dr. Carl Erb, commodore; W. J. Seaman, vice commodore; and J. L. Patton, secretary-treasurer. The club burgee was designed by F. Stanley Piper. Within three weeks the club had 50 members and a fleet of 10 boats. Members of Sea Scout Troop I, under Master H. L. Morse, with their ship *Sea Wolf*, were made junior members of the new club.

Pacific-American Fisheries allowed the new club to use its shipyard ways and a portion of the office building temporarily. Meantime, negotiations with the Whatcom County Port Commission resulted in permanent moorage on Bellingham Bay. By July 1925 the club had 80 members and was affiliated with the Pacific International Yachting Association.

During 1926 and 1927 weekend cruises, sailing and powerboat races involved some 15 boats.

In 1928 summer moorage space was obtained at Camp Perfection on Chuckanut Bay. Members built a 135-foot pier and a locker shed, which later was replaced with the first clubhouse.

Some of the BYC boats took part in the PIYA regattas during the first five years. In 1929 one predicted log race from Chuckanut to Vancouver was won by Tom Nash. During the return from Vancouver, for reasons unknown, Nash was fired upon by a Canadian fishing boat and received shotgun pellets in his back, neck and head. Fortunately the attack was not fatal.

In 1931 and 1935, BYC hosted the PIYA regatta.

The war years between 1941 and 1946 saw club membership decline because of restrictions, shortages of material and manpower, and lack of moorage space. But in 1946 BYC became active again and acquired a building on the waterfront at the foot of Cornwall Avenue, formerly the Bloedel-Donovan commissary (which served as the Coast Guard headquarters during the war).

The old Chuckanut Bay BYC clubhouse, minus the fireplace but including the lighthouse tower, was brought by barge to Cornwall where it was joined to the existing building. When the new facility was opened on Dec. 20, 1946, it featured a dining room, cocktail lounge, wardroom, kitchen, lobby, office and a storage room. Below the structure was moorage for 20 boats.

In the late 1940s ladies of the BYC decided they should have a more active role in club affairs. In January 1949, with Marge Okerland as the first president, they formed the BYC first mates' auxiliary to assist with regatta preparations. The first mates soon became indispensable in club planning, decorating, and sponsorship of style shows and an annual Christmas Party for children.

During 1950 the deck on the water side of the Cornwall building was partly enclosed to form a

1925

Opening Day races on Lake Washington resulted in Bert Jilg's *Herminia* winning the "Chance Race" for powerboats. The *Imp* won the nine-mile race for schooners. The *Dormouse*, piloted by Burns Ryan, took the catboat prize.

The Pacific International Yacht Association Regatta at Victoria July 1–5 attracted a couple of California boats. As usual *Sir Tom* earned both the Lipton and Isherwood cups, then added the Pacific Coast Challenge Cup, and in so doing bested entries from San Francisco and Vancouver.

Early in September Gil Skinner piloted his appropriately named powerboat *Gilwin* from Seattle to Victoria, arriving before five competitors to capture the Hathaway Cup. Fred Fisher won the Labor Day "Old-Timers" race to Port Madison in his *Acquila*.

ballroom and a sun deck was added. By that time the club had mushroomed to 317 boating members, 580 social members, and a staff of 21 employees. At the time there were also about 30 active junior members.

The Port of Bellingham began development of Squalicum Harbor to the north, and a place was reserved for BYC. Fred Haskell was instrumental in having the port build the original structure that is the clubhouse today. At the recommendation of the state auditor, BYC members purchased the building from the port. At that time it was necessary to raise dues from $10 to $25, and stock shares were made available to members. The move from Cornwall to the present location was made in 1965.

Membership growth created a demand for more space and a large addition to the lounge and dining area was completed in 1970.

In 1974 the PITCH (Pacific International Ton Championships) Regatta was initiated. It was an immediate success, hailed as one of the finest IOR competitions, with boats coming to Bellingham Bay from as far away as California and British Columbia. In the early 1980s the PITCH Regatta was modified to include nine handicapped divisions. It is now one of the top sailing events on the West Coast. In 1988, a total of 71 boats took part in this premier Labor Day regatta.

In an effort to expand the range of activities, the BYC membership approved an outstation fund in 1983. The club leased Inati Bay on the east shore of Lummi Island for members' use; the annual Commodore's Picnic, for example, is held there.

In 1988 the membership voted to extend scheduled activities to include more non-boating interests such as BYC world tours, and an RV Landcruiser program.

In that same year, Bellingham's Soviet Union sister city, Nakhodka, sent the 40-foot racing boat *Kapitan Panaev* to participate in local races and in the Swiftsure Classic. The visit was a result of a six-year negotiation conducted by the sponsor, Bellingham Cold Storage, and a Whatcom County delegation. The Soviet boat and crew remained for six weeks. Unfortunately, their boat suffered damage in a collision during pre-Swiftsure maneuvering and could not participate. But it was a successful visit anyway, and the Soviet crew vowed to return and invited a BYC boat to visit Nakhodka. In 1989 the reciprocal visit was made by eight yachtsmen, twelve teenagers and three counselors who went to Nakhodka for three weeks of camping and racing. In 1990 a group of Nakhodka youngsters came to Four Winds Camp on Orcas Island, and adult sailors competed in the International Pacific Rim Invitational Regatta that drew participants from USSR, Australia, New Zealand, Canada, Japan, and the United States. The racing ended just in time for the Seattle 1990 Goodwill Games.

BYC enters the 1990s as one of the finest private clubs in the Northwest and enjoys reciprocal privileges with most of the yacht clubs in the United States and Canada. The club roster now lists nearly 1,700 members and a fleet of more than 300 boats. ◇

The Who Cares, *well known in the 1920s, was owned by F. A. (Doc) Harvey. (MOHAI)*

Because of light breezes, Fritz Hellenthal's *Gwendolyn II* was the only one of five yachts to complete the 1925 Hat Island Race without resorting to power, so she took the Hat Island Trophy from *Gazeka*, which had won it the year before.

1926

Winners of Opening Day races on May 1 were *Sir Tom*; *Imp*, owned by Frank White and Henry Sander; Ray Cooke's *Claribel*; the Star *Betelgeux*, piloted by Helen Graham; and Fenton Radford's *Cat o'Nine Tails*.

Two weeks later the wind failed the annual Vashon race, forcing all but *Sir Tom* (with Jack Graham at the helm) to cruise home under power. The youthful crew of the *Sir Tom* had decided to sail home no matter how long it took. They arrived about midnight, not an uncommon occurrence for that race.

Ted Geary at the wheel of Don Lee's Invader, *which he guided to victory in the 1926 California-to-Hawaii race. Among the amateur crew was actor Douglas Fairbanks, Sr. (left). (A. Ayers Collection)*

The annual Pacific race to Honolulu attracted Ray Cooke and the crew on the

The Sir Tom *crew in 1926 usually consisted of Roy Corbett, Jack Graham, and Andy Joy. (SYC Historical Collection)*

Claribel, but adverse winds on the way south forced them to drop from the contest. Ted Geary piloted the *Invader*, a 136-foot schooner owned by Don Lee of California. Geary had redesigned the boat at a cost of $25,000. On June 12 six yachts headed toward distant Honolulu with Geary leading all the way.

The PIYA regatta was held in Seattle July 4-7. Because Ted Geary was on his way home from the Pacific race, young Jack Graham piloted the *Sir Tom* to victory. In so doing, he sailed ahead of the new and highly touted British Columbia R-boat *Riowna*, and retained the Lipton and Isherwood trophies. Graham's crew consisted of Roy Corbett, Jack Chisholm and Andy Joy.

1927

The *Post-Intelligencer* carried a lengthy article describing the wonderful sailing available to Seattle residents:

> There is no other city like it. None has so enchanting an environment. Nowhere else are there so many indescribably beautiful spots within a few hours sail of the city.
>
> Islands, almost countless in number, densely wooded and alluring, intrigue the explorer who will possess himself of a boat to embark on voyages of discovery. Hidden coves abound still unmarred in the same beauty that called forth the exclamations of Vancouver and Gray when they first beheld these shores.
>
> Our southern neighbors, Californians, are discovering the Pacific Northwest. They come with summer in an ever-increasing throng to enjoy mountains, streams, green forests, and cool cruises among the beauty spots of Puget Sound.
>
> —Post-Intelligencer, *Aug. 24, 1927*

On May 7, Opening Day of yachting season, the Rudder Cup went to Dr. J. M. Blackford in his *Sally Bruce*. The *Gwendolyn I* piloted by Ellis Provine beat out Fritz Hellenthal's *Gwendolyn II* in the sailing race.

On May 14 the 82-mile Protection Island Race attracted five yachts. The *Gwendolyn I*, again piloted by Provine, beat the other contenders. The names of the crewmen trigger many memories in the minds of old-time SYC members:

Claribel—Ray Cooke, captain; Swift Baker, Milton Benson, Jack Graham, Bob Williams, Norman J. Blanchard, and Charles Latta.

Gwendolyn I—Ellis Provine, captain; Wynn Jones, Cecil Dexter, Dr. H. E. Coe, and Jacob Nash.

Imp—Henry Sander and Joe Long, owners; Hap Allen, Jack Conway, Ed Lindberg, and G. More.

Gazeka—Colin Radford, captain; Roy Corbett, LeRoy Backus, H. L. Coe,

The Bremerton Yacht Club

In 1929 Floyd H. Phillips, who worked at the Bremerton Post Office, had a boat that often dragged anchor and ended up on somebody's beach. Though Bremerton was a small town, it was home to several pleasure craft. Floyd arranged a meeting on May 25, 1929, to discuss founding a yacht club. The group agreed to prepare bylaws, find a meeting place, and design a burgee.

On June 17 Floyd was elected the first commodore of the Bremerton Yacht Club. Ten men signed on as charter members.

The city commissioners offered the old Charleston ferry dock as a meeting place. Though the structure had been condemned, the members were not discouraged. Work parties appeared immediately to repair the place. At the first meeting on the site, held on June 25, 1929, members agreed to an initiation fee of $5 per charter member, a fee that would rise to $10 after July 1. Dues were fixed at 50 cents a month in advance. At the next meeting, bylaws were approved, and the first official BYC function was a family cruise to Brownsville.

The city dog pound shared the dock with the yacht club and early members walked past four kennels of yapping canines. Members built a landing float, but boats had to anchor out in the bay.

In March 1930, when Bob Haven was commodore, the ladies' auxiliary was formed by wives of members. Mrs. George Braendlein was chosen as their first president.

Elmer Brooks was installed as commodore in 1931. As membership increased, so did the number of boating and social events. The Queen City Yacht Club (which had helped the Bremerton Club get started and had sponsored it in the established yachting community) joined the new club for a weekend cruise and clambake on Ostrich Bay. About 120 people attended.

Members continued to seek a permanent site, but the miniscule ($60) treasury remained a problem.

In 1934 Bremerton boats for the first time entered the Capital-to-Capital Race to Nanaimo. Also that year a junior group was sponsored. The "Big Blow of 1934" is well remembered. A gale of tornado proportion struck on Oct. 21, 1934, battering a dozen boats at the Charleston moorages; only two weathered the storm. The floats were swept away and not retrieved by the Coast Guard for several days. That storm ended BYC's interest at the Charleston dock.

Captain Braendlein served as commodore in 1935, the year the club stowed its properties in a rented garage and scheduled meetings in homes of members and in downtown offices.

On June 10, 1935, the club placed a $10 down payment on waterfront property at Ostrich Bay, but a strong north wind blasted the inlet, and the wind combined with ill will from surrounding property owners blew the yacht club right out.

The big event of the 1935 season was the Everett Predicted Log Race. BYC members went to Everett en masse and captured the three top prizes plus first place in the dinghy tug-of-war.

In September members voted down the opportunity to apply for a liquor license even though prohibition had ended. The first woman member—Avadana Cochrane, a credit bureau manager—joined the club in the fall of 1935. That year the club incorporated and a past-commodores' club was formed.

In March 1935 the club agreed to make time-payments on property near the Navy Yard Highway on Sinclair Inlet. The members again voted on the divisive issue of serving liquor in the club; the motion lost by one vote. Work parties installed new floats at the property, which were financed by a $10-per-member assessment. New piling was driven.

In 1936 the club had plans to buy the old Seattle clubhouse in West Seattle and float it to their new site, but someone else bought it first. In 1937, the city agreed to install a municipal float on the club site if members would insure it and assume liability. Membership burgeoned as facilities became available.

While Elmer Brooks was commodore in 1938, a clubhouse was built under contract. The meeting of March 7 was the first in the new facility.

Monthly dances were sponsored by the club to raise money for completing the clubhouse, but at 25 cents admission, little more than headaches was generated. George Tappe and a crew of club members saw to the decorating of the interior of the club, and furniture and a piano were purchased.

On the shakedown cruise of 1938, several boats visited Fox Island. Memorial Day services that year involved Spanish-American War veterans on BYC boats. That summer the club sponsored the International Race to Nanaimo for the first time.

The state decided to build a new highway through BYC property in 1940. For the right-of-way they paid the club $400 and filled and graded the parking lot. As they were building, they had to blast a cliff near the club, and before each blast, the contractor would phone the club which, in turn, would call members to move their boats out into the bay to escape any flying boulders.

C. J. Richie took over as commodore in 1941. The last official cruise until after World War II took members to Fletcher Bay on Sept. 7, 1941, for the annual corn roast. After the December 7 attack on Pearl Harbor, many yachtsmen secured their boats for the duration. Twenty-four others joined the Coast Guard Auxiliary. During the war, no night running was allowed, many areas were off limits, and gasoline was scarce.

BYC Commodore H. D. Thompson in 1944 heard that a railroad might be built through club property. A potential new site was found on Phinney Bay where 475 feet of waterfront was purchased for $4,500—a bargain even then. On July 4, 1944, the club was ordered to vacate its premises within 30 days so railroad construction could begin. Trustees had a basement excavated on the Phinney Bay lots and space leveled for parking. An old-timer, Dr. Ray Schutt, lent the club $10,000 at no interest to ready the facility. Piling was driven in November, and the old clubhouse moved to the new site.

BYC Commodore Ray Hart named a committee in 1946 to take care of the small stores department and stock concession items including gas and oil. The first profits purchased a fine furnace for the basement. Commodore Hart outlined a comprehensive program for the year. On Washington's birthday BYC hosted every yacht club on the sound at a Heavy Weather Cruise and Dance that attracted 40 yachts and 250 visitors.

In 1953 BYC Commodore Harry Gundlach oversaw a $15,000 improvement of the moorage facilities. In 1957 while Hal Edwards was at the helm, property purchased years earlier at Point Monroe for $600 was sold for $5,500. During 1958 when Howard Huston was leading the club, a new mailing address was obtained—2700 Yacht Haven Way.

In 1964 Commodore Grady Barrentine handled the question of public access across club property. A meeting with an adjoining property owner resulted in no agreements. The club decided to close the entrance of the parking lot for one day a year to keep it from becoming a public thoroughfare. In 1966 Dr. W. E. Rownd skippered the club through a dispute with the state over waterfront rights. Chet Simpier handled the affair, and the club finally agreed to a fee of $275 a year with no retroactive rent.

While W. G. "Woody" Woodard was commodore in 1967, plans for a new clubhouse were presented by Ed Day and Stan Wardin. Authorization to spend $150,000 was secured, but in the end, V. C. Morneau presented a plan to have only the framing contracted out. Members finished the work at a total cost of $40,000. The club had a fine new home, comfortable caretaker's quarters, and no mortgage.

Over the last two decades, the Bremerton Yacht Club has continued to thrive, building on the firm foundation established back in 1929. ◇

Moritz Milburn, Jack Radford, and Dick Shaw.

Gwendolyn II—Fritz Hellenthal, captain; E. P. Dearborn, Harry Cook, Anton Pierre, Rudy Pierre, and Bert Kepfli.

The California races of 1926 were rough on *Sir Tom*; she had to be overhauled, and her planking had to be replaced after her hull was strained from being slung aboard the freighter that carried her home. However, at the PIYA races, she again brought home the Isherwood and Lipton trophies. Geary stated that his rebuilt boat was "better than ever."

In August the *Sir Tom* went south again to vie for Pacific Coast honors. At the regatta off Santa Barbara, Geary sailed her in three races in a row to win the R class championship.

Commodore James D. Hoge in September provided a barometer-chronometer prize for the sailboat race to Eagle Harbor and back. The *Gwendolyn II* came in 11 seconds ahead of the *Sir Tom* to win the prize.

1928

The Seattle Sunshine Society transported 60 "shut-ins" to Lake Washington to watch the Rudder Cup Race of June 9. Frank Seidelhuber's new *Mary Mar Ann* covered the course in lead position.

P. G. Brattstrom skippered his

Imp, *a gaff-rigged sloop, was owned by Bob White in the 1920s. (MOHAI)*

Janelva to a win in the race to Victoria in early June and took home the Norman Blanchard Trophy.

Young Bert Davis, with Chet Dawson as mate, piloted the *Banshee No. 13* and won the International-Interstate Flattie Race on Lake Washington, taking home the *Post-Intelligencer* Challenge Cup.

The first International Cruiser Capital-to-Capital Race was run from Olympia to Juneau in 1928. The grand prize of $500 in gasoline script and the Governor's Cup went to the Olympia Yacht Club's *Dell*, owned by E. J. Thompson.

At the 1928 PIYA's regatta at Vancouver, the *Sir Tom*, this year sporting a new larger jib, again retained the Lipton and Isherwood trophies for the SYC. In so doing, she defeated the new R class racer *Lady Van*. Ted Geary had earlier sent a copy of the *Sir Tom* plans to Vancouver so they could build a competitor, and the *Lady Van* looked much like the *Sir Tom*.

This prompted a *Post-Intelligencer* sports reporter to ask whether it was the craft or the skipper that wins races. Was it Ted Geary or the *Sir Tom* that won again at Vancouver? The conclusion was that since the *Lady Van* was built to beat the champion and looked much like her, the skipper must be the winning factor.

On August 26 the younger Norman Blanchard in the *Weno* arrived third in the final flattie race of the year for juniors. The single point earned by that position gave him a total of 16 points for the season. This boosted him one point above Hortense Harley for the Northwest flattie championship and the C. S. Harley Trophy.

1929

This was a year of many unhappy events—personal, financial and racing.

The personal tragedy occurred first. As the SYC Lake Washington sail race of April 7 was being completed, Ellis Provine's *Gwendolyn I* hauled into the wind toward the finish line. John Winslow, marine architect and sailing master, held the tiller. He glanced aloft to see that all sails were drawing well and asked Provine to take the stick. Winslow then stood, braced his feet for the roll of the yacht, looked to the far horizon, and crumpled to the deck, dead at age 55.

A far less tragic event occurred at the PIYA regatta at Vancouver: For the first time in 14 years the *Sir Tom* was beaten.

The third unhappy occurrence had nothing to do directly with yachting, and yet it would have great effect. The stock market crashed in October, signaling the beginning of the Great Depression.

The May 4 SYC Guest Day races were won by *Gwendolyn I* and the powerboat *Marvel*, which was owned by D. E. Helser.

In mid-June the second 1,000-mile Olympia-to-Juneau Capital-to-Capital Race for cruisers drew 10 speedsters. Among the crew members were eight women. The *Bolinder*, owned by Seattleite Richard Froboese, took overall honors.

At the PIYA Regatta off Vancouver, the sloop *Lady Van* beat the *Sir Tom*. Seattle Yacht Club had to relinquish the Lipton and Isherwood trophies to the Canadians.

On August 17, for the first time, outboards raced on Lake Sammamish. Their roar echoed from the wooded shoreline.

The 1920s were years of facilities development at the new Seattle Yacht Club on Portage Bay. Racing craft, both sail and power, were improved and auxiliary power was added to many large sailing vessels. One-design fleets multiplied and flourished. Junior members not only organized but were very active and crewed on some of the most famous racing yachts. From among these juniors of the 1920s came many leading yachtsmen, a few of whom are still active members after six decades. ☆

The Seattle Yacht Club in the early 1930s. Note the University of Washington golf links beyond the canal. (Webster and Stevens Collection, MOHAI)

FIVE

The 1930s

The new decade dawned on an America being battered by hard times. Most pundits predicted that it would be only a short recession. President Herbert Hoover did little to counter the financial depression until October 1930, when he stated the nation must prevent hunger and cold for those in real trouble. In 1932, unemployment in the United States surpassed 11 million and welfare funding had emptied state and local government coffers. Unemployed men rallied at the county-city building in Seattle and at the capitol in Olympia, demanding jobs. In November 1932 Franklin Delano Roosevelt was elected president and soon began several programs to put men to work.

Through the 1930s the Seattle Yacht Club suffered many resignations and instituted rigid economies in order to keep the doors open. Maintenance was on a patch-as-you-can-pay basis, many moorages were empty, bond payments were missed, and club services were at times almost nonexistent. However, a core of loyal members managed to keep the club afloat. Work parties were organized to make essential repairs and to paint structures.

In spite of all the hardships, the club managed to schedule many activities during every year of this depressed decade.

1930

Outboarders opened their season on April 26 with a "Puddle Jumpers Hop" at Pioneer Hall near Madison Park.

The Protection Island Race was a huge success according to the *Post-Intelligencer*:

> Bucking heavy tide rips and beating against a forty-mile-an-hour gale at times, Fritz Hellenthal's *Gwendolyn II* returned victor early today in the 120-mile Protection Island race over the weekend from the largest list of entries ever to compete in the event.
>
> —Post-Intelligencer, *May 19, 1930*

Roy Corbett and his daughter Mary

Helen received considerable publicity during the year for their sailing ability. Roy, who was mainsheet man on Ted Geary's *Sir Tom*, passed along his sailing skills to Mary Helen, who had captured the flattie championship in 1929 and would continue to demonstrate her sailing prowess.

The first annual Northwest Motor Boat Show was scheduled April 15–20 at Seattle's Ice Arena.

Famous author Stewart Edward White moored his yacht *Kuru* at the Seattle Yacht Club in 1930. So did Baron H. Long, the California racetrack and hotel man, whose boat was called the *Norab*. A third noted yacht, the new 96-foot *Electra* owned by H. W. Leonard, was launched at the Lake Union dry dock.

The club found space and funding to establish an outstation at the foot of Seaview Avenue at Shilshole.

The media gave considerable atten-

The Lake Chelan Yacht Club

The Lake Chelan Yacht Club was organized in 1930 by a group of about 40 boating enthusiasts. Bruce McKinstry was the first commodore. In 1931, under George Miller, the second LCYC commodore, several piers were built in various harbors up the lake. In 1932, with Jim Reed at the helm, the club purchased a mile of waterfront near Granite Falls from the Chelan Electric Company for $500. Later in the year the land was traded to Joshua Green, Sr., (Green-Davis Security Company) for 30 acres and 250 feet of waterfront on which was sited the Elmore Dance Pavilion. This dance hall had been forced to close because of the depression, and Josh Green held the mortgage. Two months after the trade, so the story goes, Green sent his manager over to assess the transaction and was informed that in all fairness, the Lake Chelan Yacht Club should have thrown in a mountain goat on the deal.

The Lake Chelan Yacht Club members immediately began converting the dance hall to a clubhouse. In 1933 the membership limit of 200 was reached (the initiation fee was $7.50 and annual dues were $2.50). During the 1930s, largely through volunteer labor, the clubhouse and facilities received a number of upgrades: The clubhouse was surfaced with logs; a large room with a fireplace was added; a pier and breakwater were installed; a new road was built; a concrete boat launching pad was poured, and bathhouse and restrooms were plumbed.

During the 1940s the clubhouse was re-roofed, and a new water system was developed. During the war years, a Coast Guard Auxiliary was organized on the lake, and many members of the yacht club were involved.

During the 1950s slips for moorage were added, and pilings replaced under the clubhouse.

In the 1960s upper lots were leveled for boat storage, and a camper area was added. Water mains were laid to the resident area, and by the end of the decade resident membership totaled 70.

As the 1970s began, the floating breakwater and moorage sank; however, all boats but one were freed and that one was recovered later. The club purchased 103 feet of land uplake from the clubhouse for a swimming area and additional parking.

The club has stood the test of time, an economic depression, wars, storms, sinking of the moorage, court sessions, IRS audit, recession and continued the policies laid down in the early years of its foundation—which stated the purpose: "an outlet for the boating enthusiasm and the exchange of good fellowship by boating enthusiasts. . . ."

From a sprawling, crude lake dance hall in 1932, the clubhouse and grounds have evolved into a modern nautical resort with navy trimness and neatness. The club now boasts a full membership of 250 regular, social and family members; moorage for 90 boats; camping facilities; picnic and swimming areas; and resident villa for 100 members.

—LCYC Historian

—Based on material provided by Wallace C. "Wally" Hill

tion to the 1930 PIYA Regatta in Victoria because Ted Geary had announced he would reclaim the R-boat title. This was no easy task, as it turned out. In the first race on July 1 two Canadians—Jack Crib with his *Lady Van* and Ron Maitland in *Lady Pat*, both of the Royal Vancouver Yacht Club, crossed the finish line ahead of Geary and the *Sir Tom*. However, the *Sir Tom* won the second and third races and recovered the Lipton and Isherwood cups.

Geary served as SYC commodore in 1930, and in his foreword for the SYC yearbook he wrote of progress:

> . . . In all large yachting centers in the United States the growth of racing and cruising sailboats has kept pace with the growth of motorboats, except here on Puget Sound.
>
> While this is largely a motorboat country and motorboats will always be the majority, there is a very definite reason why the racing and cruising sailboat has been kept back, and it is to be found in the present location of the Seattle Yacht Club, in fresh water behind the Lake Washington Canal Locks, and a number of bridges. It is to be regretted that with all the indentations on the shore line of Puget Sound that would otherwise be good moorings for sailing craft, there are none within thirty miles north or south of Seattle on the Seattle side of the sound. Recent events promise that this situation will be relieved.
>
> Your club will soon have a station with summer moorings for sailing craft and large motor yachts outside the locks on Shilshole Bay. We are optimistic in the belief that a mile-long breakwater will be built outside these mooring grounds as an aid to navigation, and that both sailing and motor boating will receive great impetus from the convenience afforded both branches of the sport by the outside mooring ground.
>
> —*Ted Geary, SYC Yearbook, 1930*

Late in the year, Ted Geary announced that he would seek "new moorings in Southern California." He and his draftsman, Ed Monk, Sr., moved to Los Angeles where the motion picture industry was thriving and big yachts were still in demand. They would design large yachts for John Barrymore and Donald Douglas, among others. Geary often returned to the Northwest to race in the ensuing years.

In 1930 the aging *Claribel*, skippered by Ray Cooke of SYC, captured several events—the Perpetual Challenge Trophy Race and the race for large yawls. In late August, she won the Old-Timers' Race from Point Monroe to Luna Park, finishing at the club's new outside station on Salmon Bay.

In 1930 the International Cruiser Predicted Log Race from Seattle to Prince Rupert finished on June 24. The winning boat was J. W. Power's *Madie* of the Queen City Yacht Club.

Because of the depression, volunteer help was enlisted to lay new walks from the street down past the front of the clubhouse to the piers.

As an indication of the serious financial condition of the club, the board of trustees, by unanimous vote, called for enforcement of section 11, paragraph 21 of the bylaws, which concerned delinquent accounts. At the March board meeting, 40 members were dropped from the rolls and steps were taken to immediately begin collecting the sums they owed the club; also many boat owners who were more than 90 days delinquent on moorage payments were asked to relinquish their spaces.

1931

A letter dated Feb. 10, 1931, was sent to all junior members whose accounts were overdue, requesting at least a partial payment.

During the spring of 1931, the Seattle Yacht Club board, still believing the depression would be short lived, agreed to renovate the club premises. The improvements included new chairbacks, drapes, awnings, and flower boxes for the dining room; new furniture and flower boxes for the sunroom; chairs and floor coverings for the balcony; new furnishings

L. E. (Ted) Geary
Commodore, 1930

The Seattle Yacht Club commodore of 1930 was a well-known naval architect who designed and helped build many famous yachts on Puget Sound. His name was Leslie E. (Ted) Geary.

He was born in Atchison, Kansas, on June 1, 1885, to parents who had emigrated from England. His father decided to go into the piano-selling business in Portland, Oregon. When proceeds did not live up to expectations, the Gearys moved to Seattle in 1893, where the elder Geary established a reputation as a longtime and respected music dealer at a time when home entertainment was an important part of life.

After attending Seattle's public schools, young Ted enrolled at the University of Washington, but illness interrupted his education. While recuperating, he designed the yacht *Spirit I* and with her in 1907 won the victory over the British yacht *Alexandra* in a race at Vancouver, B.C. He became known as "the boy wonder."

Once he regained his health, Ted Geary, aided by funds donated by wealthy friends, transferred to MIT where in 1910 he was awarded his degree in naval architecture. During World War I, Geary served as district naval architect, U.S. Shipping Board, Emergency Fleet, Inc., Northwest Ship Division, for which he designed the Geary class 6,000-ton wooden ships.

He is best known, however, for his racing sloops and luxury cruisers. His first motor yacht, the 100-foot *Helori*, was completed in 1912, and in subsequent years he built many sailing yachts and motorboats including the *Wanda* (1922), *Westward* (1924), *Samona I* (1924), *Malibu* (1925), *Stella Maris* (1925), *Sueja III* of James Griffiths (1926), *Principia* (1928 for L. A. Macomber), *Blue Peter* (1928 for John Graham, Sr.), *Canim* (1930 for C. B. Blethen), *Electra* (1930), *Samona II* (1931), and *Infanta*, now the *Thea Foss* (1932 for actor John Barrymore).

Geary not only designed yachts, he sailed them. His life-long hobby was racing, and he built his own boats from age 11 on. He and a friend built a 16-foot cat called *Lark* in 1899 and successfully raced her in Puget Sound regattas. He raced his *Spirit II* until 1914. He then designed his most famous racing sailboat, *Sir Tom*.

For a decade and a half, Geary sailed the *Sir Tom* as undefeated defender of the Lipton and Isherwood international cups, competing against the finest boats on Puget Sound and in British Columbia waters. He also won many outstanding victories in California and earned the Pacific Coast championship for Class R sloops.

In 1928 Geary designed the flattie. After his year as SYC commodore in 1930, Geary moved to Long Beach, California. There, during World War II, he was employed by the Navy as investigator of the stability of vessels up to 15,000-ton transports.

Geary died on May 19, 1960. The *Post-Intelligencer* obituary listed his survivors as his wife Freda; two daughters, Mrs. George Johnson of Long Beach and Mrs. Merritt Adamson of Malibu; and three sisters, Mrs. Laurence Hill of Seattle, Mrs. Archie Myers of Portland, and Mrs. Clyde Rose of San Francisco. ◇

The flattie dock in the 1930s, a site later filled to build the lower parking lot. (Photo by John B. Woodward)

and decorations for the Commodore's Room; drapes and awnings for the upper card room; enlargement of the juniors room; general shower room improvements and rewiring of the entire club. They also considered future beautification of the piers, installation of new walkways and mooring piles and painting the exterior of all structures. However, with dollars scarce, this work ended up being spread over several years, and much of it was undertaken by volunteer labor.

In spite of the deepening depression, Opening Day festivities on Lake Washington attracted 40 sailing vessels. The race, which began at the foot of Madison Street just south of the Kirkland ferry dock, fell victim to a calm and was never finished.

Racers to Hat Island on May 17 faced the opposite problem. "Many of the yachts were driven to cover with split sails and tangled rigging. Others went to the dry dock with broken planking and open seams" (*Post-Intelligencer*, May 18, 1931). Fritz Hellenthal's *Gwendolyn II* was the first to complete the race.

The Protection Island Race attracted more than 20 boats, but a calm forced most of the larger ones to abandon the race. Otto Rohlf's *Dione* was first to complete the distance. The *Preservo* arrived second, piloted by Rupert Broom, a lad still in his early teens.

On June 28, Adolph Schmidt's *Winifred* crossed the finish line with the best predicted time to win the Capital-to-Capital Power Boat Race from Olympia to Victoria. The *Mary-Mar-Ann*, belonging to SYC's Frank Seidelhuber, took second.

The PIYA Regatta, held at Bellingham beginning July 1, found the *Sir Tom* touted once again as the boat to beat. On the first day, the races for the Sir Thomas Lipton Perpetual Trophy and the Pacific Northwest Perpetual Challenge Trophy were becalmed. The *Sueja III*, owned by Commodore James Griffiths of the Seattle Yacht Club, was first to cross the finish line between Chuckanut Island and Governor's Point and won the Pacific Motor Boat Trophy.

On July 2 the *Lady Pat* bested the *Sir Tom* in a light breeze, but Seattleites remembered it took two wins to earn the Lipton Cup. On July 3 the wind again refused to stir the sails, so the second race was postponed until July 5. On July 5 the race was completed, but the results were at first contested and for good reason. As the *Post-Intelligencer* reported:

> Less than a mile from the finish buoy with the *Sir Tom* overhauling the *Lady Pat* fast in a lightening breeze, Harry Jones, member of the crew of the *Pat*, was jerked overboard by one of the lines loosened to let out a reef in a sail.
>
> The *Sir Tom*, a few hundred yards behind, hove to, and picked him up and lost precious seconds in doing so.
>
> The power yacht, the *Sueja III*, was close behind and would have picked him up a minute later. But international rules are that a boat must finish with the same crew it started with.
>
> So the *Lady Pat* finished with one less and the *Sir Tom* with one too many. The judges took the matter under advisement.
>
> —Post-Intelligencer, *July 6, 1931*

The two skippers agreed to flip a coin to decide the winner. The *Lady Pat*'s skipper called it right, but now the crews of both yachts argued that the race should be re-run. But Ted Geary refused to contest the decision and E. F. (Jack) Crib was presented the Lipton Cup, which was displayed at the Vancouver Yacht Club for the ensuing year.

1932

John H. Dreher of the *Seattle Daily Times* reported on yachting activities for much of the decade. On May 1 he wrote

Everett Yacht Club

Yachtsmen were sailing on Port Gardner Bay before the turn of the century; three yachts from Everett participated in the celebration of the Queen's Birthday at Victoria in 1895. An informal yacht club was founded at that time, but activities faltered due to the economic depression.

The Everett Yacht Club was resurrected in 1907 by several prominent citizens. Frank Newman was elected commodore. In 1909, EvYC became the newest member of the Northwest International Yachting Association, and its sloop *Rival* won a major trophy.

The first Everett clubhouse, which was located at Camp 1 south of Weyerhaeuser Mill A, could be reached only by foot (down the Great Northern tracks) or by water. Later this structure was moved to the present clubhouse location.

The *Genevieve*, designed, built and sailed by A. D. and Bob McAdam, was one of the fastest boats on the sound during the years prior to World War I. She won cups from Olympia to Bellingham and in Victoria and Vancouver races, too. Her half-hull model is preserved in the present Everett clubhouse.

Motorboat enthusiasts got together in 1910 to develop the first Everett Motor Boat Club. Arthur A. Pettersen was the first commodore. Their activities centered around an old house on floats on the Snohomish River just south of Hewitt Avenue. They later moved it downstream below Everett Avenue. This club grew rapidly and purchased a larger floathouse with lockers and dining accommodations for 42 persons.

As with many other yacht clubs, World War I stalled boating and club activities.

In 1927 the Port of Everett acquired tidal land between Piers 1 and 2 where it built a small boat landing. In 1929 fifty persons met to reorganize the Everett Motor Boat Club. In 1929 7,000 spectators witnessed a dozen boats racing on Lake Stevens. Thus the Port of Everett played a role in the yachting revival.

In 1930 the group raised funds and with volunteer labor erected a clubhouse. Howard S. Wright acted as superintendent and Nick Reinell procured the materials.

The next year, the Everett Motor Boat Club changed its name to Everett Yacht Club, and Howard S. Wright was named the first commodore.

In 1932 the club first sponsored a Sea Scout Troop, and two years later a 50-foot hull was assigned by the U.S. Navy Department to the club and its scouts. Through the generosity of Capt.

of the coming Opening Day activities of Saturday, May 7:

> With thirty-five to forty sailboats and half that number of power cruisers stretched out in long, parade-race lines; with each skipper "giving" his boat all he knows; with the crews tense and illy hiding their excitement, all of this is reflected in the shoreline audience which sits with field glasses leveled and thumbs raised as in the days of far gorier shows.
>
> —Seattle Daily Times, *May 1, 1932*

Two new sailing craft made their appearance in Opening Day races. The *Circe*, the Marconi-rigged cutter that Broadway High School student Ben Seaborn had designed (his stepfather Ray Cooke bankrolled it), won her maiden race on time allowance. The first boat across the finish line, however, was the *Mahero*, which had been christened a week earlier by her skipper, Roy Corbett.

Because of the depression, more and more attention was focused on the smaller and less expensive sailing craft—flatties and Stars. The May 15 *Seattle Daily Times* headlined the return of the Star fleet. University of Washington student Hortense Harley had moved up from her flattie to

---

Harry Ramwell, this hull became a two-masted cabin schooner with auxiliary motor.

In 1934 the Aquilonius Sailing Club affiliated itself with EvYC. The following year, the club facilities were completely remodeled and redecorated. That same year the club bought Harry Ramwell's *Black Prince*, an historic 112-foot steamer for $1. Built in 1901, she served on the Snohomish and Skagit rivers as well as on the sound. In 1936 she was pulled onto the bank, shored up on pilings and remodeled as the official meeting room. Years later she was replaced by a new addition, also named the *Black Prince*.

In 1938 the Barnacle Club was organized for women of the yacht club, and the following year the Junior Yacht Club came into existence.

In 1940 the club canceled all concessions and took over management of its refreshment and food services. This led to the building of a new clubhouse in 1941. During World War II, a U.S. Coast Guard Reserve flotilla was formed and undertook many duties. More than 100 yacht club members served in the armed forces, and the club facilities were open to servicemen of all branches. Although World War II curtailed many yachting activities, club membership increased steadily during the war years.

After the war, cruising again became popular, social activities grew apace, and a new lease from the port produced larger holdings and greater security. From then on, the club was able to operate its own moorage.

In 1951 the club purchased outstation property on Gedney (Hat) Island.

The year 1962 provided racing highlights for the Everett club when Capt. Ray Davis and crew finished first in class in the International Cruiser Race, and Dr. Ed Chase and his *Doc's Out* won the 450-mile Van-Isle Race.

In 1966 plans were made to build a new facility on 14th Street. It was built the following year, and the mortgage was retired 13 years later in 1979.

In 1973 Orv Lupton won the Bremerton Heavy Weather Race.

The year 1985 brought many changes. The members elected to close the dining facilities at EvYC, and the following year the clubhouse was sold to the Port of Everett, though social activities continued. By 1987–88 the club was an active, growing, family boating club. Bylaws were changed, creating equal membership and only one class of membership. With things going so well, in 1988–89 plans began to take shape for the Everett Yacht Club to again own a clubhouse.

In March 1991 Everett Yacht Club sent a contingent of boats to welcome home the *U.S.S. Sacramento* from the Persian Gulf War. ◇

a Star, the *Goony*, which had been launched at Norman J. Blanchard's boat works the previous Tuesday. The *Seattle Daily Times* article continued:

> The two Blanchards, Norm and Norm, father and son, worked on the *Goony*, the Junior Norm became infected; he decided he had to have a Star, too; so, Young Norm's boat eventually took form and shape and it will be launched about June 1.
>
> Then Miller Freeman and W. B. Nettleton, their Star boats laid up at Blanchard's lo these last three years, decided that, so long as there was company for their Stars, this would be a swell time to de-barnacle and re-paint. [In 1991 Norm C. Blanchard, (Jr.), explained that actually it was he who had been infected first and took the Harleys sailing on a Star, which convinced them that it was the boat that would succeed the flatties.]
>
> —Seattle Daily Times*, May 15, 1931*

Reporter Dreher explained for the "unsophisticated" that the Star was the only fully standardized sailboat class. All were 22.5 feet in length, with a six-foot beam, and carried 900 pounds of iron. In 1930 an official 34-foot mast had been ordained by the International Star Class

The christening of Hortense Harley's Star, Goony, *on May 10, 1932, found several young ladies helping to celebrate. From left are: Mary Helen Corbett, Ann Seidelhuber, Hortense Harley, Dorothy Belt, and three of Miss Harley's sorority sisters. (Hortense Harley Collection)*

Rope Yarn Sunday

"Rope Yarn Sunday" is a tradition that dates to the days of the old sailing ships. The story goes that the chief mate could ask the captain for a Rope Yarn Sunday whenever he felt that the crew needed a day of rest. Though it was always called Rope Yarn Sunday, the day off could be any time during the week that the crew needed rest from their regular chores. They would sit by and tell yarns. Much later the tradition was adopted by the U.S. Navy and, although working a rope was not necessary, a holiday at sea always seemed to find the men busy weaving hemp.

Yarns are now called sea stories, and every sailor has about a million he can tell. During SYC's earlier years members decided to bring "Rope Yarn Sunday" to life again at the club, and that it could be a wives' holiday. The plan originally called for men to meet at the club at 5:00 P.M. and have their spouses join them for cocktails and dinner if they chose.

Today Rope Yarn Sundays are sponsored by the entertainment committee and are held on Thursdays in the Marine Room from 5:00–7:00 P.M. The programs are varied, featuring subjects that are complementary to club activities or of general boating interest. The Marine Room sponsors a free light buffet with special prices for beverages.

—Adapted from an article by Jim McGinnis in Binnacle, *February 1960*

Yacht Racing Association. This mast was five feet taller and the boom four feet shorter than that previously allowed.

The Vashon Island race late in May found Roy Corbett and Carl Seitz' Marconi-rigged sloop *Winsome* beating out the *Circe* by 30 seconds.

In early June, many Seattle Yacht Club craft were moved to saltwater moorage at SYC's new outstation on Shilshole Bay. At the dedicatory race, the *Winsome* was leading until the wind carried away her jib. The *Gwendolyn II* then took first honors in the large class.

In the Capital-to-Capital Race, following modified Rudder Cup Rules and sponsored by the American Power Boat Association, Olympia Yacht Club Commodore Frank Mallory eased his *Pamanus* over the finish line at Cadboro Bay within 53 seconds of his predicted time to win overall honors.

The PIYA Regatta in 1932 was hosted by the SYC off Shilshole. The *Sir Tom* again raced against the *Lady Pat* and the *Lady Van*, both of Vancouver. The *Lady Pat* proved the faster in this series. Other PIYA winners: large sloops, *Circe*; large two-stickers, *Gwendolyn II*; small sloops, *Gypsy Heart*; small two-stickers, *Gwendolyn I*; flatties, *Alcor*, (Bob Lamson); Star class, *Blue Boot*, (Norm C. Blanchard).

It had become apparent that the *Sir Tom* was faltering after 14 years of invincibility. Ted Geary seated a new mast in her, but over Labor Day the *Lady Pat* again crossed the finish line ahead of *Sir Tom*.

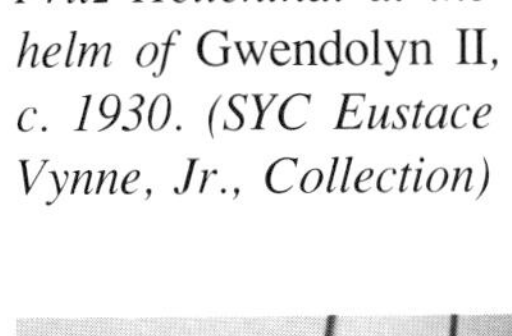

Fritz Hellenthal at the helm of Gwendolyn II, *c. 1930. (SYC Eustace Vynne, Jr., Collection)*

Bill Hedley and the Barnacle Bill Cruises

In the days of wooden ships and iron men, "sea chanteys," songs that imitated the rhythms of a sailor's movements, were sung by the crews as a means of helping them work in unison. There were certain chanteys for sweating halyards home, for swaying yards aloft, and for sheeting the braces. Some of these folk songs of the sea are well known even today—"Rolling Down to Rio," "Christofo Columbo," and "Blow the Man Down" are examples.

The words were as lusty as the men who sang them. More often than not, those used on outbound voyages were dirge-like, while those on the homeward trek had a faster and more hopeful lilt. A favorite homeward-bound chantey was "Barnacle Bill the Sailor." The words cannot be quoted here—suffice it to say that they were lusty in the more carnal sense of the word.

According to Norman C. Blanchard, his Uncle Cal (C. P. Blanchard, Jr.) told him the local Barnacle Bill Cruises started as a New England-style clambake in 1909, the year of the Alaska-Yukon-Pacific Exposition on the University of Washington campus.

The affair was at Kingston, and most of those involved were from the Elliott Bay Yacht Club, though some Seattle Yacht Club members were present (this was just as the two clubs were merging). They built a pit on the beach and roasted a whole beef critter, which actually had been cooked and basted over the coals the evening before. The locals were disappointed at the small number of Canadians in attendance. Both the Royal Victoria and Royal Vancouver yacht clubs had been invited.

Blanchard's earliest personal memory of a Barnacle Bill Cruise is that of 1930. Fritz Hellenthal with his *Gwendolyn II* and two or three of his crew left the old West Seattle moorings on Friday evening to anchor west of Port Madison Spit (Point Monroe on charts) so that they could gather three or four dinghy loads of green seaweed at the morning's low tide. On Saturday morning, they dug a trench about two feet wide and eight or ten feet long and lined the bottom with large rocks. Then they built a big fire in the hole and kept it fueled for several hours.

Prohibition was still very much in force. However, a couple of the men were busy preparing a beer dispenser, which they would load with legal "near beer" (they intended to spike it later). This was strictly an all-male event in those days.

About 5:00 P.M. the last of the embers were raked off the firepit and four inches of green seaweed were spread on the hot rocks. A layer of clams was then placed on the seaweed and covered with more seaweed. Atop this was laid three or four dozen ears of corn in the husks which, in turn, were covered with seaweed and wet gunny sacks. Then the entire mound was covered with sand; this was truly a feast in the making.

By 6:00 P.M. as many as eight or ten boats, mostly sailing craft, had anchored nearby, each with two to seven men aboard. Quent Williams was there with the *KayDee*. Harry Pigeon sailed in on his *Pilgrim*. This proved to be his last visit to Puget Sound, for he was lost somewhere off the coast of Oregon later that same fall. Other skippers present as well: Bill Hedley with *Sindbad*; Bob Moore with *Tony Boy*; Ellis Provine with *Gwendolyn I*, commonly called "Little Gwen;" Ralph Russell on *Killy Bogus*; and Swift Baker, Douglas Stansbury, Charles Frisbie, and Roy Corbett were also present.

As the Great Depression deepened, Barnacle Bill Cruises were skipped for a few years, just as they had not been scheduled during World War I. But by the late 1930s, they again were annual fall events. A few were canceled during World War II, but, to the best of Blanchard's recollection, it has been an annual event ever since.

Bill Hedley became the club's best-known Barnacle Bill. He was born in Nova Scotia in 1877, and as a young person studied violin with the best teachers in Germany, France, and Switzerland. He played professionally in England for a time, then migrated to Seattle in 1903. He became one of the original members of the Seattle Symphony and served as concertmaster for many years. He opened his own music studio in Seattle in 1928 where he taught aspiring violinists until five years before his death.

Ken Metcalf rowing ashore to collect his prizes at the finish of a Barnacle Bill sailing race at Hedley Spit (also known as Madison Spit and Point Monroe). (Photo by Ken Ollar)

He joined the Elliott Bay Yacht Club in 1909, the year it merged with the Seattle Yacht Club. He finished out C. B. Blethen's term as commodore in 1932 and was elected an honorary life member in 1945.

Bill Hedley was as lusty and enthusiastic a sailor as the Northwest has ever produced. He trained many sailors in Seattle and was noted as an exacting teacher. He was an outstanding yachtsman for 35 years and owned the yawls *Milissa* and *Norn* before acquiring the picturesque, black-hulled schooner *Sindbad*, for many years the pride of the local sailing fleet. He sailed her to Alaska and to California, and this vessel was known and respected in just about every port and cove in British Columbia waters and Puget Sound, and he carried the SYC colors on those cruises with respect and pride. His sailing ability was renowned as was his gregarious nature and storytelling ability. In his later years Hedley made his home aboard his boat, which was moored at the club.

When the Seattle Yacht Club began the tradition of a last cruise of the season, it was natural that Hedley be named to fill the role of the folk song hero, a part he relished. For the last 15 years of his life, he served as Barnacle Bill on this annual fall cruise.

Hedley made his last cruise on Jan. 31, 1948. He was 71 when he died at Marine Hospital after a 10-day illness.

Today the Barnacle Bill Last Cruise leads to the SYC outstation facilities inside Port Madison Harbor on Bainbridge Island. The tradition now is for the cruise to begin at Shilshole Bay on Saturday morning after the annual meeting, which is held the previous evening. Two members are nominated for the position of rear commodore. One member is elected, and the other becomes "Barnacle Bill." It is the responsibility of the entire membership to help Barnacle Bill erase from his memory the "agony" of being defeated in the competition for the position of rear commodore. In 1991 Barnacle Bill went co-ed.

The weekend is consumed with sailboat racing, eating and much merriment. A feast is prepared by the club staff, and entertainment is provided; many sea stories are related, and lasting friendships are founded. And Barnacle Bill lives to run for office again. ◇

The SYC crowd was forlornly admitting that the beautiful but aging *Sir Tom* R class was outclassed by newer craft.

At the clubhouse on Portage Bay, the depression kept the dining room closed for a second year. Only a small cafe counter in the galley served meals to members.

1933

According to the *Seattle Daily Times*, the Seattle Yacht Club waved goodbye to prohibition by gleefully burying "Old Man Volstead" on the first Friday in May with a "Night in the Fo'c'sle" party. A "Sun Over the Yardarm" social hour began at 6:30 P.M. with dinner at 7:00 P.M., a program at 8:00 P.M., and games and dancing later. Russell Gibson headed the entertainment committee.

Opening Day 1933 fell on May 6. Festivities began at 2:00 P.M. with the ceremonial hanging in effigy of "Old Man Depression." The parade of boats included visiting craft from the Queen City Yacht Club. Races followed off Madison Park. Among the winners were Cully Stimson and Paul Henry's 52-foot *Angelica*, Bob Lamson's Star *Alcor*, and Ann

Thursday Noon Lunches and Charles Schaak

One day in the fall of 1933 Past Commodore L. E. (Ted) Geary, a naval architect and former Seattleite who had moved to Los Angeles, was visiting in Seattle and went to lunch at the yacht club with another member. Geary was well known, so several members joined him at lunch. When asked about yachting in Southern California, he told of a certain yacht club that lacked a clubhouse and held the membership together by meeting once a week in a downtown hotel for lunch. He said it worked fine and members came, talked, had lunch, and left. He suggested the SYC do the same.

That sounded great, and the four men at the table decided to try it. They called friends and on the next Tuesday scheduled a lunch that any member could attend. About 20 gathered to talk, laugh, and promise to meet the next Tuesday. During the next few weeks, however, attendance decreased until one day only two regulars were present.

It was suggested the yacht club was too far from downtown and that the group should schedule the lunches in a downtown restaurant. This method did not work at all, so they started over again and called members for lunches at the yacht club. One of the members brought a five-gallon can of newly developed detergent oil as a prize. They issued tickets to everyone, including guests.

There was one condition to winning the prize. The winner had to bring a bottle of whiskey the next week. At the time about 15 members were attending each Tuesday, so this provided each person a free drink. This worked, and attendance picked up to the point where two conversations were going on, one at each end of the table. When the members at one end would laugh, the other half would stop talking and ask to be told what was so funny.

With the help of the prizes and the fact that the members who came regularly called up other members, attendance increased to where there was not enough whiskey in one bottle to provide everyone a free drink. So they gave up the bottle of whiskey idea, but asked the members to continue to bring prizes, which they have done ever since.

The lunches became so large that they moved from the sunroom to the main dining room. There was no head table and no emcee. If the commodore attended, he sat at the square end of the table; if the commodore began to feel his oats and tried to run things, they all got up and walked out. Once the commodore got the message, the lunch party returned to the table. Thus it was proved and established that the Tuesday members' luncheon was not a flag officer's function; they were welcome as members and tolerated as officers. Another traditional rule was that no-

Seidelhuber's flattie *Madame Jacquart*. Dr. Wurdemann's *San Toy* beat out 19 other boats to take the power prize.

By May 14 most yachts had been moved to the club's outside station at Shilshole Bay to participate in saltwater events during the remainder of the season.

Over Memorial Day weekend, older yachting folks sailed to Cadboro Bay, while the juniors took off in flatties, Stars and junior division sloops for Madison Spit (Point Monroe on the charts), directly across the sound from Shilshole Bay.

At the PIYA races off Vancouver, the *Lady Pat* again defeated the *Sir Tom* for the Lipton and Isherwood trophies. The *Angelica* won the series for sloops over 25 feet, but Vancouver craft took four of seven first-place prizes.

The so-called Capital-to-Capital Cruiser Race, this year from Olympia to Nanaimo, resulted in overall honors going to Howard Wright's *Kaleta* of the Everett Yacht Club.

The Pacific Coast Outboard Championship Regatta stirred up the waters of Green Lake Sept. 23–24, 1933, with proceeds from ticket sales going to the

body was to be introduced by profession. Bill Hedley once walked out when a guest was introduced as a banker.

In 1939 entertainment was tried with lunch but found to be more trouble than it was worth. A few times a speaker was brought in, but that fell flat. The members would rather talk and listen to each other. No singing, no fines, no speakers, no compulsory attendance, no committee appointments, and no publicity were allowed.

During the Roosevelt administration, the five-day week was enacted by Congress, which meant that the yacht club would be closed on Monday and Tuesday. It was decided by general discussion (no formal meeting) to meet on Thursdays. This continued, and the luncheons went on their merry unprogrammed way until SYC Commodore Allen B. Engle appointed Charles Schaak as chairman of a committee to run the Thursday lunches. They were strictly stag affairs.

A word about Charlie Schaak: He joined SYC in 1922, was never commodore, but his effect on the club was probably greater than that of most commodores. He kept the men's luncheons going for many years. He not only presided almost every Thursday, he did almost all of the talking. Schaak had that rare knack of being able to make anything funny, including picking up the microphone or reading illegible correspondence. Ordinary jokes became classics at his telling. He could be convincing, too. When Schaak said this was the best yacht club in the whole wide world, members believed him. It was no surprise that in 1949, the first winner of the Zecher Award was Charlie Schaak.

Commodore Carlton Powers speaks at the Feb. 21, 1963, meeting. Charles Schaak is on the left. (SYC Historical Collection)

After Schaak's retirement, his shoes at the Men's Lunches were ably filled for many years by Lon Davidson. Arden Steinhart added his indoctrination of new members, an art form in itself. The master of ceremonies job is now passed around, but it still is performed in the style created by Charlie. Charles Schaak died in 1986, but he will be long remembered.

—Based in part on SYC Yearbook, 1970

These young ladies of the club took to sailing flatties during the depression years. From left: unknown, Hortense Harley, Barbara Nettleton, Jane Porter, Ann Seidelhuber, and Alice Wanamaker. (Hortense Harley Collection)

Children's Orthopedic Hospital. Motorboats also raced on Lake Washington, Lake Sammamish, and Harrison Lake. At the latter race on Aug. 19, 1933, the speedy craft driven by Stanly Donogh, district manager of Sears-Roebuck and an outstanding race driver, overturned. Donogh, struck by a following boat, suffered a compound fracture of his left leg and was rushed to Chilliwack Hospital to be attended by a bone specialist who was flown in from Vancouver.

1934

The *Gwendolyn II* won the Opening Day race on Lake Washington and a week later captured the Vashon Island overnighter.

With the depression stifling the economy, the *Seattle Daily Times* carried a brief article titled "Yacht Swapping."

> By strange anomaly the easiest thing to get these depression days is the most extravagant of all luxuries—a private yacht.
>
> In affluent 1928 the White House had its private houseboat *Mayflower*, the secretary of the navy had the tug *Sylph* and the secretary of commerce had the yacht *Kilkenny*.
>
> But President Hoover in a sudden spasm of economy sold the *Mayflower* and made Navy Secretary Charles Francis Adams sell the *Sylph*. Only the Commerce Department yacht was left and it was sent to Florida waters for mundane service under the Bureau of Steamboat Inspection.
>
> —Seattle Daily Times, *May 20, 1934*

The article went on to explain that President Hoover preferred trout fishing, but that President Roosevelt was a yachtsman and had commandeered the *Sequoia* for use as an official White House cruiser.

At the American Lake Powerboat Regatta near Tacoma on May 20–21, Seattle drivers raced off with all first-place trophies.

As quite frequently happened during the depression years, the bulk of the publicity in 1934 went to the flatties and the Stars. Bigger boats had dominated the news until the crash. News reporters were not very interested in races where the boats were all of unique design and handicapped. The one-design boats that became popular during the '30s made match racing competitive and popular.

John Dreher, in an article on May 31, wrote of strong winds, junior sailors, and flatties.

> Such a breeze blew down two flatties flatter than pancakes, shredded the mainsails of two others and sent a Star boat, her cockpit filled with water, lumbering from the scene of two sets of Memorial Day races on Lake Washington. . . .
>
> Temple and Alice Wanamaker, in their *Teal*, were thrown clear of their boat into the lake as the boat overturned a few moments before the flattie race got its starting gun.
>
> A half-hour later the *Buccaneer*, in the same race, while running in third position before the wind, toppled over and skipper

Most of the young Star boat sailors in this 1930s photo have been identified. (Front row left to right) John Halberg, Norm C. Blanchard, Barbara Nettleton, unknown Coast Guard officer, Hortense Harley, and Bob Lamson; (back row left to right) Roy W. Corbett, honorary life commodore, Charlie Ross, Willard Skeel, Bud Henry, unknown, Jay Augustin, Philip Padelford, Garrett Horder, Otis Lamson, Dick Philbrick, and Warren Philbrick. (Hortense Harley Collection)

Hugh Caldwell and crew Bob Myers were thrown out. Caldwell was briefly entangled in the mainsheets and had to swim from under the boat and sail, while Myers retained a seat on the horizontal centerboard. . . . Everybody grinned—because the flattie can't sink. . . .
—Seattle Daily Times

Late in June, Seattle newspapers noted proudly that Portage Bay had become the major home of yacht clubs. The 90 members of the Queen City organization were moving from their Lake Union site to property they had purchased across the bay from SYC. They hoped to have a clubhouse built within three years.

Captain James Griffiths, the "grand old yachtsman" in his *Sueja III*, led the parade of Seattle craft to Vancouver for the 1934 PIYA Regatta, towing the *Sir Tom* which would be skippered by Arthur Ayers in an effort to regain the Lipton and

Flatties (Geary-18s)

The flattie was originally not a one-design class but rather a boat that kids built to sail in. These little floaters were all cross-planked on the bottom and all flat bottomed, thus the name. They were gaff-rigged and had bowsprits. Ted Geary designed the first one-design flattie in 1927. It carried a jib that added sail power forward, as well as a Marconi main, an improvement of the balance over the jibless catboat.

In January 1928 leading spirits among members of the Seattle Yacht Club realized the need for an inexpensive sailing class to create interest on the part of the younger generation in yachting. A city-wide meeting was called at the Clubhouse with a request for plans and suggestions. Over seventy young folks and their parents attended. After much discussion of at least a dozen different plans, the flattie, as designed by Ted Geary, was accepted and orders for five were placed that evening. N. J. Blanchard promised to deliver the first ten at a cost of $150 each. After that the cost would be $200.

The Royal Vancouver Yacht Club also began assembling a fleet of flatties in 1928. Newspaper headlines right after the above meeting said "Here's a Flattie . . . unsinkable sailboat provided for junior yachtsmen this year." The sail plan of the flattie was prominently pictured with comment: "Fourteen youthful enthusiasts, one of them a girl, announced their intention of securing the flattie as designed by L. E. Ted Geary." They were: Mary Helen Corbett, Douglas Stansbury, Dan

Flatties or Geary 18s racing in the 1950s. (Photo by Ken Ollar)

Isherwood trophies for SYC. But the *Lady Van* again claimed both awards. Seattle boats captured most everything else, however. Hortense Harley in the *Goony* won the Star race, and the *Madame Jacquart* of Ann Seidelhuber won the flattie contest. The *Circe* swept across the finish line four miles ahead of her competitors to win the International Team Race. Otto Rohlf's *Dione*, skippered by Cedric Gyles, handily defeated eight rivals to win the Class B cruiser event.

Ray Cooke's *Circe* took the Victoria-to-Swiftsure 150-mile race two weeks later.

In the International Cruiser Seattle-to-Nanaimo race in late July the judges declared the *Billy Bob* of W. J. Allen (QCYC) the winner. It arrived at Nanaimo closest to the 4:00 P.M. deadline and closest to its computed time.

Trefethen, Jr., Chester Dawson, Al Peterson, Jim Wilson, Roy Tierlon, Swift Baker, Bert Davis, James F. Griffiths, Fenton Radford, Fred Harley, Potter Strong Harley, and Norman Blanchard, Jr.

—*C. Fred Harley,* Binnacle, *December 1962*

Seattle newspapers generously provided coverage of flattie activities, as did *Pacific Motor Boat*, predecessor to *Sea Magazine*. The Seattle Yacht Club sponsored and supported the flattie racing fraternity all through the early years. Printed programs of those days show the flattie activities in full detail.

Geary and others quickly introduced the flattie to the South Pacific Coast, Lake Arrowhead, Los Angeles Harbor, Balboa, and Acapulco. Portland and Astoria had flattie owners interested in sailing and racing on an organized basis.

It was in the year 1935, after flatties from all over the Northwest had been sailing at Pacific International Yachting Association regattas, that Sid and Phil Miller of Vancouver, B.C., with others there, challenged Seattle skippers to a series of three boat team races July 26–28 on Lake Washington.

On Oct. 22, 1935, at the Seattle Yacht Club, Fred Harley as chairman pro-tem, Sidney Miller, secretary of the flattie division of the Kitsilano Yacht Club, and Dick Griffiths, Seattle flattie fleet captain, met to form the International Flattie Yacht Racing Association. Fred Harley was chosen commodore.

In the days around 1935 . . . we had an active flattie fleet of about 15 boats, all sailing under the SYC burgee, and racing regularly. We either sailed or paddled to races on Lake Washington, but for salt water events needed a tow. The Coast Guard in those days worked on a more liberal budget, I guess, as they provided tows through the canal and locks and to destinations on the sound. They also gave us tows to the PIYA Regattas, long trips to Victoria and Vancouver.

The guiding light of the flatties in those days was Fred Harley. [C. Frederick Harley was a paraplegic due to an auto accident and was the brother of Potter and Hortense, also great flattie sailors.] He organized the first flattie international organization and was its first commodore. Others in the earliest days of the group were Churchill Griffiths, Dick Griffiths [no relation to Churchill], Les Lewis, Conner Gray, Marybell Provine, Ferral Campbell, Harry Hoffman, Alice Wanamaker, John Dickenson, Jay McClintock, Bill Flick, Wood Lyda, Stuart Monroe and several others.

—*Dr. Bob Coe, memo, summer 1991*

The Harley Cup, presented by Clinton S. Harley and Laura Potter Harley "emblematic of the flattie championship of the junior members of SYC" was the first flattie trophy presented anywhere in the world. The Sunde and d'Evers Company also provided a trophy in 1928. Ted Geary had a trophy in mind and provided $30 for an International Championship Cup to bear his name.

A more spectacular trophy than one $30 would buy was needed so we borrowed a scale model of Bob and Otis Lamson's flattie (their mother said to be very careful of it), and took it to the foundry where we cast an aluminum hull, using the model as a pattern. Barbara Nettleton molded some clay waves from which we cast the sea supporting the hull. Dick Griffiths and his uncle machined the sails, mast, rigging, tiller and trim. N. J. Blanchard Boat Company contributed a mahogany base, and so from all of this came the famous L. E. (Ted) Geary International Flattie Championship Trophy.

—*C. Fred Harley,* Binnacle, *December 1962*

Flatties are still used today as Geary 18s. The newer models are made of fiberglass. ◇

The Inter-City Club Regatta was held at Burton on Vashon Island over the Labor Day weekend. Participating were members of the Olympia, Queen City, Seattle, Bremerton, Bellingham, Everett, Royal Victoria, and Royal Vancouver yacht clubs. The schedule: Saturday evening—bonfires on the beach, dancing at the Burton Hall, and refreshments; Sunday morning—dinghy and one-oar races and men's dinghy pole fight; Sunday afternoon—men's and women's sack races, a baseball game and men's rope-throwing contest; Sunday evening—special dance, stunt competitions with all clubs participating, refreshments, and bonfires on the beach; Monday morning—general visiting aboard boats, and skippers meeting to decide which club will sponsor the 1935 regatta, followed by up-anchor.

The 1934 Hi-Yu Celebration Regatta off Alki Point attracted 26 contestants. In the main race Roy Corbett's *Mahero* nosed out the *Circe* on time allowance. Ted Geary was a member of Corbett's crew. He had been living in California for several years and had continued honing his sailing skills in southern waters, winning the 1934 Six-Meter Pacific Coast Yachting Regatta R class title as skipper of the *Pirate*.

1935

The *Sir Tom* proved that she was not yet boneyard material. At the May 4 Opening Day Regatta on Lake Washington, guided by her owner Art Ayers and aided by a dandy breeze, she showed her stern to Cully Stimson's *Live Yankee*, the most expensive R-boat ever built. The lead in *Live Yankee*'s keel weighed more than the gross weight of *Sir Tom*. Cully Stimson's other yacht, *Angelica*, sailed in first in the big sloop race.

An article in the May 10 *Seattle Daily Times* told of 14-year-old Eustace (Sunny) Vynne, Jr., the youngest member of the Seattle Yacht Club, who was winning races with his 11-foot Moth class *Whistle Bugg*. The Moth was a birthday present from Larry Grubb, president of Philco Radio & Television Company and R. L. Heberling, president of Transitone, to the son of their Northwest representative. They sent one of these new small craft from the East Coast for young Vynne to try out. (The Moth never gained much popularity in the Northwest.)

The 1935 Vashon Island Race, called the "big drift," was won by Ray Cooke's *Circe*. The 50-mile course took 24 hours to complete. Twenty-three sailboats competed.

Barbara Nettleton entered her *Lucky Star* in many races, but it invariably arrived last. She was a great sport about it, though, and she learned a lot about sailing. For her birthday in 1935, her family commissioned Phil Spaulding and Bob Lamson to build her a surprise—a new Star racer. On May 14, the family celebrated Nettleton's birthday at the Seattle Yacht Club. After dinner, the party meandered down to the Star haul-out platform where about 50 Star owners and crew members had assembled to witness the good-natured loser as she discovered her new boat, which she promptly named *Albireo*. Her friends didn't realize how soon Nettleton and the *Albireo* would be leading them to the finish line.

At the SYC weekend outing on Bainbridge, the *Heather*, skippered by Phil Spaulding, won the Star contest, and Roy Corbett's *Mahero* took honors in larger class.

The Protection Island Race in June resulted in *Circe* beating by 18 minutes the fastest record in the 25 times the race had been run.

At the 1935 PIYA Regatta in Bellingham Bay July 2–5, the *Angelica*, owned by P. M. Henry and C. W. Stimson of Seattle, carried off the Pacific Northwest

Commodores of the Seattle Yacht Club—1930s

L. E. (TED) GEARY
1930
Born: 1885, Atchison, Kansas
Education: Massachusetts Institute of Technology
Occupation: Naval Architect
Boats: Many, but the Sir Tom *is best known*

C. B. BLETHEN
1931
Born: 1881, Maine
Education: University of Chicago
Occupation: Publisher, The Seattle Times
Boat: Canim

WILLIAM R. HEDLEY
1932
Occupation: Musician and Teacher (Concertmaster, Seattle Symphony)
Boat: 42-foot auxiliary schooner Sindbad

ROY W. CORBETT
1933
Occupation: Auto Sales
Boat: 55-foot motor-sailer Mahero

C. W. (CULLY) STIMSON
1934-1935
Occupation: Lumberman (Stimson Timber Company)
Boat: 55-foot Angelica *(owned jointly with Paul Henry)*

PAUL M. HENRY
1936-1937
Born: 1880, Minneapolis, Minn.
Occupation: Investor, Contractor
Boat: 55-foot auxiliary sloop Angelica *and 62-foot schooner* Red Jacket

C. B. WARREN
1938
Occupation: Shipping and Commission Merchant, Insurance Agent
Boat: 40-foot auxiliary sloop Loletta

MARVIN S. ALLYN
1939-1940
Occupation: Comptroller, Washington Cooperative Farmers Assoc.
Boat: 38-foot gas yacht Sandpiper II

Perpetual Challenge Trophy for cruising sloops. Roy Corbett's *Mahero* came away with the Sir Thomas Lipton Cup. During the races, a gusty wind wrecked a few masts, including those of the *Sir Tom* and *Lady Pat*. Ted Geary came north from Los Angeles to skipper the *Live Yankee* after aging former–SYC Commodore Cully Stimson insisted he was physically unable to handle the tiller. In the R-boat race, *Live Yankee* beat out the *Lady Van* and *Riowna* for the Isherwood trophy. *Live Yankee*, it appeared, had trouble in light winds and lost the final race to the *Lady Van*, but having taken the first two races, won on points. Star honors went to the *Heather*, skippered by Bob Lamson and crewed by LeRoy Caverly. Dick Griffiths' *Catspaw* finished first in all three flattie contests. Before he returned to California, Ted Geary provided a trophy for flattie races.

An Indian war canoe race at Coupeville on Aug. 10–11, 1935, attracted much attention. Ten canoes paddled by Native Americans began to race amid the cacophony of more than 60 visiting yachts' whistles. The Nooksacks won the trophy for the third year in a row.

The 1935 International Cruiser Predicted Log Race from Tacoma to Nanaimo found the Queen City Yacht Club's C. H. Bolin in *Comrade* to be overall champion.

In the annual Seattle-to-Coupeville outboard motor race, Jerry Bryant traveled the 50 miles in a new course record of 1 hour and 22 minutes.

Over Labor Day 1935 the SYC invited Northwest boats, including those from Canada, to gather on Lake Washington to witness the race for the Sir Thomas Lipton Trophy. A three-day breathless calm, however, resulted in the event being canceled.

1936

A flotilla of 60 sailboats and 17 powerboats opened the season on Lake Washington on May 1, 1936. More rain than wind filled their sails. According to the newspapers, a thunderstorm struck about halfway through the races. When the rain and mist rose enough to allow the judges to see the racers, the *Angelica* was leading the pack to the finish line.

At the Star races on June 21, Dick Philbrick in his *Argo* arrived first, with Barbara Nettleton taking second aboard her new *Albireo*.

On June 26 the juniors danced at a "cabaret style" evening at the clubhouse. At midnight a wandering minstrel led them in their favorite songs. Long after the orchestra played "Home Sweet Home," the young people sat reminiscing on the terrace overlooking the lake. Hostesses for the evening included members of Seattle's best-known families: Mesdames D. E. Frederick, Frederick Hall White, J. Irving Colwell, Otis Floyd Lamson, Thomas D. Stimson, Henry C. Field, Harry Fargo Ostrander and Dr. Walter Moore. Among the young debutantes attending were Miss Fay Frederick, just home from Vassar; Miss Betty Moran who had just graduated from St. Nicholas; and Miss Margaret Manson, just home from Wellesley. Miss Dorothea Marion, Miss Jane Calvert, Miss Diane Dickinson, Miss Dorothy Skeel, Miss Virginia Burwell, and Miss Patricia Sick were also present.

The 1936 PIYA Regatta was hosted by the Victoria club. The winds deserted on all but one of the race days. On that one day, many contestants confused the triangular course with a windward-leeward course. In the end, all races were postponed for a year except the race for the Isherwood Trophy, which was won by Eric W. Hamber's *Lady Van*.

Other outstanding racers of 1936 included Charlie Ross, who won the North American Star Championships off Shilshole; C. W. (Cully) Stimson, with *Angelica*, acquired the Pacific Northwest Perpetual Trophy, and Frank S. Bailey's *Hanko* proved to be the class of the B racers.

The Ninth Annual Power Cruiser Race from the Seattle Yacht Club's outside station to Nanaimo attracted 81 boats. W. V. Tanner of Seattle in his *Miss Elizabeth* was named overall champion with a 0.834 percent error.

The *Circe* entered the Santa Monica-to-Honolulu Race in August and crossed the finish line 13 minutes behind the *Dorade* (later an SYC boat) in the 13-day race. However, by time allowance she was officially fifth. One crew member, Frank

McHugh, complained that "We ran out of water four days from Honolulu and had only beer to drink" (*Seattle Daily Times*, Aug. 11, 1936).

The Labor Day Interclub Cruise of September 5 and 6 called all sailors to Juanita Beach for dinner, dancing, and on the final day, races on Lake Washington. This was followed by evening entertainment at the clubhouse on Hamlin Street.

With the increasing numbers of motorboats came complaints about the noise from residents near the racing areas. When the Seattle Outboard Association announced plans for a permanent race course, judges' stand and other equipment on Lake Washington near Seward Park, the Mt. Baker Community Club protested to the City Council. "The undesirability of conducting such races accompanied, as they necessarily are, by the tremendous roar of the contesting machines and on Sundays and holidays when home owners are seeking relaxation and rest in their homes, should be and is recognized by all sober-minded people." (*Seattle Daily Times*, Aug. 2, 1936) The president of the outboarders, S. V. B. Miller, responded that only two or three powerboat regattas were scheduled in Seattle each year. Others were scattered throughout the area. "Two Sunday afternoon racing programs in a whole summer certainly won't hurt property values, and on the other hand they will bring thousands of visitors to the Mt. Baker District." (*Seattle Daily Times*, Aug. 2, 1936) The city council took the dispute under advisement.

The Swinomish Yacht Club

Fifty-four years ago, several men decided it was time to gather the recreational boaters in their area together in a formal organization. One evening they met in La Conner, Washington, and formed the Swinomish Yacht Club.

The club was officially chartered with Washington State in March 1937. Its original clubhouse was a small building under the Rainbow Bridge. Two of the original officers are still living—Milo Moore (the first commodore of the club and former state fisheries director) and Ed O'Leary who served with the U.S. Army Corps of Engineers and who is still an officer in the club.

The Swinomish Yacht Club has operated continuously since its founding with the exception of the World War II years when, like many social organizations, it temporarily became inactive.

Most members live in the areas of Skagit, Whatcom, and King counties that surround La Conner. However, some hail from as far away as Alberta, British Columbia, Arizona, Idaho, Montana, California, and Hawaii.

The Swinomish Yacht Club is an active participant in "Interclub"; in fact, Swinomish Yacht Club member Jim Patterson was president of Interclub in 1991. The club sponsors Opening Day ceremonies every year with a colorful parade up and down Swinomish Channel and schedules numerous annual cruises around Puget Sound and the San Juan Islands.

—Based on materials provided by Swinomish Yacht Club Commodore Bob Longstreth

1937

The yearbook of 1937 carried a message reflecting the hard times. The house committee called attention to the many nonprofit services available to members and their friends, including a second-floor cocktail lounge with a "mixologist" on hand and an adjacent reading room, both always open even when the club had been rented by an outside organization. Three dining rooms were available if needed with dinner service from 12 noon to 10:00 P.M. Individual undercover garage space could be leased at monthly or yearly rates.

Opening Day, April 30, 1937, was described by many as "too perfect." Only a breath of a breeze rippled the lake. Of the more than 60 entries, only 15 managed to finish the race before the three-hour time limit expired. Winners included Roy Corbett's *Mahero VI* in Class A, Charlie Frisbie's new *Tola* in Class B, John Soderberg's *Lady Alice* in Class C, Art Ayers' venerable *Sir Tom* in R class, Churchill Griffiths' *Antares* in the Knockabout class. Stan Ballard in his *Davy Bill* topped the SYC skippers in powerboats. H. W. McCurdy, who had just returned from a four-month vacation in the South Seas, guided his power yacht *Moby Dick* to a second-place finish.

The Vashon Island Class A award went to Ray Cooke and *Circe*, and Class B went to Charlie Frisbie's sloop *Tola*. Cully Stimson won the Commodore's Race in *Angelica*.

The crew of the Angelica *included (from left) C. W. (Cully) Stimson, Webb Augustin, Swift Baker, Harry Fenton, and Andy Joy. (SYC D. Schmitz Collection)*

The 1937 PIYA Regatta

The 1937 PIYA Regatta officials drew a race course from the Eagle Harbor bell buoy to the West Point buoy to Duwamish Head buoy and return. Cully Stimson's old reliable single-sticker *Angelica* won in A class. The prize for the two-sticker went to SYC Commodore Paul M. Henry's *Red Jacket*. The two-stick *Armida* of Royal Van's Tom Ramsay took the Class B prize. In Class C, John Soderberg's *Lady Alice* prevailed. Vancouver's Dave Gray and W. E. Cunningham won the Snipe and dinghy races respectively. The Arrowhead winner was Everett's Virgil Gordon. Among the winners in the women's races were Dorothy Wylie (on the *Lady Van*), Mary Helen Corbett (*Debutante*), and Hortense Harley Augustin (*Lady Alice*).

The Sir Thomas Lipton trophy for R class was awarded to Lieutenant Governor Alex W. Hamber of Vancouver, B.C., and his *Lady Van*. However, it was a contested decision. The *Live Yankee*, with Jack Graham at the helm, handily won the race and series, but she was disqualified because the skipper hadn't signed in prior to the race. Graham explained in an interview that he was so upset over the results that he resigned from the Seattle Yacht Club. The Graham firm was moving to New York, anyway, he explained, and would remain there for several years. On his return to Seattle in 1946, Graham again joined SYC.

Dick Griffiths, in his green-colored flattie, brought another victory for SYC, and Don McCroskie sailed the *Nina* to a win among the Stars.

Social events during the PIYA included a "Typhoon" Blowout, the first annual "informal" sponsored by the juniors. Richard Crosby served as chairman.

Frisbie's *Tola* won another cup at the Hi-Yu Race off West Seattle late in July 1937.

Because of confusion regarding both starting and finishing times, the annual Vashon Island race of May 15 was resailed in June on a nearly windless day. John Soderberg's *Lady Alice* was named overall champion.

In June SYC Dock 1 was extended 318 feet. On the south side of the new construction, slips were marked for two 65-foot yachts. The north side was finished with no designated slips, "ready to take care of anything short of a battleship," according to SYC reports. Joe Duthie, chairman of the moorage committee, was instrumental in securing government permission for the construction.

Of the 10 participants in the Protec-

The crew of the Sir Tom *in 1937: (from left) Bob Squires, Dave Ballard, Bill Silliman, Chuck Konker, Art Ayers, and Sally Strange Ayers. (A. Ayers Collection)*

George Parson's Red Jacket, *purchased from Paul Henry's estate, captured the Opening Day Regatta Class A title in 1939. Ellis Provine was at the helm. (SYC Historical Collection)*

tion Island Race of June 1937 only half managed to complete the effort. The others cranked up their engines after drifting most of Saturday night and Sunday. John Soderberg's *Lady Alice* captured overall honors and Jack Graham's *Live Yankee*, Charlie Frisbie's *Tola*, Gardner Gamwell's *Venture*, and Paul Henry's *Red Jacket* also finished.

In July, F. A. (Doc) Harvey of Queen City Yacht Club skippered his *Kittiwake* to the overall award in the International Cruiser Race from Port Madison to Vancouver, B.C.

The winds deserted the flatties on August 7, permitting only three of the 19 young skippers to finish and only one, Dick Griffiths in his *Catspaw II*, to cross the finish line within the time limit.

Over Labor Day the *Sir Tom*, skippered by Art Ayers, captured victory in the third race. However the *Lady Pat*, formerly of Vancouver but now owned by Manson Backus of Seattle, took the first two contests and top honors. Captain F. S. Ramey received the Pacific Net & Twine Trophy in the Star races. Gregg MacDonald's *Whippet* outpaced Ben Benton's *Zircon* in the flattie class.

1938

The SYC yearbook spoke of the need for a clubhouse "modernization plan" that would allow services to be improved. The officers reported that the entire facility needed "overhauling." This remodeling was necessary if the Seattle Yacht Club was to assume its responsibilities of leadership in water sports. It was time for members to "strike eight bells and report

The Women's Interclub Council

The foundation of the Women's Interclub Council (WIC) was laid in September 1938 at the Bremerton Yacht Club when the Bremerton auxiliary Skipperettes invited the Everett Barnacles and Tacoma Shipmates to lunch. The women enjoyed themselves and agreed to exchange luncheons.

By 1949 four additional yacht club auxiliaries had been invited to join WIC. The increasing number of women at WIC meetings presented problems because of limited space and funding for lunches at some clubs. To solve these problems, a limit of 14 was placed on the number of clubs allowed to participate in WIC at any given time. In 1950 the Seattle Yacht Club Women's Group joined WIC, and that same year they invited the WIC members to SYC for lunch and a program. The SYC Women's Group has been participating in WIC on an active and continuous basis since that time.

In September 1957 a meeting was called at the suggestion of Reve Hart of Bremerton to formulate plans for Interclub luncheons. Each club sent two delegates, and at the second meeting, a president, vice president, and secretary were elected. A treasurer was added later. In 1968, bylaws were drafted and adopted. The longstanding yachting tradition, to promote friendship among boaters, was stated as WIC's objective.

The Women's Interclub Council meets six times a year between September and June on a rotating host basis.

In 1991 the 14 member clubs of WIC were: Bremerton, Day Island, Edmonds, Everett, Gig Harbor, Meydenbauer Bay, Olympia, Port Orchard, Poulsbo, Queen City, Rainier, Seattle, Tacoma, and Tyee.

Past presidents of WIC are:

1958: Trudy Baskerville, Queen City
1959: Ruth Wilson, Rainier
1960: Lucile Birdseye, Meydenbauer Bay
1961: Thelma Peterson, Port Orchard
1962: Olga Langdon, Tyee
1963: Betty Tregoning, Queen City
1964: Dorothy Scully, Seattle
1965: Mable Raab, Poulsbo
1966: Zelma Hill, Bremerton
1967: Peggy Stuckey, Ballard
1968: Helen Bixel, Day Island
1969: Georgia Grimm, Queen City
1970: Betty Ploe, Tyee
1971: Esther Dahl, Tacoma
1972: Lorraine Canterbury, Olympia
1973: Kay Williams, Edmonds
1974: Beverly Helberg, Meydenbauer Bay
1975: Marian Prater, Port Orchard
1976: Ali Street, Seattle
1977: Virginia Edwards, Bremerton
1978: Aloha Taylor, Ballard
1979: Isabel Bzdyl, Everett
1980: Joanne Stone, Day Island
1981: Jean Zeasman, Queen City
1982: Dotty Cartwright, Tyee
1983: Marge Frey, Tacoma
1984: Helen Ahola, Edmonds
1985: Joan Amos, Rainier
1986: Erna Abell, Meydenbauer Bay
1987: Janet Parker, Poulsbo
1988: Loretta Stedman, Port Orchard
1989: Jane Heinrich, Seattle
1990: Nyla Walsh, Bremerton
1991: Beverly Storkman, Gig Harbor

'All's well!'" But funding was a problem, and little was done to repair the worn premises.

This was the year the Queen City Yacht Club finally managed to build its clubhouse across Portage Bay from SYC.

Instead of scheduling only Opening Day races in 1938, the SYC planned a race series for the month of May. On May 7, 1938, Charlie Frisbie's *Tola* and Mark Mayer's *We're Here* finished one-two in the race for Class B sloops. *Tola* was awarded first overall. The next day the *Lady Pat* won the R class contest. On May 21 *Sir Tom*, with Art Ayers at the tiller, won two of the three races for special sloops. The next day Hans Otto Giese's *Oslo* managed a first-place finish.

A new racing class was established in 1938—B class for boats rating 30 or more. Although John Soderberg's *Lady Alice* raced as C class, her owner asked for an arbitrary rating of "30" so that he could compete in the Tri-Island series. The *We're Here* and *Tola* were also placed in this new class. A Canadian boat built along the same lines was believed to be a possible fourth "30 rater."

Ray Cooke's *Circe* topped A class in the Vashon Island Race, and she would have taken overall honors if she had not simultaneously lost a man overboard and had her spinnaker let go. She lost 15 minutes picking up both the crew member and the sail.

The Tri-Island champion turned out to be *We're Here*, sailed by Mark Mayer. These three overnight competitions—the Vashon Island, Protection Island and Hat Island races—found Mayer winning the first and third. Gardner Gamwell's *Venture* took the Protection Island Race.

The PIYA Regatta at Vancouver resulted in much silver for Seattle sailors, including the Swiftsure Trophy taken by Ruth Brown's *Westward Ho* with former owner Barney Johnson at the tiller, the Class AA crown captured by *Angelica*, the Star championship won by Barbara Nettleton in the *Albireo*, and the flattie title won again by Dick Griffiths in *Catspaw II*. The R class title, however, remained in Vancouver with the *Lady Van*. In the Ladies' Day R class race, Sally Strange Ayers won in the *Sir Tom*.

The Bremerton-to-Nanaimo International Cruiser Race Overall Cup was won by QCYC's F. A. (Doc) Harvey in *Kittiwake* for the second year in a row.

Late summer brought out scores of outboarders. The sectional championships were settled on Green Lake on Aug. 21, 1938, with Latham Goble and Jimmy Harland upsetting J. C. Stuart of Nampa, Idaho, who held the world's record for the F Runabout Class. Wes Loback of Seattle took overall honors for the day, winning the A class hydroplane crown. After the race, many of the boats were loaded on trailers to be hauled to Lake Harrison, B.C., for races the following weekend.

The Frisbie Trophy raced to Seattle after the Commodore's Cruise found Mark Mayer's *We're Here* again top boat. The time had to be unofficial because the race timers had not conceived of a boat traveling at that speed and were absent when she arrived. Shoreline observers, however, verified her arrival time.

H. W. McCurdy in *Moby Dick* won two of the three major powerboat events of the year—the Pacific Motor Boat and Rudder Cup races.

The depression was still taking its toll on yacht clubs, and many membership committees devised enticing lists of "Privileges and Advantages of Membership," such as this one issued by the Seattle Yacht Club in 1938.

1. Affiliation with leading yacht clubs on Puget Sound. Each membership has a book value of approximately $100.

2. Attractive clubhouse, lounge with cocktail service, and cafe, all available at rea-

Dwight Long's Journey Around the World

When Dwight Long's book, *Sailing All Seas in the Idle Hour*, was published in 1938, it immediately became a classic. In 1950 it was reprinted by the Mariners' Library and has been reprinted at least five times since.

Dwight Long, barely out of his teens, carried the SYC burgee around the world on his 32-foot *Idle Hour*. From Seattle he headed down the coast to California, then across the Pacific to Tahiti, Samoa, Tonga and on around the world.

> *Idle Hour* was built in 1921 in Tacoma, Washington. I bought her in the fall of 1932 after a long search for a suitable boat that would fit my pocketbook. Reconditioned and equipped to start the trip September 1934, she cost me 500 pounds. During the voyage to date, just a month over three years, I have spent approximately 600 pounds. This included everything—food, petrol, oil, and repairs to the auxiliary; harbour dues, food, and replacements to running gear, sails, etc. . . .
>
> Many people wonder how such a tiny craft can surmount the tremendous waves out at sea, but this is not half so difficult as getting financially stranded in some foreign port. The financing was the haphazard part of my voyage. I had no independent income, and had to rely entirely upon my writing. Occasionally I have taken paying guests from one port to another. I have given lectures, and had *Idle Hour* open for public inspection, and charged a small fee.
>
> —*Introduction of the British edition,* Sailing All Seas in the *Idle Hour*

When Long returned home on a foggy morning in 1940, he was met by a boat full of photographers and newsreel cameramen. In the last of his many columns in *The Seattle Star*, he described his homecoming after traveling 50,000 miles in his trusty little craft.

> *Idle Hour* was traveling along under power all night on a flat, glassy sea ideal for motoring. Suddenly out of the fog I sighted Ozette Island just north of La Push. We were almost to Cape Flattery . . . I had been afraid of a blow because the barometer had been dropping. That might have meant a week or ten days getting to Neah Bay and we were making it in 24 hours.
>
> We anchored at Neah Bay and I phoned home the first time I had ever phoned my folks. My mother could hardly believe her ears. . . .

During the depression years Dwight Long sailed around the world on his trustworthy Idle Hour. *(PSMHS)*

> Soon we were in Port Madison. It was like coming right back where I started, for it was here that I first sailed and decided to buy a sailboat.
>
> Coming home six years and ten days after I left, after circling the globe, I found the world changed. When I left we were just getting over a depression. Now, not a material depression is present in the general public so much as a mental depression. Because of [war] headlines, people dare not talk in positive terms about the future. . . .
>
> —*Seattle Star, undated clipping,* Sailing All Seas in the *Idle Hour*

And so Dwight Long returned to Seattle a much more mature young man than the one who had left six years earlier.

Since Dwight Long's journey more than 50 years ago, several other Northwest yacht club members have sailed their craft around the world. Among them are SYC members Richard McCurdy, Jr., Fred Lewis, John B. Kilroy, Lincoln B. Katter and Lawrence Killam (also an RVYC member). Bill Black and Chris Goodhope of CYC have also circumnavigated the globe, we are told. ◇

Young Art Ayers at the helm of Circe. *Skipper Ray Cooke, left, c. 1939. (A. Ayers Collection)*

sonable prices, with pleasing surroundings and nautical atmosphere in which to entertain visiting and local friends, being a real treat, especially to those coming from out of town.

3. Weekly yachting forum meetings through which to visit with friends and shipmates around a cheerful fireplace, and accumulate ideas on yachting.

4. Excellent moorage facilities with 24-hour watchman service, water and light connections at the slips, and attention during emergencies.

5. Laundry and supplies, including ice, beer, and groceries delivered on yachts from the clubhouse as requested.

6. Privilege of flying the club pennant, which permits courtesy mooring and use of facilities at all of the other yacht clubs on Puget Sound, British Columbia, and elsewhere.

7. Free use of unrented garage space and parking lot in which to leave cars, which also receive 24-hour watchman service.

8. Participation in all of the activities of the club including various races and events for both sailing and power yachts, entertainment functions, and other activities.

9. Inducements and opportunities to meet and fraternize with a group of live-wire, congenial yachtsmen, who are interested in this same hobby.

10. Membership in the club is not confined to boat owners, as those who do not have a vessel are always sought to man the ships of those in need of additional members of the crew.

—*SYC Flyer, 1938*

The entrance fee and yearly dues in 1938 were as follows:

- Active (must live in Seattle): Entrance fee $44, dues $25.
- Associate: Entrance fee: $27.50, dues $20.
- Non-Resident (living outside Seattle): Entrance fee $10, dues $20.
- Junior: Entrance fee $5.50, dues $11.

• Affiliate (members of other yacht clubs outside King County): Entrance fee, nothing, dues $5 per year.

1939

The 1939 yearbook mentions a commissary that had opened for members' convenience where boat supplies such as paint, varnish, sandpaper, etc. were available. A line of canned and bottled goods was also carried. Entire stores for a weekend cruise would be put aboard, including meats and poultry, merely by calling the club. The new Marine Room, the pride of the club, was promoted as "one of the finest of its type in the Pacific Northwest."

During the Opening Day Regatta, the spotlight shone on *Red Jacket*, which had been out of action for a year. Owned by George Parsons and skippered by Ellis Provine, the one-time scratch boat of the SYC big-stick fleet captured both Class A and overall honors. The *Circe*, acting scratch boat of the fleet, came in second. The clouds lay heavy and the wind blew gustily throughout the day. Among the flatties, Marya and Nancy Nordhoff sailing the *Sans Nom* suffered a knockdown and a cool soaking. They shivered atop their overturned boat until rescued by Joe Abels in his yacht *Barmina*. Among other winners were Frank Bayley's *Hanko*, which took special sloop honors, and Otis Lamson's *Vinta*, which was first in the Blanchard Knockabout Race.

Over Memorial Day, yachtsmen were busy. Most skippers headed for Eagle Harbor where the Commodore's Race was scheduled and where the big-sticks raced home for the Frisbie Trophy. SYC powerboaters sped around Bainbridge Island, finishing at Eagle Harbor. Star and flattie classes competed in their annual elimination series to determine eligibility for the PIYA.

Special notes from the 1939 season: Bill Hedley's black-hulled *Sindbad* and Captain James Griffiths' 117-foot diesel yacht *Sueja III* were not on the Memorial Day cruise because they were anchored in Victoria helping welcome England's king and queen. England was at war with Germany, and the royal couple were traveling to encourage the war effort.

Mr. and Mrs. Roger S. Stroud, who had just sailed around the world in their 37-foot ketch, were guests at the SYC moorage for a month before they headed for their San Francisco home.

The best predicted log time in the International Cruiser Race from Everett to Nanaimo was submitted by W. V. Tanner in his *Miss Elizabeth*. This SYC cruiser had also taken this cup four years earlier. Late in the season, John C. Stevenson's gas yacht *Dynamite* chugged back into commission. Months earlier, as the boat was being fueled, the gas tanks were mistakenly filled with water and the water tanks with gas. The dock attendant, when he discovered his mistake, said to Stevenson, "I doubt you'll be going any place for a while."

The Fantome Arrives

In July, one of the world's largest privately owned yachts, the four-masted schooner-rigged *Fantome*, owned by brewery mogul A. E. Guinness of London, anchored in Portage Bay. The 257-foot ship, painted like a man-o'-war of a century ago, made her stately way from a Harbor Island repair yard through the government locks to Portage Bay. Her crew of 34 watched breathlessly as her masts barely cleared the Aurora Bridge. The *Fantome* was expected to remain only until the following spring, but World War II changed the owner's plans and she would proudly rest at anchor on Portage Bay waters for more than a dozen years.

The PIYA participants assembled at Bellingham for the traditional Independence Day races. The R class results told

The *Fantome*

The black and white hull with its golden figurehead, its masts tall against the sky, became a familiar landmark in Seattle during the World War II years. The 1,260-ton, four-masted *Fantome* was anchored in Portage Bay near the Seattle Yacht Club for so long she seemed part of the family.

Her keel was laid in Italy during World War I, originally for a destroyer, but work stopped when the war ended. The Duke of Westminster bought the keel and on it built a floating palace, which was delivered in 1927. The Duke later sold *Fantome* to an American who kept her for a year and then turned her over to a ship broker who sold her to A. E. Guinness, of the famous stout brewing family. Guinness sailed her all over the world.

In the late 1930s Guinness had the *Fantome* in Alaska, and while he was there England declared war on Germany. Rather than risk his magnificent yacht to submarines or warships, he anchored her in Portage Bay. (In 1939 Seattle was a neutral port.)

The normal complement aboard the *Fantome* was 35, but while she was in Seattle, only three lived aboard her. From time to time tours were given to help worthy causes. The caretakers, Mr. and Mrs. Long, made friends with SYC members who lived aboard their boats moored at the club. These included the Cal McCunes on their *Anna Lou*, the Jim Ballards on their *Malolo* and Mary De Fries, a University of Washington professor, who lived on the *Thalia*.

In 1951, *Fantome* was sold by the Guinness estate for $50,000 to William and Joe Jones of Seattle, who moored her at various locations in Lake Union and removed her furnishings and stores. In 1953, she sailed for Montreal, supposedly to be scrapped. Instead, Aristotle Onassis rescued her, supposedly as a wedding present for Princess Grace, but *Fantome* instead spent 17 years in Spain under Onassis ownership.

Then she was purchased by Windjammer Cruises. They have restored and modernized her, and *Fantome*, beautiful as ever, today sails out of Antigua. ◇

All during World War II the Guinness yacht Fantome *was anchored in Portage Bay. (PSMHS)*

C. L. Egtvedt, president of the Boeing Aircraft Company (left), and banker Dietrich Schmitz enjoy themselves aboard Egtvedt's 62-foot motor sailer Navita. *(SYC Historical Collection)*

the same old story: The *Lady Van* retained the Lipton Cup. However, Seattleites brought home four of eight major championships: Cully Stimson sailed his *Angelica* to honors among A class yachts; Frank Bayley, in his *Hanko*, topped the special sloop division; Al Teitge, a Tacoma lad racing under the SYC banner, took all three Star division races; and Gregg MacDonald was flattie racing champion. Otis Lamson led in Spencer class and Frank Bayley was tops in the special sloop division.

The 1939 Tri-Island competition brought another cup to John Soderberg's *Lady Alice*, which the previous year had been boosted from Class C to Class B, allowing her to compete in this series.

Over Labor Day weekend, according to the society pages, Gilbert Skinner's 77-foot *Legill* returned from a 10-week sojourn in Alaska waters, C. L. Egtvedt's 62-foot motor sailer *Navita* was cruising in British Columbia waters, and Clifford Mooers' 82-foot diesel yacht *Marie Dolores* (formerly the *Sueja II*) was plying the waves of North Sound. Mooers, whose home was in Houston, Texas, maintained his boat in Seattle.

During the 1930s yachting activities were depressed. Smaller boats became popular because they provided inexpensive recreation and cost less to keep up. Sail configurations were altered as many of the leading sailboat racers changed to jib-headed (Marconi) rigs. Both the *Sir Tom* and the *Gwendolyn II* made such changes.

The Seattle Yacht Club struggled to stay afloat during the depression. By the end of the decade the facilities were badly in need of refurbishing, but funds were difficult to find. The financial picture would change quickly as the United States became involved in World War II. ☆

Six

The 1940s

By 1940 the worst clouds of the depression were lifting, thanks in large measure to increasing orders for armaments, ships, planes, and other war materials. Seattle, with one-third of one percent of the national population, attracted nearly two percent of the defense dollars spent during the war years.

As the decade dawned, though Europe was writhing beneath the Nazi boot and China was struggling to escape the Japanese bayonet, the United States was neutral. Not until after the Japanese Navy attacked Pearl Harbor, Hawaii, on Dec. 7, 1941, did the United States declare war.

1940

As the decade opened, the SYC was attempting to increase its depression-depleted membership and revenues. In promotional flyers and its 1940 yearbook, the club touted its many services, such as a dining room that served everything from a hurried snack to a full-course dinner; a game room for pool, billiards, and ping-pong; a well-stocked canteen, which would deliver ice to yachts; and a watchman on the pier who kept all boats secure. Even the yearbook advertised the advantages of club membership:

> If you own a boat,
> If you DON'T own a boat—
> You should join the Seattle Yacht Club!
>
> As beautiful a yacht club location as there is in America.
>
> A first class restaurant and coffee shop—with LOW prices.
>
> A first class bar. The Marine Room, with its view over the water, is unusual and luxurious.
>
> For your entertainment a constant round of lectures, dances and parties.
>
> The dues are LOWER than those of any other first class club in the west.
>
> —*SYC Yearbook, 1940*

A light rain fell on the 1940 Opening Day festivities, including the 100 yachts that had gathered at 1:00 P.M. for the parade from Portage Bay into Lake

Seattle Yacht Club, April 27, 1948. (SYC Historical Collection)

Washington. Skippers had been requested to decorate their vessels, and most had complied. In Opening Day races Cully Stimson's *Angelica* captured the Class A; K. G. Fiskin's *Romp II* headed Class B; Charles Padelford's *Gay Head* topped the C list for the second year in a row; Charlie Ross starred in his Star; and Gregg MacDonald won the flattie class.

Opening Day officers watched the races from the decks of the *Sueja III* with Capt. and Mrs. James Griffiths. Guests included Seattle Mayor and Mrs. Arthur B. Langlie; Capt. W. H. Munter, commander of the Seattle Division, U.S. Coast Guard, and his wife; U.S.C.G. Lt. Commander and Mrs. N. S. Haugen; Mr. and Mrs. John Curtis Blackford, Jr. (the Griffiths' daughter and son-in-law); Miss Katherine McCollister; Mr. and Mrs. W. H. (Cap'n Billy) Silliman and W. H. Silliman, Jr.; Mr. Fred H. Baxter, Miss Elizabeth Pitt, and Miss Anne Douglas. Others aboard included Mr. and Mrs. Colin Radford, Mr. and Mrs. Willis Brindley, Dr. and Mrs. W. B. Seelye and their sons Richard and Dean; Mrs. Fred Nicholson with Mrs. Philip A. Stack; Mr. and Mrs. Willard Strange, Mr. and Mrs. Wallace Campbell, Mr. and Mrs. Lowell Kuebler, Miss Peggy Andrews, escorted by Mr. Raymond Ogden, and Miss Florence Pinasco with Mr. John Lashley.

KOMO radio sent Dick Keplinger, William Vandermay, Clarence Clark, and Jerry Morris (Morrie Alhadeff) to broadcast descriptions of Opening Day; they, too, were aboard the *Sueja III*.

Late in May, Garfield High School won the Eustace Vynne Trophy for producing the best high-school flattie team.

An article in the June 9 *Seattle Times* reminded readers that many Seattle yacht owners were happy to rent their boats to visitors for charter cruises.

The Penguins arrived on Puget Sound in 1940. A regatta attracted an even dozen of these tiny craft, which raced from Portage Bay to Jerry Bryant's marina. Paul Morris' *Mike Fright* was the winner. The Seattle Yacht Club purchased a fleet of Penguins on which to teach youth how to sail. Later these classes were open to the public.

In August an experimental "power and sail race" resulted in Gardner Gamwell's *Venture* winning a wild nautical contest. This sailboat race allowed the use of auxiliary engines for a maximum

Dee Dee Danz was Miss Penguin in 1940 when the Seattle Yacht Club received a dozen of the tiny craft. (MOHAI and Seattle P-I*)*

Commodores of the Seattle Yacht Club—1940s

H. W. MCCURDY
1941
Born: 1899, Port Townsend, Wash.
Education: Massachusetts Institute of Technology
Occupation: Engineer, Shipbuilder, Owner Puget Sound Bridge and Dredge
Boats: Moby Dick *and* Blue Peter

ROBERT S. MACFARLANE
1942
Born: 1899, Minneapolis, Minn.
Education: Brown University and University of Washington
Occupation: Lawyer
Boat: 31-foot gas yacht Merrymac

E. ROY RAPHAEL
1943
Occupation: Shell Oil Co. Executive
Boat: 42-foot Stevens Bros. powerboat

ALLEN B. ENGLE
1944-1945
Occupation: President, Pacific Waxed Paper
Boat: 40-foot auxiliary sloop Neoga

JAMES F. UNICUME
1946-1947
Occupation: Manager, George A. Hormel and Co.
Boat: 30-foot gas yacht Jayma U

ARTHUR M. RUSSELL
1948
Occupation: Distributor, Johnson and Johnson Medical Supplies
Boat: The Monk design 48-foot Nan

CHARLES R. OLMSTEAD
1949
Born: 1894, Kalamazoo, Mich.
Occupation: Olmstead Opticians
Boat: 42-foot sloop Tola

of four hours, provided they were not started more than four times. The contestants stayed overnight at Hadlock Canal on Marrowstone Island.

Reporter Virginia Boren, in the August 18 *Seattle Times*, noted that "some lassies were more deft than lads in sailor roles." Women, she explained, were no longer armchair sailors but undertook a good portion of the work aboard a yacht. As examples she mentioned Mesdames Roy Corbett, Russell Gibson, Marvin S.

Allyn, James F. Unicume, Aubrey Naef, Ernest J. Ketcham, Ray Cooke, Charles J. Frisbie, Hans Otto Giese, and Martha and Barbara Nettleton, and several others.

In the 1940 PIYA contest in Cowichan, B.C., Cully Stimson's *Angelica* took Class A honors. The special sloop award went to Hans Otto Giese's *Oslo*. C class honors went to John Warren's *Cirrus* and the X class was led by Bob Thayer's *Infanta*. However, the *Lady Van*, owned by Eric Hamber, again claimed the Sir Thomas Lipton and Isherwood trophies. Harold Jones' *Spirit II* (the same *Spirit II* that caused the Alexandra's Cup dispute in 1909—see page 49) won a special cup for fast cruisers and the Key City Trophy for best handicapped time over long distance.

The 1940 International Cruiser Predicted Log Race from Tacoma to Nanaimo for the first time found a woman in front position. Margaret Rust of Tacoma Yacht Club in her twin diesel *Electra* took the prize.

A visitor to Lake Union in 1940 was the *Stranger*, always registered in the United States, which Capt. Fred Lewis called his "hobby boat." Equipped to gather rare seashells from the ocean floor, this 135-foot motor yacht cost $250,000. Its home

Day Island Yacht Club

In 1941 Fire Chief Les McGaw lived in University Place and moored his 22-foot cabin cruiser in the nearby lagoon. One of his volunteers, Horton Wilcox, lived on Day Island, down by the bridge. In 1949, Horace W. "Red" Mills of the telephone company, who also lived on Day Island, originated the idea of a yacht club. He and Wilcox started the organization but wouldn't let Chief McGaw join because he did not as yet live on the island. However, they eventually decided a few outsiders would be welcome—especially McGaw since he already moored his cruiser in the lagoon.

The founders asked the Day Island Community Club for permission to meet in their hall. At the third meeting McGaw was asked to draw up bylaws and Leslie Sulgrove oversaw the incorporation process.

At the Community Club they could not hang their burgee (which Mrs. Bringham had just designed) and were restricted in other ways from using the premises as a yacht club. As membership increased, the club began seeking a permanent meeting place.

Chief McGaw suggested money be raised to buy the old Hallen Machine Shop adjoining the 19th Street Bridge. The membership managed to raise $500 and bought the structure, which had been used to build and repair boat engines. The sheet iron building was full of holes that needed to be filled, and an oil heater was brought in to warm the interior. All members helped scrub the oil off the floor and clean the place up. An attic was sealed with plywood, and a stairway was built to make it accessible as a meeting room. Members continued to improve the downstairs, but a few years later the piling was found to have deteriorated; replacing it would be costly.

McGaw had his eye on another piece of property located west of the railroad tracks. It was covered with squatters' shacks, trees and brush. After a time, owner John S. Baker agreed to sell the land. Because the club did not have enough money for the purchase—dues were the club's only income, and they were insufficient—the club peddled $15 bonds to raise the down payment. Thus they acquired the property for a clubhouse and moorage. The squatters, some of whom had been living there since mid-depression days, were removed with some difficulty.

All the shacks on the site were destroyed except for one, which the club used as a construction shed. A road was graded and electricity acquired. McGaw bought a couple of reels of rubber-coated number 12 wire and strung the line, part of it through the water, from his home to the site.

port was the Lewises' Coal Island near Sydney, B.C. According to the late H. W. McCurdy, Lewis, a banker, had qualified for his skipper's papers while sailing around the world on an earlier yacht. As of this writing, Lewis' widow, now Mrs. Eugene (Peg) Rudow, is still a member of SYC.

1941

On December 7 the Empire of Japan attacked Pearl Harbor, drawing the United States into the conflict that had begun in Europe three years earlier. Because Canada was already at war, the PIYA Regatta was not scheduled in 1941.

With so many members on leave and serving in the armed forces, and with yachting activities curtailed, Commodore H. W. McCurdy and the three commodores who followed him had to carefully manage the club to keep it afloat.

On Opening Day 1941 all sorts of craft raced on Lake Washington: Classes A, B, C, and D, Stars, Knockabouts, dinghies, Snipes, Penguins, special sloops, and miscellaneous class. The course began and finished near the Seattle Tennis Club. A reporter suggested that "if you're down that way along about 2 o'clock, you'll see a portion of the lake that looks like a

---

To meet the need for a marine railway, some of the members built one with donated materials, anchored it to a large maple tree, and began moving their boats to and from the water.

In the meantime, the club had vacated the machine shop because of the deteriorated pilings, and they held their meetings at the University Place Masonic Hall. No moorage existed yet except for the log in the lagoon.

Another problem was evident. Skippers found it nearly impossible to maneuver a large boat under the Day Island Bridge. Even small boat helmsmen had to be very familiar with the channel. McGaw reported he had only two inches on each side of his boat going through the piling under the bridge; the tide had to be just right.

Hilding Lindberg, a board member at National Bank of Washington, secured a $25,000 loan for clubhouse construction and dredging of the moorage area. Moorages and a bulkhead replaced the old marine railway, which was torn out. City Light strung a line to the site that allowed the temporary wires from McGaw's home to be disconnected.

Securing a water supply also proved to be a problem. The squatters had been using a contaminated 50-foot well. The board decided a new deep well was needed. Nearby businesses had gone down more than 600 feet to find potable water. The Day Island Yacht Club board worried about the costs of such deep drilling but decided to proceed. At 300 feet, they began sweating over the costs, but at 450 feet, members became very concerned. McGaw figured that since they were already that deep, they might as well proceed. He told other board members that surely there would be water at 600 feet. The worried board members began meeting every night to receive reports. The driller reached 600 feet and still the hole was dry; the board told him to go down five more feet and if he did not hit water, they'd pay him off and take the loss. At 602 feet the driller yelled "There she goes!" His drill had finally struck a good stream.

As time went on, the moorages filled; the club purchased a lot south of the bridge and asked that the waterway between their two holdings be vacated. They also bought a lot on the east side of the old Hallen property, and then still another lot beyond. These additional purchases assured the club some control over the entrances to both the Hallen and government waterways.

When a second moorage was built, 104 boats could be cared for. Never was a payment missed on the several bank loans; the Day Island Yacht Club was built on a solid foundation, indeed.

—Based on an oral report recorded on tape by Les McGaw on July 9, 1971

cotton field in full bloom" (*Seattle Times*, May 3, 1941).

Though skippers frowned on Friday when it rained all day, they smiled on Saturday, which dawned sunny. Hans Otto Giese in his Six-Meter racing sloop *Oslo* took first prize. By the time Cully Stimson's *Angelica* had crossed the finish line for first in its class, the finishing gun had already boomed for Johnny Dickinson and his flattie *X*, which sailed the shorter course. John Warren's *Cirrus* captured Class B honors; Chet Dawson's *Loki* was Class C winner; Charlie Ross captured the Star class prize; Mary Jean Jordon won the junior Knockabout race, and George Spaulding was tops in dinghy sailing.

A society reporter noted that the *Sueja III*'s hostess, Mrs. James Griffiths, was attired that day in a white silk sports frock with a bright red jacket. Aboard as guests were Admiral Charles S. Freeman, commandant of the Puget Sound Navy Yard, and his wife; Capt. Guy B. Davis, U.S. Navy chief of staff of the 13th Naval District, and his wife; Capt. William H. Munter, commanding officer of the Seattle District of the U.S. Coast Guard, with his wife and daughter; and Seattle Mayor and Mrs. Earl Millikin.

Commodore and Mrs. H. W. McCurdy on their *Moby Dick* hosted Capt. Robert Thomas of the U.S. Navy and his wife, Mr. and Mrs. E. R. Hinton, Mr. and Mrs. R. L. Von Lossow with their children Jim and Janet, and young Thomas McCurdy. Most of the guests joined their hosts for dinner at the club after the races.

The contests continued on Sunday for the Mark Mayer Trophy, which was awarded to *Angelica*. The wind blew the Stars and flatties off the water.

The 1941 Vashon Island race was captured by Fritz Hellenthal's *Gwendolyn II*, and the Commodore's Cup on June 1 was awarded to *Angelica*.

The 1941 International Cruiser Predicted Log Race from Winslow to Nanaimo was captured by the Queen City Yacht Club's E. C. Guyer in his *Shangri-La*. This was the last international race until after World War II.

The first winner of the Mark Mayer Perpetual Trophy in 1941 was Cully Stimson's Angelica. *(Wallace Ackerman Photography)*

In August 1941 Seattle hosted the two-day international speedboat races on a course between Seward Park and the new Mercer Island Floating Bridge. Two hundred throttle-pushers were involved. A new world's record for outboards went into the books when Pat Cummins of Everett retained his Pacific Coast professional C-racing Runabout title. Other local winners included Art Losvar of Seattle who took first in the professional Midget class hydro division and Leonard Keller who emerged with the professional title in Class A hydroplane competition. Californians dominated in all other races.

On August 23 another Californian, a 19-year-old airplane parts machinist from Los Angeles named Roger Smythe, bagged the breeze and sailed off with the International Flattie Championship on Shilshole Bay.

The Lobby Clock

In the main lobby of the Seattle Yacht Club stands a stately grandfather clock, but many walk by without noticing until it chimes the quarter hours; then the classic tones draw interest. This chime is one-of-a-kind and can be heard only in the Seattle Yacht Club.

This valuable antique timepiece, according to the brass plate affixed inside the cabinet, was presented to the club by Joseph Blethen, G. E. Pratt, David Whitcomb, C. D. Stimson, H. F. Ostrander, and N. H. Latimer. Two generations of the Benton family, former Commodore Ben and his father Dwight, have personally maintained the working parts of the clock for more than 40 years.

A rumor, which cannot be verified, indicates the clock may have stood in the lobby of Dexter Horton's Bank (now Seafirst). When the bank building was renovated many years ago, the six gentlemen listed above thought the clock would make an excellent addition to the traditions and character of SYC. It is also claimed the clock may have originally been carried to Seattle by sailing ship.

The clock is constructed of solid oak and possesses carving and cabinet work that befits a sentinel of such stalwart character. The Gothic carvings emulate the architecture of the old English cathedrals. The finial of the cabinet depicts a fleur-de-lis shadowing Satan's head. The face of the clock is silver and brass, tooled in an ornate design that adds to the majesty of the faithful servant. The hands sweep out the hours twice a day, and a single hand marks each second within each minute. Over the face the phase of the moon is shown for each day. The works can be set to chime to the Westminster melody each quarter hour and the hourly tolling of the hours can be silenced, if desired.

The stately grandfather clock in the SYC lobby was manufactured in 1910. (Wallace Ackerman Photography)

This fine timepiece was manufactured by the Waltham Clock Company of Waltham, Massachusetts, in 1910. On the face are three shafts into which a key can be fitted; on each shaft hangs a counterweight, one for the clockworks, one for the chimes, and one for the strike. The chimes are high-quality finely tuned tubular alloy. A 1909 catalog lists the price (Model 52 with solid carved oak cabinet) at $508.50, FOB at the factory.

A popular tale, perhaps apocryphal, tells of a member who, while having a libation or two at the club one evening, called his wife on the phone in the lobby. He informed her that he would be late, that he was still slaving away at the office. In the middle of the explanation, the old clock began to chime. His wife simply replied, "I see!" and hung up. ◇

The SYC annual Labor Day regatta took club sailors to Wing Point, where John Warren's *Cirrus II* carried overall honors.

An amusing yachting story developed on the East Coast in July. According to the *Seattle Times* (Aug. 8, 1941), the U.S. Coast Guard announced that it needed 272 yachts for patrol duty on the coast. Mushky Jackson, "a social director and well-known patriot," at Jacob's Beach, New York, set about convincing his friends that "a time arrives when selfish pleasure must yield to public duty." One by one Jackson approached his friends, but he discovered not one owned a yacht "or even a dory." He had been hobnobbing with them for years, he explained, and "many of them bums have been strutting up and down the beach with their commodore hats on, pulling a roll of scratch out of their pocket and peeling off a big bill just to buy a newspaper. And what do I now find? They are bluffing. There ain't a yacht in the whole mob. I begin to suspect that some of these bankrolls I see on the beach are Michigan bankrolls. [A Michigan bankroll is a fat roll of bills with

The Christmas Ship

The Seafair Christmas Parade of Boats, one of the region's yuletide traditions, began in 1942 when Chet Gibson of the Queen City Yacht Club decorated his *Hilma III* with Christmas lights, placed Santa, his sleigh and reindeer aboard, and wired loudspeakers to play seasonal music. He then cruised Lake Union and Lake Washington to wish those on shore a Merry Christmas.

Later, after the Seattle Parks Department became involved, several yachts were enlisted, including Rod Hearne's *Sobre Las Olas*. Bedecked with holiday lights and decorations, they traveled from park to park along the lakes, where groups of citizens built bonfires and sang carols while awaiting the Christmas ships.

Closely allied to the Christmas parade is the Seafair Special People's Christmas Cruise. Back in 1960, Alice Howard, Nellie Coleman, and Howard Schroedel of SYC began the tradition of treating residents of Fircrest and Buckley—usually about 125 people each night—to a holiday cruise. Eventually the *Virginia V* was used. In 1972 Yarrow Bay Yacht Club members began organizing boat owners and members of various clubs to host these special guests. By 1980 members of Meydenbauer, Queen City, Tyee, Shrine, Everett, Bremerton, Port Orchard, Edmonds, Seattle, Elks, Seafair, Rainier, and Corinthian yacht clubs had joined Yarrow Bay members in the effort. As many as 800 developmentally disabled citizens aboard an estimated 300 vessels feasted on hotdogs, beans, potato salad and soft drinks and received Christmas stockings and other mementos. ◇

One of the early Christmas ships was the Valkyrie, *owned by Norman Berg. (PSMHS)*

One pleasure craft that served in wartime was George Stroble's Victoria *shown here in wartime colors. (MOHAI)*

a 10- or 20-dollar bill on top and nothing but ones underneath.] If the Coast Guard has got to rely on the guys on this beach," concluded Jackson, "they will have a hell of a time getting them 272 yachts." The Coast Guard would have no such trouble in Seattle.

The 20 boats of the newly formed U.S. Power Squadron volunteered in mid-September to patrol Elliott Bay and Ballard waters to keep things orderly during the finals of the *Seattle Times* salmon derby. This squadron, formed two months before Pearl Harbor, was ready to aid the Coast Guard and U.S. Navy in the event of an emergency. This group later was absorbed into Flotilla 24.

1942

The first yearbook issued after the country went to war was dedicated "to the many members of the Seattle Yacht Club who are serving their country in the Armed Forces both ashore and afloat, at home and abroad. . . ."

In spite of the conflict, the club managed to sponsor opening days each year throughout the war. True, the number of craft involved decreased noticeably, but the effort helped keep the club alive during those trying times when membership rolls were diminished. Shortages of fuel and maintenance materials also hindered or halted yachting activities.

Opening Day 1942 fell on May 3.

The Six-Meter *Indian Scout*, skippered in the special sloop class by John Locke, sailed in with the best corrected time.

On May 11 George Parsons' *Red Jacket* won a wet Mark Mayer Trophy Race on the big lake. On the same day, 42 outboards churned up the waters of Lake Sammamish as the Seattle Outboard Association held its first regatta. Two craft overturned and one caught fire during the racing, but no injuries were suffered.

The Hat Island Race was canceled because of the proximity of the course to the navy's restricted area off Point Jefferson. There would be no Tri-Island Series until the war was over.

In the August races on Lake Washington, the Puget Mill Trophy for Star class was won by Charlie Ross' *Cene*. Other winners included Charlie Frisbie's *Tola*, skippered by Jack Bowen in Class A, *Cirrus II* in Class B, and *Oslo*, in Class C.

The war was being felt increasingly by the sailing fraternity. Some boat owners had no time to act as skippers and turned the tiller over to friends or relatives. In September the Queen City Yacht Club staged a servicemen's fishing party for approximately 150 soldiers and sailors stationed in the Seattle area.

U.S. Coast Guard Flotilla 24

In July Lieutenant Commander Donald T. Adams requested owners of diesel-powered boats at least 50 feet in length to turn their vessels over to the

The SYC Women's Red Cross Unit During World War II

News of the suffering caused by World War II in Europe during the late 1930s and early 1940s caused women across America to join together through their social, religious, and service affiliations to aid victims.

The Seattle Yacht Club had no formal women's organization at the time, but women did serve on the social committee, helped decorate the club for the numerous parties and dances, and enjoyed many of the boating activities.

When the King County American Red Cross requested help in aiding war victims, the women quickly responded. In 1941 an SYC Red Cross unit was formed. Officers and chairmen were selected from among the members. Mrs. James F. Unicume was elected the first chairman. Several women served as Red Cross officers over the next five years.

The women met on a weekly basis to produce and supply clothing to war refugees and warm garments and bandages for the men and women of the armed services. Newspaper articles and the club annual listed the following as among those involved: Mrs. Roy N. Berry, Mrs. John W. Kucher, Mrs. Norman C. Blanchard, Mrs. Harold B. Murray, Mrs. B. R. Raphael, Mrs. Richard Byington, Mrs. John A. Burnett, Mrs. M. M. Rinearson, and Mrs. Noel Watson.

After the war, the women continued to meet for lunch and bridge. Some of the friendships that developed have lasted for more than a half-century. ◇

Coast Guard for offshore patrols. Work boats and pleasure craft capable of sailing 40 miles offshore were needed. Owners would be inducted into the Coast Guard Reserve and given the same pay and allowances provided regular service members. They would also receive remuneration for the use of their vessels.

Commander Adams explained that these yachts were needed to combat the submarine menace until subchasers could be constructed. Men with seafaring experience were urged to enlist in the temporary reserve for short periods, such as six

U.S. Coast Guard Flotilla 24

An undated and unsigned printed sheet of paper in the SYC archives, obviously written during World War II, provides some specific history about Flotilla 24, which was made up largely of Seattle Yacht Club members.

United States Coast Guard Auxiliary

The life story of Flotilla 24 is very similar to that of nearly all other flotillas in this district. In 1939 when it started, there were only the necessary number of boats to form a flotilla and very little interest was taken, although the Commander tried to stimulate interest.

At the first annual meeting only six members attended and three of these were the retiring officers! The result was that the other three members were elected for the following year; the choice was limited.

On the night after Pearl Harbor was bombed Commander Haugen called up the flotilla Commander and asked for five boats for patrol duty and in less than two hours six boats reported at the Repair Base. Not a bad showing for mid-winter when most yachts are supposed to be out of commission! These boats with their own skippers in command and a crew of two fully armed Coast Guard men ran all night without lights and a good part of the following day guarding vital areas.

Immediately following this there was a calm period of several months during which the flotilla started to grow, instruction in the various phases of seamanship were given and then in August of 1942 our first real assignment was given us.

That job was patrolling the Degaussing Range. For this our own boats were used and the flotilla, in the meantime, has grown to fifty-six boats. Many other tasks were given; a continuous forty-eight hour patrol of Hood Canal, carrying ammunition from the Naval Ammunition Depot to ships scattered from Seattle to Everett, boarding tugs entering the locks and examining their papers so as to save them having to tie up.

During this time classes were still being conducted and most flotilla members attended one or more very faithfully at the same time that they were devoting long and tedious hours on their various "patrols."

At the height of this activity we were, along with many other flotillas, beached without warning. This had a most demoralizing effect on the men at that time. However, when they were again called to active duty manning Coast Guard boats, they responded splendidly and past "beefs" were soon forgotten.

One phase of our work should be mentioned at this time. On Jefferson Head we were working for the Navy and the most friendly relations have always existed between the Naval officers and enlisted men and our own volunteers. They appear to go out of their way to make our lot as pleasant as possible and this spirit of co-operation is most appreciated by the "gang" who consider the Navy "tops."

It would seem that the various flotilla have proved beyond a doubt that a group of civilians can be given an assignment and carry it out in a manner that would do credit to those who call upon them. What then is to become of these flotillas when the war is over?

—*SYC Archives*

or nine months. Men with experience both on deck and below and cooks were in especially short supply.

By the end of July the Coast Guard Auxiliary had been reconstituted as a broad 13th Naval District program involving hundreds of pleasure craft and their owners. Five thousand volunteers were needed within the district, 2,000 of them from Seattle (Seattle had already supplied 600). Petty officer ratings, subsistence, and uniform allowances would be given to these volunteers when on patrol. Their yachts were to be considered Coast Guard vessels and would fly the Coast Guard ensign, but would revert to private status when not on duty. Most of them were painted Coast Guard gray so they would be hard to see on patrol. Original regulations required the auxiliary to take a Coast Guard officer with them during patrol work, but the new program eliminated this necessity. Each volunteer receiving petty officer rank was designated a recruiting officer with a quota of 20 men. Flotilla 24 was not only the largest in the United States, it logged more duty hours than any other flotilla.

Captain James Griffiths

Captain James Griffiths served as commodore of the Seattle Yacht Club in 1921, 1922, and again in 1928. Many times he rescued the club from difficult situations, financial and otherwise. His generous nature and broad sense of fairness played a major role in shaping the organization during its formative years, and he was a major support to the club during the Great Depression.

Captain Griffiths was born in Newport, Wales, in 1861. He arrived in the Pacific Northwest in 1885, settling first in Tacoma where he organized James Griffiths & Company, ship brokers and commission merchants. Later he founded the Tacoma Steam Navigation Company.

Stanley and Elsa Griffiths aboard the yacht Sueja III *at Princess Louisa Inlet in the 1920s. (A. Ayers Collection)*

He helped speed Seattle's development as a major seaport: When he learned that a Japanese steamship line was considering extending its service to the United States and was looking at a California port as its Pacific Coast terminal, Griffiths immediately wrote to James J. Hill and suggested that the Great Northern Railway arrange a traffic agreement with the Japanese. Hill came to Seattle to meet with Griffiths, and soon Griffiths was on his way to Japan to negotiate. In 1896 the *Miike Maru* arrived in Seattle, the first ship to tie Hill's Great Northern Railway to an Asian freight and passenger line.

Captain Griffiths built the first seagoing tug, the Mogul, in Tacoma. From that humble beginning, his holding increased to more than 70 vessels ranging in size from 200 tons to 8,000 tons. As he once said, "We have ships everywhere."

Captain Griffiths was an enthusiastic yachtsman. He loved the sea, and he preferred recreation near the water. He was an honorary life commodore of the Seattle Yacht Club and was commodore of the Pacific International Yachting Association. Though he never

In September the smaller craft in the auxiliary were provided a radio frequency on which the Coast Guard could warn of the presence of enemy vessels, aircraft, floating mines, and other dangers—none of which materialized. These craft could also be directed by radio to allied aircraft, merchant or commercial ships needing assistance. Eventually 300 men and 60 yachts from SYC were on active duty, patrolling throughout Puget Sound to the Pacific. They ferried ammunition, picked up target torpedoes, and provided many kinds of emergency aid.

1943

In this year of war, Opening Day races involved comparatively few boats. But the continuing of Opening Day celebrations allowed scores of wounded and convalescent sailors, marines, and coast guardsmen from the U.S. Naval Hospital in Seattle to enjoy a day's outing on Lake Washington.

Only two yachts competed in the Class A race, and Cully Stimson's *Angelica* took overall honors. John Soderberg's *Lady Alice* (with Paul Aaron at the tiller) was the best in B class.

owned a sailboat, he was interested in that type of craft as well as powerboats.

Until shortly before his death on June 29, 1943, at the age of 82, Griffiths had taken an active part in the management of three of his companies, James Griffiths & Sons, ship owners and operators; the Winslow Marine Railway and Shipbuilding Company, and the Coastwise Steamship and Barge Company.

Captain Griffiths was survived by his widow Ethel and five grandchildren, all of Seattle—James F. Griffiths, Churchill Griffiths, Miller N. Griffiths, Albert V. Griffiths, and Elizabeth Mollitor. He also left six great-grandchildren, two sisters, a brother who lived in South Wales, and two stepchildren—Mrs. John C. Blackford, Jr., and H. Arthur Ayers of Seattle. Captain Griffiths' two sons had preceded him in death: Albert V. Griffiths had died in 1933, and Stanley A. Griffiths died five months prior to his father's death. The ashes of Captain Griffiths and those of his two sons were carried north of Seattle on one of Griffiths' large freighters and cast into the waters of Puget Sound. The date was not revealed because of wartime restrictions on vessel movement. Originally, the plan had been to take the ashes out on the yacht *Sueja III*, of which Captain Griffiths was very fond, but that large vessel was in government service at the time. ◇

The Griffiths' yacht Sueja III *at Princess Louisa Inlet in the late 1920s. The 117-foot* Sueja III *was designed by L. E. Geary and built of teak in the family shipyard. (A. Ayers Collection)*

Opening Day Parade on June 23, 1943. Notice the Fantome *moored in the background. (MOHAI and* Seattle P-I*)*

Other winners were *Oslo* in special sloop class, Colonel Fred Andrews' *Sea Witch* in Class C, Holden Withington's *Scorpio* in Class D, Charlie Ross' *Cene* in Star class, Elizabeth Osborne's *Fleetwings III* in the flattie class, and Chuck Hickling's *Zipper* in the Penguin race.

Later in the month, *Lady Alice* captured the Commodore's Cup, beating out nine competitors.

Tragedy struck on July 3 when young John D. Bracken, a member of the University of Washington crew team, and Thron Riggs, a friend from the football team, were sailing a Star boat on Lake Washington. Bracken, who could not swim, fell overboard. Riggs, who had no experience sailing, tried to turn the craft to rescue his friend but to no avail. Bracken had been president of the senior honor society Oval Club and was a candidate for student body president.

Outboarders, after being criticized for using gasoline in their regatta races, explained that outboards were rationed like any other motor. They were granted 20 gallons of gasoline every three months. Furthermore, their recent race at American Lake had attracted 5,000 servicemen from nearby Camp Murray and Fort Lewis.

On July 18 the Coast Guard Auxiliary was reviewed off Madrona Park. Involved were Flotilla 11, Bellingham; Flotilla 13, Anacortes; Flotilla 15, Everett; Flotillas 21, 23, 24, 26, 27, 28, and 29, Seattle; Flotillas 41, 42, 44, and 47, Tacoma; Flotillas 46 and 49, Olympia, and Flotilla 48, Shelton. The boats passed in review before Capt. W. H. Munter, District Coast Guard commandant. Mrs. Eleanor Roosevelt, the president's wife, whose daughter Anna lived in Seattle, was a spectator. The Queen City Yacht Club's Flotilla 23 was awarded a cup for their fine seamanship. Second prize went to Flotilla 27, commanded by Jerry Bryant.

The *Seattle Times* explained that SYC Ladies Day, Aug. 8, 1943, developed from events in 1938 when the August schedule included three race days, with a fourth day set aside in case there was a need to rerun races. This fourth day had

World War II Message to Members in the Armed Services

We are exceedingly proud of the 139 furloughed members whose names are inscribed on the roll of honor. The two gold stars honoring one junior and one associate member serve as a constant reminder of the sacrifices and hardships that all of you are enduring in our behalf. [Harry d'Evers and Calhoun Watson died in the service of their country.]

You will undoubtedly be glad to know that your fellow yachtsmen on Portage Bay, along with the members of their families, are making their contributions to the war effort on the home front. Many are engaged in the production of planes, ships, tanks, and many other materials essential to the war effort. Flotilla 24 of the United States Coast Guard Auxiliary, sponsored by the Seattle Yacht Club, was actively engaged in patrolling the waters of Puget Sound and carrying out important assignments for the United States Coast Guard and Navy from the date Dutch Harbor was bombed until the recapture of Kiska on Aug. 21, 1943. Plans are now under way by the United States Coast Guard to again utilize the personnel of our organization in port security work and thereby release more men in active service for sea duty. Many of your former shipmates hold responsible positions in the organizations for civilian defense, ration boards, war bond drives, U.S. Navy manpower survey groups, war production board, draft board, and numerous other wartime agencies. The ladies of your Club, too, are unselfishly devoting their time in hours of toil for the Red Cross, the U.S.O., officers club, hospitals, and many other agencies devoted to the service and entertainment of our soldiers and sailors.

In the midst of all this wartime activity, your Seattle Yacht Club has been able to successfully carry on and preserve its treasured traditions. Our schedule for the year calls for a yachting program as complete as wartime conditions will permit. Opening Day has been set for Sunday, May 7, and we have already extended our invitation to several hundred overseas convalescent sailors from the U.S. Navy Hospital in Seattle to be aboard our yachts and participate in the races and festivities of the day.

May God speed the day when we may all join together again and sail out of Portage Bay in that grand celebration of Opening Day commemorating your victory.

—*Commodore Allen B. Engle,*
SYC Yearbook, 1944

since been established as a traditional day for ladies to race.

In the war effort, SYC women spent time at the club making shirts for refugees, knitting army scarves, and working in the Red Cross unit headed by Mrs. James F. Unicume. More than 40 SYC yachts had been either loaned or sold to the government. The government decreed that all boats had to be moored between sunset and sunrise unless being used in the war effort. Norman Blanchard, Jr., explained in the *Seattle Times* that the gasoline shortage "regulates and restricts most of the activity around the yacht club waters to sailing." Rationing for powerboats was by the quarter year. For some members, the rations for three quarters would fill a tank, which was enough to reach Canada where gasoline was not rationed.

1944

The yearbook listed the names of 139 members on active duty with the armed services. Yachting activity continued to diminish as the war effort intensified. Very little daily newspaper space was dedicated to pleasure boating activities. Opening Day, May 7, 1944, was mentioned with the emphasis placed upon the 200 convalescent sailors and cadet nurses who viewed the event from power craft of both the Queen City and Seattle yacht clubs. Unfortunately, the races flopped for lack of wind.

The 1944 yearbook carried the obituary of Honorary Life Commodore Capt. James Griffiths who died at age 82. "His loss to us is as if we were to awake one day and find Mt. Rainier or the sea gulls gone. He was as much a part of Puget Sound as the saltwater which gave it life." The tribute noted that Griffiths was the acknowledged dean of Pacific Coast yachtsmen, and that his help and counsel had endowed the Seattle Yacht Club with enduring life.

One of the most noteworthy acquisitions of the year was the *Dorade*, which Ralph James had purchased in California. The yacht had won every major ocean race, including contests to Bermuda, Norway, and Honolulu and the English Classic, the Fastnet Race.

Another famous boat changed hands in 1944. The 150-foot steam yacht *Aquilo* was purchased by Edward D. White. Among her previous owners were John W. Eddy, H. F. Alexander, and James D. Hoge. White intended to charter her for excursion cruises and fishing expeditions to Alaska.

1945

Commodore Engle's letter to members in the armed forces, which prefaced the yearbook in 1945, reported encouraging news from the battlefronts, then concentrated on the bright future for yachting.

> Your Club has been making adequate plans to continue its leadership among the yacht clubs of the Pacific Coast. The Club indebtedness, which stood at $29,750.00 in October 1943, will be paid off in full by the end of this current year. Committees are actively engaged in devising a plan to build up a cash fund that will enable us to properly finance a program involving the complete renovation of the Club House, the rebuilding and extension of the South Dock, as well as the addition of several new docks when material, supplies and labor are available following the war. The Port Madison property, acquired by the Club through donations from individual members and which was fully described in the current issue of the *Binnacle*, will prove a most valuable asset in our yachting program in the years that lie ahead. . . ."
>
> —*SYC Yearbook, 1945*

The yearbook also carried an item about Charles Willard "Cully" Stimson being named honorary life commodore. Among his many honors:

> In so much as his sailing days commenced a half century ago on Elliott Bay, and continued through the past season when he again captured the club championship Tri-Is-

Armida, *winner of the 1945 Tri-Island Series, owned by Art Ayers. (A. Ayers Collection)*

land Trophy with his *Angelica*, he probably has a wider knowledge of yacht racing and personal acquaintance with its devotees than any other individual in the club.

—*SYC Yearbook, 1945*

Cully and the late Paul M. Henry had donated the magnificent Tri-Island Trophy to the Seattle Yacht Club to encourage cruising-class racing. Cully also brought the eastern champion R-boat *Live Yankee* to Seattle in hopes of reviving interest in this once-dominant racing class.

The major story of the May 5, 1945, Opening Day concerned Charlie Frisbie and the *Chinook*. Frisbie had recently purchased this new eight-meter, the first such

Origin of the SYC Men's Oyster Feed and Auction

Longtime SYC member Con Knutson recalls how the men's oyster feed originated in 1945 during the final days of World War II and immediately after. The Seattle Yacht Club was experiencing a difficult time financially; many members were in the service, and the effect of wartime rationing was apparent in the dining room. Activities had slowed down in general. However, there were chores that needed doing around the club—replacing rotten pier planks, painting, and general cleanup, for example. To get the work done, a call would go out for a Saturday morning work party. Usually 20 or 30 members would show up to make the necessary repairs. At noon the bar would open, and the workers would have lunch.

One member (whose name Con couldn't recall these nearly 50 years later), donated some oysters to the club, and the chef made up a great oyster stew for one Saturday work party. It made such a hit that those involved resolved to duplicate the feat the next year.

Frank Morris, one of those who had been at the original oyster feed, owned a speedy 26-foot boat named the *Snuffy*. He and two others made a run over to the navy property, now Bangor, and picked up eight or ten sacks of oysters and brought them back to the club. Volunteer shuckers assembled at the Star dock where long tables had been set up. A few beers while shucking seemed to help make the job easier and remove the pain of cut fingers. On Saturday the chef not only made stew, he also served raw oysters on the half-shell, oysters Rockefeller, fried oysters, and other tasty combinations. The affair became so popular that the Saturday turnout of volunteers increased considerably, and the officers of the club manned the buffet line to do the serving.

A sailing gear auction also became a big hit at the oyster feed. Attached to the Portage Bay property in those days was a storage area called the "Canoe Shed," which provided storage for masts, spars, sails, and assorted junk. One year word was sent via the *Binnacle* that the shed was to be torn down and that anyone with gear therein should remove it or see it auctioned off at the oyster feed. Not everyone heeded the message.

The auction was a great success. Some members ended up bidding to get back their own gear! The next year, members brought in their surplus items and "white elephants" for the auction, which became an annual feature of the oyster feed.

In those simpler times, members looked forward to such events for they were a principal means of renewing friendships and developing camaraderie.

—Based on an interview with SYC member Con Knutson, 1991

Servers at a 1950s Men's Oyster Feed are (from left) Dr. Phil Smith, Howie Richmond, Dolph Zubick, Con Knutson, Ernie Watson, Frank Hiscock, and Dan Trefethen, Jr. (Photo by Dolph Zubick)

craft in Puget Sound waters. Built in Scotland, the *Chinook* was expected to show its wake to other competitors. So Frisbie sold his *Tola* to Charlie Olmstead, who asked Otis Lamson to man the tiller for Opening Day races. And what happened? The old *Tola* sailed in more than six minutes (corrected time) ahead of the *Chinook* to take Class A honors. Frisbie soon after sold *Chinook* to Howard Richmond.

The Class B bunting was awarded Bill Blethen's 35-foot sloop *Sunda*, and the special sloop award went to Hans Otto Giese's *Oslo*. As usual, Charles Ross in the *Cene* walked away with the Star class prize, and Virginia Forbes' *Breezy* topped the flatties.

Other winners during 1945: Cully Stimson's *Angelica* copped the Commodore's Race; the late Capt. James Griffiths' International Star Boat Class Trophy was brought back to Seattle by Charlie Ross; and in late August Dr. Carl D. Jensen's *Oscar IV* sailed away from the other Class A entries in the SYC Lake Washington races.

1946

For the first post-war Opening Day regatta, formal invitations were sent to other clubs to join the festivities. More than 300 gaily bedecked boats turned out for the grand parade. In special sloop class, Howard Richmond's *Polho II* (formerly Charlie Frisbie's *Chinook*) bested Dr. David W. Dale's new import from the Midwest, the *Intrepid*. John Warren's sloop *Cirrus II* finished first in Class B; Marshall Perrow's *Triki* won Class C, and J. A. Troxell's *Nymph* led Class D. Persistent winner Charles R. Ross was first in the Star race.

In the Predicted Course and Compass Race, a newcomer to SYC, Dr. W. W. Young, steered his *Alda* to a remarkable record, missing his predicted time by only two seconds. The best-dressed boats in the parade were John Locke's *Indian Scout* and Roy N. Berry's *Barbara Lee*.

With fuel again available, The Seattle Outboard Racing Association scheduled contests in Nampa, Idaho; Portland, Newport, Devil's Lake, Newberg, and Coos Bay, Oregon; and Shadow Lake (east of Renton), Moses Lake, Pasco, Anacortes, and Lake Washington in Washington State.

In June the Lake Washington International Championship Regatta drew sailboats, outboards, water skiers, Indian war canoes, and four- and eight-oared shells. In the sailing races sponsored by the Seattle Yacht Club, Cranston Paschall brought his Class X *Manana* home for overall honors, with Howie Richmond's *Polho II* winning special sloop honors and Johnny Warren's *Cirrus II* taking Class B awards. The hydroplane and runabout races were canceled because of choppy waters.

The first post-war Pacific International Yachting Association Regatta hosted by the Royal Vancouver Yacht Club was a huge success. David Dale's *Intrepid* (Corinthian Yacht Club) copped the City of Vancouver Perpetual Challenge Trophy, offered for the first time. SYC members walked off with three championships: Howie Richmond's *Polho II* in Class AA, SYC Robert Watt's *Lady Van*, in Class A, and John Warren's *Cirrus II* in Class B.

On July 14 veteran racer Dr. Wallace J. Bowles of the Seattle Yacht Club, after participating in almost every International Predicted Log Race since 1928, finally earned top honors in the 45-foot Chris-Craft cruiser *Chief Seattle*, which he borrowed from Tom Hamilton for the race. He traveled the 126-mile course from Port Madison to Nanaimo with an error of 3 minutes and 43 seconds.

The season ended with the retelling of a wartime yachting story. The 43-foot *Gometra*, with 750 feet of working sail, had been built in Scotland for a Norwegian who raced her until his country was invaded by the Nazis. The Norwegians, frantic to remove as much gold from their country as possible before it was confiscated by the Germans, sequestered $15 million in gold bullion aboard the *Gometra* and a like amount aboard another yacht and sailed them out at night to meet British destroyers, which escorted them to England. There the *Gometra*, after her hull was made almost unsinkable, was loaded aboard a freighter bound for Halifax. If submarines should sink the freighter, the yacht, it was hoped, would float free and proceed to her destination. But the freighter arrived safely, and the valuable cargo was deposited in a Canadian bank vault.

The Port Madison Outstation

The Seattle Yacht Club's most popular outstation is four nautical miles from Seattle. Located on Bainbridge Island, the Port Madison Fo'c'sle lies in a protected, snug harbor amidst tall fir trees. This idyllic site, so close to the busy metropolitan area, is easily accessible to the weekend yachtsman.

The original owner of the property was John Cosgrove, who homesteaded the 149 acres he had purchased from the government for little more than a dollar an acre on Dec. 10, 1867. Cosgrove, apparently a front man for mill owner G. A. Meigs, transferred the property to Meigs in 1874.

In the severe financial panic of 1893, the London and San Francisco Bank foreclosed on all of Meigs' property and acquired title. In the following half-century, the property went through several owners before the Seattle Yacht Club became involved.

Russell Gibson, who lived nearby, in December 1943 heard of property on Port Madison Bay that included 25 feet of waterfront and was 200 feet deep. On the property were an old building and a dilapidated wharf. The price was $750. Gibson contacted Mid Chism, and together they discussed the potential of the site with other SYC members. In the meantime Chism and his wife made an earnest money deposit to secure the property.

The SYC board minutes of March 6, 1944, mention that a letter would be sent to all members, advising them that the club had been offered property at Port Madison and that 15 members had contributed $50 each—$750 total—to acquire the property. A planning committee was named—Jerry Bryant, Russ Gibson, Roy Berry, J. C. Warburton, H. W. McCurdy, Mid Chism, and J. F. Unicume, the last two to act as co-chairmen. The committee was authorized to use its collective judgment in spending up to $1,500 to improve the building and repair the pier so that access would be available from the water side.

The scarcity of materials during those World War II years delayed the project until January 1945. Two bents were added to the pier and four pilings driven to anchor the float. The pier was redecked and a float-stair was built. Most of the materials used were leftovers from one of the contractor's wartime jobs. The club also decided to level and gravel a parking area. All this work was accomplished for the allotted $1,500. H. W. McCurdy donated creosoted pilings and a fairly new gang plank, which connected pier to float.

The building on the property, a former feed store measuring 100 x 25 feet, was refurbished and for several seasons used as a clubhouse. Many gallons of paint were daubed on the old structure, which had never seen paint until the SYC gang came along. All work was done by volunteers.

Jack Warburton suggested the name Fo'c'sle, and Opening Day at Port Madison was celebrated June 9–10, 1945.

In January 1945 John and Grace Spargur (he was a noted musician and symphony conductor) sold Russ Gibson an 18- x 25-foot parcel (southwest of the present Fo'c'sle) on which to build a garage for his auto. In May 1980 Russ Gibson's widow, Josephine, deeded the parcel to SYC, a much-appreciated gift.

Wally Ovens was chairman of the Port Madison committee in 1952. Over the next 11 years he

After this exploit, the Norwegian government sold the *Gometra* to Commander Ernest E. Bell of the Royal Halifax Yacht Club who, in turn, sold her to Gus Orentengren of the Royal Vancouver Yacht Club. She was entered in the Class A sailing competitions and finished fifth in the 1946 PIYA race. But she was best remembered for carrying the most valuable cargo ever loaded on a yacht.

1947

For the second post-war year in a row, a record number of entries (nearly 400) participated on Opening Day. The

would negotiate with Grace Spargur (who had become a widow) for additional parcels of land. Spargur was a shrewd business woman and a unique individual; she shared her home with 21 cats.

Parcel C was sold to the SYC in 1957 for $3,600. Wally had worked with Spargur for three years negotiating for this property. Spargur, at this time, liked neither SYC nor some of its members. Later, in July 1957, she conveyed parcel D to Wally and Ruth Ovens for $5,000. This parcel included 107 feet of waterfront and was 875 feet deep. Because of Spargur's friendship with Wally and Ruth, she agreed to sell parcels E-1 and E-2 in March 1959 for $7,500, with the proviso that they remain in the Ovenses' name as long as she lived, because she refused to sell them to SYC. After her death, parcels D, E-1 and E-2 were conveyed by the Ovenses to SYC in April 1963.

The first caretaker, Mr. Glastra, was hired in 1957 but stayed only a year. After a series of caretakers, Bill and Doris James took over and remained for 15 years.

A neighbor, Howard Springer, agreed to trade 150 feet of waterfront for parcel E-2 and a 30-foot easement through other parcels. The Seattle Yacht Club now owned 500 feet of waterfront.

Architect John Adams, who lived next door on the east side, designed the original heads. The first producing well was hand dug by Bob Condon, Dick Hooper, and others. Condon furnished a truck with boom and driver.

As more members began to use the new outstation, concrete floats replaced the old log floats, thanks to Fred Peterson. Under the chairmanship of Wally Ovens, showers were constructed, and a recreational area with a barbecue and picnic site was created.

Early in 1967 a new clubhouse designed by John Adams rose on the site. The major portion of the 2,800-square-foot building was devoted to a club lounge with large fireplace and a dance floor. At the after-end of the lounge was a kitchen and bar and a covered area for rainy day sailors.

Records are not complete, but among the many members who donated time and effort to Port Madison are Boris Korry, who rewired the old clubhouse and the new floats for 30-amp outlets; Randy Schmoyer, who for many years spent almost every weekend at Port Madison working on projects; and Ernie Cluck, who designed the outdoor barbecue, mixed the concrete for the foundation, and was in charge of laying the bricks.

Dick Black laid the ceramic tile and the flooring in the heads, extended the roof line and plumbed the hot water for the outdoor barbecue. He was instrumental in digging the new well and building the reserve tank 600 feet back from the original well. In commemoration of Black's service to the yacht club, a mast with a yard-arm was built and erected on the site of the old clubhouse. This project was completed with the help of George Heideman, who painted the mast and transported it to the Fo'c'sle. Ben Benton supplied the proper brass plaque.

Merrill Stewart arranged for the acquisition of two vintage 1904 cannon from the Port of Seattle. He also hand carved the Haida raven, which was placed over the mantel in the lounge.

This was the beginning of SYC's outstation program; many members donated time and effort to the improvement of the Port Madison property.

—Adapted from an article by Michele Shaw

Potlatch

Potlatch originated as a Northwest Coast Indian celebration at which wealthy Native Americans could share their bounty with other tribesmen. In Chinook jargon, "potlatch" means "gift" or "to give."

Prior to World War I, Seattleites developed a civic event called Potlatch. This late-summer celebration included a boat parade that involved SYC members, making it something of a forerunner to the current Seattle Seafair celebration.

A modern Potlatch scene. 1986 Potlach Court: (back row, from left) Princesses Kristy Briggs, Betsy Miller, Pam Lowry, Chief Yellow Belly Dick Chang, Queen Betty Chang, and Princess Leann Wilson; (front row, from left) Court Papooses John Beaty, Christine Lowry, Cara Kinsey, and Tracy Hukle. (SYC Historical Collection)

In 1947 the Seattle Yacht Club originated its own form of Potlatch at the Port Madison Outstation. At first, it was a family outing for members that was more potluck than potlatch. Among the early organizers of the event were Dr. Carlton Powers and wife Helen, Dr. Eugene Kidd and wife Elaine, John Simpson and wife Edna, Stan Youngs and wife Eleanor, and Wayne Graham and wife Nicki. Port Madison facilities at the time consisted of a float on four cedar logs that rose and fell with the tide.

Over the first three years, the event grew in popularity. Children were welcome. Gene Kidd brought toy prizes for the winners of the games and races, which included the popular three-legged and sack races, and blind dinghy races that called for the rowers to all wear paper sacks over their heads.

Beginning in 1951, the club provided food which participants transported to the Fo'c'sle. In the initial years, the men chose a Potlatch Queen. As time went on, four princesses and their papooses were added, and Chief Yellow Belly became the character who reigned over games and celebration.

Over the years, facilities at the outstation were improved, the number of participants increased, and the number of games and contests became too numerous for prizes to be awarded. Instead of prizes colored ribbons were given to first-, second-, and third-place finishers. Other aspects of the day have also changed. For example, the Women's Group now selects the Potlatch Queen, and usually it is her spouse who serves as Chief Yellow Belly.

Today, the opening ceremony features a skit around a campfire. Each of four tepees decorated by the children serve as homes for the Indian princesses and their children. Chief Yellow Belly approaches the fire and introduces the Potlatch Queen, and the Princesses are beckoned: From the east tepee, Princess Silver Birch protects all canoes; from the north, Princess Soft Zephyr brings good sailing winds; from the west, Princess Silver Fish brings good salmon fishing; from the south, Princess Fire Water keeps boating spirits high. The campfire is lit and the chief calls for the games to begin.

The modern Potlatch is the most family-oriented of the events sponsored by the SYC each year, and it is consistently a sell-out. The day's activities end with a salmon barbecue with all the trimmings.

Over the years, many generations have carried fond memories home from the SYC Potlatch.

—Based on materials provided by Jack Austin

most newsworthy result of the day was when H. E. Watson of the Queen City Yacht Club crossed the finish line in his powerboat *Halcyon* exactly on time to the specified second in the predicted log race around Mercer Island.

Overall Opening Day winner among sailing craft was John Locke's *Indian Scout*; best-dressed honors went to Howard Richmond's *Polho II* among sailboats, and to Reuben J. Tarte's *Clareu II* among powerboats. Winners of races: Class A, *Lady Van*, (Bob Watt); Eight-Meter, *Polho II*, (Howard Richmond); special sloops, *Intrepid*, (Dr. D. W. Dale); Evergreens, *Shamrock*, (Bob Lamson); CDX and Spenser, *Triki*, (Marshall Perrow).

The July 27, 1947, *Seattle Times* rotogravure section dedicated two full pages of photos to the major post-war overhaul of the SYC club facilities. Among improvements illustrated were larger windows along the west side, new trophy cases in the lobby and main lounge, doubled Star boat haul-out area, moorage for 50 additional boats, redecorated lobby and powder room, new furnishings in the main lounge, and a brightly colored bar.

SYC Commodore and Mrs. James Unicume presided over 1947 Opening Day events at a yacht club sparkling with decorations. Flags flew, Oriental lanterns swung in the breeze, search lights played over the area, and boat lights shone all night. Three orchestras took turns at the club, one of them roving along the pier to serenade aboard-ship festivities. Dinners, dances, and cocktail parties abounded.

The Memorial Day weekend brought out many SYC yachts for an informal cruise to Hood Canal. Participants mentioned on the *Seattle Times* society page included Harold Murray's *Hornet*, James Lang Hyde's *Loki*, Thomas Wheeler's *Bacardi*, Paul Wood's *Pampero*, Jack Warburton's *Sea Witch*, and Ralph Russell's *Killy Bogus*, which the paper noted was named for a tropical drink of old sailing vessel days.

The biggest news of 1947 was generated when the Seattle Yacht Club hosted the Pacific International Yachting Association Regatta, July 1–4, 1947. The University of Washington Crew Regatta was scheduled a few days earlier on Lake Washington, so Mayor William Devin designated the entire week beginning June 28 as Regatta Week. The feeling that the second World War was truly in the past was enhanced by the nine Oregon motor yachts that powered their way from Portland out over the Columbia Bar, up the coast, and in through the Strait of Juan de Fuca to Seattle for the event.

Silver cups were awarded at the July 4 evening festivities. A series of three races over three days determined the winners in the various classes. The City of Seattle Perpetual Trophy was awarded *Indian Scout* (John Locke). The Swiftsure Trophy went to *Angelica* (C. W. Stimson), the Key City Trophy to *Tola* (Charles Olmstead), the Northwest Perpetual Challenge Trophy to *Owen's Cutter* (Charlie Ross of the Corinthian Yacht Club), the Lipton Trophy to *Cirrus II* (John Warren), and the Corinthian Yacht Club Special Sloop Trophy to *Indian Scout* (John Locke). The Juan de Fuca Trophy was awarded to *Owen's Cutter* (Charlie Ross), and the City of Vancouver Perpetual Challenge Trophy went to the *Angelica* and the *Intrepid* for winning the Interclub Team Race.

For a change, Independence Day was too windy. Sails were torn and lost; rigging gave way; spreaders and masts were broken; a crew member went overboard, and a boat capsized. The most spectacular mishap occurred when the sloop *Sea Witch* and the little International 110 *Wee I* collided during the congregation of some

Interior of SYC Clubhouse

The Portage Bay clubhouse as it appeared when it opened in 1920. The Fireside Lounge, the Marine Room and the Galley. (SYC Historical Collection)

Portage Bay clubhouse lobby after 1947 inprovements. Note the posts covered with Bo'sun Eli's macrame. (SYC Historical Collection)

Above: 1991 SYC newly redecorated Marine Room bar. Right: 1991 SYC newly remodeled entry and lobby. (Both photos by Wallace Ackerman Photography)

150 boats. They hit with such force that the cast iron keel and main boom of the *Wee I* were broken and its mainsail torn. Fortunately no one was injured.

In late July the Bremerton-to-Nanaimo race drew more than 100 cruisers. The race started valiantly, but tragedy intervened when the 40-foot *Dorothy* of Seattle smashed into a barge off Possession Point on the second leg of the 145-mile race. The boat, skippered by W. T. Coy, promptly sank. Those aboard were all rescued. The winners in the various classes were Dr. F. R. Van Gilder of the Olympia Yacht Club, Leslie F. Marshall of the Burrard Yacht Club, J. C. Holstrom of the Queen City Yacht Club, and Dr. A. J. Bowles of the Seattle Yacht Club.

The Meydenbauer Bay Yacht Club

The history of the Meydenbauer Bay Yacht Club begins with a 1946 meeting of residents from the Eastside, including Marc Lagen, Gilbert Skinner, Frank Armstead, Thomas Bannon, Gail Williams, Dwight Hartman, and others.

At the first annual meeting held June 26, Gilbert Skinner was elected commodore. The board's first action was to exercise an option to purchase the property and building for a yacht club. The cost was $40,000.

The site is historic in many ways. It is on the bay named for William Meydenbauer, one of Seattle's first bakers, who homesteaded the area and built a cabin there. In 1890 he sold the property to the Kinnear family. That same year Isaac Bechtel, Sr., a well-known Bellevue pioneer, was killed in a logging accident near the clubhouse site. In the early 1900s cross-lake ferries served Meydenbauer Bay at a dock next to Wildwood Park Pavilion where dances and roller-skating were an attraction. By the 1920s, thanks to the automobile, ferry service was unprofitable and the pavilion was closed. In the early 1930s William Schupp, owner of the whaling station structures at the foot of 99th Street, purchased the Wildwood property, including what was left of the old pavilion. He began building a large frame home on the site. After he died, the building stood empty for several years. Eventually it was transformed into the present clubhouse site.

With the property in hand, the board canvassed the area and found 116 persons interested in forming a yacht club. They selected an architect to prepare plans to turn the home into a clubhouse. However, due to post-war government regulations, improvements were postponed for a time and activities were brought to a standstill.

In 1948 Commodore Skinner rallied the faithful 35 remaining members. They concluded that a yacht club was needed more than ever and named William Madden chairman. A master plan was initiated to attract potential members.

Sunday work parties under Dr. John Shori cleared the grounds around the clubhouse. Sand fill was brought in to raise the dirt floor to the level of the foundation, a concrete floor was poured, and wiring and plumbing were roughed in.

In 1949 construction was completed on a 400-foot bulkhead and 30 slips. Member Niel Jamison donated piling for the project. In August the Internal Revenue Service notified the club that it owed $3,100 in taxes on past dues and initiation fees, plus penalties. After several conferences, the IRS waived the $1,800 penalty and allowed the club to make monthly payments on the tax due plus 20 percent of all current dues and initiation fees. It took the club two years to pay this tax debt.

In September 1949 Burt Marshall was elected commodore. Work parties continued to improve the clubhouse: walling-in the lounge, installing an oil heater, and furnishing the lounge with donated furniture. During 1950 a bar was installed on the lower floor by member Bob Evans, and each board member donated a bar stool. A small access channel was dredged to the moorage area to allow yachts to reach

Labor Day weekend found many families cruising. Mr. and Mrs. Harold Murray and son Douglas on their sloop *Hornet* and Mr. and Mrs. Falcon Joslin, Jr., and their daughter Ann, aboard the *Aeolus*, sailed together. Spending the weekend in Quartermaster Harbor, according to the society editor of the *Seattle Times*, were Mr. and Mrs. John Burnett aboard the sloop *Skylark* and Mr. and Mrs. Robert Condon on the yawl *Valkyrie*. Many other names were also mentioned.

The New Year's Eve party at SYC received considerable publicity. Co-chairmen Mr. and Mrs. John Kucher and Mr. and Mrs. John Burnett arranged for dancing beneath a luminous red metal New

the slips. This was the first year that the Seattle Yacht Club invited MBYC to participate in the Opening Day parade. The club also sponsored a Sea Scout Ship and hosted the Water Ski Champions during Greater Seafair Week.

The year 1951 found membership dwindling and financial problems increasing. In October 1951 the club took on a new burst of activity. Bob Evans, the new commodore, named Doyle Fowler membership committee chairman and numbers soon doubled. The board approved the formation of a ladies' auxiliary. Plans were soon developed for children's Christmas and Easter parties.

In 1952, with 125 hardworking members backing it, the board approved expenditure of $5,000 for further improvements of the clubhouse interior. Also, $6,500 was spent for a roof over the moorage and installation of electricity and meters. This was the year of the first Commodore's Ball.

In 1953 work parties completed the interior work, improved the galley area, and installed heating units in the lower floor area. The pier committee, headed by Rolf Glerum, prepared plans for an additional 30 to 40 slips. And the club hosted its first Opening Day party for guests from other clubs.

During 1954, MBYC scheduled its first full year of social and yachting events. Junior sailors acquired two new Penguin class sailboats, and 40 of them enrolled in summer sailing classes. The first yearbook was issued in 1954.

The U.S. Army Corps of Engineers approved plans for construction of 43 new slips, which were completed for $9,012 and personally financed by member Rolf Glerum. The parking areas in front of the club and the roadways were graded and graveled, and the first of the Sunday fireside events was scheduled.

The years 1956 to 1959 brought steady growth and a full schedule. The women's auxiliary was formally organized with Geri Hill as the first president. The auxiliary later adopted the name "Meydenbauer Mates." More than 76 percent of the 1959 membership owned their own vessels.

In 1960 Meydenbauer's Fleet Chaplain Phil Baker helped dedicate Sucia Island as a Washington State marine park. Between 1960 and 1965 the clubhouse was completely remodeled and the second floor made usable for the first time with installation of a bar, paneled lounge, Commodore's Room and head.

In 1966 the old pier and bulkhead were removed, the bay was dredged, a new bulkhead was installed, and three new finger piers with 73 undercover slips and 37 slips for masted vessels were built.

In the years that followed, the second floor of the home station was completed with a board-conference room and a hallway leading to the manager's apartment.

Carol and Tommy Barber, the longtime managers, retired in 1977 and were replaced by Virginia and Bill Lowder. When the Lowders retired in 1988, Susie and Abbas Athari came aboard as managers. The Ludlow Outstation, purchased in 1967, has been steadily improved with water and electricity made available on the float and a longhouse (cook house) finished in 1978. Two other outstations are maintained at Winslow Wharf and Friday Harbor. In the nearly half-century of its existence, the Meydenbauer Yacht Club has developed into one of the most successful yacht clubs in the Seattle area. ◇

The 1948 Boat Show in the Armory (now the Seattle Center House) proved yachts again were available in many models. (MOHAI and Seattle P-I*)*

Year's sign decorated with balloons and holiday greens.

1948

Winter social events continued at the club with a family night on January 30 that featured games for children, a buffet dinner and the University Puppeteers. On Valentine's Day, the club sponsored a Shipwreck Party with Mr. and Mrs. Marshall Perrow as co-chairmen. Decorations included tropical fish and undersea marine life. Con Knutson, in an admiral's uniform and Pinocchio's nose, won the prize for the most humorous costume. On Feb. 28, 1948, the International Power Boat Association drew a crowd to a dinner dance. And all members were invited to the St. Patrick's Day dance on March 13. These are but a few of the social events of the year at the busy Seattle clubhouse.

One of the biggest opening days involved between 700 and 800 craft. Commodore Arthur Russell stood for an hour and a half saluting the boats as they passed. Top honors went to Robert Watt, who sailed his R-boat *Lady Van* to victory in the featured sailboat race. The predicted log race was won by Chet Gibson's *Hilma III* of the Queen City Club, which nosed out SYC's Phil Luther in his *Mary Jane*.

Cully Stimson had announced the previous fall that he was selling the *Angelica*, his favorite of more than 15 years, to John Locke. Then in May 1948 Cully acquired the Six-Meter *Alarm*, a boat built in Norway in 1937 that had won the International Norwegian Gold Cup. Cully hopefully notified his old crew—Ellis Provine, J. Swift Baker, Paul Harper, Herbert Coe, Carl Zecher, and Dolph Zubick—that he was sailing again.

The PIYA was sailed off Victoria in July 1948. The four-day regatta resulted in some tired sailors. Except for Howie Richmond, who took top spot among the

X class sloops, Seattleites did not fare well.

The "Bermuda Triangular" course, an innovative concept brought from the East Coast by Norm Cole, was introduced to the Puget Sound fleet in the final race of the summer series on Lake Washington. The winner of the race was Sunny Vynne's Star class *Alcor*.

After being banned for a decade from racing on Green Lake, the outboard drivers of the Northwest, California, and Utah obtained permission for a major exhibition of outboards and inboards on the

Bo'sun Eli

The posts and picture frames at our yacht club decorated with sennit work are reminders of Bo'sun Eli Ellison; his deft fingers did the delicate braiding and knotting. Bo'sun Eli was an employee at SYC from the early 1930s to the early 1950s. His home was in the old sail loft across from the club entrance (now the upper parking lot).

Born long before the turn of the century, Eli enjoyed telling how he was in the U.S. Navy when the colors were white with buff trim (the present navy colors were adopted during the Spanish-American War). While in the navy, Eli's artistic sennit work was recognized, and he was asked to decorate admirals' barges.

He retired from the navy after 36 years and came to SYC, first as a rigger for private individuals, then as a club employee. He also built the first crane lift at the club.

A true shellback in the affectionate sense, Eli loved children. He spent many hours answering their questions, showing them how to tie knots, and rewarding them with ice cream. He adhered to a strict code of behavior and did not hesitate to call attention to any breaking of rules by juniors or neighborhood kids.

[N]ot very tall, sparsely built, and wiry. He had the "rolling gait" of the proverbial sailor. Blue eyed with shortly cropped gray hair in limited amount, and craggy, well-tanned features. He wore a pleasant and somewhat whimsical expression, and while his talk and manner breathed salt and sails and just the slightest condescension to us landsmen and shallow water sailors, he was always there to help and advise on our problems.

If time was short (we worked until noon on Saturdays, remember?) a call to Eli would ice up our refrigerators and put food aboard from the SYC storeroom which, as I recall, was fairly complete with groceries.

Eli was satisfied with his somewhat unspecified job around the club—he loved it and the club and was a loyal and helpful friend to all members. When he died, we missed his salty talk and judgment of the quality of whatever spirits of fermenti happened to be available. I like to think that he is with some of our member friends who have also slipped their cable and sailed off into the mists beyond the horizon.

—Contributed by Edward E. Merges, Note in Archives

While he was a kind and gentle man, Eli did have human failings. He had a weakness for "a round of grog," and occasionally someone had to be delegated to go to the local tavern and bring Eli home. He was a "pack rat," and his room was filled with papers, magazines, bits of string, and numerous things too good to throw away.

Some people say that Eli, in spirit, still watches over the Seattle Yacht Club. ◇

lake. It was a show, they explained, not racing. Waterskiing and other entertainment were presented.

Overall winner of the IPBA's International Cruiser Race from Tacoma to Vancouver, B.C., was SYC's Dr. Al Bowles in *Aldon*.

The major story of 1948 concerned the North American Star Class Sailing Championships held in Seattle Aug. 23–28, 1948. Each Star fleet in North America had been invited to enter two boats that qualified as championship contenders. Seattle's entries were Charlie and Bob Ross' *Cene* and Bjarne Jensen's *True Luff*. Of the 11 crack contenders, the Ross brothers took the crown. Second place went to *Yellow Jacket*, the San Francisco Star skippered by former Seattleite Dean Morrison. Jensen's *True Luff*, with Milt Flaten as crew, picked up third prize. These standings placed a bright feather in the cap of the sponsoring Puget Sound Star Fleet and hosting Seattle Yacht Club.

1949

The SYC yearbook indicated a membership of 752 and an equity in the clubhouse worth $154,115.10. Commodore Charles Olmstead praised the club.

> Your Club holds an enviable position among yacht clubs as it has always led in yachting activities. It is also the yacht club in the Pacific Northwest which furnishes com-

The Rainier Yacht Club

On the evening of Jan. 14, 1948, in the workshop of Little's Marina at the south end of Lake Washington, about 20 boat owners attended the first official meeting of the Rainier Yacht Club. Art Chitty served as temporary chairman and Harry Beck as secretary.

The Rainier Yacht Club was created out of a desire to serve boat owners on the south end of Lake Washington, specifically those at Rainier Beach, where four small marinas were located. Renton, Kennydale, and contiguous areas were also represented.

At a meeting on Jan. 28, 1948, bylaws were adopted and the first permanent officers elected. The bylaws were patterned after those of Queen City Yacht Club, thanks mainly to Dale Cogshall, a Queen City member who served as an advisor to the Rainier group. At this meeting Art Chitty was elected commodore. On February 3 bylaws were endorsed that would limit club membership to males only. On February 10 the design for a burgee was adopted and on March 2 the necessary steps were taken to incorporate as required by state law. All applications received and approved on or before April 6 were accorded the status of charter members.

The first club cruise attracted 12 boats to Lake Washington on April 25. That month a ladies' auxiliary was also formed; however, the name "Rainierettes" was not adopted until 1951.

The next few months were dedicated to building a clubhouse. A site was leased at Little's Marina, financing was procured, and the basement floor of a clubhouse was planned.

The groundbreaking occurred on August 25 and during the next year work parties completed the basement facility. In the meantime regular twice-monthly meetings were held at the Bryn Mawr Club House. In September 1948 the incumbent officers were re-elected. In November, Rainier Yacht Club boats participated in the first running of the Seattle Yacht Club's Interclub Challenge Race. This was the start of Rainier Yacht Club's history of racing participation.

The story of any club is really a record of people and the early commodores: Art Chitty, Roy Palm, Cal Eddy, Harold Wilson, and Ed Tuttle all made major contributions to the establishment of the Rainier Yacht Club. Possibly the most active was Ev

plete club services, with first class meal service six days per week. This requires a well trained staff of employees under efficient management. Your regular use of these club services makes it possible to continue them.

—*SYC Yearbook, 1949*

The yearbook carried a chart with the names and locations of all boats moored at the Portage Bay station piers.

Commodore Olmstead saluted the yacht parade on Opening Day, April 30, which included participants from Tacoma, Bremerton, Everett, Bellingham, and Canada, as well as Seattle.

The 1949 PIYA Regatta was held at Bellingham Bay beginning on July 2. Bob Sutton wrote in the *Seattle Times*:

The skippers of the big expensive 50-footers generally get the recognition, yet they're outnumbered more than ten to one by those who must content themselves with one- and two-man craft and small cruising-type sailboats in which family outings and racing must be combined.

It was an unheralded skipper and boat from the latter group who stood out head and shoulders above the others today as the four-day championship regatta drew to a close. He is Bert Hyde of Seattle and his boat is the 26-foot cruising sloop, *Lady Jane*, which triumphed in the "C" cruising class again yesterday to become the only boat of the some 150 competing here to win all three of its races so far.

—Seattle Times, *July 7, 1949*

More than two dozen Seattle skippers brought home first-place silver from

Henry, commodore in 1952. It was Henry who persuaded the fledgling club, along with IPBA, that Rainier Yacht Club could and should sponsor the start of the 1952 International Cruiser Race. Largely through Henry's efforts and contacts with the yacht clubs from Olympia to Bellingham, a record 182 boats entered that race; a number never since equaled.

In September 1952 Past Commodores Chitty, Palm, Eddy, and Henry organized the Blue Gavel Club as an organization for past commodores. This has since grown into the International Order of the Blue Gavel with chapters across the United States and in Australia, Canada, Mexico, New Zealand, the Philippines, and Singapore.

In 1954, RYC sponsored its first Invitational Course and Compass Race on Lake Washington. This race in later years was transferred to Puget Sound and is now jointly sponsored by Rainier and Poulsbo yacht clubs. The year 1954 is also remembered by this young club as the year it swept the major races with RYC skippers winning the Bremerton Heavy Weather Race, Tyee Ladies' Day Race, overall in the IPBA International Race, the RYC Invitation Course and Compass, and at the end of the year the Seattle Yacht Club Invitational Challenge Race.

In 1956 Commodore Randy Rockhill headed a successful fund-raising effort, and in 1957 the plans and drawings for the building were completed by Past Commodores Alex Thompson and Wes Wilkes, along with Eric Kinnard. Permits were obtained and in early 1958 construction began. That fall the first Commodore's Ball in the new clubhouse honored Commodore Stan Stevenson.

The club by now was well established and a very active member of the Northwest boating fraternity. Two major events occurred in 1975: The mortgage on the clubhouse was burned, and the bylaws were changed to allow wives and/or spouses to become full-fledged members of RYC.

The club continues to serve the south end of Lake Washington. In 1986, due largely to the efforts of Past Commodore Bert Ward, lighted and decorated boats paraded for Christmas around the south end of the lake for the first time.

RYC distinguished itself by electing Carlene Striker to serve as its commodore in 1991—the first woman commodore of an Interclub member.

The Rainier Yacht Club, a family club and a cruising fraternity, is looking forward to many more happy years as part of the Northwest marine activities picture. ◇

Bellingham, including the Lipton Challenge Cup for the Six-Meters, two of which ended up tied for the prize. *Risken*, owned by Bob Ross, and *Light Scout*, belonging to Don Amick, shared first place.

Sunny Vynne and Bob Watt made yachting headlines in August when they guided the 17-year-old Star *Alcor* to a qualifying win in the *Seattle Times* Puget Sound Star Fleet Championship Series. They then drove to Chicago with the Star on a trailer and competed in the Lake Michigan series for the national title. They finished 18th among 38 competitors.

On Sept. 9, 1949, a fatal collision between the racing sloop *Bacardi* and a cabin cruiser off Laurelhurst resulted in the sinking of the smaller boat owned by architect Lester P. Fey. Robert Olds, a Boeing engineer aboard Fey's boat, was lost in the collision.

Racing on Green Lake attracted 86 outboard and inboard racers. In addition, the show on July 10, 1949, included waterskiing demonstrations by Don Ibsen's Skiquatic Follies.

The Olympia-to-Nanaimo IPBA International Overall Award went to the Queen City Yacht Club's M. G. Hopkins in *Grif Ann*. The first IPBA Alaska Race in 1949 suffered strong winds and rough seas. The Overall Trophy was awarded George H. Patton of the Nanaimo Club in his 48-foot *Aileen*.

The Carl Zecher Award

Carl Zecher came to Seattle from San Francisco where he was an enthusiastic sailor. He joined the SYC in 1942 and soon became a prominent member of the crew of the yacht *Angelica*, owned by C. W. Stimson.

He was a bachelor, and a good portion of his spare time was spent working on the *Angelica* and around the Seattle Yacht Club, where he was affectionately known as an outstanding sailor and a man's man.

Carl Zecher died suddenly on the *Angelica* during the Hat Island Race in May 1948. It seems that in coming about sometime during the night, an overriding turn of one of the Genoa sheets became fouled on a windlass. Zecher made one desperate attempt to free the overriding turn, and apparently that strain led to his fatal cerebral hemorrhage.

Zecher was a born sailor and loved the sport. He died doing what he enjoyed most. SYC members wanted to find an appropriate memorial for him. A committee consisting of Zecher's friends and shipmates was selected by the commodore to work out the details. C. W. Stimson, Ellis Provine, Anderson S. Joy, Jack Warburton, and Harold B. Murray were appointed.

The committee commissioned an oil painting from the well-known Northwest artist Eustice Ziegler.

The Carl Zecher Award displays this scene by famous Northwest artist Eustice Ziegler. (Wallace Ackerman Photography)

The Aug. 21, 1949, races on Lake Washington were described as "ghosters." Seventy boats competed. Phil Smith's *Gossip*, Bill Buchan's *Heather*, Warren Meyer's *Sea Chase*, Cully Stimson's *Alarm*, Hans Otto Giese's *Oslo*, Sandy Prentice's *Linda*, and Dave Nurse's *Fury III* were proclaimed winners of various races, as were Van Butler's Knockabout *Pepper*, Norm Cole's International 14 *Li'l Luffer*, and Don Graham, Jr.'s International 110 *Dart*.

In December 1949, for the sixth year, Norman Berg's gaily lighted 106-foot *Valkyrie*, sponsored by the Seattle civic Christmas ship committee and carrying an 18-piece orchestra and 20-voice chorus, made the rounds of Lake Washington. Chet Gibson's 40-foot *Hilma III*, sponsored by Flotilla 21, also serenaded during the Christmas season.

So ended one of the most historic, trying, and exciting decades in Seattle Yacht Club history. During the first half of the decade, attention focused on the war effort, but during the last half, yachtsmen made up for lost time.

The decade saw the growth of small sailing boats and around-the-buoy racing. As the 1940s came to a close and the Corinthian Yacht Club was formed to service the new sailboat enthusiasts, SYC membership declined, and the club was again scrambling for new members. ☆

This abstract marine scene is titled *The Yacht Race*. It now hangs over the mantelpiece in the main lounge of the club. On the base of the painting, in addition to a small plate on which is engraved the memorial name, there is added each year a small plate bearing the name of the person to whom the award is made.

The award is SYC's highest honor and goes to the member who has contributed the most to the club during the year.

The memorial was dedicated on April 30, 1949, and the first recipient was Charlie Schaak, whose wit and tenacity made the Thursday lunches so popular.

Dolph Zubick took a photograph of the painting in 1949 and sent it to Zecher's mother in California. Since then, each recipient has received a framed photo of the painting.

Members who have received the award:

1991—A. Gilman Middleton
1990—Arden C. Steinhart
1989—George W. Heideman
1988—Robert Berst
1987—Jack Allen
1986—Dick Chang
1985—David L. Williams
1984—William E. Bradshaw
1983—Charles E. Erickson
1982—Townley W. Bale
1981—John C. Rottler
1980—Ben Benton
1979—Walter B. Little
1978—Phil Duryee
1977—Garrett Horder
1976—Robert W. Condon
1975—Arthur M. Russell
1974—Eustace "Sunny" Vynne, Jr.
1973—H. W. McCurdy
1972—Ray L. Eckmann
1971—Howard E. Richmond
1970—Stanley S. Martin
1969—Frank E. "Jimmy" James
1968—Peter J. McTavish
1967—Harold B. Murray
1966—James D. Sparks
1965—Norman C. Blanchard
1964—Frank Morris
1963—Chester C. Adair
1962—Jerry Bryant
1961—Wallace Ovens
1960—James H. Moffett, Jr.
1959—Tom W. Wheeler, Jr.
1958—Russell G. Gibson
1957—James Scully
1956—Conrad Knutson
1955—Quent Williams
1954—Anderson S. Joy
1953—Jack Warburton
1952—John W. Kucher
1951—Allen B. Engle
1950—Middleton M. Chism
1949—Charles G. Schaak

—Taken in part from material prepared by Anderson S. Joy in 1960

4
M

Seven

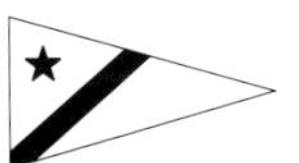

The 1950s

On June 25, 1950, North Korean Communist troops invaded South Korea. Five days later President Truman and the United Nations ordered ground troops to Korea. In the nasty three-year conflict that followed, 54,000 young Americans died. Several SYC members, among them World War II veterans, were called to active duty. SYC's membership roster was reduced again and services were curtailed by wartime restrictions. The truce ending the conflict was signed July 27, 1953.

The decade ended with the country in a peaceful and productive mode. Seattle and its suburbs boomed as the GIs of World War II finished college and started families. The late 1950s were good years for the Seattle Yacht Club, as well.

The method of electing the commodore became more democratic. Instead of being nominated by a committee of the board of trustees, the commodore was elected to two preliminary positions—rear commodore and vice commodore—before being nominated for the top job. Perhaps more important, SYC's members worked to make the club more family oriented. Wives' names were added to the club roster, and family activities multiplied. The wives of members organized a women's social group that created a warmer club atmosphere. Vi Banner, wife of Junior Advisory Chairman Ernie Banner, attended junior social activities and helped the younger members develop their plans.

Early in the decade, because of other club developments and the Korean War, the SYC struggled to increase membership and improve its financial situation.

Tom Tyrer, commodore in 1950, died while in office. Vice Commodore Dr. R. Philip Smith, one of Seattle's best-known obstetricians, was promoted to commodore for most of 1950 and was reelected in 1951 and 1952. He and others successfully went after new members,

Two old-timers were still racing over the waters in 1950—the Royal Van's Spirit II *and SYC's* Angelica, *owned by John L. Locke. (*Seattle Times*)*

History of the Seattle Yacht Club Women's Group

In the 1920s, the Seattle Yacht Club was the site of many parties, dinner dances, and tennis games. The women participated in the party preparations and helped entertain guests, and they enjoyed the lounge, sun porch, and dining room. The club advertised for their patronage in the yearbook, stating that "mothers, wives, and daughters . . . are welcome to the club at all times." Women gathered for bridge, teas, and luncheons. Back then, women did not feel the need to organize as the club membership was small enough to know nearly everyone.

By the 1930s several women were participating in boating activities. Junior women were invited to join in club races. Mary Helen Corbett, Hortense Harley, and Ann Seidelhuber brought home coveted trophies. (The first trophy for women was a powerboat trophy given to the club by William M. Meacham in 1929.) Women's names began to appear in the yearbook as active and associate members. In 1928 the first woman's name, that of Mrs. J. W. Wheeler, appeared as an active member. In 1934 Hortense Harley, Katharine C. Buschmann, and Mrs. H. F. Ostrander were the first women listed in the yearbook as associate members.

In the 1940s SYC women organized to assist with social events such as potlucks and special holiday affairs. The 1940 yearbook listed husbands and wives as co-chairmen of the social affairs committee for the first time. The women also organized the SYC Red Cross unit that year. Toward the end of the 1940s, emphasis was placed on increasing membership and family participation. General changes in society were felt at the club. Many members wanted more time with their families, so they included them in club activities.

By 1950 SYC membership had grown to several hundred. The women found it difficult to meet new members' wives, and coordinating activities and problem solving became cumbersome without the structure of a formal organization. Other Puget Sound yacht clubs had organized women's auxiliaries, and now the SYC women had decided to organize.

In September 1950, Margaret Marlatt, Norma Russell, Cora Condon, and Jo Gibson called together the wives of members for the purpose of forming a group. At the second meeting, with 15 to 20 women gathered, they agreed to formally organize. Among those present were Anne Foster, Elaine Kidd, Alfy Berry, Eunice Blanchard, Eleanor Fiorito, Jean Harthorn, Ann Knutson, Kitty Chism, Meg Byington, and Jeanette Wood. Margaret Marlatt was elected the first president. They decided against becoming an auxiliary and against choosing a nautical name. They would be known as the SYC Women's Group.

According to Margaret Marlatt, at first there was no secretary, no treasurer, and no money. "We were told we could get together if we didn't carry things too far," said Marlatt. The SYC's Women's Group began with no funds and elected two standing committees to plan programs and to contact members. The group's influence was soon felt: Improvements were made to the ladies' lounge; organized luncheons were scheduled; and the south end of the bar, formerly a men-only area, became less restrictive.

"This was the beginning of women's lib at the Seattle Yacht Club," remarked Marlatt in a recent interview. "Women joined the Power Squadron and many of us learned to skipper the family boat."

Exchanges with women from other yacht clubs began that first year, and the Women's Group joined Women's Interclub. They invited other club auxiliaries to SYC. They organized a luncheon and fashion show, then raised money to redecorate the powder room.

Floral decorations at meetings came from the gardens of members. Speakers and entertainment were arranged. The group began to grow and enjoy the programs and to recognize one another when cruising. "We were building friendships," recalls charter member Elaine Kidd, president in 1968–69.

Even though Commodore Phil Smith supported

the SYC Women's Group, some opposition continued. "We were not very popular with the men then," recalled Anne Foster, 1955–57 president. "But each year we grew in numbers, and the men began to appreciate our efforts." A camaraderie developed across the social fiber of the club.

The 1950s and 1960s continued to usher in changes. An increase in membership brought in many new wives. By 1953 the Women's Group had six standing committees, and a secretary and treasurer had been added to the board of officers.

During the 1950s, when the club was sponsoring Gold Cup Races, the Women's Group entertained the wives of raceboat owners, drivers, and dignitaries. Club receptions, garden luncheons at the members' homes on Lake Washington, and boating parties provided the backdrop for an exciting era.

When Anne Foster's term as president was ending in May 1956, she decided to go out in style by scheduling a Women's Day Cruise. Husbands were asked to skipper sixty members in six host boats to Port Madison for a luncheon and elections. Foster was reelected president, and ever since, the May cruise has remained an annual highlight for the Women's Group. Foster was the third president to serve two consecutive terms in office. The early-day presidents provided the needed strength and leadership for the new organization.

Beginning with the 1957 yearbook, the names of wives were included, which greatly facilitated the organization of Women's Group committees and activities.

The women integrated with the club traditions and included the commodores and their wives as special guests of honor at the Christmas luncheon. The group began honoring the admiralty with invitations during the 1950s. In 1959, the admirals invited a member of the Women's Group to join their Opening Day ranks as the admiralette. These practices became part of the traditions of today.

With the membership growing in the 1960s, bridge and bowling became popular activities. The luncheon program included prominent speakers, educators, and personalities. Fashion shows were a popular luncheon program as well. Whimsy was not forgotten. An occasional award was given for the most elegant or outrageous chapeau worn by guest or member. Evening dinner programs were added to accommodate the variety of lifestyles and the professional women.

As juniors became seniors with voting rights, the young women became active in the club and the Women's Group and assumed roles of greater responsibility.

The Women's Group members entered the 1970s with a new burgee, sweepstake trophies for best-dressed boats in the Opening Day parade, an increase in membership, and additional committees. Drama, exercise, and dance classes were added to the list of activities. In addition to Potlatch, Easter and Santa parties for children, the women were involved with other volunteer activities. But many found time for boating instructions in classes taught by Denny Johnson, Sally Laura, Eunice Blanchard, and Barbara Benton. Women were encouraged by one another and their families to be involved and take an active part in boating. Seamanship skills were being honed and women were bringing home prized trophies.

The decade of the 1980s brought Mah Jong classes and a new travel group for women called "The Dinghy Group," which takes trips away from the club. A second burgee was designed, similar to the SYC burgee but with the star replaced by the biological sign for women. The Women's Group has donated mooring buoys to state parks and dinghies to a children's camp, started a new sport for SYC women—rowing, produced a cookbook, and added the names of SYC women to state, national, and international trophies through yachting competitions.

As the Women's Group approaches the centennial of SYC, its membership stands at 250 members, and it takes some 33 committees to handle all the activities. In September of the year 2000 the Women's Group will celebrate its 50th anniversary.

—Based on material provided by Ann F. Bayless

Commodore Phil Smith's 46-foot Pacific Coast Class sloop Gossip *frequently showed up in the winner's column. (Photo by Ken Ollar)*

increasing the number from 625 to about 1,000. For a time the initiation fee was dropped entirely. As a result, membership jumped, and the club's financial picture improved quickly.

During part of the decade, the historic schooner *Gracie S* floated at the end of Pier 2. Photographer and SYC member Ed Kennell had purchased the former San Francisco Bay pilot schooner from actor Sterling Hayden. Hayden later bought her back, took his children from his former wife, and made headlines by sailing away to the South Seas with them on the *Gracie S*. Later, he returned to Hollywood to appear in such movies as *The Godfather*.

The Unlimited Hydroplanes

During the early years of the decade, a little-known Seattle unlimited racing hydroplane, *Slo-mo-shun IV*, captured the American Power Boat Association's "Gold Cup" in Detroit and brought the national race to Lake Washington, where it was sponsored by the Seattle Yacht Club from 1951 to 1956.

The hydroplanes generated increased interest in powerboats. The SYC members and, indeed, the entire Pacific Northwest came down with Gold Cup fever. The club gained a reputation as a national competitor during those years.

In 1955 the Gold Cup was lost to a Detroit hydroplane, the *Gale V*, when the Detroit boat took two seconds and a third in the three heats. The Seattle competitor, *Miss Thriftway* owned by Willard Rhodes, took two firsts and a third, but the *Gale V* was awarded 400 points for the lowest aggregate time for its three heats.

Following the loss, the Seattle Yacht Club was asked by the Greater Seattle organization to sponsor an unlimited hydroplane race for the Seafair Trophy in 1956. That year, back in Detroit, Seattle's *Miss Thriftway*, still owned by Willard Rhodes and driven by Bill Muncey, recaptured the Gold Cup for Seattle. In 1957 Greater Seattle Incorporated co-sponsored the race with SYC, and the American Power Boat Association assumed responsibility for liability insurance. The increasingly commercial aspects of hydroplane racing, plus the massive amount of volunteer time required, began to concern members and the club gradually pulled back from sponsoring the races.

1950

Opening Day, celebrated on April 29, attracted more than 500 craft, about half of them sailboats. SYC Commodore Tom Tyrer reviewed the parade from his cruiser *Lady Grace*, saluting smartly as Charlie Frisbie's *Alatola* sailed by, for Frisbie had pretty "sidegirls" standing at attention on deck while the boys and the crew stood at attention high in the rigging. This was one of Commodore Tyrer's final duties before his untimely death a few months later.

Opening Day featured an unusual SYC-sponsored predicted log race. Instead of an exact finish time, the powerboats, which started between 3:00 P.M. and 3:45 P.M., were permitted to finish any time

Stan Sayres' speedy Slo-mo IV *and* V *show their stuff in the early 1950s. (Photo by Ken Ollar)*

Hydroplane Reminiscences

The early Seattle Gold Cup Races focused a national spotlight on the Seattle Yacht Club and brought it a prominence it may never experience again. Many Seattleites became interested in the competitions after watching race preparations on the then-new medium of television. In the few taverns equipped with television, many customers gathered around a small screen, watching the racing news. Many did not know a hydroplane from an airplane, but most quickly became experts. The television coverage of the first heat of the first race on Lake Washington was so enticing, that an estimated 50,000 more spectators streamed down to the lake to view the second heat.

When SYC's Stan Sayres and *Slo-mo IV* showed up in Detroit in the summer of 1950, nobody paid much attention until he qualified for the Gold Cup Race. The win gave Sayres the right to bring the next race to his yacht club. A meeting at SYC attracted about 100 people, and the club agreed to take on the responsibility. The first chairman was Jerry Bryant, owner of the largest marina in the area and veteran outboard racer. He opened the meeting with: "We don't know the first damn thing about putting on an unlimited hydroplane race, but we are going to do it." Because the race was to be part of the Seafair celebration, Greater Seattle, Inc. provided about $30,000; today it take hundreds of thousands. Greater Seattle also took care of most of the coordination with the city police, fire, park, and street departments. The committees for that first race were concerned with security, registration, communications, officials' barge, judges and timers, course and survey, trophy and awards, publicity, log boom, and course patrols.

The U.S. Army Corps of Engineers surveyed the course, the Coast Guard set the sinkers, and Foss Tug and Barge furnished the buoys and log boom. Much of the material for cribbing and fencing was acquired in exchange for pit passes. Gasoline companies bid on the right to be exclusive provider of fuel and donated fuel for the patrol boats. Most of the food was donated in exchange for the right to display a little advertising.

About three weeks prior to the race, the club began building cribs for cranes and cradles for boats. Cranes were supplied by the Port of Seattle, the U.S. Navy, and private companies. The official barges—one each for VIPs, press, and the officials' crews—were provided by the navy. The army brought a portable bridge from Fort Lewis for use between shore and barges. A tower was built for drivers' reps, course safety officer, timers, judges, and referees. If the Blue Angels were performing, a representative from the FAA was on the barge.

The club focused on the race. The Commodore's Room was occupied for weeks by Sis Cooney and Jo Gibson and other committee wives taking log boom reservations. The clubhouse was decorated with pictures of *Slo-mo IV* and its rooster tail. A large number of members delayed San Juan Island cruises so that they could take friends to see the race. It was a thrill to view the famous Gold Cup Trophy on display in the lobby and to see famous people such as Guy Lombardo, Lou Fageol, Wild Bill Cantrel, and Horace E. Dodge roaming about the club. The Thursday luncheons during August time trial week were always packed by members interested in meeting drivers and owners.

The Gold Cup committee was also responsible for other events. That first year the Gold Cup Race was followed the next day by the Seafair Trophy Race. In subsequent years, when Seattle owners lost the Gold Cup Races, the Seafair Trophy Race was the big one. During Seafair week, the committee scheduled outboard and limited hydroplane races on Green Lake and a night parade of lighted boats in Andrews Bay for which outboard patrol boats were provided. On Monday following the Gold Cup, the committee operated an American Power Boat Association–sanctioned one-mile course on the east side of Mercer Island so that people with large and small hydroplanes could attempt to set new world records in their classes. *Slo-mo IV* and other unlimiteds over the years set new world straight-away records on this course.

An important and enjoyable part of Gold Cup

week was the social side. In addition to the Thursday lunch where drivers and owners would make brief speeches, there was a women's brunch for wives of the hydroplane drivers and crew members, a Thursday night cocktail party for members and guests, a Friday night barbeque on the lawn to which media celebrities were invited, a Saturday night banquet at the Olympic Hotel where trophies were awarded, and finally the party for the committee at Stan Sayres' home on the end of Hunts Point. In addition, there were deluxe parties on beautiful yachts during race week.

Service on the committee was the precursor of greater things for many of the members involved. Some became commodores of SYC—Howie Richmond, Mid Chism, Andy Joy, and Don Amick, for example. Chism, Joy, Knutson, Gibson, Wheeler, Bryant, Morris, Martin, Richmond, Vynne, Duryee, and Williams were later presented the Zecher Award, SYC's highest honor.

The first Unlimited Hydroplane Committee of 1951-52. From left, standing: Stan Donogh, Stan Sayres, Con Knutson, Chuck Jones, Latham Goble, Paul Morris, Charles Stipp, and Jerry Bryant, the chairman. Seated: Linton Ivey, Art Shorey, Frank Morris, Commodore Phil Smith, and Ross Merrill. (Paul Morris Collection)

The *Slo-mos* put Seattle on the map, but the *Hawaii Kai* was also a famous SYC hydroplane. Edgar Kaiser entered her in every race in the 1957 season (see photo on page 200), and with Jack Regis as driver, she won five of the eight. The Kaiser family donated all their memorabilia to the club for preservation. Edgar Kaiser was born and raised in Seattle and graduated from Queen Anne High School. Stan Sayres was the first local resident in the Unlimited Class, but Peter Woeck was one of the first sponsors. He underwrote the *Miss Burien* and the first Bardahl boats. Willard Rhodes owned the Thriftway boats which Bill Muncey drove to fame, and Bill Boeing, Jr., owned the *Wahoo* boats driven by Mira Slovak. Pay 'n Save also sponsored a boat. There was a boat called the *Maverick* out of Lake Mead, brought here by Bill Waggoner who moved his headquarters to Seattle. SYC members Lin Ivey and Chuck Hickling were behind the *Miss Seattle*, formerly the *Slo-mo V*. All these boats flew the SYC burgee. There were other local boats such as Austin Snell's *Miss Rocket*, and *Coral Reef* from the Tacoma Yacht Club, and the *Miss Spokane*. Willard Rhodes changed the names of the Thriftway boats to *Century 21* in order to promote the World's Fair in 1960 and 1961. Shirley Mendelsohn owned the Notre Dame Unlimiteds and belonged to SYC.

About 1956 the Seattle Yacht Club began to bow out of the Gold Cup Races, and Greater Seattle became the major sponsor. Powerboat racing, once a gentleman's sport, had always been very expensive. With television and advertising and commercial sponsorship, the sport changed and became much more of a commercial venture. When the races began to be run for purses rather than trophies, the true yachtsmen began to pull back.

While SYC was involved with the hydroplane races, new vitality was pumped into the club, because many new members joined during this time. And to this day SYC members who were involved in the Gold Cup Races enjoy many fond memories.

—Based on an interview with Jim Stirrat and material provided by Dave Williams

For many years former Commodore H. W. McCurdy on Opening Day hosted Navy and Coast Guard brass on the 96-foot Blue Peter, *designed by Ted Geary and built by Lake Union Drydock Co. for John Graham, Sr. (PSMHS)*

between 4:30 P.M. and 5:00 P.M. The race started off Webster Point, continued clockwise around Mercer Island, and finished under the east arch of the first floating bridge. Ray Stroble of the Queen City Yacht Club garnered top honors.

Opening Day inaugurated two days of racing that produced several double winners. These included Charlie Frisbie's *Alatola* in A class, Hugh Watt's *Lulu* in Six-Meter, Sunny Vynne's *Alcor* in Star class, Steven Chadwick's *Wild Flag* in International 110, and John Abel's *Holgazen* in Lightning class.

In the International Cruiser Race from Everett to Victoria, Dr. George Knowles, in *Seachum*, beat out 132 entrants. Buel Hannum placed first in the fast boat class with his *Candy*, Dr. Al Bowles took first in the large cruiser class with his *Aldon*, and Dick Byington brought his *Kaleta* in ahead of others in family cruiser class.

SYC's new commodore, Phil Smith, won the Swiftsure in his *Gossip*. J. Franklin Eddy's *Dorade* captured the Tri-Island Series.

The club's 1950 Winter Frostbite Series for International 14 dinghies matched activities of any small boat fleet in the country. The establishment of the new park board moorage at Leschi in 1950 paved the way for even greater racing activity for this fleet.

The biggest headlines of the year were captured by Stan Sayres and his new *Slo-mo IV*. In April he tested this Ted Jones–designed and Anchor Jensen–built hydroplane. In September he won the Harmsworth Trophy and was on the way

History of Opening Day

As far back as 1879, a Seattle yacht club was sponsoring regattas, but the first mention we could find of the term "Opening Day" was in 1909 when the Elliott Bay Yacht Club opened the boating season on May 1. That day the club featured a contest for its three fastest yachts. Later that year, the Elliott Bay and Seattle yacht clubs merged, taking the name of the latter.

News releases in 1914 mention an "annual opening day," which that year occurred on May 16. In 1915 Opening Day was shifted back to May 1. Apparently, no Opening Days were celebrated during World War I, but following the 1920 dedication of the new clubhouse on Portage Bay, Opening Day became an annual event on the first Saturday in May. The first parade through the Montlake cut in 1920 consisted of 30 yachts. Several hundred spectators were seated on the sloping banks; the Montlake Bridge was still a decade in the future.

In 1940 race instructions dictated that a parade of boats start at 1:00 P.M., and that all boats be decorated. Regatta chairman that year was Eustace Vynne, Sr.

During World War II Opening Day was shifted to Sunday. Though participants were few, races were held. Recuperating veterans were given a Sunday outing as part of the celebration.

In 1946 formal invitations were sent to Queen City and other yacht clubs to join in the Opening Day parade and festivities. That year Larry Calvert was named the first "Admiral of the Day" (general chairman). The events concluded with dinner and dancing at the clubhouse.

In the 1950s a more organized parade format was instituted. The proposal to include other yacht clubs was promoted, and the clubs responded. In the mid-1950s, a flag-raising ceremony and a few short speeches were added to the day's events. A military band, the hoisting of the burgees of visiting clubs and the honoring of their commodores became part of the ritual. Somewhere along the line, a New England seaman remembered the tradition that sent fishing fleets to sea and suggested a ceremonial prayer; this became tradition once again. An Opening Day theme was first utilized in 1959.

As the ceremonies became more complex, the starting time for boats to assemble on Portage Bay was gradually moved from 12:00 noon to 9:30 A.M. Over the years the competition for the best-decorated boat, selection of parade themes, assigning judges, and awarding prizes became part of the day. In 1970, crew racing was added to the festivities.

Opening Day 1991 was typical of what the event has become. Daily newspapers on the day previous gave it front page coverage. Hundreds of pleasure craft assembled, bands played, flags were hoisted, crew races preceded the parade of boats, awards were given to the best-decorated yachts, and thousands of spectators ashore and afloat enjoyed the event.

A 1940s crowd enjoying Opening Day festivities from Denny Blaine Park. (Photo by Ken Ollar)

More changes will come, but since the day has finite length, something will have to go. We hate to give up anything so good so we'll find a way to work it in; but when eventually the fleet includes seaplane cruisers as well as powerboats and sailboats, the spirit of that Opening Day will have to be pretty clever.

—Don Finlay, Binnacle, *May 1979*

to winning the Silver Cup in Detroit when the propeller shaft was damaged, compelling *Slo-mo IV* to limp from the race. Driver Lou Fageol had her speeding as high as 106 miles per hour in the first heat.

According to the *Seattle Times*, Seattle boats shone at the 1950 PIYA Regatta:

> Vancouver, B.C., July 5—Seattle yachtsmen headed home today with approximately 60 elaborate trophies in recognition of their outstanding performance in the five-day Pacific Coast Yachting Association Regatta which wound up at the Royal Vancouver Yacht Club here yesterday.
>
> Of the 21 class championships established, Seattle boats came out the winners in 11 of the series. In addition, they won some four dozen silver awards for other victories in "seconds."
>
> —Seattle Times, *July 6, 1950*

Because the host committee apparently became overwhelmed by the huge turnout of 237 boats, it wrongly awarded 11 trophies, which had to be recalled. They also failed to complete the posting of final results at the designated time. Among the winners from SYC were Doug Sherwood in *Coho*; J. Franklin Eddy in *Dorade*; Bill Boeing, Jr., in *Wahoo*; and from the Corinthian Yacht Club, Bill Buchan, Sr., in *Heather*.

Late in the year, word was circulated that the *Fantome*, the huge four-masted schooner that had been anchored in Portage Bay since 1939, was about to be sold by the estate of the late Irish brewer, Arthur Ernest Guinness. The *Fantome* had originally cost more than $1 million.

In 1950 the Norwegian-built Dragon was suggested as the official one-design racing-cruising class of this area, pending PIYA board approval. The committee—Bill Jaynes, Bob Withington, and Norm

Bylaws of the SYC Women's Group

Article II of the Women's Group bylaws states:

The purpose of this organization is to encourage social and other activities and friendship among its members.

The membership is open to women members of the Seattle Yacht Club, to any woman whose husband is a member, and to women who are surviving members.

The bylaws are written to provide a broad opportunity for members to participate in the selection of leaders and in the decision-making processes of the organization.

Article IV, Section 1, gives members the right to select officers. The election of president, vice president, secretary, and treasurer takes place at a general meeting of the membership by voice vote. The board is composed of elected officers, who serve for one year. The board of officers and the committee chairmen serve as the executive committee which, in turn, appoints members to the 31 committees. These committees are concerned primarily with social activities, as indicated in the bylaws.

The founding members in 1950 established a means of expansion. Their major purpose was to encourage social and other activities and to increase the membership. The organization has grown in complexity since then. Amendment of the bylaws over the years has allowed for the traditions of the past to coexist with current social settings and to allow the SYC Women's Group to retain its vitality. ◇

The 1950 roster of officers and board of trustees was made up of well-known members. Back row, from left: Frank James, Frank Calvert, Mid Chism, Stan Sayres, John Kucher, Russ Gibson, and Dolph Zubick. Seated: Andy Joy, Larry Calvert, Phil Smith, Jack Warburton, and Howard Richmond. (Photo by Dolph Zubick)

Cole of Seattle—soon heard protests from supporters of other candidates, such as the Blanchard Senior Knockabout and Bill Nightingale's Cub.

In 1950 Hedley Spit, also known as Madison Spit and Point Monroe, was used as the site of many boating rendezvous and Barnacle Bill parties.

The first year of the decade also brought the first Ladies' Predicted Log sponsored by the Tyee Yacht Club. TYC member Mrs. Ted Baker won the contest.

1951

Commodore Phil Smith wrote in his yearbook message:

> This year will be memorable in our yacht club's history for the diversification of our activities—powerboating, sailing, racing and cruising, and, for the first time, the opportunity to defend and stage the Gold Cup race for unlimited hydroplanes.
>
> —*SYC Yearbook, 1951*

Opening Day brought out more than 700 boats. Chet Gibson served as grand marshal, assisted by Jerry Bryant and Doc Harvey. The best decorated sailboat was *Jandy*, owned by Gordon C. (Sandy) Prentice. The powerboat award for decoration went to Ray Stroble's *Nina Ray* of the Queen City Yacht Club.

Among the race winners were the following: Big Sticks—Charlie Frisbie's *Alatola*; Class B and C, Cruising—John Warren's *Cirrus II*; X and Y class—Hans Bebie's *Hecate*; Z class—Lars Lynges' *Butterfly II*, and Evergreens—Bob Withington's *Kuon*.

Among outstanding boats of the year were Dr. Carl Jensen's newly acquired *Amorita*, which won the Swiftsure Lightship Race and the Tri-Island Series. Frank Morris' *Snuffy* won the 1951 International Cruiser Race, which was run in reverse from Vancouver to Seattle so that

Commodores of the Seattle Yacht Club—1950s

TOM D. TYRER
1950
Occupation: President, Washington Asphalt Co.
(Died in Office)
Boat: Lady Grace

DR. R. PHILIP SMITH
1950-1952
Born: 1908, Massachusetts
Education: Kansas University Medical School
Occupation: Physician and Surgeon (Ob-Gyn)
Boats: Gossip, Gossip Too

FRANK D. JAMES
1953
Born: 1907, Seattle, Wash.
Education: University of Washington Law School
Occupation: Lawyer, King County Superior Court Judge
Boats: Kohovasan, Amicus Curiae, *and* Footloose

MIDDLETON M. CHISM
1954
Occupation: Orchardist, Philanthropist
Education: West Point
Boats: Cheri

JOHN A. SODERBERG
1955
Born: 1911, Seattle, Wash.
Education: University of Washington
Occupation: Insurance Broker
Boats: Lady Alice *and* Eugenie

HOWARD E. RICHMOND
1956
Born: 1914, San Francisco, Calif.
Education: University of Washington
Occupation: Wholesale Grocer: Northern Commercial Company
Boats: Polho I *through* V

ANDERSON S. JOY
1957
Born: 1900, Colorado Springs, Colo.
Education: University of Washington (Mechanical Engineering)
Occupation: Boeing Engineer, Insurance (Retired as head of fire and marine division, Travelers Insurance Co).
Crewed on Sir Tom, Circe, *and* Alarm

T. DAYTON DAVIES
1958
Born: 1903, Seattle, Wash.
Education: University of Washington
Occupation: Automobile Dealer (Davies' Chevrolet)
Boats: 42- and 54-foot Chris-crafts called Sea Cookie

ROBERT W. CONDON
1959
Born: 1907, Seattle, Wash.
Education: University of Washington
Occupation: Mgr., Graystone Seattle Plant, Consulting Engineer
Boats: Lively Lady, Valkyrie, *36-foot Hunter powerboat called* Tahsis

The Swiftsure Race has been a major event for decades. A Swiftsure class sloop can be seen in the background at the stern of the lightship. (Photo by Ken Ollar)

it would end as part of the Seafair activities. Charlie Frisbie's *Alatola* continued her winning ways by earning Class AA Protection Island Race honors. Harbine Monroe's Class A *Nautilus III* sailed in first in the Vashon Island Race.

During 1951 the SYC burgee was carried to Hawaii in the Honolulu Race by three Seattle boats—Commodore Phil Smith's *Gossip*, Ed Kennell's *Gracie S*, and Cranston Paschall's *Revenge*. *Gossip* placed seventh and *Revenge* was ninth.

The 1951 International Cruiser run from Bremerton to Juneau was won by Ray Hart, Jr., in *Donolie*.

1952

Dr. Phil Smith in his second yearbook message as commodore wrote:

> For more than fifty years the Seattle Yacht Club has forged ahead and today holds an enviable position as one of the finest yacht clubs in America. Our physical plant is once again in excellent repair; our moorage is safe and adequate; our clubhouse facilities and services are unmatched by any other yacht club on the coast.
>
> But above all this, club spirit today is at its highest peak in years. . . . This year will be memorable in our club's history for the diversification of our activities—power boating, sailing, racing and cruising, and, for the first time, the opportunity to defend and stage the Gold Cup race for unlimited hydroplanes. The combined efforts of all of us are necessary to make this the most outstanding year of our history. . . .
>
> —*SYC Yearbook, 1952*

The 1952 Pacific Coast Yachting Championship Regatta was raced in the waters off Seattle under a committee chaired by Mid Chism. Local papers reported that the event attracted craft from every club on the Pacific Coast. Among winners mentioned: *Dorade* (F. Eddy, SYC); *Gossip* (P. Smith, SYC); *Lady Van* (R. Watt, SYC); *Serada* (C. Goodhope,

CYC); *Nixie* (M. Perrow, SYC and TYC); *Sunny* (F. LeSourd, CYC); *Ganessa* (A. Nyblom, RVanYC); *Ishkoodah* (Russell, RVicYC); *Subdeb* (McTavish, SYC); *Pinafore* (Holmes, CYC); *Oslo* (O. Giese, CYC); *Kuon* (Withington, SYC and CYC); *Manana* (J. Ellis, SYC); *True Luff* (Jensen, SYC); *Oceanide* (M. Rattray, SYC); *Siwusin* (Dr. C. Coleman, CYC); and *Maskee* (G. Horder, SYC).

At the PIYA Regatta, five member associations agreed to race each other in 46-foot Pacific Cruising Class sloops with selected crews. The winner was *Bolero* under helmsman Charlie Ross.

Boats that showed their winning ways during 1952 include Dr. R. N. Rutherford's PCC *Hussy*, overall winner of the Hat Island Race; Dr. A. J. Bowles' *Aldon*, a winner in class and John Rottler's *Jadon II*, overall winner of the Bremerton Heavy Weather Race; Cranston (Bo) Paschall's *Revenge*, winner of the Tri-Island Series; Dr. Herbert Day's K-38 *Ono*, winner of Swiftsure Race; Douglas Sherwood's K-38 *Rebel*, overall winner of Vashon Island Race; and Jack Graham's *Maruffa*, winner of the Protection Island Race.

The overall winner of the Port Madison-to-Nanaimo powerboat contest was H. L. Salvesen's *Sea Tramp* from the Tyee Yacht Club.

1953

SYC Commodore Frank D. James, with tongue in cheek, commented in his commodore's message that "certain irresponsible elements in the club," his wife included, had accused him of being stuffy; therefore, he would squelch this "base canard" by presenting his yearbook message in the form of a poem.

May your winds be fair
But not *too* strong.
Your petrol pure,
Your vacations long.
May your ship be blessed
With sober crews.
But don't forget
To pay your dues.
—*SYC Yearbook, 1953*

The Serada, *owned by Dr. Chris Goodhope of the Corinthian Yacht Club, flies over the waves, though heavily reefed, c. 1952. (Photo by Ken Ollar)*

The week-long PIYA Regatta was hosted jointly by the Vancouver and Kitsilano yacht clubs. Phil and Sid Miller of the Royal Vancouver club took Star class awards by edging out Kitsilano and the Royal Victoria boats in the three-race series. In an exciting race for the City of

Volunteers Made Gold Cup Races Possible

The involvement of Seattle Yacht Club volunteers in the Gold Cup Races is truly astounding. Literally hundreds of members of yachting families were involved.

It would take a mammoth pot full of money to purchase the amount of man and woman hours devoted to putting on the gigantic Gold Cup Regatta.

Instead, hundreds of men and women give unstintingly of their time and effort to make this outstanding event a success. Committees and sub-committees perform many and varied jobs; they pick out the trophies, they lay out the course, they see that pit facilities are available. They arrange entertainment for the "visiting firemen." They see that the finest press facilities possible are made available, so that nation-wide coverage of this great event is assured.

A thousand and one minute details are taken care of by these unselfish people.

They get little or no recognition for their efforts, nor do they ask for recognition; what they do ask is that the Gold Cup Regatta shall be remembered by one and all—participants and spectators—as the finest racing event ever run.

Jerry Bryant, the general chairman of the Gold Cup Committee, summed up everyone's feelings when he said, "The Gold Cup is an example of unselfish devotion on the part of a great many people to a very great sport. Everyone owes these people a tremendous vote of thanks."

—Seattle Yacht Club Gold Cup Regatta Program, 1952

As an example of the numbers of SYC members involved, here is a list of the 1953 committees.

General Chairman: Howard Richmond

Vice-Chairmen: Ross Merrill and Lin Ivey

Advisory Committee: Paul Brown, Jerry Bryant, Lawrence Calvert, Frank James, Larry Norton, and Stanley Sayres.

Budget Committee: Allen P. Green, Jr. (chairman), Dave Grey, Kenneth A. Metcalf, John C. Warburton.

Course and Survey: Arthur Shorey (chairman), Phil Bessor, Bob Spearman, J. A. Troxell.

Entertainment Committee: Mr. and Mrs. Conrad Knutson (chairmen), Mr. and Mrs. Charles Stipp (vice-chairmen), Mr. and Mrs. Victor Beck, Mr. and Mrs. John Day, Mr. and Mrs. Jack Eyler, Dr. and Mrs. Cordell Jarrett, Dr. and Mrs. Michael Kennedy, Mr. and Mrs. E. Nowogroski, Dr. and Mrs. Dean Parker, Dr. and Mrs. Robert Rutherford, Mr. and Mrs. Dolph Zubick.

Log Boom Committee: Russ Gibson (chairman), Phil Duryee, Jo Gibson, Alice Holcomb, John Rottler, Mary Thomas.

Official Barge Committee: Joseph B. Mesdag (chairman), William E. Boeing, Jr., Gilbert L. Duffy, George Morry, and Gordon A. Prentice.

Patrol Committee: Eustace Vynne, Jr. (chairman); Lt. Comdr. R. N. Norris, USCG; Captain Bruce Temple, USCG Reserve; David Williams.

Judges and Timers: Middleton Chism and Anderson Joy (co-chairmen)

Referees: Mel Crook, Stanly Donogh, F. W. Fredericks, Mildred Barber.

Measurers: Al Hart, Jim Harland

Starters: Middleton Chism, Don Dunton

Gunners: Conrad Knutson, Ray Ogden, Jr.

Flag Man: Don Dunton

Clock Men: Richard Crosby, R. O. Burns

Timers: Otto Crocker, Art Shorey

Recorder: Betty Shorey

Computers: Bob Spearman, Al Pond

Weston Timer: Doc Watson, Ray Watson

Scorers: Anderson Joy, Betty Sundine (and nine assistants)

Course Judges (starting line): Paul Brinson, John Ford, Herman Green

Field Judges: Jimmy Cain, Jim Perrine, Bill Rumins

Course Surveyor: Phil Bessor

Announcers: Bob Engler (Gold Cup), Carl Blackstock (Green Lake)

Pits: Don Cooney (chairman), Don Amick (assistant), Sam Bartell, Paul Brown, Dick Cahan, Bill Cooper, Church Griffiths, Ron Johnson, Comdr. Jack London, George Orovitz, Bill Seaborn, Herb Sears.

Program: Clyde A. Robinson (chairman), Jack Gordon, Cliff Harrison, Kent Powell, Ray Murray, Jr., Don Hesler.

Publicity, Press, Radio: Art O'Laughlin (chairman), Bob Engler, Bob Priebe, Cliff Harrison, Bob Walters, Kent Powell.

Registration and Accommodations: Frank Calvert (chairman), Dr. Irving Anderson, Mrs. Don Cooney, Jack Glidewell, Kenneth C. Gordon, Dr. Eugene L. Kidd, Dr. Dean Parker, Harold Tolford, Tom Wheeler, Neil S. Sanborn, John E. Graham.

Olympic Hotel Booth: Miss Clara Stenstrom, Mrs. Henry Wood.

Trophies: Stanly Donogh (chairman).

Carl Jensen's Adios *competing in the 1954 Pacific International Yachting Association Race. (Photo by Ken Ollar)*

Vancouver Diamond Jubilee Trophy, Seattle's Doug Sherwood sailed the *Pompero* to a first place finish in "smart, heady" style.

At the annual meeting in Los Angeles, Ken Kraft of Seattle was elected commodore of the International Flattie Yacht Racing Association. Kraft, in his *Small Kraft*, won the L.A. Yacht Club Invitational and finished fifth in the International.

Among other noted yachtsmen of the year were SYC's Maurice (Mose) Vining who, in his *Benign*, captured overall honors in the 1953 Heavy Weather Race. Gordon (Sandy) Prentice in *Jandy* won the Tri-Island Series. Quite a story goes with Howard Cruver's win in the 920-mile Alaska Cruiser Race. His *Wahineui* hit Carne Rock in Reid Channel, demolishing one shaft and propeller. He took her on one engine to Butedale where repairs were possible, then continued to the finish line with only a 1.15 percent error, which won the race.

Ernest Banner's Blanchard Knockabout *Rival* was overall winner on Opening Day; Frank Morris' *African Queen* earned overall honors at the Interclub Challenge Race; and Howard Richmond's *Polho III* won the Swiftsure Lightship Race. T. W. Ayres' *Senarieta II* of the Royal Vancouver Yacht Club won the International Powerboat Race from Poulsbo to Vancouver.

1954

SYC Commodore Middleton M. Chism in 1954 called for members to concentrate on the development of young people—"encourage them to acquire nautical skills, learn to play and compete and take to the water whenever or wherever they can. Support our juniors and the junior instruction and sailing program. For only through our young people will we perpetuate the great traditions of our club." (SYC Yearbook, 1954)

Memorable yachts of 1954 include Dr. Carl Jensen's *Adios*, which won the Tri-Island Series Trophy. Among AA class boats in the Tri-Island contest, Franklin Eddy's world-famous yawl *Dorade* was best of class; in BB class, Doug Sherwood's *Rebel* covered the distances most rapidly; Jack McKenzie in his *Indian Scout* carried away Six-Meter honors; and in Dragon class, Gary Horder's *Maskee* was triumphant.

Dick Byington's *Kaleta* captured the Opening Day Predicted Log Race, and the *Nixie*, owned by Marshall Perrow, was awarded the Gamwell Trophy.

In the IPBA International Cruiser contest from Bremerton to Nanaimo, QCYC's Dale Cogshall in his *Hawkeye* took the honors with an error of only 0.88 percent.

In November, old-timers met at the Seattle Yacht Club to reminisce. Six of those present—C. P. Blanchard, Jr., Dietrich Schmitz, John Graham, Sr., Miller Freeman, Edward Cunningham and Quent Williams—could remember the 1909 merger of the Seattle and Elliott Bay yacht clubs.

1955

John Soderberg, 1955's commodore, speaking like a true sailor, noted in the annual:

> Thanks to distinguished past skippers and hearty cooperation from mates and forem'st hands, the good ship Seattle Yacht Club is a tight craft, ready for any weather. With all sails pulling, our quarters attractive, our galley shining anew, our lobscouse and plum duff the best, the grog cask broached on the upper deck and a ship's chest with sufficient pieces-of-eight, our craft is sound below and aloft.
>
> —*SYC Yearbook, 1955*

A hardy group of yachtsmen cruised year-round on Puget Sound waters. Jim Moffett's yawl *Mrs. Pettibone* was one of these. Several joined a Cruise-of-the-Month Series, which developed a schedule that found them at Port Blakely in January, on the way to Manzanita (with Bob Priebe leading them in his cruising sailboat *Taruga*) in February, and so on through the winter months.

Commodore Soderberg in 1955 received a worrisome letter from the Washington secretary of state: The club was informed that its 50-year corporate life had expired, and the law provided for liquidation. Judge Advocate Chet Adair and attorney-member Harry Jones, Jr., were asked to determine what the club response should be. They found that the Seattle Chamber of Commerce had been similarly challenged two years earlier and had arranged for the legislature to pass an enabling act granting it unlimited corporate life. Adair, Jones, and Commodore Soderberg made their plans, visited Olympia with a check to pay the penalty for not rechartering on time, and eventually the Seattle Yacht Club received a corporate charter for an unlimited number of years.

Dr. George Horton and Donol Hedlund were very active on the 1955 House Operations Committee. They planned a needed modernization of the galley and Ward Room. To overcome the charge that they were getting too fancy, when the work was completed they covered several tables with oilcloth and advised that all members who lunched in work clothes would be given a free martini. Business boomed until the club ran out of gin.

John Ford, chairman of the publicity committee, was excited when *Life* magazine agreed to cover Opening Day of 1955, but no one from the magazine showed. He was chided by members who

Totem Yacht Club

The Totem Yacht Club of Tacoma came into being on June 16, 1955, and in the first six months 175 people were drawn into its midst. At the outset, meetings were held in the public library and social functions were scheduled in rented quarters. The club began to save money toward the purchase of property on which to build a clubhouse.

Many activities conceived during those first years are still enjoyed by the members—yearly boating activities, the Dockton breakfast, the fishing derby, the land cruises, seasonal dances and parties, and fund-raising programs. On the other hand, a number of functions enjoyed during those early days are now, for various reasons, no longer part of the calendar. Among them are the Vashon Island Marathon Race, which started at Dash Point and ran around the island, and the Puyallup River Race, which started at the old port yacht basin owned by two club members and ran up the river and back. This race drew thousands of spectators to the riverbank who bought food from various stands set up by the club to raise funds. For a time members were part of the hydroplane scene, sponsoring a boat for three years, trekking to Lake Chelan each year for the race, chartering buses and grandstands for members and friends at the famed Gold Cup when it was held in Seattle.

In 1958, after two years of searching, the club purchased waterfront property a few yards west of Cummings' Boat Company. Piling was driven, and the clubhouse was started. Materials were scrounged, begged for, salvaged, donated, and borrowed. Over the course of 10 years, volunteers built the clubhouse. The first meeting in the new facility was held in July 1961. Only the framing was up and the roof on, so the wind blew through, but everyone enjoyed the potluck and the good fellowship. By the following spring, the outside walls were up and the heating system installed, and from then on all functions were scheduled there.

Then on Jan. 30, 1970, just as the clubhouse was completed, some deranged person forced his way inside, took what he wanted, and set fire to the building. It was reduced to a burned-out hulk. The club immediately started negotiations to rebuild, but the city planning commission and city council had developed new rules regarding off-street parking, beautifications, and other cost factors, which took the total expenses beyond the club's means; the only alternative was to sell the property and relocate. Insurance money plus sale of the property would allow a new clubhouse to be built elsewhere. After considering many sites, the club's present location, North High Lane, was found, purchased, and a new clubhouse erected. In 1976, six years after the fire, the new facility was completed.

Membership soon surpassed 220, and a limit had to be established because the clubhouse could accommodate no more. The last few years have been much like those preceding. Membership is full, activities are well attended, the club is solvent, and the enthusiasm and good fellowship seem to grow with each passing year. The parking lot has been enlarged, the clubhouse interior redecorated, the exterior painted, and a handsome cover installed over the walkway. All of this was accomplished by the members.

In 1988 the Totem Yacht Club elected its first woman commodore—Sharon Nell. Totem Yacht Club continues to prosper and is what the founders envisioned: A group of people who further the sport of boating and all its related activities, a snug haven in which to congregate, a good fellowship among members, and a constantly growing membership.

—Based on an history composed by former Totem Yacht Club Commodore Frank Boers

Blanchard Sr. Knockabouts racing in the mid-1950s. Skippers were as follows: B 75, Ernie Banner; B 7, Rev. Plettenmaier; and B 81, Maurice Rattray, Jr. (SYC Historical Collection)

told him if he didn't slow down a bit, they'd elect him commodore (which they did later).

In 1955 Phil Butler offered the club a gift of building materials left over from one of his highway jobs. The commodore was so pleased he asked Butler to chair the moorage and docks committee. That same year Butler's son Mike was elected by the juniors to serve as their commodore.

Greater Seattle and SYC co-sponsored the 1955 Gold Cup Race on Lake Washington. After considerable disagreement between Detroit and Seattle owners on how the race should be conducted, Melvin Crook, the designated referee, resigned as a result of a dispute over Stan Sayres' team's "under-the-bridge flying start." He was replaced by Stanly Donogh who, with his positive attitude, extensive experience in motorboat racing, and belief in sportsmanlike conduct, managed to get things straightened away. *Gale V* took the Gold Cup back to Detroit, but Seattle reclaimed it the next year and the race continued under the sponsorship of Greater Seattle.

Because the wind often refused to blow in the traditional race around Vashon Island, a substitute race was inaugurated in 1955 on Admiralty Inlet. It would count as part of the Tri-Island Series. Dr. Herb Day's *Ono* placed first overall in the Tri-Island Series and Maurice Rattray, Jr., in *Oceanide* placed first among the Knockabouts in the same series.

The juniors began planning for the 24th Annual Shipwreck Party in February, choosing a motif of "Shipwrecked in the Government Locks at Ballard." It sounded like so much fun that senior members took over the planning and invited mature members to join the juniors at the affair.

It so happened that 1955 turned out to be the year of the cannon. Byron Fish, the well-known *Seattle Times* columnist, wrote of the "search" for the Seattle Yacht Club's ancient Chinese pirate cannon. It had disappeared in September 1954, the club reported. Fish received a telephone tip that contained enough "vagueness as to details to make the business properly mysterious." It seems the cannon had been discovered in the wilds of Mercer Island. So Fish and various other reporters accompanied CHAOS (Cannon Hunters Association of Seattle) to the predetermined site. Fish reported that "the build-up was rather spoiled by somebody who charged right into the woods and shouted: 'Here it is.'" A large photo accompanied his column showing Donald H. Clark, head hunter of CHAOS; John Harvey, vice admiral of the day; Dean Parker, admiral of the day; and John Soderberg, commodore, hauling the cannon from the leaves. As Fish indicated, "The recovery of the cannon couldn't have been more timely. It will be back at the Seattle Yacht Club just in time for the ceremonies, a week from tomorrow, opening the yachting season."

Opening Day 1955 brought out the largest field of pleasure craft ever assembled for the occasion—more than 900. Charlie Frisbie's *Alatola* led the big boats around the triangular course on Lake Washington. Henry Kotkins' *Totem* took an easy first among the K-38s. Fred Sundt's Norwegian-built Six-Meter *Ylliam VIII* was best of the Six-Meter class. Other winners were Howie Richmonds' *Polho III*, Fran LeSourd's *Sunny*, and Bob Cram's Star, *Scram*.

Powerboats winning Opening Day Races included two Queen City racers—*Tomara*, belonging to George Knight, and *Hilma III*, belonging to Chet Gibson. A third place went to Dr. A. J. Bowles' *Aldon* of Seattle Yacht Club.

The Masthead Trophy Race

The first Masthead Trophy race was held in 1955. In this unique race, all contestants must pilot the same boat, which eliminates the usual arguments over relative speed of various boats, failure to follow course, errors in time, etc. Any member of the club—boat owner or not—may participate.

The name of the race originated during the first contest. The boat used was Campbell Church's *Deer Leap*. At the end of the race, as the yacht was headed for the clubhouse, it came to the Fremont Bridge. The hour was late, past the time when the bridge would open. The *Deer Leap*'s mast was too high to pass under the bridge. In order to reach the clubhouse at the designated time, Campbell Church had the top of the mast sawed off, and this later became part of the Masthead Trophy. Usually two legs of the race were run before lunch and the other two legs after lunch on the way back to the locks. When he reports aboard, each contestant receives all the essential information regarding boat speed, time required to make turns, the length of each separate segment of each leg and other necessary information to make his predictions. Each contestant must be prepared to do his own computing, which includes making allowances for currents, weather, etc.

Over the years, all categories of predicted log racers, novice to expert, have participated in this contest.

—Based on an article in
The Binnacle, *March 1967*

Alatola was Charlie Frisbie's 57-foot racing sloop. She won the Opening Day Races in 1955. (SYC Historical Collection)

Judges gave best-decorated awards to Victor Beck's sailboat *Vixen*, William Rowan's powerboat *Windrush*. The novelty class was won by Tom Wells and Dr. David Law.

Swiftsure Race rules were amended in 1955. The ban on the use of auxiliary power was changed to allow the motor to be started if anyone fell overboard and to allow the boat to continue in the race if the use of the motor had not contributed to the advantage of the yacht. The first six finishers in the 1955 Swiftsure were from the Seattle Yacht Club. First overall in corrected time was *Serada*, owned by Dr. Chris Goodhope. The first over the finish line was Jack Graham's *Maruffa*, in spite of the fact she lost 10 feet of her mast to a wind gust just before finishing. Her corrected time was 8 hours, 47 minutes and 34 seconds, placing her second and 11 minutes behind *Serada*. Other finishers in order were *Westward Ho* (John Helsell), *Kate II* (D. E. Skinner), *Adios* (Carl Jensen), and *Red Jacket* (George Parsons).

On the Bellingham-to-Genoa Bay International Cruiser Predicted Log Race, Carl Saluzzi of the Rainier Yacht Club, with his broken leg in a cast, piloted *Coconito* to an overall win.

1956

Commodore Howard E. Richmond, in his yearbook message, emphasized the fact that on August 5, "thousands of people from all over the United States and Canada will come to Seattle to see the Seafair Trophy Race, the successor to the famous Gold Cup Race, which is administered entirely by the committee made up of Seattle Yacht Club members." (SYC Yearbook, 1956)

He reminded members that during the week of September 10, in conjunction with the Corinthian Yacht Club, the North American Sailing Championships (the Mallory Cup Series) would be conducted again by the SYC. On top of this, he stated with pride: "We have a full season of both sail and powerboat racing and cruising activities, topped by the Pacific Coast Yachting Association championships, which will be held this year in Victoria simultaneously with the Annual PIYA Regatta from July 1 to July 6."

Opening Day attracted 1,143 boats, the biggest turnout ever in the West. Seattle writer Emmett Watson wrote an article about Opening Day for *Sports Illustrated*. Burt Thomas, the burly

Tacoma long-distance swimmer, dived in the water to stroke ahead of the boat parade. The historic *Thea Foss* went through Montlake cut, carrying the tootling bagpipes of the Keith Highlanders' Bagpipe Band. Twelve Star class boats sailed by, each representing a different country, and a pair of kayaks and a couple of outriggers darted in and around the parading craft. The best-decorated boats were D. E. Skinner's *Kate*, Frank Metz's *Tipsy Too*, and Dr. David Law's *Gloucester Hesperous*. Stan Youngs' *Arlene* captured the predicted log race for powerboats with a percentage error of 0.67.

In 1956 Max Wyman, accompanied by George M. Olsen and Raleigh Chinn, sailed his 72-foot yawl *Diamond Head* to the Virgin Islands.

This was the year that both Seattle and Queen City yacht clubs filed for rezoning to allow covered moorage facilities. Residents protested that such moorage was unsightly; however, the Seattle Planning Commission ruled that the clubs could proceed with the proposed changes.

Slo-mo IV was retired in October

Poulsbo Yacht Club

On a chilly day in February 1956 Ed Neimier and Clarence "Gundy" Gunderson were admiring Neimier's new boat. For a shakedown cruise, they decided that Everett, the home of their mutual friend, Harold, might be a good destination. They called Harold and he invited them and their wives to dinner at Everett Yacht Club.

As they docked the new boat, snow began to fall and the temperature dropped. Ed and Jean Neimier and Gundy and Alma Gunderson scurried up to the clubhouse only to find a sign on the door, reading "MEMBERS ONLY."

Neimier simply pushed his group right on into the warm interior. "What yacht club are you from?" the clerk asked. "Poulsbo Yacht Club," Neimier blurted and quickly signed the registration book. As they sat at a table, waiting for friend Harold to arrive, the smiling waiter informed them that all drinks were on the house because EvYC never entertained anyone from the Poulsbo Yacht Club before. Needless to say, by the time Harold arrived, the four "Poulsbo Yacht Club" members were truly enjoying the hospitality.

All the next week, Jean Neimier's conscience bothered her. "You shouldn't have done that," she chided her husband. Then she got the idea of creating a yacht club. She secured a copy of the Tyee Yacht Club's incorporation papers (Tyee was the only club at the time that accepted both men and women as members). The proper forms were completed and the Neimiers had Fred Hill, Leif Ness and Clarence Gunderson sign them. When they inquired as to what they had signed, Ed told them they were founders of the Poulsbo Yacht Club. All agreed it was a fine idea. Ed sent the forms to Olympia with a $25 check. Two weeks later, back came the official certificate. Now they needed members. Jean suggested putting a note in the local newspaper inviting anyone interested in a yacht club to come to a potluck dinner at their house. Luckily the scheduled date turned out to be a nice May evening, because 75 people showed up! They had a noisy, merry time, and before the evening was over, Hill Sawyer had been elected commodore. Jim Brix would attend to the finances, Kline Jagger would handle the public relations, and Betty Shephard would work up a bulletin, which evolved into the club's *Springline*. Mrs. Sawyer submitted the design for a unique burgee. When it came to talking finances, dues were set at $9.50 each ($19.00 a couple), because if memberships were $10.00 or more, there was a federal tax to pay.

Right away folks started talking about a clubhouse. In clearing up legal descriptions for some

1956, and the American Power Boat Association retired her registration number (U-27). The Harmsworth Trophy was brought to SYC, thanks to the win of *Shanty I* and William T. (Bill) Waggoner.

A. Douglas Sherwood's *Rebel* won the Tri-Island Trophy (and would repeat the win in 1957). Donol F. Hedlund's *Eugenie* of SYC was the overall winner of the International Powerboat Association International Cruiser Race from Poulsbo to Nanaimo. M. Phil Butler's *Paramour* was in a winning mood throughout the year, capturing the Capital-to-Capital Race, the Seattle-to-Prince Rupert Race and the Prince Rupert-to-Juneau Race. On the return trip from Alaska, *Paramour*, while at anchor in Behm Canal, floated onto a reef and listed 45 degrees. The skipper's concern was that the trophies, which were lashed to the deck, might be lost overboard. Fortunately, they weren't.

Karl Hostetter's *Karen IV* of the Corinthian Yacht Club won overall in the Hat Island Race. Carl Jensen's *Adios* added the 1956 Mark Mayer Trophy to its shelf.

The North American Sailing Cham-

Poulsbo property, Ed found a piece of tideland belonging to the city. The city agreed to lease this mudflat property to the Poulsbo Yacht Club for $1 a year if members would clean up the site. If nothing else, a small boat landing area could be prepared there. That met with everyone's approval, but the club still needed upland property on which to build a clubhouse. Since nobody wanted to sell such a site, in the spirit that prevails to this day at the club, members agreed to "make some land." The men corralled logs and Clarence Paulson, the town's engineer, drove pilings in his spare time. But soon waves driven by a southwest wind washed through and over the logs, collapsing them in a jumble.

"Has to be rocks," said John Epkland, an old deep-sea diver who knew blasting and heavy construction. Ed Neimier had the proper equipment, so he and Epkland drove all over Kitsap County looking for rocks. When they spotted a big one, they would offer to remove it free of charge. Folks were usually delighted to get rid of the rocks; but one man wanted an especially difficult boulder removed, and after it was broken into manageable pieces, his wife got excited about those lovely rocks and would not let them be hauled away. The first rocks dumped into the mud were the big boulders Jean had been saving for her rock garden. Ed thought the club needed the rocks more than Jean did. Sadly, when dumped into the muck, they slowly sank from sight. Finally, enough broken concrete and rock were added to create a piece of dry land on which to build.

When that fill became firm enough to support a building, the members sold non-interest-bearing $50 bonds, to be redeemed partially each year by lot. When nearly every member family was participating in the bond purchases, it was time for the site to be leveled. When Hal Hoover and Jerry Almos laid out the Panabode housing that had been ordered, everyone got into the act. After the boards were assembled, the wiring strung, the plumbing in, and the painting done, the people of Poulsbo were invited to visit their new yacht club, which had replaced an unsightly mudflat.

And so, from one woman's disturbed conscience, a new yacht club was formed. It soon took its place among the others already established around Puget Sound. Today the Poulsbo Yacht Club has about 350 members, which will increase as soon as larger, more comfortable quarters are completed at the marina uplands. Tentative plans call for the addition of 32 more slips to the recently completed 120-slip marina.

The Poulsbo Yacht Club continues to be marked by the highest caliber of volunteer services from its industrious members. Building on lessons of the past and retaining the original spirit and enthusiasm, members enjoy the achievement, recognition, and camaraderie so evident beneath the PYC burgee. ◇

The Port Orchard Yacht Club

The Port Orchard Yacht Club was formed in 1956 with Russell Sweany as the first commodore.

The women's auxiliary became active in 1958, with Ann Hannah serving as their first president; members were called "Commodears." The original clubhouse was a Mosquito Fleet ferry boat called the *Concordia* and was used until it was sold in 1973.

The club met in various places around Port Orchard until the present clubhouse was finished and dedicated on Sept. 9, 1978.

The moorage was enlarged and concrete floats were installed in 1986. At present this moorage accommodates about 159 boats.

—From materials submitted by Past Commodore William G. Palmer

pionship Races for the Mallory Cup, begun in 1952, were held in Seattle waters for the first time in 1956. The Corinthian *Helmsman* carried a report of the event in which Dick Marshall told of such oddities as an awards banquet with no award, steady "north-southerly" winds of practically zero velocity, a mark being rounded the wrong way by the eventual winner of the series, six out of the eight competing crews winning at least one race, and two members on one crew named Quail and Nightingale who were immediately dubbed the Bird Boys. In spite of it all, Fred E. (Ted) Hood of Marblehead, Massachusetts, scored two firsts, three seconds and a third to win the cup in a manner that fulfilled the motto on the beautiful 144-year old tureen, "May the Best Man Win." Norman Baess, representing the Northwest, came in third. Other notables raced, including: Buddy Melges, who has become a leading world sailor, a designer of world-class boats and sails and a defender of the America's Cup; and Bus Mossbacher, who later won the America's Cup in 12-Meter

The Shelton Yacht Club

The Shelton Yacht Club was founded in October 1956 and incorporated the following year. Membership now numbers 200, and about 90 boats call the Shelton Yacht Club their home port. Twenty of the former commodores are still living. The clubhouse is located at the Shelton Port.

The club schedules many events each year, among them an oyster/ham dinner, a Labor Day clamfest, a Christmas dinner and a First Mates' Cruise and Brunch.

Among the traditions are a lighted cruise at Christmas, a St. Patrick's Day Cruise, and a Ragbagger's Weekend, which is combined with a New Members' Cruise.

Obviously, Shelton residents, as do their compatriots all around Puget Sound, enjoy the sheltered waters of our great inland sea.

—Based on material supplied by Donna Davidson

sloops and was also remembered as a member of President Nixon's cabinet.

1957

The yearbook was dedicated to Stanley St. Clair Sayres who died at age 60 on Sept. 17, 1956. In 1950 Sayres set the world one-mile straight-away record of 160.323 miles per hour, then in 1952 broke his own record with a speed of 178.497 miles per hour. It was in 1950 also that he captured the American Power Boat Association's Challenge Cup (the Gold Cup) with his *Slo-mo V* and brought it to the Seattle Yacht Club. For the next four years, he successfully defended the Gold Cup against all challengers. He also brought the Harmsworth Trophy and the President's Trophy to the club. One result of his accomplishments was the stimulation of Seafair. As a result of his contributions to Seattle he was named the city's "Man of the Year."

Andy Joy, in his commodore's message, noted that the SYC trophy locker was the fullest it had ever been with national and international prizes.

At its annual meeting, the club hon-

Stanley St. Clair Sayres

Stan Sayres in the cockpit of the retired Slo-mo-shun IV. *Note SYC burgee on the tail fin. (SYC Historical Collection)*

No member brought more renown to the Seattle Yacht Club than did Stan Sayres. He was truly a gentleman sportsman. Sayres sought perfection in his boats, recognition for his championship crew, and honors for his club and city. He was a tough competitor, but a most generous and gracious champion.

Sayres, with his *Slo-mo-shun* boats, revolutionized hydroplane speedboat racing, and his achievements made Seattle the speedboat capital of the world. In 1952 he broke his own mile straight-away record with a run at 178.497 miles per hour. In 1950 he captured the American Power Boat Association's Challenge Cup, commonly called the Gold Cup, and brought it to SYC for the first time. He alone defended the Gold Cup against all challengers for the next four years. He is also credited with bringing the British International Trophy for Motor Boats (the Harmsworth Trophy) and the President's Trophy to the club, in addition to winning five consecutive Gold Cup championships.

Stan Sayres' achievements with his famous *Slo-mo-shuns* stimulated the organization of Seattle Seafair, gaining national prominence for this community; it was most fitting that these efforts earned him Seattle's "Man of the Year" title.

Sayres also received worldwide recognition with the award of the Bronze Medal of Honor from the Union of International Motorboating in Belgium.

With the passing of Stan Sayres on Sept. 17, 1956, the Seattle Yacht Club lost one of its most distinguished members. His friendliness, his eagerness to help others, and his loyalty are still remembered. ◇

ored its half-dozen 50-year members—L. E. (Ted) Geary, Dietrich Schmitz, Quent Williams, Harold Lee, Edward Cunningham, and Dr. Henry Schmitz.

In June the dining room was refurbished and the waitresses donned new uniforms. Meal prices were raised, but the scale remained slightly below comparable commercial restaurants; the management believed that because members paid dues they were entitled to a slight advantage on prices. State law at the time did not permit sale of liquor-by-the-drink in restaurants. However, post-war consumption of the hard stuff was considerable enough at the bar to make up for the deficit in the SYC dining room.

The Marine Room also was

The Story of the Junior Yachtsmen

In the years since the Seattle Junior Yacht Club was founded in 1921, many things have changed. The first members were aged 14 to 26, but when prohibition was repealed, the age was changed to 14 to 21. The first members paid a $50 initiation fee and $50 per year for dues. Trustees have always been aware of the fact that the junior yachtsmen are the future of the club. Even during the years of the Great Depression the SYC juniors were active. Though many things have changed, one thing has not—the spirit that prompted the charter of the junior club, the joy of "just messing around in boats."

Junior yachtsmen enjoying the 1975 Junior Summer Series. Back row (from left): Charlie Footh, Mark Laura, Frank Heffernan, and Lee Ann Hobble. Middle: Wade Cressman and Carol Hyde. Front: Jim Anderson, Mark Robinson, Mike Sibold, and Karen Hamilton. (Wallace Ackerman Photography)

Junior meetings in 1956 were held the first Thursday of every month. Also that year it was decided to reestablish the custom of junior dinners before the meetings. The club provided a fine meal for a nominal fee, and dining together gave juniors a chance to exchange gossip and boat talk. A short business meeting followed, and the evening was usually completed with a sailing movie or talk.

Under the direction of senior advisors the sailing program flourished. The Winter Frostbite Series was more popular than ever before after the renovation of the Junior Station at the end of Pier 2. The station gave contestants a place to warm up and enjoy hot coffee between the races. John Ford III won the Captain H. B. Lovejoy Trophy in 1956. This was awarded annually to the junior with the most points in the winter series and could be won by any competing junior, regardless of club affiliation. Seattle Junior Yacht Club was host to the McCurdy International Challenge Cup Trophy in November 1956, which was won by Corinthian Yacht Club juniors. Other standings were Royal Vancouver Yacht Club, second; University of Washington Yacht Club, third; Seattle Yacht Club, fourth; Royal Victoria Yacht Club, fifth. The contestants from Seattle Junior Yacht Club always have many tales to tell about the fine time they have when attending the Royal Vancouver Yacht Club's annual Christmas Regatta.

refurnished and its former 16- and 10-foot bars, stainless steel bar sink, refrigerators, and large photo mural were auctioned off on June 26 at the family buffet.

The PIYA Regatta, hosted by SYC June 29–July 4 at Port Townsend, had two parts—small-boat races on Saturday and Sunday with two final races on Monday, and larger-yacht races Sunday through Wednesday. Powerboat chairman Dick Black arranged a predicted log race for Saturday from Port Townsend to Marrowstone Point.

All during yachting season, the limited parking at the club caused problems. Members were requested to leave their keys in their cars if they were forced to park in a manner that might block other vehicles.

Early in the spring of 1957, the juniors raced among themselves for the Stimson Memorial Trophy. Competition for the trophy was keen, as the winner was acknowledged the best junior skipper in the club. In the interest of producing more and better skippers, Seattle Yacht Club juniors sponsored 10 weeks of sailing instruction in 1956. Classes were held all day Saturday through April and May, and 72 students took advantage of this opportunity to better their sailing skills. Much to the delight of many would-be members, the age limit for entrance into the Junior Yacht Club was lowered from 14 to 12 in an effort to increase the number of enthusiastic sailors.

The 1957 junior social calendar was a full one. The Junior Commodore's Ball came first. Spring brought the annual "Waterfront Brawl," a costume dance with a nautical theme, and all through the year there were informal mixers, splash parties (in conjunction with the University of Washington Yacht Club), ski trips, and an occasional pajama dance. Juniors also took an active part in the proceedings on Opening Day and during the Gold Cup Regatta.

It is impossible to imagine Seattle Yacht Club without junior members. In 1957 juniors were noted for gathering in the club lobby after a rainy Winter Frostbite race and dripping large puddles on the clean linoleum from their baggy foul-weather gear. It was the juniors who crowded to the largest table in the dining room, dirtied the napkins, spotted the tablecloth, disarranged the silver, then ordered coffee! It was the juniors who were miraculously transformed into sophisticated young men and women for the one night a year at their annual Commodore's Ball. And it was the juniors who pledged to you, senior members, that they would be the sportsmen, the yachtsmen, the club members of whom you may be proud in the coming years.

—Based in part on an article by Joy Lusty McFarlane in the SYC Yearbook, 1957

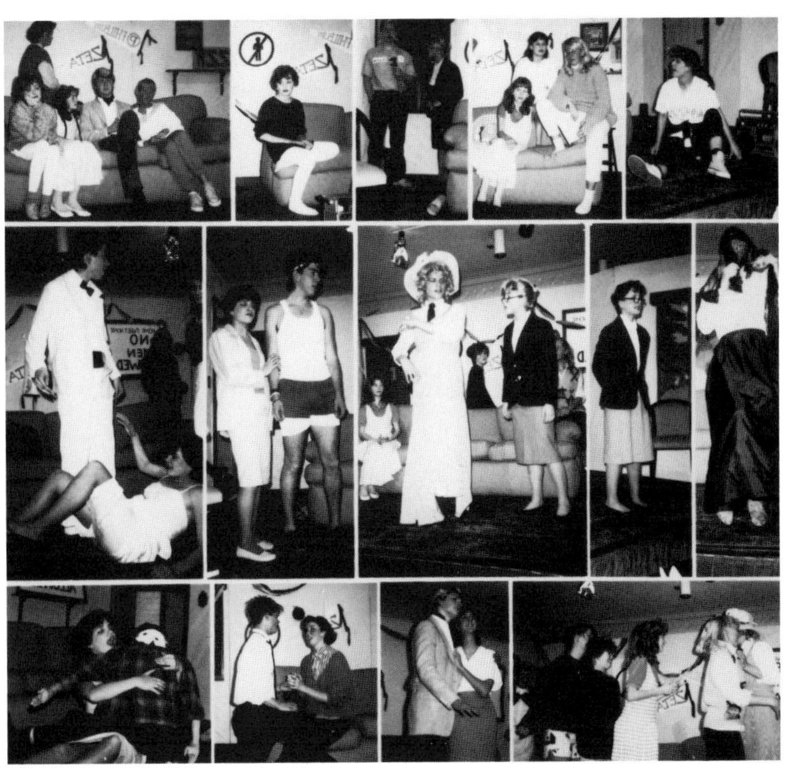

Juniors at play. (SYC Historical Collection)

With all these hydroplane trophies, the Seattle Yacht Club trophy cases were full in 1957. Behind the awards are driver Jack Regis of Edgar Kaiser's Hawaii Kai III *and Mike Welsch, crew chief of the* Slo-mo. *(SYC Historical Collection)*

Gold Cup chairman Ross Merrill predicted the 1957 Gold Cup Race would be a one-day event. Log boom chairman Russ Gibson advised all boats to be securely moored to the log boom prior to 10:30 a.m. on the day of the race. Paul Brown, city parks director, reported that the parks board would have the new Stanley S. Sayres Memorial Pits completed and in full operation by August 2 and that the first hydroplanes would move in on August 3.

Members were requested to carry their Class H Liquor Scrip Books with them when utilizing the club's liquor facilities; this would allow the extra help employed for Seafair week to render speedier service. Any member not using his moorage space during that busy week was requested to advise the club office so that it might accommodate guests' vessels.

The 1957 IPBA International Cruiser Overall Award went to Willis Crossett of Queen City Yacht Club, who brought his *Winabu* over the finish line with a percentage error of only 0.4558.

1958

Commodore T. Dayton Davies wrote in the yearbook of the well-rounded program at the club and added:

> Membership has been kept at a high level with due care being given to our standards, the renovation of the club house has greatly improved our quarters and facilities, Port Madison has seen the start of what should be a great, long-range development program; and, while accomplishing this, the financial

condition of our club remains in an exceedingly sound and healthy condition.

—*SYC Yearbook, 1958*

Willard Rhodes' *Miss Thriftway*, driven by Bill Muncey, kept the Gold Cup in Seattle that year.

Outstanding boats of 1958 include *Sea Fever*, designed by Ben Seaborn, built by Vic Franck, and owned by Otis Lamson, Jr., Dr. R. C. Philbrick and B. H. Gardner of SYC, which captured five firsts among AA class craft, including Opening Day, Mark Mayer, Vashon Island, Protection Island and Tri-Island overall. Charles Olmstead's *Tola* equaled this feat in A class, taking the Mark Mayer, Vashon Island, Frisbie, Mark Mayer overall and Tri-Island overall awards. The BB class winner was Dr. Byron Ward's *Seaward*, which also claimed first in five races—Vashon Island and its overall, Commodore's, Tri-Island overall, and Tri-Island BB overall. In B class, James G. McCurdy's *Yum Yum* took four firsts—Vashon Island, Frisbie, Hat Island and Little Tri-Island overall. In C class, Norm Cole's *Halavo* did proud work, taking firsts in the Mark Mayer, Vashon Island, Marrowstone Island, Hat Island and Little Tri-Island races. Six-Meter champion was Hans Otto Giese's *Oslo*. Doug Wilson won the overall Frisbie Trophy Race in his PC *Illusion*.

The International Cruiser Trophy from Olympia to Nanaimo, for the second year in a row included a mandatory overnight stop at Reuben Tarte's new Roche Harbor facilities. Winner was Harold D. Fowler's *El Phileen II* of Meydenbauer Bay Yacht Club.

The 1958 Alaska Race, with 13 boats entered, set a record for participation. The race from Prince Rupert to Juneau called for radar in fog-bound Cascade Harbor. As he did in the International, Harold Fowler took the overall trophy.

The Gig Harbor Yacht Club

Gig Harbor Yacht Club, organized in 1957 by 28 original members, presently has a membership of about 180. Approximately 168 of these are boat owners. One unique feature of the club is that spouses of members have the right to vote at the monthly meetings.

The club's first full-term commodore was Walt Williamson; as of 1991, 27 of the club's past commodores are living. GHYC has a new clubhouse located on Stinson Avenue in downtown Gig Harbor.

In addition to monthly cruises, the club annually holds a salmon bake, a newcomers' dance, and a New Year's Eve party. The club also hosts a Special People's Parade and a Merchants' Parade in December, participates in SYC Opening Day activities, and enters a float in the Tacoma Marine Daffodil Parade.

GHYC, a founding member of the Tacoma Area Racing Council, maintains a lively competitive program for sailors, which includes sponsoring the Lemans Race in November, the Islands Race in March, the Spring Regatta, and an in-harbor series on Thursday evenings in May. The club is rebuilding its predicted log racing program and sponsors a race for powerboaters in March.

—Based on materials submitted by Ellie Johnson, Gig Harbor Yacht Club secretary

The "In Memoriam" column was included for the first time in the 1958 yearbook. Members lost during the year:

Thomas Autzen, Arthur L. Bobrick, Lt. Richard H. Boyce, Edward K. Dawson, Hawthorne K. Dent, Harry B. Fay, Mrs. James Griffiths, John L. Holcomb, Mildred Hubbard, Nelson J. Leonard, Carl Marts, Giffort G. Neil, L. R. Phillips, E. S. Ramey, and James S. Scully.

1959

Barnacle Bill Night at the Port Madison clubhouse was a huge success. Cy Cornell added a race and other nautical competitive events for the first time. Doug Sherwood won the single-handed Sea Fever Trophy Race. Ralph Russell of SYC, in his self-built, double-ended steel *Rust Bucket*, showed his stern to Ben Benton and Norm C. Blanchard.

The *Binnacle* carried a "Ladies Only" column that exposed the "Men's Stag Program." A reporter had supposedly investigated the masculine mind—Mentus Americanus—by attending the meeting of the Men's Stag Party Committee. She reported that the program included the following:

8:00 to 9:30 P.M. Tea and crumpets served.
9:30 p.m. Program begins.
1. Colors and dedication—Cub Troop 105
2. Demonstration of Indian Weaving—Brownies' Circle 20
3. Harp Solo—Minerva Broadbilge

The Des Moines Yacht Club

The Des Moines Yacht Club was first registered in 1957 as the Vagabond Outboard Association. The name was changed to the Vagabond Yacht Club in 1963, and in 1970 it became the Des Moines Yacht Club.

Today, club membership stands at 275 active members and 33 life members. These members own 230 boats. The club has no outstations but has moorage reciprocity with 24 yacht clubs between Olympia and Nanaimo. The clubhouse is located within the Des Moines City Marina.

Among the club's special traditions is the South Sound Opening Day in May, usually one week after the Seattle Opening Day. This event started in 1963, the year the Vagabond Outboard Association became the Vagabond Yacht Club.

The DMYC encourages its members to join in work parties at the marine state parks.

Every year on the first Sunday in December the first mates organize a Tom and Jerry party with hors d'oeuvres to thank the outgoing bridge officers and to welcome the new officers. The club also arranges for six dinner dances each year.

Special events include an annual special people's Christmas party, during which the guests are taken out in a parade of boats. While cruising South Sound, each person speaks to Santa by radio. The club also joins in the South Sound Christmas Lights boat parade.

Members of DMYC have always been staunch supporters of Interclub. Warren Elfstrom, 1984 commodore at DMYC, is an Interclub trustee and 1991 Commodore Bernard L. Murray is also an Interclub member.

—Based on material submitted by Commodore Bernard L. Murray

4. Lecture: "The Case Against Sin" by Abigale Hodtree
5. Slide Pictures: "Andean Folk Dances 1807–1809"
6. Community singing.

The notice ended with these words. "Those are the things your husband and loved one will be doing and thinking on the night of November 13. Encourage the poor old guy to go. A little culture won't do him no harm at all." (*Binnacle, 1959*)

A December *Binnacle* article on "Winter Boating" reminded members that weather charts prove Seattle has winter temperatures comparable to El Paso, Texas, much of Arizona, and New Mexico. Many powerboaters went out every weekend all winter long, the article explained. If the predictions were for bad weather, they stayed on the lake, if the

The Tyee Yacht Club

The Tyee yachtsmen organized in 1946. From the outset, women members have had equal rights, possibly because they found they always received an equal share of the work.

For several years, the club existed without a building in which to meet. In 1950, for example, the Commodore's Ball honoring Past Commodore Dr. William L. Thompson and the incoming Commodore J. D. Williamson and their wives, was held at the Forty and Eight Club. The Commodore's Ball of 1956 was at the Norselander.

That same year, the Tyee members remodeled the old steamship *Manitou* to use as a floating clubhouse at 2501 Northlake Way.

In 1953 Tyee began sponsoring the International Cruiser Race. They also feature a Ladies' Day Race each spring which, so the story goes, originated when one member challenged another with the words "My wife can beat your wife." The men may assist in planning this race, but women take over controls and navigation. In 1957 Dorothy Willis of the Rainier Yacht Club in *Pal-O-Mine* won the first women's predicted log race from Eagledale to Poulsbo. By 1962 Tyee women members had won six firsts in the 12 years the race had been run.

In 1957 Tyee Yacht Club sponsored the first annual mid-winter land cruise to the Puget Hotel at Port Gamble, flying club burgees from their auto aerials.

In 1959 because of the low level of Lake Union, the *Manitou* sank at its mooring. By May the members had dedicated a new clubhouse.

In 1968, on the Santa Claus boat, Tyee member Chet Gibson's *Hilma III*, Jack Meyer played Santa, a role he filled for many years. Meyer held membership number one at Tyee and served as commodore in 1953.

Another annual event at Tyee is the exchange cruise with the Portland Tyee Yacht Club. Every other year the Seattle group charters a bus and travels to Portland where their hosts provide boat cruises through local waters. On the other years, the Portlanders come north and are likewise treated to a good time.

Tyee also has a program for junior members, Valentine's parties, and Halloween activities. ◇

Opening Day

Left: "Happy Birthday, U.S.A." was the theme for Opening Day in 1976. Pictured here are Admiral Jerry Caldwell, Vice Admiral Gary Ritner and Admiralette Margie Williams. SYC officers are in the background. (Thurston Lane Collection)

Visiting commodores. (Thurston Lane Collection)

In 1969 the Opening Day theme was "Salute Your Flag." The admiral was Bull Dawson; vice admiral was Phil Tebb and Harriet Vesoja was the admiralette. Visiting commodores are in the background. (Thurston Lane Collection)

Opening Day, 1977. Boats from Royal Vancouver Yacht Club are moored at guest dock. Right, Old Man IV, *13th Naval District Admiral's yacht, sits at the mast hoist pier. (SYC Historical Collection)*

Above: Opening Day, 1967. Jack Allen, admiral; Vern Hammer, vice admiral; Betty Musson, admiralette.
Left: 1977 Opening Day parade judging line in Union Bay.
(Both photos from the SYC Historical Collection)

Doug Wilson's Pacific Class Illusion *(right) in 1959 raced Sunny Vynne's* Risken *in the Commodore's Race. In 1959* Illusion *placed first in the Vashon Island, Hat Island, Little Tri-Island, and Humphrey and Hostetter races and second in the Marrowstone and Quartermaster Harbor races.* Illusion *was built in 1946 at Kettenberg Boat Works, San Diego. The Pacific Class was one of the most active one-design classes on the Pacific Coast. Among former local PC owners one found Commodore Bill Bradshaw, Gov. Dan Evans, David Faires, Charlie Mabee, Bud Peterson, Bill Whipple, Bowen Scarff, James Houston, Peter Schmidt, Dick Gilbert, George Martin, C. Fain Sutter, Harvard Palmer, Glenn Botsford, and Karl Hostetter. (Photo by Don Miller)*

forecast was more encouraging, they headed for outports on Puget Sound. Sailboat racing often continued on the lake through mid-December. But the author advised that rubberized clothing was required; quilting was fine for warmth, but if damp it could be cold and miserable.

The staff at the club in 1959 included William "Willie" Washington, department head over the seven employees in the bar department; Daphne O'Brien, in charge of the dining room department with 14 employees; Head Chef Alfred Eiseman, with 10 employees; Gunnar Algren in maintenance, with eight full- and part-time employees; and Carpenter Herman Borgmaster headed up the repair and construction efforts. In the front office, Mildred Matson directed five employees, and Leonard Slye worked in the printing department.

Powerboat 1959 awards went to, among others, T. Dayton Davies' *Sea Cookie*, winner of the International Everett-to-Vancouver Cruiser Race and the Pacific Motor Boat Trophy; James H. Moffett's *Nelsie*, tops among Interclub Challengers; and George W. Heideman's *Vittoria*, best SYC boat in the Bremerton Heavyweather contest and also recipient of the La Conner Cup. The Rudder Trophy

The Viking Yacht Club of Tacoma

In the summer of 1959 several pleasure boat owners invited those interested in forming a family-oriented boating club to a meeting at the Redondo Marina. Several formative meetings later the Viking Yacht Club was born. Eldred Pilant, who had been the primary mover, was elected the first commodore. Under his leadership, the club developed a solid set of bylaws that have changed little over more than 30 years.

Most of the charter members owned outboard boats from 16 to 22 feet in length. Undoubtedly, most recognized a boater's built-in desire for "just a little more room," a desire also known as "two footitis."

In October 1960, the first monthly newsletter was printed. It is called *The Lur*, the name of the long, flat horn used by the Vikings to call their bands together and to send messages from one group to another.

The Viking Yacht Club members met with the Tacoma Beachcombers, a small boat-oriented group that had the shell of a clubhouse constructed on property owned by Harbor Marina of Tacoma. In 1962 the two groups merged, and the VYC members were able to assume the debts of the Beachcombers and to complete the building.

The club entered a float in the April 1964 Tacoma Marine Daffodil Parade and captured the Sweepstakes Award for best float. In 1965 they repeated the feat. The next year, vying for a record third Sweepstakes Award, the Viking float had to settle for second place. During the next 11 years, the Viking entry was a leading competitor. Then in 1977, with expenses for the float proving too much, the club dropped from the parade.

In 1964 Rear Commodore Ken Wilson, who was chairman of the cruise committee, thought Tacoma should have a Christmas ship to cruise its harbor and nearby communities, decorated like a Christmas tree and playing seasonal music. Invitational letters were sent to local yacht clubs, but none seemed interested. Viking members voted to proceed anyway, and they decorated Don and Dee Bangert's 33-foot *El Dondee* and sailed it around the harbor. For the next 19 Christmas seasons, VYC's Christmas ship traveled various routes and schedules. Not until 1978, after Mayor Mike Parker of Tacoma convinced the Tacoma Yacht Club and the city council to jointly sponsor a Christmas ship parade, did other clubs join in.

The Viking Yacht Club had been a member of the Northwest Boating Council (NBC) for many years, and in 1962 and 1963 the Vikings won the attendance trophy at the annual NBC cruise for having the largest percentage of member-owned boats present. In 1964, at Whitman Cove (now J. F. Kennedy State Marine Park), 43 Viking boats were rafted together right in front of the registration area, and with that win the trophy was theirs permanently.

The 1960s were good years at VYC. An active cruise and social schedule kept members busy every weekend year-round. Members participated in many Puget Sound yachting functions such as Opening Day at Seattle and Des Moines, and at the Shelton Forest Festival, to name a few. During this period, the membership stabilized at around 75 members.

Then came the 1970s, which were "bad years" at VYC. A financial recession caused most yacht clubs to suffer. The energy shortage caused gasoline prices to rise from 35 cents to nearly $2 per gallon; the side effects were felt well into the 1980s. The club membership bottomed out at about 20 families. In November 1976 the club members felt the limited use of the clubhouse did not justify the increasingly high rent. Since then, the club has held meetings in a variety of public and private meeting rooms.

What began as a family club more than 30 years ago, when most members had school-age children, has matured into a group where many have school-age grandchildren. All through these years the Viking Yacht Club has continued to be active in Northwest yachting events.

—Adapted from material supplied by Historian Hazel Doxon

went to Dr. Mike Kennedy's *Neomar*; the Pacific Marine Supply Trophy to Chester Green's *Bendora*; and the Masthead Trophy to Harold Hovland's *Sea Breu*.

Top sail craft: in AA class, George Olsen's *Wild Goose*, which took three firsts; in A class, T. Harbine Monroe's *Nautilus IV* captured a first plus a pair of seconds and a pair of thirds. In BB races, Byron Ward's *Seaward* came in first six times, twice second and third once and won the Mark Mayer Perpetual Trophy. The *Alarm* (Six-Meter), owned by Kiefer Fobes, H. McGuane, and W. Teeter took four firsts, a second and a third, and Phil Spaulding's *Ylliam VIII* took home three first-place awards, including the Frisbie

The Robert Condons sailing their 41-foot auxiliary yawl Valkyrie *during the 1950s. (Cora Condon Collection)*

The SYC Admiralettes

The title of "Admiralette" was given to the newly created position of hostess for the 1959 SYC Opening Day festivities. According to Virginia Cluck, the second admiralette, the tradition was initiated by the Opening Day Admiral Jim Stirrat and Vice Admiral Jim Bryant, who suggested the club add some glamour to the admiralty by appointing a woman to serve during the biggest SYC event of the year. They asked a popular member of the SYC Women's Group—Jean Harthorn—if she would do the honors.

The following year Harthorn and the president of the SYC Women's Group asked Virginia Cluck to serve.

Each year the Women's Group sponsors a luncheon in honor of the Opening Day officers. Before an admiralette was added, the luncheons honored the admirals.

As hostess for the club, the admiralette promotes the Opening Day events, invites the participation of women from all area clubs, greets guests, and attends all social functions related to Opening Day.

Jean Harthorn enjoyed her experiences, and the new position and title received an enthusiastic acceptance from the club. Over time the job description has expanded. Beginning in 1960, the commandant of the Sand Point Naval Air Station invited the past admiralettes and admirals to be his guests aboard the "crash boat" for the Opening Day parade. This was continued until 1990 when a change in naval operations prevented use of the craft. Since then, private boats have been made available to the officers.

An admiralette of the 1990s will find herself co-chairman of and responsible for one-third of the Opening Day committee activities. She can expect to be asked to share the workload and leadership with the admiral and vice admiral and to help coordinate the work of 30 sub-committees and scores of member volunteers.

Throughout the year, she participates in promotional events, speaks before many groups, and attends many community social affairs leading up to the grand finale during which she reviews the boat parade aboard a designated vessel.

The admiralette must be a member in good standing of the SYC Women's Group, demonstrate leadership qualities, and have served as chairman of activities for both the SYC Women's Group and the Seattle Yacht Club. Personal qualities and abilities

and Commodore's trophies. Douglas Wilson's PC class *Illusion* was a winner five times, came in second once, and was awarded both the Humphrey and the Hostetter trophies. In Z class, the *Thunderbird* of J. McKenzie was almost unbeatable, arriving first five times.

Six hydroplanes flew the SYC burgee in 1959—*Miss Seattle*, *Miss Seattle Too*, *Miss Wahoo*, *Hawaii Kai*, *Miss Thriftway*, and *Miss Thriftway Too*—but none won a major race.

In Memoriam 1959: Ray C. Anderson, Elmer O. Beardsley, Frank Calvert, Latham Goble, Howard R. Henderson, Richard W. Jones, Lawrence J. Jurick, A. W. Leonard, Ben C. Seaborn, Dwight Ware, and Dr. J. N. Wilkinson.

The latter years of the 1950s were peaceful and financially rewarding ones for Americans in general and the Seattle Yacht Club in particular. It was a decade of rejuvenation and of change. Under the leadership of Commodore Philip Smith, the "good old boys" yacht club became a family boating club. Potlatch was initiated at Port Madison. A new format was adopted for Opening Day. The Northwest was enchanted with hydroplane racing, and the SYC sponsorship brought the club worldwide recognition. Many new members were added, and the club demonstrated much vitality all through this decade. ☆

SYC Admiralettes (front row, from left): Betty Chang, Sally Laura, Barbara Leslie, Audrey Salkield, Virginia Cluck, and Molly Cadranell; (middle) Pam Thurman, Margaret Botsford, Barbara Benton, and Harriet Ford; (back) Joy McDonald, Michele Shaw, Linda Blondin, Diane Sweezey, Diane Benson, Betty Stewart, Diane Hagen, and Betty Bostick. (SYC Women's Group Collection)

are a consideration, as well. She serves as co-chairman of the Opening Day committee and is spokesperson and in charge of elections and social engagements the following year for all past admiralettes.

The admiralette is elected in May by a majority vote of past admiralettes who are members of the SYC Women's Group. It is a closed meeting and is attended by the president of the SYC Women's Group, who serves in an advisory capacity. Suggestions for candidates come from past admiralettes and from the women's group membership. All submitted names are given consideration.

The admiral and vice admiral wear nineteenth century–style uniforms complete with cocked hat, admiral's boards with fringe, brass buttons, and gold braid. The admiralette wears white skirt, shoes, gloves, a hat adorned with a fine feathered plume, and a fitted navy blue waistcoat with brass buttons and sleeves decorated with bands of gold braid.

There have been 33 admiralettes since 1959. All are listed among club officers and committee chairmen in the appendix.

—Based on material provided by Ann F. Bayless

In this Joseph Scaylea photo from the 1962 CYC Windjammer Series, the three closest boats have been identified as (from left) Windward, *belonging to John W. Ellis, CYC; K-38,* Excalibur *of Westin B. Albiston, SYC; and the* Meteora *of Donald L. Thompson, SYC. (Photo by Joseph Scaylea)*

EIGHT

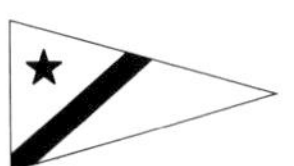

The 1960s

The 1960s brought social unrest and rapid change to America. At the outset of the decade, black Americans and their supporters were demanding equality via sit-ins, boycotts, and riots. The volatile atmosphere permeated most large cities.

These societal pressures affected all organizations. For example, the state of Washington license allowing liquor to be served in private clubs could be rescinded if race or religion were used as a membership screening device. Also, ecological concerns became major factors in acquiring building permits. Many young people "opted out" of what they considered a greedy society. By the end of the decade, anti-Vietnam War activists were attracting large numbers of followers and demonstrations were common occurrences.

Following the Soviet Union's success in placing *Sputnik* in orbit, the 1960s brought increased interest in science and space exploration. The 1962 Seattle World's Fair, with its Space Needle and scientific exhibits, highlighted the importance of science.

At the 1968 Olympic Games in Mexico the United States won gold medals in Star and Dragon class yacht racing. The next year, the short-lived "Boeing Recession" hit the Northwest, following cancellation of federal contracts for Boeing work on the C5A and SST. During the 1960s the Seattle Yacht Club continued to develop as a family organization and its membership began to reflect the changing society around it.

Throughout the 1960s, *Binnacle* editor Frank E. "Jimmy" James was aided by several columnists. Robert E. Street wrote a series on club trophies, Serge Becker described activities in what he called "The Starting Line," and Harriet Vesoja (now Ford) introduced new members. Katherine Rau wrote "The Captain's Lady," a column in which she discussed items of interest to women, while Vi

The annual Potlatch at Port Madison provides play for persons of all ages. Here the younger set demonstrates rowing skills in a race under the pier. (SYC Historical Collection)

Banner Corlis, Judy Brighton and others prepared a column headed "Women."

1960

Early in the year a picnic area, barbecue, and large play field were added to SYC's facilities at Port Madison.

Howard Richmond served as president of an organization of past Pacific Northwest yacht club commodores. Their annual stag party at the Rainier Yacht Club attracted more than 120 former commodores.

The yacht *Sueja III*, so familiar to SYC members when it was owned by Capt. James Griffiths, ran onto a reef near the Bermuda Islands while under English registry. It was repaired and as of this writing, is still in service.

In Northwest waters, Harold Fowler of Bellevue, a most careful and competent SYC member, lost his boat to fire and explosion off the west coast of Vancouver Island. No one was injured.

Permission was received in September from the federal government for SYC to fill in approximately 25,000 square feet of wetlands south of the clubhouse as a site for badly needed parking space. Chet Adair successfully arranged for this land to be leased from the state and Jim McCurdy worked to secure a permit from the U.S. Army Corps of Engineers. John Graham and Company produced plans. The canoe shed was relocated, and Butler Construction built a parking lot to hold 85 cars.

Commodore M. Phil Butler reported

that the club was considering installation of a swimming pool and enlargement of the galley and dining room. The swimming pool idea was soon dropped.

SYC entrance fees were increased on Aug. 1, 1960:

	From:	To:
Active (Boat owner, 30 years or older, voting)	$150	$250
Associate (Non-boat owner, 30 or older, non-voting)	75	150
Non-Resident (in state, not in King County)	75	100
Intermediate Active (21 to 30 years, voting)	37.50	50
Junior (12 to 21 years, non-voting)	5	25

At the annual meeting in October, an assessment of $4 a month for active and associate members and $2 a month for intermediate-active members was approved. This assessment, which became known as the Graham fund, provides income for the purchase of additional outstations. Commodore Butler reported membership had increased by 80 during the year to 1,480. The piers had been improved at a cost of $9,000. The club was solvent with $45,000 in the bank, an amount said to be needed to purchase the wetlands property south of the clubhouse for additional parking.

The Women's Group at their yuletide luncheon invited past presidents Ruth Harlan, Hazel Bloss, Anne Foster, Jo Gibson, Norma Russell, and Margaret Marlatt. The traditional wassail bowl provided by the commodore was enjoyed by all at the social hour prior to the luncheon.

The Norpac Race from Astoria to Port Angeles resulted in another trophy for *Sea Fever*, owned by Otis Lamson, Dick Philbrick, and Bob Coe.

The Swiftsure trophies awarded on November 17 went to: Jack Graham (*Maruffa*) for finishing first, to Otis Lamson (*Sea Fever*) for first in AA class; two awards were given to David E. Skinner's *Kate II* for first in Class A and overall handicap.

Sucia Island

Thanks to the members of the various yacht clubs making up the Interclub Boating Association of Washington, Sucia Island is preserved as a marine park.

"Sucia," the island paradise that Puget Sound boating people bought without the aid of governmental funds, will be publicly turned over to the Washington State Department of Parks on Sunday, May 29, 1960, at 2:00 p.m. in ceremonies at one of this island's major harbors—Fossil Bay.

The donor of Sucia Island is the Puget Sound Interclub Association, a service group of 42 Washington State boating organizations.

It has been a refreshing acquisition of a recreational playground. In an age when public bodies at all levels are besieged with requests for funds to buy lands, build roads, improve parks, and other worthy-enough projects, this group of Northwest boating people is probably the only group in the country today which decisively walked out, signed sizable notes to insure a major purchase, raised the funds from its own, then turned the island over to the state to maintain as a boating playground forever. It has been a monumental five-year effort.

Sucia Island is one of the most beautiful of the 174 islands in the San Juan Archipelago. Comprising 362 acres of land, it is directly north of Orcas Island. It is not as large in land-area as the other major islands, but is an ideal marine park with extensive water boundaries, four harbors, many beaches and other tiny islands and indentations.

—Binnacle, *June 1960*

The Tri-Island winners were AA class *Aurora* (John Schlagel), A class *We're Here* (Dr. R. Smith), and BB class *Seaward* (Dr. Byron Ward).

The SYC yearbook listed the following trophy and award winners for 1960. Winners are SYC members unless otherwise noted.

Mark Mayer Trophy: *Calypso* (Henry Garrigues); Mayer Cup: first, *Khorasan* (Robert Sylvester); second, *Yum Yum II* (Jim McCurdy); third, *Serene* (Bob Bollong); Gardner Gamwell Trophy: *Halavo* (Norm Cole); Humphrey and Hostetter trophies: *Pompero* (Bill Bradshaw and Bud Peterson); Frisbie Trophy: *Zingara* (Bob Cadranell); Commodore's Trophy: *Calypso* (Dr. Garrigues); Osprey Single-Handed Trophy: *Killy Bogus* (Ralph Russell)

Consistent winners: four firsts, *We're Here* (Dr. C. Robert Smith); five firsts, *Seaward* (Dr. Byron Ward); six firsts, *Calypso* (Henry Garrigues); three firsts, *Jaunty* (S. Thordarson, TYC); four firsts, *Risken* (Vynne/Perry, CYC); other firsts, *Halavo* (Norm Cole), *Blue Jacket* (Jack Lidral), *Saga* (Kirk Hull, TYC), *Pinta* (T. Bushnell)

The International Cruiser Award: *Paramour* (Phil Butler); Capital-to-Capital Race: *Jadon* (Jack Rottler); SYC Lake Washington Predicted Log Race and Rudder Trophy: *Cheri* (Mid Chism); Pacific Motor Boat and La Conner Cup trophies: *Sea Breu* (Harold

The Fircrest Yacht Club

In October 1961 boating enthusiasts from the town of Fircrest organized a boating club. In December officers were elected, and by March 1962 "The Fircrest Boating Club" was incorporated. In 1969 the name was changed to Fircrest Yacht Club. At that time the club entered into an agreement with the Narrows Marina to provide guest moorage for members of visiting yacht clubs and provide certain advantages in acquiring permanent moorage for members. This has long since changed, and FYC boats now moor all over Puget Sound.

The purpose of the Fircrest Yacht Club is to stimulate boating interest, courtesy, safety, education, and unified family fun and adventure.

Membership in the club is a family affair. Husbands and wives share equally in the meetings, business, and committees, and have individual votes.

A full schedule of activities is enjoyed by a very active membership. For the past several years members have participated in the clean-up of Blake Island, taking Boy Scouts along to help. By doing so, the scouts earn an historical trails badge and help make one of the special Puget Sound boating parks a cleaner place for all to enjoy.

Fircrest Yacht Club has participated in the Daffodil Marine Parade since its inception and has been awarded several trophies in different categories over the years.

For the past several years, Fircrest members made and sold Christmas candy rings as a main source of club income; the family activity has become a tradition in the Pierce County area.

As of June 1991 FYC has 36 members and 14 boats. They have no specific water moorage but are very active in all areas of boating on Puget Sound.

The Fircrest Yacht Club meets on the third Tuesday of each month at 8:00 P.M. in the Fircrest Community Building. ◇

Hovland); Masthead Trophy: Fred Peterson on Jim Moffett's *Nelsie*.

Charles A. Sparling of Meydenbauer Bay Yacht Club and his boat *Saga* won the overall trophy in the International Cruiser Race from Port Madison to Ladysmith. The race to Juneau resulted in Arthur Church, aboard his 75-foot former Coast Guard boat *Twanoh*, capturing overall honors for the Rainier Yacht Club.

Seattle Yacht Club members accumulated 100 points to win the Interclub Challenge Race for the second year in a row. The Bremerton Yacht Club was second, just 10 points behind.

In Memoriam, 1960: Edward Cunningham, Frank Dupar, Sr., Lou Fageol, Mrs. Miller (Betsy) Freeman, W. L. Gazzam, L. E. (Ted) Geary, Dr. John Wayne Graham, R. M. Hardy, Carl Haubrock, Glenn C. Lazar, C. W. Maryatt, and Mrs. Clifford Mooers.

1961

In March, after serving 14 years as the amiable head maintenance man at the club, Gunnar Algren retired.

The year 1961 brought some unusual cruising restrictions. In the January *Binnacle*, mariners were advised that work was progressing on the I-5 freeway bridge over the ship canal. Progress was from each shore toward the center, and large barges were anchored at the construction sites. Mariners in the vicinity were urged to use extreme caution. In anticipation of the Evergreen Point Bridge construction, the Opening Day parade route was shortened to extend only to Webster Point rather than to Madison Park as before. The Coast Guard warned in August that construction of the Hood Canal Floating Bridge had resulted in an anchor cable being laid across the navigable channel on the centerline of the bridge.

The U.S. Navy in 1961 asked pleasure craft owners to realize that Dabob Bay was unique in that it contained the only essentially landlocked deep sea water within the lower 48 states. The navy had installed more than $1 million worth

The Elk Yacht Club

The Elk Yacht Club was organized in 1961 and incorporated in March 1962. Membership was open to any member in good standing of Elk Lodge 92. A women's auxiliary, the "Elkettes," was formed in May 1964.

In 1968 the bylaws were revised to open eligibility to any Elk in good standing, which greatly expanded the membership. In 1991 there were 88 members of the Elk Yacht Club and a total of 64 boats in the fleet.

The outstation at Hat (Gedney) Island was purchased in 1969 and is the location for many club activities. The Elk Yacht Club observes Opening Day with a gathering for dinner, following the parade. The annual Commodore's Ball is held in November and all 28 reciprocal club officers are invited to attend.

There are generally nine club cruises during the year. Many club boats participate in the Christmas Parade and the Special People's Christmas Cruise. Other activities include the annual Christmas party, past commanderette luncheon, golf tournament, and crab feed. ◇

of underwater instrumentation on the bottom of the bay to test its deep water torpedoes. Because a boat propeller could distort data gathered by the acoustical tracking equipment, whenever the navy's red warning lights installed along the test indicated a torpedo test was underway, all boats in the vicinity were to stop.

The popular measured mile course marked on the Mercer Island Floating Bridge was reduced to one-half nautical mile at center bridge after shoreside residents complained that wakes of speeding boats testing the mile course were eroding the shoreline.

Member Bob Graham warned that yachtsmen should be prepared to write to their legislators to counter a move calling for a state excise tax on pleasure craft.

Mr. and Mrs. Dick Hoyt, properly attired in coonskin coat and flapper dress, posed in a vintage auto to help promote the Roaring Twenties Party scheduled at the club for September 29. Throughout 1961 family activities were increasingly popular at SYC. For example, sailing classes for women were in great demand. Jim Coon was the instructor. Other classes at the club included boys' boxing, macrame, bridge, and instruction in Latin American and ballroom dancing taught by Marge and Ross Werner. Informal modeling of holiday fashions graced the dining room on Sunday and Thursday evenings in December.

On a memorable evening at the club, Charlie Frisbie and Ronald Ramsey regaled members with reminiscences of their recent voyage to Europe on the *Alatola* and of their exploration of the Mediterranean Sea on the way home.

The February 5 predicted log race on Lake Washington resulted in four boats finishing with less than one percentage error: Jim Moffett in *Nelsie* (0.28), Dr. Carlton Powers in *Nautilus* (0.39), Charlie Erickson in *Manna* (0.69) and Fred Peterson in *Molly Shannon* (0.74).

At Opening Day ceremonies on April 29, 20 visiting commodores stood at attention as their club burgees were raised. More than 800 boats paraded in review while another 200 stood by loaded with spectators. Commodore Butler's *Paramour* proudly displayed Charlie Schaak at the bow and a full-throated pump organ astern. Arthur Ayers' *Barbara Lee* was selected as the best-dressed powerboat and John Ford's *Watauga* as best-dressed sailboat. Among notables enjoying SYC hospitality on Opening Day were Gov. Albert D. Rosellini, Rear Admirals William A. Dolan, G. C. Towner and Allen Winbeck, Col. R. P. Young, City Councilwoman Mrs. Harlin Edwards, and Police Chief Frank Ramon.

The SYC yearbook listed the following trophies and award winners for 1961.

Mark Mayer Trophy: *Kate II* (Ned Skinner); Mark Mayer Cup: first, *Interlude* (L. Mercille); second, *Khorasan* (R. Sylvester); third, *Serene* (D. Bollong)

Tri-Island Race: AA class, *Sulaire* (K. Furnell); A class, *We're Here* (Dr. Robert Smith); BB class and Tri-Island Overall Trophy, *Calypso* (Dr. Henry Garrigues)

Humphrey and Hostetter trophies: *Easy* (Dick Gilbert); Ben Seaborn Trophy: *Shadow* (Stefan Thordarson); Gamwell Trophy and Osprey Single-Handed Trophy: *Osprey* (Ben Benton); Commodore's Trophy: *Shamrock* (Bob Lamson); Frisbie Trophy: *Bobtail* (Bob Allen); Captain Hoyt Trophy: *Falcon* (Henry Kamstra); Sea Fever Single-Handed Trophy: *Rebel* (Doug Sherwood)

Also in 1961 a new award to further ocean sailing was announced: the Haida North Pacific Sailing Trophy. It was donated by Jack Graham, Philip D. Graham, Henry Kotkins, Otis F. Lamson, Jr., John L. Locke, Norm McCarvill, Max H. Wyman, Cranston P. Paschall, Dr. Richard Philbrick, and John A. Soderberg. The initial race was sponsored by the Corinthian

Yacht Club in 1960 from Astoria to Port Angeles and was won by *Sea Fever*, owned by Dr. Dick Philbrick, Dr. Bob Coe, and Otis Lamson, Jr. (The Seattle Yacht Club was planning to sponsor the next race from San Francisco to Seattle as part of the World's Fair festivities.)

On award's night, Bill Buchan, Jr., and Doug Knight were honored for winning the World's Star Championship.

During 1961 Dr. Garrigues' *Calypso* and K. Furnell's *Sulaire* each finished first in seven races.

In the International Cruiser Race from Seattle to Vancouver, Joe A. Park of Meydenbauer Yacht Club in *Potlatch* was tops in overall performance.

The Rudder Trophy was awarded Jim Moffett's powerboat *Nelsie*, the Pacific Motor Boat Trophy to Richard Shorett's *Nelsonia*, and the La Conner Cup went to Dr. Carlton Powers' *Nautilus*.

The Shilshole Bay Yacht Club

The Shilshole Bay Yacht Club was formed in September 1961 as a recreation-oriented boating organization with an emphasis on member participation and informality. A. W. (Monty) Morton, a principal founder, was the first commodore. He owned the 101-foot *Adventuress*, which is now used by one of the local youth groups.

The first meetings of the club were scheduled in the Port Authority Administration Building at Shilshole Bay, but these quarters were soon outgrown so the meetings were moved to local restaurants. Sufficient reserves were accumulated in 1965 for the club to purchase the *Chimacum*, a retired ferry-freighter that was moored at J Dock and used as a meeting place. However, maintenance and moorage became increasingly costly, and the club sold the *Chimacum* for $1 in 1977, and it was towed to La Conner.

The club moved its sessions to a large meeting room in the Shilshole Bay Marina's administration building, but again, with membership doubling to 100, this facility was too small, and the club transferred sessions to the Seafair Room, largest space in the port building. When these restaurant facilities were sold in 1979, SBYC negotiated to continue holding dinner meetings in the Seafair Room.

In the early 1980s, the club's number of racing enthusiasts increased to include nearly half the 160 members and the first official race instruction booklet was published. A Tuesday night series, the Jack-'n-Jills and the Snowbird Race series became traditional. In 1982, the club sponsored its first Trans-Puget Classic Open Race for PHRF boats. Five years later this race was recognized as a qualifier for the Grand Prix. The club's cruising program expanded, too, with cruises scheduled for virtually every month of the year.

A junior program was established in 1981. In 1982 and 1984, during some of their first major efforts, the young people won second-place trophies for decorated theme boats in Seattle Yacht Club's Opening Day parade. In 1985 they took first place in the junior division.

In 1986 the club celebrated its 25th anniversary with a dinner cruise on Elliott Bay aboard the chartered *Sightseer*.

In 1987 the Shilshole Bay Yacht Club installed its first woman commodore—Ms. Peggy Willis. The year 1988 witnessed some outstanding cruises: The Kingston Valentine Cruise, Port Ludlow in May, Poulsbo for the June Dinner Dance, and Port Orchard. That year the club recaptured the Port Madison Challenge Cup.

Activities multiply as the years go by, and membership at the Shilshole Bay Yacht Club continues to increase.

—Based on material provided by former
Shilshoe Bay Yacht Club Commodore
David Bordewick

SYC Sailing Yachts Active in the 1950s and 1960s

Gracie S *(named for Gracie Spreckles), owned by Ed Kennell, is shown here on the Strait of Juan de Fuca, c. 1955. (Photo by Ken Ollar)*

The Kate II *was designed by Ben Seaborn for Keith Fisken and later owned by Ned Skinner. (Photo by Ken Ollar)*

The African Star *was built by Schmidt Marine Construction and Design for Rupert Broom and later owned by Doug Fryer. (Photo by Ken Ollar)*

The Helene *was designed by Ben Seaborn and built by Vic Franck for Rod Scheuman who named it for his wife. It was later owned by Rod's son Dick. (Photo by Ken Ollar)*

In Memoriam, 1961: Elmer O. Beardsley, Thomas L. Bushnell, Fred Huey, Robert Landweer, Lee Moran, J. Lenhart Reese, and James Spinner.

1962

SYC Commodore John Ford announced a $172,000 remodeling of the club that included enlarging the kitchen and dining room and building an entrance from the new south parking lot to the lower floor. This expansion, the largest in club history, was made possible by moving the south wall of the clubhouse out 10 feet and extending the dining room west wall to take over the former Sun Room.

Commodore Ford explained to the members in July that Docks 2, 3, and 4 were affected by the state's recent platting of wetlands under the waters of Lake Union and Portage Bay. He reported that "Years ago these docks were built with permission of the U.S. [Army Corps of] Engineers. The platting makes these areas state lands and the parks department of our city has preference to buy them at the amount of the state's appraisal." The commodore named Bob Graham, Chet Adair, and others to negotiate with the city council.

The SEABACS Boat Club

The SEABACS Boat Club was founded in 1961 as a Boeing-sponsored recreational club with membership available to Boeing Company employees and retirees. Now, 30 years later, the club conducts many organized activities that are enjoyed by a very active membership of more than 100 members. Activities are scheduled for both power and sailing members. The club motto, "SEABACS have more fun," proclaims a love of boating.

Old-time traditional activities such as the annual Commodore's Ball, South Sound Opening Day, and New Year's Eve party remain SEABACS favorites. Among the more recent traditions providing us with enjoyment and interesting cruises are the Blake Island Work Party, scavenger hunts, dinghy rafts, the First Mates' Cruise, and the Christmas Parade.

The members support many community events, especially during the Christmas season, with food donations and stuffed animal parties, and they join fellow clubs for lighted and decorated boat parades. SEABACS maintain memberships in The Interclub Boating Association, the Northwest Boating Council and the Princess Louisa Society.

Each year SEABACS members plan and organize a schedule of more than 25 cruises and events, beginning in February with a Sweetheart Cruise and culminating in a New Year's Eve party on the water. Parties, potlucks, dances, raffles, auctions, and contests add fun to club gatherings and strengthen friendships. Summer and vacation time bring long cruises and rendezvous in distant San Juan and Canadian waters. The club's friendship is extended to all fellow boaters, whether their craft is a runabout, a fish boat, a fine yacht, a dinghy, or just a fond dream for the future.

—Based on material provided by SEABACS Boat Club Publicity Chairman Edd Lahar

The Women's Interclub Council met for their January meeting at the Seattle Yacht Club. The luncheon program featured guest speaker British Consul-General Geoffrey Jackson, who spoke about Queen Elizabeth. Included at the head table was the wife of the speaker, Mrs. Jackson, and the president of the host club women's group, Mrs. Richard C. Hooper. Program chairman for the event was Mrs. Charles E. Erickson.

Seattleites were busy in 1962. The biggest headlines were awarded Seattle Century 21 World's Fair, although the Evergreen Point Floating Bridge approach, then being constructed in the Yacht Club's back yard, received its share of attention. The bridge, completed in 1963, disrupted the major boat routes on Lake Washington. This, combined with the opening of the Shilshole Marina, resulted in many members moving their yachts to Shilshole, leaving numerous vacancies in the Portage Bay moorage. Not until former city councilman Ray Eckman obtained permission to cover most of the slips did the Portage Bay moorage fill again.

When the National Conference of the Coast Guard Auxiliary attracted about 600 visitors to Seattle during the first week in May, club members provided courtesy cruises. On May 24, Rear Admiral Willard J. Smith, superintendent of the Coast Guard Academy at New London, Connecticut, visited SYC and presented certificates to young persons who had finished the basic seamanship course.

During the year, Dave Buttles of SYC traveled to Australia where he viewed the Aussies' America's Cup *Challenger* under construction.

At a November 15 theater party, honored guests Dr. and Mrs. Henry Schmitz accompanied other members to the opening performance of *Little Mary Sunshine* at the renovated Showboat Theater at the University of Washington. Price, including dinner, was $5 per person.

Membership Rates in 1962:

	Entrance Fee	**Dues/ month**
Active (Boat owner, 30 years or older)	$300	$10.80
Associate (Non-boat owner, 30 years or older)	180	9.60
Intermediate (21 to 30 years)	60	4.20
Junior (12 to 21 years)	6	1.50

Opening Day, May 5, found Boris Korry's *Borealis* (power), D. E. Skinner's *Kate II* (sail), and Chet Green's *Bendora* (novelty) to be best-dressed.

By virtue of two firsts, two seconds, and a third, Paul Morris, running his *Skipalong* in all five races counting toward the "Overall Skipper of the Year Award," amassed 1,503 points out of a possible 1,550 to put the SYC on the predicted log map. Second and third standings also went to SYC members: Merne Dougherty, skipper of *Another World*, and Jim Moffett, skipper of *Nelsie*.

Bill Buchan, Jr. added to his World's Star Championship in 1962 by winning the North American Championship, which was staged by the Puget Sound fleet with the assistance of the Seattle and Corinthian yacht clubs.

Dwight and Michele Shaw were the only mainland sailors to place in the Hawaiian International 110 Class Regatta, and they took first. The International Powerboat Race from Victoria to Seattle resulted in another overall win for SYC's Dr. A. J. Bowles in his *Aldon*. The La Conner Cup went to Paul Morris' *Skipalong*, which also won the Interclub Challenge Race.

The SYC yearbook listed the following trophies and award winners for 1962.

Mark Mayer Trophy: *Thetis* (Robert Regan); Mark Mayer Cup: *Meteora* (Don Thompson); Tri-Island Race: AA class, *Sulaire* (E. H. [Ted] Halton); PAA class,

We're Here (Dr. Robert Smith); B class and Overall Tri-Island Trophy, *Seaward* (Dr. Byron Ward)

Humphrey and Hostetter trophies: *Easy* (Dick Gilbert); Seaborn Trophy: *Bobtail* (R. F. Allen); Gardner Gamwell Trophy: *Svanten* (Fred Plum); Commodore's Trophy: *Risken* (Sunny Vynne); Frisbie and Osprey Single-Handed trophies: *Blue Jacket* (Jack Lidral); Sea Fever Single-Handed Trophy: *Falcon* (Stan Martin)

Winners of four or more races in 1962: Z class, *Bobtail* (R. F. Allen); BB class *Thetis* (R. Regan); AA class, *Sulaire* (E. Halton); B class, *Cirrus* (R. B. Gregory)

In Memoriam, 1962: Robert J. Acheson, Dr. E. F. S. Chambers, Mary DeVries Earthy, Dick Eisinga, Allen B. Engle, Paul C. Harper, Theron H. Hawkes, Sr., Tony Jensen, Captain Fred E. Lewis, John Mauk, Mrs. L. R. Phillips, Paul J. Pigott, John N. Ritter, H. D. Sargent, William Waggoner, and Ross Wood.

1963

During the year that Dr. Carlton J. Powers was SYC Commodore, the new moorage covers were installed over Piers 1, 3, and 4, and enlargement and modernization of the Portage Bay clubhouse was completed. By June members were utilizing their larger quarters. The *Post-Intelligencer* carried an interesting article about a bit of this additional space.

> There are 1,500 active and junior *male* members of the Seattle Yacht Club, but it took one persevering, enterprising woman with a Texas drawl to guarantee a sundeck for the club's new $200,000 addition.
>
> Mrs. Ernest Cluck was not about to take "no" for an answer. Members had been told that a deck above the new dining room was impossible; Ginny Cluck didn't think so.
>
> She trekked down to the city building superintendent's office, and as a result of her efforts, Seattle Yacht Club members have a new sundeck overlooking their moorage; it's appropriately called "Ginny's Poopdeck."
>
> Today the members will view their new facilities during a "Sundown Cruise."
>
> Of most interest is the new dining room, the first major addition to the building since it was built in 1920. Other new facilities include the sundeck, small private dining room, and a well-equipped galley.
>
> —Post-Intelligencer, *(undated clipping)*

Two German frigates arrived on April 11 for a four-day stay in Seattle. Aboard were 80 cadets from the West German Naval Academy. The Seattle Chamber of Commerce asked that the yacht club's powerboat committee arrange for short rides for the visitors.

The *Binnacle* carried this definition of a commodore, a contribution of Bruce Calhoun who borrowed it from the Royal Vic's *Main Sheet.*

> A commodore is a cross between a humidor and a matador. He has to be kept damp like a humidor and bullthrowing like a matador. Being a commodore entitles you to wear a motorman's coat, white duck pants, and a cap with a monogram, wreaths, and flags on it. In most clubs, a commodore's boat must draw at least seven feet of water, and the commodore must draw at least six feet of gin.
>
> —Binnacle, *June 1963*

The fall activities at SYC included a luncheon before the Kansas City Chiefs–Oakland Raiders football exhibition game at the University of Washington stadium. Bridge and dancing classes were also planned.

In December the members were invited to a club showing of a NASA movie of the recent John Glenn journey around the world in a space capsule.

The junior racers, according to the February 1963 *Binnacle*, brought home the Clark Gibson Trophy from the annual Winter Regatta in Vancouver. Bill Nicolai, John Goodrich, and Eric Swanson participated with Gary and Rae Ellen Syverson as coaches. John Goodrich reported that weather conditions were miserable but there was a fine wind.

The February 10 SYC Predicted Log Race on Lake Washington and the Bremerton Heavy Weather Race both ended with the *Nelsie*, owned by SYC's Jim Moffett, in first place. The IPBA In-

Commodores of the Seattle Yacht Club—1960s

M. PHIL BUTLER
1960 and 1961
Born: 1899, Indianapolis, Ind.
Education: University of Washington
Occupation: Contractor (M. P. Butler Construction)
Boats: Paramour, Hyades III, Phil's Folly

JOHN FORD
1962
Born: 1910, Denver, Colo.
Education: Denver Art Student's League
Occupation: Epcon Company, Electromatic Corp.
Boats: Jakie, Watauga, Jake

DR. CARLTON J. POWERS
1963
Born: 1898, Marshall, Mich.
Education: University of Michigan
Occupation: Dentist
Boats: Nautilus, Nautilus II

DON H. AMICK
1964
Born: 1913, Seattle, Wash.
Occupation: self-employed (Amick Metal Fabricators)
Boats: 38-foot Hattaras Cruiser and five others

HAROLD HOVLAND
1965
Born: 1904, Colsax, Wisc.
Education: University of Washington
Occupation: self-employed (Industrial X-Ray)
Boats: Gala II *(owned nine boats through the years).*

BEN BENTON
1966
Born: 1921, Seattle, Wash.
Education: University of Washington
Occupation: Jeweler
Boats: Owned a flattie, a lightning, a Blanchard, two different Ospreys *and a cruiser* Otter.

FREDERICK C. PETERSON
1967
Born: 1909, Hoquiam, Wash.
Education: University of Washington Law School
Occupation: Lawyer
Boat: Molly Shannon *(38-foot powerboat)*

CHESTER (CHET) C. ADAIR
1968
Born: 1907, Seattle, Wash.
Education: University of Washington Law School
Occupation: Lawyer
Boats: Ichiban *(28-foot ketch)*

WALLACE (WALLY) L. OVENS
1969
Born: 1899, Seattle, Wash.
Occupation: X-Ray Sales (Western X-Ray)
Boats: Islander *(42-foot Monk/Jensen)*

ternational Race, from Keyport to Vancouver, found W. E. Fowler of Burrard Yacht Club in his *Kedaro* with best overall score. The SYC powerboats retained the Meydenbauer Bay Yacht Club Boomerang Log Race Trophy with the four best boats in the race of May 25. They were *Another World* (Merne Dougherty), *All Dunn IV* (Frank Dunn), *Skipalong* (Paul Morris), and *Lauren J.* (Fred Haight).

The Royal Vancouver Club hosted the PIYA Regatta on English Bay. Many a Seattleite shared in the glory of winning, including Henry Kotkins, Sunny Vynne, Bob Regan, Bob Sylvester, Jack Lidral, Ray Cooke, Sandy Prentice, Bob Cadranell, and Ted Watkins. In the small boat series, 102 craft participated in nine classes. Only Ed Cotter in a Cougar catamaran brought home a small boat trophy for SYC.

The Tri-Island awards went to *Diamond Head* (Henry Kotkins) in AA class, and *Falcon* (Henry Kamstra) in B. *Falcon*, which placed in 10 races, was named sailing yacht of the year.

The SYC yearbook listed the following trophies and award winners for 1963.

> Outstanding sailboats: Lightning, *Black Magic* (Don Clark); OK Dinghy, *Turmoil* (Al Vandevanter); BB class, *Stormy Weather* (Govnor Teats, TYC); B class, *Mistral* (J. C. Baillargeon, Jr.); C class, *Blue Jacket* (John Lidral); Thunderbird, *Frappe* (George Valentine); PC class, *Canto* (Pete Eising); Blanchard with Spinnaker, *Raven* (Carl Doherty); Blanchard Without Spinnaker, *Verada* (Frank Francisco); Six-Meter, *Risken* (Sunny Vynne); Y class, *Shamrock* (Bob Lamson); International 110, *Bobtail* (Bob Allen) and *Skatt* (Al and Dana Voorhees)
>
> Ole Bardahl's *Miss Bardahl*, driven by Ron Musson, captured the 1963 Gold Cup Race in Detroit while flying the SYC burgee, bringing that national contest to Seattle the following year.

In Memoriam, 1963: Robert S. Butler, Garland D. Connor, Ray Cooke, Robert S. Green, Harold Lee, William Meacham, Foster Pratt, William Reely, A. V. Shorrock, Dr. William Stellwagon, Donald C. Taylor, and Clarence M. Tuck.

1964

While SYC Commodore Don Amick was in office, the new parking lot and massive club alterations began in previous years were finally wrapped up. During renovation, Commodore Amick championed the larger doorway between the two dining rooms.

The membership committee in the January *Binnacle* advised new members that they could spread their initiation payment over nine or 12 months. Active membership, for example, could be paid at $60 down and $20 per month for 12 months, which totaled the $300 initiation fee.

The membership was also reminded that Hamlin Street was now one-way heading west and the exit was via Shelby.

The Seattle International 14 Fleet elected CYC's Joe Norman captain and SYC's John Hyde secretary. The fleet was organized in 1948 by two SYC members—Norm Cole and Gary Horder—and now totaled a record 36 boats.

This was the year that H. W. and Catharine McCurdy gave an anemometer to the club to be mounted beside the barograph given earlier in memory of their son Tom, junior commodore in 1949.

The May cruise of the SYC Women's Group to the Fo'c'sle attracted 115 women. Jean Harthorn was the outgoing president of the SYC Women's Group. The installation of new officers highlighted the program for the day. Shirlee Liberman was elected as the group's new president. Eight cruisers skippered by SYC members provided transportation for the annual event.

The month of June brought a double dose of sadness when the members learned of the death of two of the club's most noted yachtsmen—Charles Frisbie and F. C. (Fritz) Hellenthal. Then, the very next issue of the *Binnacle* carried the notice of the death of Quent Williams.

The 1964 Potlatch celebration at Port Madison offered a typical good time for SYC families. The outstation was a hive of activity June 20 and 21. Potlatch Queen Inger Heideman reigned over the festivities. Sailboat men arranged a Crooz N Snooz Race. The Blindfold Dinghy Race was enjoyed by all with Commodore Don Amick and wife Betty leading the field. Jim Bryant and wife Fran put together an incomparable dinner, and the games committee did a bang-up job. Jim and Ginny O'Brien were chairpersons.

The July 30 Rope Yarn featured the Blue Angel aviators as guests. They were in town to fly during Seafair week.

In early summer, the Evergreen Point Bridge offramp to Montlake Boulevard was opened, improving access to the club from downtown.

In 1964 Swiss-born Fritz Buehler took over as host in the Ward Room. In December the club gave itself a present—a color television set for the men's bar.

The SYC yearbook listed the following trophies and award winners for 1964.

Mark Mayer Trophy: *Lady Van* (Phil and Sam Peoples); Mark Mayer Cup: *Seaward* (Dr. Byron Ward); Tri-Island Race: Class A, *Lady Van* (Phil and Sam Peoples); Class BB and Overall, *Calypso* (Dr. Henry Garrigues); Hooper and Commodore trophies: *Goose* (Stephen F. Chadwick, Jr., and Donald G. Graham, Jr.); Humphrey and Hostetter trophies: *Canto* (Peter W. Eising); Seaborn: *Yare* (Victor Smith); Gamwell: *Indefatigable* (Richard H. Hasse and John D. Anderson)

Frisbie Trophy: *Eros* (Ron McFarlane); Single-Handed races: J. C. Baillargeon, Jr.; John G. Schlagel, who won two races; Victor R. Smith

Consistent winners, Class A: *Odusa*

The Cruising Club of America

The Cruising Club of America (CCA) was launched on the East Coast of the United States in 1921–22 as an organization comparable to the Royal Cruising Club of Great Britain. Yacht clubs at the time were organized around the principal activity of sailboat racing; none were primarily focused on cruising and the development of the wholesome type of cruising yacht.

Membership in CCA is a mark of cruising achievement and is by invitation only. Club members reside in North America and hold their membership through one of the geographically located stations or posts.

The Pacific Northwest station of the CCA was organized in 1964–65, largely through the efforts of the late Jack Graham, SYC member. Graham had a branch office of his architectural firm in New York City at the time, and he had become acquainted with many CCA members through his membership in the New York Yacht Club. For the past 15 years the Pacific Northwest CCA station has held its regular meetings in the SYC Portage Bay station clubhouse.

Objectives of the club, according to the charter, are

To promote cruising by amateurs, to encourage the development of suitable types of cruising craft, to stimulate interest in seamanship, navigation and handling of small vessels, to gather and keep on file all information which may be of assistance to members in cruising. ◇

(Eric H. Zahn); Class BB: *Calypso* (Dr. Henry B. Garrigues) and *Thunder* (Bill Buchan); PC class: *Canto* (Pete Eising); Dragon class: *Skatt* (Al and Don Voorhees); Thunderbird: *Yare* (Vic Smith) and *Wisp* (Bob Hughes); C class: *Blue Jacket* (John P. Lidral); B class: *Seaward* (Dr. Byron Ward) and *Falcon* (Henry Kamstra); OK Dinghy: *Feather* (Connie Van Deventer)

Swiftsure Race: City of Victoria Trophy, *Hussy* (Robert Page); Lipton Trophy: *Adelante* (E. Bates McKee); Sailboat of the Year: *Aurora* (John G. Schlagel)

In the powerboat spotlight Jack Allen's *Alley Oop*, which won the Course and Compass Race and finished third in the Bremerton Heavy Weather and Lake Washington races; A. William Pratt's *Coho*, first in the Bremerton Heavy Weather, second in the Lake Washington Race, and winner in class IV of the International Cruiser Race; Frank M. Dunn's *All Dunn IV*, which won three contests—

The History of the Henry Island Outstation

In the fall of 1965 SYC Commodore Ben Benton appointed a committee of six members to find the next desirable location for an outstation, preferably in the San Juan Islands.

The committee investigated 30 suggested locations; committee member Frank Morris suggested Henry Island (he had a vacation home about a half mile from the proposed site).

Morris invited the five other members of the committee—Bob Graham, George Heideman, Wally Ovens, Harold Hovland, and Peter McTavish and their wives—to be guests at his Mosquito Pass home early in March 1966. They were ferried by small boat to Henry Island where they found the weather-beaten remains of an old pier. They tramped over the 22 acres and inspected the house on the property.

Though vacant for four years, this building was of superior construction and the dry climate had preserved it as though it had been vacated the week before. It had been built in 1929 by Frank M. Dever, who had operated a dairy on this site since early in the century. The house had ceramic tile, hardwood floors, and a 110-volt direct-current generator that powered lights, refrigeration, etc. The furnace and stove were wood fueled.

The house was owned by Mr. and Mrs. Henry Bressler, who had purchased it from Dever in 1926 and had lived in it until 1962. They placed it on the market when they moved to a smaller house they had built around the corner on Mosquito Pass.

The committee expressed their interest in the 22 acres, but Bressler had given an option on the property to a man named Thatcher, who turned out to be a friend of Frank Morris. He was willing to turn the option over to the committee provided the property would not be used for commercial purposes. The option had six days to run.

The committee knew they could never get the SYC board to act within that time, so, feeling the property was underpriced at $61,500, they decided to buy it themselves and hold it until they had time to persuade the club to buy it from them at that price. They each put up $2,000 cash, a total of $12,000, and from this paid $7,500 down. The remainder went for miscellaneous expenses.

Back in Seattle, though most members thought it was a great deal, a small and vocal minority did not agree. Further, the committee got the impression that some suspected they were trying to make a fast buck out of the club. Through the rest of 1966 and 1967 the members were encouraged to visit the property and decide for themselves.

As time went by, money for taxes, contract payments and other expenses was needed. So more members—among them Gordon Ingman, Bob Camber, Jerry Bryant, Harry Emmel, Paul Morris, Marco Magnano, and Thurston Lane—were taken in as partners. They were soon joined by George Heideman, Frank Morris, Bob Graham, Wally Ovens, Peter McTavish, and Harold Hovland. Since some members felt that the entire 22 acres was not needed for an outstation, the committee had the

the Opening Day, Crooz N Snooz, and Single-Handed races.

The International Cruiser Predicted Log Race was won by the Royal Vancouver Yacht Club's Len Sewell in his *Dorle*. The overall winner of the Alaska Race from Vancouver to Juneau was the Royal Van's Les and Babe Simmers sharing honors in *Walithy*.

In Memoriam, 1964: Mrs. R. J. Acheson, Allan Edmunds, Arthur C. Foss, Charles Frisbie, Russell H. Green, Dr. Hale Haven, F. C. Hellenthal, B. N. Hutchinson, Mrs. George McVey, Ralph L. Rush, Emil G. Sick, George Stroble, Paul Webb, William H. Wesphal, Charles West, and Quent Williams.

1965

Throughout the year, SYC Commo-

property surveyed and platted. One piece, approximately two acres, with about 200 feet of waterfront and the buildings, was offered to the yacht club at a bargain price. The remainder was divided into 20 lots, averaging one acre each, with a common waterfront of 216 feet. The partners intended to build on the lots or hold them for investment; they then incorporated, and since someone had referred to them "as a bunch of pirates," they called themselves the Henry Island Privateers (HIPpies, for short). They offered the unclaimed lots to the membership, but no one came forward, probably because the best lots had been claimed or perhaps the "Privateer" label scared them off.

In the meantime, pressure was building for the board to make a decision on the offered property. In June 1967, after all options had been aired, the board voted 13 to 1 to buy the two acres with the waterfront and buildings.

A Henry Island Outstation committee was formed to put the property in shape for the members to use, with Les Eastman as the first chairman.

The Privateers and the club formed a joint venture to share equally in the cost of bringing electric power to the island. The Orcas Power and Light Company demanded a large deposit before they would lay the submarine cable. Though some neighbors intended to utilize the power, they refused to help fund the deposit. Again the club went to the Privateers, and each of them put up $200 and a lien on their waterfront property and the club came up with $850. Finally electric power came to Henry Island.

By this time some work had been done on the house: The wood furnace had been removed, electric baseboard heat installed, the kitchen rewired, the basement rebuilt, and two bathrooms and two shower rooms had been added.

Securing a water supply proved difficult. First the club contracted for a deep well to be drilled through rock, but when no water showed after 208 feet, a second 401-foot well was drilled; it, too, remained dry. After consultation, high explosives were placed along the bottom 100 feet of the first well, and the top part was filled with sand. The explosion that followed blew vaporized rock into the air for 15 seconds. The driller estimated a hole 15 feet wide and 90 feet deep had been created in the rock, with perhaps 50 feet of shattered rock at the bottom. Slowly the hole filled with water, which for a few years amounted to about 400 gallons per day.

The original primitive sewage system was upgraded as more of the membership discovered Henry Island. In the winter of 1975–76, SYC negotiated to purchase the remainder of the tract, some 20 acres and 216 feet of waterfront, from the Privateers at the initial cost and without interest. New moorage was added in 1977. That same year, on a high spot about 100 yards south of the main building, a 20,000-gallon water storage tank was installed. In 1978, this tank was enlarged to store just over 60,000 gallons.

Finally in 1985, a telephone cable was laid to Henry Island, now one of the jewels in the SYC outstation holdings.

—Based on material supplied by Peter McTavish

The 1965 Gold Cup Committee reunion—(from left) Howard Richmond, Anderson Joy, Con Knutson, Middleton Chism, and Joe Mesdag. (Con Knutson Collection)

dore Harold Hovland and his various committees worked toward gaining ownership of the all-important wetlands.

In January the genial club manager Russ Hoppe resigned to take over at the Jonathan Club in Los Angeles. Dick Reardon was chosen as his replacement.

A Mexican theme brought flavorful food and bright decorations to the club's big annual party in March. An added attraction for the dinner dance included a piñata, which was stuffed full of favors from Mexico. Among other events, a bean-counting contest drew several contestants. The committee responsible for the party included Mr. and Mrs. Scott Fields, Mr. and Mrs. Bill Stewart, and Mr. and Mrs. George Heideman.

The March 25 Rope Yarn Sunday featured the Seattle Banjo Band.

The March Women's Group meeting featured Mrs. William J. Luhr, curator of education at the Seattle Art Museum. She spoke about the "Romance of Jade."

In December 1965 the Women's Group held its annual Christmas Party with the traditional commodore's punch bowl. The past presidents presented a program of songs and a skit as entertainment for members and guests.

This was the year of the *Mintos*, the handy fiberglass shoreboat that sailed in a lively manner and could be rowed easily. It was light enough to launch alone from the dinghy dock and didn't need a crew to hold down the high side. It had room for a second adult or two children. Several Minto races were scheduled during the year.

Seattle Yacht Club's team of four powerboats won the Interclub Predicted Log Challenge Race with 79 points, besting Queen City Club's 74. The four boats were *Coho* (Bill Pratt), *Alexa* (Jerry

Bryant), *All Dunn IV* (Frank Dunn), and *Skipalong* (Paul Morris).

The Bremerton-to-Nanaimo International Cruiser Race winner was Don Bancroft, representing the Port Orchard Yacht Club in *Hoot.*

A clever and unusual predicted log race was enjoyed by seven contestants on Power-Sail Day. The skippers were not told the course until one minute before each of the five legs where they were then given the next control point. All hands agreed it was a most interesting and tough race. First place went to Paul Morris in *Skipalong* with 1.8618 percent error.

The *Miss Bardahl* was heralded as the top hydroplane of 1965. She established a new 45-mile world's record of 115.064 miles per hour, a new world heat record of 116.079 miles per hour and a new world one-lap (three-mile) record of 117.87 miles per hour. Furthermore, she returned the Gold Cup Trophy to SYC for the third consecutive time. Ron Musson was her driver, and Ole Bardahl was the owner of this record-breaker.

Sailboat of the year was Henry Kamstra's *Falcon.*

The SYC yearbook listed the following trophies and award winners for 1965.

> Consistent sailboat winners, Class AA: *Kialoa* (William C. Brazier), *Nor'wester* (William Hofius and Kenneth Browne), and *Sea Fever* (Otis Lamson, Richard Philbrick, and Robert Coe); Class A: *Kate II* (D. E. Skinner, II); Class BB: *Salute* (Phillip and Sam Peoples), *Warrior* (John Buchan), *Thunder* (William Buchan), *Calypso* (Dr. Henry Garrigues), and *Stormy Weather* (Dr. Govnor Teats); Blanchard Senior Knockabouts: *Frantic* (Bill Barnard) and *Raven* (Carl Doherty); PC class, *Puff* (Nils Rosenberg), *Wahine* (Arthur Henry), *Canto* (Peter W. Eising), and *Mandra* (Gary Syverson); Division 1: *Shamrock* (Robert T. Lamson); Z Class: *Bobtail* (Bob Allen); Thunderbird: *Rev II* (Pat Lettenmaier); B class: *Ghost* (Max Agather), *Mistral* (J. C. Baillargeon, Jr.), and *Seaward* (Byron Ward); C class: *Seaquin* (Richard S. Marshall) and *Blue Jacket* (Jack Lidral); Six-Meter, *Goose* (Stephen Chadwick and Donald Graham) and *Risken* (R. O. Anderson and Karl Hostetter)

In Memoriam, 1965: Ernest Banner, Hugh Cawsey, A. James Cook, Truman Cragin, William H. Curtis, William P. Ellis, Lynn O. Foster, Sidney Gerber, R. Kline Hillman, Harry Jensen, Earl Kennell, John I. MacNichol, Henry S. Russell, Dr. Henry Schmitz, Ray Schutt, J. B. Stalnaker, and David Whitcomb, Sr.

1966

In 1966 Margaret Haight prepared entertaining *Binnacle* columns about club activities. This sample is from the January issue.

> Commodore Benton's wife Barbara hosted our annual Ball in a gown of moss green and oyster white—with orchids to match! Joann Field, hard-working committee member, almost stole the show with a black lace mantilla and Spanish comb in her lovely tresses. I could go on and on but in the words of one happy sailor, "all of you galley queens looked gorgeous."
>
> —Binnacle*, January 1966*

The ladies enjoyed a spring fashion show on April 20 with summer outfits presented by James Crosby of Mercer Island and University Village. Pants by Vera ($16.95), zepell seersucker costume suit by California Girl ($36.00), and a paisley shirtwaist dress by Mac Shore were a few of the outfits shown.

Throughout the year Norman J. Blanchard, II, sent letters to the club monthly, describing his navy duty off the coast of Vietnam.

SYC member Everett Henry received the Latham L. Goble Memorial Award for 1965 as the individual outside the marine industry deemed to have made the outstanding personal contribution to boating in the area. His leadership in the Interclub Association, in founding the Blue Gavel Association of past commodores, and in

Traditions of Seattle Yacht Club

Any yacht club that has existed for an entire century is rich with traditions; the Seattle Yacht Club is no exception. Each of the diverse interest groups has formed a committee to shepherd its causes. Thirty-five committees are officially authorized by club bylaws. The club management notes that more than 70 different committees have met during a one-year period, which indicates that there are many active ad hoc and rump committees in existence. Collectively they support the traditions that make up SYC's uniqueness. Here are a few of the memorable traditions that evolved over the past century.

The Annual Meeting: A legal requirement of all Washington chartered corporations. On the first Friday evening in October, such business as election of officers and revision of bylaws occurs. No other members meetings are held during the year unless a special meeting is called by the trustees to obtain a vote of the membership as required by the bylaws. The board members carry on the business of the club at their 11 regularly scheduled meetings spaced throughout the year.

Barnacle Bill Cruise: During the process of electing officers, two well-qualified members are nominated for the position of rear commodore. One is elected to office and the loser is designated Barnacle Bill. The morning after the annual meeting, Barnacle Bill is joined by his fellow members on a cruise across Puget Sound to Port Madison, where Barnacle Bill is entertained in an effort to make him forget the election.

Commodore's Ball: This is normally held the first weekend in December and honors the newly elected commodore, his officers and staff. This is the most formal and posh event held at the club during the year. Officers from all the major yacht clubs in the Northwest are invited to attend. This is one of the outstanding formal dinner dances held in Seattle during the social year.

Junior Officers' Ball: By special invitation, junior officers from many of the Puget Sound yacht clubs gather for a formal dinner dance each year. This is an opportunity for the junior leadership of the boating community to get acquainted socially; it promotes close working relationships for the betterment of boating throughout the year.

Junior Commodore's Ball: Junior members join together to honor their elected leaders for the year at a dinner dance each year in the fall after school has begun.

End-of-the-Season Awards Dinner: The sailboat, powerboat, and rowing committees each schedule a night at the end of the season of competition to award the individual and perpetual trophies won by the outstanding performers throughout the year.

Thursday Noon Stag Lunch: Every Thursday noon except for Thanksgiving the male members of the club gather in the Ward Room for lunch. This tradition has now been celebrated for more than 50 years. After a few jokes and discussion of upcoming events, reports are given by the powerboat and sailboat chairmen. Women are seldom invited to attend; however, the admiralette is always asked to report on Opening Day plans.

Men's Oyster Feed: This annual event benefits the Junior Members' Sailing Program. An auction of new and used boating equipment is featured before the feed begins. Traditional stag entertainment is provided during the luncheon.

Men's Christmas Party: This extended Thursday noon luncheon features donated merchandise that is given as gifts under a raffle format. Several bottles of booze are included as gifts. There is always a lot of laughter and a good time.

Employees' Christmas Party: The club is closed to the membership on the last Thursday before Christmas for this special party at which gifts and bonuses are given to employees. Cocktails and dinner are served by trustees and officers.

The Children's Christmas Party: This event is held the Sunday before Christmas for the children of club members. The party consists of a special menu dinner in the Ward Room, a program of entertainment consisting of Santa Claus and his elves. Each child is invited to sit on Santa's lap and to receive a gift from one of the elves.

The Tom and Jerry Party: On the Sunday between Christmas and New Year's, the bar is closed for the afternoon and the active intermediate members host the annual Tom and Jerry party. All members are invited in for a cup of cheer before the roaring fireplace.

The Commodore Christmas Punch Bowl: The commodore is invited to attend the December meeting of the SYC Women's Group on the condition that he bring with him a large punch bowl filled with good cheer. It is rumored that a commodore arrived dressed as Santa and invited the ladies to sit on his lap and tell him what they wanted for Christmas.

Christmas Ships and Special People's Cruises: SYC yachtsmen always participate in the two Christmas cruises. The first is the parade of lighted and decorated Christmas ships and the second is the cruise led by Santa Claus for handicapped people.

New Year's Parties: The New Year is rung in at two locations at SYC. The more formal black tie event is held at the Portage Bay station where a posh dinner dance is enjoyed by all. This party has grown to the point that the festivities are scheduled on the three decks with three bands. A less formal event is scheduled for the Port Madison Outstation where families enjoy potluck.

Children's Easter Party: This party is held each Easter Sunday for the children of club members. The party consists of a special menu dinner in the Ward Room, a program of entertainment, and the traditional egg roll on the lawn west of the club.

Gourmet Cruises: Sometime between Labor Day and Opening Day, inspiration strikes the club. There are many reasons to journey across Puget Sound to the protected inlet known as Port Madison. One of these is to just cruise over to eat. The club sponsors chili cook-offs, garlic cook-offs, clambakes, salmon barbecues, or whatever members can think up. One way or another, these are traditions. But most important of all is that each occasion starts with the traditional "Green Box Party."

Special Dinner Parties: There are many special dinners during the year, including October Fest, a crab feed, an oyster feed, Mexican Night, Italian Night, wine tasting, and other special parties staged by the entertainment committee for the enjoyment of gourmets.

Ladies' Cruise: Always in the month of May there is the Ladies' Day Cruise to Port Madison. Several members are invited to ferry the SYC Women's Group across Puget Sound to the fo'c'sle for a day in the sun. Along with good food and entertainment, the new SYC Women's Group officers for the coming year are introduced.

Special Cruising Events: Sailboat Rendezvous, Powerboat Rendezvous and the Golf Cruise are held annually.

Rope Yarn Thursdays: The entertainment committee plans a special event for each Thursday evening for the Marine Room. Members gather there to enjoy a specially priced libation and complementary hors d'oeuvres along with an entertaining program.

Dinner Theater: Those members who possess the thespian urge join together each winter to prepare a theatrical work of art that they share with the rest of the membership in a dinner theater presentation.

Potlatch: This event in the middle of June at the Fo'c'sle Outstation at Port Madison is a family affair where parents and children join together in races and games.

July 4 at Henry Island: Over the last few years it has become a tradition for members cruising in the American San Juan Island area to gather at the Henry Island Outstation for a good old-fashioned Fourth of July celebration. The format includes a picnic and softball game and everyone shares their fireworks and enjoys the Roche Harbor displays.

Port Madison Fishing Derby: In September each year, the members gather at the Port Madison Outstation for some "fishin'." Prizes are given for most anything that can be caught on a hook and line. Most prized is the largest salmon, but bullheads and rock crabs can also win a prize if caught by the little members off the float.

Football Buffet Brunches: Before each Husky home football game, SYC hosts a buffet brunch for members and their guests. The club provides a relaxed atmosphere and excellent parking for members who attend football games in Husky Stadium, an easy walk from the club.

Some traditions live on while others fade. When shipwreck parties are mentioned, old-timers remember them, but such parties are no longer scheduled. Traditions are a strength of the club and help make SYC a comfortable and friendly place.

—From material supplied by Jack Austin

his personal contributions to the work of the Seattle-King County Safety Council were behind this recognition.

This was the year the yacht club purchased one of the Dunsmuir islands in Ladysmith Harbor. To SYC members, it is commonly known as Ovens Island for Wally Ovens, the former commodore largely responsible for its acquisition.

During the year, work on the parking lots was completed.

SYC Commodore Ben Benton's message in the March newsletter read in part:

> We are located in the exact center of Seattle activities and with the advent of the freeway we are only a few minutes from anywhere in town. Our club is bursting with activities and because of this we must do all that we can to give our members adequate service, parking, etc. Your Board and Flag Officers, because of this, placed a limit of 1,500 on our membership and are asking that all visitors be properly identified. . . . This means we will not be able to serve some people who may have used our Club in the past. We are not being high-hat but are just doing our best to see that the facilities will be always available to the members. We also must operate this way because of our liquor laws.
>
> —Binnacle, *March 1966*

Featured in the June *Binnacle* was the story of the *Preston*, the familiar flat-

The 1966 Long-Range Plan

In 1966 a committee chaired by Peter McTavish, with Phil Butler, Bob Graham, George Heideman and Wally Ovens as members, presented a long-range plan to the board of trustees. It was based on an extensive questionnaire to which members had responded.

The committee made certain assumptions about the club: It is first and foremost a boating club with equal interest in sailboat and powerboat activities; it is essentially a family-oriented organization; there is little membership demand for luxury or ostentation, but there is firm insistence on high quality.

The 1965 board of trustees had limited club membership to 1,500 not counting out-of-state members. The committee believed that if this number were to be increased, the physical plant, even if enlarged as suggested, would be overcrowded.

The clubhouse needed improvement; the dining and bar facilities were fairly adequate but the entire building needed redecorating. Other suggestions included replacing the existing workshop and storage building, improving the parking lots and the new driveway entrance, enlarging the clubhouse, renovating the interior spaces to provide improved circulation and more efficient use of the building, and installing new carpeting, draperies, and furnishings.

The membership wanted to stay at the 1807 Hamlin site, but two factors might affect that desire: First, the club did not have permanent title to the land under the docks or the new parking lot and should immediately seek ways to purchase the property (this was accomplished); second, in all probability, the University of Washington would eventually take over most of the property facing East Shelby Street and East Hamlin Street for one block on either side of Montlake Boulevard. However, the university did not contemplate a need for the shorelands and considered the club to be a compatible entity in the area. (The university later found expansion space elsewhere.)

Members indicated a need for fencing, erosion control on the bank, a new clubhouse and a swimming pool at Port Madison. They also expressed keen interest in acquiring an outstation in the San Juan Islands.

The estimated cost of these plans was $710,000 for the Hamlin Street property and $54,000 for the Port Madison property.

As is apparent in the pages that follow, many of these goals were realized. ◇

bottomed snag boat operated by the Corps of Engineers in waters from Blaine to Olympia and in Lakes Washington and Union.

All the club mourned hydroplane racers Ron Musson and Rex Manchester, who died in tragic accidents during the running of the President's Cup Race on the Potomac in June. Both belonged to the club and were well known to the members.

According to the 1966 yearbook, the following were employed at the club during the year: Chester Smith was chef, Fritz Buehler was maitre d' in the dining room, beverage department head was Willy Washington, and the office manager was Mildred Matson. James Torrance was maintenance head and Herman Borgmaster was the carpenter.

Bruce Calhoun, Northwest manager of *Sea* and *Pacific Motor Boat* magazines, donated a handsome trophy in memory of his father Charles H. Briggs. The trophy was to be awarded to the skipper earning the most points in a schedule of 12 races sailed on or adjacent to Puget Sound, Strait of Juan de Fuca, Strait of Georgia, or offshore ocean races.

Frank J. Sando's *Gerhild* was the SYC sailboat of the year.

The SYC yearbook listed the following trophies and award winners for 1966.

Consistent winners, small boats: *Breeze Bandit* (Dwight Shaw); *Habel* (W. R. Davies); *Tadpole* (S. Breuer); *Whippet III* (F. Moitoret); *Thistle 2142* (R. D. Clark); Division A: *Aurora* (John Schlagel); *Kialoa* (W. Brazier); *Nor'wester* (Kenneth Browne); *Odusa* (Eric Zahn); Division B: *Blue Jacket* (John Lidral); *En Garde* (Stewart/Agather); *Maelstrom* (E. Miller); *Mistral* (J. C. Baillargeon, Jr.); *Salute* (Phil and Sam Peoples); *Topic* (Irv Smith); *Mandra* (G. Syverson); *Maybe VII* (Sunny Vynne); *Privateer* (B. Fiander/L. Johnson); Division D: *Aeolus* (D. Ridgeway); *Domino* (R. Rawson); *Frantic* (Bill Barnard); *Rev* (P. Lettenmaier); *Trinket* (G. Sutherland); *Yare* (V. Smith); Division E: *Gerhild* (F. Sando); *Moonglow II* (D. Nielsen)

Overall Tri-Island Series: *Goose* (Chadwick/Graham, CYC); *Gerhild* (F. Sando, SYC); *Nor'wester* (K. W. Browne, SYC); *Warrior* (John Buchan, CYC); *Canto* (Peter Eising, CYC); *Aeolus* (Dave Ridgeway, CYC); Protection Island/Point Hudson Race: *Kialoa* (William Brazier, TYC); *Sea Bird* (R. Theriault, CYC); Frisbie Trophy Race: *Hussy* (R. Page, SYC); Commodore Trophy Race: *Maelstrom* (E. Miller, CYC); Single-Handed Race: *Lancer* (Norman Larabee, CYC); *Mandra* (Gary Syverson, CYC); *Gerhild* (F. Sando, SYC); Hat Island Race: *Trinket* (Glen Sutherland, CYC); *Gerhild* (F. Sando, SYC); *African Star* (Doug Fryer, SYC)

Standout powerboats of 1966: *Alexa* (Jerry Bryant); *Coho* (A. William Pratt); *Skipalong* (Paul Morris); Jerry Bryant Trophy: *High Cotton* (Gordon Shotwell)

International Cruiser Race from Tacoma to Tree Island: *Driftwood* (C. A. [Pete] Ross, BremertonYC); Alaska Race: Juneau Yacht Club Bear, *Alaska Hunter* (Don Bancroft)

In Memoriam, 1966: Wilden H. Baldwin, Homer Bale, Richard M. Black, Lincoln Bouillon, Richard H. Byington, Lawrence Calvert, Coburn Crosby, O. D. Fisher, Robert Green, William C. Greer, John C. Hagen, Jr., C. Frederick Harley, Clinton S. Harley, L. F. "Dick" Harthorn, J. B. Headley, Karl Heideman, John G. Holmstrom, Jr., A. West Johnson, Rex Manchester, William R. McRae, Ron Musson, Aubrey Naef, John Rumsey, Emmett B. Schmidt, Earl Staley, William Stead, John L. Wilfong, and Dolph Zubick.

1967

SYC members taught several spring maritime classes: Phil Duryee provided information on "Communications" and the equipment to have on your boat; Art Russell taught "First Aid at Sea"; Phil Luther spoke about "Boat Handling"; Harold Hovland taught the "Decor of Yachting," which included boat etiquette; Frank Morris gave forth on "Tides and Currents"; and Paul Morris spoke about "Piloting."

At the Women's Group luncheon in

February it was announced that Betty Musson would become the 1967 Opening Day admiralette. Mrs. Musson, widow of the famed unlimited hydroplane driver, was excited about her appointment but wanted everyone to know that should they see her fine feathered hat afloat, they should give immediate aid as she couldn't swim a stroke.

On May 14, 1967, the *Seattle Times* mentioned that the annual cruise of the Seattle Yacht Club Women's Group to the Port Madison Outstation for a luncheon and election of officers was coming up the following Wednesday. Club members who transported the women aboard their cruisers were: C. R. Wilcox (*Blacktop*), Phil Butler (*Paramour*), Ralph Chambers (*Flyer*), Fred Peterson (*Molly Shannon*), Wally Ovens (*Islander*), Stanley Youngs (*Seafari*), Albert Bloss, Jr. (*Sea Swallow*), Howard Lovejoy (*Tolo*), Larry Norton (*Westlake*), Mrs. John Holmstrom (*Island Stream*) and Frank Dunn (*All Dunn IV*).

Anton Z. "Tony" Pos took over in the Ward Room. An Austrian by birth, he was educated in Yugoslavia and France. He arrived in Seattle in 1951 with experience in many of the world's finer hotels and restaurants. He is remembered for the enjoyable after-working-hours piano concerts he provided. Darleen Lane, also a new employee, was hired as social director, a position that lasted only a few years.

Frederick C. Peterson, while commodore, watched over the Port Madison fo'c'sle where carpenters were busy adding 2,500 square feet to the clubhouse, including a spacious lounge with a large fireplace and a floor suitable for dancing. Past Commodore Peterson, who lived near the Port Madison Outstation, kept a fond eye on fellow members as they enjoyed this favorite weekend destination.

On June 18 the new memorial flagstaff was dedicated at Port Madison. A plaque was attached that read: "In memory of Dick Black from his many Seattle Yacht Club friends."

Jandy *was designed by Sparkman and Stevens and built by Vic Franck in 1963. She was inspired by a famous Sparkman and Stevens centerboard yawl* Finnesterre. Jandy *was owned by Janet and Gordon "Sandy" Prentice, Jr. in the 1960s when this photo was taken. The boat is now owned by Past Commodore Bill Bradshaw and Bud Peterson and has been renamed* Trio. *(Photo by Ken Ollar)*

The sailboat committee, concerned with the aging of the membership, reported that adults over 40 accounted for 68 percent of the membership, juniors for 10 percent and adults under 40 for 22 percent. Several suggestions were made which, it was hoped, would increase the number of younger members.

Late in the year, Roy W. Corbett was presented an Honorary Life Commodore Flag by the new SYC Commodore Chet Adair, who mentioned Corbett's unswerving devotion to the club of which he had been a member for 47 years. From 1925 to 1932 Corbett had been a crew member aboard the famed *Sir Tom.*

At a special meeting on June 20, the voting members of SYC agreed to confirm the trustees' decision to purchase property on Henry Island for an outstation in the San Juan Islands.

The 1967 race results found Don Bancroft of the Port Orchard club in first place, winning the Jerry Bryant Skipper-of-the-Year Trophy, with SYC's Gordon Shotwell just a few points behind him.

The International Cruiser Race from Victoria to Edmonds, one of the few times the boats headed south, was won by Chuck King of the Edmonds Yacht Club who was participating for only the second time in a predicted log race.

Sailboat of the year in 1967 was Ron McFarlane's *Eros*, which in Division 1, Class D, won the following races: Vashon, Point Hudson, Scatchet Head, Frisbie, Hat Island, Tri-Island and Commodore's.

The SYC yearbook listed the following trophies and award winners for 1967.

Consistent winners, Division 1, Class A: *Windward* (John Ellis); *Miss Chiff* (Charles

SYC's Historic Anchor

During the summer of 1967, Merrill Stewart was master of the Alaska Steamship Company's motorship *Tanana*. One day he anchored the ship in 30 feet of water in the Naknek roadstead at the confluence of the Kvichak and Naknek rivers, where shallow waters force vessels to anchor several miles off shore. They took on a load of salmon and then attempted to weigh anchor. Chief Mate Jose Franco called to the captain on the bridge that the anchor was fouled. When they finally managed to hoist it to the surface, it brought with it a huge old sailing ship anchor and chain.

SYC's historic anchor was brought down from Alaskan waters. (SYC Historical Collection)

Captain Stewart remarked to the mate that the bark *Charles Moody* had burned and sank in the vicinity and joked that perhaps they had the remains of the old ship on the other end of the chain. Happily only one shot (90 feet) of chain was secured to the old anchor. The anchor could have been lost anytime between 1885 and 1920, when the last of the old square riggers sailed north.

Because of the anchor's historical value, Stewart considered giving it to the Puget Sound Maritime Historical Society, but the president of that organization, Wilbur Thompson, suggested it be displayed at the Seattle Yacht Club where it would be appreciated by all sorts of sailors.

After member D. E. "Ned" Skinner, II, a veteran sailing and racing enthusiast, donated all freight charges, wharfage, and handling, the huge old artifact was brought to the club and installed on the lawn. ◇

Schiff); *White Squall* (Gov Teats); *Brigadoon* (Charles Guildner); *Pursuit* (Don Fleming); *Swallow* (Phil Johnson); *Aye Aye* (Dick Gilbert); Division 1, Class D: *Seaquin* (Richard Marshall); *Mistral* (J. C. Baillargeon, Jr.); Division II, Class A: *Goose* (Steve Chadwick); *Eros* (Ron McFarlane); Division II, Class B: *Trelawney* (James Marta); Division II, Class E: *Hi Hat* (Dr. William Jaquette); *Seabird* (Robert Theriault); *Volenti* (Stevens and Brink); Division II, Thunderbirds: *Kiwa* (Mrs. Ted Pape); Dragons: *Bluenose* (Ron Farrell); PHRF: *African Star* (Douglas Fryer); Tri-Island and Commodore's cups.

In Memoriam, 1967: William K. Blethen, David R. Bollong, Dr. Emory J. Bourdeau, Mrs. Scott Calhoun, Middleton M. Chism, Charles J. D'Amico, Dr. Herbert W. Day, George V. Eastes, Dan R. Fisher, Dr. William M. Godefroy, Dr. A. W. Van Kirk, and J. Dennis Wick.

1968

SYC Commodore Chet Adair mentioned in the January *Binnacle* that new bylaws had changed the procedure for processing membership applications. Henceforth, no person was to be given an application for membership without first being sponsored by an active member of the club, and members should not bring friends to Thursday luncheons and introduce them

Measurement and Handicapping

Sailboats are of all sizes, shapes, rigs, and speeds. If there is to be competition between sailboat owners on a man-to-man format, then there must be corrections included in the calculated race results to equalize the inherent speed differences between boats. These corrections are known as "handicaps."

These corrections are not easily made. For the past 120 years numerous attempts to determine appropriate handicaps have been made, all of them usable but not entirely satisfactory. Here is a list of such attempts known as "rules" (handicap rules, that is), up to 1965.

1. Hull speed rule (v=1.33 waterline)
2. Universal rule
3. International rule
4. Royal Ocean Racing Club rule (British)
5. Off-soundings rule (Northeast United States)
6. CCA rule (Cruising Club of America)

Generally, the approach to the problem by all rules is to measure hull and rig dimensions when the sailboat is in static mode; then, with suitable mathematical procedures to arrive at a rating number representing the racing speed of the sailboat when sailing, that is, when in dynamic mode. This is difficult, for a sailboat is a complicated dynamic machine. It operates in two fluids—air and water—with a wave-making, energy-losing interface. There are probably 20 to 30 physical variables that affect the speed of the sailboat. The mathematical linkage between static measurements of a sailboat and its dynamic moving performance are not well established.

Most of the rules oversimplify the problem by using only three of the variables—waterline, displacement, and sail area. This increases the probability of error in the ratings.

In the Pacific Northwest, the Pacific International Yacht Racing Association (PIYA) is an association of several of the Northwest yacht clubs. Seattle Yacht Club has been a longtime member of PIYA and coordinates and manages sailboat racing where it involves more than one club. In 1966 and before, PIYA sailboat racing used handicaps as determined by the CCA rule, which had been adopted many years previously.

In 1966 the Seattle Yacht Club organized a week-long sailboat regatta called Norpac Race Week. The location was the west coast of Vancouver Island. The format was to race each day to a new rendezvous that night. Thus, in a week, it included five races and five destinations. Thirty boats registered, but 12 of these were cruisers that did not have CCA ratings and didn't plan to get them. What to do?

as "potential new members." The proper action, the commodore explained, was to bring the friend to the club as a guest and introduce him to members, especially those of the membership committee; never indicate that this friend is being considered for membership. New membership proposal forms were being printed.

During 1968, the startling display of trophies in the two large cases on the main floor caused many members to stop and stare. Exhibited were the Gold Cup and the Indiana Governor's Cup won by *Miss Bardahl* in 1967, the Seafair Trophy won by *My Gypsy* in 1966, and the Alabama Governor's Trophy donated by George Wallace, but apparently never awarded nor engraved. On the lower shelf were the Martini and Rossi Trophy, the Atomic Cup and the Dakota Cup, all three won by *Miss Bardahl*. In the second case were the Suncoast Cup, Harrah's Tahoe Trophy and the San Diego Cup, all three also belonging to *Miss Bardahl*.

Margaret Botsford in the February *Binnacle* reported on the Women's Group luncheon and activities. The Opening Day admiralette for 1968 tried on her new hat at the ceremonial events. Betty Musson was presented with her own past

In Southern California there had evolved a different method of figuring handicaps. According to a possibly apocryphal story, several owners dissatisfied with their CCA ratings assembled in a bar and agreed that they could do better by arbitrarily assigning ratings by committee. Thus was born the Arbitrary Ocean Handicap Fleet, later renamed the Pacific Handicap Racing Fleet (PHRF). Bob Baslam, chief handicapper, furnished the necessary data to the Seattle committee and PHRF ratings were assigned to the sailboats in cruising class. It was a very successful experiment.

Back in Seattle Tom Wheeler, Ralph Russell, and Walt Little, over a drink or two, decided that Puget Sound needed a PHRF fleet and that they would start it. PHRF of Puget Sound grew slowly at first, but by about 1970 the CCA rule was having difficulties. More and more boats reported non-competitive competitive ratings. Cruising clubs were getting tired of the increasing administration and there was a developing demand in England and on the U.S. East Coast for a single rating rule that hopefully would be adopted for world-wide racing. The United States Yacht Racing Union (USYRU) in 1970 adopted a new rule, the International Offshore Rule (IOR) and discontinued use of the CCA rule.

It soon became apparent that most of the sailboats that had been racing under CCA would not receive competitive ratings from IOR. Later on, it also became apparent that early boats designed to fit the IOR became non-competitive in two years or so because of being outdesigned by newer boats.

At present the USYRU is the governing body for the PHRF. However, the "P" now denotes "Performance" instead of "Pacific."

So a great expansion in PHRF was begun, and as of 1991 PHRF has spread to all of the United States and Canada and is used extensively in New Zealand; estimates are that 18,000 sailboats are now registered with PHRF ratings.

PHRF-Northwest expanded also and as of 1991 had members registered in British Columbia, Washington, Idaho, Oregon, and Montana; its registered memberships now number about 1,600 sailboats.

Seattle Yacht Club members too numerous to list have contributed to the birth and growth of PHRF-Northwest. They have functioned as officers, handicappers, administrators, and registered sailboat owners, and should be credited with a job well done.

Walt Little, the father of PHRF Northwest, served as chief handicapper for 19 years and has prepared a book that contains the rules, an explanation of the handicapping system, and a brief history. Little is considered by all who know of his work as a credit to the sport of sailboat racing.

—Based on information supplied by Walt Little

admiralette hat to keep. The March luncheon, it was announced, would feature Ellie Austin wearing her Ukrainian costume and demonstrating the technique of decorating Ukrainian Easter eggs. Chef Otto Dinkenger was scheduled to demonstrate the art of braiding dough for the special breads of the Easter season.

The Women's Group also made the newspaper in May when the *Seattle Times* reported that they decked out the *Blue Water* as a Venetian Carnival Boat for

Stanwood-Camano Yacht Club

The Stanwood-Camano Yacht Club was organized in 1968 by a group of boating enthusiasts who lived in the area. Over the next 10 years, they purchased property for a clubhouse on Skagit Bay, but the cost of maintaining a deep-water channel through the mud flats proved too expensive.

In 1985, this property was sold, and waterfront property was purchased on Saratoga Passage at Madrona Beach, Camano Island. An existing building on the site was remodeled with almost 100 percent volunteer labor. Meetings and potlucks were held there beginning in February 1987.

Since that time, members have furnished the clubhouse and completed the galley. The upper floor, with its magnificent view of the water and the Olympic Mountains, houses the dining-meeting room. On the lower floor is a cocktail bar with a hardwood dance floor plus an office and storage area.

An old boathouse, once used for boat launchings, storage, and repair, was demolished and a picnic/barbecue area and boat launching site are being built there. Four buoys anchored in front of the property are used by members and guests as moorages.

In 1991 the Stanwood/Camano Yacht Club had 378 members (168 couples and 42 singles), and 141 of these members owned boats. The club cruisemaster schedules monthly cruises in spring, summer, and fall to destinations ranging south to Hood Canal and north to Canadian waters. In spring 1991 a ladies' auxiliary was formed. A "mosquito squadron" is being organized for day cruisers 15 feet and over. One-day cruises are planned, as well as overnighters to moorages with nearby motels and restaurants.

The club schedules social activities at least once a month. There are dinners and dances, barbecues and brunches, salmon bakes and crab feeds. A luau each July offers a wonderful buffet and authentic Tahitian/Samoan entertainment. The club's first fishing derby was sponsored in 1991. So far, the clubhouse is opened only for specified social events. A monthly newsletter is published. Members participate in Opening Day and Christmas parades sponsored by neighboring yacht clubs.

Commodore Robert Howlett reported that a major goal of the Stanwood/Camano Yacht Club is to maintain a quality facility for the use of members, guests, and neighboring reciprocal yachting friends.

—Based on material prepared by Martha Young, Stanwood-Camano Yacht Club historian

The 32-foot sloop Mistral, *a frequent Division B winner, has been owned since the mid-1960s by J. C. "Bill" Baillargeon, Jr. Formerly it was* Romp II, *owned by Keith Fisken;* Cirrus II *owned by John Warren; and* Yum Yum, *owned by James McCurdy. All were from SYC. (*Yacht Soundings*)*

Opening Day. Margaret Botsford wrote that when gale force winds reached 75 knots, all aboard were asked to hold onto crepe paper streamers, glittering crowns, plumed hats, fluttering standard, castle wall, balloons and giant-sized oars. Cheers met Queen Ellie Hammer, Esquire Bobbie Dunstan, and Rowers Janet Matson, Benny Robinson, and Ellie Austin. Paul Dunstan was captain of the ship. The *Blue Water* won first-place honors.

In September SYC and the Queen Anne–Magnolia Lions Club sponsored the 21st Annual Blind Fishing Derby. The Lions Club provided auto transportation, tackle, bait, and prizes. Up to 50 blind persons were taken on yachts to fish off Jefferson Head and then treated to a free lunch provided by Clark's Windjammer Restaurant.

During the year the Henry Island moorage received new piling, electric power was installed via submarine cable, and the three-story brick clubhouse near the beach was opened. Furthermore, water from the 18,000-gallon water cistern had tested out pure. The club was seeking caretakers for the recently acquired station.

Perhaps the most exciting race of 1968 was the Scatchet Head contest, third in the year's Tri-Island Series. It started in sail-popping winds that exceeded 25 knots. Many of the 145 entries suffered broken spars, booms and blown out sails. Three crewmen went overboard when one yacht attempted to round the leeward mark. Another yacht lost one crewman. All were recovered safely.

The SYC yearbook listed the following trophies and award winners for 1968.

Mark Mayer Race: *Moonglow* (D. Nielsen, TYC); Commodore's Trophy: *LuLu* (Charles Ross, CYC); Frisbie Overall Trophy: *Satin Doll* (Tom Bush, CYC); Single-Handed Race: *Salute* (Phil Peoples, CYC); *Norn* (Olav Ekrom, SBYC); *Mondo Cane* (J. Williams, CYC); Vashon Island Race: *Seaquin* (D. Marshall, CYC); Protection Island Race: *Warrior* (J. Buchan, CYC); Hat Island Race: *Mara* (Bill Buchan, Jr., CYC)

Smith Island/Hat Island Race: *Warrior* (J. Buchan, CYC); *Indefatigable* (Haase/Anderson, CYC); *Risken* (Jensen/Ambrose, CYC); *Pow Wow* (Burdick/Blanchard, CYC)

Overall Tri-Island Series: *Warrior* (J. Buchan, CYC); *Theory* (Bill Fander, CYC); *Maybe VII* (Vynne/Nichols); *Windsong II* (S. Kiesling, TYC); *Swift* (G. Gunby, SYC); *Virada II* (F. Francisco, CYC); *Serena* (C. Keaton, CYC)

Consistent winners, Category III, Class A: *Ylliam VIII* (Hugh Watt/Anderson); *Maybe VII* (Sunny Vynne/Brent Nichols); Category I-II, Class A: *Moonglow III* (Dave Nielsen); *Navita* (Art Hemenway); *La Ruina* (Mike Gibbons); Dragon: *Antigone* (Stephen Tupper); Category III, Class B: *Serena* (Clark Keaton); Category I-II, Class B: *Mara* (Bill Buchan, Jr.); *Warrior* (John Buchan); *Ta'aroa* (Charles Mabee); Category I-II, Class C: *Tschitah* (Ken Brostrom); *Theory* (Bill Fiander); Category I-II, Class D: *Indefatigable* (Haase/Anderson); *Norn* (Olav Ekrom); *Blue Jacket* (Jack Lidral); Category I, II, and III, Class D: *Satin Doll* (Tom Bush); Category III, Class D: *Pow Wow* (William Burdick); *Windsong II* (Stan Kiesling); Category III, Thunderbirds: *Frappe* (G. Valentine); PHRF: *Vigilant* (Jack Voll); *Swift* (George Gunby); Category III, Class E: *Volenti* (Bob Stevens/D. Brink)

The 55-foot Viboco *was the last wooden yacht of this design. It was built in 1968 by owner and builder Vic Franck. It marked the end of an era for the famous design of seaworthy wooden yachts which were at home in the roughest of seas or calm waters. (Photo by Bob Carver)*

In the contest to be named one of the top 20 powerboat skippers of the year, SYC's Fred Haight managed a second place behind Olympia's Carl Kaiser. In fourth and seventh positions were SYC's Les Lewis and Gordon Shotwell.

Among the trophies won during 1968, the following were on display at SYC: the City of Prince Rupert Perpetual Speedboat Trophy won by Gordon Shotwell in his cruiser *High Cotton*; the Rudder Cup awarded Fred Haight in his *Lauren J*; the Swiftsure Overall Trophy brought back after a year at CYC by J. C. (Bill) Baillargeon, Jr. and his *Mistral*; the

West Vancouver Yacht Club Thunderbird Trophy won by Wil Anderson's *Foresta* in the PIYA Long Distance Race; and the IPBA trophies for first place overall in the International Powerboat Race to Alaska won by Gordon Shotwell's *High Cotton*, Chet Johnson's *Mercer Girl*, and Don Bancroft's *Alaska Hunter*. Dr. Arthur C. Jordan won the Masthead Trophy Race, Jerry Bryant was first overall in the Edmonds Round the Isle Race, Fred Haight was overall winner in the Boomerang Race, and Edward A. Dunn won first place in Class V of the International Cruiser Race. Carl Kaiser of the Olympia Yacht Club was awarded overall in the International Cruiser Race from Olympia to Bedwell Harbour in his boat *Lucky Star IV*. Fred Haight won the Lake Washington Predicted Log Race, missing his predicted time by just 20 seconds.

In Memoriam, 1968: Nick Bez, Ralston R. Cunningham, Dr. F. L. Flashman, Charles C. Hall, C. A. Hansen, Mrs. R. M. Hardy, F. A. Harvey, Warren W. Iverson, Henry H. Judson, Sr., John L. Locke, Jr., Mrs. John S. Mauk, George J. Morry, John S. Pape, Dr. Lawrence M. Penny, Willard E. Rhodes, James L. Robertson, John L. Salladin, Reuben J. Tarte, Mrs. Dwight Ware, and Fred Zylstra.

1969

SYC Commodore Wally Ovens continued his support of the various outstations, several of which he had a hand in acquiring. He also approved installation of a second-floor fire escape and a sprinkler fire suppression system in the Portage Bay clubhouse.

Opening Day was a big success. KOMO Radio assigned their "Man in the Sky," Ted Garlatz, to be a flying commentator and Buddy Weber to broadcast descriptions from Parade Marshal Jim Stirrat's boat. The Women's Group won the grand sweepstakes award for best-decorated boat, the *TNT* belonging to the Thurston Lanes. The theme was "Show Your Flag," and the women surely did. Aboard the boat were Betsy Ross, George Washington, Uncle Sam, and several continental soldiers along with a 56-foot handmade flag and several smaller ones. Also aboard were Mesdames Gus Robinson, Eugene Kidd, Vernon Hammer, Clifford Liberman, Robert West and Thurston Lane.

Junior members had a good year in 1969. The club presented them with four additional C-Larks, making a total of eight. These, along with eight Penguins, were put to good use the year round by the younger set. The junior C-Larkers defeated a team from Shawnigan Lake School in Canada and the following weekend took their third consecutive McCurdy Cup victory against five teams.

Randy Schmoyer, chairman of the Port Madison committee, reported that in 1969 more than 1,500 boats carried 4,210 adults and 1,215 children to the Fo'c'sle. Wall-to-wall carpeting was installed in the Port Madison clubhouse during the year. Captain Merrill Stewart, one of the last steamship captains on the Alaska Steamship Company, donated a "Haida Raven," which he had handcarved in his shipboard quarters over the summer. It now hangs over the mantel. Stewart also arranged for the Port of Seattle to contribute two fine 1904 cannon to be placed on the lower grounds. Another donor, Don Finlay, hung a 100-year-old chart of Port Madison in the clubhouse. And the 20-foot totem pole from the Portage Bay clubhouse was refinished, repainted, and installed at Port Madison, thanks to the efforts of Mr. and Mrs. George Heideman and Bill James. The August *Binnacle* featured Doris and Bill James, the custodians of the Port Madison Outstation. A photo showed the two standing before the terraced walls Bill had constructed be-

SYC Decorated Parade Boats

The SYC Women's Group won the Grand Sweepstakes award with their 1969 Opening Day parade entry shown here aboard the TNT *owned by Thurston Lane. (SYC Women's Group Collection)*

The SYC Junior Yacht Club members carried a Bicentennial theme into the Opening Day parade shown here in 1976 aboard Jim England's Pajlo. *(Thurston Lane Collection)*

The Miriki II, *owned by SYC members Marol and Dick Johnson, carried a theme familiar to Northwest boaters in this 1975 Opening Day parade. (SYC Historical Collection)*

The Sea Bliss, *owned by Dick Davidson, displayed the Seattle Yacht Club's popular motto in the Daffodil Festival parade of boats. (Thurston Lane Collection)*

tween the colorful flower beds his wife had cultivated.

At the annual meeting, architect Heideman disclosed plans to remove the three homes adjoining the parking lot to the east to make room for more parking.

Among the women members' fall activities were a fashion show presented by Anson A. Littler and the organization of a women's bowling league.

In August, SYC hosted the C-Lark National Championship Races on Shilshole Bay. Of the 47 entries from all over the Northwest, the final standings were:

1. George Morrell, Corinthian Yacht Club
2. Don Clark, Corinthian Yacht Club
3. Flip Wingrove, Corinthian Yacht Club

SYC Memorials

Many years ago a group of dedicated SYC members—Allen Engle, F. A. "Doc" Harvey, Dietrich Schmitz, Aubrey Naef, Paul Cressman, Sr., Keith Fisken, Horace McCurdy, and sometimes Russ Gibson—met every Friday for lunch at the club. They all would take turns paying for the tureen of pea soup they all enjoyed. When the club menu was changed to a Friday clam chowder, this dyed-in-the-wool pea soup group drifted apart, but only lunchwise.

As each of these gentlemen went on that last cruise to the Great Beyond, the remaining members would erect a memorial at the club in his honor.

The SYC memorial beacon sits atop the Seattle Yacht Club. (Photo by Betty Chang)

The plaque on the stairway to the clubhouse tower reads: "The flashing beacon light was installed by friends in memory of Aubrey Naef, Life Member of the Seattle Yacht Club. . . ." The "souper" group purchased the beacon from the Coast Guard, which assisted in the installation. The beacon flashes, in Morse code, the letters A and N for Aubrey Naef. The group also arranged to have the beacon listed on charts as a private stationary aid to navigation.

In the club lobby on the east wall is a Geochron, an attention getter to all who pass by. It was donated in 1969 in memory of F. A. "Doc" Harvey by his friends.

The Seattle Yacht Club guest book rests upon a pedestal that was presented to the club in 1971 by the surviving members of the pea soup group in memory of Dietrich Schmitz, the longtime treasurer of the club.

Although there is no plaque on the picture of the *Neoga* that hangs in the club, the picture was presented by the three surviving members of the "souper" assemblage—Keith Fisken, Russ Gibson, and H. W. McCurdy—in memory of the yacht's owner, Allen Engle, SYC commodore 1944–45.

In the years since, those three survivors have gone to join their friends. Of the original eight, the last to leave us was H. W. McCurdy, who died in 1990 at the age of 90.

—Based on material supplied by H. W. McCurdy

4. Ro Pearsall, Seattle Yacht Club
5. Stan Ruble, Seattle Yacht Club
6. Dave Motherwell, Seattle Yacht Club
7. Mark Laura, Seattle Yacht Club
8. Sid Hays, American Lake
9. Bob Kearns, Corinthian Yacht Club
10. Laurie Wilcox, Corinthian Yacht Club

Ed Dunn, with a crew of Ed Dunn, Jr., Jack Allen and Vern Hammer, won the Bremerton Heavy Weather Race. George Delaney was the best guesser in the Masthead Trophy Race which was raced on Casey Jones' new *Blue Heron* with Jack Allen as race master. Fred Haight was first on his *Lauren J* in the Meydenbauer Bay Yacht Club's annual Boomerang Predicted Log Race. Haight also finished first in the Bremerton Heavy Weather, the Lake Washington, and the International Cruiser races. The 120-mile International Cruiser Race from Everett to Vancouver overall award went to Howard Wilson of the Queen City Yacht Club who arrived with a .6582 percent error.

The SYC yearbook listed the following trophies and award winners for 1969.

Commodore's Trophy: *Miss Chiff* (Charles Schiff, MBYC); Single-Handed Race: *Six Pack* (Bruce Hedrick, UWYC); *Holiday* (D. Barr/J. Ford, CYC); *Pompero* (John Svensson, CYC); *Red Baron* (Mike Lund, CYC); Vashon Island Race: *Nor'wester* (Brown, Footh, Williams, SYC); *Rev* (Pat Lettenmaier, CYC); Protection Island Trophy: *Indefatigable* (R. Hasse/Anderson, CYC); Point Hudson Trophy: *Hokus* (J. Kevorkian, CYC); Scatchet Head–Hat Island Trophy: *Eagle* (L. Shorett, CYC); Scatchet Overall Trophy: *Yare* (V. Smith, CYC); Blakely-Scatchet Head Race: *Pompero* (J. Svensson, CYC); *Red Baron* (M. Lund, CYC)

Tri-Island Series: Mark Mayer Cup, *Maelstrom* (Earl Miller, CYC); Bob Bollong Trophy, *Holiday* (Dan Barr/John Ford, CYC); Humphrey Trophy, *Serena* (Clark Keaton, CYC); Seaborn Trophy, *Canopus* (Fred Fenske, CYC); Three-Island Trophy, *Maelstrom* (Earl Miller, CYC); Gardner Gamwell Trophy, *Windsong II* (S. Kiesling, TYC); Hooper Six-Meter Trophy, *Goose* (S. Chadwick, CYC); First President's Trophy, *Altair* (Kjell Dale); Walt Little Trophy, *Haida* (Bob Dawson); T-Bird Trophy, *Yare* (V. Smith); Hostetter Trophy, *Serena* (C. Keaton, CYC)

Crooz N Snooz: Captain Hoyt Trophy, *Aurora* (J. Schlagel, SYC)

Consistent winners, large boats, Category 1, Class A: *Aurora* (John Schlagel, SYC); *Maelstrom* (Earl Miller, CYC); Category 1-B: *Lancer* (Norm Larabee, CYC); Category 1-C: *Teaser* (Dr. D. Houtz, TYC/S. Thordarson, CYC); Category 1-D: *Holiday* (Dan Barr and J. Ford, CYC); Class III-X: *Pompero* (J. Svensson, CYC); *Serena PC57* (Clark Keaton, CYC); Class III-Y: *Canopus* (Fred Fenske, CYC); Thunderbirds: *Yare* (Victor Smith); Six-Meters: *Eros* (Ron McFarlane, SYC); *Goose* (S. Chadwick, CYC); PHRF-ALPHA: *Haida* (Bob Dawson, PMYC); *African Star* (D. Fryer, SYC); PHRF-BETA: *Altair* (Kjell Dale, CYC).

In Memoriam, 1969: Warren W. Adams, Merritt E. Benson, Elmer Doll, E. A. Eastman, Commander Edward F. Ferguson, E. C. Fiedler, Mrs. Tony (Bessie) Jensen, O. M. Henderickson, Dr. Edward D. Hoedemaker, Michael S. Lafromboise, J. Glen Liston, J. Elroy McCaw, Dr. Frederick Moll, Past Commodore Charles R. Olmstead, Mrs. E. S. (Ellie) Ramey, Lawrence M. Riches, and George Watt.

The 1960s were unusual years for Seattle. The world's fair and the new Supersonics basketball team brought national headlines. The decade was also a time of continued growth for the Seattle Yacht Club in membership and outstations. The club was remodeled, and the moorages were renovated and covered. Participation in both sailboating and powerboating was intense. Fiberglas hulls began to replace wood in both sail and power craft. Late in the decade, the social unrest reached private clubs as federal and local governments pressured organizations to guarantee equal opportunities. These pressures would increase in the years that followed. ☆

The Seattle Yacht Club in the late 1970s. (Photo by Sally Laura)

NINE

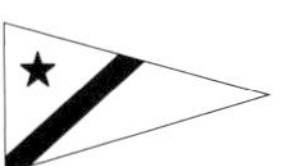

The 1970s

The 1970s had hardly dawned when President Nixon sent combat units into Cambodia, broadening the Vietnam conflict. This heated up the anti-war protests on campuses throughout the country. From time to time, anti-war parades blocked Seattle streets and even the I-5 freeway. The friction continued until April 1975, when the United States withdrew from the Vietnamese conflict.

In 1971 U.S. astronauts traveled across the moon's surface in a lunar buggy made by The Boeing Company.

In 1973 the Watergate Affair dominated national news. Four of President Nixon's aides, including Domestic Advisor John Ehrlichman of Bellevue, resigned in April. In August 1974 Nixon resigned the presidency rather than face impeachment proceedings.

All this turmoil seemed to contrast with the pleasures of sailing on peaceful Puget Sound. The 1970s were busy years at the Seattle Yacht Club.

1970

Commodore Don Thompson oversaw phase one of improvements that included work on the upper parking lot, Star dock, and shop-locker building. The SYC Henry Island Outstation also was improved during the year, and Ted and Jane Grunerud moved in as caretakers.

Later in the year, plans for enlarging the moorage at Port Madison ran into opposition from neighbors and certain public agencies. The club solved the problem by agreeing to install a new sewage disposal system to meet new Kitsap County Board of Health standards and by canceling plans for a landfill.

In May the cover of the *Binnacle*, in color for the first time, featured the smiling faces of the Opening Day Admiral Paul Morris, Admiralette Ellie Hammer, and Vice Admiral Peter McTavish. Inside was an article written by Arden Steinhart about member Ray Eckmann's recent suggestion to hold the Washington-

UCLA crew race down the Montlake cut just before parade time on Opening Day. This move would allow more spectators to view the contest than was the case with the traditional location off Madison Park. Commodore Don Thompson and Eckmann worked out the details with University of Washington Coach Dick Erickson.

Once again the Women's Group took the Sweepstakes Trophy for best overall decorated boat in the Opening Day parade. *Jake*, belonging to Jake and John Ford, was the boat of choice. The designer and producer of costumes and decor was once again Alice West. The futuristic sailors aboard the 2070 A.D. *Flying Dutchman* wore costumes of shimmering fabrics in bright colors, which, according to the *Binnacle*, "dazzled the judges into making the right decision."

A major topic among yachtsmen in 1970 involved new state and federal regulations requiring boat owners to install

The Corinthian Yacht Club

Following the end of World War II, a number of developments precipitated a general discontent among the sailing community, including the Seattle Yacht Club. First, there was an increased emphasis on powerboating. Second, the number of one-design small boats had increased, and the owners wanted more competitive events and around-the-buoy racing on Lake Washington. Third, the Seattle Yacht Club seemed reluctant to expand its racing program beyond traditional and long-distance races. And last, but not least, the SYC facilities and organization at the time were not adaptable to including a large number of small sailboat owners with limited means.

World War II had taken many of the younger members away from established traditional yacht clubs where racing programs had been eroded during the war years. There was a need for an organization that could absorb the more serious older sailors and the aggressive new younger sailors into a tightly operated racing program. A corps of dedicated sailboat owners held a number of meetings in 1944 to form a new association of amateur sailors to be available to all who wanted to sail and were dedicated to enhancing the art of sailing through a comprehensive competitive racing program.

At war's end, Charlie Frisbie and Charlie Ross gathered a group to discuss the formation of a pure sailing club patterned along the lines of the successful Corinthian Yacht Club in San Francisco. The idea became very popular and a large number of Seattle Yacht Club sailors transferred their allegiance to the new club or held dual membership.

Jan. 26, 1945, is officially registered as the date of inception of the new Corinthian Yacht Club of Seattle. Charlie Frisbie was elected the first commodore and served two terms. Hans Otto Giese followed with two terms. Gosta Erickson was elected as the third commodore but left Seattle for a crew-coaching position at Syracuse University. Bob Withington filled the vacated position, then was elected to a full term as the fourth commodore. The 1946 yearbook lists 248 members and indicates the initiation fee was $20 and annual dues were $20.

Hans Otto Giese was a controversial character and played a major role in the formation of CYC. An aggressive and competitive sailor and skier, he always wanted to win at anything he undertook, but he respected anyone good enough to beat him. Giese's skiing ability continued to improve along with the better equipment available in the 1940s and 1950s. He was a difficult man to beat on a downhill run. A group of younger people formed an alliance that became known as the "I beat Giese" group after they had crossed the finish line before the older man. It was all in good fun and demonstrated his competitive spirit and the respect others held for him.

The proliferation of one-design boats was a major cause of expansion of the racing program. The

holding tanks in order to prevent pollution of the sound.

In the September *Binnacle* the interim committee for the Salt Water Facility Program presented a plan that included recommendations to (1) add facilities to allow future expansion of membership, (2) add SYC moorage at Shilshole, (3) locate a regatta facility near a desirable sailing area, and (4) establish a designated after-race meeting and socializing place.

The North American Six-Meter Championship Races, held August 29–31, involved such SYC members as Bill Teeter, Kiefer Fobes, Minor Pelly, Wood Lyda, Ron McFarlane, Ray Wester, Charlie Ross, Bill Button, and Carl Jensen. Eustace "Sunny" Vynne, Jr., was the defending champion, but the *Francis IV* of the St. Francis Yacht Club of San Francisco ran off with the honors.

The winner of the first leg of the Masthead Trophy Race was Dr. Rodney Hearne with a 16-second error. Ed Messett

"one designs" were very competitive in their own fleets, and they wanted to be competitive in class. Owners of Stars, Blanchards, Dragons, flatties, and others were interested in the development of a well-run racing program. SYC seemed uninterested in providing support for such an expanded sailboat schedule, and many of the new boat owners were less interested in the social aspects of SYC or were unable to afford to belong; all of this factored into the formation of CYC.

So CYC was born as a low-overhead organization dedicated to the spartan aspects of sailing. The first clubhouse and meeting room were in the old ferry terminal building at Leschi. Charlie Frisbie, through his downtown connections, arranged free use of the space. The races were run from the top of the old cold storage building, now the site of the Leschi Cafe.

CYC was a solid club from the beginning; the Wednesday night racing series drew a lot of interest. CYC sailors also competed in all other major races in the area, contributing to and participating in the annual PIYA Regatta each summer. An annual club cruise was held during the remainder of the two weeks following the PIYA events. The annual banquet, where awards were made and new officers introduced, was the wrap-up for the sailing year.

When CYC was forced to move from the ferry terminal building, their next meeting rooms were in a community center in south Seattle. Members definitely needed a home port location. In 1953 there was talk of a moorage and new clubhouse at Duwamish Head, then meeting rooms were reestablished at Leschi. CYC Commodore Bill Lieberman, in his 1970 message, noted that Sunny Vynne, Dick Marshall, John Ellis, Tom Hickman and Peter Eising were the members most responsible for the completion of the Shilshole Bay clubhouse station. Twenty-five years after formation, CYC occupied its own home, a major milestone.

Commodore Phil Smith of SYC in 1950 recognized that SYC membership needed a boost. A "good old boys" men's club could no longer serve the evolving pleasure craft community, for boating was rapidly becoming a family sport and popular recreational activity. Sailing, as demonstrated by CYC, needed to be highly organized and supported by the club administration and structure. So in 1950 Dr. Smith extended SYC membership at no initiation fee to any Corinthian member who wished to join. Many took advantage of this dual-membership opportunity; this membership boost did much to restore the sailing program at SYC.

For many years, CYC and SYC have jointly coordinated their racing programs. A warm relationship developed as SYC conducted the major distance races on both Lake Washington and the sound, and CYC conducted the evening series on Lake Washington and at Shilshole Bay.

—Based on a May 1991 interview with Holden W. (Bob) Withington, who was official club measurer for many years and developer of the XYZ classes for light displacement boats

won the second leg, Phil Luther took the third leg, and Ed Donohue captured the fourth leg, but the overall winner was Rod Hearne, whose accumulated error was 168 seconds. The contest was held aboard Art Woodley's twin-screw diesel yacht *North Star*.

Overall winner of the IPBA International Cruiser Race was Les Summers of Vancouver in *Vandal* with a .2865 percent error after correction for his handicap. This was the first year a handicapping system was used and it proved controversial.

In the Vancouver-to-Juneau Race, the *Largo* of Thol Simonson, one of four California entrants, won the Juneau Bear Pennant and placed first overall for the entire run.

Serge Becker described another race in the November *Binnacle*:

Familiar Names and Familiar Faces

Jim Torrance was hired at SYC on Opening Day 1953, when he was 14 years old; soon after he was offered a job as bus boy in the dining room. He worked through a number of positions before becoming assistant manager. He served many years as maintenance engineer, and still knows every nail, pipe, wire, and board in the club's buildings.

In 1953 Torrance was hired by Manager Dick Jones and reported to Head Bookkeeper, Receptionist and General Roustabout Elsie Palmer. His supervisor was Gunner Algren, chief of maintenance. His first duties were in the maintenance department, though he also worked for Luncheon Hostess Levey as bus boy, table waiter, and dishwasher.

In the early 1950s the office staff consisted of Elsie Palmer and Leonard Sly, the printer. Sly ran his print shop in an area that is now the men's bar. He printed everything, including the *Binnacle*. He later began his own printing business in Alaska and was replaced by Harvey White. White was concerned that every child know how to read and volunteered much time teaching remedial reading.

While Millie Matson was in charge of the office, she had a helper named Diane Malone who, among other duties, helped Walt Little with the PHRF sailboat handicapping and race results work. Malone later married retired Coast Guard CWO Denny Johnson, who is now skipper of the club's *Portage Bay* and in charge of the club's many small boats. Matson and Malone ran the phones, put out the mailings, set up all the parties, typed the *Binnacle* and handled many other duties. They were so busy the office was like a zoo most of the time, Torrance recalled.

Millie Matson was also the first assistant manager of operations. In fact, she served as manager of the club in the interim between Fred Taylor and Frank O'Gara. Frank Smith is now banquet manager and Diane Malone Johnson is now the assistant banquet manager.

Following Matson, the office managers have been Linda Ives, Noreen Daniels, and now Nan Peterson.

Maintenance supervisors have been Gunner Algren and Jim Torrance, with Torrance taking over the position in 1960. Herman Borgmaster, a carpenter who worked at the club in the 1950s and 1960s, was a true artist with wood. He built special sets for events such as the shipwreck parties. He built the bulkhead for the Star dock and the walkways to the piers. He installed the teak in the Marine Room, built the roof-mounted hoist that serves the Marine Room bar and built a nice table with anchor legs for the chart room, which is now over in the fisheries building conference room.

Chefs who have served at SYC include Ron West, Manfred Stumpf, Bruce Marsh, Otto Dinkenger, Chet Smith, Alfred Eisman, Gene Meuller, Hilda Dolozycki, Francis Ramey, Costa Lazanti, Carl Reinholt, and Josephine Morgenroth. Francis Ramey was at the club for more than a quarter-century. Hilda was famous for her banana cream pies that were served only on Wednesdays.

No matter how you look at it, the Seattle Salts' Smith Island Race, and its companion, Seattle Salts' Blakely-Scatchet Race, lived up to the synonym that is part of their title! They're not salty so much as hairy. . . .

An imposing list of statistics record the gear and other failures: 10 dismastings. This is not confirmed, it is merely the count taken on boats that came within range of the R.C.; two broken booms, confirmed. Uncounted blown spinnakers, genoas, and assorted sails. Two strandings, the most romantic one being Bob Hurlow's *Balaka* which perched on Minor Island until the following high tide. Story has it that U.S. Coast Guard patrol boat ordered all crew except one to abandon ship and stay on Minor Island. There *is* a story there, if we could get it!! Just how was removal effected in the first place, and boarding completed when the water came back! Also, how effective is stud poker in whiling away time between tides on a Light House station? A more prosaic one was Henry Garrigues' pile-up of his *Calypso* somewhere

Names of those who worked the Ward Room include Tony Pos, Renado, Bunny, Daffney O'Brien, Ila Menne, Levey, Fritz Meuller, Martin Roberts, Tim Rooke, Ted Johnson, Barbara Pomeroy, Erma Jean Gordon, Lona Wehling, Shawn Chriest, and Margie Gibson. There were others whose names could not be remembered.

Bookkeepers through the years include Elsie Palmer, Kay Reitslag, Eddie Abellera, Betty Nermi, Mary Cerosklags, and Phyllis Mohr. The club's current bookkeeping staff includes: Eddie Abellera, controller, Marie Douglas, Gilbert Martelino, and Julie Moore.

Over the past 70 years at the Hamlin Street location, the Marine Room staff has included chief bartenders Frank Edwards, Willie Washington, Elzie Taylor, Mary Berry, and Bing Kimble. Vera Washington and Caroline Benning served as hostesses.

The club has never had a dock master, but does employ a night watchman to check the boats in each slip every night, 365 nights a year. Chris Johnson worked on the docks for a time. He painted the Portage Bay station masthead from a bosun's chair. A fellow named Jimmy Meyers helped on the piers for a time. Doug Goodspeed worked at the club several years and was well-liked. Byron Knight was a good worker and stayed about six years. (He is now a television station manager in Milwaukee, Wisconsin.) Keith Dearborn, who once worked for the club, is now a yacht club member. Terry Foxum, now an architect, also worked at the club.

Dave Thomas is the present chief of maintenance. He plans and supervises most club maintenance and keeps up the grounds. He came on board in 1970 and has really improved the landscaping. He is responsible for the flowers in the gardens. Kevin Fleetwood is Thomas' assistant and has been with the club for six years.

The club has had one employee for 28 years that few members have ever met. Harold Taylor works on Mondays, and his job is to completely clean the kitchen. He scrubs everything and cleans filters and grease traps. He is the reason the SYC restaurant has established such a high standard with the King County Health Department.

The club also has a longtime dishwasher and pots and pans man in the kitchen. Dick Hammond is a former brick layer, whose pay was reduced by about half when he took the job. But his job at SYC is steady and has benefits, and he is a very loyal employee. His cousin Benny, also a brick layer, worked for the club for several years.

Many years ago a barber worked at the club. In the 1940s and early 1950s, members could get a shave, haircut and shoeshine at the barbershop, which was located at the north end of the lower deck hallway about where the employees' lounge is now located.

And those are some of the memorable names and faces that have served through the years at the Seattle Yacht Club as recalled by Jim Torrance.

—From an interview with Assistant Manager Jim Torrance who has been employed at SYC for nearly 40 years. We regret any misspelling of names or the overlooking of employees. Unfortunately club records are scarce for years prior to the 1970s.

in the vicinity of Port Townsend.

Calypso's rudder carried away, and she had to be towed back to moorings.

—Binnacle, *November 1970*

Powerboat race results were dominated throughout the decade by Donovan Bancroft's *Alaska Hunter*. Other boats that won often included Dr. Rodney B. Hearne's *Keewaydin*, Townley Bale's *Blue Chip* and Lester Lewis' *Desert Queen*.

The SYC yearbook listed the following trophies and award winners for 1970.

Commodore's Trophy: *Pursuit* (Don Fleming, CYC); Mark Mayer Trophy: *Virada II* (Frank Francisco, CYC); Single-Handed Races: Sea Fever Trophy, *Lancer* (Norm Larabee, CYC); Nautilus Trophy, *Wildwind* (G. William Ososke, CYC); Quent Williams Trophy, *Pompero* (John Svenson, CYC); Osprey Trophy, *Prelude* (K. Magleby, PMYC); Vashon Island Race: Vashon Trophy, *Mara* (Bill Buchan, Jr., CYC); Category III Overall, *Goose* (Stephen Wertheimer, CYC); Protection Island/Point Hudson Race: *Mara* (Bill Buchan, Jr., CYC); Category III Overall, *Margueritha* (William Button, SYC); Scatchet Head Race: Hat Island Trophy, *Mara* (Bill Buchan, Jr., CYC); Category III Overall, *Rev* (P. S. Lettenmaier, CYC); Smith Island Race: Gwendolyn II and Bob Gibbons Memorial trophies, *Moonglow III* (Dave Nielson, TYC); Lady Medina Trophy, *Swallow* (Phil Johnson, SYC); Blakely-Scatchet Head Race: Jerry Bryant Old Salts' Trophy, *Serena* (Clark Keaton, CYC); Horder-Provine Old Salts' and Kennell Midwatch trophies, *Canopus* (Fred Fenske, CYC)

Tri-Island Series: Mark Mayer Cup and Three-Island Trophy, *Mara* (Bill Buchan, Jr., CYC); Bob Bollong Trophy, *Firecracker* (Richard Gilbert, SYC); Humphrey and Hostetter trophies, *Serena* (Clark Keaton, SYC); Seaborn, Gardner Gamwell and Tri-Island T-Bird trophies, *Rev* (Pat Lettenmaier, CYC); PHRF Walt Little Trophy, *Kaiulani* (Paul

The Three Tree Point Yacht Club

In 1969, five men named Cole, Harper, Anderson, Puckett, and Wintermute decided to enter a dinghy derby contest sponsored by a Seattle radio station. They became involved with a *Lusty Wench* on the Lake Washington Ship Canal. The *Wench*, of course, was an especially seaworthy, six-horsepower bed complete with night-shirted, cacophonous minstrels and an ornamental "wench." The raft, being sufficiently peculiar, won $50 for first place in the dinghy derby. What better use of the $50 prize money than to organize a yacht club? Thus the Three Tree Point Yacht Club was formed.

In 1970, with the opening of the Des Moines Marina, the club was expanded to include sailboaters. From the original 32 charter members, the club had grown to 327 members and 133 boats by May 1991.

The highlights of the TTPYC include the entrance of *Cherokee* in the 1977 Victoria-to-Maui Race; the win by Explorer Post 950 in the Swiftsure Race aboard *Heather*; the 1980 SYC Sailor of the Year Award to Jim Chilton (TTPYC commodore at the time); the Sea-Tac recording of 28.755 inches of mercury the morning of the 1980 Duwamish Head Race, which 122 boats entered and only 50 finished; and the presentation of the 1980 Tug Boat Annie Award to Jo Anne Walderon.

Major events of the club include the traditional crab feed and cruise to Blake Island in March, the Minto Mingle Dinghy Race in July, and the Sleep and Creep Cruise to Dockton in October. The Windjammer series of sailboat races is a Grand Prix qualifier, as is TTPYC's biggest race—Duwamish Head—which is run in January as part of the South Sound series.

The Three Tree Point Yacht Club has no clubhouse or outstation and yet offers well-attended races, cruises, and social get-togethers throughout the year. This yacht club has come a long way since the days of the *Lusty Wench* and her small crew.

—Based on material supplied by Phil Rhodes and Dory Hamlyn

McCullough, BremertonYC); PHRF First President's Trophy, *Freedom* (Dan Barr, CYC); Captain Hoyt Trophy, *Gamin* (Lon Robinson, CYC)

Consistent winners, Category I, Class A: *Aurora* (John Schlagel, SYC); *Moonglow* (Dave Nielson, TYC); *Six Pack* (Bruce Hedrick, UWYC); *Olympian* (Peter Schmidt, SYC); Category I, Class B: *Gamin* (Lon Robinson, CYC); *Mara* (Bill Buchan, Jr., CYC); Category I, Class C: *Eagle* (Larry Shorett, CYC); *Hooligan* (Tom O'Brien, SYC); *Swallow* (Phil Johnson, SYC); Category I, Class D: *High Life* (Don Miller, CYC); *Mistral* (J. C. Baillargeon, SYC); *Quest* (Alan Rutherford, CYC); Category III, Class X: *Bobtail* (Bob Allen, SYC); Category III, Class Z: *Canopus* (Fred Fenske, CYC); *Drakkar* (Fred Krabbe, CYC); *Prelude* (K. Magleby, PtMYC); Thunderbirds: *Rev* (Pat Lettenmaier, CYC); *Sonata* (R. J. MacLean, CYC); *Williwa* (Bernard Swenson, CYC); PHRF-Alpha: *Kaiulani* (Paul McCullough, Bremerton YC); *Keema* (Russ Schulke, CYC); *Swanhilde* (W. L. Mercier, CYC); PHRF-B: *Freedom* (Dan Barr, CYC); Coronado 25: *Cristobal* (Lee Buse, CYC); *Encore* (Don Campbell, CYC); *Scotch Mist* (C. Sandborn, CYC); PHRF-Gamma: *Otter* (H. Preusser, SBYC)

In Memoriam, 1970: Jerry C. Bryant, Edward E. Clapp, Vern A. Cole, Dexter W. Dimmock, Richard W. Gilbert, Donald F. Grandston, Allen P. Green, Jr., Winslow Jones, Dr. Michael E. Kennedy, Charles W. Latta, L. Burns Lindsey, Mrs. Gerald P. (Helen) McManama, Dr. McCormick Mehan, M. M. Mossman, P. J. Perry, Mrs. Carl A. (Eva May) Sandquist, Dietrich Schmitz, J. Harold Sparkman, and William A. Stancer.

1971

Commodore Richard Shorett appointed Serge Becker as editor of the *Binnacle*, but Becker resigned in June, and Hugh Blackwell took over with Ed Donohue as managing editor.

In March the commodore wrote:

> Our legislature is now in session and many bills have been introduced. There are five bills having to do with boat operation, numbering, taxes, and police powers, and another bill dealing with holding tanks. In addition, there are several bills involving shoreline and still another concerning our liquor permits.
>
> —Binnacle, *March 1971*

He urged each member to become acquainted with these bills and to send letters to legislators, with copies submitted to Interclub representatives Ray L. Eckmann and Hartney Oakes.

The *Wild Goose* was seen often in Northwest waters during the summer of 1971 with its owner, movie star John Wayne, aboard. He posed for *Binnacle* pictures and noted that the San Juan Islands were the finest cruising waters in the world. Wayne's boat was a 136-foot mine sweeper that had been converted after World War II to the luxury yacht *La Beverie* by SYC honorary member Harold A. Jones of Vancouver, B.C. SYC member Max Wyman owned it for a time before it was acquired by John Wayne.

New Commodore Joseph L. Williams' first message in the *Binnacle* noted how busy the past year had been.

> We have seen the completion of our new [upper] parking facility and the renovation of our Star dock, a new disposal system at Port Madison and the development of additional moorage floats there and the completion of a variety of improvements here in our clubhouse. In addition to all this we have passed a milestone in meeting our final payment on the tidelands under our piers.
>
> Our activities have been equally successful and were beautifully handled by our competent committees. We gained national notice in co-hosting the World Star Championships and have added the Dragon Gold Cup to our trophy case.
>
> —Binnacle, *November 1971*

The *Binnacle* pictured the club's office staff at work. In the front office were Lee Arnold, Millie Matson (who was starting her 20th year at the club), and Ruth Meranda. In the bookkeeping office were the club accountant Kay Retschlag, her assistant Hazel Gordon, and "burroughs operator" Janet Dickinson.

Activities of the Women's Group

During the 1950s few committees were needed to coordinate the activities of the Women's Group. Today, however, women serve on the entertainment, opening day, powerboat, trophy, racing, rope yarn, *Binnacle*, club boats, membership, historical, and finance committees to name a few of the nearly 50 club committees. In addition they serve on many Women's Group Committees.

The Women's Group column in the *Binnacle*, the club newsletter started by the juniors in 1928, keeps the members informed of dates, times, activities and general news; it is vital to the functioning of the club. The *Binnacle* committee chairman is responsible for preparing this column.

The women's bridge group was started during Shirlee Liberman's presidency in 1964. From the outset, a variety of bridge classes for all skill and interest levels have been offered. Even the men found time to take lessons and play. From a small group of a few tables the group has increased to 40 or 50 players a month. The regular gathering is the fourth Wednesday of the month from September to June with "passes" in November and December. After 28 years, bridge is still going strong at SYC.

Such is not the case with bowling, a popular women's activity for many years, which was started by Judy Brighton in 1968. Four teams of four players each began playing at the University Village Lanes, which were convenient because parking was free, free lessons were available, and a nursery was available for child care and babysitting while mothers bowled. The next year Queen City and Rainier yacht club women were invited to join the Interclub Yacht Club Bowling League, which eventually had 12 teams. But after 20 years, the bowling teams disbanded.

The women's golf group meets the second and fourth Thursday each month. Some 12 to 15 women have always played together since this group formed in 1990, with players at various skill levels. The women began by hitting balls at Puetz Driving Range on Aurora. They have since played on the Jefferson and Jackson courses and have taken lessons from Ken Greenway. After their games of nine holes they return to the club for lunch followed by a meeting in the Commodore's Room. On rainy days they meet in the Heritage Room, watch golf movies, and practice putting on the plush carpet. The group is still in the developing stages and has not yet selected a name. The committee heads are Betsy Greenway, chairman; Ann Weber, assistant; Libby Oswald, secretary; Betsy Sunich, treasurer; Norma Cochran, luncheons; and Fran Barnard, trophies.

Mah Jong, a game first popular in the United States during the 1920s, was introduced to the Women's Group in 1980 by member Betty Chang, who had learned the Chinese game in her home as a child. The western version is played with 144 ivory or plastic tiles about the size of dominoes, which are painted with symbols, characters, and flowers. The object of the game, played with four players, is to obtain sets of tiles. It is similar to the game of rummy. Betty taught Mah Jong lessons at the club for several years. Over the last decade, such members as Lou Bradley, Barbara Benton, Phyllis Parsons, Eleanor Black, Lucy McHolland, Jeanne Kelly, Gertrude Palmer, and Jan Freitag have been heard clicking tiles in the Marine Room on Mondays. The Mah Jong welcome mat is always out.

The dinghy group was organized in 1980 by La Rue Gove for the purpose of taking excursions away from the club. This monthly excursion group is open to all SYC women. Instrumental in organizing the planned activities were Diane Sweezey and Pat Saxon. The group's journeys took members to the waterfront, art galleries, and museums, as well as to Leavenworth, Tahoe, Reno, and other destinations. An April 1991 article written for the *Binnacle* by Lola Smith describes a dinghy group trip to Victoria.

> Double occupancy for one night with continental breakfast and a champagne cocktail. Transportation to and from the Empress Hotel . . . a two-and-a-half hour trip on the Clipper. Activities included museums, Butchart Gardens, shopping, dining, gambling, and much more . . . Grab a partner and bring your dough. Off to Victoria we go. All for the price of $132.
>
> —*Lola Smith,* Binnacle, *April 1991*

The drama group was organized by Lou Bradley in the mid-1970s. Members of the drama group have received both amateur and professional guidance and have performed for luncheons, holidays, club inaugurations,

Rope Yarn Thursdays, and at the Fo'c'sle. Among the early actors were Eleanor Black, Margaret Botsford, Peggy Gould, Rae Schmoyer, Ellen Ward, Joan Goodwin, Vicky Johnston, Barbara Benton, Sally Laura, Diane Sweezey, and Betty Chang. Past productions have been written, produced, and directed by members. Productions of *Cynthia* and *Four for the Money* received applause from *Binnacle* critic Lola Smith, who wrote: "The Drama Group always exudes an aura of great good humor and camaraderie, and their productions are always a delight for everyone." Thespians of recent years include Donna Rodda, Marlee McKibbin, La Rue Gove, Betty Stewart, Virginia Cluck, Jeanne Kelly, Margo Miller, and music major Lola Smith. The drama group meets monthly between September and June.

The cookbook committee was formed in 1989 when the Women's Group decided to publish *Extraordinary Cuisine for Sea and Shore*. The effort was to raise funds to help support nonprofit boating organizations by sharing private recipes adapted to boating. Unlike cooking in a kitchen which is furnished and equipped much like others in the neighborhood, galleys vary greatly. This cookbook takes those differences into consideration and was a great success. To date the proceeds have allowed the women to purchase two rowboats, which they donated to Children's Hospital for the summer camp program. The women continue to promote the cookbook, which sells for $12.95 and contains 200 recipes including appetizers, beverages, salads, soups, vegetables, entrees, pasta, rice, potatoes, eggs, breads, and desserts. Committee co-chairmen are Gail Johnson and Carol Kessi. Committee members are Barbara Endrody, Mary Fox, Judy Johnson, Elaine Kidd, Debby Koch, Sally Laura, Penny Pilant, Bev Romano, Mary Shirley, and Linda Wyman.

Exercise and dance classes have been available through the Women's Group since the 1970s. Margaret Tapping Eastman, former director and choreographer of Northwest Ballet and owner of the Margaret Tapping School of Dance, teaches the classes. It was no accident that classes in fitness and exercise expanded to ballet, tap dance, and a few interpretive hulas, which find their way from time to time to the Fo'c'sle dance floor in May. Classes change to reflect the popular culture and members' interests.

The Seanotes, a Women's Group choir organized by Sally Laura in 1990, joined with SYC men under the direction of Tamara Still with accompaniment by Rae Schmoyer to prepare for their first holiday appearances but snow interrupted. They did perform at Rope Yarn Sunday (Thursday) and received considerable acclaim, and they were a smash hit in their spring musical review. Seanote members include Maxine Bailey, Lee Hillman Brown, Laura Boone, Gail Dupar, Krissie Hayes, Jette Hammer, Susan Laura, Donna Rodda, Natalie Roush, Polly Russell, Audrey Salkield, Bonnie Sharpe, Sharon Strong, Mary Williams, Gordon Boone, Norm Cole, Jim Chilton, Dr. Ernest Frolund, Don Hillman, Stan Laura, Doug Sherwood, Bruce Smith, Brian Thomas, and Dave Williams. All members are invited to try out with the Seanotes.

The Women's Group historian is charged with the duty of collecting and preserving newspaper articles, photographs, and other memorabilia representative of the Women's Group activities. At the time of this writing, six large scrapbooks have been filled with programs, clippings, and photos illustrating the variety of activities, projects and adventures undertaken by the members. Historian chairman and past president Elaine Kidd has kept the collection on a continuous basis for more than 20 years.

The grants-in-aid committee researches the opportunities for placement of excess funds from membership dues. These funds have been used to assist women in competitive racing and to purchase three mooring buoys which were donated to the parks department for use by the public.

The water-at-large committee arranges courses related to boating. In the past classes offered have covered navigation, first aid, lockage, anchoring, and electronics. Barbara Benton, Eunice Blanchard, Sally Laura, and Molly Cadranell have been among those who volunteered as instructors for both youth and adult classes. Denny Johnson, skipper of SYC's *Portage Bay* has served as instructor for the Women's Group committee.

Other Women's Group committees include those involved with decorations, dinner meetings, hospitality, membership, menus, newcomers, photography, foreign language classes, publicity, reservations, sunshine, and telephone.

—From materials provided by Ann F. Bayless

Women's Group Activities

Eleanor Black (left) and Margaret Botsford joined the popular bowling activities offered through the SYC Women's Group in the 1970s and 1980s.

Women's Group historian, Elaine Kidd.

Lola Smith (left) and Helene Becker brought out their hats for the September 1981 Fashion Show, an annual event.

The Drama Group provides entertainment for the Women's Group. From left, Shirlee Liberman, Betty Stewart, and Barbara Benton share the spotlight as drama members.

From left, Jeanne Kelly, Lou Bradley, Suzanne Ward, and Gertrude Palmer combined the pleasure of cruising with the fun of playing Mah Jong during a Women's Group outing.

La Rue Gove and Diane Sweezey, organizers of the Dinghy Group.

SYC Women's Dinghy Group off to Reno, January 1987. From left: Elizabeth Meier, Margaret Boruki, Ellen Ward, Doris MacRae, Donna Rodda, Marlee McKibbin, Judy Fisher, and Betsy Luther.

Above: Michele Shaw (left) and Barbara Leslie. At left: Sally Laura (left) and Virginia Cluck on an annual May cruise to Port Madison.

SYC Women's Group dance class. Standing, from left: teacher Margaret Eastman, Muriel Clark, Barbara Benton, Diane Benson, Kit Ford, unknown, and Suzanne Ward. In front, from left: Nona Lippert, Margie Williams, and Peggy Gould.

(Photos courtesy SYC Women's Group)

A note from *Binnacle* writer Judy Brighton to the SYC general membership called for support of the Women's Group. "Comfort those few among you who are shuddering in trepidation of 'Women's Lib' as a potential threat from the Women's Group," she wrote. "Fear not." She explained that the ladies of the Seattle Yacht Club truly wished only to be a complement to all members in every way, at all times. "But the Women's Group is here and it doesn't plan to go away. . . . Perhaps more generous recognition of the Women's Group endeavors could reflect on all of you." (*Binnacle*, November 1971)

The December *Binnacle* carried a fascinating report from Bob Carter who was sailing his yacht *Cynthia R* across Europe via the river and canal system.

Two SYC members—Norman C. Blanchard and Robertson Ross—were named by U.S. Secretary of Transportation John A. Volpe to the new national Boating Safety Advisory Council. This council advised the Coast Guard on performance and construction standards for boats and accessory equipment.

Conrad Knutson was up to his epaulets in organizational details as Opening Day approached. He had help from Admiralette Trudy Lane, Vice-Admiral Frank G. Bourque, and Mickey Mouse, who served as grand marshal of the Opening Day parade, which had a Disney World theme. John Ford's *Jake* won a first prize among the decorated sailboats, and Howard Lovejoy's *Tolo* captured the overall award.

The Swiftsure Race was something special in 1971 because KOMO-TV's Don McCune, with his production crew headed by Joel Schroedel, went along to capture the race for an episode of "Exploration Northwest."

During the week of September 11 Seattle hosted "Star Worlds," the first time this prestigious sailing event was scheduled in Northwest waters. It was sponsored by the International Star Class Yacht Racing Association, the Puget Sound Star Fleet and the sixth district (PIYA area) and hosted by the Seattle and Corinthian yacht clubs. The races attracted boats from Sweden, Brazil, Argentina, Bahamas, Australia, Canada, and the United States. Bill Buchan, Jr., and Carl Sutter, who won the world championship in Sweden in 1970, were the defending champions. The best showing by a Seattle racer was Bill Buchan's fourth place. He was topped by two boats from San Diego and one from Sweden.

John "Bud" Peterson reported on the Norpac Race, which took place July 25–August 4 in three sounds—Barkley, Clayoquot, and Nootka. After each race day, the boats would rendezvous in some nearby bay. He reported that the Turtle Island rendezvous was a disaster:

> The chart showed a rock on one side of the entrance but someone moved it and it was in the middle of the channel. Serge Becker's boat *Ocean Cape* gave it a good whack at six knots but couldn't move it and it resulted in cut and bruised legs for Serge when he was thrown against his wheel. Les Eastmen, one of the crew, was thrown about ten feet and crashed through a safety glass window in the rear of Serge's cabin. Another crewman on his boat fell hard on the deck and his head missed the anchor by inches. Two more sailboats crashed on the rock and, then, not to be outdone, the *Lauren J*, a powerboat piloted by owner Fred Haight, piled on the rock. However, he didn't just dent a keel, he bent a shaft and has two shiny new props on this boat to show for it.
>
> —Binnacle, *September 1971*

The Seattle Yacht Club yearbook listed the following trophies and award winners for 1971.

Commodore's Trophy: *Six Pack* (L. C. Hedrick, RCYC); Mark Mayer Trophy: *Warlock* (R. Spanfelner, SBYC); Single-Handed Races: Sea Fever Trophy, *Outrageous* (Vern Day, CYC); Nautilus Trophy, *Firecracker* (Dick Gilbert, CYC); Osprey Trophy, *High*

Commodores of the Seattle Yacht Club—1970s

DONALD L. THOMPSON
1970
Born: 1918, Seattle, Wash.
Education: University of Washington
Occupation: Insurance Broker (P.J. Perry Co., Fred S. James Co.)
Boats: Meteora I, II, Spray *(36-foot sloop)*

RICHARD H. SHORETT
1971
Born: 1909, Seattle, Wash.
Education: University of Washington
Occupation: Founder, Metropolitan Savings and Loan, also Seattle Home Mortgage Corporation
Boats: Safari, Seamew, Nelsonia

JOSEPH L. WILLIAMS
1972
Born: 1931, Los Angeles, Calif.
Education: University of Washington
Occupation: Architect (Williams & Associates, Inc.), Legislator
Boats: Maria *(Cal 40 sailboat),* Nor'wester *(K-50)*

PETER J. MCTAVISH
1973
Born: 1919, Calgary, Alberta, Canada
Education: University of British Columbia
Occupation: Marine Electronics, Insurance Broker
Boats: Amigo *(3 different powerboats)*

STANLEY S. MARTIN
1974
Born: 1908, Spokane, Wash.
Occupation: Insurance Agency
Boat: KT, *(Thunderbird class sailboat)*

HOWARD E. LOVEJOY
1975
Born: 1916
Education: University of Michigan and University of Washington
Occupation: Marine Architect and Naval Engineer (CEO, Puget Sound Freight Lines and founded Puget Sound Truck Lines
Boat: Tolo

FRANK G. BOURQUE
1976
Born: 1918, Vancouver, B.C.
Education: University of British Columbia
Occupation: Banker, Bank of Nova Scotia, People's National Bank.
Boat: Mam'selle

HOWARD C. BRONSON
1977
Born: 1916, Sacramento, Calif.
Education: University of California, Davis
Occupation: Pacific Northwest Bell, then Self Employed
Boats: Ponga

WILLIAM (BILL) E. BRADSHAW
1978
Born: 1922, Seattle, Wash.
Education: University of Washington
Occupation: Self-employed Manufacturer's Agent
Boats: Elohe *(Sr. Knockabout 39),* Pompero *(PC),* Trio *(35-foot yawl)* Trio *(48-foot sloop)*

ARDEN C. STEINHART
1979
Born: 1906, Bucoda, Wash.
Education: University of Washington
Occupation: Architect
Boat: Seawagon

Life (Don Miller, CYC); Vashon Island Race: Vashon Trophy, *Adios* (Carl Jensen, SYC); Category III Overall, *High Life* (Don Miller, CYC)

Tri-Island Series: PHRF First President's Trophy, *Swift* (George Gunby, SYC); PHRF Walt Little Trophy, *Shalom* (Gary Watson, WL); Protection Island Trophy, *Eagle* (Larry Shorett, CYC); Category III Overall, *Bobtail* (Bob Allen, SYC); Scatchet Head Race: Hat Island Trophy, *Ambush* (Stan Kiesling, TYC); Category III Overall, *Marauder* (Baillinger and Anderson, CYC); Smith Island Race: Gwendolyn II Trophy, *Moonglow III* (Dave Nielsen, TYC); Lady Medina and Bob Gibbons Memorial trophies, *Firecracker* (Dick Gilbert, CYC); Mid-Sound Race: Horder-Provine Old Salts' and Kennell Midwatch trophies, *Reliant* (T. Uerling, EYC); Tri-Island Series: Mark Mayer Cup, *Olympian* (Pete Schmidt, SYC); Bob Bollong and Three-Island trophies, *Firecracker* (Dick Gilbert, CYC); Seaborn, Gardner Gamwell and T-Bird trophies, *Foresta* (Wil Anderson, SYC); Crooz N Snooz: Captain Hoyt Trophy, *Gamin* (Lon Robinson, CYC).

The IPBA decided to encourage family participation in the International Cruiser Race by making it a two-day affair with an overnight stop at Roche Harbor. The 1971 racers traveled south from Dodd Narrows to Jefferson Head. Howard Wilson of QCYC, the 1969 winner, picked up his second overall trophy.

Top powerboats of the year were Don Bancroft's *Alaska Hunter*, Townley Bale's *Blue Chip*, Lester Lewis' *Desert Queen*, J. Gordon Shotwell's *High Cotton*, Dr. Rodney B. Hearne's *Keewaydin*, Ed Dunn's *Runaway*, and Richard Shorett's *Safari*.

On Nov. 5, 1971 two longtime members were named honorary life members. James H. Moffett, Jr., who had joined SYC in 1948, died two months after being so honored. Frank Morris' membership dated from 1947.

In Memoriam, 1971: George B. Buchan, Ernest R. Cluck, Mrs. A. J. (Anne) Cook, W. Ward Davison, Ralf E. Decker, Dr. William P. Dodge, Elmer E. Green, Mrs. Paul C. (Jean) Harper, E. E. Kennell, Jr., Mrs. William O. (Leah) McKay, and Russell R. Pretlow.

1972

A reminder in the August *Binnacle* read:

> Seattle Yacht Club membership is limited by the Board of Trustees to 1,500. At this writing we are only 35 short of that number and there are that many applications to be processed. However, on the assumption that not all will be accepted, it is in your friends' interest that you submit his or her application immediately to Paul D. Dunstan, chairman of the Membership Committee. Thereafter, applications for membership will be considered on a waiting list pending resignation or demise of a present member.
>
> —Binnacle, *August 1972*

SYC Commodore Joseph L. Williams informed *Binnacle* readers in September that the Department of Ecology had decided the boating public would, in the near future, be faced with the installation of either primary treatment facilities or, after three years, holding tanks.

In his first message to members, incoming Commodore Peter J. McTavish wrote:

> The past year has been a memorable one for Seattle Yacht Club. We co-hosted a superb Pacific Coast Yachting Association sailing regatta, and in addition put on many fine racing events. The new docks and lower level heads at Port Madison are completed. . . . The Seattle clubhouse has had several improvements including the office area, the front lobby, the Marine Room deck, and virtually ready for use is the newly remodeled Men's Bar.
>
> —Binnacle, *November 1972*

At the time, a contest was announced to name the area formerly called "the men's bar." Several names were suggested at a Thursday men's luncheon before someone shouted "To hell with the women—let's call it the 'Men's Bar!'" A loud voice vote left no room for argument, even though the group had no power to decide. (Eighteen years later, the bar would be declared an open area, and women would be welcome at all times rather than just after 6:00 P.M. as was the case previously.)

Outgoing Commodore Joseph L. Williams called 1972 a memorable year. "For the first time in many, many years," he said, "we are totally free of debt, owing nothing to anyone. For the first time in our history we can proudly claim a net asset value in excess of one million dollars!" (*Binnacle*, November 1972)

At the end of the year, Executive Chef Otto Denkinger retired after six years at the club. Manfred Stumpf returned after two years at the Everett Golf and Country Club.

Opening Day was made memorable by John Ford's *Jake*, which won the Sweepstakes Award. The theme was the Alaska Gold Rush and Ford's boat depicted the "Cremation of Sam McGee," with the hero being warmed on a burning sled pulled by six dogs (people disguised as such).

The first Great Equalizer Race in April was a big hit. In level class racing, yachts with similar handicap ratings are grouped together to compete without handicaps. The first boat to cross the line is the winner. The sections do not race against each other. Ed Gove in *Pow Wow* took first in IOR Section 4. Dorr Anderson in his *White Mist* came in first in PHRF Section A. Several other SYC members placed second or third in the race.

The PIYA was considering instituting a new format providing for four "offshore racing" categories compared with the present three in use at the club. Rear Commodore Stan Martin reported that Bob Theriault, safety committee chairman, had volunteered to hold a series of meetings with members and to carry a consensus to the PIYA in the fall.

The basis for awarding the Jerry Bryant Skipper of the Year trophy was altered to allow each contestant to discard two of the six contests: the Bremerton Heavy Weather, the Everett Invitational, the Meydenbauer Bay Boomerang, the Rainier-Poulsbo Course and Compass, the Edmonds Round the Lake, and the International Cruiser races. Each contestant was to complete five of the races. The winner would be decided by adding total running times and errors to determine a seasonal percentage of error.

Les Lewis won the Barusch Trophy Race, topping contestants from five areas of the Pacific Coast. Contestants were not allowed to use their own boats. Lewis used a Queen City craft called the *Carrie Ann*.

Of the 147 boats in the Bremerton race, the best Seattle skipper placed 13th, and that was Rodney Hearne in his *Keewaydin*.

Howard Wilson won the International Cruiser overall award in the predicted log race from Keyport to De Courcy Island in British Columbia. This was his third win in four years. The race on to Alaska found Jim Hanna in *Jamal*, Jim Clapp in *Nothing More*, and Herb Schaefer in *Margy M. III* taking overall trophies. Jim Clapp won the Iceberg Goof Trophy for putting his boat on a reef in Silva Bay and dumping his wife Pam into the ocean off Egg Island as she tried to pass 70 pounds of gas to the *Co-Ca*.

The annual awards banquet on December 6 attracted an overflow crowd of 260. Many reservations were turned down for lack of space. "As a very large percentage of the people attending belong to other yacht clubs, we tried very hard to put our best foot forward, and with the staff of the SYC and the members of the trophy committee this was accomplished." (*Binnacle*, January 1973) There were many awards: Ten plaques were awarded to SYC powerboat and sailboat owners for donating their craft at races; 150 take-home race plaques, 33 take-home silver mint julep goblets, 18 take-home small boat awards, and 16 perpetual trophies were also given.

SYC junior Mark Laura, who won the Douglas Trophy with his University of Washington crew at the Inter-collegiate Match Boat Championships, was honored. So was Phil Brazeau whose *Kathy* was named SYC Boat of the Year. Beginning in 1972 a picture of the SYC Boat of the Year was displayed at the club.

The SYC yearbook listed the following trophies and award winners for 1972.

Vashon Island Race: *Jubilee* (Steve Crary, CYC); Commodore's Race: IOR, *Maysie* (Mike Meachan, CYC); PHRF, *Keema* (Russ Schulke, CYC); Frisbie Race: IOR, *Six Pack* (Bruce Hedrick, SYC); PHRF, *Helios* (Ralph Morgan, CYC); Protection Island Race: IOR Overall, *Tonic* (Dan Brink, CYC); Smith Island Race: Gwendolyn II A and B trophies, *Camelot* (R. R. Smith, TYC); Lady Medina C, D, and E trophies, *Starwagon* (Dick Gilbert, CYC); Jerry Bryant Old Salts' A and B PHRF trophies, *Nina Del Mar* (C. T. McCann, OYC); Bob Gibbons Memorial IOR Overall Trophy, *Camelot* (R. R. Smith, TYC)

Mid-Sound Race: Kennell Midwatch Trophy, *Wiki Wiki* (D. Clark, SYC); Horder/Provine Old Salts' PHRF Gamma/Delta Trophy, *Intrepid* (J. A. Herbert, CYC); Crooz N Snooz Races: Captain Hoyt IOR Overall Trophy, *Gamin* (Lon Robinson, CYC); PHRF Overall Trophy, *Rubicon* (Watkins, CYC); Scatchet Head Hat Island Trophy, *Moonglow IV* (Dave Nielsen, TYC).

Tri-Island Series: Mark Mayer Classes A and B cups and Three-Island Category I and II trophies, *Camelot* (R. R. Smith, TYC); Bob Bollong Memorial Class C Trophy, *Starwagon* (Dick Gilbert, CYC); Humphrey Class E Trophy, *Tonic* (Dan Brink, CYC); Seaborn Tri-Island Category III and Tri-Island Thunderbird trophies, *Galadriel* (John Kelly, CYC); Gardner Gamwell Class C Trophy, *Gem* (Ray Fiedler, CYC); First President PHRF Gamma/Delta Trophy, *Intrepid* (J. A. Herbert, CYC); PHRF Walt Little A and B trophies, *Panacea II* (John Daughters and Stone Parker, SYC)

Outstanding powerboats: *Alaska Hunter* (Donovan S. Bancroft); *Blue Chip* (Townley Bale); *Desert Queen* (Lester Lewis); *Keewaydin* (Dr. Rodney Hearne); *Nothingmore* (James Clapp)

In Memoriam, 1972: Bruce H. Bettcher, A. L. Blessing, John A. Burnett, Robert F. Campbell, Mrs. Truman C. (Margaret) Cragin, A. J. Duthie, Ev G. Henry, Howard F. Keeler, Otis F. Lamson, Jr., Mrs. J. Glen (Llo) Liston, Jr., James H. Moffett, Jr., R. Stuart Moore, Jr., Paul W. Neuman, Dr. E. B. Parmelee, John S. Radford, Mrs. James S. (Dorothy) Scully, and Mrs. H. C. Stimson.

1973

SYC Commodore Peter J. McTavish served during a comparatively quiet year and, as he put it, "we spent no money recklessly."

The Arab oil embargo was being felt in Seattle. Fuel for pleasure boating grew scarce and prices tripled. Several Seattle Yacht Club skippers switched from power to sailing craft.

February 2 and 3 brought the second annual Groundhog Day Cruise and Unpredictable Log Race which awarded a suitable plaque to the skipper of any boat that found its way to the fo'c'sle at Port Madison.

This year most Washington recreational motorboats, regardless of engine size, were required to have Coast Guard certificates of number by July 1. Previously only engines of more than 10 horsepower had to display numbers.

Bill and Florence Burke gave a specially mounted noon cannon to SYC to be used as a trophy for some type of boating competition. It became the SYC perpetual powerboat trophy known as the Noon Cannon Award and in February 1974 Andy Joy's name was the first to be appended.

Frank Piddington of the Royal Victoria Yacht Club announced that the

PIYA Regatta would begin its three-year residence at the "Royal Vic" in 1973 and that about 400 competitors were expected for the traditional annual event.

Charlie Ross garnered many a chuckle on Opening Day when his boat *Crok*, disguised as a crocodile, featured a live struggling female form in the gaping maw. He won first prize in the novelty class.

Sunny Vynne, manager of the *Intrepid* group to which many SYC members had contributed, spoke at the Sailboat Awards Banquet; his subject was the 12-meter yacht *Intrepid*, which now belonged to the Seattle Sailing Foundation and would race for a chance at the America's Cup. Among her crewmen were three SYC members—Gary Philbrick, Cappy Neu, and Steve Koch. Bill Buchan and Jim Caldwell were also from the Seattle area. The *Intrepid*, being the only wooden contender, adopted the motto "Knock on Wood." The failure of a turnbuckle at a

The Noon Cannon Perpetual Power Boat Trophy

The unusual Noon Cannon Trophy. (Wallace Ackerman Photography)

A noon cannon is a working model of a cannon with a lens suitably mounted as part of a sundial so that the sun's rays at noon are focused on the powder hole of the cannon, thus firing the cannon at high noon. The first ones were made in Europe in the early 1700s for royalty and are very rare today.

The Noon Cannon Trophy was donated to the Seattle Yacht Club by Florence and William Burke in March 1973. This handsome trophy was first presented to Andy Joy at the Seattle Yacht Club Power Boat Award Banquet the same year.

The Noon Cannon Trophy is a perpetual prize that may be awarded annually. The recipient is chosen by the noon cannon committee.

Criteria for selection of a winner may include, but not be limited to, (a) excellence in predicted log competition in any capacity; (b) participation in all phases of powerboat activities; (c) promotion of powerboat activities; (d) conduct as a member of the Seattle Yacht Club as to enhance the image and prestige of the club.

Winners of the Noon Cannon Award

1991 William A. Freitag
1990 James P. Erickson
1989 James R. Vaupell
1988 Jack M. Jorgeson
1987 Charles T. Cravens, Jr.
1986 Paul W. Sunich
1985 John R. Allen
1984 Phil Duryee
1983 A. Gilman Middleton
1982 Richard Chang
1981 Ralph Buseman
1980 Gerald Johnson
1979 Lester Lewis
1978 Harold B. Murray
1977 Frank M. Dunn
1976 Townley Bale
1975 Edward R. Donohue
1974 Donovan S. Bancroft
1973 Anderson S. Joy

crucial time knocked the *Intrepid* out of the running during the preliminary trials of the America's Cup.

The SYC sailing craft of the year was *Hooligan II*, owned by Tom O'Brien.

The SYC yearbook listed the following trophies and award winners for 1973

Vashon Island Race, Categories I and II IOR: Vashon Trophy, *Midnight Special* (S. Crary, CYC); Commodore's Race Trophy (IOR), *Jubilee* (B. Watkins, CYC); PHRF, *Moshulu* (Bob Sylvester, CYC); Mark Mayer Race: IOR Overall, *Mogombo Extravaganza* (Don Clark, SYC); Frisbie Race: IOR, *Viking* (F. Thorp, CYC); PHRF, *Tolo Tolo* (E. E. Woodson, CYC); Protection Island Race: IOR Overall, *Windward* (John Ellis, CYC)

Smith Island Race: Gwendolyn II A and B trophies, IOR Overall, *Race Passage* (P. McCullough, BYC); Lady Medina Trophy, C, D, and E, IOR, *Bydand* (William Buchan, CYC); Jerry Bryant Old Salts' Trophy (no finishers); Bob Gibbons Memorial Trophy, IOR Overall, *Race Passage* (P. McCullough, BYC)

Mid-Sound Race: Kennell Midwatch Trophy, IOR, *Easy Raider* (Stan Kiesling, TYC); PHRF Horder/Provine Old Salts' Trophy, *Chantey* (M. Minnich, EYC); Crooz N Snooz races: Captain Hoyt Trophy, IOR, *Jubilee* (B. Watkins, CYC); PHRF, *Sorcery* (N. Riebe, SHYC); Scatchet Head Race, Hat Island IOR Overall: *Bydand* (William Buchan, CYC)

Tri-Island Series: Mark Mayer Cup, A and B—IOR and Three-Island Trophy Categories I and II—IOR, *Windward* (John Ellis, CYC); Bob Bollong Memorial Trophy, C—IOR, *Bydand* (William Buchan, CYC); Humphrey Trophy, E—IOR, *Desiderata* (Tom Geisness, SYC); Seaborn Tri-Island Trophy, Y-IOR, *Gambit* (P. Wamsley, CYC); Gardner Gamwell Trophy, D—IOR, *Reliant* (Ted Uerling, EYC); Thunderbird Trophy, *Au Soleil* (P. B. Grytness, TYC); First President's Trophy, PHRF, *Rauha* (George Palo, GHYC); Walt Little Trophy, PHRF, *White Squall* (Gov Teats, TYC)

The Port Ludlow Yacht Club

The Port Ludlow Yacht Club was founded and incorporated in 1973. There are presently 181 member families and 139 boats equally divided between power and sail, and most of them are moored in Port Ludlow harbor. Commodore Cletus Gasson leads the club at the present time.

Seven social events are scheduled each year, including a crab feed, a clambake, an officers' open house, a salmon bake, a barbecue, a nomination-of-officers cocktail party, and a change-of-watch Christmas dinner and dance. Member meetings are held in conjunction with these social events. These and the monthly meetings of the board of trustees are held in the beach club at Port Ludlow.

The club sponsors five cruises, ranging from three- to ten-days' duration during the spring, summer, and fall. Up to 15 sail races and a fishing derby complete the list of annual boating activities. The club does not currently have an outstation but does offer reciprocal mooring privileges to 53 other clubs in Puget Sound and Canadian waters.

Opening Day ceremonies on the second Saturday in May have become a tradition. A flag ceremony, a cannon firing, a new-boat-in-the-club christening, a decorated boat parade, and a rafted boat party in the inner harbor are among the festivities.

The *Jib Sheet*, a monthly newsletter, is published and sent to all members.

—Based on material submitted by Howard A. Slack

The powerboat of the decade, Don Bancroft's Alaska Hunter. *(SYC Historical Collection)*

Tri-Island Series Overall Winners: IOR Long Course, *Windward* (John Ellis, CYC); *Assault* (John Buchan, SYC); *Bydand* (William Buchan, CYC); PHRF Long Course, *White Squall* (Gov Teats, TYC); *Mariah* (R. E. Brown, SHYC); *Bright Star* (D. Pennell, SYC)

Single-Handed Race: Sea Fever Trophy, A and B—IOR, *Olympian* (P. Schmidt, SYC); Nautilus Trophy, C—IOR, *Starwagon* (Dick Gilbert, CYC); Osprey Trophy, D—IOR, *Marrowstone Light* (R. A. Cairns, CYC); Quent Williams Trophy, E—IOR, *Barefoot* (J. Ward, SYC); SYC Trophy, Half-Ton, IOR, *Climax* (M. D. Smith, CYC); SYC Trophy, Gamma/Delta/Omega—PHRF, *Intrepid* (John Herbert, CYC).

Top powerboat races included the Masthead contest on Wells McCurdy's *Canim*, aboard which Les Lewis won the prize. Gerry Johnson captained Les Lewis' *Desert Queen* into first position in the SYC Lake Washington race. J. G. Shotwell's *High Cotton* earned a first in the Edmonds Race.

From Shilshole Bay to Cadboro Bay, the predicted log racers in the International Cruiser event found strange tidal currents, but old "pro" Don Bancroft steered his *Alaska Hunter* over the two-day course with an error of only 1.1946 percent. Bancroft was named Skipper of the Year for bringing his *Alaska Hunter* in first in this race and the Bremerton, Everett, Rainier-Poulsbo, Tacoma-Olympia and SYC End of the Season races.

In Memoriam, 1973: George W. Babcock, Forester Bradford, Lyle E. Branchflower, James H. Clapp, Mrs. Vern

Cole, Dewey Estey, John H. Gould, Robert Lee Hudson, Schubert S. Inch, Frank E. James, Sr., Herbert B. Johnson, Falcon Joslin, Jr., Mrs. Henry H. (Martha) Judson, Sr., Joseph R. Manning, James R. Martine, Jack Nettleship, Albert W. Olson, Mrs. Robert Paysee, Congressman Thomas M. Pelly, Sr., James J. Prendergast, Emery T. Putnam, Former Commodore Richard H. Shorett, Sr., John B. Stirrat, Mrs. George

Ovens Island

The Dunsmuir Islands rest within Ladysmith Harbour, an inlet on the eastern side of Vancouver Island about 40 miles north of the city of Victoria. The island is named for James Dunsmuir, formerly the president of the Esquimalt and Nanaimo Railway Company. Dunsmuir was born on July 8, 1851, in the United States at Fort Vancouver, Washington Territory, while his parents were enroute from Scotland to Victoria. Dunsmuir operated several coal mines on Vancouver Island during his lifetime.

Wally Ovens was active over many years in efforts to secure outstation properties. (Photo by Sally Laura)

Dunsmuir Island Number 6 is affectionately known to SYC members as Ovens Island in memory of Past Commodore Wally Ovens, who was instrumental in the acquisition of the properties for the Seattle Yacht Club. In 1965 Wally and his wife Ruth discovered the availability of the properties and traveled to Puerto Vallarta, Mexico, to obtain title from the owners.

This outstation has retained the natural setting and original charm of the adjacent Canadian Gulf Island archipelago. The island, roughly 200 feet wide and 800 feet long, sits on a foundation of solid rock with a mantle of earth that supports light vegetation and a cap of conifer trees. There is no water on the island, therefore no smoking and no fires are allowed. The island has no electricity, garbage service, or sanitation facilities. The shoreside lands to the east are inhabited by North American natives, one of whom is hired as the caretaker. The harbourmaster in Ladysmith serves as the club's representative in the area and occasionally patrols the outstation.

In 1974 a picnic area was prepared and, under the direction of Stuart Oles, a 150-foot float was constructed on the easterly or Sibell Bay side of the island. In 1986 Wally Ovens directed construction of 300 additional feet of float. The floats are attached to the island by a gangway and several stiff-leg braces. Walking these braces is a challenge even to the more daring, and it often results in a dunking.

Ovens Island is a popular stopping place for SYC members as they travel to and from destinations in the northern Straits of Georgia. As has become a tradition at most SYC outstations, two or more boats tied to the floats means a "Green Box Party,"* where old friends meet and new friends are made.

*The "Green Box Party" takes its name from the green box on the float at the Fo'c'sle at the Port Madison outstation. A tradition originated there that calls for 5:00 p.m. hors d'oeuvres and drinks to be shared atop the green box by those aboard any two or more boats moored at any outstation. ◇

Stroble, John A. Troxell, Walter A. Van Camp, Henry B. Wheeler, and David E. Wyman.

1974

The January Women's Interclub Luncheon was a sold-out affair with a record 100 guests from Queen City, Edmonds, Day Island, and Tyee yacht clubs. Pat Wilson, wife of member Chester Wilson, presented a program called "Cooking Afloat." She came well qualified as women's editor of *Nor'westing* magazine and as a teacher in the Department of Home Economics at the University of Washington.

Neither rain nor wind could keep the SYC women from their March luncheon. The program was titled "Joy of Cooking," and the guest speaker was Edgar Rombauer, son of the author of the best-selling cookbook of the same title.

SYC Commodore Stan Martin chose Paul Dunstan to be editor of the *Binnacle*. Dunstan, in turn, appointed reporters who filed appropriate stories for each issue. (Dunstan resigned in August and was replaced by Stan Laura.)

The commodore in his June message to members spoke highly of the Opening Day committee and their work. And he warned that "funnelators, those oversized slingshots loaded with water-filled balloons" were dangerous and had caused injuries on Opening Day.

The Sinclair Inlet Yacht Club

The first organizational meeting of the Sinclair Inlet Yacht Club was held on Sept. 25, 1974. Three meetings followed, and a name was chosen, bylaws were written, and officers were elected. Those who attended the three meetings were considered to be the charter members. It was decided that boats of members were to be considered members of the yacht club and that women would be considered active voting members; there was to be no auxiliary.

Sinclair Inlet Yacht Club was chartered as a nonprofit organization in February 1975. The first officers were: Commodore Ted Cobb, Vice Commodore Omar Neshem, Rear Commodore James Lambion, Secretary Loa Cobb, Treasurer Dianne Engebretson, and Trustees Bill Barton, Ron James, Bruce German, and Jack Minger.

The first club function was "Christmas Lane," a display of decorated boats moored at the Port Orchard breakwater on Dec. 21–22, 1974. This display, open to the public, has been a yearly event since. *The Dinghy*, the club newsletter, is published monthly. Members have actively promoted boating safety and have sponsored one of the West Sound Sailing Association series races each year.

SIYC sponsored Sinclair Inlet Opening Day of the boating season in 1979.

The first woman commodore of the club, Charlotte Mossman, was elected in 1984.

Although at the outset members began building a clubhouse, an internal reorganization caused them to assume the current non-household form of club. Membership at SIYC has increased from 20 to 125 boats, and the club's reciprocal arrangements have expanded to include 65 yacht clubs. ◇

Seattle sailboats *Jake*, *Cloud 9*, and *Lenore*, belonging to John Ford, Robert Hass, and Wells Ostrander, respectively, won the first three places for being best-dressed or decorated on Opening Day. Among powerboats, the *Miriki II* (Dr. Richard Johnson) took first prize.

The historic *Groote Beer* was part of the Opening Day parade in 1974. This 52-foot vessel owned by Stuart Anderson was originally built in Amsterdam for Reichsmarschall Hermann Goering of Nazi

Now *This* is Cruising!

Bob and Cynthia Carter, SYC members since 1952, have cruised more than 62,000 miles in their 44-foot Pearson Custom Countess. After being launched in Maine the spring of 1967, *Cynthia R* took the Carters along the coast of Maine and then to the Bahamas for the winter. In the summer of 1968 Bob sailed from South Carolina to Gibralter via Bermuda and the Azores. His crew for the trip included SYC member Skip Kotkins (Bob had earlier crewed on Henry Kotkins' *Diamond Head*).

Bob and Cynthia Carter's Cynthia R *on Canal L'Est in Europe in 1969. (Carter Collection)*

For the next 13 years, Bob and Cynthia explored European waters, most with guests who shared expenses. They circled the Mediterranean, crossed Europe on the canal and river system, emerged into the North Sea from the Frisian Islands, then into the Baltic for parts of two seasons, including six weeks in the Finnish islands. They crossed Sweden on the Gota Canal and spent another summer on the outer coast of Norway, then crossed Europe again, this time via the Rhine to Switzerland and then by canals and the Rhone back to southern France.

The years 1974 through 1980 were spent in the Mediterranean, concentrating on Greece and Turkey, where the Carters became involved in archaeological discoveries. In 1980 they sailed back to the United States via Puerto Rico, the Dominican Republic, Haiti and the Bahamas and traveled north on the Intercoastal Waterway to Maine.

Since then, they have spent considerable time in the Canadian Maritime Provinces, visiting the outer coast of Newfoundland, the French islands of St. Pierre-Miquelon, the Magdalen Islands of Quebec in the Gulf of St. Lawrence, and Minas Basin in the Bay of Fundy, site of the world's highest tides (50 feet plus).

At the close of the 1990 season, Bob and Cynthia had sailed over 62,000 miles and had entered 30 countries aboard the *Cynthia R*. Bob swears they have never been caught in a storm at sea.

Bob has been published repeatedly in many leading yachting periodicals, and his book *Sail Far Away* was a main selection of the Dolphin Book Club when it came out in 1978. The SYC library has a copy. Bob, by the way, is a life member of SYC. ◇

notoriety. It was moored on the south side of Pier 1, adjacent to the parking lot. This monstrous, wide-nosed, varnished sailboat with its gigantic up-raised leeboards made quite a conversation piece for several years.

Boat owners were receiving from their insurance companies' oil anti-discharge placards. By law these placards had to be posted by July 1, 1974, in the machinery spaces or at the bilge and ballast pump control stations of all vessels 26 feet or longer.

The board of trustees in July approved a plan to standardize all the club's moorage power supply systems using the OSHA-approved 30-amp, 125-volt receptacles and plugs.

As the summer months faded, hammers, blasting, and buzz saws disrupted the peaceful atmosphere of Henry Island as sewage and water systems were enlarged and showers and heads rearranged. During the year, Ovens' Island received a new 150-foot float, a fireplace and picnic facilities.

At the November annual meeting, Chairman John Harding of the Henry Island committee reported new floats would be ready in 1975 and recommended purchasing 20 acres adjacent to club property. Mike Gibbons of the sailboat committee reported 14 main sailing events attracted 1,578 starting boats. SYC also sponsored the 1974 Mallory Cup Regatta.

SYC finances, according to J. C. Baillargeon, Jr., of the finance committee and club treasurer Irvin Matson, were in fine shape since fees for club services had been increased.

During 1974 the Princess Louisa International Society erected a monument at Princess Louisa inlet with places for plaques in memory of those who frequented and loved the pristine beauty of the inlet. This effort also helped raise funds to pay for the property. SYC members involved in the construction included Norm C. Blanchard, Philip Stewart, Bob Bulmer, Howard King, Tom Snyder, Will Dearborn and designer George Heideman.

The Puget Sound Vessel Traffic System, operated by the U.S. Coast Guard under the authority of the Ports and Waterways Safety Act, became mandatory in September 1974.

Gerry Johnson of the powerboat committee reported that fuel shortages had affected the turnout for events. The Bremerton Heavy Weather Race course was shortened and speed was restricted to between 5 and 7 knots.

This was the year that William F. Niemi, Jr., skippered the *Joli* and Robert Alexander skippered the *Scaramouche* in the race from Victoria to Maui. *Joli* was awarded fifth place and *Scaramouche* third.

Seattle skippers did well at the PIYA Regatta at Victoria. Bob Connor's *Brer Rabbit* took a first, second, and a third in three days to dominate the Large Boat Wind Pennant Series. Bruce Hedrick's *Warrior* was third. John Buchan's *Assault* was first in the Long-Distance Race. In the Six-Meter, *Joli II*, belonging to Sunny Vynne, took first place.

Mark Laura won the Area H. Mallory Cup semi-finals, which were raced off Shilshole. In the North American Yacht Racing Union finals, which were hosted by the Seattle and Corinthian yacht clubs, young Laura skippered the Washington boat to 40 1/2 points in eight races, fewer than eight points behind the leading California and New Jersey boats. In October he also captained the University of Washington racing team at the national invitational race for the Douglas Cup at Long Beach, California, finishing third behind the University of Southern California and University of California Berkeley.

The Seattle Yacht Club Sailboat of 1974 was Larry Shorett's *Citation*.

The SYC yearbook listed the following trophies and award winners for 1974.

Mark Mayer IOR Overall Trophy: *Assault* (John Buchan, SYC); Hostetter Trophy, PHRF Overall, *Osprey* (Ben Benton, SYC); Vashon Island Trophy, Categories I, II IOR Overall and Commodore's Trophy, IOR Overall, *Brer Rabbit* (Bob Connor, SYC); PHRF Crooz N Snooz Trophy, *Captain America* (Carl DeGrazia, SYC); Frisbie Trophy, IOR Overall, *Warrior* (Bruce Hedrick, SYC)

Single-Handed Race: Sea Fever Trophy, A/B—IOR, *Warrior* (Bruce Hedrick, SYC); Nautilus Trophy, C—IOR, *Citation* (Larry Shorett, SYC); Quent Williams Trophy, E—IOR, *Soul Catcher* (Caspar Clarke, SYC); SYC Trophy, Alpha/Beta PHRF, *Starwagon* (Dick Gilbert, SYC); SYC Trophy, Gamma/Delta/Omega, Epsilon PHRF, *African Star* (Doug Fryer, SYC)

Scatchet Head Race: Hat Island Trophy, IOR Overall, *Brer Rabbit* (Bob Connor, SYC); Smith Island Race: Gwendolyn II Trophy, A, B—IOR, and Bob Gibbons Memorial Trophy, IOR Overall, *Warrior* (Bruce Hedrick, SYC); Jerry Bryant Old Salts' Trophy, Alpha/Beta PHRF, *Starwagon* (Dick Gilbert, SYC)

Tri-Island Series: Gardner Gamwell Trophy, D—IOR, *Ghost Rider* (Tom Geisness, SYC); Humphrey Trophy, E—IOR, *Soul Catcher* (Caspar Clarke, SYC); Three-Island Trophy, Categories I, II—IOR, *Epic* (Chuck Schiff)

Large-boat plaques, IOR-Class A: *Warrior* (Bruce Hedrick, SYC—three firsts); IOR-Class C: *Brer Rabbit* (Robert B. O'Connor, SYC—three firsts); *Citation* (Larry K. Shorett, SYC—a first and three seconds); *Soul Catcher* (Caspar Clarke, SYC—placed in nine races); IOR-Class D: *Ghost Rider* (Tom Geisness, SYC—placed in six races); PHRF-Delta: *Impossible* (Dwight Shaw/L. Walcott, SYC—a first and second); PHRF-Epsilon: *African Star* (Doug Fryer, SYC—placed in five races); 1/4 Ton: *Piglet* (Gary Wood, SYC—placed in six races); T-Birds: *Aeolus* (Don Cooney, SYC—placed in three races)

The IPBA bi-annual Alaska Cruiser Race/Cruise resulted in Townley Bale in *Blue Chip* taking overall honors. Tragedy struck the California contestant *Margy M.* on her way north to take part in the race. She was lost off Bodega Bay with all hands.

In the Century 21 Race, a couple of SYC skippers teamed with a couple from the Edmonds Yacht Club to beat the Canadian team and bring the prestigious trophy south of the border.

The IBPA International Cruiser Race (Burroughs Island to Nanaimo) spotlighted Queen City log racers who took all class prizes except Class 4, which was won by Bill Lanphear of Edmonds in his *Omega*. Overall was won by Don Bancroft who predicted so well that he totaled 52 seconds of error over two days of racing. He called this the best race he had ever run.

Bancroft and his yacht won six races during the year. He received the Jerry Bryant Skipper of the Year award and also the Noon Cannon Award. Townley Bale's *Blue Chip* won three firsts, a second and two thirds. Rod Proctor's *Monitor* placed in four races.

In Memoriam, 1974: Dr. Ralph E. Allen, Edward A. Black, Mrs. M. P. (Jeannette) Butler, Frank C. Calvert, Jr., Roy W. Corbett, Chester E. Gunderson, Boris V. Korry, John W. Kucher, Dr. Fraser McDonald, Frank Morris, Dr. Herbert R. Pearsall, Jack C. Warburton, Harry E. Wilson, and Robert G. Zener.

1975

In the February *Binnacle* Staff Commodore Stan Martin described three proposed boating legislation bills pending in Olympia. The Interclub of Washington had worked with the parks committee on its drafted legislation and felt it was now less objectionable. Martin promised to report further as the bill progressed.

Sally Laura was invited to join the men's luncheon of January 16, for on that day she, her husband Stan, daughter Susie and son Mark received the National Maritime Association's Boating Family of the Year Award.

Maitre d' Tony Pos retired at the end of March after eight years with the club. Lloyd Lamb replaced him.

The Juniors' 1975 milk carton entry is proudly displayed by Dan McGinnis (holding the tip of the SYC burgee), Charlie Pickle, John Stoddard, Gwen Perry, Marianne George, and Frank Heffernan. (SYC Historical Collection)

Two new committees became active in March—the major improvements or long-range priorities committee and the building committee to oversee construction and completion of projects. Both were to complement the permanent planning committee.

The north side of the Evergreen Point Bridge was marked to allow speedboat calibration despite concern of residents at each end of the bridge over possible wake damage.

Earl Fessler, *Binnacle* outstations editor, noted, "With the improvements which have been made, use of the outstations has doubled and quadrupled over several years. There is no question that we must continue to improve our existing sites and obtain additional new sites." (*Binnacle*, March 1975)

June Anderson Almquist wrote in the *Seattle Times* about the fashion show presented for the SYC Women's Group by Littler's. This was the first women's event scheduled after the clubhouse refurbishing. After describing the new color schemes, the reporter noted that the principal change in the cocktail lounge was the removal of a wall that separated an area for the men. "This wasn't a case of the women objecting to the men having their own bar," explained one of the Women's Group members, "but rather of the men not wanting it anymore. They were always coming into the main cocktail lounge to sit with the ladies, so they just decided they might as well take out the wall."

Late in the year, SYC purchased property for an outstation in Gig Harbor across the bay from the town. The holding featured 300 feet of waterfront and 200 feet of depth, and all of it was heavily forested. A new committee cochaired by Bob Pace and Frank Sando was named to establish a plan and begin development.

Claudia Rombauer, *Binnacle* Women's Group editor, while reporting on December's Christmas luncheon for members wrote: "What do you think happens when you place Michele Shaw on Santa's lap to have her picture taken in front of

Michele Shaw's December 1976 gift from Santa was the Admiralette's hat she would wear for 1977 Opening Day. (SYC Women's Group)

The Sequim Bay Yacht Club

In the summer of 1975, 10 Sequim residents, while cruising in the San Juan Islands, decided to form a Sequim Bay Yacht Club. The founders invited boating friends to meetings, and on April 3, 1976, a charter night was scheduled at the Dungeness Inn. Fifty members present heard Port Commissioner James Dick and Port Manager Tom Neal speak on the progress of the proposed Sequim Bay Marina. Actor John Wayne had donated acreage at Pitship Point on Sequim Bay to the Port of Port Angeles as the site for the marina.

The first commodore of the Sequim Bay Yacht Club was Jim Tallman. Dues were set at $12 per year. The first annual Sequim Bay Yacht Club picnic was held at Pitship Point and at that time free steaks to all members became a tradition. The first annual small boat regatta on Oct. 10, 1976, saw El Toros being launched at a minimal ramp at the end of the spit.

In 1977 the port decided portions of the Environmental Impact Statement for the marina needed replanning. During 1979 the Sequim Bay Yacht Club members instigated and worked with the port to install and operate grounding floats at the existing boat launch ramp at Sequim Bay State Park.

The first SBYC fishing derby was held Dec. 2, 1979, with first prize going to Daryl Davis. Margaret Lewis printed up the first newsletter *The Scuttlebutt*. In March 1980 the 80-foot pier was finally in place at the state park, thanks to SBYC.

The port allowed SBYC to rent an old house on Pitship Point for $11 per meeting, and this became the club's first temporary home. In April 1981 Don Berry programmed the year, making use of the clubhouse on Friday evenings and weekends. Dues were increased to $25 per single and $35 per couple with a $35 initiation fee. On May 10 that year the Opening Day ceremonies featured a new flag and pole.

At a special meeting in September 1981 forces were coordinated to speak at another hearing on the proposed marina. Petitions were signed and a newspaper ad was run. In that same year the first Sequim Coast Guard Auxiliary Unit was chartered.

In 1982 SBYC sent a letter to the port commis-

The King Olav Cup was first presented in 1975 to the Six-Meter Razzle Dazzle. *(Wallace Ackerman Photography)*

the members? Why, he hands her a package to open and surprise! It contains an admiralette's hat."

On October 19 King Olav V of Norway in his name dedicated a silver trophy to the Puget Sound Six-Meter Fleet. The King had raced and built a number of Six-Meter craft over a 50-year sailing career. The cup is held in perpetual guardianship by the Seattle Yacht Club.

Biggest racing news of the year was generated by Don Bancroft and Les Lewis at the North American Powerboat Association races in St. Petersburg, Florida, where they beat out many racers from the United States and Canada. Those they defeated were so amazed at their low error that they swarmed around to see how it was done. Their trophy was a noon cannon similar to the one SYC presents to

---

sioners requesting them to consider space for the club in the new marina facilities. In April Commodore Schroeder, Jack Day, and Chuck Hinkley attended their first Interclub meeting. The first annual "Don't Fall in the Water, Raft Up, Spaghetti Feed" was held at the state park pier. October 1982 brought the first Oktoberfest at the clubhouse.

In December the County Shoreline Advisory Board again approved the plans for Sequim Bay Marina, which included an overhead launcher for small boats. In May 3,000 signatures were gathered by SBYC members in favor of the proposed marina. In September 1983 the port selected architects to design the marina and canceled SBYC's lease of the house, which would be used as offices for contractors. On October 4 the ground was finally broken. Members voted to set aside $1,000 for a new clubhouse development fund.

In March 1984 the purposes of the club were reworded to read "shall promote and encourage boating, water sports, and the science of seamanship, navigation, and other matters." Dues were raised to $48 per couple with $100 initiation fee. Membership climbed to 177.

The drawing of the completed marina building included rooms and offices for SBYC. In July 1984 the marina moorages opened. In September the floats became available. That December 15 and 16 the first annual Christmas boat parade around Sequim Bay attracted six boats and rain and snow.

On Sept. 14, 1985, the port dedicated the John Wayne Marina Building with all the Wayne family present. At noon, SBYC held the Duke Cup Races with many out-of-the-area ocean racing class sailboats as well as Thistles, Pelicans, and Open class.

In November SBYC hosted a meeting for area sailors to help found a local chapter of the Sailing Foundation, dedicated to the promotion of sailing in the Pacific Northwest.

The most recent Christmas parades involved more than 20 boats while Opening Day 1991 had 27 boats in the parade. The latest project is to form a goals committee to look into the possibilities of building a clubhouse on other port property at the John Wayne Marina.

—Based on material provided by Annette Kuss, historian

the Powerboat Man of the Year; the 1975 Powerboat Man of the Year, by the way, was Ed Donohue.

In competition off Los Angeles, Larry Shorett received the Carr Trophy awarded by the Pacific Coast Yachting Association. Seattle would host the races in 1976.

Joli, skippered by W. F. Niemi, Jr., of SYC, finished first in Division I to take the Governor of Hawaii Trophy in the Victoria-to-Maui Ocean Race. Earlier *Joli* had won the Mazatlan Race in Mexico.

Mark Laura, supported by SYC crew members Lee Ann Hobble and Brian Thomas, won the top individual award in the Intercollegiate Yacht Racing Association of North America competition in Chicago. The Seattleites sailed a 14-race series in the 410 dinghy competition, edging the Tulane crew by one point.

The SYC yearbook listed the following trophies and award winners for 1975.

Vashon Island Trophy, IOR Overall: *Brer Rabbit* (R. Connor, SYC); PHRF Overall: *Starwagon* (R. Gilbert, SYC); Protection Island Trophy, PHRF Overall: *Regal Eagle* (R. Allen, SYC); Frisbie Trophy, PHRF, *Jubilee* (W. Watkins, SYC)

Single-Handed Race: Sea Fever Trophy, *Heather* (John Buchan, SYC); Nautilus Trophy, *Surprise* (G. Maurer, SYC); Quent Williams Trophy, *Soul Catcher* (C. Clarke, SYC). Smith Island Race: Bob Gibbons Memorial Trophy, IOR, *Chinook* (R. Spanfelner/R. Perry, SYC); Gwendolyn Trophy, IOR-A and B, *Heather* (J. Buchan, SYC); Lady Medina Trophy, IOR—C, D, and E, *Chinook* (R. Spanfelner and R. Perry, SYC); Scatchet Head Race, Hat Island Trophy, IOR *Heather* (J. Buchan, SYC); PHRF, *Gamin* (L. Robinson, SYC)

Tri-Island Series: Walt Little Trophy, PHRF Long Course, *Starwagon* (R. Gilbert, SYC); Mark Mayer Cup, IOR-A and B, *Brer Rabbit* (R. Connor, SYC); Best Performance trophies: Vashon Island, Long, *Starwagon* (R. Gilbert, SYC); Protection Island, *Regal Eagle* (R. Allen, SYC); Scatchet Head, Long, *Starwagon* (R. J. Gilbert, SYC)

Sailboat of the Year: *Starwagon* (R. Gilbert, SYC); Consistent winners, IOR Class A: *Scaramouche* (Robert M. Alexander); IOR Class B: *Brer Rabbit* (Robert Connor, Jr.); IOR Class E: *White Mist* (Dorr Anderson and Irv Matson); PHRF—Alpha: *Gamin* (Lon Robinson); PHRF—Beta: *Starwagon* (R. Gilbert, SYC); PHRF—Epsilon: *African Star* (Doug Fryer)

As in previous years, one powerboat won a lion's share of awards in 1975—*Alaska Hunter*, the 45-foot diesel cruiser owned by Don Bancroft. Chet Wilson's *Lady Patricia* also came in first in a couple of contests. In the SYC Lake Washington Race Alaska Hunter ran the course in 58 minutes and 45 seconds, resulting in an error of only nine seconds or 0.2553 percent. This, of course, won the trophy. The winner of overall honors in the 1975 IPBA International was Edmonds Yacht Club's Bob Brubaker in his *Yolo*. He finished the 76-mile race from Skyline Marina to Vancouver, B.C., (with an overnight at Bedwell Harbour) with a .3584 percent error. He went on to win the coveted Jerry Bryant Skipper of the Year Award.

In Memoriam, 1975: Bruce G. Baldus, Captain Edward E. Brighton, Richard H. Cahan, Fred W. Clark, Richard (Dick) Conner, John H. Gaffney, William L. Green, George W. Hixson, Mrs. John G. (Marjorie) Holstrom, William P. Joslin, Otto D. Leonhardt, Edmund Locke, Wallace J. Osborn, R. Albert Osborne, John A. Ruggles, John H. Simpson, William E. Stinson, Mrs. Henry V. (Margaret) Wheeler, Sam W. Wilcox, and Mrs. Robert G. (Irene) Zener.

1976

SYC Commodore Frank G. Bourque's term extended over most of the bicentennial year of U. S. independence, and he helped raise funding for the marine section of the local celebration. In the February *Binnacle* the commodore asked that members be patient with the inconvenience caused by the Marine Room remodeling, which would be completed in May.

While the Marine Room was being remodeled, the operations of the bar were moved downstairs to a storage room adjacent to the present Heritage Room. This was dubbed "Bourque's Bar." Some members wish it was still there.

The 1976 SYC Boating Family of the Year, that of Mr. and Mrs. Richard Gilbert, often sailed together on their boat *Starwagon*. Their crew during races usually consisted of son Scott, daughter Phoebe Ann, and her husband Bruce Stocker.

At the annual meeting, mooring and docking Chairman Bob Gilmore reported 28 moorage cancellations during the year from among the 224 locations, a turnover of 12 1/2 percent.

Treasurer Eric Van explained that inflation had forced the raising of membership dues and entrance fees. The club treasury had produced $300,000 to fund additions to club facilities, additional land at Henry Island, acquisition of the Gig Harbor property, and Marine Room remodeling. The treasurer assured members that the club remained solvent.

The Gig Harbor outstation committee was having a problem with the Eastside Gig Harbor Association, and development plans were placed on hold until the dispute could be solved.

The Cal 40 *Blue Marlin*, skippered by Mark Laura and crewed by Gene Baker, Nick Blattner, Brian Gallagher, Kurt Lillibridge, Mark Schlosser, Mike Sibold, and Brian Thomas, captured the Tacoma Cup.

SYC member Shannon Morris and her crew qualified for the Women's Intercollegiate Yacht Racing Association Championship at M.I.T. in early June.

Carl Buchan won the overall honors in the SYC-sponsored Soling North American Championships raced in July off Shilshole.

Julie Rattray, with Maria Buchan and Julie Lightfoot as crew, won the Soling

The Fidalgo Yacht Club

The Fidalgo Yacht Club was formed in 1976 and incorporated the following year. The club is located at Skyline in Anacortes, Washington, and the members' boats are located throughout the city.

In 1991 the club had 130 family memberships and 92 boats in its fleet. Ten social and business meetings each year attract about a 50 percent attendance. The fleet captain organizes seven three- or four-day rendezvous each year, ranging from Port Ludlow to the Canadian Gulf Islands. These are attended by 20 to 30 boats and up to 100 people.

The club sponsors a cruiser navigation contest each spring and a First Mates' Exchange Breakfast at Friday Harbor in April. In this the ladies eat breakfast on one boat while the men do all the cooking and dishwashing on another. In 1982 the club and the Capital City Yacht Club of Sidney, B.C., established a home-and-home meeting called "Capidalgo" whereby the members have a fun-filled weekend of dinners, skits and get-togethers.

—Based on material supplied by Past Commodore and Historian Allen E. Hill

Jack Graham's 67-foot Maruffa *driving hard in the Swiftsure Race. This SYC boat was in the Bermuda races, sailed to Greece, up the Atlantic Coast, and in the races to Hawaii. After Jack sold her she was lost in a storm in New Zealand. (Photo by Ken Ollar)*

semi-finals in the Women's Adams Cup North American Championship in Hawaii. They moved on to Rochester for the finals and were awarded the Battleaxe Plaque.

SYC junior Jonathan McKee captured the Canadian National Laser Championship in Vancouver in September.

The Dragon North American Championships held in Vancouver resulted in a win for Seattle's Martin Godsil. His crew included Bob Vynne and Bob Cairns.

SYC juniors were in fine fettle throughout the year and won the McCurdy Cup, and SYC won its own trophy in the End of the Season Predicted Log Race.

The Crooz N Snooz overall winner was William W. Watkins' *Jubilee*, which also was named Sailboat of the Year. Townley Bale was named Powerboat Man of the Year.

The SYC yearbook listed the following trophies and award winners for 1976.

Opening Day Race, Overall: *Spirit* (Eustace Vynne); Vashon Island Race, IOR Overall: *Ladybug* (Alan Holt); Best Performance Trophy, Long Course: *Heather* (John Buchan); Protection Island Race, IOR Overall: *Prospector* (Larry Shorett, Tom Geisness); PHRF Overall: *Olympian* (Peter Schmidt); Point Hudson Best Performance: *Skinnydipper* (Joe Ireland); Single-Handed: Sea Fever Trophy, *Surprise* (Gerry Maurer); Nautilus Trophy, *Roo* (John Powell, Rob Fleming, skipper); Osprey Trophy, *Soul Catcher* (Cappy Clarke); Hat Island Race, IOR, *Heather* (John Buchan); Best Performance, *Soul Catcher* (Cappy Clarke); Smith Island Race: Bob Gibbons Memorial Trophy, IOR Overall and Gwendolyn Trophy, IOR-A and B, *Heather* (John Buchan); Lady Medina Trophy, IOR-C, D, Half-Ton, *Prospector* (Larry Shorett and Tom Geisness); Best Performance Trophy, *Heather* (John Buchan)

Tri-Island Series: Three-Island Trophy, IOR Long Course, and Mark Mayer Cup, IOR—A and B, *Heather* (John Buchan); Bob Bollong Memorial Trophy, IOR—C, *Prospec-*

Carver Cruisers

Carver Cruisers, a club for owners of Carver boats, was the inspiration of Dorian Halvorson of Anchor Boats and was formed on March 13, 1976. Halvorson had the help of several owners, including Don and Ruth Martin. An organizational meeting was held March 12, 1976, and at the first club meeting on May 7, officers were elected. The first club cruise was a wet success, with 12 boats traveling to Port Ludlow on June 12–13, 1976.

At the first annual membership meeting in October 1976, the burgee designed by Dorian Halvorson was adopted. At the meeting Commodore Audrey Lunde presented a plaque from the board, the "Dorian Halvorson Inspirational Award," which is presented each year to the member who has most inspired the club. Judy Halvorson was given lifetime membership at that meeting.

Though Carver Cruisers does not have a clubhouse, they have developed several traditions. At the annual dinner meeting in October of each year, officers are elected and annual awards are presented to members, among them the Inspirational Award and the award to the Boating Family of the Year. Also presented are the New Membership Award and others not quite so serious, such as the Stiff Rope Award, the Bent Prop Award, and the Rubber Duckie Award. A Carver Cruisers Officers' Reception is scheduled each November in Seattle. Members congregate for the annual smelt derby each January at La Conner. Schack's Shack is a land and water cruise along the Skagit River each July. There is a cruise to the John Wayne Marina in Sequim Bay and an annual Labor Day Weekend golf tournament.

Members participate in the annual Blake Island work party, enter a decorated flag ship in the Daffodil Regatta in Tacoma and participate in the South Sound Opening Day festivities held in Des Moines.

Carver Cruisers is a member of the Northwest Boating Council and Interclub Boating Association of Washington. Past commodores are eligible to join the Blue Gavel Past Commodores' Club where Carver Cruisers Commodore Mary Eiffert served as 1991 district one president.

—Based on material submitted by Commodore Clarence Ausbun

tor (Larry Shorett and Tom Geisness); Humphrey Trophy, IOR Half-Ton, formerly E class, *Ladybug* (Alan Holt); Joe Duthie Memorial Trophy, Lisa Sando; Ruptured Eardrum Trophy, Phil Duryee

Don Bancroft successfully defended his title as North American Powerboat champion in Boston in August. His navigator was Les Lewis. His *Alaska Hunter* was again a standout power racer in the Northwest along with Harold Murray's *Bluenose* and William Pratt's *Newport Belle*, each of which also claimed three or four races.

The Masthead Trophy Race ended in a tie between Don Bancroft and Rod Willis.

In Memoriam, 1976: Mrs. Thomas (Marvel) Autzen, Woodford B. Baldwin, Dr. Albert J. Bowles, Albion E. Crayne, Robert C. Detrich, V. L. (Vic) Downing, Robert R. Fox, Jr., Frank L. Hawkins, Arthur Launder, John L. Locke, William H. McColloch, Jr., C. A. (Bud) Newell, K. Gerald Norby, A. J. (Bert) Proctor, Charles W. Stewart, and William S. Teeter.

1977

Under Commodore Howard C. Bronson the reorganization of accounting for the Marine and Ward rooms was begun. Also the manner of contracting services by the committees was changed.

The value of outstations had been proven over the preceding years, and several would be added during the decade. At Eagle Harbor, 138 feet of dock space was acquired from the Winslow Wharf Company to be used as an outstation. In June the club purchased 1.3 acres at Moss Point, including 350 to 400 feet of beach with a common area behind for condo-

The Shelter Bay Yacht Club at La Conner

The Shelter Bay Yacht Club was founded in 1976 and incorporated the following year. The club now has 234 members (not counting spouses), 160 powerboats and 40 sailboats.

Among their major boating season activities are monthly cruises to other islands in the San Juan Archipelago for weekends or for a full week and mid-week cruises for both powerboats and sailboats. There is a monthly social night at the Shelter Bay clubhouse, usually a potluck dinner.

During the winter months—November through February—there are monthly social dinners and other activities at the clubhouse such as live-band dancing, bingo, and theme nights.

Traditions at Shelter Bay include the Commodore's Ball, Thanksgiving dinner, Christmas dinner, the Flotilla/Fleet blessing, an Opening Day event (actually three days of boarding parties, cruises, salmon barbecues), plus annual fishing derbies, club birthday parties, chili cook-offs, and crab feeds.

Although not a service club, the Shelter Bay Yacht Club members collect food to give to Friendship House. Also, all members take a day to clean, mow the grass, trim the shrubs, and in other ways beautify Cornet Bay or some other favorite boating destination frequented by boaters from all over Puget Sound.

—Based on material provided by Kathy Fleet

Barbara and Gerry Maurer's Surprise *competed in the 1977 Swiftsure Race. In 1981* Surprise *was named Sailboat of the Year. (Photo by David King)*

miniums, but sold it several years later after the moorage was found to be impractical. Over at Port Madison, new heads and showers were completed and all floats had been replaced.

At the annual meeting in November, Bill Bradshaw, chairman of the grants in aid program, reported $4,423 had been expended on 11 races and regattas for junior members. In response, Rear Commodore Steinhart read a letter written by the Junior Commodore Kristin Kennell:

> Seattle Yacht Club's Junior Sailing Program is hailed as one of the most complete and competitive of its kind. Out of the six team racing regattas held this past year, we

sailed off with top honors from all but two. Plus first place in Junior Big Boat race-cruising championship. In most youth regattas, the name of at least one Seattle Yacht Club junior appears in the top 10 and locally the top three. A recent visitor to our club for Fall McCurdy Cup stated, "You have an advantage over any other yacht club on the coast. You're the best, you train the best, you send the best and you show the best. Your sailors are said to be untouchable . . . and they are." We have an on-going program of both sailing and social activities which creates an opportunity for all our members to get involved. This past year we put on two theatrical performances, decorated boats for the Opening Day and Christmas parades, and had dances. It's not a coincidence that the successful sailors between the ages of 15 and 25 in our area owe a portion of their success to the Seattle Yacht Club's Junior program.

—Kristin Kennell, 1977

The SYC yearbook listed the following trophies and award winners for 1977.

Opening Day Races: Hostetter Trophy, IOR, *Foulweather Bluff* (Scott Rush, CYC); SP, *Tinuviel* (Allen Hughes, HHYC); Vashon Island Trophy: IOR, *Island* (Bill Buchan, CYC); SP, *Soul Catcher* (Cappy Clarke, SYC); Best Performance, *Salty Tiger* (John Herbert, CYC) and *Tinuviel* (Allen Hughes, CYC); Protection Island Trophy: IOR, *Island* (Bill Buchan, CYC); SP, *Starwagon* (Dick Gilbert, SYC); Best Performance, *Destiny* (James Christensen) and *Errant* (Dave Ridgway); Commodore's Trophy, IOR: *Airpower* (Dave Campbell, CYC); SP, *Jubilee* (Bill Watkins, SYC); Frisbie Trophy and Crooz N Snooz Trophy: *Jubilee* (Bill Watkins, SYC)

Single-Handed Race: Sea Fever Trophy, *Warrior* (Bruce Hedrick, SYC); Nautilus Trophy, *Roo* (R. Fleming, skipper, SYC); Osprey Trophy, *White Mist* (Dorr Anderson, SYC); Quent Williams Trophy, *Skinnydipper* (Joe Ireland, SYC); SYC Trophy, *Return* (Chris Johnson, CYC); Hat Island Trophy, IOR and Best Performance, *Heather* (Bill Buchan, skipper, CYC); SP, *Blackwatch* (Bill Nelson, CTYC); Best Performance, *Carefree* (R. G. Bell); Smith Island Race: Bob Gibbons Memorial Trophy and Lady Medina Trophy, *Outlaw* (Tom Hukle, SYC); Gwendolyn Trophy, *Warrior* (Bruce Hedrick, SYC); Jerry Bryant Old Salts' Trophy and Best Performance, *Maria* (Joe Williams, SYC); Best Performance, *Sorcery* (N. Reibe); Mid-Sound Race: Horder-Provine Old Salts' Trophy, *Cold Milk* (Dean Erickson, EDYC)

Blue Marlin *with Mark Laura at the helm won the Tacoma Cup in 1977. Her owners: Eugene Baker and Mark Schlosser. (Photo by Alan S. Rutherford)*

Tri-Island Series: Three-Island Trophy, *Outlaw* (Tom Hukle, SYC); Walt Little Trophy, *Night Fighter* (Don Stabbert, SYC); First President's Trophy, *Talisman* (Joel Clark, EVYC); Mark Mayer Cup, *Heather* (John Buchan, SYC); Bob Bollong Memorial Trophy, *Lepsoya* (Jon Runstad, SYC); Gardner Gamwell Trophy, *Flamenca* (John Michael, CYC); Humphrey Trophy, *Outlaw* (Tom Hukle, SYC); Tri-Island Thunderbird Trophy, *Luffly* (J. Thompson, TYC)

The Joe Duthie award went to Libby Johnson; the Ruptured Eardrum Trophy to

Walt Little; the Marymount Trophy for SYC Sailor of the Year was awarded Carl Buchan, and the SYC Boat of the year was Bill Watkins' *Jubilee*. The Tacoma Cup was returned to SYC thanks to Mark Laura and the crew of the *Blue Marlin*.

Two SYC members—Carl Buchan and Brian Thomas of the University of Washington sailing team—were named "All Americans." Buchan was also awarded the Everett Morris Trophy as the outstanding collegiate sailor of the year. Then Brian Thomas, with Keith Whittemore and Kevin Downey as crew, sailed to a second-place finish, three points behind Texas, in the annual Mallory Cup race at Sandy Hook, New Jersey.

Robert Alexander's *Scaramouche* was the Class B winner in the 1977 Los Angeles-to-Honolulu Race, the first SYC boat to win in this division since 1906.

A new trophy was donated during 1977—a magnificent Franklin Mint Bicentennial Bowl of solid sterling with a 24-carat gold lining. The name of the winner of the Grand Prix Invitational Regatta is to be inscribed on this 44-inch perpetual trophy, which was donated by Mr. and Mrs. Robert J. Cadranell. The first race on November 11–13 was a grueling endurance contest. Among the SYC finishers was the *Ladybug* of Alan Holt, winner of the IOR division with a record of 3-1-1. (It also received a two-foot gash on the hull near the waterline as a result of trying to kiss the Possession Head Point buoy.)

The major powerboat race winner was Don Bancroft's *Alaska Hunter*, which captured seven firsts, a second, two thirds and a fourth in races through the season. In the SYC-sponsored North American Invitation Contest, Bancroft lost first place by two one-thousandths of a second. For the sixth time he was named Puget Sound Skipper of the Year.

Harold Murray's *Bluenose* placed in six races, Townley Bale's *Blue Chip* placed in four races, taking two firsts; Bill Pratt's *Newport Belle* and Gerry Johnson's *Helga N.* placed in four races. Al Dubie won the Masthead Trophy.

In Memoriam, 1977: Mrs. William E. (Bertha) Boeing, Sr., Dale Bumstead, Jr., C. Noel Caldwell, N. Peter Canlis, George W. Crippen, Charles S. Dunn, Ray L. Eckmann, Mrs. Frances Edris, Frank E. Freshwater, Thomas F. Gleed, Charles F. Hanson, Robert W. Isaacson, Mrs. Richard (Kathie Ann) Jones, Mrs. Earl (Irene) Kennell, Mrs. Nelson J. Leonard, Marvel S. Morgan, William L. Noon, Albion I. Ostlund, Mrs. Stephen (Frances) Phipps, Stephen C. Phipps, Bruce William Roemer, Lowell A. Wakefield, Edward D. White, and Urgel O. Wintermute.

1978

This was the year Ray Pullen became the manager of the Henry Island Outstation, and after 24 years Doris and Bill James retired as resident managers of the Port Madison Outstation. A site for the club's seventh outstation was purchased at Port Ludlow.

Craig Westlin came aboard as the new maitre d'. Chief Warrant Officer (retired) Dennis Johnson of the Coast Guard was named skipper of the club's newly acquired committee boat *Portage Bay*.

In February Sally Laura of SYC and Herb Cleaver of QCYC held a press conference to promote the formation of a Pacific Northwest fleet of classic yachts.

At the SYC annual meeting chaired by Commodore William E. Bradshaw, powerboat committee Chairman Ralph Buseman reported that the club had participated in the Tacoma Daffodil Parade, had inaugurated a Port Madison rendezvous and fishing derby and planned on working with the IPBA in renewing interest in predicted log racing.

Sailboat committee Chairman Gerry

Maurer reported the new fee schedule for sailboat races had not hindered registration, which had increased 20 percent for the year.

At the meeting, Phil Duryee, chairman of the marine traffic and safety committee, explained the comprehensive traffic program which involved the Coast Guard, Puget Sound pilots, tugboat operators, and the ferry system. Duryee had spent thousands of hours patrolling sailboat races on Puget Sound and was very active in both SYC and CYC in promoting race course safety. Largely due to his efforts, sailboats and commercial ships were kept out of each other's way. Representatives of the Coast Guard and Puget Sound Pilots were often seen as guests aboard his boat as they studied the situation on the main waterways.

Phil Johnson reported that the new in-house computer was being loaded with the club's accounting system. SYC had enjoyed a 27 percent increase in business over the previous year, with a reduced payroll cost and a 60 percent reduction in operating deficits.

Also at the annual meeting, Robert Wheeler, chairman of the mooring and docks committee, discussed the continuing milfoil problem. Jim England of the membership committee reported the club had added 56 new juniors, 20 new intermediates under age 30, 22 new intermediates

The Missing Caulking
A David Romano Mystery

On July 17, 1978, Bev and I were headed for Desolation Sound on our 40-foot Monk/Vic Franck cruiser. After an afternoon stop we left Silva Bay to cross the Georgia Straits and spend the night at Secret Cove. We had enjoyed a hot afternoon on our flying bridge, and when the setting sun cooled the air, Bev went below to change out of her bathing suit. She immediately rushed back up to tell me that our carpet in the aft stateroom was under six inches of water. Bev and I took turns with the strenuous task of bailing. As we headed for Merry Island, I considered the possibility of beaching my boat rather than seeing it sink in deep water on the way to Secret Cove. However, Bev and I were able to bail fast enough to keep it afloat.

We slowed the boat to idle speed when we reached Secret Cove Marina. This dropped our bow from our planing position, which allowed the seawater in the boat to rush forward, killing the engine. We quickly threw a lock line to a person standing on the end of the pier and were pulled in. Several people came to help and two portable bilge pumps were brought aboard to pump out the seawater as our bilge pumps had shorted out on the straits when they were not able to keep up with the saltwater coming into the boat.

Our next job was to look for the water leak. In the lazerette we discovered water streaming in where the caulking was missing between two planks just below the waterline. Then Bev and I realized why the boat had sprung a leak: Shortly after we had left Silva Bay to cross Georgia Strait we had heard a thud; we now realized we had hit a deadhead that knocked the caulking out of the seam.

In order to make a temporary patch, about 20 people stood on the starboard edge of our boat long enough to bring the port chine out of the water to patch the seam. The next morning we headed to Pender Harbor for a permanent chine repair at Penga Marina. With the chine repaired, we continued our trip to Desolation Sound.

Little did I know that five years later the repair spot at Penga Marina would become the Seattle Yacht Club Garden Bay Outstation.

—David Romano, 1991

over 30, 5 non-residents, 1 out-of-state, and 71 new actives.

The Powerboat of the Year was Frank M. Dunn's *All Dunn IV*; Graham Anderson's *Baccarat* captured Sailboat of the Year. The Marymount Trophy for Sailor of the Year went to Mark Laura. His mother, Sally Laura, was named Woman of the Year and received the Tug Boat Annie Award. The Briggs Trophy from the PIYA went to John Buchan. The Endeavor PIYA Team Trophy was awarded the Seattle Yacht Club. The Ruptured Eardrum Trophy went to Bill Bradshaw, Bob Cadranell, Bob Allen, Dick Gilbert, Gerry Maurer and Bates McKee.

The SYC yearbook listed the following trophies and award winners for 1978.

Vashon Island Trophy: Long Course IOR, *Sachem* (Bill Buchan, CYC); SP, *Baccarat* (Graham Anderson, SYC); Short Course, *Flasher* (Daril Hahn, CYC); Best Performance Long Course, *Warrior* (Bruce Hedrick, SYC); Best Performance Short Course, *Chimera* (Ken Waters, TTP); Protection Island Trophy, Long Course IOR, *Merlin* (Doug Fryer, SPC); Long Course, SP, *The Phoenician* (Chris Schilbach, PYC); Point Hudson, Short Course, *Foxfire* (P. Strandjord, CYC); Best Performance, Long Course, *The Phoenician* (Chris Schilbach, PYC); Best Performance, Short Course, *Sundown Express* (Ian Christopher, SSSS)

Commodore's Trophy: IOR, *Rat Bite* (Bryce Ecklein, CYC); SP, *Roo* (John Powell,

The Eagle Harbor (Winslow) Outstation

In 1978 SYC member Barrie Arnett was anchored near Mac's Tavern (now the Saltwater Cafe) in Winslow when he noticed a group of men repairing the old fuel off-loading float. Recognizing friend Kent Miller among them, he rowed in and struck up a conversation. Miller explained that a marina would be built there in two stages; the first half was to be completed later in the year. Arnett asked if they might rent the end of the largest pier to the Seattle Yacht Club. Miller replied that they would be pleased to have SYC members at their marina.

By the time the first floats were built, the SYC trustees had approved a year-long lease for the outside 80 feet and two inside slips, which gave members access to the friendly town of Winslow. Over the next few years, the second phase of the marina was completed, and SYC moved its moorage to a longer pier end.

In the early 1980s, the Wharf Company decided to "condominiumize" some of the moorage slips, including the pier end leased by the Seattle Yacht Club. Though the SYC acquisition committee had depleted the outstation reserve fund with the acquisition of Pender Harbor property, they sought a way for the club to buy this Winslow moorage. In the end, Barrie Arnett's friend Nick Nicolai bought both the 90-foot pier end and a 53-foot space on the inside slip and leased the larger space back to SYC.

When, in 1985, Nicolai decided to sell both slips, the SYC acquisition fund had been replenished to where the board decided the club could purchase the properties. Marty Crowder worked out the details and was able to talk the owners into some concessions. The taxes and condo fees were less than the rent had been and, in the purchase, the club gained an additional 53 feet of moorage. ◇

SYC); Frisbie Trophy: SP, *Epic* (Charles Schiff, CYC); Crooz N Snooz Trophy, *Surprise* (Gerry Maurer, SYC); Single-Handed Race: Sea Fever Trophy, *Roo* (John Powell, SYC); Nautilus Trophy, *Flamenca* (John Michael, CYC); Osprey Trophy, *White Mist* (Dorr Anderson, SYC); Quent Williams Trophy, *Skinny Dipper* (Joe Ireland, SYC); SYC Trophy, *Return* (Chris Johnson, CYC)

Hat Island Trophy: Long Course IOR, *Heather* (John Buchan, SYC); SP, *Harpoon* (William Brasier, TYC); Short Course, *Sundown Express* (Ian Christopher, SSSS); Best Performance Long Course, *Heather* (John Buchan, SYC); Best Performance Short Course, *Impulse* (J. Kevorkian, CYC); Smith

The Betty Meacham Powerboat Trophy

The Betty Meacham trophy was donated to the Seattle Yacht Club by William M. Meacham in 1929 to be awarded to the outstanding junior girl connected with powerboating. However, because of the small number of women powerboaters, the trophy was awarded to women outstanding in competitive sailing events. They were:

1929—Ann Seidelhuber
1931—Hortense Harley
1932—Mary Helen Corbett
1933—Barbara Nettleton
1934—Hortense Harley Augustin

The Meacham trophy was unofficially retired after 1934 for some unknown reason.

The Betty Meacham Women's Powerboat Trophy. (Wallace Ackerman Photography)

Nearly 45 years later the trophy, a silver loving cup, was rediscovered, polished, and given new life. It was taken before the fleet captain-power and his committee by Sally Laura with a request from the trophy committee that it be used as the powerboat service award for women.

Since 1978 the trophy has been awarded annually at the November Awards Banquet. The fleet captain-power selects the trophy recipient. It serves to honor the committee woman who has greatly enhanced the efforts and goals of the powerboat committee through her deeds and services.

Recipients of the Betty Meacham Powerboat Trophy Award for Women are:

1978—Betty Chang
1979—Lou Bradley
1980—Sally Laura
1981—Carol Buseman
1982—Donna Kline
1983—Maggie Jorgeson
1984—Pam Nichols
1985—Sharon Marless
1986—Mary Ellen Quigley
1987—Elaine Kidd
1988—Gail Johnson
1989—Bonnie Sharpe
1990—Patty Frary
1991—Mary A. Williams

Island Race: Bob Gibbons Memorial Trophy and Gwendolyn Trophy, *Warrior* (Bruce Hedrick, SYC); Best Performances, Long Course, none; Short Course, *Candyman* (Guy and Dawn Bockus, PMYC); Mid-Sound Race: Kennell Midwatch Trophy, *Outlaw* (Tom Hukle, SYC); Horder-Provine Old Salts' Trophy, *Candyman* (Guy Bockus, PMYC); Tri-Island Series: Three-Island Trophy, *Warrior* (Bruce Hedrick, SYC); Walt Little Trophy, *Baccarat* (Graham Anderson, SYC); First President's Trophy, *Willy Willy* (James Chilton, TTP); Mark Mayer Cup, *Warrior* (Bruce Hedrick, SYC); Bob Bollong Memorial Trophy, *Siris II* (George King, SYC); Gardner Gamwell Trophy, *Flamenca* (John Michael, CYC); Humphrey and Northwyn Trophies, *Ladybug* (Alan Holt, SYC); Tri-Island Thunderbird Trophy, *Talisman* (Joel Clark, EVYC); Roaring Forties Trophy, *Hooligan* (Tom O'Brien, SYC); Norpac Race: Haida Trophy, *Arrow* (Cappy Neu, SYC); Corinthian Offshore Trophy, *Loon* (Tom Schneide, CYC); Spinnaker Trophy, *Paraphernalia* (Stan Marcus, BLYC); Grand Prix Race: IOR, *Ladybug* (Alan Holt, SYC); SP, *Hooligan* (Tom O'Brien, SYC)

Don Bancroft's *Alaska Hunter* again dominated the powerboat races, placing 17 times and arriving first nine times. Among others it won the Victoria-to-Juneau 50th Anniversary Capital-to-Capital Race and the 1978 North American Invitational Predicted Log Championship at Newport, Rhode Island. Townley Bale's *Blue Chip* and Harold Murray's *Bluenose* each placed seven or more times.

Betty Chang was awarded the Betty Meacham Powerboat Trophy for women. Charles Cravens took the Masthead Trophy.

In Memoriam, 1978: Laurent E. Belcourt, Mrs. Middleton M. (Catharine) Chism, Irving M. Clark, Alton L. Collins, Mrs. Edward E. Cunningham, J. Franklin Eddy, William N. Ferguson, Jr., Sylvester F. Fink, Keith G. Fisken, Harold D. Fowler, Otis Harlan, Chauncey E. Hazen, Mrs. Andrew R. (Frances) Hilen, Sr., Dr. James Keenan, Mrs. Edmund (Betty) Locke, Clive W. McDonald, Henry B. Morris, Nathaniel Paschall, Arthur R. Taylor, Arne Vesoja, and Clayton K. Watkins.

1979

Commodore Arden Steinhart's goals for the year included (1) To complete installation of the computer system which would provide prompt billings and give the manager a tool for daily cost control information; (2) Enlarge the opening between the lounge and the Ward Room to provide interim relief to the over-taxed dining facilities; (3) Refurbish the lounge in a decor that would subtly relate to the Ward Room; (4) Make a comprehensive study of club facilities to result in more efficient use of the present structure and to look at possible additions; (5) Update mooring and docking regulations; (6) Improve the club's position relative to continued use of the mudlands under Piers 3 and 4; and (7) Reevaluate the outstation program to determine value of existing stations and to locate potential new acquisitions.

The property under the parking lot and some of the moorages remained a problem. The club's plan was to postpone the reverter clause indefinitely or extend that clause beyond the year 2002. This change would require approval from the neighborhood, the parks board and the city council. The majority of neighbors, the club discovered, were supportive, and SYC began hosting two annual parties for them.

SYC's float in the Tacoma Daffodil Festival was awarded the Queen's Trophy.

The resident manager's house at Port Madison was completed at a cost of about $70,000. SYC member and engineer Van Caples spearheaded the drive for funds and oversaw the construction of this first-class modified pre-fabricated home.

The Women's Group was as busy as ever. The September 1979 *Binnacle* mentioned activities such as exercise-dance groups, bridge, French lessons, Ellie Austin's Ukrainian Easter Egg workshop, a floral design course, and the Littler's fashion show luncheon.

In December SYC members volunteered for the annual Handicapped Children's Christmas Cruise. In all, about 150 yachts from various local clubs were involved.

At the annual meeting in October, the membership committee recommended limiting membership to 1,200 active, each class of intermediate to 200 and juniors to 200. Entrance fees would be raised to $50 for juniors 12 to 15 and $100 for juniors 16 to 20. Intermediates 21 to 25 would pay $300, intermediates 26 to 30 would pay $800, and intermediates 31 to 35 would pay $1,500. Active members would pay $5,000. To compensate for rampant inflation, the monthly dues ceiling was raised from $25 to $30.

At the Women's Group November meeting, Dr. Virginia Scholls, fellow in the American College of Surgeons, spoke about reconstructive surgery. The drama group scheduled a workshop for "frustrated stage stars," and the dinner theater group presented a melodrama. Announcements were made concerning bridge dates and plans for the upcoming Interclub luncheon at Port Orchard.

The juniors were happy to receive delivery of eight new Vanguard 420s.

Thomas C. Hukle's *Outlaw* was the SYC Sailboat of the Year.

The Marymount Trophy went to Sunny Vynne as the Sailor of the Year. Bill Chubb, writing in the *Binnacle*, described the Mark Mayer Race:

> Johnny Buchan with family and friends on *Heather* tore across the starting line, brushing by the floating starting buoy to make certain it was properly inflated. Upon executing this generous deed and re-starting, he propelled *Heather* through the course in one hour and fifty-two minutes, taking first in IOR I and first overall. *Coho II*, Pete Hanson's sleek Spencer 1330, captured first in SP-I and first overall in PHRF.

Of the Hat Island Race, he wrote:

> A healthy northerly greeted over 300 boats, with apparent winds in the 15-22 knot range. Generally those boats that beat up the east side fared well just past Possession Point, where the wind characteristically softens in the lee of Whidbey Island. After ghosting around Hat Island down past Possession again, the northerly reappeared to push the early starters home at a comfortable pace.
>
> —Binnacle, *June 1979*

Among the SYC winners were Tom Hukle's *Outlaw*, Chris Brain's *Saturday's Child*, Don Flynn's *Beluga*, Steve Leonard's *Orca*, and Joe Ireland's *Skinnydipper*.

Bill Chubb was at it again when he described an October race:

> This year's Smith Island Race . . . recorded gale winds up to 67 knots. Unfortunately this blow was confined to various saloons in Port Townsend, Kingston, Edmonds, etc, which were generated by well-oiled crews who had retired from a windless course.
>
> A pathetic southerly building up to a roaring three or four knots doomed any boat from finishing within the 33-hour limit. After this fiasco, the sailboat committee will doubtless seriously consider purchasing several gigantic fans to be strategically placed throughout Puget Sound. . . .
>
> Incredibly, seven boats completed the Mid-sound Race within the 27-hour limit. Tom Hukle in *Outlaw* took first place honors.
>
> —Binnacle, *November 1979*

At the Six-Meter World Cup Races held in Seattle, SYC's Brian Wertheimer in his *Warhorse* took a respectable third. Out of the 25 international skippers, eight were SYC members. Pat Goodfellow received the Henry Morgan trophy for best performance in an aged Six-Meter—the *Ylliam VIII*, which had been launched in 1954.

In the Great Equalizer Race, Graham Anderson's *Whistle Wing V* led the IOR-1 class. John Buchan's *Heather* came in first in IOR-2, M. Cahan's *Serada* in IOR-5, J. Murray's *Madrugador* in SP-B, and Dorr Anderson's *White Mist* in SP-J.

The SYC yearbook listed the following trophies and award winners for 1979.

Mark Mayer Race: IOR, *Heather* (John Buchan, SYC); SP, *Coho II* (Pete Hanson, SYC); Vashon Island Race: IOR, *Pachena* (John Newton, WVYC); SP, *Coho II* (Pete Hanson, SYC); Protection Island Race: IOR, *Weatherly* (Alan Buchan, TYC); SP, *Epic* (Charles Schiff, CYC); Commodore's Trophy Race: SP Overall, *Surtsey* (Bates McKee, SYC); Frisbie Trophy Race: SP Overall, *Adversary* (Duane Vergeer, SYC); Crooz N Snooz Race: Overall, *Outlaw* (Tom Hukle, SYC); Single-Handed Race: Sea Fever Trophy, *Flamenca* (John Michael, CYC); Nautilus Trophy, *Draco* (N. Brangsholt, CYC); Osprey Trophy, *Orange Juice* (S. Blackbourn, SYC); Quent Williams Trophy, *Bumper* (Dennis Clark, SYC); SYC Trophy, *Grauer Geist* (Wayne Berge, CYC)

Hat Island Race: IOR and SP Overall, *Weatherly* (Alan Buchan, TYC) and *Saturday's Child* (Chris Brain, SYC); Midsound Race: Horder-Provine Old Salts' Trophy, SP Overall, *Tamure-Tamure* (Sheridan Halbert, PMYC); Tri-Island Series: Three-Island Trophy, IOR Overall, Long Course, *Warrior* (Bruce Hedrick, SYC); Walt Little Trophy SP Overall, Long Course, *Epic* (Charles Schiff, CYC); First President's Trophy, SP Overall, Short Course, *Nasty Jack* (Dave Brink, CYC); Mark Mayer Cup, IOR A and B, Overall, *Warrior* (Bruce Hedrick, SYC); Bob Bollong Memorial Trophy, IOR C, Overall, *Anomaly* (William Elmer, CYC); Gardner Gamwell Trophy, IOR D, Overall, *Sachem* (Bill Buchan, CYC); Humphrey Trophy, IOR Half-Ton, Overall, *Ladybug* (Alan Holt, SYC); Tri-Island Thunderbird Trophy, SP Thunderbirds, Overall, *Aozora* (John Monk, CYC)

SYC Sailboat of the Year in 1979 was Thomas C. Hukle's *Outlaw*.

In powerboating circles, Don Bancroft again won just about everything—the Masthead Trophy, the Barush Trophy, the North American Championship, the Century 21 and Tacoma Olympia races. He was first in the Bremerton Heavy Weather, and the Lake Washington Rudder Cup and was with the winning team in the SYC-QCYC Challenge Race.

Townley Bale's *Blue Chip*, Jerry Caldwell's *Manana* and Ralph Buseman's *Gaika* placed in several races.

The Betty Meacham Powerboat Award for Women went to Lucille Bradley. SYC member Robert L. Steil was named Sportsman of the Year by the Unlimited Hydroplane Racing Commission for his work with *Squire Shop*.

Dick Chang proudly reported that SYC racers brought back all the trophies in the Stimson Trophy Powerboat Race. The best four boat team was made up of Don Bancroft, Bob Hawley, Sr., Frank Kline and Jerry Caldwell.

In early December 1979 the U.S. Yacht Racing Union held its annual meeting in Seattle. This was the first time in its 82-year history that the organization had met in a city on Puget Sound. About 200 attended.

In Memoriam, 1979: Starr H. Calvert, C. Spencer Clark, Mrs. Caspar W. Clarke, Mrs. Charles Clise, Russell Gibson, Mrs. Elizabeth S. Gustison, J. J. Harris, John W. Harvey, George P. Horton, Gordon G. Ingman, Mrs. Richard R. Loynes, Dr. Wood Lyda, W. W. Mitchell, Herbert M. Nichols, Howard Thorpe, and Homer Wickerd.

As the decade was closing, yachtsmen were bemoaning the increasing costs of fuel and many were switching to sail, an effect still felt to this day. More yachts were used for cruising and fewer for racing, for racing was becoming increasingly expensive as prices escalated for sails, equipment, maintenance, and other necessities. Outstation acquisition received a high priority during the 1970s, and this concern would continue into the 1980s. In spite of the inflation of the 1970s, SYC operational budgets were balanced, though to accomplish this, dues and initiation fees were increased. ☆

Aerial view of the Seattle Yacht Club Portage Bay Station taken in 1981. (MOHAI)

TEN

1980-1991

The decade opened with an explosion in Washington State that was heard round the world. On May 18, 1980, Mt. St. Helens, dormant since 1857, erupted and sent ash and hot gases 60,000 feet into the atmosphere, killing at least eight people.

At the 1984 Olympics in Los Angeles, American yachtsmen won gold medals in Finn, Flying Dutchman, Soling and Star classes and a silver in Finn class. Local sailors Carl Buchan, Jonathan McKee, Bill Buchan and Steve Erickson brought honor to their yacht clubs.

During the decade Seattle's skyline punctured the clouds with new structures, the highest being the 954-foot, 76-story Columbia Center. Increasing trade with Pacific Rim countries escalated the tonnage through the Port of Seattle. The Boeing Company sold hundreds of jetliners during the decade.

The Pacific Northwest was one of the last regions to feel the pinch of the financial recession that greeted the 1990s. In early 1991, the United States declared war on Iraq for invading Kuwait, a conflict that quickly gained Kuwait its freedom but left that volatile Mideast region in turmoil.

1980

There were several personnel changes at the club during the year. Assistant Manager Millie Matson retired in January. Al Bosch, manager of the Port Madison Fo'c'sle, died, and Clarence and Eve Ellis took over at the outstation.

In 1980 SYC members owned 520 sailboats and 650 powerboats. Moorage fees totaled about $250,000 a year, and a $100 deposit was required before a member's name was added to the moorage waiting list.

Jack Austin and his moorage committee concluded an effort started three years earlier by Commodore Bill Bradshaw. They made recommendations on how to improve procedures for moorage assignments, which had been a problem in years past. Austin reported that the more than 240 members waiting for moorage space could now note their positions on the posted computerized list.

Late in the year, the long-range planning committee headed by Jim McCurdy released the findings of a membership survey, the first since the one undertaken a decade earlier by Peter McTavish. With the help of Gilmore Research Group, the committee discovered that a majority of the members favored acquisition of additional moorages in both salt- and freshwater and expansion of existing moorages. The club's membership was about at maximum, they believed, and the present clubhouse was the right size and in the right location. A majority agreed that an additional outstation in the San Juan or Gulf Islands with floats, moorage buoys, and garbage facilities was a priority item.

At the annual meeting, Commodore Phil Johnson introduced Dick Chang, fleet captain, power. Chang reported that SYC members had participated in all but two of the IPBA-sanctioned predicted log races for the season.

Later in the agenda, Commodore Johnson explained that Graham Anderson, Fleet Captain, Sail, had put together an excellent program. But Anderson had been appointed to an Olympic Games skiing committee; he asked to be relieved and suggested Bob Kaczor take over his duties. Kaczor made this report:

> This year the Tri-Island series tried out a new format and the idea was to run all the races in the spring. It was a tremendous idea. We ran off the Vashon and Smith Island races and then were ready to do Protection. The wind didn't cooperate, so now the race is being held next weekend [first week in October].
>
> The program we instituted this year was family cruising and family cruising racing using the idea of the Crooz N Snooz, Commodore's, and Frisbie trophy races and we added a Henry Island Rendezvous to which all the membership was invited. Ten boats showed up and we had a tremendous time. . . .
>
> The One-design Fleet this year had two very successful regattas. . . . The *Portage Bay* received probably the best use it has had since we acquired the boat. It was used by the Powerboat Committee; it was used by the juniors for Opening Day; for the Daffodil Parade; worked last year with handicapped people during the Christmas season; took the Seafair queen and court around during Seafair; and was used by the Women's Rendezvous at Port Madison. . . .
>
> —*Bob Kaczor, Oct. 3, 1980*

This was the year that SYC's Dick McCurdy, Jr., circumnavigated the globe on his 36-foot auxiliary cutter *Active Light*. And Denny and Elaine Morgan left in August for a three-year cruise of the South Pacific on their 43-foot ketch *Contagious*.

Closer to home, John Schlagel and Dr. Frank Henry spent many evenings during the year attending public meetings in an effort to find how to control the Eurasian milfoil weed that was encroaching on SYC moorages.

The U.S. Coast Guard required a Federal Waterway Closure Permit for the Opening Day parade. Only registered entrants could participate.

The races of 1980 were colorful and often close. They also began early. On January 5 and 6, the SYC 420s raced in the first post-war Frostbite series. As Bill Chubb reported:

> The boats (including spinnaker gear) proved themselves to be built to hold up to the test although some of the crews found themselves to be better suited to friendlier weather. The first day of racing was the real test of endurance as the wind gusted to 18 knots while temperatures hovered around freezing. Five races were sailed on the lake with five of the eight boats capsizing before everyone agreed it was cold enough to call it a day.
>
> —Binnacle, *February 1980*

The next day six more races were sailed beneath cold blue skies, and no one

Sally Laura received the Betty Meacham Award for outstanding service by a woman in 1980. The presenter was Dick Chang. (SYC Historical Collection)

could catch SYC juniors Jonathan McKee and Sarah Steel.

Powerboats also were scheduling races in January. On January 19 the fifth annual running of the 28-mile Queen City Trophy Contest attracted 37 powered craft from nine yacht clubs. Townley Bale in his *Blue Chip* finished with a score of .7484, which earned a third overall behind two Queen City Yacht Club competitors—Bernard Butler and Pat Fricks.

On March 30 on Lake Lawrence in Thurston County, SYC's John Fox broke the existing world's record in the Region 10 APBA-sanctioned ski-jet drive class circle boat competition by running the course at 85.960 miles per hour. Then on July 12 he broke his own record in his 17-foot Rogers, *Mistaken Identity*, by averaging 88.977 miles per hour.

Dave Bingham in *Zip* brought in the first-place score in the Puget Sound Powerboat Association Offshore Juan de Fuca Race on April 13 by covering the 67.9-mile course at an average speed of 48.85 miles per hour. This was Bingham's first attempt at the sport.

In the Victoria-to-Maui race, which began June 28, six boats were from SYC. *Katana*, skippered by Vladimir Plavsic of the West Vancouver Yacht Club, won the Division II and overall corrected time race. D. Bruce Adams' *Virginia Dare* placed highest among the SYC finishers—third place in Division III and fifth overall.

The 1980 races for the Barush and Carr trophies were hosted by SYC. The Carr award went to a Southern California team under skipper Butch Cassidy with SYC's Sunny Vynne a very close second. The Barush went to Queen City's Al Smith for the second year in a row. SYC's team of Don Bancroft and Les Lewis were second.

At year's end, Gil Middleton and his *Far Out* captured the Bale Trophy as SYC's number one predicted log racer. In all he captured five first places—the Rudder, Everett Invitational, Meydenbauer Bay Boomerang, Rainier-to-Poulsbo and Stimson trophies. The coveted Noon Cannon Award went to Gerry Johnson for his work in furthering the powerboat program. The Betty Meacham Award was presented to hard-working Sally Laura.

Sailboat of the year was Lawrence (Lon) Robinson's *Gamin*. Jonathan McKee was acclaimed the Sailor of the Year. The Ruptured Eardrum Trophy went to Marilyn and Bill Bradshaw.

The SYC yearbook listed the following trophies and award winners for 1980.

Mark Mayer Race: SP, *Foxy Lady* (Pat and Bill Park, CYC);

IOR, *Whistlewing V* (Graham Anderson, SYC); Crooz N Snooz: Overall, *Gamin* (Lon Robinson, SYC); Frisbie: *Innamorata* (Cliff Lanzinger, CYC); Single-Handed: Nautilus Trophy, *Draco* (Tom Drangshold, CYC); Hat Island: SP, *Olympian* (Pete Schmidt, SYC); IOR, *Chiron* (Bryan Archer, TYC); Short, Kennell Wind Pennant, *Nasty Jack* (Dave Brink, CYC); Smith Island: Jerry Bryant SP, *Gamin* (Lon Robinson, SYC); Horder Provine Old Salts' Trophy, SP, *Soul Catcher* (Cappy Clarke, SYC); Lady Medina, *Rhapsody* (Jim Smith, EdYC); Protection Island: SP, *Circe* (Tom Geisness and Bob Bartleson, SYC); IOR, *Rhapsody* (Jim Smith, EdYC); Pt.

Hudson: *Phyrxix* (Stan Clark, CYC); Vashon Island: IOR, *Draco* (Tom Drangsholt, CYC); *Moonglow IV* (Dave Nielsen, TYC); Rawson Trophy, *Z-26* (Greg Hedrick, CYC)

Tri-Island Series: Cal 40s, *Legend* (Chuck Steward, SYC); Walt Little Trophy, SP, *Moonglow* (Dave Nielsen, TYC); First President's Trophy, *Fastbreak* (Gerald Lawrie, PO); Bob Bollong Trophy, IOR C, *Prospector* (Larry Shorett, SYC); Gardner Gamwell Trophy, IOR D, *Rhapsody* (Jim Smith, EdmYC); Humphrey and Northwyn trophies, *Lady Bug* (Alan Holt, SYC); Tri-Island Thunderbird Trophy, *Foreigner* (F. and M. Eykel, TTPYC); PIYA Trophies: Briggs Trophy, IOR, *Dream Machine* (Wink Vogel, RVYC); Key City Trophy, SP, *Moonglow IV* (Dave Nielsen, TYC); Endeavor Team Series: Seattle Yacht Club

In the Swiftsure races Alan Holt of SYC raced his half-ton *Ladybug* to a first overall in IOR, winning the Swiftsure and the Royal Vancouver Yacht Club trophies for first in Division IV. Bill Burdick managed a first in Division III in his *Wotan*, thus winning the City of Seattle Trophy. Both the Pacific Rim Trophy, awarded to the overall handicap winner, and the Corinthian Yacht Club Trophy, for finishing first in Division B, went to SYC's Dr. Roy Gunsolus in his *Delicate Balance*. Tom Hukle came away with overall honors and the Royal Canadian Navy Trophy for first in Division VI in the Juan de Fuca Race. The other two top trophies in this race—the Royal Victoria Yacht Club Trophy and the San Juan Trophy—went to Jerry Duncan's *Hagar*. SYC racers collected 11 of the 24 major trophies.

The Masthead Trophy went to Frank Kalberer, Jr.

In December, 22 SYC members joined other yachtsmen at the Royal Vancouver Yacht Club and later at the Bayshore Inn for the IPBA meeting and awards banquet. Don Johnson of the Poulsbo Yacht Club received the Jerry Bryant Man of the Year Trophy. Don Bancroft was given the PCYA Commodore's Award.

The Suma Trophy, the Japanese treasure ship Takarabune worked in silver, was provided by the Suma Yacht Club of Kobe, Japan, to be awarded every other year in a home and home series of J-24 races. (Wallace Ackerman Photography)

In Memoriam, 1980: Jay Adams, Alvin W. Anderson, Dr. Arthur S. Biddle, Mrs. Lincoln (Louise) Bouillon, Duane Culbertson, Mrs. Charles (Martha) Dunn, Mrs. John C. (Mary) Hagen, Charles R. Hartman, Ernest H. Haynes, Dr. Raymond Hellickson, Hugh C. Klopfenstein, Jr., Roy L. Maryatt, Sr., Mrs. Henry B. (Isla) Morris, Richard B. Newell, Dr. Dean Parker, Manuel E. Stevens, Daniel B. Trefethen, Jr., John O. Warren, and Mrs. Paul Webb.

1981

In January, 23 SYC members joined together to form a ham radio group, and they planned to secure current licenses for all members who wished to join. A special burgee was designed to be carried on any yacht with an SYC ham radio aboard.

Early in the year a Thursday luncheon was held at the Museum of History and Industry. Director James Warren spoke to the group and led them on a tour

The Red Fleet was the first SYC group to win the Wilson Seamanship Trophy. The group was organized by Audrey Salkield in 1981. (SYC Historical Collection)

of the area where artifacts were stored. Over the previous year Seattle Yacht Club members participated in the successful effort to purchase the 50,000 maritime photographs of the Williamson Collection that were preserved by the Puget Sound Maritime Historical Society at the Museum of History and Industry.

The Suma Yacht Club of Kobe, Japan, and Seattle Yacht Club became sister clubs in 1981. The Kobe group sent a Japan treasure ship (Takarabune) trophy to be awarded the winners of J-24 boat races to be scheduled every other year in the home-and-home series. The first race was scheduled for Seattle in 1982.

Opening Day was made memorable in part thanks to "the Great Red Fleet." Eight sailing vessels were involved, all with red hulls and crews attired in red tops and white trousers. They won the Wilson and Mariner Friedlander trophies. The eight vessels belonged to Dwight Shaw, Thomas Hukle, William Weaver, Ken Briggs, Larry Salkield, Larry Hills, Gerry Maurer, and Peter Huwiler. Ed and Claudia Rombauer helped with the Red Fleet idea, and it was organized by Audrey Salkield. The theme for Opening Day was "Lifesaver, a Salute to the U.S. Coast Guard."

In June Admiral Charles Hunter, commandant of the Whidbey Island Naval Air Station, provided a bus to transport 24 yacht club members to Whidbey for the day. A briefing titled "War at Sea" was delivered by several officers. A tour, lunch, and films filled the rest of an interesting day.

Commodore Jack Sylvester in the September *Binnacle* mentioned that the club had hosted the Blue Angels at a salmon barbecue on the lawn on August 11 after the fliers had performed on Gold Cup Sunday.

August 29 was memorable as the day the club reroofed Pier 3. Andy Smith of Pacific Northwest Bell provided names of the best roofing contractors. When the bids arrived, the figures showed that removing the old roof would cost $40,000. The club decided to ask volunteers from the membership to do the work. Though 165 signed up to help, 217 eventually showed up. They were assigned to work teams led by Bob Berst, Gus Robinson, Eric Van, Hugh Blackwell, Doug Sherwood, and Jimmy James. In addition, a safety team was headed by Charles Cummins and the dumpster loading team by Bull Dawson. Tools and wheelbarrows were rented, and some members brought their own. All the gravel was swept up, and the tar paper removed and placed in the dumpsters by 4:30 P.M. The only casualties were blisters galore and several feet punctured by roofing tacks. John Scott won the blister prize with one the size of a silver dollar. Charlie Erickson ruined a $15 pair of leather gloves and still earned a blister. The workers were fed a continental breakfast, a hefty lunch, and, once the work was done, a salmon barbecue. The replacement roof was commercially installed.

In November the club presented the play *Never Trust a Tattooed Sailor*. Paul Dunstan, who had the lead, was taken ill two days before the event, and the faithful director, Dee Sanwick, filled in for him. The *Binnacle* reported that this caused a bit of added glee for the audience. The drama was presented again in January. The juniors' presentation of the year was *Heaven Can't Wait*.

The 1981 Sailboat of the Year was Gerry Maurer's *Surprise*, and the Predicted Log High Point winner was Ralph and Carol Buseman's *Gaika*. Charlie McKee was Sailor of the Year. The Ruptured Eardrum Award went to Bob Kaczor for his race committee service.

The Wood Lyda Trophy awarded at the CYC Commodore's Ball went to *Ylliam VIII*, owned by Pat Goodfellow and Harry F. Ostrander.

The Dragon World Championship (using Olympic scoring) found a Seattle team in the boat *Vim* with Martin Godsil, helmsman, Davy Jones, tactician, and Patrick Dore, foredeck hand. Max Godsil replaced Dore for the last races. At the Travemunde Woche held on Lubecker Bay, 35 Dragons competed; *Vim* finished fifth. The following week, vying for the world championship, *Vim* again finished fifth among 49 Dragons from 12 nations.

The SYC yearbook listed the following trophies and award winners for 1981.

Mark Mayer Race: IOR, *Glory* (John Buchan, SYC); SP, *Melaine* (Bill Bruch, CYC); Smith Island Race: Jerry Bryant Trophy, SP Long, *Olympian* (Pete Schmidt, SYC); Bob Gibbons Trophy, IOR Long, and Gwendolyn Trophy, *Pachena* (John Newton, WestVanYC); Mid-sound Race: Horder Provine Old Salts' Trophy, SP Short, *Blue Moon* (Elliott Jones, SYC); Kennell Midwatch Trophy, IOR Short, *Christopher Robin* (Gary Morgan, SYC); Vashon Island Race: IOR Long, *Sachem* (Bill Buchan, CYC); SP Long, *Stinger* (Stan Kiesling, TYC); Rawson Trophy, IOR Short, *Aquaratarus* (N. Steward/B. Kruger, CYC); SP Short, *Mrs. Olson* (Brian Gallagher)

Protection Island Race: IOR Long, *Glory* (John Buchan, SYC); SP Long, *Blackwatch* (Bill Nelson, CTYC); Point Hudson Race: Golden Potlatch Protection Island Trophy, IOR Short, *Sly* (Rick Moeller, CYC); SP Short, *Prism* (Bob McPake, SYC); Hat Island Race: IOR Long, *Sachem* (Bill Buchan); SP Long, *Bald One* (KLAYC); Kennell Wind Pennant Trophy, IOR Short, *The Heeling Art* (Jim Sylvester, SYC); Lady Medina Trophy, SP Short, *Vandal* (Stephen Stoller, CYC)

Tri-Island Series: Three-Island Trophy, IOR Overall Long, *Sachem* (Bill Buchan, CYC); Walt Little Trophy, SP Long, *Blackwatch* (Bill Nelson, TCYC); First President's Trophy, SP Overall Short, *Blue Moon* (Elliott Jones, SYC); Mark Mayer Cup, IOR 1 and 2 Short, *Sachem* (Bill Buchan, CYC); Bob Bollong Memorial Trophy, IOR 3, *Made in Japan* (CYC); Gardner Gamwell Trophy, IOR 4, *Rhapsody* (Jim Smith, EYC); Humphrey Trophy, IOR Short, *Christopher Robin* (Gary Morgan, SYC); Tri-Island Thunderbird Trophy, *Luffly* (Jon Thompson, TYC); Roaring Forties Trophy, *Olympian* (Pete Schmidt, SYC)

Alan Holt designed Ladybug, *shown here on its way to one of several Swiftsure Race victories.* Ladybug *took first in the Swiftsure IOR in 1976 and first again in 1980 in the Swiftsure Overall and IOR. She continued her winning record with a 1986 first Overall and first IOR in the Cape Flattery Race in 1986 and 1987. Holt was also a top Star-class sailor through the years. (Photo by Kelly O'Neil)*

Crooz N Snooz Race: *Outlaw* (Tom Hukle, SYC); Commodore's Race: John Graham Cup, IOR, *Rhapsody* (Jim Smith, EYC); SP, *Tonic* (Dan Brink, CYC); Half-Ton Overall Season Winner: *Ladybug* (Alan Holt, SYC); All Islands—Overall Short Cruise: SP, *Poisson Soluble* (Robert Horsley, CYC); Norpac Race Week: Haida Trophy, *Golden Apple* (Bob Kershaw, SYC); Corinthian Trophy, Overall, *Scrambler* (Robin and Mike Bookey, SYC, CYC); Spinnaker Trophy, *Rhub Runner* (Ken C. Wilson, TTPYC); Dovkie Trophy, Overall, *Scrambler* (Robin and Mike Bookey, SYC, CYC)

Jeray Holmes was awarded the new Half Vast Trophy. The Briggs Trophy (for high point IOR winner at PIYA) went to Bill Buchan's *Sachem* and the Key City Trophy (SP) to Bill Nelson's *Blackwatch*.

Outstanding service plaques were awarded Mike Bookey, Peter Z. Cahan, Pat Goodfellow, Henry Helliesen, Ned Rawn, Doug Sherwood, Roger Werner, Peter Thorlakson, Miles Miller, Mike Duffy, Bill Mains, Bill Niemi, Bill Watkins, Corey Anderson, Carol Buchan, Tom Hukle, Mike Sharpe, Bill Bradshaw, Sally Laura, Wil Anderson and Phil Duryee.

Powerboat awards were presented to Gil Middleton's *Far Out*, which captured five firsts (Queen City, SYC Rudder Cup, Meydenbauer Bay Boomerang, Rainier-Poulsbo Seat of the Pants, and Edmonds Round the Isle), and placed in four other races. Other powerboat winners included Ralph Buseman's *Gaika*, which was given the Bale Trophy as Predicted Log Racer of the Year (*Far Out* was ineligible since she had won previously). Jerry Caldwell's *Manana* also did well during the year.

The Betty Meacham Powerboat Trophy for Women was awarded to Carol Buseman.

In Memoriam, 1981: Mrs. Raymond C. (Thelma) Anderson, Donald Baldwin, Mrs. Ray (Helen) Blackstock, Thomas C. Bostic, Eugene Clark, Flora Comstock, Mrs. Roy W. (Helen) Corbett, Edgar E. Cushing, Mrs. Theron (Christina) Hawkes, Peter Johnston, Welcom Johnston, Edgar F. Kaiser, Harry L. Marshall, Michael C. McKinney, J. Edmund Messett, William E. Muncey, Harold B. Murray, John Riach, Mrs. Sanford (Doris) Skilton, and Richard A. Smith.

1982

The Women's Group programs for the year included opportunities to learn more about antiques and fashions. The

Commodores of the Seattle Yacht Club—1980s

PHILLIP G. JOHNSON
1980
Born: 1930, Seattle, Wash.
Education: Seattle University
Occupation: Industrial Engineer (Crown Zellerbach), Contractor
Boats: Inisfail *(48-foot ketch),* Swallow II

JOHN (JACK) N. SYLVESTER
1981
Born: 1909, Pasco, Wash.
Education: University of Washington Law School
Occupation: Lawyer
Boats: Jane's Fighting Ship *(50-foot Chris-Craft)*

ROBERT (BOB) A. BERST
1982
Born: 1930, Seattle, Wash.
Education: University of Washington Law School
Occupation: Lawyer
Boats: Just Blue, El Cid, *and* Visa, *(32-foot Islander sloop)*

ROBERT (BOB) W. SCARFF
1983
Born: 1917, Seattle, Wash.
Education: University of Washington
Occupation: Ford Dealer (Scarff Motors, Inc.)
Boats: Sunliner *(four different ones)*

DONALD H. SIMPSON
1984
Born: 1935, Seattle, Wash.
Education: University of Washington
Occupation: Self-employed, Ballard Sheet Metal Works, Inc.
Boats: Bar le Duc, Bandit *(47-foot sailboat)*

RALPH H. BUSEMAN
1985
Born: 1929, Seattle, Wash.
Education: University of Washington
Occupation: Dentist
Boats: Gaika *(43-foot Hatteras)*

JERAY A. HOLMES
1986
Born: 1934, Seattle, Wash.
Education: Central Washington State University
Occupation: Self-employed, Holmes' Electric
Boats: Kaleo *(53-foot cruiser),* Limbo *(45-foot Heritage cutter).*

BILL T. STEWART
1987
Born: 1921, Fort Worth, Tex.
Education: University of Texas
Occupation: Publisher's Representative, Advertising Director for Post-Intelligencer
Boats: Billet *(42-foot Chris-Craft)*

LARRY SALKIELD
1988
Born: 1939, Wendell, Idaho
Education: University of Washington, Willamette and New York University Law Schools
Occupation: Lawyer
Boats: Sockeye *(34-foot C and C sloop),* Molly Anne, Pepe.

WILLIAM (BILL) A. FREITAG
1989
Born: 1940, Milwaukee, Wis.
Education: Michigan State University
Occupation: Veterinarian
Boats: Cat's Meow *(36-foot Uniflite Double Cabin)*

group also enjoyed a visit behind the scenes of the television program "A.M. Northwest."

The club installed a new garbage compactor and dock-side dumpsters and warned that any oil dumped in with other garbage would ruin the equipment. The compactor would be paid for in a year and a half on money saved from collection charges.

Commodore Bob Berst reminded members that Jim Torrance had started working at the Seattle Yacht Club in 1954 when he was 14 years old and now, 28 years later, was the much appreciated department head of maintenance and grounds. (As of this writing, he is the club's assistant manager.)

In March the Women's Group heard Jennifer James, Ph.D., columnist for *The Seattle Times*, speak on the topic "Be Kind to Yourself." This was followed by a social hour and dinner for members and their guests.

In April the SYC sailboat committee adopted this addition to the general sailing instructions for the race handbook: "The skipper of a registered yacht is responsible for unsportsmanlike actions of his/her crew. Violation of the fundamental rule—fair sailing—may exclude a competitor from further participation in the SYC racing program."

During the spring, a mother goose made her nest on old coats in a shelf on the club's Pier 3. Wally Ovens took her picture, which appeared in the *Binnacle* along with the note from the editor: "A gosling was hatched and at last report was doing fine."

At the Daffodil festival in Tacoma, Bob Gilmore furnished his speedboat *Annie*. The Busemans, Nichols, and Scarffs arrived by boat.

Charlie (Outstation) Erickson acted as auctioneer at the oyster feed, which was an outstanding event.

Commodore Bob Berst recalled that the first Suma Regatta was a highlight of his year as Commodore.

> Don "Suma Slammer" Oakland "found" a keg and shared it with his Suma buddies. This was the international gesture that contributed to the success of the first Suma Regatta. Our team, led by Keith Lorence, Charlie McKee, and Carl Buchan, won this exciting series. The last day, after the outcome was settled, the U.S. and Japanese teams split up and joined each other for some excellent competition. Words cannot describe the electricity in the air at the Awards Banquet. All the Suma racers called our SYC team forward and gave them their special regatta ties. The banquet closed with final words of our own Dorothy Sprinkle [a waitress who spoke Japanese]. Her words in a Japanese "Sayonara" brought tears to many eyes. Rear Commodore Don Simpson headed up the committee putting on the first Suma Regatta.
>
> —Binnacle, *June 1982*

Another highlight of the year, according to Berst, was the re-activation of Rope Yarn Sunday every Thursday evening from 5:00 to 7:00 P.M. Rope Yarn continues to this day, sometimes with programs and sometimes with just good "Rope Yarn Sunday" fellowship.

At the annual meeting, Commodore Berst called on Treasurer Dave Rice to give the financial report. After preliminaries, a question came from the floor about the cost of the Suma Regatta. The response was that it was expensive, about $6,000. Another member questioned the costs of the *Portage Bay*, the yacht club–owned boat. It, too, was expensive—with about $11,000 worth of capital equipment installed. Nonetheless there was no thought of abandoning either.

A new committee was mentioned—the active-intermediate. Barbara Bradshaw reported that three major functions had been a success with good turn-outs.

Sixty-year pins were presented to five life members—Charlie Schaak, Harold Helliesen, Reginald Parsons, J. Swift Baker, and Andy Joy. All had joined the club in 1922 except for Parsons, who had joined in 1920. In a speech to the club in 1982, Andy Joy told how much easier it had been to purchase a life membership "in ancient history." It was possible, according to Joy, "to buy a life membership for one thousand dollars, and at that time, the Seattle Yacht Club still had several depression-era $1,000 bonds out. The bonds went kind of sour and you could buy one for maybe fifty cents on the dollar and then you could trade it in for a life membership. That's what was done by

History of Rowing at the Seattle Yacht Club

After the Portage Bay station of the Seattle Yacht Club was dedicated in 1920, rowing was added as a boating activity. Several graduates of rowing programs from the nearby University of Washington and other universities became SYC members, including Sunny Vynne, Mac McCurdy, and Ray Eckmann.

Most of SYC's rowing contests in the 1920s involved sculling singles. The famous mentor and shell builder George Pocock won one of these contests and was awarded a handsome silver trophy that his family kept for years.

SYC women's rowing team and winners of the 1988 FISA Veterans World Championships D8, Scotland. From left, Pamela Blake (bow), Gretchen Boe, Sue McKain, Michelle Day, Ellie Austin, Jane Baldwin, Irma Erichson, Artha Shelver (stroke), and Susan Stein (coxswain). (SYC Historical Collection)

For the 1972 Opening Day celebration Ray Eckmann invited University of Washington Huskie coach Dick Erickson to stage a rowing race prior to the boat parade. This event gradually expanded to include as many as 12 races (all conducted in less than one hour), often with international competitors.

Rowing became an official activity of the Seattle Yacht Club in the spring of 1982 when Kathy Snyder, Lou Bradley, and Sally Laura asked honorary member Dick Erickson to provide boats and rudimentary training for women members of Seattle, Meydenbauer, Queen City and Royal Vancouver yacht clubs. These women would compete in a masters class race on a course laid out between Queen City and SYC on the Friday afternoon before the traditional Saturday Opening Day boating parade. The race was intended to provide good-natured competition following the Opening Day Friday luncheon; the training turned out to be fierce and the competition intrepid.

The following year these women talked Dick Erickson into continuing the event and expanding it to other yacht clubs. On Opening Day 1984 the race was held in the Montlake cut. In 1985, heat races determined which of the increasing number of crews would compete for the championship. Many of the more active rowers competed through the rowing season. An elite group, composed mainly of SYC members, became known as "Dick's Chicks."

In the fall of 1984 an ad hoc committee chaired by Laura Boone, with members Janet Footh, Kit Ford, Joann Aberle, Sue Donaldson, Randy Pratt, Peg Marckworth, Sally Laura, CiCi Engle, Irma Erickson, some of the life members who are no longer around here."

The December women's luncheon presented a festive array of activities. Included were holiday caroling by the Forest Ridge Glee Club, the commodore's punch bowl, and the announcement by the past admiralettes that Betty Chang had been chosen admiralette for the 1983 Opening Day celebrations.

Late in the year Pat Goodfellow headed up a syndicate to purchase *Chi-*

Ellie Austin, Rae Jean Measer, Dottie Simpson, and Gerie Clark, presented a plan to the board of trustees that called for the club to purchase two four-oared shells and two training ergometers. The board approved immediate purchase, and storage space was prepared in the old mast storage building.

At the annual meeting in 1986, the bylaws were amended to include a standing rowing committee, which was to have charge of the club shells and equipment. Laura Boone was chairman until the fall of 1987 when Larry Shelver agreed to take the chairmanship with the proviso that Jack Austin be vice chairman. In 1989 Brian Vickers took over. Serving on the rowing committee beside the original founders were Barbara Bradshaw, Artha Shelver, Dorothy Anderson, Butch Ford, John Aberle, Jim Vaupell, Guy Harper, Keith Johnson, Mary Anderson, Gretchen Boe, Dick Hagen, Celeste Rose, Leslie Albertson, Mari Jalbing, Scott Graham, Dave Slepyan, and Kane Fenner.

By spring 1991 a launching float south of the lower parking lot and a floating storage rack had been attached to Pier 2. By then the club owned 3 eights, 2 fours, 2 pair/doubles, 2 singles and a recreational double, all with oars bearing the now-familiar "star and bar" of SYC. A trailer, ergometers, support slings, and a training dock-box with sliding seat were part of the equipment. The club boats committee supplied a launch for use by the coaches hired by the club to train the crews. Coaches' salaries are paid from training fees collected from rowing members.

The rowing program has been competitive from the beginning. In the first decade of racing, besides winning the U.S. Nationals, SYC crews won races in Canada, Scotland, France, and Italy.

SYC junior members also have a rowing program, and their crews have competed successfully in the Northwest and Canada. A junior crew composed of Crissy Marshall, Ali Gates, Rokelle Mead, Danielle Wright, Jenny Hunter and P. J. Austin (captain) and coached by Susan Stein won the 1987 Virginia Stillwell Memorial Perpetual Trophy Race for varsity fours with coxswain. Many members of this junior crew went on to compete in college, and Allison Gates became a member of the U.S. Junior National Rowing Team.

The rowing program is successful because of the voluntary help and dedication of club members. Rowers arise at 4:30 each morning, are on the water by 5:30, winter and summer, to practice. Their rewards are the exhilaration of communing with nature and the satisfaction of competing as a team members. ◇

SYC rowing trophies and medals. (Wallace Ackerman Photography)

Women's Rowing in the 1980s

Green Lake Extravaganza 1985 Women's Masters 4+. Cox, Bob Miles; stroke, Gretchen Boe; 3, Ellie Austin; 2, Artha Shelver; and bow, Sue Donaldson.

Masters Women's Nationals Green Lake 1985 Master Women's 4+, second place (First National metals for SYC rowers). From left: Janet Footh, stroke; Irma Erickson, 3; Laurie Parrott, cox; Artha Shelver, 2; Jean Elmer, bow.

(Ellie Austin Collection)

Junior Women's Varsity 4+, 1987. Junior rowers won first rowing trophy. From left: Susan Stein, coach; Patricia Austin, 2; Christine Marshall, cox; Jennifer Hunter, stroke; Allison Gates, 3; Danielle Wright, bow; Rokelle Mead, spare.

Opening Day Mixed Master 1987 winners. cox, Leslie Albertson; stroke, Dick Hagen; 7, Jim Vaupell; 6, Gretchen Boe; 5, Jean Elmer; 4, Guy Harper; 3, Brian Vicker; 2, Ann Barker; bow, Mary Anderson.

nook, a $60,000 Pele Patterson design boat to race in the 1983 Six-Meter World Cup Contest at Newport Beach, California. In all, he estimated $100,000 would be needed. Bill Buchan was asked to take the helm and organize the proper crew. The boat would belong to the Sailing Foundation and contributions were tax deductible.

The Opening Day theme was "Ports of the Pacific." The women rowed for the first time in the University of Washington "Tub 4s" as an Opening Day Friday luncheon activity.

The Sailboat of the Year in 1982 was Gerry and Kathy Maurer's *Surprise*, which among other wins took first in class and first overall in PHRF in the Swiftsure. Bill Buchan of Corinthian Yacht Club took the Marymount Trophy for Sailor of the Year. The Bellwether Trophy went to D. Paul Thorlakson of SYC, and the Briggs Trophy (PIYA High Point Winner) was taken by Bill Buchan's *Sachem* (IOR). John Buchan took the Half-Vast Trophy, and Don Oakland enjoyed the Ruptured Eardrum Trophy that year.

The SYC yearbook listed the following trophies and award winners for 1982.

Mark Mayer Race: IOR, *Scrambler* (Robin and Mike Bookey, SYC, CYC); SP, *Sakura* (Tal and Carol Godding, CYC); Smith Island Race: Jerry Bryant Trophy, SP Long, *Tsunami* (Conrad Moran, CYC); Bob Gibbons Trophy, IOR Long, *Promises* (Dave Ballaine, EHW); Gwendolyn Trophy, IOR 1 and 2, *Flash* (Ken Briggs, SYC); Point Hudson Race: Horder Provine Old Salts' Trophy, SP Short, *Honeysuckle Rose* (Gene Hoefling, CYC); Kennell Midwatch Trophy, IOR Short, *Sasquatch* (Greg Prothman, CYC); Vashon Island Race: Vashon Island Trophy, IOR Long, *Feelings* (Breck Adams, TCYC); SP Long, *Cayenne* (Gene Baker, SYC); Point Dalco Race: Rawson Trophy, SP Short, *Cool Change* (Nick Alvanos, SH); IOR Short, *Sasquatch* (Greg Prothman, CYC)

Protection Island Race: Protection Island Trophy, IOR Long, *Desperado* (Guyman/Blackbourn, SYC); SP Long, *Auspicious* (Mike Nilson, EYC); Point No Point Race: Protection Island Potlatch Trophy, IOR Short, *Rhapsody* (Smith/Smith, CYCE); SP Short, *Honeysuckle Rose* (G. Hoefling, CYC); Hat Island Race: Hat Island Trophy, IOR Long, *Sachem* (Bill Buchan, CYC); SP Long, *Draco* (Tom Drangshold, CYC); Kennell Wind Pennant Trophy, IOR Short, *Hagar* (Pete Strelinger, CYC); Lady Medina Trophy, SP Short, *Thunder Chicken* (Judy and Gordy Cole, CYC)

Tri-Island Race Series: Three-Island Trophy, IOR Overall, *Sachem* (Bill Buchan, CYC); Walt Little Trophy, SP Overall, *Surprise* (Gary Maurer, SYC); First President's Trophy, SP Short Overall, *Honeysuckle Rose* (G. Hoefling, CYC); Mark Mayer Cup, IOR Long and IOR 1 and 2, *Sachem* (Bill Buchan, CYC); Bob Bollong Memorial Trophy, IOR 3, *Promises* (D. Ballaine, EHW); Gardner Gamwell Trophy, SP, *Beluga* (Don Flynn, SYC); Humphrey Trophy, IOR Short, *Outlaw* (Tom Hukle, SYC); Tri-Island Thunderbird Trophy, *Honeysuckle Rose* (G. Hoefling, CYC); Roaring Forties Trophy, *Hooligan II* (Tom O'Brien, SYC)

Crooz N Snooz Race: Cannon Trophy, *Surtsey* (Bates McKee, III, SYC); Commodore's Race: John Graham Trophy, *Surtsey* (Bates McKee, III, SYC); Frisbie Race: Potlatch Trophy, *Stargazer* (Bill Headden, SYC); Half-Ton Overall Season Winner: *Bumper* (Dean Erickson, CYCE); All Islands Race: (All Islands Trophy, SP, *Antiqua* (Stef Thordarson, CYCT); Single-Handed Race: Sea Fever Trophy, *Surtsey* (Bates McKee, III, SYC); Nautilus Trophy, *Kuon II* (Martin Withington, SYC), Osprey Trophy, *Hot Tomato* (Steven Tindall, ST); Quent Williams Trophy, *Rough Draft* (Roger Werner, SYC); Seattle Yacht Trophy, *Zee-Boli* (Kent Powley, CYCE)

Outstanding 1982 Powerboats:

Far Out, owned by Gil Middleton, took first in the Everett Race, Rainier-to-Poulsbo Race, SYC Stimson Race, International Cruiser Race, and SYC Rudder Cup Race; it also took second in the Queen City Race, third in Bremerton Heavy Weather Race and fourth in the Meydenbauer Bay Boomerang. Don Bancroft's *Alaska Hunter* won the Queen City Race, the Bremerton Heavy Weather, Meydenbauer Bay Boomerang and Masthead Trophy races, and it came in third in the Rainier-to-Poulsbo contest. Jack Jorgeson's *So So Mo* won the Edmonds race and came in second in the Rainier/Poulsbo, SYC Rudder Cup, and International Cruiser races and fifth in four other races. Because both the *Far Out* and the *Alaska Hunter* had been powerboats of the year, the *So So Mo* was powerboat of the year for 1982.

In Memoriam, 1982: Mrs. Wilden H. Baldwin, Hugh Brady, Mrs. Hugh (Mary) Brady, Kenneth B. Colman, Christine Dameyer, Mrs. Sylvester Fink, Dr. Frederick Harvey, Mrs. Russell (Gretchen) Hawkins, Andrew Hilen, Col. Frances R. Hoehl, Hendrik G. Kamstra, John C. Laughlin, Mrs. John L. (Irene) Locke, Robert S. Macfarlane, Mrs. Charles W. (Lela) Maryatt, Joseph Mattes, E. Bates McKee, Dr. Ira O. McLemore, Mrs. Lee F. (Margaret) Miller, J. Rance Morris, Edward Patton, Randy Raden, Arthur Russell, A. Leslie Simmers, Mrs. Orville (June) Smith, Dr. Caleb S. Stone, Jr., James Unicume, Ernest G. Watson, Ray C. Wilcox, and Charles C. Wyatt.

1983

Commodore Bob Scarff in the January *Binnacle* explained that phase one of the redecorating, including permanent furnishings for the ladies' lounge off the lobby, was completed. Phase two was about to begin, and he asked members to excuse any inconveniences.

This was the year Congress passed a bill transferring ownership of Jones Island in the American San Juans to the Wash-

The Chinook Syndicate

In June 1979 the Six-Meter World's Regatta was staged at Shilshole. Many boaters remember it because Ted Turner skippered the *Ranger* in those races. Pelle Peterson's *Irene* was top boat, and *Warhorse*, the boat designed and built by Brian Wertheimer of Seattle, placed third.

At the time, Pat Goodfellow and George Schuchart wanted the classic Six-Meter yacht to maintain prominence in racing and, more important, wanted Seattle to maintain its leadership in the Six-Meter competition. Historically, Seattle boasted the largest and most competitive fleet of Six-Meters in the United States.

The two decided to put together a "Seattle Syndicate" to ready a boat for the 1983 Six-Meter World Cup scheduled for California. George Schuchart was the leading force behind the Sailing Foundation, which was approached to sponsor a Six-Meter campaign similar to their earlier *Intrepid* venture.

Founding members and major contributors of what became known as the "Chinook Syndicate" were David Buntz, Patrick Goodfellow, Jack Graham, Robert Helsell, Henry Kotkins, Mike Mumm, Harry Ostrander, Minor Pelly, Charlie Peterson, Howard Richmond, Jon Rose, Jon Runstad, George Schuchart, Hunter Simpson, and David C. Wyman.

Goodfellow researched the possibility of having a new Six-Meter designed and built, but the time and cost involved made that approach unrealistic. Jon Rose then located a Six-Meter in Sweden, a Pelle Peterson design built by Sune Carlsson Boatyards, Stockholm. It was purchased and outfitted specifically for the 1981 World Cup in Switzerland.

The boat was shipped to Seattle on Dec. 1, 1982, from Stockholm and arrived on December 23, badly damaged from escaping its cradle during the rail trip across the country. Five weeks later, the insured yacht was released, beautifully repaired, from the Cadranell yard.

Carl and Bill Buchan organized the crew of Keith Whittemore, Mark Rodgers, Pat Dore, and Eric Kowanki; Carl took the helm. Charlie Footh was chosen boat chief and assisted by Kevin Callaghan, who was responsible for the care and feeding of boat and crew. Christened *Chinook*, the boat, after a few

ington Parks and Recreation Commission for use as a marine park. Interclub, which had worked closely with the Parks Commission for many years building shelters at several marine parks, actually owed its origin to the campaign to raise funds from boaters to purchase Sucia Island and donate it to the Parks Department.

On January 8 the Black and White Masked Ball honored Vice Commodore Don Simpson and wife Mary and Rear Commodore Ralph Buseman and wife Carol. Helping in the festivities were the vice and rear commodores of 13 other clubs in the area.

The February Women's Interclub luncheon at SYC included women members from Day Island, Everett, Port Orchard, Poulsbo, Tyee, and Gig Harbor yacht clubs. The entertainment included songs of the 1890s vocalized by Rhinestone Rosie.

On Feb. 28, 1983, the club purchased a marina in Pender Harbour near the community of Madeira Park, B.C., to be known as the Garden Bay Outstation. Existing facilities included a clubroom, caretaker cottage, and 1,400 feet of moorage.

The Permanent Planning Committee chaired by Don Thompson recommended that the upper limit of assessments be $15 and that the monthly assessment be raised from $5 to $10 to build the Graham fund to buy outstations.

Commodore Scarff in April announced that full reciprocal privileges had

---

weeks of being used in training, was trailered to Newport Harbor, California, to prepare for the nationals and the 1983 World Cup. The *Chinook* was sailed superbly in both regattas, placing a strong second in each, only seconds behind world champion Pelle Peterson in *Irene*.

In 1985 *Chinook* was renamed *Belle* and readied for the World Cup campaign of April 1985. The major contributor, Pacific Northwest Bell, made it possible for Jon Rose and Pat Goodfellow to race the yacht in Cannes, France. The new crew was Mark Laura, skipper, and Larry Klein, tactician, with Dr. David Jones, Pat Dore, Brent Foxall, and David Buntz.

The boat arrived safely. The campaign took 10 days, and when the mist had settled, *Belle* had placed seventh, just ahead of George Schuchart's *Sockeye*, skippered by Brian Thomas.

The *Belle* next was scheduled for the North American Championships on San Francisco Bay. But 30 miles from Sausalito, the trailer broke an axle and the Six-Meter slid down the California highway and was badly scuffed up. It was returned to Seattle for repairs.

Dave Lewis, a Bainbridge Island shipwright, purchased *Belle* from the foundation in 1985 and rebuilt her. The next year, Jon Rose and Pat Goodfellow raised enough through the syndicate to repurchase the yacht and went on to win two Lipton Cups with Mark Brink at the helm.

The boat was structurally sound and competitive with the purchase of another set of hi-tech sails. She raced on Long Island Sound, scene of the earliest Six-Meter regattas of the 1920s, at Seawanaka Yacht Club on Oyster Bay. This time, commercially trailered, she arrived in perfect condition. Again renamed *Chinook*, she was crewed by Mark Brink, skipper; Bob Pistay; Arne Hammer; Paul Frederickson; and Jamie Stewart. But new boats dominated the regatta and the eight-year-old *Chinook* finished 14th. The boat was left at Seawanaka for sale to the highest bidder. A Swedish group bought her and returned her to her birthplace in Stockholm.

The Puget Sound Six-Meter Fleet has been almost inactive the past few years, but as of this writing a fleet of seven or eight "Sixes" of various ages are racing again out of Port Madison under the dedicated direction of Fleet Captain Harry Hoffman and his son Peter.

—Based on material supplied by Pat Goodfellow

been arranged with the Royal Hong Kong Yacht Club.

During the year, the club thespians presented the comedy *Harvey*, with the talented George Heideman cast as the rabbit-seeing Elwood P. Dowd.

At the annual meeting, five pages of bylaw corrections and updates were enacted. This legitimized several committees that had been active for years and made other changes.

The 1983 Washington State Legislature passed a one percent excise tax on boats over 16 feet.

President Diane Sweezey of the Women's Group began her fall membership meeting with a luncheon speaker on mental health. The annual dinner meeting the following week included a trip on the *Goodtime* to Tillicum Village for an authentic Indian salmon bake and an opportunity to learn more about the heritage of the North Coastal Indians.

In Powerboat awards, the Bale Trophy went to Gil Middleton as Best Predicted Log Racer of the Year. The Betty Meacham Powerboat Trophy for Women was awarded Maggie Jorgeson and the 8-Ball Trophy (blooper award) went to Bruce Peterson.

At the annual meeting, Dr. Gil Middleton reported on the powerboat races.

Garden Bay Outstation

In the early 1980s Charlie Erickson and his outstation acquisition committee evaluated more than 60 potential outstation properties. Charlie and wife Mildred spent seven weeks cruising to and inspecting these sites. In 1982 a realtor friend dealing in Canadian holdings told the Ericksons of a property in distress on Garden Bay of Pender Harbour. After considerable negotiation, an agreement was reached. This former marina would become yacht club property for $500,000, which was about half the going rate for waterfront.

Commodore Bob Scarff explained the action to the trustees in January 1983:

> We had to make a quick decision in regard to buying a piece of property at Garden Bay in Pender Harbour which was in bankruptcy court. The decision was to go for it, and earnest money was put down. Charlie Erickson and his outstation acquisition committee had been looking at properties for another outstation for a couple of years. It was hoped that we could acquire this new property and have it ready for use by SYC members for the 1983 spring and summer cruising season. A debt of gratitude is owed to Charlie, Wayne Murray, Bob LaBow, Arden Steinhart, Don McCausland, and John Osberg, all of whom had a piece of the assistance in acquiring our new outstation.
>
> —*Board minutes, January 1983*

Much renovation and cleanup work was necessary. Arden Steinhart prepared drawings. Rear Commodore Ralph Buseman bet Charlie that he'd be back for more money, so to be sure that repairs were done right and within budget, Charlie and Mildred rented a nearby house, and Charlie personally supervised all renovation work while Mildred coordinated the decoration.

Shortly after repairs began, a misleading article in the local weekly paper stirred up nearby residents who feared the club would begin competing with local businesses. The Ericksons soon convinced them that yachtsmen are good neighbors and that the outstation would not be a commercial competitor.

Where once a decrepit marine railway had been located, a riprap wall was installed. The caretaker's house was gutted down to the studs and renovated; 1,400 feet of moorage space was prepared; and electricity, water, and a pay phone were installed. The clubhouse was furnished with washer, dryer, ice machine, showers, toilets, and a small meeting room. A social area was prepared on the deck. For this major undertaking, Charlie found good workmen and some committee members willing to volunteer their help.

He said the most spectacular race was the first race, Queen City Yacht Club. Don Bancroft, even with a broken neck and paralyzed, with the help of his brother and son won first overall.

The 1983 Powerboat of the Year was Gil Middleton's *Far Out*, which captured firsts in the SYC Rudder Cup, the Everett Invitational, and the Rainier-Poulsbo races and seconds in the International Cruiser, Queen City and Meydenbauer Bay Boomerang races.

Other outstanding power racers included Townley Bale's *Blue Chip* (first overall in the Stimson Race), Don Bancroft's *Alaska Hunter* (first overall in the Queen City Race), Roy Bumstead's *Concrete Queen* (first in the Meydenbauer Bay Boomerang), Frank Kalberer's *Kalico* (first in the International Cruiser Race), Rod Willis' *Sea Spice* (first in Bremerton Heavy Weather Race), and the Masthead Race was won by Jim Vaupell. Jerry Caldwell in *Manana* came in second once and third five times.

The Sailing Foundation's Six-Meter *Chinook*, with Carl Buchan at the tiller, almost won first place in the world competitions in California. As it was they came in second by seconds.

At the Flying Dutchman class sailboat races in Sardinia, Italy, usually domi-

The popular Garden Bay Outstation. (SYC Historical Collection)

When Charlie and Mildred returned to Seattle, Norm C. Blanchard, chairman of the Garden Bay Outstation committee, and his wife Eunice, moved in to do some of the finishing work and to welcome the hundreds of yachtsmen who stopped there during that first season of 1983. Norm, after interviewing a score of persons, hired Werner and Gerda Born to manage the facility, which has become one of the most popular of all the outstations.

By the way, Charlie reports that all those improvements came in under budget, and he collected on the bet from his friend Ralph Buseman. ◇

Importance of the SYC Bylaws

For most clubs, bylaws are hardly more than a legal formality. In order to provide officers flexibility, bylaws frequently go no further than to restate some of the basics of corporation law. In SYC's bylaws, the most important legal feature identifies who runs things. Thus the first sentence of Article VII, Section 1, reads:

> The corporate powers of the Club and control and management of business funds, activities, and affairs of the Club are vested in the Board of Trustees.
>
> —*Bylaws of the Seattle Yacht Club*

This concept of board control is crucial to the success of a large and complex organization such as the Seattle Yacht Club. Many of the members are businessmen and used to the idea that the boss is the one who runs things and board members act as advisors. At SYC, however, the board runs things subject to the restrictions detailed in the bylaws.

Three factors mark SYC as different from many clubs: (1) direct election of officers; (2) widespread participation of members in decision-making groups; (3) frequent amendment by the members of the club's detailed bylaws.

Dave Williams, a lawyer-member, points to the fact that in many other clubs, the officers are elected by the board and the number of bylaws and committees are kept to a minimum in order to make control of the club more efficient.

Detailed bylaws like those at SYC relieve the board of the need to reinvent the wheel. SYC members may alter the bylaws by calling a special meeting and passing an amendment. In practice such an amendment is rare, but the fact that it can be done keeps the board more attentive to the desires of the members.

Detailed bylaws allow members to learn quickly how to participate simply by reading. On the other hand, the great complexity of the bylaws also makes them difficult to remember. Even the SYC judge advocates have to look things up frequently.

Another SYC feature is the many committees that make it possible for any member to participate. Literally hundreds of SYC members serve on committees each year. These committees are busy with duties and responsibilities that are clearly delineated.

The 1991 amendments formalized the eligibility of spouses of members to participate in and chair most committees. Within the last decade spouses have been appointed to such offices as librarian and fleet chaplain. This spousal participation is a recent development. Reflecting changes in our society, activities at SYC have become much less male dominated. The increasing equality of the sexes resulted in changing part of Article III, Section 6 (a) to replace the words "conduct unbecoming a gentleman . . ." with simply ". . . unbecoming conduct. . . ." as a basis for disciplining a member.

Custom also plays a role in governing an institution such as a yacht club. For example, a fleet chaplain is appointed although this office is not mentioned in the bylaws.

With complex operations and a changing institution, the bylaws need frequent modification. For example, the club eliminated the "associate" membership in the 1960s, divided the race committee into powerboat and sailboat committees in the 1970s, and provided for a quartermaster in the 1980s.

By 1983, the SYC bylaws had fallen behind some practices at the club. Many committees had become standing committees even though they weren't mentioned in the bylaws. A few conflicting descriptions of committee authority were also discovered. Commodore Berst, trying to conclude what committee chairmen he had to appoint, compared lists in the bylaws, in the *Binnacle*, and in the yearbook and found discrepancies.

With the age of word processors at hand, the 1983 bylaw committee chairman, who had worked as a bill drafter in the legislature, cleaned the bylaws up. At the 1983 annual meeting, the largest group of amendments ever presented passed without discussion and the list of committees and functions was simplified and brought up to date. ◇

nated by European racers, Jonathan McKee and Carl Buchan became the first Americans to capture first place.

At the annual meeting, Don Flynn explained that though it was another year of declining participation, the club managed to start nearly 2,000 boats in races. It was also an outstanding year for international competition. As for the Flying Dutchman race mentioned above, he said:

> Carl and Jonathan so dominated this event that they were able to watch the last race from the beach. No Americans have ever won this event in this class before. It has traditionally been the private reserve of the Europeans and it was really kind of tantamount to the U.S. hockey team beating the Russians. . . .
> —*Annual Meeting Minutes, Oct. 7, 1983*

The Bates McKee Memorial Trophy was awarded to Robin and Mike Bookey's *Scrambler*. The Marymount Trophy for Sailor of the Year went to co-sailors Carl Buchan and Jonathan McKee. The Bellwether Trophy went to Dick Rose of Corinthian, the Briggs Trophy for PIYA High Point Winner went to John Buchan and *Glory* (IOR). The Half-Vast Award was claimed by Evan Schwab and the Ruptured Eardrum Trophy by D. Paul Thorlakson.

The SYC yearbook listed the following trophies and award winners for 1983.

Mark Mayer Race: IOR, *Delicate Balance* (Roy Gunsolus, SYC); SP, *Surprise* (Gerry Maurer, SYC); Smith Island Race: Jerry Bryant Trophy, SP Long, *Coyote* (Kristian Overby, CYCT); Bob Gibbons Trophy, IOR Long, *Pachena* (John Newton, RVYC); Gwendolyn Trophy, IOR 1 and 2, *Pachena* (John Newton, RVYC); Point Hudson Race: SP Short, Horder Provine Old Salts' Trophy, *Shooter* (Stephen Stroller, CYC); Kennell Midwatch Trophy, IOR Short, *Scrambler* (Mike and Robin Bookey, SYC, CYC); Vashon Island Race Trophies: IOR Long, *Glory* (John Buchan, SYC); SP Long, *Bonnie* (Badgley/Callahan, CYC); Point Robinson Race: Rawson Trophy, SP Short, *Tyrone Shoelaces* (Rich Walz, CYC); IOR Short, *Katana* (Davis/Suzuki, CYC); Protection Island Trophy: IOR Long, *Audacious* (A. Hoffman/Anderson, CYC); SP Long, *Pegasus* (John and Diana Becker, CYC); Point No Point Race: Protection Island Potlatch Trophy, IOR Short, *Scrambler* (Mike and Robin Bookey, SYC, CYC); SP Short, *H2B2* (Allen McInnis, CYC); Hat Island Trophy, IOR Long, *Miura* (Carl Frederickson, QMYC); SP Long, *Juggernaut* (Randy Pittman/Sloop Tavern); Kennell Wind Pennant Trophy, *Sweet Cheeks* (Jack Sinton, SYC); Lady Medina Trophy, SP Short, *Hobi-Kenobi* (Mar/Ing, CYC)

Tri-Island Race Series: Three-Island Trophy, IOR Overall, *Glory* (John Buchan, SYC); Walt Little Trophy, SP Overall, *Coyote* (Kristian Overby, CYC); First President's Trophy, SP Short Overall, *Shooter* (Stephen Stoller, CYC); Mark Mayer Cup, IOR Long 1 and 2, *Glory* (John Buchan, SYC); Bob Bollong Memorial Trophy, IOR 3, *Delicate Balance* (Roy Gunsolus, SYC); Gardner Gamwell Trophy, IOR 4, *Hagar* (Peter Strelinger, CYC); Humphrey Trophy, IOR Short, *Scrambler* (Mike and Robin Bookey, SYC, CYC); Tri-Island Thunderbird Trophy, Overall, *NR1172* (Stan Clark, CYC); Roaring Forties Trophy, Cal 40s Overall, *Hooligan II* (Tom O'Brien, SYC)

George Barclay Perry Race: Best Performance Tri-Island and Hat Island, *Oz* (Marda Runstad, SYC); Crooz N Snooz Trophy, *Scrambler* (Mike and Robin Bookey, SYC, CYC); Frisbie Race: Potlatch Trophy, IOR, *Delicate Balance* (Roy Gunsolus, SYC); McKee Memorial Rendezvous: Beaver Trophy, Best Performance Overall, *Hooligan II* (Tom O'Brien, SYC); Half-Ton Overall Season Winner, Northwind Trophy, *Sea Beater* (Glen Boudon, CYC); All Islands Race: SP Short Course and Hat Island, Gwendolyn Cannon, *Katana* (Davis/Suzuki, CYC); Single-Handed Race: Sea Fever Trophy, *Coyote* (Kristian Overby, CYCT); Sir Thomas Lipton Race: Lipton Cup, *Sockeye* (George Schuchart, SYC); Key City Race Trophy, PIYA High Point Winner—SP, *Cohort* (Verne Lawrence, CYCP)

Outstanding service plaques went to Maxine Bailey, Marilyn and Bill Bradshaw, Carol Buchan, Norm Cole, Phil Duryee, Don Flynn, Doug Goodspeed, Henry Helliesen, Pat and Keith Johnson, George Kuchenbecker, Cappy Neu, Marilyn and Roger Priem, D. Paul Thorlakson, Lynn Ward, and John Woodley.

In Memoriam, 1983: Marvin S. Allyn, George B. Berry, Mrs. David R. (Beth) Bollong, Mrs. Albert J. (Lillian)

Seattle Yacht Club Activities

From left: Guests of honor Commodore Phil Johnson, Vice Commodore Jack Sylvester, and Rear Commodore Robert Berst at the Women's Group Christmas punch bowl. (SYC Women's Group Collection)

Paul and Betsy Sunich make the prize catch at the 1989 SYC fishing derby. (SYC Historical Collection)

Junior participants in 1976 Opening Day activities dressed in Minuteman gear. (Thurston Lane Collection)

A happy party-goer at the club's 1977 New Year's celebration. (Thurston Lane Collection)

Dick Chang, Chief Yellow Belly, at 1986 Potlatch at Port Madison. (SYC Women's Group Collection)

Pam Thurman, 1982 Potlatch queen. (Thurston Lane Collection)

One of the family events featured at Potlatch at Port Madison is a sack race by boat. (SYC Historical Collection)

Potlatch, June 1976. (Thurston Lane Collection)

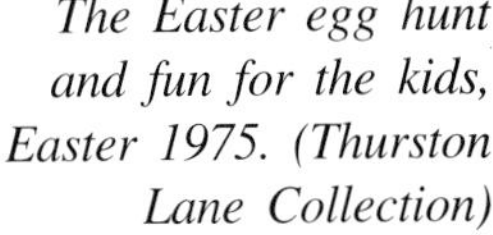

The Easter egg hunt and fun for the kids, Easter 1975. (Thurston Lane Collection)

Bowles, Robert B. Davis, Jr., Don W. Emerick, William H. Ferguson, Mrs. Louis (Patricia) Ford, John H. Hale, John B. Harris, Dale M. Huling, Mrs. Walter J. (Jean) Kennedy, Mrs. Kenneth A. (Ethel) Metcalf, R. Brent Nichols, J. Gordon Shotwell, Bernard J. Westlund, and Alfred W. White.

1984

Commodore Don Simpson in his January *Binnacle* message announced that the deficit of the 1983 fiscal year (nearly $97,000) required an increase in dues from $34 to $40 per month.

In the fall, Coach Erickson's "Dick's Chicks" entered the Canadian-American Masters' Challenge and raced in the Lake Washington Regatta. Three shells raced two miles, from the Mercer Island Floating Bridge to Seward Park. SYC was represented in the winning shell by Robin Bookey, No. 7 oar; Laura Boone, No. 6; Irma Erickson, No. 5; Ellie Austin, No. 3; and Cici Engle, No. 2. Corrected time: 14:39:94.

At a Women's Group meeting in September, Diane Sweezey interviewed Alfy Berry and Eunice Blanchard, two of the original members of SYC's World War II Red Cross Unit. They recalled their work and the camaraderie that developed among the volunteers. After the war they continued to meet at the club socially. They usually met monthly to play bridge and sip wine with lunch in the galley or potluck. Sweezey's efforts created further interest in the history of the Women's Group. A second interview took place with Jo Gibson, 1953–55 president, and Anne Foster, 1955–57 president. Both Jo and Anne were charter members of the Women's Group.

Betty Stewart, chair of the history committee, reported that Mrs. Wanda (Hensel) Daman presented four trophies to SYC that had been won by the *Xora* prior to 1900. The *Xora* belonged to Henry Hensel, first commodore of the Elliott Bay Yacht Club, which in 1909 merged with and took the name of the Seattle Yacht Club.

The July *Binnacle* carried this from Commodore Simpson:

> Last month I ended my column by stating "The Suma Yacht Club of Kobe will never be the same." How wrong I was. I should have said, "Seattle Yacht Club members going to Japan will never be the same." I won't try to list all of our members who made the trip, we numbered about 60.
>
> I believe I speak for all of the travelers when I say, the Japanese people are the friendliest, the cleanest, the most hospitable, the most accommodating in the world. The trip was an experience we will never forget.
>
> SYC also won the Takarabune Regatta. The winning skippers were as follows: first, Brian Thomas; second, Peter Shorett; third, Mark Laura; fourth, K. Ohtuka; fifth, K. Koi; and sixth, Stuart Archer.
>
> We are all proud of our sailors. They represented our club in great fashion in all respects.
>
> —Binnacle*, July 1984*

Simpson also thanked Pat Goodfellow for raising $500 to send to the Prickly Bay Yacht Club of Grenada, West Indies, to rebuild their junior sailing fleet now that the Grenada incursion had ended.

The commodore went on to congratulate Jonathan McKee and Carl Buchan, two SYC sailors, for winning the gold in the Flying Dutchman class races of the Summer Olympic games. He also saluted two Corinthian Yacht Club sailors—Carl's father Bill Buchan and Steve Erickson—for capturing the gold in the Star class races.

As the year was about to end, the efforts of Dave Williams and others to exchange property owned by SYC on Lake Union for the mudlands under Piers 2, 3, and 4 bore fruit when the Seattle City Council approved unanimously. The final transaction occurred in 1985.

The Sailboat of the Year (Bates

Carl Buchan and Jonathan McKee in their Flying Dutchman class boat with which they won an Olympic Gold Medal. (SYC Historical Collection)

McKee Memorial Trophy) was *Surprise* owned by Gerry Maurer. The Sailors of the Year (Marymount Trophy) were the Olympic Gold Medal winners—Carl Buchan and Jonathan McKee of SYC and Bill Buchan and Steve Erickson of Corinthian.

The Briggs Trophy awarded the PIYA High-Point Winner-IOR went to *Flying Machine* of Chuck Walsh (CYC).

The Key City Trophy, PIYA High-Point Winner—(SP), was won by Kristian Overby of CYC in *Coyote*.

The Half-Vast Trophy went to Larry Hills and his *Savage*. The Ruptured Eardrum Trophy was awarded to SYC's Bill Watkins, and the Brent Nichols Inspirational Trophy was given to Samantha Walls of SYC.

The SYC yearbook listed the following trophies and award winners for 1984.

Smith Island Race: Jerry Bryant Trophy, SP Long, *Bohemia* (Robert Helsell, SYC); Bob Gibbons Trophy, IOR Long, *Glory* (John Buchan, SYC); Gwendolyn Trophy, IOR 1 and 2, *Glory* (John Buchan, SYC); Point Hudson Race: Horder Provine Old Salts' Trophy, SP Short, *Honeysuckle Rose* (Gene Hoefling, CYC); Kennell Midwatch Trophy, IOR Short, *Sea Beater* (Glen Boudon, CYC); Vashon Island Race Trophy, IOR Long, *Glory* (John Buchan, SYC); SP Long, *Pro Tanto*, (Bob Strange, CYC); Point Robinson Race: Rawson Trophy, IOR Long, *Cygnet* (Mike Milburn, CYC); IOR Short, *Ladybug* (Alan Holt, SYC); Protection Island Race: IOR Long, *Sachem* (Bill Buchan, CYC); SP Long, *Windbird* (Glen Utgaad, CYC); Point No Point Race: Protection Island Potlatch Trophy, IOR Short, *Tyrone Shoelaces* (Rich Waltz, CYC); SP Short, *Sea Spirit* (Bill and Barb Shaug, QC/TT); Hat Island Race: IOR Long, *Glory* (John Buchan, SYC); SP Long, *Cats Paw* (Bob and Andi Pistay, CYC); Kennell Wind Pennant Trophy, IOR Short, *Mo Bettah Two* (Chuck Pepka, SYC); Lady Medina Trophy, SP Short, *Interface* (Dillner/Gould Neumann, CYC)

Tri-Island Race Series: Three-Island Trophy, IOR Overall, *Glory* (John Buchan, SYC); Walt Little Trophy, SP Overall, *Bohemia* (Robert Helsell, SYC); First President's Trophy, SP Short Overall, *Steamer* (Bauer/VanderHoek, SH); Mark Mayer Cup, IOR Long 1 and 2, *Glory* (John Buchan, SYC); Bob Bollong Memorial Trophy, IOR 3, *Saga* (Joann Erickson, CYC); Gardner Gamwell Trophy, IOR 4, *Hagar* (Peter Strelinger, CYC); Humphrey Trophy, IOR Short, *Hagar* (Peter Strelinger, CYC); Tri-Island Thunderbird Trophy, *NR1172* (Clark/Lettenmair, CYC); Roaring Forties Trophy, Cal 40s Overall, *Maria* (Jake O'Brien, Sloop Tavern)

Tri-Island Perpetual Trophy: Classes C and D, *Bohemia* (Robert Helsell, SYC); All Islands Race: SP Short Course Overall, Hat Island, All Islands Trophy, and Gwendolyn Cannon, *Dynamo Hum* (Mike Schaeffer,

SYC); Crooz N Snooz Race: Cannon Trophy, *Surprise* (Gerry Maurer, SYC); Half-Ton Overall Season Winner: Northwind Trophy, *Mo Bettah Two* (Chuck Pepka, SYC); George Barclay Perry Trophy, Best Performance Tri-Island and Hat Island: *Glory*, *New Wave*, *Bohemia*, *Gilliean*, *Wisp*, *Mo Bettah Two*, *Wind Bird*, and *Tillicum*; Commodore's Race Trophy: *Surprise* (Gerry Maurer, SYC); SYC Cruising Boat of the Year: *Kim III* (Bob Simmonds, SYC); Single-Handed Race: Sea Fever Trophy, *Katana* (Bruce Davis, CYC); Nautalux Trophy, *Kuon II* (Martin Withington, SYC); Seattle Yacht Club Trophy: *Grauer Geist* (Wayne Berge, CYC); Six-Meters: King Olaf V Trophy and Wood Lyda Trophy, *Chinook* (Pat Goodfellow, SYC); Seattle Cup, *Chinook* (Carl Buchan, SYC); Sir Thomas Lipton Cup, *Sockeye* (Brian Thomas, SYC); Classic 6, *Hanko* (Dick Shively, CYC)

Big winners among the powerboats were Gil Middleton's *Far Out*, which took six first places, two seconds and a third; Bill Watkins' *Anthem* which won three firsts, three seconds and a third; and Paul Sunich's *Solace*, which came in second three times and third once.

The Bale Trophy for predicted log racer of the year went to Gil Middleton. Pam Nichols was awarded the Betty Meacham Powerboat Trophy for women and the 8-Ball Trophy went to Bruce Peterson.

In Memoriam, 1984: Mrs. Ralph E. (Esther) Allen, Dr. Gayton S. Bailey, Albert Bloss, Jr., M. Phil Butler, Mrs. E. F. Chambers, Fred Cookman, Mrs. Fred (Betty) Cookman, George F. Cropp, Richard Dilling, Mrs. Robert (Mary) Fox, Mrs. Thomas F. (Mary) Gleed, Edward Gove, Steven E. Hilson, James Hoffar, Mrs. Aubrey (Sue) Naef, Mrs. Russell T. (Grace) Pretlow, Howard Schroedel, John H. Sellen, Mrs. John B. (Rita) Stirrat, Norman A. Stockland, Mrs. G. A. (Ellen) Truesdell, Dr. G. A. Truesdell, and Mrs. George (Marguerite) S. Watt.

1985

The Women's Group scheduled a typically busy year. In January alone they presented their second annual Boncho! auction and luncheon, scheduled a bowling league, took bridge lessons, organized bridge luncheons, volunteered for decoration work parties, organized a drama group, offered French lessons, played Mah Jong and gave lessons, and activated the dinghy group.

Commodore Ralph Buseman in the March *Binnacle* wrote:

> March finds Bob Maurer and his wife Pepper well settled into the Port Madison manager's house. Bob has spent many hours painting, repairing and catching up following Clarence's illness and passing. Jim Erickson and his Port Madison committee have a well planned program for this favorite outstation and are working closely with Bob. Eve Ellis is now settled amongst her family in Everett. A special thanks to Paul Sunich who had his crew working on the galley at the Fo'c'sle to make it more functional for large group meals.
>
> —Binnacle, *March 1985*

As an indication of how busy Port Madison was, the 1985 schedule of events included a ladies' cruise, sailboat rendezvous, powerboat rendezvous, Potlatch, sailboat Crooz N Snooz, fishing derby, Stimpson Trophy race, Barnacle Bill, Grand Prix sailing race, and the New Year's party. In addition members were constantly dropping by and staying overnight.

This was the year the Gig Harbor outstation moorage materialized after prolonged negotiations with the neighbors and the county.

The Women's Group celebrated their 35th anniversary with an old-fashioned birthday party, including party hats, clowns, bright colored balloons, party dresses and a large birthday cake decorated with roses and candles. The group's earliest presidents were honored guests. Entertainment, a play presented by the past presidents, followed; the drama was called *Roberts Rules Ordered Out*.

On March 19, the board approved purchase of two Pocock four-oared rowing shells for members' use. This was done after members responded to a questionnaire with an 80 percent majority supporting a club-sponsored rowing program. University of Washington coach Dick Erickson volunteered to take charge of the instructional program. The two shells were named for Ray Eckmann and Eustace "Sunny" Vynne.

The SYC candidates for the Boating Family of the Year award were Dick and Betty Chang. Dick's father came to America from China in a 64-foot junk as a Protestant missionary to give stability to Chinese workers in the logging and railroad camps. Dick and Betty joined the Seattle Yacht Club in 1969. Both are deeply involved in club activities and community agencies such as Children's Hospital.

John Buchan skippered his new *Glory* to a second overall in both fleet and class in the Southern Ocean Racing Conference race. He informed the Thursday Nooners that he credited his success to the strong, all-around performance of his French-built One-Tonner and his predominately Northwest crew. He joked about the crew, who apparently did not properly respect a catered quiche and roast beef dinner he had arranged; he said he fed them Snickers bars and peanut butter sandwiches thereafter.

At the annual meeting, three 50-year members—Horace W. (Mac) McCurdy, Milton Flaten and Sunny Vynne—were introduced by Commodore Buseman.

At the December meeting, the board of trustees directed the moorings and docks committee to propose an appropriate moorage rate increase to help offset a serious budget shortfall caused by four factors: a decision to decrease the active intermediate dues in order to increase the numbers of members in this category; an unbudgeted expense underwriting the Women's Sailboat Championships; an increase in rental fees for the mudlands under Pier 1 and the lower parking lot, and an increase in the cost of completing the re-roofing of Piers 1 and 4 because of increases in costs of labor, material, and insurance.

The SYC-owned fleet in 1985 consisted of the *Portage Bay* (a 40-foot Universal trawler); the *Eli*, a 17-foot Boston whaler used to set racing marks in deep water, a speedboat at Henry Island, a dozen Lasers, eight 420 sailboats, and several Sealarks and racing shells.

Anthem was named Powerboat of the Year, and her owner Bill Watkins was acclaimed the Predicted Log Racer of the Year and received the Bale Trophy. Sharon Maples was awarded the Betty Meacham Powerboat Trophy for Women. The 8 Ball Trophy went to Paul Sunich.

Power racing activities resulted in the *Anthem* developing the best record. She won the Rudder, Edmonds, and Rainier-to-Poulsbo races and came in second at the Queen City, Bremerton Heavy Weather, and Meydenbauer races. The *So So Mo*, with John Brooke and Jack Jorgeson at the helm, won the Everett Race and took second in the Rudder Cup and the Rainier-to-Poulsbo. Paul Sunich piloted his *Solace* to second in both the Everett and the Stimson races and a third in the Queen City. Bill Freitag's *Cat's Meow* came in third in the Meydenbauer, Everett, and Stimson races.

The Sailboat of the Year (the Bates McKee Memorial Trophy) was awarded to *Bohemia*, proudly owned by Robert Helsell of SYC. The Sailor of the Year (Marymount Trophy) went to Bruce Davis of CYC. The PIYA High Point Winner—IOR (Briggs Trophy) was the *Glory* of John Buchan. The PIYA High Point Winner—SP (Key City Trophy) was *Bohemia* owned by Robert Helsell. The Half-Vast Trophy went to Don Simpson, the Ruptured Eardrum Rifle Trophy to Fran and

SYC's public sailing classes for youth promote safe boating and practices. Here, Lasers sail on Portage Bay. (SYC Historical Collection)

Bill Barnard, the Brent Nichols Inspirational Trophy to Patricia Austin, and the Ernest Gann Trophy to Alan Johnson. John Brooke was awarded the Masthead Trophy.

The SYC yearbook listed the following trophies and award winners for 1985.

Smith Island Race: Jerry Bryant Trophy, *Surprise* (Gerry Maurer, SYC); Bob Gibbons Trophy, *Promises* (Dave Bellaine, SYC); Gwendolyn Trophy, *Promises* (Dave Bellaine, SYC); Point No Point Race: Horder Provine Old Salts' Trophy, *Hobi-I-Kenobe* (Mar/Eng, CYC); Kennell Midwatch Trophy, *Mo Bettah Two* (C. Pepka, SYC); Vashon Island Race: *Sachem* (B. Buchan, CYC); *Coyote* (K. Overby, CYCT); Point Robinson Race: Rawson Trophy, *Scrambler* (Robin and Mike Bookey, SYC, CYC); *Coruba* (R. Fleming, CYCT); Protection Island Race: *Delicate Balance* (R. Gunsulos, SYC); *Babe* (R. and C. Moeller, CNST); Point Hudson: Protection Island Potlatch Trophy, *Ladybug* (Alan Holt, SYC); *Whippet* (Keller/Carpenter, CYC); Hat Island Race: *Wisp* (J. Caslon, CYC); *Melange* (Robert Thib, STYC); Kennell Wind Pennant Trophy, *Ladybug* (Alan Holt, STYC); Lady Medina Trophy, *Katana* (Davis/Suzuki, CYC);

Tri-Island Race Series: Three-Island Trophy, *Sachem* (Bill Buchan, CYC); Walt Little Trophy, *Bohemia* (Robert Helsell, SYC); First President's Trophy, *Katana* (Davis/Suzuki, CYC); Mark Mayer Cup, *Sachem* (Bill Buchan, CYC); Bob Bollong Memorial Trophy, *Cetus* (Bogdan Sawicki, CYC); Gardner Gamwell Trophy, *Mo Bettah Two* (C. Pepka, SYC); Humphrey Trophy, *Ladybug* (Alan Holt, SYC); Tri-Island Thunderbird Trophy, *Redwing* (Clemens/House, CYC); Roaring Forties Trophy, *Legend* (Steward/Zener, SYC); Tri-Island Perpetual Trophy, *Bohemia* (Robert Helsell, SYC); Quent Williams Trophy, *Surprise* (G. Maurer, SYC)

All Islands Race: Short Course and Hat Island, *Katana* (Davis/Suzuki, CYC); Crooz N Snooz Race: *Ladybug* (Alan Holt, SYC); Half-Ton Overall Season Winner: Northwind Trophy, *Mo Bettah Two* (C. Pepka, SYC); George Barclay Perry Trophy: Best Performance Tri-Island and Hat, *Legend* (Steward/Zener, SYC); SYC Cruising Boat of the Year: *Elusive* (Steve Shea, SYC); Single-Handed Race: Sea Fever Trophy, *Katana* (Bruce Davis, CYC); Nautalux Trophy, *Surprise* (G. Maurer, SYC); Quent Williams Trophy, *Thunder Chicken* (G. Cole, CYC); Seattle Yacht Club Trophy: Whidbey Island, *Dynamo Hum* (M. Schaeffer, SYC)

Six-Meters: King Olaf V Trophy, *Steverino*; Wood Lyda Trophy, *Maybe VII*; Seattle Cup, *Arunga*; Sir Thomas Lipton Cup, *Sockeye*; Classic VI, *Maybe VII*

In Memoriam, 1985: Conrad Carlson, Marshall L. Doty, Jr., Oscar Glaeser, Clarence S. Howell, Jr., Henry C. Issacson, Sr., Bjarne M. Jensen, Ernest J. Ketcham, Mrs. Leroy C. (Dorothy) McCormick, Dr. Carlton J. Powers, Evan S. Prichard, Mrs. William R. (Pat) Saxon, Charles G. Schaak, Van Roger Scheumann, Mrs. Dietrich (Peggy) Schmitz, J. Al Smiley, Mrs. James R.

The SYC Centennial Celebration

In 1984 Commodore Don Simpson directed the historical committee to plan for the 1992 Centennial Year. Each year following, the commodores charged the historical committee with continuing the planning. In 1989 Commodore Freitag named Past Commodore Bill T. Stewart as centennial chairman. The centennial committee developed a plan for a six-month Centennial Celebration—April through September 1992. As of this writing, the schedule is as follows:

April: A tribute to the U.S. Coast Guard with special tours of their bases and several of their vessels, which will be moored at SYC. A special Coast Guard dinner and dance are planned.

May: A special Opening Day will salute the other yacht clubs in the area, including those in Canada.

June: A salute to the maritime industry. A Victoria-to-Seattle predicted log race is planned. Racers will be honored at a Centennial Victory Dinner-Dance.

July: This will be celebrated as SYC Family Month. On July 12, at the 100th birthday party, a big show "SYC Under the Big Top" will feature magic shows, jugglers, games of skill, clowns, plus free beer and soft drinks. An old-fashioned picnic with all the trimmings will also be featured. There will be free hats and balloons for all and dancing in the Marine Room. The SYC Centennial Memorial will be dedicated and a time capsule embedded within it.

August: A salute to the U.S. Navy. A trip is planned for a large number of SYC members from Port Angeles to Elliott Bay aboard Navy ships at the start of Seafair Week. Several Navy ships will tie up to the club's piers while members are welcomed aboard. Festivities will be topped off with a big Men's Thursday Luncheon and a Navy Dinner-Dance on Saturday.

September: A big climax with two major sailing races recreating the famous 1892 races between SYC and the Royal Victoria Yacht Club (which is celebrating its 100th year, also). One race will be in Victoria waters, the other in SYC waters. SYC members will follow the race team to Victoria for a big weekend at the RVYC, and the RVYC members will come to the SYC the following week for a weekend of racing, plus a big Saturday night dinner-dance and Centennial Cup presentation.

An official Centennial Crest has been designed for use on stationery, buttons, pins, shirts, etc. KOMO Radio and TV has committed to covering the six months of activities.

A major design focal point, a 25- x 30-foot hot air balloon will be stationed on the lawn by the anchor, displaying the club's colorful burgee, as well as a reference to the club's centennial birthday. At night, the balloon will be lighted from the inside for the best visibility.

A major history of the Seattle Yacht Club is being prepared and will be available for purchase during the Centennial year. ◇

The SYC Centennial Committee planned different events for each month of the Centennial year. This poster, designed by Mary Blanchard, advertises the official Birthday Party in July 1992. (Wallace Ackerman Photography)

(Jacqueline) Tenneson, S. Bruce Tobin, Mrs. Don C. (Katie) Whitworth, C. R. Wilcox, and Mrs. Quent (Jean) Williams.

1986

Under the leadership of Commodore Jeray A. Holmes, several improvements were made to the clubhouse. The Ward Room received a new ceiling, lighting, and an improved air conditioning and heating system. The controversial compass rose chandelier was removed; its removal caused more controversy. The Junior Room (lower lounge) had cabinets installed around the perimeter to display historical memorabilia of the club and was renamed the Heritage Room. The outside of the clubhouse was painted for the first time in nine years.

SYC member Walt Little was honored by yacht clubs of Oregon, Washington, and British Columbia as he retired as chief handicapper of PHRF, a position he had held since the founding of the organization 19 years earlier. He wrote the rule book that is used all over the world.

Commodore Frisbie weekend was moved from mid-July 1985 to February 1986, and then the sailboat committee reconsidered and voted to cancel the event for 1986. Jack Lidral, fleet captain, sail, reported that no decision had been made about the future of the once-popular weekend.

The Ancient Mariner Sailing Society, comprised of vintage sailboats built in 1950 or before, held their tenth annual gathering at the Seattle Yacht Club.

The 1986 United States Yacht Racing Federation Women's Double, Single-Handed, and Sail Board Sailing Championships, hosted by the Seattle Yacht Club, were contested off Shilshole in June. Top women sailors from all over the country competed in Lasers, 470s and Mistral Superlites.

Commodore Jeray Holmes in the May *Binnacle* reported that the club's insurance coverage had become a monster. SYC was turned down for liability coverage by 11 of the nation's top companies. Food, bar, and water-related risks were too much for them. By summer, the problems were ironed out, but the cost for liability insurance rose from $67,000 to $173,000 for the year.

Members of the SYC Centennial Committee gathered to sign the contract to write this book. Though the announcement was made in 1986, the signing did not take place until 1988. From the left: Norm C. Blanchard, Jim Warren, Don Whitworth, Teresa Dowell, and Bill Stewart. Seated are Commodore Larry Salkield and Mary Ann Mangels, president of board of trustees, Museum of History and Industry. (SYC Historical Collection)

Moorage rates were increased during 1986 to $2.85 per foot for open moorage and $3.36 per foot for covered moorage.

Club thespians were busy during the year. The Junior Dinner Theater presented the play *Omen, Amen!* and the Adult Dinner Theater delighted its audience with *Arsenic and Old Lace*.

Eric Wall, centennial chairman, reported planning was well under way for the celebration in 1992 and that Dr. James Warren, director of the Museum of History and Industry, had been appointed to research and write the history of the Seattle Yacht Club.

The historic Washington State Centennial '89 flagships involved many SYC members. Adventuress, *a 101-foot youth training schooner built in 1913, is owned by Ernestine Bennett. The* S.S. Virginia V *was built in 1922. Phil Spaulding and Web Anderson were* Virginia V *Foundation founders and early presidents. The* M.V. Arthur Foss, *built in 1889, was restored under the chairmanship of George A. Bayless, representing Northwest Seaport. All three vessels are on the National Historic Register and served as good will ambassadors to Expo '86 in Vancouver, B.C. These three historic craft which participated in the 1989 state centennial were preserved with the help of many volunteers, including several from SYC. (CM3 Associates)*

On Opening Day the Wilson Seamanship Trophy, which is awarded the yacht club showing the best seamanship during the parade, was won by a fleet of Tollycraft organized by Gil Middleton and Paul Sunich. This was the second time since the award was originated in 1977 that SYC members had claimed it. The first SYC win was when the "Red Fleet" took the prize in 1981. In all other years, the Royal Vancouver Yacht Club took top honors.

The SYC sailors outsailed their Japanese sister city visitors from the Suma Yacht Club by capturing the first five positions in the Takarabune Regatta during Opening Week.

The SYC oarswomen raced on Opening Day Weekend. Led by Cici Engle, they took a second place behind the Corinthian crew.

The Royal Vancouver Yacht Club invited Seattle Yacht Club members to cruise north to the downtown Coal Harbour station to visit the Expo '86, which was just a short distance away. Many SYC members took advantage of the Royal Van hospitality.

Canada's most famous sailing vessel, the schooner *Bluenose*, which had been on display at the opening of Expo '86 in Vancouver, visited Seattle soon after. Built in Nova Scotia in 1921 to race for the International Fisherman's Trophy, she won on her first try and never relinquished the award during her 20-year racing career.

The SYC running team took on other clubs in the eight-kilometer run across Lake Washington. The eight members—Neil Riebe, Mike O'Brian, Steve Blackbourn, Foster Radford, Greg Guyman, Martin Withington, Skip Kotkins and Bob Kaczor—did well. The accumulative time of these fastest six of the SYC members was 204 minutes and 28 seconds, which established the team time and event record.

In rowing, Janet Footh, Irma Erickson, Laurie Parrot, Artha Shelver and Jean Elmer won second place in the Masters Nationals Rowing Championship for Women 45 plus, Four with Coxswain, held in Seattle in September. Also, the SYC junior rowers—Rokelle Mead, P. J. Austin, Allison Gates, and Jennifer Hunter with Crissie Marshall as coxswain—took first in the Greenlake Summer Extravaganza.

Commodore Bill Stewart alerted members that the membership at the annual meeting had approved an increase in dues that amounted to a 23 percent boost for active, non-resident, out-of-state, and remarried survivor members. But to soften this increase, the board reduced the Graham Fund assessment from $10 to $5 per month.

At that October annual meeting the following 50-year members were recognized—Dwight Benton, Joe Mesdag, Larry Norton, and Bob Schoen. And 60-year members Art Ayers and Swift Baker were introduced. Wally Ovens was presented a Distinguished Service Award at the meeting.

Awards for sailors of 1986:

Sailboat of the Year (Bates McKee Memorial Trophy) went to *Hooligan* and owners Tom O'Brien and family.

The Marymont Trophy for Sailor of the Year was awarded to Mark Brink of the Corinthian Yacht Club.

The Cruising Sailboat of the Year Trophy was awarded to Jeanne and Dave Kelly of SYC and their *Kazan*.

The Key City Trophy (PIYA) High Point Winner—SP was given to Mike Milburn of CYC and his boat *Cygnet*.

The Briggs Trophy for PIYA High Point Winner—IOR was won by Paul Jones and Max Decker and *Madame X* of TTP.

The annual Half-Vast Award went to Seattle's John (Butch) Ford. The Ruptured Eardrum Trophy went to Sunny Vynne.

The Tug Boat Annie Trophy was awarded to Carol Hyde Buchan of SYC-CYC. Buchan had an outstanding racing record and could sail small center board boats, keel boats, or just about anything. She was the first woman to serve as a voting member of the sailboat committee.

The Ernest Gann Award to the outstanding junior sailing instructor was awarded to Peter Flynn of SYC.

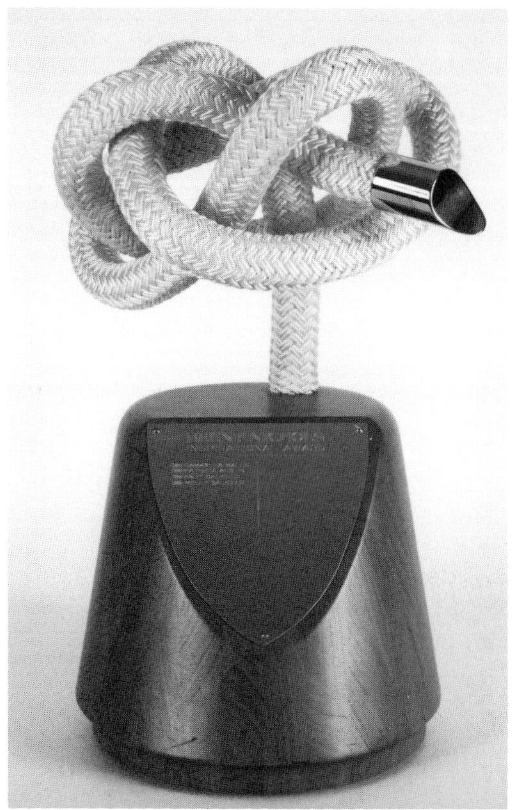

The Brent Nichols Inspirational Award is presented each year to the most outstanding junior member. (Wallace Ackerman Photography)

The Brent Nichols Inspirational Trophy for the most outstanding junior of the year was presented to Andy Salkield. The Bellwether Award went to former Commodore Bill Bradshaw.

The SYC yearbook listed the following trophies and award winners for 1986.

Mark Mayer Race: IOR, *Oz* (Marda Runstad, SYC); SP, *Hooligan* (Tom O'Brien, SYC); Smith Island Race: SP, Jerry Bryant Trophy, *Epic* (Ed and Nancy Baumueller, SH/CYC); IOR, Bob Gibbons Trophy, *Glory* (John Buchan, SYC); IOR 1 and 2, Gwendolyn II Trophy, *Glory* (John Buchan, SYC); Point Hudson Race: SP, Horder Provine Old Salts' Trophy, *Prairie Home* (Ken McCarty, CYC); IOR, Kennell Midwatch Trophy, *Mo Bettah Two* (Chuck Pepka, SYC); Vashon Island Race: SP, *Surprise* (Gerry Maurer, SYC); IOR, *Lobo* (Roger Livingston, SYC); Point Robinson Race: SP, Rawson Trophy, *Coruba* (Rob Fleming, CYC); IOR, *Madam X* (Paul Jones and Max Decker, TTP);

Protection Island Race: SP, *Surprise* (Gerry Maurer, SYC); IOR, *Sachem* (Bill Buchan, CYC); Point No Point Race: Golden Potlatch Trophy, SP, *Vesper* (Douglas Swihart, ST); IOR, *Ladybug* (Alan Holt, SYC); Hat Island Race: Hat Island Trophy, IOR, Long, *Sachem* (Bill Buchan, CYC); SP, *Juggernaut* (Randy Pittman, CYC); Kennell Wind Pennant Trophy, IOR Short, *Madam X* (Paul Jones and Max Decker, TTP); Lady Medina Trophy, SP Short, *Coruba* (Rob Fleming, CYC)

Tri-Island Race Series: Three-Island Trophy, IOR Overall, *Sachem* (Bill Buchan, CYC); Walt Little Trophy, SP Overall, *Teddy Bear* (Gray Hawken, CYC); Mark Mayer Cup, IOR 1 and 2, *Sachem* (Bill Buchan, CYC); Roaring Forties Trophy, SP Overall, *Madrugador* (Madrugador Syndicate, SYC, CYC)

Tri-Point Race Series: First President's Trophy, SP Overall, *Coruba* (Rob Fleming, CYC); Humphrey Trophy, IOR Overall, *La-*

The Tug Boat Annie Woman of the Year Award

The Tug Boat Annie trophy was donated to the Corinthian Yacht Club by Serge J. Becker in 1973. It is a perpetual trophy which may be awarded annually to the woman who has distinguished herself in outstanding achievements and service.

The Tug Boat Annie Woman of the Year Award may be given to a woman who has served or performed in any field associated with yachting but primarily has achieved some or all of the following:

The Tug Boat Annie Award. (Wallace Ackerman Photography)

. . . sailing mastery in local waters, performances in Area Eliminations and area Final in NAYRU events, skippering or navigating a powerboat in the Women's Predicted Log contests, seamanship and boat handling, committee work, administrative and organizing ability accomplishments, teaching and coaching juniors and adults, any other outstanding performances.

—*Deed of Gift, Tug Boat Annie Woman of the Year Award*

The recipient is chosen by a nominating committee that is made up of women members from the Corinthian and Seattle yacht clubs. Nominations may come from any yacht club in the Pacific Northwest that is a recognized member of the PIYA or IPBA. A club may submit more than one name for consideration. Through 1990 six Seattle Yacht Club women have been honored with this award.

The Tug Boat Annie Women of the Year are:

1973—Renate (Red) McVittie, CYC
1974—Jerie Clark, CYC
1975—Kathleen Ball, PSYC
1976—Marilyn Thordarson, TYC
1977—Connie Matteson, EYC
1978—Sally Laura, SYC
1979—Jo Pape, CYC
1980—Jo Anne Walderon, TTPYC
1981—Robin Bookey, CYC-SYC
1982—Alice E. Pettengill, GHYC
1983—Sarah Steel, CYC-SYC
1984—Dianne Cox, CYC
1985—Marge Frey, TYC
1986—Carol Hyde Buchan, SYC-CYC
1987—Kathie White-Fryer, CYC
1988—Laura Boone, SYC
1989—Patty Ambrose, BYC
1990—Molly Benton Cadranell, SYC

dybug (Alan Holt, SYC); Bob Bollong Memorial Trophy, IOR 3, *Ladybug* (Alan Holt, SYC); Gardner Gamwell Trophy, IOR 4, *Mo Bettah Two* (Chuck Pepka, SYC); Tri-Island Thunderbird Trophy, T-Bird Overall, *Aozora* (John Monk, CYC); Tri-Island and Hat Island Overall, All Islands Trophy, SP, *Coruba* (Rob Fleming, CYC)

Best Performance for Island Races: George Barclay Perry Trophy, Tri-Island and Hat Island Best Performance Overall, *Coruba* (Rob Fleming, CYC); Smith Island, Long, *Delicate Balance* (Roy Gunsolus, SYC); Short, *Phantom* (Al and Jane Johnson, CYC); Vashon Island, Long, *Lobo* (Roger Livingston, SYC); Short, *Banjo Music* (Armond Marion, CYC); Protection Island, Long, *Challenge* (Peter Jennings, CYC); Short, *Ladybug* (Alan Holt, SYC); Hat Island, Long, *Quicksilver* (Dave and Diane Veltkamp, CYC)

Single-Handed Race: Sea Fever Trophy, Class A, *Downtown* (Marty Blanchard, SYC); Nautilus Trophy, Class B, *Surprise* (Gerry Maurer, SYC); Half-Ton Season Overall Winner: Northwind Trophy, *Mo Bettah Two* (Chuck Pepka, SYC); Crooz N Snooz: Cannon Trophy, *Hooligan* (Tom O'Brien, SYC); Norpac: Dovekie Trophy, Class 1, *Harmony* (Tad Lhamon, SYC); Corinthian Trophy, Class 2, *Ladybug* (Alan Holt, SYC); Serge Becker Spinnaker Trophy, Class 3, *Tonic* (Dan Brink, CYC); Haida Trophy, *Kellogg* (Miller/Watkins, SYC); Whidbey Island Race Week: Seattle Yacht Club Trophy, Best SYC Boat, *Mo Bettah Two* (Chuck Pepka); Swiftsure Race: Endeavor Trophy, Team Trophy, *Oz*, *Lobo*, *Glory* (SYC); Cape Flattery Race: Ned Ashe Juan de Fuca Team Trophy, *Surprise*, *Gamin*, *Dynamo Hum* (SYC); Adams Cup: Mary Rattray Trophy, Local, and Battle Axe Trophy (Carol Buchan, SYC); Victoria-to-Maui Race, Seattle Yacht Club Winners: *Madrugador* (John Kelly); *Night Runner* (Doug Fryer); *Citius* (Mark Schlosser); *Boomerang* (Michael O'Byrne)

Six-Meters: King Olaf V Trophy, *Frenzy* (Bill Buursma, SYC); Sir Thomas Lipton Cup, *Chinook* (Skipper: Mark Brink); Gary Horder Trophy, North American Champion, *Steverino* (Brian Wertheimer, SYC); Wood Lyda Trophy, Overall Participation, *Frenzy* (Bill Buursma, SYC); Classic 6, Overall Points for Wooden 6, *Saga* (Bjorn Sundt); Jesse Carr Trophy, PCYA Invitation, SYC (Pat Goodfellow, Tom O'Brien, Joe Williams, Sr., Willard Rosing)

For the second time in the 35-year history of the Mallory Cup competition, a Seattle sailor crossed the finish line first. Jack Christiansen took the lead after two days and six races of the eight-race series and sailed to two second places on the final day to win the prestigious event.

Outstanding Service for 1986 recognition was given to Dennis Clark, Sunny Vynne, Dick Marshall, Mike Duffy, Larry Bailey, Gerry Maurer, Norm Cole, Don Hillman, Ken Kellogg, Bill Bradshaw, and Marilyn Bradshaw.

The Predicted Log Racer of the Year (Bale Trophy) was won by Jack Jorgeson. The Betty Meacham Powerboat Trophy for Women went to Mary Ellen Quigley. The 8 Ball Blooper Award went to Charlie Cravens.

Among the outstanding powerboats was *So So Mo* which, skippered by Jack Jorgeson, placed in races all year long, including first in the Stimson, Edmonds, and Rainier-to-Poulsbo races. Bill Freitag's *Cat's Meow* also did well, winning the Bremerton Heavy Weather and placing second in the Meydenbauer and Stimson races. Jerry Caldwell's *Manana* was first in the Queen City, Meydenbauer and Everett races and placed in four others.

In Memoriam, 1986: Dwight Benton, Mrs. Norman C. (Eunice) Blanchard, Norman Charleson, Dan Fiorito, Mrs. L. E. Geary, Hans Otto Giese, George LeBlanc Green, Marion M. Harrell, Mrs. F. A. (Willa) Harvey, Mrs. Howard R. (Lee) Henderson, Donald L. Holman, Garrett Horder, Harold Hovland, Mrs. Welcom Johnston, Dr. David B. Law, Joseph Marshall, Mrs. Ruth Norton, John S. Pankratz, Frederick C. Peterson, Henry J. Rahe, William K. Ryan, Sr., Mrs. Ray C. (Sara) Wilcox, and Roderick M. Willis.

1987

The Women's Group in February heard Sam McKinstry relate anecdotes about his many travels to China, which he illustrated with slides.

Right*: SYC sailboats and powerboats in competition for the Wilson Seamanship Trophy, Opening Day, 1987. (SYC Historical Collection)*
Below*: The Wilson Seamanship Trophy, an ancient Spanish naval cannon, was presented to the Seattle Yacht Club in 1977 by Chet and Pat Wilson. (Wallace Ackerman Photography)*

The Classic Yacht Association, organized by Sally Laura, met at SYC to enjoy Norm Blanchard's discussion and slides of famous yachts. The group enjoyed viewing the display of half-models on the walls leading to the Ward Room and the trophies and memorabilia in the Heritage Room.

During this year of the America's Cup Race in Australia, Commodore Bill Stewart led a contingent of 54 Seattleites to the far continent for the occasion. He reported in the *Binnacle*:

> Our task force assembled after a two-hour delay at the Sea-Tac airport for the long trip to the continent down under. We made our first land-fall at Cairns and immediately planted our SYC burgee in the sandy shore, claiming it our first possession. After a devious trip with a stopover in Sydney to test the waters, we proceeded to Perth and then to Fremantle, the site of the great face-off. We established our most distant outstation in Fremantle. . . .
>
> After watching Conner and his outstanding crew completely wax the *Kiwi Magic* in the Louis Vuitton Series, we knew that victory was in hand. It was an incredible experience being aboard the press boat *Sunbird* and seeing a racing spectacle the likes probably never to be duplicated. . . .
>
> —Binnacle, *March 1987*

Stewart arranged for the America's Cup to be on display and the winning boat *Stars and Stripes* to lead the Opening Day Parade through the Montlake cut.

Also on Opening Day in May, a Soviet crew, in Seattle on a goodwill tour, rowed in the Windermere Real Estate–sponsored Crew Regatta with the University of Washington in the Montlake cut on May 2. The Seattle Yacht Club was co-host.

The Powerboat Committee arranged for the SYC members to tour the Trident Submarine Base at Bangor on June 27.

Air Force Pilot (retired) Frank Newton and his wife Lynda took over as Port Madison caretakers after the Maurers retired.

Summer at SYC found members enrolling in windsurfing classes, using the six O'Brien Freesail sailboards owned by the club.

Commodore Stewart in September

The *Moshulu* Cruising Award

The *Moshulu* Cruising Award was presented to the Seattle Yacht Club by Robert O. and Irene V. Sylvester in 1987 to encourage and honor extended recreational cruising by SYC yachts, both sail and power. The name of the honored yacht is inscribed on a plate on the award, and a take-home brass plaque is provided the skipper.

The name of the award comes from the original *Moshulu*, an historic 335-foot ship built in Glasgow in 1904 for German owners. Originally she was called the *Kurt*. Her three main masts carried 45,000 square feet of sail.

In 1917, when the United States entered World War I, the *Kurt*, moored at Astoria, Oregon, was seized and renamed *Dreadnought*. When the president's wife, Mrs. Woodrow Wilson, was asked to rename all seized German ships, she chose Indian names. Thus the former *Kurt* became the *Moshulu*, a Seneca Indian word meaning "fearless."

The Moshulu *Cruising Award. (Wallace Ackerman Photography)*

After the war the *Moshulu* was declared surplus and laid up in Lake Union and at Eagle Harbor from 1928 to 1935. Then she was placed in the grain trade under Finnish owners. In World War II, she was seized by the Germans when they invaded Norway; they converted her to a barge. Later she was re-rigged and outfitted and moored in the Delaware River in Philadelphia, serving as a maritime museum and floating restaurant.

Bob Sylvester saw her for the first time when she was moored in Lake Union, and he named his 42-foot yacht in her honor. In their own *Moshulu* the Sylvesters traveled on many long voyages to the South Pacific, Hawaii, Alaska, through the Panama Canal, the Mediterranean, the Caribbean, and on and on. They've logged more than 60,000 nautical miles.

In honor of their yacht, they donated the *Moshulu* Cruising Award for extended recreational cruising. ◇

summed up his year as follows:

> New docks at Henry and Ovens. Gig Harbor is now a GO! The Pier 2 program should be ready for 27 added boats by next summer. A food service elevator for the club's three floors and a new men's room on the second floor. The Heritage Room with new furniture and rugs is outstanding. The juniors have a new summer meeting room and our grounds at Port Madison, Portage Bay and Henry Island have never looked better and a tennis court is planned for Henry Island.
>
> —Binnacle, *September 1987*

Past Commodore Jeray Holmes organized a group of members who donated their time and money to build the tennis courts at Henry Island. This project was completed at no cost to the club. A brass plaque was mounted at the courts to recognize all those members who made this facility possible.

Commodore Larry Salkield, in his *Binnacle* message, mentioned that

> One important issue your board of trustees is considering concerns membership size. Presently we are at or above the 1,300 active membership cap and either we will have to raise it or establish a waiting list. In addition to the actives, we have another 1,000 or so members in the life, surviving, non-resident, out-of-state, active-intermediate or junior categories. If we all wanted to use our club at the same time there would be no way, but we do not believe you build a church based on the attendance on Easter Sunday. The board of trustees as your elected representatives would like any input you may have on the issue.
>
> —Binnacle, *November 1987*

The SYC Women's Group provided a generous donation to the deputy director of the Washington State Parks and Recreation Commission with which to purchase two mooring buoys for Blake Island State Park.

In September two SYC Six-Meter craft were trucked to Long Island's Oyster Bay to take part in the Eighth International World Cup and Seawanaka Cup races. Pat Goodfellow and Jon Rose orchestrated the *Chinook* campaign, placing Mark Brink at the helm. Brian Wertheimer modified his *Steverino* and skippered the boat with SYC member Bob Cadranell at his side. Of the 23 boats in the races, the Seattle entry *Chinook* placed second best of the eight U.S. entries and fourteenth overall. *Steverino* placed eighteenth overall.

Late in the year, the Gig Harbor Outstation opened but with restrictions. Members were warned that pre-registration was absolutely necessary and only four yachts in any configuration could be moored at the float at the same time.

At the annual meeting, the following were honored for 50 years of membership: Bill Bradshaw, Howie Richmond, Jim McCurdy, Greg McDonald, and Russell Hawkins.

Predicted Log Racer of the Year (Bale Trophy) went to Gil Middleton. The Betty Meacham Powerboat Trophy for Women went to Elaine Kidd. The 8 Ball Blooper Award went to John Rasmusson. The Stimson Race Team Trophy Skippers were Christel Blackwell, Gil Middleton, Paul Sunich, and Dave Williams. The Wilson Trophy Powerboat Skippers were Dick Davidson, Don MacRae, and Dave Romano.

The Rudder Cup overall winner was Paul Bradley. The Little Rudder Cup for Ladies was presented to Mary Williams, and the winner of the Log Class Trophy (Novice) was Ed Olsen. The winner of the Masthead Race was Paul Sunich.

Outstanding among the powerboat participation awards were Gil Middleton and his *Far Out*, which took first overall in the Rainier-to-Poulsbo Race and in the I.C.R. and Stimson Trophy races and participated in many others. Paul Sunich and his boat *Solace* also entered many races and took firsts in the Bremerton and Stimson races. Others given participation awards were Robert Anderson, Jack Austin, Dick Beselin, Christel Blackwell,

Hugh Blackwell, Paul Bradley, John Brooke, Roy Bumstead, Ralph Buseman, Ben Cozadd, Jerry Caldwell, Dick Chang, Jim Clark, Charlie Cravens, Richard Davidson, Jack Dressler, George Fliflet, William Freitag, Gail Johnson, Gerry Johnson, Richard Johnson, Pat Goodfellow, Roy Gunderson, Jack Jorgeson, Carol Kessi, Roy Malm, Dave Maples, Leroy McCormick, Harry McGuane, Peter McTavish, Ed Olsen, John Quigley, Gus Robinson, David Romano, Loren Rudd, Bruce Smith, Bill and Betty Stewart, Betsy Sunich, Jim Vaupell, Eric Wall, Robert Walls, Pem Nichols-Weeks, Steve Weeks, and Dave Williams.

Sailboat of the Year (Bates McKee Memorial Trophy) was *Surprise*, Barbara and Gerry Maurer, SYC; Cruising Sailboat of the Year was *Cloud Racer*, Neil Riebe, SYC.

The Moshulu Trophy went to *Diva*, Kenneth and Nancy Seright, SYC, and *Etesian*, James and Julie Dersham, SYC. The PIYA High Point Winner-IOR (Briggs Trophy) was awarded to *Deliverance*, Steve Tuck, CNT; PIYA High Point Winner-SP (Key City Trophy) was given to *Delicate Balance*, Roy Gunsolus, SYC. Ruptured Eardrum Trophy went to Marilyn Bradshaw, SYC; Half-Vast Trophy, Larry Bailey, SYC; Tug Boat Annie Trophy, Kathy Ann Fryer, CYC/SYC;

The Gig Harbor Outstation

Late in 1975 the Seattle Yacht Club purchased a site for an outstation on the east shore of Gig Harbor. This beautiful wooded acreage has 282 feet of waterfront and is about 225 feet deep. Almost immediately it became apparent that a pier would be required if the property were to be used by yachtsmen.

The desire for a pier and floats was conveyed to officers of the East Gig Harbor Improvement Association in January 1982. This was the beginning of a relationship that can best be described as a three-year war.

At a meeting in April 1982 the East Gig Harbor Improvement Association voted unanimously against permitting construction of the SYC pier and float. This was followed by a hearing at the Peninsula Advisory Council which voted 12 to 4 against the float. The local newspaper, the *Peninsula Gateway*, headlined the result: "PAC Rejects Precedent-Setting East Gig Harbor Yacht Club Dock."

Subsequently, SYC presented this request for a pier and float to Robert J. Backstein, a Pierce County hearing examiner, on Feb. 1, 1984. He listened closely during the five-hour hearing. His finding was that the request should be denied, but "because of the excellent presentation by the Seattle Yacht Club, that in the final analysis, a test period may be a possibility. . . ." SYC decided to request a test period for a float that would not be attached to the shore; if the test was unsuccessful, the float could be easily removed.

The *Peninsula Gateway* then editorialized that the harbor did not need the outstation. The East Gig Harbor Improvement Association attorney said, "In spite of good-faith offerings [by SYC], this is a case of the camel having his nose in the tent . . . of a rural residential environment." The SYC attorney responded, "The camel's nose is already in the tent" with all of the other boats anchoring or rafting in the harbor.

The battle escalated through the summer of 1984. The Pierce County Council heard the appeal of the ruling of Examiner Robert Backstein in October 1984. A further hearing was set for Dec. 4, 1984. The many SYC members in attendance at that hearing heard the county council vote four to two to allow a float for a two-year test period. There was some talk by both sides of appealing to the State Shoreline Hearings Board or possibly the Pierce

Ernest Gann Award for Outstanding Junior Sailing Instructor, Jon Henderson; Crooz N Snooz Cannon, *Delicate Balance*, Roy Gunsolus, SYC.

The SYC yearbook listed the following trophies and award winners for 1987.

Smith Island Race: Jerry Bryant Trophy, SP, *Deliverance* (Steven Tuck, CYCT); Bob Gibbons Trophy, IOR, *Glory* (John Buchan, SYC); Gwendolyn II Trophy, IOR 1 and 2, *Glory* (John Buchan, SYC); Point No Point Race: Horder Provine Old Salts' Trophy, SP, *Coruba* (Rob Fleming, CYC); Kennell Midwatch Trophy, *Bullet* (Gerald Leggett, CYC); Vashon Island Trophy: SP, *Surprise* (Gerry Maurer, SYC); IOR, *Aquila* (Ben Dembart, CYC); Point Robinson Race: Rawson Trophy, SP, *Thunder Chicken* (G. and L. Cole, CYC); IOR, *Aurora* (David and Kay Lattimer, CYC); Protection Island Race: SP, *Surprise* (Gerry Maurer, SYC); IOR, *Aquila* (Ben Dembart, CYC); Point LipLip Race: Golden Potlatch Trophy, SP, *Tioga* (Kim Bottles, SH); IOR, *Ladybug* (Alan Holt, SYC); Hat Island Race: Hat Island Trophy, IOR Long, *Delicate Balance* (Roy Gunsolus, SYC); SP Long, *Paddy Wagon* (Bill Lenihan, SYC); Kennell Wind Pennant Trophy, IOR Short, *Lady Bug* (Alan Holt, SYC); Lady Medina Trophy, SP Short, *Roxy* (Tom Hukle, SYC)

Tri-Island Series: Three-Island Trophy, IOR Overall, *Aquila* (Ben Dembart, CYC); Walt Little Trophy, SP Overall, *Surprise* (Gerry Maurer, SYC); Mark Mayer Cup, IOR 1 and 2, *Aquila* (Ben Dembart, CYC); Roaring Forties Trophy, Overall Cal 40s, *Madrugador* (Mad Syndicate, SYC, CYC); Tri-Point Series: First President's Trophy, SP Overall, *Coruba* (Rob Fleming, SYC);

County Superior Court to see whether the test period concept was legal.

Instead, peace came quickly. After a lengthy series of negotiation meetings, SYC and the East Gig Harbor Improvement Association entered into a comprehensive agreement permitting the pier and float that now exist at Gig Harbor. The *Peninsula Gateway* summarized the result: "Both Sides Benefit Through Compromise."

Armed with the agreement from the East Gig Harbor Improvement Association and a rough plan for a pier and float, the club began to obtain approval from the various governmental agencies. Pierce County gave its permission. After negotiations and a meeting with their fisheries biologist, the Puyallup Tribal Council granted approval. Hydraulic project approval was received from the State of Washington Department of Fisheries. The Fish and Wildlife Service of the U.S. Department of Interior strongly objected to the small amount of dredging required by the plan, but after a year of negotiation and club agreement to test for impact upon marine life, a dredging agreement was obtained. With approval from all these agencies, the final request went to the U.S. Army Corps of Engineers. On July 1, 1987, the final permit was granted.

The SYC Board of Trustees at a meeting on April 21, 1987, authorized funds to build the pier and float, which Manson Construction completed on Oct. 12, 1987.

Word was sent through the *Binnacle* to SYC members.

> This outstation is located in a residential community, and for that reason special rules and limited use are required. Our use of the dock and pier is limited to approximate the use that our neighbors may make of their own individual docks. . . .
>
> Two rules are of particular importance. The first rule requires preregistration because of the limited space.
>
> The second rule limits moorage at the dock to a maximum of four yachts in any configuration, including rafting.
>
> —Binnacle, *November 1987*

The Seattle Yacht Club is now a member of the East Gig Harbor Improvement Association, and the two organizations meet at least once a year to discuss the successful operation of the Seattle Yacht Club facility and an agenda of items for the betterment of the Gig Harbor community. In the meantime, SYC members are enjoying this outstation in South Puget Sound.

—Adapted from material signed by Robert Berst and placed in the time capsule at the Gig Harbor Lighthouse on April 29, 1989

The Sailing Foundation team of (from left) Mark Rodgers, Carl Buchan, Keith Whittemore, Eric Kowanki, Pat Dore, and Pat Goodfellow is shown aboard the Chinook *at the 1983 Six-Meter World Championships, Newport Beach, California. (SYC Historical Collection)*

Humphrey Trophy, IOR Overall, *Ladybug* (Alan Holt, SYC); Bob Bollong Memorial Trophy, IOR 3, *Ladybug* (Alan Holt, SYC); Tri-Island Thunderbird Trophy, T-Bird Overall, *Aozora* (John Monk, CYC); Tri-Island and Hat Island Overall, All-Islands Trophy, SP Short, *Coruba* (Rob Fleming, CYC); Best Performance for Island Races: Smith Island Long, *Tin Man* (Ned Flohr, SYC); Short, *Coruba* (Rob Fleming, CYC); Vashon Island, Long, *Surprise* (Gerry Maurer, SYC); Short, *Jolly Roger III* (Lauren Anstead, CYC); Protection Island, Long, *Imago* (Dearborn/Moss/Lumpkin, SYC, CYC); Short, *Tioga* (Kim Bottles, SH); Hat Island, Long, *Endurance* (Hugh Minor, EV); Short, *Willawa* (Bob Hale, CYC); George Barclay Perry Trophy, *Jolly Roger III* (Lauren Anstead, CYC)

Whidbey Island Race Week: Xzora Trophy, Best SYC Boat Overall, *Lucille* (Kevin and Colleen Stamper, SYC); Single- and Double- Handed Race: Sea Fever Trophy, *Strait Shot* (Stacey Wilson, SYC); Quent Williams Trophy, *Thunder Chicken* (G. and L. Cole, CYC); Nautilus Trophy, *Ladybug* (Alan Holt, SYC)

The SYC rowing teams did well in 1987; for example, the SYC "A" boat took first place in the Mixed 8 Event on Opening Day. The junior women's team was also victorious in the Junior 8 "B" event; they won in the Brentwood Regatta in Victoria in April and in November won the Head of the Lake race, as well. The men's Masters 4 took first in the same race.

In Memoriam, 1987: Mrs. Chester (Alberta) Adair, Mrs. Barrie (Florence) Arnett, Mrs. Curley P. (Dorothy) Blanchard, Eric O. Brown, Mrs. Dorothy Chambers, Frederick Dobbs, Edward A. Dunn, Sr., Frank M. Dunn, Donald W. Finlay, Bennett I. Fisher, John M. Goodfellow, Capt. Richard B. Hadaway,

Mrs. Raymond A. (Agnes) Hellickson, Raymond Hellickson, Mrs. Harry L. (Mary Ann) Jensen, Mrs. Meder (Peggy) Johnson, Mrs. Anderson (Gertrude) Joy, Paul Kalmanovitz, Dr. George O. Kennaugh, Mrs. John W. Kucher, Mrs. Marjorie Lundin, Hartney Oakes, William Rudolph, Phillip A. Stewart, Dr. J. Irving Tuell, Ray Utterstrom, Benjamin E. Weeks, Mrs. David (Mary Louise) Whitcomb, Glen A. Widing, and Dr. Joseph T. York.

1988

Commodore Larry Salkield mentioned that the club was honored to have been presented the Adams Cup Trophy by Carol Buchan and her crew—Cheryl Lanzinger, Libby Johnson, and Jean Trucano. They won the award in Florida, competing against women from all other areas of the United States, and they did it with such a commanding lead that they did not have to sail the last race; they raced it anyway and won over their nearest competitor by a total of about 20 points. The Adams Cup has been presented for 60 years, and this is only the second time it has been won by Northwest sailors.

Buchan and her teammates captured the Adams Cup for the second year in a row in 1988.

Kathie White-Fryer was recognized as the recipient of the prestigious Tug Boat Annie Yachting Woman of the Year award presented by the Corinthian Yacht Club. This award originated in 1973 as a way of honoring "women who have exhibited outstanding seamanship and who have given generously of their time to further yachting activities." White-Fryer was selected by a committee comprised of

The West Bay Yacht Club

In the summer of 1988, a group of boaters gathered to consider the possibility of establishing a new yacht club for the south Puget Sound area. The resulting constitution located the club at the West Bay Marina, Olympia, Washington. The object of the club is "to afford good fellowship, promote group cruising for fun and safe yachting, to stimulate a greater interest in boating and other water-related recreation among all citizens of the area . . ." (Constitution of West Bay Yacht Club).

While this small group realized the difficult task ahead, they would not be discouraged. With spirit, enthusiasm and determination, they began to turn ideas and dreams into reality. On Nov. 1, 1988, the West Bay Yacht Club was officially established with 48 charter members. By December, many members had attended the first official club cruise, the club burgee had been designed, the constitution and bylaws had been written, and the club had been granted state incorporation.

By June 1991 West Bay Yacht Club membership had increased to 86 boats and 166 members. Reciprocal agreements had been established with 48 clubs throughout the entire Puget Sound area, the San Juans, Canada, and Alaska and as far away as the Fiji Islands.

A flagpole has been erected on the shore overlooking West Bay Marina from which proudly flies the club burgee along with the American, Washington State, and Canadian flags. ◇

five women members of the Seattle and Corinthian yacht clubs.

Lisa Niece and Pat Raymond finished second in the Women's 470 World Championships in Brazil in March, and hoped to continue on to the Olympics. Many yacht club members contributed to the Sailing Foundation which supported them. Pacific Northwest Bell and Pemco each donated $12,500 for the cause.

Also working toward the Olympic Sailing contest was Charlie McKee, who learned to sail at SYC. He was teamed with John Shadden from California in a 470 sloop. They captured a bronze medal at the Olympics in Seoul, South Korea.

The SYC Masters Women's crew team won the gold medal at the FISA World Championships in Strathclyde, Scotland.

The 1988 membership committee recommended and the trustees approved a new membership application form and procedure. The form is more explicit about information desired. The goal of the new procedure is to provide the membership a more complete profile of prospective members and to make it easier for the committeemen to complete their investigations.

Dave Romano, "milfoil removal chairman," signed a contract with Metro's Water Quality Department for a milfoil removal project around the SYC Portage Bay piers. Metro will pay 50 percent of the costs.

The Women's Group was entertained

The Port Ludlow Outstation

The history of the Port Ludlow Outstation begins in the early 1970s when SYC member Dr. Dick Philbrick offered to sell the club his two lots on the south side of Port Ludlow's outer harbor. The area had been platted for development by the Pope and Talbot Timber Company, but the surrounding area was still largely wooded.

Port Ludlow is a one-day sail from Shilshole and provides the only good harbor between Port Madison and Port Townsend. In earlier years a large sawmill and ferry dock were located there. Before the area was developed, SYC ran its annual Commodore's Sailboat Race to Ludlow. A salmon barbecue with rum punch was served on the old mill property.

At the time the Philbrick lots were offered, the north side of the harbor had been developed. The woods, mill, and ferry dock had been replaced by multi-unit condominiums, a commercial marina, tennis courts, lawns, a swimming pool, restaurant, and bar. An outstation located on the south shore would be a distance from the commercial activity but still close enough to use the facilities. However, the club's financial condition was not conducive to expansion at that time. The two Philbrick lots were sold to the Meydenbauer Bay Yacht Club.

In 1978 SYC purchased an 85-foot lot in tract 5 for $47,500 from Howard Cole. A permit to construct a pier and floats was submitted the following year, but opposition developed. Neighbors were concerned about noise, insufficient supply of fresh water, and damage to their views if permanent floats were installed.

Under a new Shoreline Management Act, the requested pier and floats were considered a "marina" and required an Environmental Impact Statement. An engineer was consulted, and advised SYC that the EIS would cost $10,000, and the county would deny the permit anyway.

In order to accommodate members and establish a usage pattern at Port Ludlow, SYC leased 180 feet of dock space at the Pope Resources' marina. Many members used this space, but it lacked satisfactory restrooms, was often noisy, and non-members sometimes moored there.

It appeared that an SYC outstation on the south shore would be enhanced if SYC purchased a lot adjacent to the one already owned. This $80,000 prop-at its March meeting by a vocal trio from Vashon Island. The women's renditions of popular and original songs have been inspired by their community on the edge of Puget Sound. Their three-part harmony was enjoyed by all.

Jane Heinrich, past president of the SYC Women's Group was elected to serve as president of the Women's Interclub Council, a group of women's organizations from 14 yacht clubs in western Washington. Heinrich is the third SYC woman to serve in this position, the others being Dorothy Scully (1964) and Ali Street (1976).

A new general manager—C. Vaughan Mason, Jr.—came aboard during the summer. He brought with him experience in like positions at the Harbor Club and Bellevue Athletic Club.

The SYC Women's Group for the second year in a row donated money to the Washington State Parks Department. As a result of their assistance, two new mooring buoys have been installed at the Sucia Island Marine State Park.

On Opening Day, the SYC juniors won for best-decorated boat, and the Wilson Seamanship Trophy was returned to the SYC after display at the Royal Vancouver Yacht Club over the past year. This year the winning entry was a fleet of 10 powerboats, which proceeded in two echelons of five through the cut until they were opposite the judges' boat. The boats then changed formation and honored the judges.

---

erty, which the club purchased in April 1980, provided area for a well and drain field. In December still another tract was purchased for $88,000 from member Ernie Frolund, making a total of 255 feet of waterfront and 1.72 acres of land. In 1985 public water lines were extended to the point and later a sewer and paved roads were added, allowing Pope Resources, successor to Pope and Talbot, to develop and sell the remaining lots on the peninsula.

In 1985, under Chairman Bob Sylvester, the outstation committee petitioned for a permit for buoys, a pier, and a dinghy float, but a newly formed "Protect Ludlow Bay Committee" fought the application. In 1987 an engineering firm was employed and an application submitted for a substantial development permit that included a 20-boat, three-fingered float and pier, a clubhouse, and a manager's house.

On May 17 and 19, 1986, the property was partially cleared by an SYC work party using a backhoe.

In 1988, under Chairman Don Simpson, the draft EIS was filed. A hearing before the Jefferson County Shoreline Committee was scheduled for April 19, 1989. The results were negative.

After the county commissioners, on the advice of the shoreline board, denied the permit, SYC appealed to the Washington State Shoreline Hearings Board. Commodore Bob Sylvester, who had been largely responsible for developing the permit application, was SYC's leading witness. He also was an expert on water quality, having taught classes on the subject for many years at the University of Washington. At the week-long hearing, which began in Port Townsend and ended in Olympia, he explained the SYC rules governing conduct at all its outstations. Neighbors at Henry Island and Port Madison added favorable testimony. The SYC attorney, Peter Buck, argued that a main purpose of the Shoreline Management Act was to preserve the shoreline for water-dependent uses such as yachting.

On July 2, 1990, the board ruled four to one in favor of SYC. Even the dissenting member said that the outstation would be acceptable if there were a guarantee it would be operated only by SYC. The county and the interveners appealed the decisions on the basis that the board had been "arbitrary and capricious." The superior court judge affirmed the decision of the state board on July 8, 1991. The county has appealed to the state supreme court, so SYC will not be able to start work until 1993.

—Based on material provided by David L. Williams

Commodore Larry Salkield paid tribute to the SYC team of Carol Hyde Buchan, Cheryl Lanzinger, Jean Trucano, and Libby Johnson McKee who won the Adams Cup (U.S. women's sailing championship) in 1987. The women were named SYC Sailors of the Year. (SYC Historical Collection)

The 10 skippers who inspired the event were Gil Middleton, Jim Erickson, Ralph Buseman, Jerry Horrobin, Frank Young, Bob Simpson, Pete McTavish, John Quigley, Paul Sunich, and Dave Romano.

Joe Williams penned a long report for the August *Binnacle* about the races hosted by sister city Kobe's Suma Yacht Club. For the first time in the biennial series, a Japanese yacht finished first; SYC's team finished second, third, fourth, and fifth, retaining the Takarabune Trophy. Representing SYC at the event were 54 racers and spectators.

The Royal Thames Yacht Club of London exchanged burgees with SYC and extended reciprocal privileges to SYC members who are visiting London.

The Masters Rowing Dinner was held May 7 with 82 rowing enthusiasts on hand. The evening featured Dick Erickson, Stan Pocock, Charlie McIntyre and Frank Cunningham. Coach Erickson presented the SYC Opening Day Trophy to Coxswain Leslie Albertson. Charlie McIntyre from the Seattle Tennis Club received the SYC Masters Inspirational Award for his efforts in reintroducing the "Pocock" stroke into Northwest rowing circles.

At the annual meeting in October, Treasurer Hal Wolf explained that the club had spent more than $810,000 on capital improvements during the year. Dock 2 revision had required $525,000 to date, and $210,000 was spent on main station improvements, including a dumb waiter, a new men's head, laundry facilities and air conditioning in the kitchen. The computer system was also upgraded. About $75,000 went into outstation improvements. Nonetheless, the budget showed a small surplus at year's end.

Concluding his term as commodore, Larry Salkield listed some of the firsts at the club during the previous 12 months: The first time in history the club had a $3 million operating budget; first time SYC won the Adams Cup twice; first time the club had a sailor on a winning America's Cup boat (Carl Buchan); first time an SYC

Carol Buchan (Mrs. Carl) was awarded the coveted Adams Cup in 1988 for the second time and also holds an Olympic gold medal for sailing and was recipient of the Tug Boat Annie Award. (SYC Historical Collection)

sailing protege became an Olympic bronze medalist had learned sailing at SYC (Charlie McKee); first time a woman had been a board member (Theresa Dowell); first time the club had a Women's World Masters Rowing championship; first time for a tennis court at Henry Island; first time the Commodore's Ball was held on two floors, and the first time the commodore and the junior commodore came from the same family.

Member Guy Harper, a talented wood carver, donated several of his pieces of art to the club. His cedar carvings are based on themes of the Northwest Coast Indians, and he uses authentic symbols to depict his message. His pieces serve as identification signs at Cortez Bay, Port Madison, Henry Island, Ovens Island, and Garden Bay outstations.

A popular journey in 1988 took members to the Trident Nuclear Submarine Base at Bangor. The tour, hosted by the U.S. Navy, was so popular that three different weekends were devoted to the event. Participants were given first-hand views of the support facilities for nuclear submarines, a most impressive and educational experience.

The Sailor of the Year Award was not awarded in 1987, for not all United States Yacht Racing Union events had taken place at the time of the SYC Annual Awards Banquet. For example, the 1987 Adams Cup (U.S. Women's National Championship) was not completed in Florida until January 1988. Later, after the SYC team of Carol Buchan, Libby Johnson, Cheryl Lanzinger, and Jean Trucano won the cup easily, the committee reopened the Sailor of the Year nominations and the four women were named Sailors of the Year for 1987. At the 1988 Summer Olympics in Seoul, Charlie McKee earned a bronze medal sailing a 470. He was named Sailor of the Year for 1988.

Stacey and Leann Wilson, sailing *Strait Shot*, earned the prestigious Sailboat of the Year Award for their tremendous racing season. Stacey went on to win the not-so-prestigious Half-Vast Award for hitting a rock while Leann was on the foredeck setting the spinnaker during the Norpac Regatta in the cold water of Barkley Sound. *Strait Shot* stopped but Leann didn't. Stacey recovered Leann, and they went on to win the regatta.

Other outstanding sailors for 1988 included: High Point Winner-IOR (Briggs Trophy), *Salute*, Daryl Delmotte, RVYC; PIYA High Point Winner-SP (Key City Trophy), *Long Shot*, Barry Richmond, SSSS.

At the 1988 Awards Banquet, two cruising awards were presented. Sharing the Cruising Sailboat of the Year Award were Mik and Barbara Endrody and their

Wanderbird and Larry and Maxine Bailey and *Shingebiss II*. The Endrodys cruised for six weeks on Queen Charlotte Strait, Seymour Inlet, Hecate Strait, and adjacent waters. The Baileys sailed to Queen Charlotte Islands and explored the east and west coasts of Vancouver Island. The Moshulu Award went to Roy and Barbara Greening of SYC for a voyage from Maine to the Bahamas and return to the Great Lakes via Northeast Canals—6,000 miles in all.

That year the Ruptured Eardrum Trophy went to Ray Rairdon, SYC, and the Outstanding Junior Sailing Instructor was Scott Holt. Cruising Sailboats of the Year were *Wanderbird*, Mik and Barbara Endrody, SYC, and *Shingebiss II*, Larry and Maxine Bailey, SYC.

The West Vancouver Yacht Club Alan Award went to Michael Duffy, and the Serge Becker Tug Boat Annie Award went to Laura Boone in 1988

Predicted Log Racer of the Year (Bale Trophy) went to Gil Middleton, and the Betty Meacham Powerboat Trophy for Women was awarded to Gail Johnson. The 8 Ball Blooper Award went to Tom MacBride.

Rudder Cup winners for 1988 included: Overall, Gil Middleton; Little Rudder Cup for Ladies, Judy Middleton; Winner Log Class Trophy (Novice), Tom MacBride; Masthead Race winner, Jim Vaupell.

The powerboat participation awards went to Bob Anderson, Paul Bradley, Hugh Blackwell, John Brook, Roy Bumstead, Ralph Buseman, Ben Cozadd, Dick Chang, Charlie Cravens, Dick Davidson, Jim Erickson, Phil Erickson, George Fliflet, Bill Freitag, George Heideman, Jerry Horrobin, Gerry Johnson, Mike Johnson, Don MacRae, Roy Malm, Dave Maples, Pete McTavish, Gil Middleton, Judy Middleton, Tom MacBride, Ed Olsen, John Quigley, Dave Romano, Loren Rudd, Bob Simpson, Paul Sunich, Jim Vaupell, Steve Weeks, Dave Williams, and Frank Young.

The SYC yearbook listed the following trophies and award winners for 1988.

Smith Island Race: Jerry Bryant Trophy, SP, *Challenge* (Peter Jennings, CYC); Bob Gibbons Trophy, IOR, *Airpower* (Derek Campbell, CYC); Gwendolyn II Trophy, IOR 1 and 2, *Airpower* (D. Campbell, CYC); Point No Point Race: Horder Provine Old Salts' Trophy, *Whippet* (L. Keller/D. Carpenter, CYC); Kennell Midwatch Trophy, *Ladybug* (Alan Holt, SYC); Vashon Island Race: SP, *Palm Tree Express* (Gordy and Judy Cole, CYC); IOR, *Glory* (John Buchan, SYC); Point Robinson Race: Rawson Trophy, SP, *Strait Shot* (Stacey Wilson, SYC); IOR, *Ladybug* (Alan Holt, SYC); Protection Island Race: SP, *Harmony* (Tad and Joyce Lhamon, PMYC, SYC); IOR, *Glory* (John Buchan, SYC); Point Liplip Race: Golden Potlatch Trophy, SP, *Cathexis* (Brian Reid, EHYC); IOR, *Ladybug* (Alan Holt, SYC); Hat Island Race: Hat Island Trophy, IOR Long, *Glory* (John Buchan, SYC); SP Long, *Gadzooks* (Peggy Willis/Ted Willhite, SBYC); Lady Medina Trophy, SP Short, *Coruba* (Rob Fleming, CYC)

Tri-Island Series: Three-Island Trophy, IOR Overall, *Airpower* (Derek Campbell, CYC); Walt Little Trophy, SP Overall, *Harmony* (Tad and Joyce Lhamon, PMYC, SYC); Roaring Forties Trophy, Overall Cal 40, *Maria* (O'Brien/Cowen/Rattray, SYC, SSSS, CYC)

Tri-Point Series: First President's Trophy, SP Overall, *Strait Shot* (Stacey Wilson, SYC); Humphrey Trophy, IOR Overall, *Ladybug* (Alan Holt, SYC); Bob Bollong Memorial Trophy, IOR 3, *Ladybug* (Alan Holt, SYC); Tri-Island Thunderbird Trophy, T-Bird Overall, *1172* (Dennis Lettenmair, CYC); Tri-Island and Hat Island Overall, All Islands Trophy, SP Shorts, *Strait Shot* (Stacey Wilson, SYC)

Best Performance for Island Races: Smith Island, Long, *Challenge* (Peter Jennings, CYC); Short, *Ladybug* (Alan Holt, SYC); Vashon Island, Long, *Harmony* (Tad and Joyce Lhamon, PMYC, SYC); Short, *Ignitor* (Mel Marshel, CYC); Protection Island, Long, *O My God* (Rob Adler/David Ames, SSSS); Short, *Coruba* (Rob Fleming, CYC); Hat Island, Long, *O My God* (Rob Adler/David Ames, SSSS); Short, *Coruba* (Rob Fleming, CYC); George Barclay Perry Trophy, Best Performance Tri-Island and Hat Island Over-

J35 Hound Dog, *owned in 1988-89 by Bill Headden. (Photo by Doug Brusig)*

all, *O My God* (Rob Adler/David Ames, SSSS); Whidbey Island Race Week: Xzora Trophy, Best SYC Boat Overall, *Delicate Balance* (Roy Gunsolus, SE); Single- and Double-Handed Race: Sea Fever Trophy, *Surprise* (Gerry Maurer, SYC); Quent Williams Trophy, *Tabasco* (Craig Mackey, PAYC); Nautilus Trophy, *Challenge* (Peter Jennings, CYC); Seattle Trophy, *Seahawk* (Ken and Sandy Robbins, STYC); Mark Mayer Race: *Victory* (Vic and Patti Kihara, CYC); Crooz N Snooz Cannon: *Strait Shot* (Stacey Wilson, SYC); Grand Prix Awards: Cadranell Cup, *Sachem* (Bill Buchan, CYC); *Gadzooks* (Peggy Willis/Ted Willhite, SBYC); *Rev* (Jon Thompson, CYC); Norpac Results: I., *Pusillanimous* (Robert G. Alexander); II., *Strait Shot* (Stacey Wilson); III., *Harum Scarum* (John Hyry)

In Memoriam, 1988: Donald J. Adams, Roy N. Berry, Ken Browne, Anthony Callison, Frank W. Cole, Mrs. George W. (Dorothea) Crippen, Dr. David W. Dale, Dr. G. E. Deer, William L. Dierickx, Ward M. Doland, Frank H. Draper, Mrs. Frank A. (Ethel) Dupar, Sr., Mrs. Oscar (Mary) Glaeser, Mrs. R. Kline (Margerita) Hillman, Dr. A. C. Jordan, Andy Joy, Mrs. Harold Kauffman, Lawrance H. Killam, Mrs. Philip H. (Betsy) Luther, Lex McAtee, Tobe Reed, Mrs. Willard E. (Edith) Rhodes, Mrs. Charles Schaak, David E. Skinner, Mrs. Richard A. (Gertrude) Smith, Capt. M. D. Stewart, Tom Wheeler, Thomas T. White, M.D., Mrs. Homer F. (Doris) Wickerd, Mrs. C. R. (Mary) Wilcox, Joe Williams, and Chester G. Wilson.

1989

The increasing popularity of the outstations caused the club to produce a written set of rules to govern their use. Above all, use of the stations was restricted to boats operated by an SYC member or spouse.

Over at the Gig Harbor outstation relations with the community warmed considerably when SYC, as a member of the Gig Harbor Lighthouse Association, contributed to the new Centennial Lighthouse project, which included installation of several time capsules. The SYC capsule was filled with contemporary memorabilia and trivia from the club.

In February Carolyn and Eric Van wrote at length in the *Binnacle*'s cruising column about their experiences crossing the Pacific from Acapulco to New Zealand in their *Skamokawa*. After enjoying the Marquesas, they sailed on around the world.

Doug Sherwood and wife Frances sailed down the Atlantic Ocean Intercoastal waterway during the year. This was a nostalgic five-week trip for Sherwood because he had made the same trip 30 years earlier. His boat this time was the 37-foot Cooper-built Seabird *Wind Seeker*, owned by Keith Gilmore of Boise, Idaho. Sherwood was helping Gilmore bring the boat to the West Coast. The trip was from East Greenwich, Rhode Island, to Charlestown, South Carolina. The Sherwoods saw many familiar places; some were drastically changed and some unchanged from 30 years earlier.

Commodore Freitag reported that the membership committee had evaluated the numbers of members and the services they would require and concluded that the club should maintain active membership (age 35+) at the 1,350 cap. Active-intermediate (ages 30 to 35) would remain capped at 160, but active-intermediate (ages 21 to 25 and 26 to 29) would increase from 305 to 350 each. Caps for the juniors (ages 12 to 16) and intermediates (ages 17 to 21) would also increase from 305 to 350 each.

Under Commodore Freitag a club manager review process was established in the bylaws, and a new budgeting process calling for development of the next year's budget well in advance was instigated.

In July, 18 members of the Royal Akarana Yacht Club from Auckland, New Zealand, came to Seattle to join with SYC members in 10 days of cruising on Puget Sound. This is the first of a home-and-home cruising exchange between the two clubs. SYC planned to journey to New Zealand for a winter exchange cruise in 1991. The Kiwis were hosted on 23 Seattle yachts, which cruised through the San Juan Islands, stopping off at several SYC outstations.

The first sailboat to travel to the United States from the Soviet Union since the end of the Cold War tied up to SYC Pier 2 on July 20, 1989. The boat was thoroughly inspected by agents of the Customs and Immigration Service. The 42-foot *Nadezdha*, out of Vladivostok, carried a crew of six men. SYC formed an ad hoc committee headed by Stacey Wilson to welcome the Soviets to SYC and Seattle. They had little cash, so SYC members were generous with their gifts and entertainment.

The christening of the fountains on both sides of the Evergreen Point Bridge was added to Opening Day festivities on May 5. Fireworks and music followed the dedication.

Opening Day featured a flotilla of SYC powerboats, the lead four transporting the entire Husky Band playing grandly. Rear Commodore Dave Romano deserved a lot of credit for the entertaining results.

The theme for the Opening Day Parade of Boats was "Centennial at Sea," which corresponded with Washington's centennial year of statehood. The Seamanship Trophy went to the Royal Vancouver Yacht Club; the Grand Sweepstakes Award or Admiral's Trophy for Best Overall Decorated Yacht was given to SYC's David Rosenquist and his *Sea Rose*. The best community-sponsored entry, recipient of the Alaska Airlines Trophy was Henry Kotkins' *Diamond Head*. The best junior-sponsored entry was the Miller 44 *Saturday's Child*, owned by SYC's Christopher and Romney Brian.

Late in the year building permits were received and work began on the clubhouse elevator which, when completed, made all floors accessible to the handicapped.

In November new Commodore Bob Sylvester complimented Michele Shaw and Duse McLean for the new look of the *Binnacle*.

In December, as he completed his first year at SYC, General Manager Vaughan Mason introduced a new chef, Ron West, who joined SYC after three years as executive chef at the Bellevue Athletic Club.

At the Annual Meeting, two 50-year members were introduced: Harold Stack and Harris Bremmer. Arthur Robinson had become a 60-year member, and Swift Baker had joined 69 years previously. Chet Adair was made an honorary life commodore.

SYC rowing crews won many races in 1989. The cover of the May *Binnacle* pictured the women who won the San Diego Crew Classic: Ellie Austin, Laurel Case, Mari Jabling (Roberts), Michelle Day, Jane Baldwin, Cathy Loeffler, Carlene Striker, Gretchen Boe, Coxswain Rachel LaMieux, and Coach Susan Stein.

At the Greenlake Spring Rowing Regatta, SYC oarswomen won firsts in Women's Masters' 8+, Women's Masters' Novice 8+, and in Women's Masters' 4+ (ages 27 to 40) and a third in Women's Masters' 4+ (ages over 41). The Men's Masters' 8+ took a second.

At the National Rowing Championships on Lake Merritt in Oakland, California, Seattle Women (8-oared) took a silver medal as did the 4-oared crew. Another 4-oared Seattle shell took a bronze medal. And the Mixed 8 captured a gold medal.

In Vichy, France, in September, competing against crews from 27 countries, SYC's Women's B 4 won a first and a second; Women's C 4 won a first and third, and the Women's B, C, and D 8s captured seconds. Women's A Double came in sixth. The men's crews took a third, a fourth, and a fifth place.

The SYC Women's Masters crew then proceeded to win the World's Championship in Scotland.

Undoubtedly the biggest powerboat racing success of the year occurred in August in Chicago at the North American Invitational where Gil and Judy Middleton of SYC won with a predicted time error of .565 percent.

The Queen City First-of-the-Season Race got off on January 14. Nine clubs were represented and SYC members entered nine boats. The Middletons won here, too, with just 18 seconds total error. Dave Romano had an error of 19 seconds, but his observer made a mistake that cost him 20 seconds and second overall. He was still first in Class V.

The Predicted Log Racer of the Year (Bale Trophy) went to Gil Middleton. He was also the overall winner of the Rudder Cup races and was the Best SYC finisher in the Bremerton Heavy Weather Race. His *Far Out* was the 1989 Power Boat of the Year.

The Jerry Bryant Trophy for top predicted log racer from IPBA North Puget Sound Region was awarded to Howard Klock of Queen City Yacht Club. He used the same boat his father used to win the trophy many years previously. Klock beat out Gil Middleton by just a few points.

The Betty Meacham Powerboat Trophy for Women went to Bonnie Sharpe and the Tug Boat Annie Award to Laura Boone. Phil Luther received the 8 Ball Trophy (Blooper Award). Sally Johnson won the Little Rudder Cup and Ken Kester was winner of the Log Race Class Trophy for Novices. Steve Sunich was top Masthead racer. Tom Yarrington managed the best SYC finish in the International Cruiser Contest.

Outstanding boats of the year were Paul Sunich's *Solace*, Tom Yarrington's *Endurance*, and Ken Kester's *Mockingbird*; but none could match Gil Middleton's *Far Out*, which had a list of a dozen race wins below its name.

As for sailboat records, the second annual Primadonna Race in April resulted in Helen Schlagel in *Aurora* winning overall. In Division SP-A the winner was Roberta Riebe and in SP-C, it was Pam Thurman.

The Sailboat of the Year award (Bates McKee Memorial Trophy) went to *Strait Shot*, which belonged to Stacey Wilson.

SYC sailor Charlie McKee won a bronze medal in the 470 sailing class in the 1988 Olympics in Seoul, Korea. SYC's Carol Buchan and crew won the Adams Cup.

The SYC yearbook listed the following trophies and award winners for 1989.

Smith Island Race: Jerry Bryant Trophy, SP, *The Boss* (E. Barrett/W. Berge, CYC); Bob Gibbons Trophy, IOR, *Aquila* (Ben Dembart, CYC); Gwendolyn II Trophy, IMS, *Flim Flam* (Fred Creitz, CYC); Point No Point Race: Horder Provine Old Salts' Trophy, SP, *Strait Shot* (Stacey Wilson, SYC); Kennell Midwatch Trophy, IMS, *Traveling Jack* (Jim and Leslie Kerr, SYC); Vashon Island Race: SP, *Deliverance* (Steve Tuck, QMYC); IOR, *Delicate Balance* (McKee/Gunsolus, SYC); IMS, *White Squall* (R. Deitz/G. Teats, TYC); Point Robinson Race: Rawson Trophy, SP, *Penetration* (Chris Johnson, CYC); IMS, *Sloop De Jour* (Dick and Carolle Rose, CYC); Protection Island Race: SP, *Windbird* (Glen Utgaard, CYC); IOR, *Aquila* (Ben Dembart, CYC); IMS, *Maria* (O'Brien/Cowen/Rattray, SYC, SSYC, CYC)

Point Liplip Race: Golden Potlatch Trophy, SP, *Surfbird* (Ivan Brown, PMYC); IMS, *Ladybug* (Alan Holt, SYC); Hat Island Race: SP Long, *The Boss* (E. Barrett/W. Berge, CYC); IOR Long, *Glory* (John Buchan, SYC); IMS Long, *Audacious* (A. Hoffman/L. Anderson, CYC); IMS Overall, *Satyr* (Kent Forman, SYC); Lady Medina Trophy, SP Short, *Sidewinder* (M. and B. Jones/D. Clark, GHYC); IMS Short, *Satyr* (Kent Foreman, SYC)

Tri-Island Series: Walt Little Trophy, SP Overall, *Chimo* (Conor Boyd, CYCT); Three-Island Trophy, IOR Overall, *Aquila* (Ben Dembart, CYC); Roaring Forties Trophy, Overall Cal 40s, *White Squall* (R. Deitz/G. Teats, TYC); Tri-Point Series: First President's Trophy, SP Overall, *Surfbird* (Ivan Brown, PMYC); Bob Bollong Memorial Trophy, IMS Overall, *Ladybug* (Alan Holt, SYC); Best Performance for Island Races: Smith Island, Long, *Chimo* (Conor Boyd, CYCT); Short, *Whippet* (L. Keller/D. Carpenter, CYC); Vashon Island, Long, *Deliverance* (Steve Tuck, QMYC); Short, *Sloop De Jour* (Dick and Carolle Rose, CYC); Protection Island, Long, *Chimo* (Conor Boyd, CYCT): Short, *Coruba* (Rob Fleming, CYC); Hat Island, Long, *The Boss* (E. Barrett/W. Berge, CYC); Short, *Young Lust* (B. Larson/D. Lindley, STYC); George Barclay Perry Trophy, Best Performance Tri-Island and Hat Island Overall, *Chimo* (Conor Boyd, CYCT)

Whidbey Island Race Week: Xzora Trophy, Best SYC Boat Overall, *Strait Shot* (Stacey Wilson, SYC); Single- and Double-Handed Race, Sea Fever Trophy, *Zephyr* (Kay Jones, SYC); Quent Williams Trophy, *Airloom* (Tim and Gail Morgenroth, STYC); Nautilus Trophy, *Steamer* (Ken VanderHoek, STYC, SHYC); Six-Meter Races: Sir Thomas Lipton Cup (Kris Bjornerud and Crew); Wood Lyda Trophy (Dave Buntz and Crew for the Sail Foundation); Mark Mayer Race: *Chicken Little* (R. Shorett, Jr., SYC); Cruise 'n Snooze Cannon: *Surprise* (Gerry Maurer, SYC); Grand Prix Awards: *Snook* (Erik Bentzen, FHYC); *Teddy Bear* (Gray Hawken, CYC); *Keladi* (Ray Fiedler, CYC); *Ladybug* (Alan Holt, SYC)

Junior Awards: Ernest Gann Award, Outstanding Junior Sailing Instructor, Rusty Lhamon; Brent Nichols Trophy, Most Outstanding Junior, Molly Salkield, SYC

Cruising Sailboat of the Year: Diva (Ken and Nancy Seright, SYC); Race Committee Ruptured Eardrum Trophy (Paul Bradley, SYC); Half-Vast Trophy (Mike Duffy, SYC)

In Memoriam, 1989: Carey Anderson, James M. Brown, Jr., Ole Bardahl, Cortlandt T. Clark, Woodworth B. Clum, Mrs. E. E. (Ruth) Cushing, Louis H. Ford, Mrs. Angelo F. (Isabelle) Ghiglione, Churchill Griffiths, Frederick J. Hagen, Russell Hawkins, Jr., Thomas E. Hayes, John W. Hite, Mrs. Ernest J. (Blanche) Ketcham, Ray Krantz, Walter M. Lembke, G. Stewart Marlatt, Mark Mayer, Mrs. John (Katherine) McCollister, H. W. McCurdy, Ronald L. McHolland, Moore M. McKinley, Reginald B. Parsons, Mrs. Evan S. (June) Prichard, William H. Robertson, Gordon F. Rogers, E. B. Sargent, Mrs. Richard H. (Kathryn) Shorett, C. W. Snedden, William R. Snyder, Fred H. Tolan, Malcolm Villesvik, John W. White, David Whitcomb, Eric Zahn, and Dr. Von Zanner.

1990

The new decade found the Seattle Yacht Club undertaking considerable construction and remodeling of not only the

The J40 Tiger Rag *as she appeared in 1990, owned by Bill Headden. (Bob Ross, CYC Photo Collection)*

main clubhouse but outstations as well. General Manager Vaughan Mason listed the following activities in March: installation of an elevator to service all three floors, new double-wide doors to enhance the decor and make it easier for handicapped members and guests to enter the clubhouse, new carpets, skylight and lighting in the lobby. The Star dock was being rebuilt and the canoe shed storage areas were being remodeled. A larger Junior Room and dressing rooms for the staff were being planned. Basement level storage areas were moved and those areas converted to committee work rooms and meeting rooms. Lockers were being installed for the boats on Pier 2.

By May Manager Mason could list refurbishing projects such as the Fireside Lounge where new carpet, window coverings, loveseat and easy chairs, new ceiling lights, new windows and air conditioning had been installed. In the Commodore's Room renovation included new ceiling and lights, removal of the center column (which held up part of the club and thus took some engineering to accomplish), new tables and window coverings. In the Ward Room there were new windows, new carpet, refinished table bases, and raised chair heights to add comfort. In the Marine Room were new windows, new tables, new chairs, trim moldings, swing patio door. The Men's Bar received new windows, back bar glassware cabinet, refinished bar tops, and awning for south windows. There were also new carpets and lights in the main stairway, lobby hallway, and lower deck hallway and a complete remodel of the men's lower deck head.

The Henry Island outstation was being cleaned up after several severe wind storms. Dave Pratt had built extra rails for the side supports to make the ramps safer for children. At Port Madison, Kathy and Mike Norris had repainted the heads and the halfway house.

The drama group presented the play *The Odd Couple* in March with Jim Vaupell as Felix and Rick Minogue as Oscar. The "standing room only" sign was brought out for two presentations.

Late in the year, Norine Daniels, who for nine years had worked as office manager, announced her resignation to pursue a new career.

The year also brought the first "Cheechako Pennants" to SYC, thanks to the new member activities committee. "Cheechako" is Chinook jargon meaning "newcomer," and the pennants are to be flown by Seattle Yacht Club's new members for one year. This will help longer-time members recognize the newcomers and help them feel at home.

As SYC approached its centennial year, total membership stood at 2,800. Active membership numbered 1,350 and there were 215 life members and 267 surviving spouses.

Past presidents of the Women's Group at Port Madison 1990 May cruise event. From left, standing: Shirlee Liberman, Mary Fox, Ann DeLaurenti, Doris Marshall, Diane Sweezey, La Rue Saddler, Diane Benson, Trudy Lane, Barbara Benton, Elaine Kidd, Rae Schmoyer, Gail Johnson, and Jane Heinrich. In front: Pam Thurman and Marlee McKibbin.

The appeal hearings on SYC's Port Ludlow property resulted in a "Shoreline Substantial Development Permit." This, however, was appealed to a higher court and any construction at this outstation was again delayed.

Commodore Robert O. Sylvester remarked that club management learned a great deal during the year about construction in Canada: There, too, permit requirements, regulations, and relations with neighbors were part of the learning curve in efforts to enlarge the Garden Bay outstation moorage. Pier 3 was installed but had to be removed because of a misunderstanding with local government. As the commodore noted, "Times have changed in British Columbia, just as they have in the United States."

Commodore Sylvester was pleased with the smooth operations during the Fifth Takarabune Trophy Race, which was hosted by the Seattle Yacht Club just prior to Opening Day (the well-chosen theme for Opening Day was "Celebrate International Good Will"). The sailors from Suma Yacht Club in Kobe, Japan, showed they were improving their skills each contest. Suma brought a 24-man sailing team and 40 observers. SYC members hosted the Suma visitors during Opening Day weekend and during the regatta held the following week. Seattle Yacht Club again retained the Takarabune Trophy, but one Suma racing team attained a second overall standing. Jack Lidral was chairman of the host committee for the event. The only sour note, according to the commodore, was heard one evening while entertaining the Suma Club officers and their wives in the Commodore's Room. Commodore Sylvester recalled: "After a series of loud noises and screeching of tires, I learned that my new car was one of those severely damaged in the commotion. So much for having your own prominent parking space."

The powerboat year extends over all 12 months. On January 13 the Queen City Yacht Club's First-of-the-Season Cruiser Contest on Lake Washington brought out boats from five yacht clubs, including nine from SYC. Best scores earned by SYC members included Gil Middleton with 0.8633 percent error, Craig Hopkins with 1.0956 percent, Jim Vaupell with 1.2471, and Bill Freitag with 1.4304. By reason of the standard scoring methodology, the three top SYC boats wound up in Class 5, taking first through third in that class. Bill Freitag took third in Class 4. Overall winner was Ray Pond of TYC.

Predicted Log Racer of the Year (Bale Trophy) was awarded to Murray Dorsey, and his *Solara* was the powerboat

The Cortes Bay Outstation

During the summer of 1990, Rear Commodore John Rasmussen laid the groundwork for expansion of SYC's northern holdings. As a result, Rankin Smith, developer and operator of the marina at Cortes Bay in Desolation Sound, British Columbia, called Rasmussen during the winter to discuss the sale of this property. The outstation committee, chaired by William Morse, sent Ken Hammer, Bob Landau and Ray Goad to look over the site and report back. The three recommended the club acquire the property.

Ray Goad was delegated the task of negotiating and closing the transaction, which was complicated by international tax and accounting issues. Accounting whiz Duane Boe and Finance Chairman Mike Riley filled out the acquisition team. Staff Captain Paul Sunich and construction pro Al Harrison also visited Cortes to inspect the physical aspects of the property. The board of trustees closely monitored the effort and, with SYC Commodore Dave Romano's leadership, authorized decisive action when needed. Their vision and foresight will be appreciated by visitors to this wonderful outstation for generations to come.

John and Helen Schlagel's *Aurora* was the first SYC yacht to arrive at the new Cortes Bay Outstation. They carried with them instructions to hoist the club burgee and spread the word that the rest of the members were on the way.

The first thing yachtsmen notice after rounding the Cortes Bay harbor buoy is the 1,000 linear feet of well-constructed floats conveniently configured in a large "U," ideal for varying hull lengths. It will also accommodate rafting both inside and outside. The floats have fresh water and electrical service.

An aluminum gangway leads to a series of graduating decks overlooking the bay, perfect for sunning and green box parties. At the head of the decks is the Crow's Nest, which is a full kitchen permitting food service for group functions or crew barbecues. The pathways along the landscaped rockeries lead to the store and manager's residence, part of which have been converted to a Club Room overlooking the bay.

Beyond the store, the ice machine, and ample ice storage bins are the shoreside heads and showers. The laundry facility is in a separate building and includes three washers and three dryers. A full shop and several utility buildings round out the main two-acre compound.

On the hillside are four cabins that will be available to members on an advance reservation basis. Cortes Island can be reached by car via ferry from Campbell River, and a concrete boat ramp is available adjacent to the floats.

Across the road from the cabins is a beautiful crescent public beach with spectacular views and world-class beachcombing opportunities.

The only concern of the Cortes Bay committee is that once you arrive, you won't want to leave.

—Based on the report by Ray Goad in the Binnacle, *June 1991*

of the year. The Betty Meacham Powerboat Trophy for Women went to Patty Frary. The 8 Ball Blooper Award was given to Bonnie Sharpe.

Rudder Cup winners: overall, Sandy Skeel; Little Rudder Cup, Christel Blackwell; and Predicted Log Race Class Trophy (Novice) went to Sandy Skeel.

Best SYC Finish at Queen City First of Season Race (January) was Gil Middleton, at Bremerton Heavy Weather Race (February) was Tom MacBride, at Meydenbauer Bay Boomerang Race (March) was Gil Middleton, at Everett Invitational Race (April) was Murray Dorsey, at Rainier/Poulsbo Race (May) was Murray Dorsey, at the International Cruiser Contest (July) was Craig Hopkins and Steve Sunich, at the SYC Stimson Trophy Race (September) was Ed Nelson, and at the Port Orchard Fall Round Up Race (October) the best finish belonged to Murray Dorsey.

Participation awards were presented to Jack Allen, Bob Anderson, Eleanor Black, Maggie Jorgerson, John Brooke, Charlie Cravens, Dick Davidson, Murray Dorsey, Phil Erickson, Mike Wade, Lynn and Patty Frary, Bill Freitag, Jerry Greenway, Dick Johnson, Gerry Johnson, Dave Kalamer, Dave Maples, Gil and Judy Middleton, Ed Nelson, Bonnie Sharpe, Sandy Skeel, Jim Vaupell, Bob Walls, and Frank Young.

The 1990 Opening Day Cruising Classic concluded with *Grimalkin* (John and Sue Donaldson) winning first place. *Roxy* (Mike, Tom and Karen Hukle) was second and *Cynosure* (Bill and Martha Davis) was third.

In rowing, the SYC crews did well at the April Greenlake Regatta. The Masters Men's 8+ came in first as did the Mixed Masters 8+ and the Masters Women's 8+. The Masters Women's 4+ had four entries and finished second, third, and fourth. The Masters Men's 4+ took a pair of fourths.

George and Eileen Maillot are shown cruising home in 1990 on their Bonne Vie. *(Photo by Norman C. Blanchard)*

At the Tri-Mountain Regatta, the Women's 4+ took a first and a second and their 8+ crew came in second. The Men's 4+ rowed in first and the 8+ took third. At the Fremont Four Miler at Seattle Pacific University, the women's crews took two firsts and a third. At the Head-of-the-Lake races, the women took two seconds and the men a first and a second.

The sailboats had another busy year. An interesting contest developed at the United States Yacht Club Challenge Regatta, which invited the 12 top yacht clubs in the nation to compete. In the Schock 35 class, in eight races, Seattle came in fourth. In the overall results without juniors, Seattle ended up seventh. The co-skippers from Seattle were Keith Lorence and Mark Laura.

The Bates McKee Memorial Trophy for Sailboat of the Year went to *Paddy Wagon*, belonging to Bill Lenihan of SYC.

The SYC yearbook listed the following trophies and award winners for 1990.

Smith Island Race: Jerry Bryant Trophy, SP, *Paddy Wagon* (Bill Lenihan, SYC); Gwendolyn II Trophy, IMS, *Audacious* (A. Hoffman/L. Anderson, CYC, SYC); Point No Point Race: Horder Provine Old Salts' Trophy, SP, *Steamer* (Ken VanderHoek, ST, SHYC); Kennell Midwatch Trophy, IMS, *Ladybug* (Alan Holt, SYC); Vashon Island Race: SP, *Wasp* (John Piety/Cory Smith, CNW); IMS, *Olympian* (Peter Schmidt, SYC); Point Robinson Race: Rawson Trophy, SP, *Synergy* (Eric Hurlburt, SSYC); IMS, *Satyr* (Kent Foreman, SYC); Protection Island Race: SP, *Paddy Wagon* (Bill Lenihan, SYC); IMS, *Audacious* (A. Hoffman/L. Anderson, CYC, SYC); Point Liplip Race: Golden Potlatch Trophy, SP, *Coruba* (Rob Fleming, CYC); IMS, *Ladybug* (Alan Holt, SYC); Hat Island Race: Hat Island Trophy, SP Long, *Paddy Wagon* (Bill Lenihan, SYC); IMS Long, *Audacious* (A. Hoffman/L. Anderson, CYC, SYC); Lady Medina Trophy, SP Short, *Impulse* (Ken Robbins, STYC); IMS Short, *Kiwi Express* (Larry Hoppe, CEYC)

Tri-Island Series: Walt Little Trophy, SP Overall, *Paddy Wagon* (Bill Lenihan, SYC); Roaring Forties Trophy, Overall Cal 40s, *Olympian* (Peter Schmidt, SYC); Tri-Point Series: First President's Trophy, SP Overall, *Sidewinder* (Mike and Brad Jones, GHYC); Bob Bollong Memorial Trophy, IMS Overall, *Ladybug* (Alan Holt, SYC)

Best Performance for Island Races: Smith Island, Long, *Audacious* (A. Hoffman/L. Anderson, CYC, SYC); Short, *Sidewinder* (Mike and Brad Jones, GHYC); Vashon Island, Long, *Jackrabbit* (Don Hebard, PM); Short, *Penetration* (Chris Johnson, CYC); Protection Island, Long, *Audacious* (A. Hoffman/L. Anderson, CYC, SYC); Short, *Williwa* (Bob Hale, CYC); Hat Island, Long, *Paddy Wagon* (Bill Lenihan, SYC); Short, *Kiwi Express* (Larry Hoppe, CEYC); George Barclay Perry Trophy, Best Performance Tri-Island and Hat Island Overall, *Audacious* (A. Hoffman/L. Anderson, CYC, SYC)

Whidbey Island Race Week: Xzora Trophy, Best SYC Boat Overall, *Satyr* (Kent Foreman); Norpac Race Week: Haida Trophy, First Overall, *Sachem* (Carl and Carol Buchan, SYC); first in Class A, *Sachem* (Carl and Carol Buchan); first in Class B, *Cloud Racer* (N. and R. Riebe, SYC); first in Class C, *Strider* (K. Johnson/P. Crockett, SYC); Single- and Double-Handed Race: Seafever Trophy, *Steamer* (Ken and Kathy VanderHoek, T/SHYC); Quent Williams Trophy, *Cetus* (Bogdan Sawicki, CYC); Nautilus Trophy, *Windbird* (Glen Utgaard, CYC); Mark Mayer Race: *Neptune Bullet* (Neptune Sailing Club)

Crooz N Snooz Cannon, *Gamin* (Lon Robinson, SYC); Grand Prix Awards: Cadranell Cup, *Jackrabbit* (Don Hebard, PM); *Starfire* (B. Nelson/M. Benjamin, TA); *Impulse* (Ken and Sandy Robbins, ST); IMS Grand Prix Trophy, *Mo Bettah Two* (Chuck Pepka, SYC)

Peter Schmidt's Cal 40 Olympian, *running before the wind in the Swiftsure Classic. Designed in the early 1960s, Cal 40s have won ocean races all over the world, and still are active in the 1990s. (Peter Schmidt Collection)*

Commodores of the Seattle Yacht Club—1990s

PHOTO BY YUEN LUI STUDIO

ROBERT SYLVESTER
1990
Born: 1914, Seattle, Wash.
Education: University of Washington, Harvard Graduate School
Occupation: University Professor, Consulting Engineer.
Boats: Yawl North Star, *Sloop* Khorasan, *Sloop* Moshulu

DAVID ROMANO
1991
Born: 1927, Seattle, Wash.
Education: University of Washington
Occupation: President/ Owner, North American Enterprises; Chairman, Romano Surgical Instrumentation, Inc.
Boats: Beachcomber I, II, III, *(the last a 48-foot Tollycraft)*

P. GERRY MAURER
1992
Born: 1942, Long Beach, Calif.
Education: Stanford, Columbia (MBA)
Occupation: Insurance and Estate Planning
Boat: Surprise *(35-foot C and C MK II sloop)*

Cruising Sailboat of the Year, *Skamokawa* (Eric and Carolyn Van, SYC); PIYA High Point Winner, SP, Key City Trophy, *Paddy Wagon* (Bill Lenihan, SYC); Moshulu Award (Doug Fryer, SYC)

In Memoriam, 1990: Mrs. Albert (Shirley) Bloss, Sr., Mrs. William E. (Marcy) Boeing, Jr., Mrs. George B. (Edith) Buchan, Chester Burdic, William F. Dawson, Stanly Donogh, Captain Harry Dudley, Mrs. George (Grace) Eastes, Carl Elwood Fryer, Ralph J. (Mike) Gibbons, Kenneth C. Gordon, Robert Graham, Mrs. Donald F. (Emily) Granston, Mrs. William H. (Linda) Green, Jr., James F. Harper, Al Horn, Mrs. Robert F. (Kathryn) Hyde, Mrs. Frank E. (Mary) James, Mrs. A. C. (Anne) Jordan, Mrs. John C. (Doris) Keatts, Jr., Hugh C. Klopfenstein, Howard E. Lovejoy, Mrs. Robert (Vivian) MacFarlane, Mrs. R. Stuart (Margaret) Moore, Paul Nemours, Robert S. Norman, Arthur Norris, Dave Palin, Mrs. J. Lenhart (Peggy) Reese, Robert E. Richardson, William Ritter, Connie Robbins, Nat S. Rogers, William Rosen, David Rowley, Mrs. James M. (Lillian) Ryan, Alfred A. Smith, Mrs. Reuben J. (Clara) Tarte, Girton R. Viereck, Mrs. Clayton (Maggie) Watkins, Mrs. Alfred (Ingfrid) White, William D. White, Don Whitworth, Dick Willard, Arthur G. Woodley, Frank E. Wood, Jr., and Max Wyman.

1991

The year dawned with a siege of the coldest weather on record.

A problem was noted in Lynn Wingard's *Binnacle* column, "Sailboat News," which concerned the decreasing number of boats entering races. This phenomenon was being felt by all yacht clubs.

At this time there are approximately 420

The J24 has replaced the Blanchard Sr. Knockabout as the most popular one design racing class. Owner Bob Ross, CYC, raced his Plane Crazy *on Puget Sound during the National eliminations. (Photo by Bob Arney)*

cruising sailboats, 20 handicap racing sailboats, and 30 one-design sailboats. A lot of members feel strongly about commercialism and that is why we need to address it. To what extent should we allow it? What problems will it solve or create? Who will it benefit?

. . . Where has everyone gone? Are racers no longer interested in the long, overnight races? Has the sport become too expensive? Is there a better rating system? (No doubt!)

Those in favor of introducing corporate commercial sponsorship feel that providing more gifts and/or better prizes will attract more competitors as well as showcase sailing as a sport to get involved in. Also by introducing the resources of a large corporation we would be able to use their expertise in marketing to better present our product (our races). We are lagging behind the rest of the country in what is an inevitable solution to our financial woes. It would also be a great vehicle for raising funds for charitable organizations and promoting civic involvement.

Those against it feel the cost of selling what is left of our Corinthian sport is too high. There is a better solution to the lack of attendance. We should continue to implement creative racing programs and reduce the number of races we sponsor using the theory of quality not quantity. . . . Your opinions and concerns on this or any item that the sailboat committee is addressing would be greatly appreciated.

—Binnacle, *January 1991*

Commodore Dave Romano, in remarking on his year in office, noted that after nine years of SYC outstation acquisition committee work, and after dozens of properties had been examined, the SYC board of trustees approved the purchase of Cortes Bay Marina. This acquisition provides members an exemplary outstation in Desolation Sound with a clubhouse and four cabins, plus facilities for moorage, power, water, ice, laundry, and showers. The commodore concluded that "the Seattle Yacht Club has the finest collection of outstations in the world."

At the behest of Commodore Romano, the trustees approved the formation of a gifts and bequests fund. This would allow members to give something back to the club such as living gifts or bequests in their wills. All gifts are to be appropriately recognized by the board of trustees.

On Jan. 1, 1991, the SYC implemented a monthly minimum food charge for the first time in the history of the club. This was necessary to support the club's restaurant services. An elegant weekly dinner buffet in the Ward Room allows members to utilize the minimum food charge in an enjoyable manner. He explained that maintaining a successful quality restaurant in a private club is almost impossible since it is not open to the public. The minimum food charge would ensure that SYC could continue providing quality food and service for members.

During the spring of 1991, the club installed a new and elaborate state-of-the-art computer system with point-of-sale accounting for the food and beverage operation. All areas of the club, including accounting and office, function more efficiently with this added computer capability.

Women's Group President Sally Laura and her board provided a variety of programs for the members as well as for the general club membership. Several new activities were introduced, including morning coffees at which boat decor, health, golf, the new chorus (Seanotes), and other subjects were discussed.

The Primadonna Regatta of April 13 and 14 provided a weekend for the women. Started by Mik and Barb Endrody, this unusual event finds the men doing all the work, while the women do all the racing and are later wined and dined by their husbands.

Also in April the women enjoyed a day on Lake Washington, which had been arranged by dinghy chairmen Molly McGuane and Penny Goodfellow. Leisurely hours were spent visiting friends, playing bridge, and admiring the newly redecorated yacht.

Lola Smith reported that the May 1991 cruise to Port Madison was enhanced by the presence of four men. This year the theme was Hawaiian. Two of the men—Bruce McKibbin and Stan Laura—played the ukulele. Warren Ceely performed as "Gung Ho," the singer, and Bruce Smith and Ceely gave hula lessons to the new officers of the Women's Group. Ina Mae Ceely evoked happy memories with her impression of Hilo Hattie and Barbara Benton regaled the group with her rendition of the Hawaiian War Chant. If audience reaction is an indication, the event was a great success. Elected as Women's Group officers for 1992 were President Pat Graffius, Vice President Margo Miller, Secretary Marlene Foster and Treasurer Bev Mahoney. Admiralette for 1992 is Tammy Erickson.

Art Ayers and Norm C. Blanchard spent many hours identifying and recording historic photos for this book. (Photo by Ann F. Bayless)

The 1991 Opening Day Boat Parade was one of the best ever. Two changes in rules made by the Opening Day committee were effective. Every boat in the parade had to be decorated or dressed in accordance with rules. This reduced the number of parading boats from 450 to 250, and allowed the parade to conclude at a more reasonable time.

The Garden Bay Outstation foreshore lease was renewed through the year 2021. Commodore Romano noted that Vice Commodore Gerry Maurer did the heavy work. The club had first pursued the lease renewal in 1990, when the old lease had expired. As Commodore Romano phrased it, "After overcoming considerable neighborhood opposition to our lease request, with patience, diligence, and perseverance, we were gratified to be granted a 30-year extension. We were most appreciative of the cooperation and approval of the various Canadian Government Agencies involved."

As this book was being completed in July 1991, the commodore informed the

Pat Grafius served as president of the Women's Group in 1991-92. (SYC Women's Group Collection)

club that in June the board approved in principle the leasing of 180 slips plus a 1,500 square-foot free-standing shoreside building at the Elliott Bay Marina. This provides saltwater moorage that has long been desired by many members. Originally the club was going to pay for any slip vacancies in order to hold the lease. Commodore Romano and a contingent of three commodores and the sub-committee had lunch with the four principals of the Elliott Bay Marina. The commodore explained that because SYC members had signed on for only 95 of the 180 slips; the vacant slips would cost about $375,000 annually; the club was in no position to incur such an expense. An agreement was reached whereby the Elliott Bay Marina would not require the club to pay for the vacant slips. This enabled the commodore to later recommend to the board that the plan for saltwater moorage be approved.

At the 1990 All-Japan J-24 Championship Races, the SYC team of Joe Williams, Eric Stelter, Fritz Lanzinger, Garth Olsen, and Steve Boyle secured a "loaner" boat from the sister Suma Yacht Club in Kobe. Housing was also arranged. Continental Airlines provided transportation. This five-race series is scored on the Olympic System. The SYC entry, *Cen-*

The 1991 Opening Day theme of Broadway Musical Salute resulted in Oz *winning the Sweepstakes Award. Here are owner Marda Runstad and crew. (Marda Runstad Collection)*

tennial Spirit, won the series in four races, scoring 11.7 points. The next closest challenger out of San Francisco scored 35.7 points. Mark Laura sailed on a Suma Yacht Club entry, which came in fourth with 51.4 points. The SYC team accepted the championship trophy, but then awarded it to the top Japanese boat.

Molly Cadranell was selected to receive the Tug Boat Annie Award for 1990. Cadranell, a very active third-generation member is the granddaughter of the late life member Dwight Benton and daughter of Ben and Barbara Benton.

The second biannual SYC–Royal Arkana Yacht Club summer-winter cruising exchange took place in March 1991. Fifty SYC members traveled to Auckland, New Zealand, where their hosts provided tours of the local area and a five-day cruise to Great Barrier Island. All participants had a most enjoyable time, and an

The Calendar of the SYC Women's Group

The calendar of the 1990s for the Seattle Yacht Club Women's Group is filled with a variety of activities; some are traditional, and some are special to our times. More than 30 committees organize, coordinate, and financially manage the group's calendar year.

In September the members are welcomed back from summer boating and vacation activities. A "welcoming" luncheon is preceded by the traditional social hour and followed with a program speaker. The new admiralette is introduced, and the activities rosters are distributed, detailing plans for chorus, language classes, Monday coffees, Mah Jong, Tuesday dance and exercise programs, Wednesday drama and dinghy outings, and Thursday golf and bridge events. The committee chairmen call for volunteers and announce meetings.

The fall fashion show follows the social hour and luncheon in October. Honored guests include the club managers. Reservations are a must for this popular event.

In November the monthly luncheon and special program sets the stage for the holidays. Topics cover fashion, food, and festivities.

At the Women's Group traditional Christmas party the commodore and vice commodore serve the great Yuletide punch bowl. The dining room is decorated and holiday music fills the air.

The January luncheon features the past commodore as the honored guest and a guest speaker.

The Women's Interclub (WIC) annual meeting held in February includes luncheon and program. Seven of the 14 WIC member clubs are honored guests on a biannual basis. It is a popular monthly luncheon and social exchange between the neighboring yacht club women.

In March the Opening Day admiralty are presented to the membership. Flanked on either side by an honor guard of past admiralettes, they make their entrance into the club dining room. They are among the honored guests for the luncheon and program, which includes a guest speaker.

Several traditions take place in April. Guests may be invited to the spring fashion show; ballots are cast for the following year's slate of officers, and rosters are prepared for the historic May Cruise.

The last meeting of the club year is held in May and includes a boat trip through the locks to Port Madison. This practice began in 1957 when outgoing President Anne Foster wanted to celebrate the end of her term with a special party and boating event. It was an immediate success. Foster was reelected for another term as president. At Port Madison, a day of fun and celebration is enhanced by entertainment from the drama group, a party, and the announcement of the newly elected officers. This final luncheon is filled with merriment and good cheer. The spirit of the day reflects the objective of the SYC Women's Group—to encourage social activity and friendship among members. ◇

In the May 1991 CYC Center Sound Series, Martin Godsil's Invader *won its division in the Pully Point Race on Puget Sound and took first place for the series with three wins overall. (Photo courtesy of* Nor'westing*)*

invitation was extended by SYC for the New Zealanders to join them on Puget Sound in 1993.

In Memoriam, 1991: J. Swift Baker, Lawrence V. Brown, Cecil P. Callison, Van R. Caples, Mrs. Cortland Clark, Gordon Clauson, Larry Clein, Mrs. George Cropp, Mrs. Frank Dunn, Mrs. John H. Gaffney, John T. Gillespie, Mrs. John (Ruth) Gould, John (Jack) Graham, Jr., George Hawkins, Harold S. Hellieson, Mrs. Albert Horn, Jr., David S. Ingram, III, Max O. Jensen, Lloyd W. Johnson, Henry D. Knowles, Mrs. David Law, Albert Lilygreen, Mrs. Marco (Darlene) Magnano, A. I. Ostlund, Mrs. Wally (Ruth) Ovens, Wallace L. Ovens, Charles E. Peterson, Mrs. Carlton Powers, Dr. Max Schoonik, Dr. R. Phillip Smith, George H. Stebbins, Mrs. Alice Street, A. Harold Tomlinson, Lawrence D. Wade, and Frederick Wirtz, and Lysle Wood.

So we close this chronicle of more than a century of history of the Seattle Yacht Club and the boating community of the Puget Sound region. The foundations are in place for the next century of boating. We bequeath to those future boaters of this region our rich heritage, with the hope that they will honor, preserve and expand those manifest traditions. In the words of our beloved Charlie Schaak, "It is the duty and obligation of every member to work toward keeping the Seattle Yacht Club the BGDYCITWWW!"

Epilogue

The Seattle Yacht Club will be led through its Centennial Year by P. Gerry Maurer as commodore, John Rasmussen as vice commodore, and William A. Bain as rear commodore. During the Centennial year, the SYC will take note of traditions and will sponsor many Centennial events.

It has been an exciting one hundred years, at the Seattle Yacht Club, thanks to the energetic and imaginative people, officers, and others who have led the way. Who can forget the early races with sailors from Canada, the fight with the lumber company over the West Seattle site, the move to the Portage Bay site, the sponsorship of hydroplane races which drew the world's largest assembly of spectator craft, the building of the world's best chain of outstations, our unique opening day, the accumulation of championships in crew, sailing, log and speed boat racing, the fun we have had at Thursday lunch, Potlatch, various rendezvous, and a vast variety of other social events. We don't know what the next one hundred years will bring, but with the ambitious and inspired sort of person who is attracted to SYC membership the next one hundred years is likely to be as exciting as the past has been. ☆

Officers and Board Members of the Seattle Yacht Club

The first mention of a Seattle Yacht Club occurs in 1879. No records exist from those early days of yachting on Puget Sound other than what can be found in the old newspapers. It appears the club was not only informal but may have ceased to exist from time to time.

An early *Intelligencer* mentions the "Commodore" of the July 4, 1878, Elliott Bay Regatta was a Captain Winsor.

In 1879, the paper reports on the founding of the Seattle Yacht Club and the election of shipbuilder William Hammond as the Commodore of the new organization.

In 1880, 1886, and in 1890, newspapers and/or the City Directory name Dr. Frederick W. Sparling the Commodore of the Seattle Yacht Club. Apparently he served off and on for a decade. *The Seattle Times* listed the officers of 1890.

1890:

Commodore:	Fred W. Sparling
Vice Commodore:	George E. Budlong
Secretary:	Charles W. Thornton
Treasurer:	John W. Brauer
Measurer:	R. S. Clark
Race Committee:	Joseph Green
	William Howe
	M. J. Johnson
Membership:	C. P. Blanchard
	William McIntyre
	H. W. Morrison
House:	George C. Bartlett
	G. A. Zeiger
	D. M. Simonson

1891

The Commodore was Joseph Green (according to the City Directory).

1892-94

The Commodore was Fred E. Sander (City Directory).

The Seattle Times, on December 26, 1954, published a list of officers of the Seattle Yacht Club for the year 1892:

Commodore:	Fred E. Sander
Vice Commodore:	J. H. Johnson
Secretary:	W. W. French
Treasurer:	A. R. Pickney
Port Captain:	Carl Siebrand

1895

The Commodore was J. H. Johnson (City Directory)

1901-09

The Commodore was C. D. Stimson (City Directory)

The Elliott Bay Yacht Club from its 1894 founding to its amalgamation with the Seattle Yacht Club in 1909 operated as a separate entity until 1909 when the two yacht clubs became one. The Elliott Bay Club yearbook for 1909 was printed just prior to the amalgamation and lists the officers of EBYC between the 1894 founding and 1904. Apparently the officers remained the same for the next five years, a time when the club had no boathouse. The list picks up again in 1909, the year of amalgamation. Only the EBYC Commodores prior to 1909 are honored in the present SYC Commodore's Room. The pre-1909 SYC Commodores are largely forgotten.

1894 (Elliott Bay Yacht Club)

Commodore:	Henry Hensel
Vice Commodore:	A. M. Towle
Secretary:	R. J. McClelland
Treasurer:	Amos Brown
Measurer:	Amos Goodell
Fleet Captain:	Harvey Nugent

1895 (Elliott Bay Yacht Club)

Commodore:	Henry Hensel
Vice Commodore:	W. D. Wilson
Secretary:	R. J. McClelland
Treasurer:	Amos Brown
Measurer:	Leigh Coolidge
Fleet Captain:	Dave Boyd

1896 (Elliott Bay Yacht Club)

Commodore:	Henry Hensel
Vice Commodore:	George E. Thompson
Treasurer:	Amos Brown
Measurer:	Leigh Coolidge
Fleet Captain:	H. J. Turlow

1897 (Elliott Bay Yacht Club)

Commodore:	Henry Hensel
Vice Commodore:	George E. Thompson
Treasurer:	Amos Brown
Measurer:	Amos Goodell

1898 (Elliott Bay Yacht Club)

Commodore:	George E. Thompson
Vice Commodore:	H. J. Turlow
Secretary:	R. J. McClelland
Treasurer:	Amos Brown
Measurer:	Amos Goodell

1899 (Elliott Bay Yacht Club)

Commodore:	George E. Thompson
Vice Commodore:	A. H. Rohlfs
Secretary:	R. J. McClelland
Treasurer:	Amos Brown
Measurer:	Amos Goodell

1900 (Elliott Bay Yacht Club)

Commodore:	George E. Thompson
Vice Commodore:	A. H. Rohlfs
Secretary:	L. A. Keating
Treasurer:	Amos Brown
Measurer:	Amos Goodell

1901 (Elliott Bay Yacht Club)

Commodore:	George E. Thompson
Vice Commodore:	A. H. Rohlfs
Secretary:	L. A. Keating
Treasurer:	Amos Brown
Measurer:	Amos Goodell

1902 (Elliott Bay Yacht Club)

Commodore:	George E. Thompson
Vice Commodore:	A. H. Rohlfs
Secretary:	L. A. Keating
Treasurer:	Amos Brown
Measurer:	Amos Goodell

1903 (Elliott Bay Yacht Club)

Commodore:	George E. Thompson
Vice Commodore:	A. H. Rohlfs
Secretary:	L. A. Keating
Treasurer:	Amos Brown
Measurer:	Amos Goodell

From here on, the officers and committee chairmen are taken from lists in the yearbooks. Where there are blanks, either no yearbooks were published or no copy could be found.

1904

Commodore:	George E. Thompson

1905

Commodore:	George E. Thompson

1906

Commodore:	George E. Thompson

1907

Commodore:	C. W. Wiley

1908

Commodore:	C. W. Wiley

1909

Commodore:	H. W. Gocher
Vice Commodore:	S. A. Hoyt
Rear Commodore:	H. W. Starrett
Secretary:	Dr. C. Benson Wood
Treasurer:	George T. S. White
Board of Directors:	William Farr
	W. D. Wiley
	H. C. Moss
	Dr. F. E. O'Connell
	A. H. Rohlfs
	W. B. Allison
	H. W. Starrett
	Miller Freeman
	Dr. C. Benson Wood
Fleet Captain:	James V. Pellitier
Judge Advocate:	George Clinton Congdon
Fleet Surgeon:	Dr. R. D. Forbes
Measurer:	Frederick S. Brinton
House Committee:	E. W. Rogers
	O. D. Rohlfs
	Ivan Hyland
Regatta Committee:	T. W. Wynn-Jones
	Dr. F. E. O'Connell
	O. D. Rohlfs
Press Committee:	Miller Freeman
	James V. Pellitier
Investigating Committee:	W. B. Allison
	Dr. C. Benson Wood

1910

Commodore:	S. A. Hoyt
Vice Commodore:	Miller Freeman
Rear Commodore:	A. Hambach
Secretary:	Dr. C. Benson Wood
Treasurer:	George T. S. White
Directors:	H. W. Starrett
	Dr. C. Benson Wood
	G. E. Butts
	Edward Kellogg
	M. Robert Guggenheim
	W. J. Alexander
	W. B. Allison
	H. W. Gocher
	Capt. B. B. Whitney
Judge Advocate:	George Clinton Congdon
Fleet Surgeon:	Dr. R. D. Forbes
Measurer:	Frederick S. Brinton
House Committee:	Vince Faben
	John Mungall
	Dr. George E. Thompson
Regatta Committee:	W. B. Allison
	A. H. Rohlfs
	Dr. H. V. Wurdemann
Press Committee Chairman:	Miller Freeman
Investigating Committee:	Dr. C. Benson Wood
	W. B. Allison

1911
Commodore: H. W. Starrett

1912
Commodore: H. V. Wurdemann
Vice Commodore: B. R. Lewis
Rear Commodore: Lloyd Johnson
Secretary: A. V. Comings
Treasurer: E. L. Kellogg
Directors: B. B. Whitney
R. E. Magner
E. B. Moore
Dietrich Schmitz
H. W. Gocher
A. F. Russell
J. F. Jacoby
Henry Hensel
A. V. Comings

1913
Commodore: John Graham
Vice Commodore: Robert E. Magner
Rear Commodore: C. P. Constantine
Secretary-Treasurer: C. L. Burt
House Secretary: A. F. Comings
Judge Advocate: G. C. Congdon
Directors: H. V. Wurdemann
Henry Hensel
Q. H. Williams
D. L. Pratt
J. F. Jacoby
H. V. Chutter
D. H. Schmitz
W. A. Deering
H. C. Moss
R. F. Broadaway
B. B. Whitney

1914
Commodore: Robert E. Magner

1915
Commodore: William G. Norris
Committee Chairs
Powerboat: Quent Williams
Sailing: Dr. F. E. O'Connell
Investigating: B. B. Whitney
Dr. A. F. Comings
House: Henry Hensel
J. F. Jacoby
Press: C. P. Constantine
Entertainment: Charles T. Boyd

1916
Commodore: J. E. Chilberg

1917
Commodore: N. H. Latimer

1918
Commodore: N. H. Latimer

1919
Commodore: N. H. Latimer
Vice Commodores: R. R. Fox
Capt. James Griffiths
Rear Commodore: W. G. Norris
Secretary: George C. Congdon
Treasurer: Henry Hensel
Directors: J. E. Chilberg
J. T. Heffernan
Scott Calhoun
Francis G. Frink
David Whitcomb
Miller Freeman
B. B. Whitney
Frank McDermott
A. W. Leonard
Committee Chairs
Powerboat: John Graham
Sailboat: Quent Williams
Finance: J. S. Gibson
Entertainment: Raymond Frazier
Membership: Fred Baxter
Judge Advocate: Vince Faben
Fleet Captain: J. F. Blain
Press: Dan L. Pratt
House: George W. Allen

1920
Commodore: Capt. J. S. Gibson
Vice Commodore: Capt. James Griffiths
Rear Commodore: Fred H. Baxter
Secretary: George C. Congdon
Treasurer: N. H. Latimer
Directors: B. B. Whitner
Frank McDermott
A. W. Leonard
Joseph Blethen
Frank Waterhouse
David Whitcomb
J. E. Chilberg
Francis G. Frink
Reginald H. Parson
Committee Chairs
Powerboat: John Graham
Sailboat: Quent Williams
Finance: Henry Hensel
Entertainment: Dr. V. A. Kelly
Membership: Stanley Griffiths
Press: Daniel Pratt
Judge Advocate: D. B. Trefethen
Fleet Captain: David Whitcomb
House: F. G. Frink

1921
Commodore: Capt. James Griffiths
Vice Commodore: Fred H. Baxter
Rear Commodore: Reginald H. Parsons
Secretary: George C. Congdon
Treasurer: C. M. Latimer
Directors: Joseph Blethen
Frank Waterhouse
David Whitcomb
J. E. Chilberg
Francis G. Frink
D. W. Branch
N. H. Latimer
C. D. Stimson
A. W. Leonard
Committee Chairs
Powerboat: John Graham
Sailboat: Quent Williams
Finance: Capt. J. S. Gibson
Entertainment: William H. Silliman
House: William T. Isted
Membership: Stanley Griffiths
Press: Daniel Pratt
Judge Advocate: D. B. Trefethen
Fleet Captain: David Whitcomb

1922
Commodore: Capt. James Griffiths

1923
Commodore: Henry Seaborn

1924
Commodore: None listed (May have been change of fiscal year dates.)
Committee Chairs
Membership: Henry K. Sander
Junior Commodore: J. G. Swift Baker

1925
Commodore: F. C. Hellenthal

1926
Commodore: F. C. Hellenthal

1927
Commodore: James Hoge

1928
Commodore: James Griffiths
Vice Commodore: Quent Williams
Rear Commodore: C. S. Waddingham
Secretary: Colin O. Radford
Treasurer: Dietrich Schmitz
Directors: F. G. Frink
W. H. Silliman
Roy Corbett
F. H. Baxter
A. S. Eldridge
H. G. Seaborn
Stanley Griffiths
J. von Herberg
Rollin Sanford
Fleet Captain: Bert Jilg
Judge Advocate: D. B. Trefethen
Fleet Surgeon: Dr. Wurdemann
Committee Chairs
House: W. H. Silliman
Sailboat: Quent Williams
Powerboat: John Blackford
Finance: W. J. Lake
Entertainment: C. S. Harley
Membership: W. T. Isted
Press: A. Shannon
Docks and Moorings: L. E. Geary
Junior Commodore: Robert K. Hodges

1929
Commodore: John Graham
Vice Commodore: Ray Cooke
Secretary: Colin O. Radford
Committee Chairs
Sailboat: J. Swift Baker
Powerboat: W. M. Meacham
Finance: Francis G. Frink
Entertainment: F. C. Hellenthal
House: T. W. Nash
Mooring: L. E. Geary
Junior Commodore: C. Frederick Harley

1930
Commodore: L. E. Geary
Vice Commodore: Col. C. B. Blethen
Rear Commodore: C. W. Wiley
Secretary: C. W. Broom
Treasurer: Dietrich Schmitz
Directors: Stanley Griffiths
J. von Herberg
Rollin Sanford
Dr. J. M. Blackford
C. S. Harley
J. S. Baker
Colin O. Radford
Harry B. Lear
Roy W. Corbett
Fleet Captain: Russell Gibson
Judge Advocate: D. B. Trefethen
Fleet Surgeon: Dr. W. J. Jones
Measurer: N. J. Blanchard
Librarian: James F. Hodges
Committee Chairs
House: R. M. Boykin
Powerboat: Richard Froboese
Sailboat: A. J. Duthie
Finance: F. G. Frink
Entertainment: Roy W. Corbett
Membership: A. W. Webb

Publicity: Peter Salvus
Docks: F. C. Hellenthal
Junior Officers
Commodore: Douglas C. Stansbury
Vice Commodore: Bert Davis
Secretary-Treasurer: Dan Huntington, Jr.
Committee Chairs
Entertainment: Arthur Ayers
Membership: Potter S. Harley
Fleet: Bert Davis
House: Vernon Latimer
Publicity: Peter Salvus

1931

Commodore: C. B. Blethen
Vice Commodore: Stanley A. Griffiths
Rear Commodore: William Hedley
Secretary: Colin O. Radford
Treasurer: Dietrich Schmitz
Directors: Jack W. Power
Fred H. Baxter
Francis G. Frink
Junior Commodore: Bert Davis

1932

Commodore: C. B. Blethen
Vice Commodore: William R. Hedley
Rear Commodore: F. J. Seidelhuber
Secretary: R. F. Peier
Treasurer: Dietrich Schmitz
Directors: Colin O. Radford
Roy W. Corbett
Harry B. Lear
F. G. Frink
F. H. Baxter
Jack Power
James Ballard
Russell Gibson
H. C. Rolfe
Fleet Captain: Capt. James Griffiths
Judge Advocate: F. R. Jeffrey
Fleet Surgeon: Dr. J. M. Blackford
Measurer: Anderson S. Joy
Librarian: James F. Hodges
Committee Chairs
House: C. S. Harley
Finance: Dietrich Schmitz
Sailboat: A. J. Duthie
Powerboat: R. S. Moore
Entertainment: Roy W. Corbett
Membership: C. O. Radford
Docks: F. C. Hellenthal
Breakwater: F. C. Hellenthal
Advisory: John Graham
Junior Advisory: Douglas S. Egan
Press: Edward H. Peltret

1933

Commodore: Roy W. Corbett
Vice Commodore: Robert W. Moore
Rear Commodore: A. J. Duthie
Secretary: Anderson S. Joy
Treasurer: Dietrich Schmitz
Directors: F. G. Frink
F. H. Baxter
Jack Power
James M. Ballard
Russell G. Gibson
Hamilton C. Rolfe
F. A. Harvey
W. H. Silliman
Clinton S. Harley
Fleet Captain: John T. Harrison
Judge Advocate: James M. Ballard
Fleet Surgeon: Dr. J. Howard Snively
Measurer: John M. Beaufort
Librarian: James F. Hodges
Committee Chairs
House: P. J. Perry
Finance: Dietrich Schmitz
Sailboat: Ellis Provine
Powerboat: Jack Power
Entertainment: Russell G. Gibson
Membership: Colin O. Radford
Moorings: C. W. Wiley
Advisory: Capt. James Griffiths
Junior Advisory: Douglas S. Egan
Press: Gordon Strewart
Junior Officers
Commodore: Charles H. Konker
Honorary Commodore: J. Swift Baker
Vice Commodore: Norman Blanchard, Jr.
Secretary-Treasurer Walter M. Lembke

1934

Commodore: C. W. Stimson
Vice Commodore: Robert S. Moore
Rear Commodore: Jack Power
Secretary: Anderson S. Joy
Treasurer: O. W. Tupper
Directors: James M. Ballard
Russell G. Gibson
F. A. Harvey
Hamilton C. Rolfe
W. H. Silliman
Clint S. Harley
C. M. Poncin
A. J. Duthie
Roy W. Corbett
Fleet Captain: C. M. Poncin
Judge Advocate: James M. Ballard
Fleet Surgeon: Dr. H. V. Wurdemann
Measurer: Ellis Provine
Assistant Measurer: Robert T. Lamson
Librarian: Chester Dawson
Committee Chairs
House: Clint S. Harley
Finance: O. W. Tupper
Sailboat: Roy W. Corbett
Powerboat: Russell G. Gibson
Entertainment: Robert S. Moore
Membership: Colin O. Radford
Moorings: A. J. Duthie
Advisory: Capt. James Griffiths
Junior Advisory: Charles G. Schaak
Press: Gordon Stewart
Junior Officers
Commodore: Arthur Ayers
Honorary Commodore: James Hodges
Vice Commodore: Norman Blanchard, Jr.
Secretary-Treasurer: Bert Davis

1935

Commodore: C. W. Stimson
Vice Commodore: Russell G. Gibson
Rear Commodore: Ellis Provine
Secretary: Anderson S. Joy
Treasurer: Paul C. Harper
Directors: Charles G. Schaak
W. H. Silliman
Clint S. Harley
C. M. Poncin
Roy W. Corbett
A. J. Duthie
James M. Ballard
Hamilton C. Rolfe
J. E. Frost
Fleet Captain: Robert S. Moore
Judge Advocate: James M. Ballard
Fleet Surgeon: Dr. A. O. Tucker
Measurer: Ellis Provine
Assistant Measurers: Robert T. Lamson
Ben Seaborn
Librarian: Charles G. Schaak
Committee Chairs
House: J. Swift Baker
Finance: Paul C. Harper
Sailboat: Ray Cooke
Powerboat: Dr. R. T. Pretlow
Entertainment: Stanley A. Griffiths
Regatta: Clint S. Harley
Membership: Russell G. Gibson
Moorings: A. J. Duthie
Advisory: Capt. James Griffiths
Junior Advisory: Chester Dawson
Ballard Breakwater: Charles G. Schaak
Press: C. W. Stimson
Junior Officers
Commodore: Garret Horder
Honorary Commodore: William R. Hedley
Vice Commodore: John F. Dore, Jr.
Secretary-Treasurer: Robert T. Lamson

1936

Commodore: Paul M. Henry
Vice Commodore: C. B. Warren
Rear Commodore: W. V. Tanner
Secretary: Ellis Provine
Treasurer: Paul C. Harper
Directors: C. M. Poncin
Roy W. Corbett
A. J. Duthie
James M. Ballard
H. C. Rolfe
J. E. Frost
Chas. I. Frisbie
Russell Gibson
Aubrey Naef
Fleet Captain: Middleton M. Chism
Judge Advocate: James M. Ballard
Fleet Surgeon: Dr. Torleif Torland
Measurer: E. G. Monk
Librarian: Charles Konker
Committee Chairs
House: Roy W. Corbett
Finance: Paul C. Harper
Sailboat: Leland J. Clark
Powerboat: R. S. Moore
Entertainment: J. Swift Baker
Regatta: Professor C. W. Harris
Membership: Capt. E. F. Eckhardt
Moorings: A. J. Duthie
Advisory: Capt. James Griffiths
Junior Advisory: Anderson S. Joy
Press: Jack M. Chisholm
Junior Officers
Commodore: John F. Dore, Jr.
Honorary Commodore: C. W. Stimson
Vice Commodore: Robert T. Lamson
Secretary-Treasurer: John F. Amsberry

1937

Commodore: Paul M. Henry
Vice Commodore: C. B. Warren
Rear Commodore: H. W. McCurdy
Secretary: Anderson S. Joy
Treasurer: James G. Thwing
Directors: James M. Ballard
Dr. H. V. Wurdemann
Dr. Torleif Torland
W. V. Tanner
Russell Gibson
Aubrey Naef
Roy W. Corbett
Paul C. Harper
A. J. Duthie
Fleet Captain: Roy W. Corbett
Fleet Surgeon: Dr. H. E. Coe
Judge Advocate: James M. Ballard
Measurer: E. G. Monk
Librarian: Charles H. Konker
Committee Chairs
House: W. V. Tanner
Finance: James G. Thwing
Sailboat: Paul C. Harper
Powerboat: Raymond C. Krueger
Entertainment: Dr. Albert J. Bowles
Regatta: Roy W. Corbett
Membership: James M. Ballard
Moorings: A. J. Duthie
Advisory: F. C. Hellenthal
Junior Advisory: Chester Dawson

Press: Charles H. Konker
Forum: John F. Snapp
Reception: Walter Gerke
Junior Officers
Commodore: Norman Blanchard, Jr.
Honorary Commodore: Ellis Provine
Vice Commodore: Richard W. Griffiths
Secretary-Treasurer: Fred Moe

1938

Commodore: C. B. Warren
Vice Commodore: H. W. McCurdy
Rear Commodore: James W. Thwing
Secretary: Charles Konker
Treasurer: Charles W. Schaak
Directors: J. L. Hyde
Russell G. Gibson
Aubrey A. Naef
Roy W. Corbett
Paul C. Harper
A. J. Duthie
William R. Hedley
Marvin S. Allyn
Anderson S. Joy
Fleet Captain: Roy W. Corbett
Fleet Surgeon: Dr. H. E. Coe
Judge Advocate: James M. Ballard
Measurer: Edwin Monk
Librarian: J. Swift Baker
Committee Chairs
House: Russell G. Gibson
Finance: Middleton M. Chism
Sailboat: John A. Soderberg
Powerboat: Bruce Bartley
Entertainment: James F. Unicume
Regatta: Paul D. Clyde
Membership: Richard Froboese
Moorings: A. J. Duthie
Advisory: C. W. Stimson
Junior Advisory: W. J. Rhodes
Press: Henry J. Olschewsky
Forum: John F. Snapp
Reception: Dr. McCormick Mehan
Modernization: Roy W. Corbett
Junior Officers
Commodore: Ben Seaborn
Honorary Commodore: Ray Cooke
Vice Commodore: Mark Mayer, Jr.
Secretary-Treasurer: Ferrall Campbell

1939

Commodore: Marvin S. Allyn
Vice Commodore: Middleton M. Chism
Rear Commodore: John C. McCollister
Secretary: James F. Unicume
Treasurer: John W. Rumsey
Fleet Captain: Ray Cooke
Fleet Surgeon: Dr. Albert J. Bowles
Judge Advocate: James M. Ballard
Measurer: Edwin Monk
Librarian: Dr. Ralph E. Allen
Committee Chairs
Membership: Gardner Gamwell
Entertainment: C. S. Cumins
Press: M. M. Rinearson
House: C. M. Ponsin
Regatta: Capt. E. F. Eckhardt
Powerboat: Russell Rathbone
Sailboat: Ellis F. Provine
Finance: John W. Rumsey
Moorings: A. J. Duthie
Advisory: C. B. Warren
Junior Advisory: John A. Soderberg
Junior Girls Advisory: Mrs. Virginia Gibson

1940

Commodore: Marvin S. Allyn
Vice Commodore: Middleton M. Chism
Rear Commodore: Gardner Gamwell
Secretary: E. G. Watson
Treasurer: M. M. Rinearson
Directors: William R. Hedley
Anderson S. Joy
John Soderberg
John F. Snapp
Richard Froboese
Raymond C. Krueger
C. L. Egtvedt
Tom Owen
James F. Unicume
Fleet Captain: John Soderberg
Fleet Surgeon: Dr. Albert J. Bowles
Judge Advocate: James M. Ballard
Measurer: Edwin Monk
Assistant Measurer: Ben Seaborn
Librarian: Dr. Ralph Edgar Allen
Committee Chairs
Membership: Richard Froboese
Social: Mr. and Mrs. George Parsons
Men's Affairs: Charles Schaak
House: John Snapp
Regatta: Eustace Vynne
Powerboat: James F. Unicume
Sailboat: C. S. Cumins
Finance: M. M. Rinearson
Moorings: Tom Owen
Advisory: Roy W. Corbett
Junior Advisory: Anderson S. Joy
Junior Officers
Commodore: Eustace Vynne, Jr.
Vice Commodore: Richard Philbrick
Honorary Commodore: Thomas W. Owen
Secretary-Treasurer: Frank Hiscock

1941

Commodore: H. W. McCurdy
Vice Commodore: Aubrey A. Naef
Rear Commodore: William W. Warren
Secretary: E. G. Watson
Treasurer: M. M. Rinearson
Directors: John F. Snapp
Richard Froboese
Dr. Albert Bowles
James F. Unicume
C. L. Egtvedt
J. Swift Baker
Tom Owen
George Parsons
Eustace Vynne, Sr.
Fleet Captain: Roy W. Corbett
Fleet Surgeon: Dr. Herbert E. Coe
Judge Advocate: Robert S. Macfarlane
Measurer: Edwin Monk
Assistant Measurer: Ben Seaborn
Librarian: Ross Brattain
Committee Chairs
Membership: Richard Froboese
Social: Mr. and Mrs. J. Swift Baker
Entertainment: C. S. Cumins
House: John Kucher
Regatta: Harold S. Allen
Powerboat: Arthur M. Russell
Sailboat: Ralph S. Russell
Finance: M. M. Rinearson
Moorings: Tom Owen
Advisory: Marvin S. Allyn
Junior Advisory: Eustace Vynne, Sr.
Forum: John Snapp
Bylaw Revision: Robert S. Macfarlane
Yearbook: George Stroble
Publicity: John Cannon
Barnacle Bill: William R. Hedley
Junior Officers
Commodore: Eustace Vynne, Jr.
Honorary Commodore: Tom Owen
Vice Commodore: John Dickinson
Secretary-Treasurer: Janice Rumsey
Fleet Captain: Frank Moegling

1942

Commodore: Robert S. Macfarlane
Vice Commodore: James F. Unicume
Rear Commodore: John F. Snapp
Secretary: John E. Cannon
Treasurer: M. M. Rinearson
Directors: E. R. Raphael
C. L. Egtvedt
J. Swift Baker
Tom Owen
George Parsons
Eustace Vynne, Sr.
John Kucher
William Warren
M. M. Chism
Fleet Captain: John Warren
Fleet Surgeon: Dr. C. D. F. Jensen
Judge Advocate: Lowell P. Mickelwait
Measurer: Edwin Monk
Assistant Measurer: James Paterson, Jr.
Librarian: Dwight Benton
Committee Chairs
Membership: Richard Froboese
Social: John O. Warren
Entertainment: E. R. Raphael
House: John Kucher
Regatta: McCormick Mehan
Powerboat: E. G. Watson
Sailboat: Allen B. Engle
Finance: C. L. Egtvedt
Moorings: Tom Owen
Advisory: H. W. McCurdy
Junior Advisory: Eustace Vynne, Sr.
Publicity: M. M. Rinearson
Yearbook: George Stroble
Barnacle Bill: William R. Hedley
Binnacle Editor: J. Swift Baker
Junior Officers
Commodore: Eustace Vynne, Jr.
Vice Commodore: Ames Cohan
Secretary-Treasurer: Patricia Parker
Fleet Captain: Frank Moegling
SYC Unit of King County American Red Cross
Chairman: Mrs. J. F. Unicume
Secretary-Treasurer: Mrs. M. M. Rinearson
Sewing Co-Chairmen: Mrs. E. R. Raphael
Mrs. John W. Kucher
Knitting Chairman: Miss Noel Watson

1943

Commodore: E. Roy Raphael
Vice Commodore: Allen B. Engle
Rear Commodore: E. G. Watson
Secretary: Eugene Kolb
Treasurer: John C. Warburton
Directors: Thomas W. Owen
George H. Parsons
Eustace Vynne, Sr.
John W. Kucher
Jerry Bryant
Middleton M. Chism
Roy N. Berry
Arthur M. Russell
J. F. Unicume
Fleet Captain: Raymond C. Krueger
Fleet Surgeon: Dr. Charles B. Ward
Judge Advocate: Lowell P. Mickelwait
Measurer: Edwin Monk
Librarian: William Hedley
Committee Chairs
Membership: Harold Murray
Social: Mrs. J. F. Unicume
Entertainment: L. A. Robinson
House: J. W. Kucher
Regatta: Norman Blanchard, Jr.
Powerboat: R. C. Krueger
Sailboat: Bill Blethen, Jr.
Finance: Paul Webb
Moorings: J. D. Sparks
Advisory: R. S. Macfarlane
Junior Advisory: Eustace Vynne

Publicity: M. M. Rinearson
Yearbook: R. S. Moore
Barnacle Bill: William R. Hedley
Binnacle Editor: Miles S. Johns
Junior Commodore: Miss Patricia Parker
Red Cross Unit Chairman: Mrs. J. F. Unicume

1944

Commodore: Allen B. Engle
Vice Commodore: E. G. Watson
Rear Commodore: Roy N. Berry
Secretary: Harold B. Murray
Treasurer: Jack C. Warburton
Directors: John W. Kucher
Jerry Bryant
Middleton M. Chism
John L. Locke
Arthur M. Russell
J. F. Unicume
Lawrence C. Calvert
Keith G. Fisken
Aubrey A. Naef
Fleet Captain: Ralph James
Fleet Surgeon: Dr. H. E. Nichols
Judge Advocate: Robert S. Macfarlane
Measurer: Edwin Monk
Assistant Measurer: Norman Blanchard, Jr.
Librarian: William Hedley

Committee Chairs

Membership: Aubrey A. Naef
Entertainment: Arthur M. Russell
Dining Room: E. G. Watson
Club Grounds: John W. Kucher
Clubhouse: Roy N. Berry
Marine Room: Jack C. Warburton
Regatta: Jerry Bryant
Powerboat: J. F. Unicume
Sailboat: John L. Locke
Moorings: Lawrence Calvert
Finance: Keith G. Fisken
Advisory: E. R. Raphael
Junior Advisory: Middleton M. Chism
Publicity: Middleton M. Chism
Club Luncheon: Charles G. Schaak
Yearbook: Roy N. Berry
Binnacle Editor: C. S. Cumins
Barnacle Bill: William Hedley
Red Cross Unit: Mrs. James Unicume

Junior Officers

Commodore: Roy Raphael, Jr.
Vice Commodore: Don Rottler
Secretary-Treasurer: Eugene Corbally
Fleet Captain: Davie Stomberg

1945

Commodore: Allen B. Engle
Vice Commodore: Roy N. Berry
Rear Commodore: John L. Locke
Secretary: Harold B. Murray
Treasurer: John C. Warburton
Directors: Norman Blanchard, Jr.
Arthur M. Russell
J. F. Unicume
Lawrence C. Calvert
Keith G. Fisken
Aubrey A. Naef
Jerry Bryant
H. W. McCurdy
C. E. McKillop
Fleet Captain: Albert E. Horn, Jr.
Fleet Surgeon: Dr. Torleif Torland
Judge Advocate: Robert S. Macfarlane
Measurer: Edwin Monk
Assistant Measurer: Norman Blanchard, Jr.
Librarian: B. K. Campbell

Committee Chairs

Membership: Aubrey A. Naef
Social: Mr. and Mrs. Arthur Russell
Dining Room: Jerry Bryant
Grounds: James F. Unicume
Maintenance: Roy N. Berry
Marine Room: Carl F. Zecher
Regatta: Norman Blanchard, Jr.
Powerboat: Lawrence C. Calvert
Sailboat: John L. Locke
Moorings: H. W. McCurdy
Finance: Keith G. Fisken
Advisory: Robert S. Macfarlane
Junior Advisory: Norman Blanchard, Jr.
Publicity: Jerry Bryant
Club Luncheon: Charles G. Schaak
Yearbook: C. E. McKillop
Binnacle Editor: Richard Byington
Barnacle Bill: William Hedley
Port Madison: Middleton M. Chism
J. F. Unicume
Red Cross Unit: Mrs. James F. Unicume

Junior Officers

Commodore: A. W. Pratt
Honorary Commodore: Frederick C. Harley
Vice Commodore: John Rottler
Secretary-Treasurer: Eileen Berry

1946

Commodore: James F. Unicume
Vice Commodore: John L. Locke
Rear Commodore: Albert Horn, Jr.
Secretary: Harold B. Murray
Treasurer: John C. Warburton
Directors: Lawrence C. Calvert
Keith Fisken
Aubrey A. Naef
Jerry Bryant
H. W. McCurdy
C. E. McKillop
John O. Warren
Orville Borgerson
Norman Blanchard, Jr.
Fleet Captain: John Soderberg
Fleet Surgeon: Dr. A. C. Jorden
Judge Advocate: Robert S. Macfarlane
Historian: Daniel Pratt
Measurer: Edwin Monk
Assistant Measurers: J. A. Troxell
Marshall Perrow
Librarian: Calmar M. McCune

Committee Chairs

Membership: Aubrey A. Naef
Social: Mr. and Mrs. Orville Borgersen
House: Albert Horn, Jr.
Regatta: Norman Blanchard, Jr.
Sailboat: John Warren
Powerboat: Jerry Bryant
Mooring: H. W. McCurdy
Finance: Keith Fisken
Advisory: Allen Engle
Publicity: Richard Crosby
Club Luncheon: Charles G. Schaak
Clubhouse: John L. Locke
Yearbook: Charles McKillop
Binnacle Editor: Paul Wood
Barnacle Bill: William R. Hedley
Port Madison: Russell Gibson
Middleton Chism
Red Cross Unit: Mrs. F. A. Harvey
Junior Advisory: Norman Blanchard, Jr.

Junior Officers

Commodore: A. W. Pratt
Vice Commodore: Joe Pendergast, Jr.
Secretary-Treasurer: Patricia Woodruff
Social Chairman: Eileen Berry

1947

Commodore: James F. Unicume
Vice Commodore: John W. Rumsey
Rear Commodore: Keith Fisken
Secretary: Paul E. Wood
Treasurer: Jack C. Warburton
Directors: Jerry Bryant
H. W. McCurdy
C. E. McKillop
John O. Warren
Orville Borgersen
Norman Blanchard, Jr.
Aubrey A. Naef
J. Adron Troxell
Eustace Vynne, Jr.
Fleet Captain: J. Lang Hyde
Fleet Surgeon: Dr. Philip R. Smith
Judge Advocate: Robert S. Macfarlane
Historian: Daniel Pratt
Measurer: J. Adron Troxell
Assistant Measurers: Marshall Perrow
Frank Blumberg
Librarian: Ben Campbell

Committee Chairs

Advisory: Allen B. Engle
Junior Advisory: Eustace Vynne, Jr.
Barnacle Bill: William R. Hedley
Binnacle Editor: Paul Wood
Club Grounds: Norman Blanchard, Jr.
Club Lunch: Charles Schaak
Club Plans: Mr. and Mrs. John Burnett
Finance: Kenneth Metcalf
House: Keith Fisken
Maintenance: Ralf Decker
Marine Room: Arthur Warnell
Membership: Aubrey A. Naef
Mooring: H. W. McCurdy
Port Madison: John W. Rumsey
Powerboat: Jerry Bryant
Publicity: Ray Krantz
Regatta: Eustace Vynne
Sailboat: John Warren
Howard Richmond
Social: Mr. and Mrs. Orville Borgerson
Yearbook: Marvin S. Allyn

Junior Officers

Commodore: Frederic Graff
Vice Commodore: Robert Cloes
Secretary: June Hill
Social Chairman: Dorothy Barrett
Honorary Commodore: R. A. Osborne

1948

Commodore: Arthur M. Russell
Vice Commodore: Jack C. Warburton
Rear Commodore: John Soderberg
Secretary: Joseph E. Pendergast
Treasurer: John E. Cannon
Directors: John O. Warren
Orville Borgersen
Norman Blanchard, Jr.
Aubrey A. Naef
J. Adron Troxell
Eustace Vynne, Jr.
Anderson S. Joy
Howard Richmond
G. Stewart Marlatt
Fleet Captain: F. A. Harvey
Fleet Surgeon: Dr. Merrill Shaw
Judge Advocate: Frank D. James, Jr.
Historian/Librarian: Daniel L. Pratt
Measurer: Ralph S. Russell
Assistant Measurers: Ames Cohan
Jack Lidral
Robert Olds

Committee Chairs

Advisory: James F. Unicume
Junior Advisory: Eustace Vynne, Jr.
Barnacle Bill: William R. Hedley
Binnacle Editor: Paul E. Wood
Club Grounds: Richard Byington
Club Luncheon: Charles Schaak
Club Plans: Mr. and Mrs. John A. Burnett
Finance: Keith Fisken
House: Ralf E. Decker
Dining Room: Joseph E. Pendergast
Marine Room: Ronald J. Frizzell
Membership: Charles Schaak

Mooring:	J. Adron Troxell
Port Madison:	Russell Gibson
Powerboat:	Philip Luther
Publicity:	Ray Krantz
Regatta:	Conrad Knutson
Sailboat:	Robert Denny Watt
Social:	Mr. and Mrs. Robert Condon
Yearbook:	Marshall W. Perrow
Junior Officers	
Commodore:	Frederic Graff
Vice Commodore:	Douglas Foster
Secretary:	Marilyn Hovland
Social Chairman:	Anne Byington
Honorary Commodore:	Eustace Vynne, Jr.
Rear Commodore:	Frank Hopkins
Treasurer:	Gibson Gholson
Fleet Captain:	C. Harrington Schiff

1949

Commodore:	Charles R. Olmstead
Vice Commodore:	Orville Borgersen
Rear Commodore:	John O. Warren
Secretary:	Robert W. Condon
Treasurer:	Frank D. James
Directors:	Eustace Vynne, Jr. Frank Hawkins Aubrey A. Naef Anderson S. Joy Howard E. Richmond G. Stewart Marlatt Joseph Pendergast Conrad Knutson Tom Tyrer
Fleet Captain:	Conrad Knutson
Fleet Surgeon:	Dr. Robert Rutherford
Judge Advocate:	Calmar McCune
Historian/Librarian:	Daniel Pratt
Measurer:	Ben Seaborn
Committee Chairs	
Advisory:	Arthur Russell
Junior Advisory:	Eustace Vynne, Jr.
Binnacle Editor:	Marshall Perrow
Club Operation:	G. Stewart Marlatt
Finance:	Keith Fisken
Club Plans:	Ralf Decker
Club Luncheons:	Charles Schaak
Membership:	Charles Schaak
Mooring:	Aubrey A. Naef
Port Madison:	Russell Gibson
Powerboat:	Tom Tyrer
Public Relations:	Jerry Bryant
Publicity:	Frank Hiscock
Regatta:	Anderson S. Joy
Sailboat:	John O. Warren
Social Affairs:	Dr. and Mrs. William E. Merrill
Yearbook:	Norman Blanchard, Jr.
Junior Officers	
Commodore:	Tom McCurdy
Vice Commodore:	Gibson Gholson
Rear Commodore:	Bill Laney
Secretary:	Margaret Hovland
Treasurer:	Margery Graff

1950

Commodore:	Tom D. Tyrer
Vice Commodore:	Dr. R. Philip Smith
Rear Commodore:	Robert Condon
Secretary:	John W. Day
Treasurer:	Jack Warburton
Trustees:	Anderson S. Joy Howard Richmond G. Stewart Marlatt Joseph Pendergast Conrad Knutson Kenneth Metcalf Russell Gibson John W. Kucher Dolph Zubick
Fleet Captain:	Conrad Knutson
Fleet Surgeon:	Dr. Carl D. Jensen
Judge Advocate:	James M. Ballard
Measurer:	Middleton M. Chism
Assistant Measurers:	Edwin Monk Ralf Decker Norman Blanchard, Jr. Nils Rosenberg
Historian/Librarian:	Quent Williams
Committee Chairs	
Advisory:	Charles R. Olmstead
House:	Robert W. Condon
Membership:	Joseph Pendergast
Press:	Ray Krantz
Regatta:	Dr. R. Phil Smith
Powerboat:	Frank Morris
Sailboat:	Howard Richmond
Junior Advisory:	Eustace Vynne, Jr.
Entertainment:	Mr. and Mrs. Stewart Marlatt
Finance:	Keith Fisken
Mooring/Dock:	Allen B. Engle
Yearbook:	Paul Wood Frank Calvert
Clubhouse Plan:	John W. Kucher
Club Luncheons:	Charles G. Schaak
Port Madison:	Harold Murray Russ Gibson
Binnacle Editor:	W. Eyrle Day
Bylaw Revise	Irving Linnell
Lipton/Isherwood Races:	Anderson S. Joy C. W. Stimson Row W. Corbett
Opening Day:	Lawrence Calvert
Junior Officers	
Commodore:	Louis William Roebke
Vice Commodore:	James England
Rear Commodore:	Des Kreger
Secretary:	Donna Cooney
Treasurer:	Joyce Wiley
Fleet Captain:	William Crayne
Social Chairman:	Margery Graff

1951

Commodore:	Dr. R. Philip Smith
Vice Commodore:	Lawrence Calvert
Rear Commodore:	Howard Richmond
Secretary:	Frank Hiscock
Treasurer:	Jack Warburton
Trustees:	Joseph Pendergast Conrad Knutson Frank D. James Russell Gibson John W. Kucher Dolph Zubick Middleton M. Chism Anderson S. Joy Stanley S. Sayres
Fleet Captain:	Conrad Knutson
Fleet Surgeon:	Dr. A. J. Bowles
Judge Advocate:	Daniel B. Trefethen, Jr.
Measurer:	Middleton M. Chism
Historian:	Daniel L. Pratt
Librarian:	Quent Williams
Committee Chairs	
Advisory:	Charles R. Olmstead
House:	Russell Gibson
Membership:	Joseph Pendergast
Press:	Frank Hiscock
Regatta:	Howard Richmond
Sailboat:	Middleton M. Chism
Powerboat:	Frank Morris
Junior Advisor:	E. Edison Kennell
Entertainment:	Mr. and Mrs. John W. Day
Finance:	Kenneth Metcalf
Mooring/Dock:	R. H. Byington
Clubhouse Plans:	John W. Kucher
Yearbook:	Paul Wood Frank Calvert
Club Luncheon:	Charles G. Schaak
Port Madison:	Dan Trefethen
Public Relations:	Frank D. James
Binnacle Editor:	Paul E. Wood
Leschi Station:	Ernest Banner
Photographic:	Dolph Zubick
Lipton and Isherwood:	Anderson S. Joy C. W. Stimson
Opening Day:	Lawrence Calvert
Gold Cup:	Jerry Bryant
Women's Group President:	Norma Russell
Junior Officers	
Commodore:	C. James England
Vice Commodore:	Thomas Dupar
Rear Commodore:	Denny Thorlakson
Treasurer:	Evelyn Schmidt
Secretary:	Janet Halder
Fleet Captain:	Miles McCoy
Social Chairman:	Margery Graff
Honorary Commodore:	Middleton M. Chism

1952

Commodore:	R. Philip Smith
Vice Commodore:	Lawrence Calvert
Rear Commodore:	Conrad Knutson
Secretary:	Anderson S. Joy
Treasurer:	Jack Warburton
Directors:	Russell Gibson John W. Kucher Dolph Zubick M. M. Chism Frank D. James Stanley S. Sayres Ray C. Anderson Jerry Bryant Frank Calvert
Fleet Captain:	Howard Richmond
Fleet Surgeon:	Dr. Dean Parker
Judge Advocate:	Daniel B. Trefethen, Jr.
Measurer:	J. Adron Troxell
Historian:	Daniel Pratt
Librarian:	Quent Williams
Committee Chairs	
Advisory:	Charles Olmstead
Audit:	John Simpson
House Planning and Operations:	John W. Kucher
Press and Publicity:	Conrad Knutson
Regatta:	Middleton Chism
Sailboat:	Howard Richmond
Powerboat:	Larry Norton
Membership:	Lawrence Calvert
Junior Advisory:	Eustace Vynne, Jr.
Entertainment:	Mr. and Mrs. John W. Day
Finance:	Ken Metcalf
Mooring and Dock:	Russ Gibson
Port Madison:	Ralf Decker
Opening Day:	Ray Anderson Dolph Zubick
Gold Cup:	Jerry Bryant
PIYA and PCYA:	Conrad Knutson
Interclub Association Representative:	F. A. Harvey
Trophy:	Ken Metcalf
Small Boat Race:	Robertson Ross
Leschi Station:	Reidar Gjolme
Yearbook:	Paul Wood Frank Calvert
Large Boat Race:	James H. Moffett, Jr.
Protest:	Anderson S. Joy
Women's Group President:	Norma Russell
Junior Commodore:	Denny Thorlakson

1953

Commodore:	Frank D. James
Vice Commodore:	Frank Calvert
Rear Commodore:	Larry Norton
Secretary:	Anderson S. Joy
Treasurer:	Jack Warburton
Directors:	M. M. Chism Stanley S. Sayres Ray C. Anderson Jerry Bryant James H. Moffett, Jr.

	Dr. Carlton Powers
	John H. Simpson
	Howard Richmond
	Conrad Knutson
Fleet Captain:	Lawrence Calvert
Fleet Surgeon:	Dr. Eugene L. Kidd
Judge Advocate:	Harry B. Jones, Jr.
Measurer:	John P. Lidral
Historian:	Daniel Pratt
Librarian:	Quent Williams
Committee Chairs	
Advisory:	Dr. R. Philip Smith
Audit:	John Simpson
House Planning and Operations:	Frank Calvert
Press and Publicity:	Conrad Knutson
Regatta:	Kenneth Metcalf
Sailboat (Steering):	Dr. George Horton
Large Boat:	James H. Moffett, Jr.
Small Boat:	Dr. Irving Anderson
Women's Group President:	Mrs. Arthur M. Russell
Powerboat:	Reuben Tarte
Membership:	Larry Norton
Junior Advisory:	Paul Morris
Entertainment:	Dr. and Mrs. Charles Stipp
Finance:	Dietrich Schmitz
Mooring and Dock:	Arthur Hedderly Smith
Port Madison:	Robert W. Condon
Opening Day Admiral:	Reuben Tarte
Vice Admiral:	T. W. Wheeler, Jr.
Gold Cup:	Howard Richmond
PIYA Council:	M. M. Chism
Interclub Association Representative:	Dr. R. Philip Smith
Trophy:	Daniel B. Trefethen, Jr.
Leschi Station:	Hollis Farwell
Yearbook:	Thomas E. Wood
Protest:	Holden Withington
Thursday Luncheon:	Charles G. Schaak
Binnacle Editor:	Paul E. Wood
Women's Group President:	Norma Russell
Junior Commodore:	Don Calvert

1954

Commodore:	Middleton M. Chism
Vice Commodore:	Reuben J. Tarte
Rear Commodore:	Howard E. Richmond
Secretary:	Anderson S. Joy
Treasurer:	Jack Warburton
Trustees:	Ray C. Anderson
	Jerry Bryant
	Dr. Charles Stipp
	James H. Moffett
	Dr. Carlton Powers
	John H. Simpson
	Lawrence Calvert
	C. Spencer Clark
	Conrad Knutson
Fleet Captain:	Dr. George Horton
Fleet Surgeon:	Dr. R. N. Rutherford
Judge Advocate:	Harry B. Jones, Jr.
Measurer:	John P. Lidral
Historian:	John Graham
Librarian:	Quent Williams
Club Manager:	Ralph E. Rider
Committee Chairs	
Advisory:	Judge Frank D. James
Audit:	John Simpson
House Planning:	John Graham, Jr.
House Operation:	Dr. Carlton J. Powers
Press and Publicity:	Conrad Knutson
Regatta:	A. D. Sherwood
Sailboat Steering:	Harbine Monroe
Large Boat:	Tom W. Wheeler, Jr.
Small Boat:	Frank Hiscock
Jr. Educational Program:	Frank Hiscock
Powerboat:	Maurice Vining
Membership:	Lawrence Calvert
Junior Advisory:	Paul Morris
Entertainment:	Mr. and Mrs. Don Cooney
Finance:	Dietrich Schmitz
Mooring and Dock:	J. A. Troxell
Port Madison:	Robert W. Condon
Opening Day:	Tom W. Wheeler, Jr.
Gold Cup:	Howard Richmond
PIYA Interclub Association:	Frank Morris
Trophy:	Daniel B. Trefethen, Jr.
Yearbook:	Thomas E. Wood
Protest:	A. Talcott Ostrander
Thursday Luncheon:	Charles G. Schaak
Binnacle Editor:	Paul E. Wood
Barnacle Bill:	F. C. Hellenthal
Junior Commodore:	John Hyde
Women's Group President:	Jo Gibson

1955

Commodore:	John A. Soderberg
Vice Commodore:	Russell Gibson
Rear Commodore:	Daniel B. Trefethen, Jr.
Secretary:	Anderson S. Joy
Treasurer:	James H. Moffett, Jr.
Trustees:	Harry B. Jones, Jr.
	Dr. Carlton Powers
	John H. Simpson
	Middleton M. Chism
	C. Spencer Clark
	Conrad Knutson
	Dr. George P. Horton
	Dr. Charles G. Stipp
	Don Cooney
Fleet Captain:	Marco J. Magnano
Fleet Surgeon:	Dr. William J. Stellwagen
Judge Advocate:	Chester C. Adair
Measurer:	John P. Lidral
Historian:	John Graham
Librarian:	Quent Williams
Club Manager:	Ralph E. Rider
Women's Group President:	Jo Gibson
Committee Chairs	
Advisory:	Middleton M. Chism
Audit:	Melvin Borgersen
House Planning:	John Graham, Jr.
House Operation:	Dr. George P. Horton
Press and Publicity:	John Ford
Sailboat Steering:	Robert W. Hubner
Large Boat Regatta:	Robert W. Condon
Small Boat Regatta:	Eustace Vynne, Jr.
Junior Program:	Robert D. Watt
Powerboat:	Stanley E. Youngs
Membership:	Lawrence Calvert
	C. Spencer Clark
Junior Advisory:	Ernest A. Banner
Social Affairs:	Mr. and Mrs. Richard Cahan
Finance:	Dietrich Schmitz
Mooring and Dock:	M. Phil Butler
Port Madison:	Wallace L. Ovens
Opening Day Admiral:	Dr. Dean Parker
Vice Admiral:	John Harvey
Gold Cup:	Don Cooney
PIYA Interclub:	Dr. J. Wayne Graham
Trophy:	John W. Day
Yearbook:	J. Lang Hyde
Protest:	Don H. Amick
Thursday Luncheon:	Charles Schaak
Greeters:	Dr. Michael Kennedy
Binnacle Editor:	Daniel B. Trefethen, Jr.
Barnacle Bill:	F. C. Hellenthal
Junior Commodore:	Michael Butler

1956

Commodore:	Howard E. Richmond
Vice Commodore:	Anderson S. Joy
Rear Commodore:	Dr. Carlton J. Powers
Secretary:	Daniel B. Trefethen, Jr.
Treasurer:	James H. Moffett, Jr.
Trustees:	C. Spencer Clark
	Conrad Knutson
	Chester C. Adair
	Dr. George P. Horton
	Dr. Charles G. Stipp
	Don L. Cooney
	Marco Magnano
	Keith Fisken
	M. Phil Butler
Fleet Captain:	T. W. Wheeler, Jr.
Fleet Surgeon:	Dr. Henry B. Garrigues
Judge Advocate:	Harry B. Jones, Jr.
Measurer:	John P. Lidral
Historian:	Roy W. Corbett
Librarian:	Quent Williams
Club Manager:	Ralph E. Rider
Committee Chairs	
Advisory:	John A. Soderberg
Audit:	John H. Simpson
Barnacle Bill:	Fritz C. Hellenthal
Binnacle Editor:	Daniel B. Trefethen, Jr.
Entertainment:	Mr. and Mrs. Dale Gaeth
Finance:	Dietrich Schmitz
Greeters:	Michael Kennedy
House Operations:	Marco Magnano
Interclub Association:	Middleton M. Chism
Junior Advisory:	J. Rance Morris
Membership:	C. Spencer Clark
Mooring and Docks:	James G. McCurdy
Opening Day Admiral:	Sidney D. Campbell
Vice Admiral:	Lloyd Johnson
Port Madison:	Wallace L. Ovens
Powerboat:	M. Phil Butler
Press and Publicity:	John Ford
Race Committee:	Anderson S. Joy
Large Boat Regatta:	Don Amick
Small Boat Regatta:	Eustace Vynne, Sr.
Protest:	John C. McKenzie
Sailboat Steering:	Robert W. Condon
Seafair Regatta:	Don L. Cooney
Thursday Luncheon:	Charles G. Schaak
Trophy:	Peter J. McTavish
Yearbook:	J. Lang Hyde
Women's Group President:	Anne Foster
Junior Commodore:	Michael Butler

1957

Commodore:	Anderson S. Joy
Vice Commodore:	T. Dayton Davies
Rear Commodore:	T. Harbine Monroe
Secretary:	Daniel B. Trefethen, Jr.
Treasurer:	Chester C. Adair
Trustees:	Dr. George P. Horton
	Dr. Charles G. Stipp
	Don L. Cooney
	Marco Magnano
	Keith Fisken
	M. Phil Butler
	William E. Boeing, Jr.
	Robert H. Hyde
	Wells F. Ostrander
Fleet Captain:	A. Douglas Sherwood
Fleet Surgeon:	Dr. Frank C. Henry
Judge Advocate:	Harry B. Jones, Jr.
Measurer:	Ralph Russell
Historian:	Roy W. Corbett
Librarian:	Quent Williams
Club Manager:	V. Russ Hoppe
Junior Commodore:	Alfred H. Hyde
Committee Chairs	
Advisory:	Howard E. Richmond
Audit:	John H. Simpson
Barnacle Bill:	Fritz C. Hellenthal
Binnacle Editor:	Daniel B. Trefethen, Jr.
Entertainment:	Mr. and Mrs. Don C. Whitworth
Finance:	Dietrich Schmitz
Gold Cup:	L. Ross Merrill
Greetings:	Albert J. Lilygren
House:	Don L. Cooney
Interclub:	M. Phil Butler
Junior Advisory:	Ben Benton
Membership:	Conrad Knutson
Mooring/Docks:	James G. McCurdy
Opening Day Admiral:	Joseph Mesdag
Vice Admiral:	James Stirrat

PIYA Regatta: T. W. Wheeler, Jr.
Port Madison: Wallace L. Ovens
Powerboat: R. M. Black
Publicity: T. W. Wheeler, Jr.
Race Committee: T. Harbine Monroe
Large Boat: Dr. Charles G. Stipp
Small Boat: James S. Scully
Protest: Judge Frank D. James
Sailboat: A. Douglas Sherwood
Slo-Motion
Preservation Fund: Dr. R. Philip Smith
Thursday Lunches: Charles G. Schaak
Trophy: Peter J. McTavish
Yearbook: Daniel B. Trefethen, Jr.
Women's Group President: Anne Foster

1958

Commodore: T. Dayton Davies
Vice Commodore: Robert W. Condon
Rear Commodore: Michael E. Kennedy
Secretary: Daniel B. Trefethen, Jr.
Treasurer: Chester C. Adair
Trustees: M. Phil Butler
Marco Magnano
D. E. Skinner
William E. Boeing, Jr.
Robert H. Hyde
Wells F. Ostrander
James G. McCurdy
Wallace L. Ovens
A. Douglas Sherwood
Fleet Captain: John Ford
Fleet Surgeon: Dr. Eugene L. Kidd
Judge Advocate: Robert Graham
Measurer: Ralph Russell
Historian: Roy W. Corbett
Librarian: Quent Williams
Club Manager: V. Russ Hoppe
Junior Commodore: Alfred Hyde
Committees Chairs
Advisory: Anderson S. Joy
Audit: John H. Simpson
Barnacle Bill: F. C. Hellenthal
Binnacle Editor: R. H. Byington
Budget: Chester C. Adair
Entertainment: Mr. and Mrs. Paul S. Morris
Finance: Dietrich Schmitz
Gold Cup: Robert H. Hyde
Greeters: A. Linus Pearson
House: Donol F. Hedlund
Interclub: Middleton M. Chism
Junior Advisory: Ben Benton
Marine Traffic and Safety: D. E. Skinner
Membership: Herbert B. Johnson
Mile Trails: Arthur S. Shorey
Mooring and Docking: James G. McCurdy
Opening Day Admiral: James R. Stirrat
Vice Admiral: Jim McGinnis
Port Madison: Wallace L. Ovens
Powerboat: Allen P. Green, Jr.
Press: William M. Burke
Race: Robert W. Condon
Large Boat: Don Whitworth
Small Boat: Wayne Murray, Jr.
Protest: John C. McKenzie
Sailboat: John Ford
Speed Boat: Robert H. Hyde
Thursday Luncheon: Charles G. Schaak
Trophy: Lawrence E. Wick
Yearbook: Dr. Carlton J. Powers
Zecher Memorial: Lawrence Calvert
Women's Group President: Anne Foster

1959

Commodore: Robert W. Condon
Vice Commodore: M. Phil Butler
Rear Commodore: Dr. Byron Ward
Secretary: John Ford
Treasurer: Peter J. McTavish
Fleet Captain: James H. Moffett
Staff Captain: Marco J. Magnano
Trustees: Robert Hyde
Wells F. Ostrander
Paul Morris
James G. McCurdy
Wallace Ovens
A. Douglas Sherwood
Chester C. Adair
C. E. Cornell
Frank Hiscock
Fleet Surgeon: Dr. William E. Merrill
Judge Advocate: Robert Graham
Measurer: John P. Lidral
Historian: Roy Corbett
Librarian: Quent Williams
Club Manager: V. Russ Hoppe
Junior Commodore: Robert L. Pace
Women's Group President: Hazel Bloss
Committee Chairs
Advisory: T. Dayton Davies
Audit: John Simpson
Barnacle Bill: Daniel B. Trefethen, Jr.
Binnacle Editor: Harry H. McGuane
Budget: Peter J. McTavish
Entertainment: Mr. and Mrs. Stanley Youngs
Finance: Dietrich Schmitz
Greeters: Bill T. Stewart
Gold Cup: Don Amick
House: James J. McGinnis
Interclub: Middleton Chism
Junior Advisory: Ben Benton
Marine Traffic and Safety: D. E. Skinner
Membership: Don Kennedy
Mooring and Docking: V. R. Scheumann
Opening Day Admiral: James R. Stirrat
Vice Admiral: Jim Bryant
Admiralette: Jean Harthorn
Permanent Planning: Donol Hedlund
Port Madison: Frederick C. Peterson
Powerboat: Harold Hovland
Press: Richard E. Pulver
Race: Don Cooney
Large Boat: Stanley S. Martin
Small Boat: Frank Hiscock
Protest: Maurice Rattray, Jr.
Sailboat: Don Whitworth
Speed Boat: Don Amick
Thursday Luncheon: Charles Schaak
Trophy: Lawrence Wick
Yearbook: Robert L. Hass

1960

Commodore: M. Phil Butler
Vice Commodore: A. Douglas Sherwood
Rear Commodore: Harold Hovland
Secretary: Harry McGuane
Treasurer: Peter J. McTavish
Fleet Captain: Otis Lamson, Jr.
Staff Captain: Frederick C. Peterson
Trustees: James G. McCurdy
Wallace Ovens
Paul S. Morris
C. C. Adair
Cy Cornell
Frank Hiscock
Don Amick
Ben Benton
John Ford
Fleet Surgeon: Dr. Randolph P. Pillow
Judge Advocate: Robert W. Graham
Measurer: John P. Lidral
Historian: Roy Corbett
Librarian: Quent Williams
Club Manager: V. Russ Hoppe
Junior Commodore: Sheldon Bennett
Women's Group President: Ruth Harlan
Committee Chairs
Advisory: Robert W. Condon
Audit: John Simpson
Barnacle Bill: C. E. Cornell
Binnacle Editor: Ernest R. Cluck
Budget: Peter J. McTavish
Entertainment: George Heideman
Finance: Dietrich Schmitz
Greeters: Larry Wick
House Operations: James W. O'Brien
Interclub Delegate: Larry Wick
Junior Advisory: Phil S. Groves
Marine Traffic and Safety: Paul S. Morris
Membership: Don Kennedy
Mooring and Docks: Dr. Carlton J. Powers
Opening Day Admiral: Al J. Lilygren
Vice Admiral: Al McNichol
Admiralette: Virginia Cluck
Permanent Planning: M. M. Chism
Port Madison: Frederick C. Peterson
Powerboat: Harold D. Fowler
Press/Publicity: Bill T. Stewart
Race: Stan Martin
Large Boat: Dr. Richard Philbrick
Small Boat: Dr. Pierre R. Dow
Protest: Wells F. Ostrander
Sailboat: T. W. Wheeler, Jr.
Seafair: Don Amick
Speed Boat Race: Don Amick
Thursday Luncheon: Charles G. Schaak
Trophy: Charles Olmstead, Jr.
Yearbook: Sanford Skilton

1961

Commodore: M. Phil Butler
Vice Commodore: James G. McCurdy
Rear Commodore: Dr. Carlton Powers
Secretary: John Rottler
Treasurer: P. J. McTavish
Fleet Captain: Dr. Richard Philbrick
Staff Captain: Wallace Ovens
Trustees: C. C. Adair
Cy Cornell
Paul S. Morris
Don Amick
Ben Benton
John Ford
J. W. O'Brien
Harold Hovland
Otis Lamson, Jr.
Fleet Surgeon: Dr. Henry Garrigues
Judge Advocate: Robert W. Graham
Measurer: Ron McFarlane
Historian: Roy W. Corbett
Librarian: Quent Williams
Club Manager: V. Russ Hoppe
Junior Commodore: Dick Lilly
Women's Group President: Helen Ring
Committee Chairs
Advisory: Robert W. Condon
Audit: John H. Simpson
Barnacle Bill: R. B. Parmelee
Binnacle Editor: Jay B. Adams
Budget: P. J. McTavish
Entertainment: Mr. and Mrs. L. F. Harthorn
Finance: T. Dayton Davies
Greeters: Noel Caldwell
House: Harold Stack
Interclub: Sanford Skilton
Intermediate: Don Calvert
IPBA Delegates: T. Dayton Davies
Howard E. Richmond
Junior Advisory: Louis Pace
Large Boat: Walt Little
Marine Traffic: Wells Ostrander
Membership: Don Kennedy
Mooring/Docks: George Heideman
Opening Day Admiral: A. Linus Pearson
Vice Admiral: Noel Caldwell
Admiralette: Betty Stewart
Permanent Planning: C. C. Adair
Port Madison: Duane Culbertson
Powerboat: Howard E. Richmond
Publicity: Charles Erickson

Protest: Robert O. Sylvester
Race: Stan Martin
Small Boat: Dr. Pierre Dow
Thursday Lunch: Charles Schaak
Trophy: Charles Olmstead, Jr.
Yearbook: Muriel McLaren

1962

Commodore: John Ford
Vice Commodore: Dr. Carlton J. Powers
Rear Commodore: Dr. Richard C. Philbrick
Secretary: Frederick C. Peterson
Treasurer: John C. Rottler
Fleet Captain: Stanley S. Martin
Staff Captain: Wallace Ovens
Trustees Peter J. McTavish
Dr. Byron Ward
Paul S. Morris
James W. O'Brien
Harold Hovland
Otis Lamson
Don Amick
Ben Benton
George Morry
Fleet Surgeon: Dr. A. H. Bill, Jr.
Judge Advocate: Robert W. Graham
Measurer: Ron McFarlane
Historian: Roy W. Corbett
Librarian: Quent Williams
Club Manager: V. Russ Hoppe
Junior Commodore: Mary Hiltner
Women's Group President: Dorothy Hooper
Committee Chairs
Advisory: M. Phil Butler
Audit: John H. Simpson
Barnacle Bill: Daniel B. Trefethen, Jr.
Binnacle Editor: David S. Storey
Budget: John C. Rottler
Entertainment: Mr. and Mrs. Dick Croy
Finance: Aubrey A. Naef
Greeters: James D. Sparks
House: George Morry
Interclub: Harold Hovland
Intermediate: Michael R. Butler
IPBA Delegates: T. Dayton Davies
Frank Dunn
Dr. Carlton J. Powers
Junior Advisory: Louis Pace
Large Boat: Walt Little
Marine Traffic and Safety: Robert J. Cadranell
Membership: Cy Cornell
Moorings/Docks: Russ Gibson
Opening Day Admiral: James J. McGinnis
Vice Admiral: Tom Ables
Admiralette: Suzy Ward
Permanent Planning: R. W. Condon
PIYA Regatta: Robert O. Sylvester
Port Madison: Boris V. Korry
Powerboat: Frank Dunn
Press/Publicity: Charles Erickson
Protest: John C. McKenzie
Race: Wells F. Ostrander
Real Estate Advisor: John Schlagel
Sailboat Steering: Dr. Byron H. Ward
Small Boat: Howard Herrigel
Speed Boat: Con Knutson
Thursday Luncheon: Charles Schaak
Trophy: Al Crayne
Yearbook: Muriel McLaren
Club Activities, SYC Flotilla 24, USCG: Arthur Launder

1963

Commodore: Dr. Carlton J. Powers
Vice Commodore: Don Amick
Rear Commodore: James H. Moffett, Jr.
Secretary: Frederick C. Peterson
Treasurer: John C. Rottler
Fleet Captain: Ben Benton
Staff Captain: Wallace Ovens
Trustees: Stanley S. Martin
Con Knutson
Robert W. Graham
Peter J. McTavish
Dr. Byron Ward
Paul S. Morris
James W. O'Brien
Harold Hovland
Otis Lamson
Fleet Surgeon: Dr. C. S. Stone, Jr.
Judge Advocate: W. C. Anderson
Measurer: Ron McFarlane
Historian: Roy W. Corbett
Librarian: Quent Williams
Club Manager: V. Russ Hoppe
Women's Group President: Dorothy Scully
Junior Commodore: Dick Peterson
Committee Chairs
Advisory: John Ford
Audit: John Simpson
Barnacle Bill: Dr. E. B. Parmelee
Binnacle Editor: Ernest Cluck
Budget: John C. Rottler
Entertainment: Mr. and Mrs. George Heideman
Finance: Aubrey Naef
Greeters: Michael E. Kennedy
House: Andrew Hawley
Interclub Delegate: Robert W. Graham
Intermediates: Allan (Skip) Stewart
IPBA Delegate: Harold Hovland
Junior Advisory: Eustace Vynne, Jr.
Stanley E. Youngs
Marine Traffic and Safety: Sanford Skilton
Membership: Cy Cornell
Mooring/Docks: Russ Gibson
Opening Day Admiral: Bill T. Stewart
Vice Admiral: Dick Hoyt
Admiralette: Alice Korry Clark
Permanent Planning: Robert W. Graham
Port Madison: Vernon B. Hammer
Powerboat: Frank Dunn
Press, Publicity: Donald L. Thompson
Sailboat: Serge Becker
Thursday Luncheon: Charles Schaak
Trophy: Al Crayne
Yearbook: Muriel McLaren
Club Activities, SYC Flotilla 24, USCG: Phil Duryee

1964

Commodore: Don Amick
Vice Commodore: Harold Hovland
Rear Commodore: Ben Benton
Secretary: Frederick C. Peterson
Treasurer: John C. Rottler
Fleet Captain: Jerry Bryant
Staff Captain: C. C. Adair
Trustees George Heideman
Henry Kamstra
Frank M. Dunn
Stanley S. Martin
Con Knutson
Robert W. Graham
Peter J. McTavish
Dr. Byron Ward
Paul S. Morris
Fleet Surgeon: C. Robert Smith, M.D.
Judge Advocate: W. C. Anderson
Measurer: Ron McFarlane
Historian: Roy W. Corbett
Librarian: Quent Williams
Club Manager: V. Ross Hoppe
Women's Group President: Jean Harthorn
Junior Commodore: Kenny Fielding
Committee Chairs
Advisory: Carlton J. Powers
Audit: John Simpson
Barnacle Bill: James K. Bryant
Binnacle Editor: Ernest Cluck
Covered Moorage: Dr. C. J. Powers
Budget: John C. Rottler
Entertainment: Mr. and Mrs. James J. McGinnis
Finance: Clayton K. Watkins
Greeters: Herbert B. Johnson
House: Andrew D. Hawley
Interclub Delegate: Robert Graham
Intermediates: Frank Baker
Junior Advisory: D. B. (Ted) Martin
Marine Traffic and Safety: Ralph S. Russell
Membership: Charles G. Schaak
Mooring and Docks: Russ Gibson
Opening Day Admiral: Eric Wall
Vice Admiral: Skip Skinner
Admiralette: Betty Newell
Permanent Planning: Robert W. Graham
John Ford
Port Madison: Richard M. Black
Powerboat: Frank Bourque
Press and Publicity: Stanley E. Youngs
Sailboat: Dr. Richard C. Philbrick
Large Boat: Don L. Thompson
Small Boat: Howard Herrigel
Protest: Charles Olmstead, Jr.
Thursday Luncheon: Charles Schaak
Trophy: Robert J. Cadranell
Yearbook: David Storey
Club Activities, SYC Flotilla 24: Dr. J. W. Gallagher

1965

Commodore: Harold Hovland
Vice Commodore: Ben Benton
Rear Commodore: Frederick C. Peterson
Secretary: Paul S. Harris
Treasurer: Frank G. Bourque
Fleet Captain: Dr. Byron H. Ward
Staff Captain: Clayton K. Watkins
Trustees: George Heideman
Henry Kamstra
Frank M. Dunn
Stanley S. Martin
Conrad Knutson
Robert W. Graham
Richard M. Black
James J. McGinnis
Donald L. Thompson
Fleet Surgeon: Charles G. Stipp
Judge Advocate: Chester C. Adair
Measurer: Ron McFarlane
Historian: Roy W. Corbett
Librarian: R. H. Byington
Club Manager: Richard R. Reardon
Women's Group President: Shirlee Liberman
Junior Commodore: Jim Kearnes
Committee Chairs
Advisory: Donald H. Amick
Award (Zecher Memorial): Wallace Ovens
Barnacle Bill: Bill T. Stewart
Binnacle Editor: Frank E. James
Budget: Peter J. McTavish
Club Activities, Flotilla No. 24: Charles D. Cummins
Entertainment: Mr. and Mrs. Irvin F. Matson
Greeters: C. James England
House: John C. Rottler
Interclub Delegate: Robert Graham
Intermediates: James P. Erickson
IPBA Delegate: Robert Graham
Junior Advisory: Eric H. Wall
Marine Traffic and Safety: Charles D. Cummins
Measurer: Ronald A. McFarlane
Membership: Wallace L. Ovens
Models: Robert S. Carter
Mooring and Docking: Dr. Carlton J. Powers
Opening Day Admiral: James K. Bryant
Vice Admiral: Ralph Chambers
Admiralette: Eleanor Young
Permanent Planning: John Ford
Port Madison: John G. Schlagel
PIYA Representatives: Serge J. Becker

Garrett Horder
Tom Wheeler, Jr.
Powerboat: John R. Allen
Press and Publicity: Stanley E. Youngs
Sailboat: Wilbert C. Anderson
Large Boat: Walt Little
Small Boat: Robert M. Alexander
Protest: George C. Gunby
Speed Boat: Dr. Randolph P. Pillow
Trophy: John A. Baillargeon
Yearbook: Arthur Launder
Military Advisor to the Commodore: Cmdr. Otto R. Noetzelman, USNAS

1966

Commodore: Ben Benton
Vice Commodore: Frederick C. Peterson
Rear Commodore: Chester C. Adair
Secretary: Paul S. Morris
Treasurer: Frank G. Bourque
Fleet Captain: Wilbert C. Anderson
Staff Captain: Stanley Youngs
Trustees: George Heideman
Frank M. Dunn
Norman Blanchard
Richard M. Black
James J. McGinnis
Donald L. Thompson
John Rottler
Eric Wall
C. R. Wilcox
Fleet Surgeon: John P. Sauntry
Judge Advocate: C. M. McCune
Measurer: Ron McFarlane
Historian: Roy W. Corbett
Librarian: Richard H. Byington
Club Manager: Richard R. Reardon

Committee Chairs

Advisory: Harold Hovland
Barnacle Bill: Scott Field
Binnacle Editor: Frank E. James, Jr.
Budget: Peter McTavish
Club Activities, SYC Flotilla 24: Frank M. Dunn
Entertainment: Mr. and Mrs. Ev. Henry
Greeters: James D. Sparks
Albert J. Lilygren
House: Bill T. Stewart
Interclub Delegate: Robert Graham
IPBA Delegate: Jerry Bryant
Junior Advisory: Wayne Schuh
Marine Traffic and Safety: Frank M. Dunn
Membership: Wallace L. Ovens
Models (Half-Hull): Norman Blanchard
Mooring and Docks: Dr. Carlton J. Powers
Opening Day Admiral: Ralph F. Chambers
Vice-Admiral: J. Edmund Messett
Admiralette: Trudy Kamstra
Permanent Planning: Peter J. McTavish
Port Madison: Harold Murray
PIYA Reps: Serge Becker
Garrett Horder
Tom Wheeler, Jr.
Ron McFarlane
Powerboat: John R. Allen
Press and Publicity: Paul Dunstan
Sailboat: George Gunby
Large Boat: Joseph L. Williams
Small Boat: Robert M. Alexander
Protest: Caspar Clarke
Speed Boat: Dr. Randolph P. Pillow
Trophy: John F. O'Brien
Yearbook: Allen Stewart
Military Advisor to Commodore: Cmdr. Otto R. Noetzelman, USNAS
Women's Group President: Ann De Laurenti
Junior Commodore: Rick Martin

1967

Commodore: Frederick C. Peterson
Vice Commodore: Chester C. Adair
Rear Commodore: Wallace L. Ovens
Secretary: Paul S. Morris
Treasurer: Paul G. Bourque
Fleet Captain: J. C. Baillargeon, Jr.
Staff Captain: George Heideman
Trustees: James J. McGinnis
Donald L. Thompson
Stanley E. Youngs
John Rottler
C. R. Wilcox
Ray L. Eckmann
Peter J. McTavish
Harold B. Murray
Fleet Surgeon: Rodney Hearne, M.D.
Judge Advocate: Ernest R. Cluck
Measurer: Robert G. Page
Historian: Roy W. Corbett
Librarian: Dr. McCormick Mehan
Club Manager: Richard R. Reardon

Committee Chairs

Advisory: Ben Benton
Barnacle Bill: Jim Bryant
Binnacle Editor: Frank E. James, Jr.
Budget: Frank Bourque
Club Activities, SYC Flotilla 24: Dr. A. C. Jordan
Entertainment: Mr. and Mrs. Ev. Henry
Greeters: James D. Sparks
House: Homer F. Wickerd
Interclub Delegates: Robert Graham
Harold Hovland
Russell D. Amick
IPBA Delegate: Jerry Bryant
Junior Advisory: Wayne Schuh
Marine Traffic and Safety: Frank M. Dunn
Membership: John B. Stirrat
Models (Half Hull): Otis Lamson
Mooring and Docks: Dr. Carlton J. Powers
Opening Day Admiral: John R. Allen
Vice Admiral: Vernon B. Hammer
Admiralette: Betty Musson
Permanent Planning: Peter J. McTavish
Port Madison: C. R. (Cotton) Wilcox
PIYA Representatives: Serge Becker
Garrett Horder
Tom Wheeler, Jr.
Powerboat: Fred Haight
Press and Publicity: Dr. Michael E. Kennedy
Sailboat: Joseph L. Williams
Large Boat: Joseph L. Williams
Small Boat: Norman Cole
Protest: Caspar Clarke
Trophy: Earl Powell
Publicity: Harry McGuane
CYC Liaison: James Marta
Race Book: Ken Browne
Sailboat Advisory Board Delegate: Serge Becker
Speed Boat: Dr. Randolph Pillow
Trophy (Powerboats): Fred Haight
Trophy (Small Boats): Earl Powell
Yearbook: Allan Stewart
Women's Group President: Trudy R. Lane
Junior Commodore: Rowland Pearsall

1968

Commodore: Chester C. Adair
Vice Commodore: Wallace L. Ovens
Rear Commodore: Donald L. Thompson
Secretary: Paul S. Morris
Treasurer: Frank G. Bourque
Fleet Captain: Joseph L. Williams
Staff Captain: Richard Shorett, Sr.
Trustees: John R. Allen
John Rottler
C. R. Wilcox
Ray L. Eckmann
Peter J. McTavish
Harold B. Murray
W. C. Anderson
J. C. Baillargeon, Jr.
George Heideman
Fleet Surgeon: Jack Docter, M.D.
Judge Advocate: John Sylvester
Measurer: Robert G. Page
Librarian: Dr. McCormick Mehan
Historian: Roy W. Corbett
Armed Forces Advisor: Capt. William F. Dawson

Committee Chairs

Advisory: Frederick C. Peterson
House: Vernon B. Hammer
Membership: Robert R. Fox
Press: Donald W. Finlay
Trudy Lane
Ann Knutson
Sailboat: Philip G. Johnson
Powerboat: Edward R. Donohue
Speed Boat: Randolph P. Pillow
Junior Advisory: Keith W. Dearborn
Entertainment: Mr. and Mrs. Ev. Henry
Finance: E. E. Cushing
Mooring and Docking: Dr. Carlton J. Powers
Yearbook: Allan Stewart
Permanent Planning: George W. Heideman

Special Committees and Activities

Barnacle Bill: Jack Warburton
Binnacle Editor: Frank E. James, Jr.
Greeters: Brent R. Johnson
Models (Half Hull): James G. McCurdy
Marine Traffic and Safety: Frank M. Dunn
Men's Oyster Feed: Ernest R. Cluck
Men's Stag: Ralph F. Chambers
Opening Day Admiral: Fred Haight
Vice Admiral: Jack Chambers
Admiralette: Lois Dawson
Outstations: Leslie W. Eastman
Ropeyarn Sundays: James K. Bryant
Interclub Association: Harold Hovland
Russell D. Amick
IPBA Delegate: Jerry Bryant
PIYA, Vice Commodore: Wells Ostrander
Port Madison: Randall L. Schmoyer
U.S. Coast Guard Auxiliary, Commander: Robert C. Ellis
Women's Group President: Ellie Hammer
Junior Commodore: Rory Martin

1969

Commodore: Wallace L. Ovens
Vice Commodore: Donald L. Thompson
Rear Commodore: Richard H. Shorett, Sr.
Secretary: Paul S. Morris
Treasurer: Frank G. Bourque
Fleet Captain: Philip G. Johnson
Staff Captain: Fred H. Haight
Trustees: Ray L. Eckmann
Peter J. McTavish
Harold B. Murray
W. C. Anderson
George Heideman
John R. Allen
Don Cooney
Edward R. Donohue
Henry L. Kotkins
Fleet Surgeon: Robert L. Camber, M.D.
Judge Advocate: John Sylvester
Measurer: Robert G. Page
Librarian: Dr. McCormick Mehan
Historian: Roy W. Corbett
Armed Forces Advisor: Capt. William F. Dawson

Committee Chairs

Advisory: C. C. Adair
House: Walter S. Parks
Membership: William R. Neill, Jr.
Press: Donald Finlay
Trudy Lane
Ann Knutson
Sailboat: Robert M Helsell
Powerboat: Jack Henningsen

Speed Boat: Randolph P. Pillow, M.D.
Port Madison: Randall Schmoyer
Junior/Intermediate: Keith Dearborn
Entertainment: Mr. and Mrs. Cliff H. Liberman
Finance: E. E. Cushing
Mooring and Docks: Frank M. Dunn
Yearbook: William M. Burke
Permanent Planning: Peter J. McTavish
Special Committees and Activities
Barnacle Bill: Stephen Weeks, George Delaney
Binnacle Editor: Frank E. James
Greeters: Arden Steinhart
Models (Half Hull): James McCurdy
Marine Traffic and Safety: Dr. J. W. Gallagher
Men's Oyster Feed: Ernest R. Cluck
Men's Stag: Ernest R. Cluck
Opening Day Admiral: William F. (Bull) Dawson
Vice Admiral: Philip T. Tebb
Admiralette: Harriet Vesoja
Outstations: Leslie W. Eastman
Trophy: Robert E. Street
Interclub Association: Ray L. Eckmann, Hartney Oakes
IPBA Delegate: Richard Shorett
PCYA Commodore: Tom Wheeler, Jr.
PIYA Vice Commodore: Donald L. Thompson
U.S. Coast Guard Auxiliary Commander: Edward R. Donohue
Women's Group President: Elaine E. Kidd
Junior Commodore: Jan M. Kennaugh

1970

Commodore: Donald L. Thompson
Vice Commodore: Richard H. Shorett, Sr.
Rear Commodore: Joseph L. Williams
Secretary: Thurston I. Lane
Treasurer: Frank G. Bourque
Fleet Captain: Douglas M. Fryer
Staff Captain: Walter S. Parks
Trustees: W. C. Anderson, George Heideman, John R. Allen, Don Cooney, Edward R. Donohue, Henry L. Kotkins, Fred Haight, Philip G. Johnson, Elmer Nordstrom
Fleet Surgeon: Robert L. Camber, M.D.
Judge Advocate: John Sylvester
Measurer: William E. Stinson
Librarian: Dr. McCormick Mehan
Historian: Norman C. Blanchard
Armed Forces Advisor: Capt. William F. Dawson
Women's Group President: Violet L. Corlis
Junior Commodore: John Kearnes
Committee Chairs
Advisory: Wallace L. Ovens
House: Frank H. Jefferson
Membership: Philip Luther
Press: Erik Peterson
Powerboat: Dr. Rodney B. Hearne
Speed Boat: Randolph P. Pillow, M.D.
Port Madison: Randall Schmoyer
Junior Advisory: Richard W. Peterson
Entertainment: Mr. and Mrs. Thurston Lane
Mooring and Docks: Frank M. Dunn
Yearbook: Edward R. Donohue
Permanent Planning: Ben Benton
Special Committees and Activities
Barnacle Bill: Stephen Weeks
Binnacle Editor: George Delaney
Greeters: Howard Bronson
Henry Island: E. E. Kennell
Models (Half Hull): Norman Blanchard, Richard Hooper
Opening Day Admiral: Paul S. Morris
Vice Admiral: Peter J. McTavish
Admiralette: Ellie Hammer
Outstations: Leslie W. Eastman
Trophy: Robert E. Street
Interclub Association: Ray L. Eckmann, Hartney Oakes
IPBA Delegate: Fred Haight
PCYA Rear Commodore: Serge Becker
PIYA Vice Commodore: Donald L. Thompson
U.S. Coast Guard Auxiliary Commander: Larry Mickelson
Carl F. Zecher Memorial Award: Frank Morris

1971

Commodore: Richard H. Shorett, Sr.
Vice Commodore: Joseph L. Williams
Rear Commodore: Peter J. McTavish
Secretary: Howard E. Lovejoy
Treasurer: Irvin F. Matson
Fleet Captain: Garrett Horder
Staff Captain: Leslie W. Eastman
Trustees: Don Cooney, Edward R. Donohue, Henry L. Kotkins, Fred Haight, Philip G. Johnson, Elmer Nordstrom, Loren C. Davidson, William F. Dawson, Douglas M. Fryer
Fleet Surgeon: Paul Betzold, M.D.
Judge Advocate: John Sylvester
Measurer: William E. Stinson
Librarian: George P. Horton
Historian: Norman C. Blanchard
Armed Forces Advisor: Capt. William F. Dawson
Women's Group President: Doris Marshall
Junior Commodore: Mark Laura
Committee Chairs
Advisory: Donald L. Thompson
House: Raymond J. Wachter
Membership: Philip Luther
Press: Donald Finlay
Sailboat: Douglas M. Fryer
Powerboat: John R. Allen
Speed Boat: Randolph P. Pillow, M.D.
Finance Committee: E. E. Cushing
Mooring and Docks: Frank M. Dunn
Permanent Planning: Harold Murray
Port Madison: Randall Schmoyer
Junior Advisory: Richard W. Peterson
Entertainment: Mr. and Mrs. Thurston Lane
Binnacle Editor: Serge Becker
Greeters: J. Del McCracken
Henry Island: G. Stewart Marlatt
Models (Half Hull): Norman Blanchard
Marine Anti-Pollution: Barrie Arnett, Harold Hovland
Marine Traffic and Safety: Phil Duryee
Men's Oyster Feed: Con Knutson
Opening Day Admiral: Con Knutson
Vice-Admiral: Frank G. Bourque
Admiralette: Mrs. Trudy Lane
Outstations: Philip G. Johnson
Trophy: William E. Bradshaw
Interclub Association: Ray L. Eckmann, Hartney Oakes
IPBA Delegates: John R. Allen, Anderson S. Joy
PCYA Vice-Commodore: Serge Becker
U.S. Coast Guard Auxiliary Flotilla #24 Commander: Bob O. Austin
PIYA Vice-Commodore: Richard H. Shorett
Barnacle Bill: Edward R. Donohue

1972

Commodore: Joseph L. Williams
Vice Commodore: Peter J. McTavish
Rear Commodore: Stanley S. Martin
Secretary: Howard E. Lovejoy
Treasurer: Irvin F. Matson
Fleet Captain: Thomas D. O'Brien
Staff Captain: Howard C. Bronson
Trustees: Fred Haight, Philip G. Johnson, Elmer Nordstrom, Loren C. Davidson, William F. Dawson, Douglas M. Fryer, Frank G. Bourque, Leslie W. Eastman, John N. Sylvester
Fleet Surgeon: John L. Cahill, M.D.
Judge Advocate: Henry L. Kotkins
Measurer: William E. Stinson
Librarian: William N. Ferguson
Historian: J. Swift Baker
Armed Forces Advisor: Capt. William F. Dawson
Women's Group President: Eleanor Agner
Junior Commodore: Brian Gallagher
Committee Chairs
Binnacle Editor: Hugh Blackwell
Greeters: William O. Master, Jr.
Henry Island: G. Stewart Marlatt
Models (Half Hull): Norman Blanchard
Marine Anti-Pollution: Barrie Arnett
Marine Traffic and Safety: Phil Duryee
Men's Oyster Feed: Loren C. Davidson, William D. Bacon, M.D.
Opening Day Admiral: Ron Rawson
Vice Admiral: John Russell, III
Admiralette: Ellie Austin
Outstations: Philip G. Johnson
Trophy: William E. Bradshaw
IPBA Delegates: Don Bancraft, Anderson S. Joy
PCYA Vice Commodore: Joseph L. Williams
Barnacle Bill: Edward L. Williams
Employees Welfare and Pension: John R. Allen
Advisory: Richard H. Shorett
House: Richard L. Hasselquist
Membership: Paul D. Dunstan
Press: Erik V. Peterson
Sailboat: John P. Lidral
Port Madison: Randall Schmoyer
Junior Advisory: Robert L. Pace
Entertainment: Mr. and Mrs. Gary Ritner
Small Sailboat: Michael R. Dooley
Powerboat: Donovan S. Bancroft
Speed Boat: James R. Stirrat
Finance: E. E. Cushing
Mooring and Docks: John R. Allen
Yearbook: Edward R. Donohue
Permanent Planning: C. C. Adair

1973

Commodore: Peter J. McTavish
Vice Commodore: Stanley S. Martin
Rear Commodore: Howard E. Lovejoy
Secretary: Howard C. Bronson
Treasurer: Irvin F. Matson
Fleet Captain: W. C. Anderson
Staff Captain: Arden C. Steinhart
Trustees: Loren C. Davidson, William F. Dawson, Douglas M. Fryer, Frank G. Bourque, Leslie W. Eastman, John N. Sylvester, Richard L. Hasselquist, Peter G. Schmidt, Jr., Robert O. Sylvester
Fleet Surgeon: Harry E. Emmel, M.D.
Judge Advocate: C. C. Adair
Measurer: William E. Stinson
Librarian: William N. Ferguson
Historian: Philip H. Luther
Flotilla 24 Commander: Charles Cummins
Women's Group President: "Benny" Robinson
Junior Commodore: Brian Thomas

Committee Chairs
Advisory: Joseph L. Williams
House: John M. Peterson
Membership: Paul D. Dunstan
Press: Wallace Ackerman
Junior Advisory: Robert L. Pace
Entertainment: Mr. and Mrs. Gary Ritner
Powerboat: Townley Bale
Sailboat: John P. Lidral
Large Boat: Van R. Caples
Small Boat: William N. Ferguson, A. W. Henry
Protest: G. Lawrence Salkield
Inspection and Technical: Robert D. Theriault
Finance: C. E. Hazen
Mooring and Docking: M. Phil Butler
Yearbook: Edward R. Donohue
Speed Boat: James R. Stirrat
Permanent Planning: C. C. Adair
Port Madison: Randall Schmoyer
Henry Island: G. Stewart Marlatt, Donald W. Finlay
Binnacle Editor: James P. Hannon
Greeters: James W. Clyne, Jr.
Models (Half Hull): Norman Blanchard
Marine Anti-Pollution: Barrie Arnett
Marine Traffic and Safety: Phil Duryee
Men's Oyster Feed: Loren C. Davidson
Opening Day Admiral: James P. Hannon
Vice Admiral: Loren C. Davidson
Admiralette: Joy McDonald
Outstations: Philip G. Johnson
Trophy: William E. Bradshaw
Barnacle Bill: Edward R. Donohue
Interclub: Ray L. Eckmann, Hartney Oakes
IPBA: Townley Bale, Anderson S. Joy
PIYA Vice Commodore: Peter J. McTavish

1974

Commodore: Stanley S. Martin
Vice Commodore: Howard E. Lovejoy
Rear Commodore: Frank G. Bourque
Secretary: Howard C. Bronson
Treasurer: Irvin F. Matson
Fleet Captain: Henry L. Kotkins
Staff Captain: Loren C. Davidson
Trustees: Leslie W. Eastman, P. Gerry Maurer, John N. Sylvester, Richard L. Hasselquist, William E. Bradshaw, Robert O. Sylvester, Townley W. Bale, Thomas D. O'Brien, Arden C. Steinhart
Fleet Surgeon: Dr. Ernest L. Frolund
Judge Advocate: Russell W. Newman
Measurer: John W. Ward
Librarian: Robert R. Fox, Jr.
Historian: Philip H. Luther
Women's Group President: Claudia Rombauer
Junior Commodore: Karen Dawson
Flotilla 24 Commander: J. W. Gallagher
Committee Chairs
Advisory: Peter J. McTavish
House: Robert M. Hawley
Press: Wallace Ackerman
Junior Advisory: Roger Dunham
Entertainment: Gary Ritner
Powerboat: Gerald E. Johnson
Sailboat: Ralph J. (Mike) Gibbons
Large Boat: Bates McKee
Small Boat: D. Paul Thorlakson
Protest: G. Lawrence Salkield
Inspection and Technical: Robert D. Theriault
Finance: J. C. Baillargeon
Mooring and Docking: M. Phil Butler
Yearbook: Edward R. Donohue
Permanent Planning: C. C. Adair
Port Madison: Randall Schmoyer
Henry Island: John Harding
Binnacle Editor: Paul D. Dunstan
Greeters: C. James England
Models (Half-Hull) Norman Blanchard
Marine Anti-Pollution: Barrie Arnett
Marine Traffic and Safety: Phil Duryee
Men's Oyster Feed: William D. Bacon, M.D.
Opening Day Admiral: William M. (Bill) Burke
Vice Admiral: Philip B. Rollins
Admiralette: Margaret Botsford
Outstation Acquisition: Larry G. McQuarrie
Ovens Island: Stuart G. Oles
Trophy: Phillip S. Brazeau
Barnacle Bill: George A. Delaney
Interclub: Ray L. Eckmann, Hartney Oakes, A. M. Russell
IPBA: Gerald E. Johnson, Anderson S. Joy
PIYA Commodore: Stanley S. Martin

1975

Commodore: Howard Lovejoy
Vice Commodore: Frank G. Bourque
Rear Commodore: Howard C. Bronson
Treasurer: Irvin F. Matson
Secretary: Loren C. Davidson
Staff Captain: G. Lawrence Salkield
Fleet Captain, Sail: Bates McKee
Fleet Captain, Power: Rod L. Proctor
Trustees: Richard L. Hasselquist, William E. Bradshaw, Robert O. Sylvester, Townley W. Bale, Thomas D. O'Brien, Arden C. Steinhart, Phil Duryee, John F. Leutzinger, P. Gerry Maurer
Fleet Surgeon: Dr. Ernest L. Frolund
Judge Advocate: John R. Allen
Librarian: Robert R. Fox, Jr.
Historian: Philip H. Luther
Women's Group President: Margaret Botsford
Junior Commodore: Fritz Johnston
Committee Chairs
Advisory: Stanley S. Martin
House: Gary Ritner
Membership: Capt. Edward E. Brighton
Press: Bill T. Stewart
Junior Advisory: C. James England
Entertainment: Mr. and Mrs. Lawrence Salkield
Powerboat: Rod L. Proctor
Sailboat: Bates McKee
Large Boat: Philip G. Johnson
Small Boat: Larry K. Shorett
Protest: Harry Helliesen
Inspection and Technical: Alan S. Rutherford
Finance: Louis H. Ford
Mooring and Docking: Robert L. Anderson
Yearbook: Edward R. Donohue
Permanent Planning: Winston D. Brown
Port Madison: Randall Schmoyer
Henry Island: John Harding
Binnacle Editor: Sally Laura
Models (Half Hull): Norman Blanchard
Marine Anti-Pollution: Capt. W. H. Buxton
Marine Traffic and Safety: Richard J. Chang
Men's Oyster Feed: Steve Weeks
Opening Day Admiral: Jerry Johnson
Vice Admiral: Gerry Maurer
Admiralette: Kit Ford
Outstations Acquisition: Harold B. Murray
Ovens Island: Wallace L. Ovens
Trophy: Townley Bale
Barnacle Bill: Jerry Caldwell

1976

Commodore: Frank G. Bourque
Vice Commodore: Howard C. Bronson
Rear Commodore: William E. Bradshaw
Secretary: Loren C. Davidson
Treasurer: Eric P. Van
Fleet Captain, Power: Donald N. Kopp
Fleet Captain, Sail: Russell W. Newman
Staff Captain: Robert H. Hyde
Trustees: Townley W. Bale, Thomas D. O'Brien, Arden C. Steinhart, Phil Duryee, John F. Leutzinger, P. Gerry Maurer, Irvin F. Matson, Rod L. Proctor, G. Lawrence Salkield
Fleet Surgeon: Frederick G. Lippert, III, M.D.
Judge Advocate: John R. Allen
Librarian: Robert R. Fox, Jr.
Historian: Philip H. Luther
Women's Group President: Carol Weeks
Junior Commodore: Frank Heffernan
Committee Chairs
Advisory: Howard E. Lovejoy
House: Andrew D. Hawley
Membership: Robert L. Anderson
Press: Bill T. Stewart
Junior Advisory: Robert L. Pace
Entertainment: Mr. and Mrs. Guy O. Foss, Jr.
Powerboat: Don Kopp
Sailboat: Russell W. Newman
Large Boat: Donald F. Pennell
Small Boat: Scott Rohrer
Protest: Henry Helliesen
Race Registration: Mr. and Mrs. Bates McKee
Finance: Louis H. Ford
Mooring and Docking: Robert H. Gilmore, Jr.
Yearbook: Edward R. Donohue
Permanent Planning: Peter J. McTavish
Port Madison: Randall Schmoyer
Henry Island: Fred Stolz
Building: Joseph L. Williams
Binnacle Editor: Stan Laura
Models (Half Hull): Norman Blanchard
Marine Anti-Pollution: Capt. W. H. Buxton
Marine Traffic and Safety: Frank M. Dunn
Men's Oyster Feed: John Q. Blondin
Opening Day Admiral: Jerry N. Caldwell
Vice Admiral: Gary R. Ritner
Admiralette: Margie Williams
Outstation Acquisition: Earl J. Fessler
Ovens Island: Wallace L. Ovens
Trophy: Townley Bale
Barnacle Bill: John Peth
Gig Harbor: Robert L. Pace, Frank J. Sando

1977

Commodore: Howard C. Bronson
Vice Commodore: William E. Bradshaw
Rear Commodore: Arden C. Steinhart
Secretary: Robert H. Gilmore, Jr.
Treasurer: Eric P. Van
Fleet Captain, Power: Gerald E. Johnson
Fleet Captain, Sail: Richard O. Gilbert
Staff Captain: Frank M. Kalberer, Jr.
Trustees: Phil Duryee, John F. Leutzinger, P. Gerry Maurer, Irvin F. Matson, Rod L. Proctor, G. Lawrence Salkield, Gordon Bass, A. S. (Stan) Laura, Russell W. Newman
Fleet Surgeon: Eugene L. Kidd, M.D.
Judge Advocate: Robert A. Berst

Librarian: Robert R. Fox, Jr.
Historian: Philip H. Luther
Women's Group President: Ray Schmoyer
Junior Commodore: Carol Thomas
Committee Chairs
Advisory: Frank G. Bourque
Binnacle Editor: Peggy and Charles Steward
Building: Robert Theriault
Entertainment: Mr. and Mrs. John Q. Blondin
Finance: Louis H. Ford
Gig Harbor: Barrie Arnett
Grants and Aid: William Bradshaw
Greeters: James M. Scott
Henry Island: Fred Stolz
House: Frank M. Kalberer
Junior Advisory: Phil Robbins
Marine Anti-Pollution: Capt. W. H. Buxton
Marine Traffic and Safety: Glenn R. Botsford
Membership: Hugh C. Klopfenstein
Models (Half Hull): Norman Blanchard
Mooring and Docking: Jerry N. Caldwell
Opening Day Admiral: Gary R. Ritner
Vice Admiral: Russell Newman
Admiralette: Michele Shaw
Outstations Acquisition: Earl Fessler
Ovens Island: Wallace L. Ovens
Permanent Planning: Peter J. McTavish
Personnel: Raymond J. Wachter
Port Madison: Randall Schmoyer
Powerboat: Gerald E. Johnson
Press: Bill T. Stewart
Sailboat: Richard O. Gilbert
Large Boat: William M. Nye
Small Boat: Scott Rohrer
Protest: John P. Ford
Race Registration: Mr. and Mrs. Bates McKee
Trophy: David G. King
Yearbook: Walter J. Reid
Barnacle Bill: Loren C. Davidson
Bylaws Revision: John R. Allen
Men's Oyster Feed: Loren C. Davidson

1978

Commodore: William E. Bradshaw
Vice Commodore: Arden C. Steinhart
Rear Commodore: Philip G. Johnson
Secretary: Robert H. Gilmore, Jr.
Treasurer: Eric P. Van
Fleet Captain, Power: Ralph H. Buseman
Fleet Captain, Sail: P. Gerry Maurer
Staff Captain: Rod L. Proctor
Trustees: Irvin F. Matson
G. Lawrence Salkield
Barrie Arnett
A. S. (Stan) Laura
Robert W. Scarff
Russell W. Newman
Robert M. Alexander
Robert L. Anderson
Norman C. Blanchard
Fleet Surgeon: John L. Cahill
Judge Advocate: David G. King
Historian: Philip H. Luther
Women's Group President: Joyce Endrody
Junior Commodore: Kristin Kennell
Flotilla 24 Commander: Richard J. Chang
Committee Chairs
Advisory: Howard C. Bronson
Binnacle Editor: Fran and William Barnard
Building: Larry Waldron
Entertainment: Gary Ritner
Finance: David Duryee
Gig Harbor: Don L. Cooney
Grants in Aid: Arden Steinhart
Greeters: James M. Scott
Henry Island: Philip Miller
Fred Stolz
House: Lester B. Lampman
Junior Advisory: Phil Robbins
Marine Anti-Pollution: Frank M. Dunn
Marine Traffic and Safety: Phil Duryee
Membership: James England
Models (Half Hull): Norman Blanchard
Mooring and Docking: Robert W. Weber
Moss Point: William K. Ryan, Sr.
Opening Day Admiral: Russell W. Newman
Vice Admiral: Mark Strope
Admiralette: Pat Saxon
Outstations Acquisition: Earl Fessler
Ovens Island: Frank Rosenquist
Wallace L. Ovens
Permanent Planning: Howard E. Richmond
Port Madison: Howard Schroedel
Powerboat: Dr. Ralph Buseman
Press: Joel Schroedel
Sailboat: Gerry Maurer
Large Boat: Robert Spanfelner
Small Boat: Norman Cole
Trophy: David King
Yearbook: Peggy and Walter Reid
Barnacle Bill: Howard C. Bronson
Bylaws Revision: Anderson S. Joy
Men's Oyster Feed: Philip R. Fuller

1979

Commodore: Arden C. Steinhart
Vice Commodore: Philip G. Johnson
Rear Commodore: John N. Sylvester
Secretary: Robert H. Gilmore, Jr.
Treasurer: Eric P. Van
Fleet Captain, Power: Richard J. Chang
Fleet Captain, Sail: Larry C. Hills
Staff Captain: Bill T. Stewart
Trustees: A. S. (Stan) Laura
Robert W. Scarff
Russell W. Newman
Robert M. Alexander
Robert L. Anderson
Norman C. Blanchard
Robert A. Berst
Ralph H. Buseman
Miklos Endrody
Fleet Surgeon: Dr. Robert Camber
Judge Advocate: David Williams
Historian: Philip H. Luther
Women's Group President: Jane Heinrich
Junior Commodore: Laurie Weeks
Flotilla 24 Commander: Frank M. Dunn
Committee Chairs
Advisory: William E. Bradshaw
Binnacle Editor: Alita and Jan Kiaer
Building: Larry Waldron
Entertainment: Mr. and Mrs. Peter Z. Cahan
Finance: David Duryee
Grants in Aid: Philip G. Johnson
Greeters: Brent Johnson
House: Lester B. Lampman
Junior Advisory: Robert Ranzenbach
Marine Anti-Pollution: Robert F. Peterson
Marine Traffic and Safety: Phil Duryee
Membership: C. James England
Models (Half Hull): Russell McComb
Mooring and Docking: Robert W. Weber
Opening Day Admiral: Miklos Endrody
Vice Admiral: Joel Schroedel
Admiralette: Barbara Benton
Outstation Acquisition: Robert W. Graham
Eagle Harbor: Richard Haugan
Gig Harbor: Robert Bourgaize
Henry Island: Jack Minkler
Moss Point: Steve Heinrich
Ovens Island: Richard Swan
Wallace L. Ovens
Port Ludlow: John E. Rasmussen
Port Madison: Donald H. Simpson
Howard Schroedel
Permanent Planning: Louis Ford
Powerboat: Richard J. Chang
Press: Joel Schroedel
Sailboat: Larry Hills
Trophy: James Sylvester
Yearbook: Peggy and Walter Reid
Barnacle Bill: Lon Davidson
Bylaws Revision: Anderson S. Joy

1980

Commodore: Philip G. Johnson
Vice Commodore: John N. Sylvester
Rear Commodore: Robert A. Berst
Secretary: Bill T. Stewart
Treasurer: David W. Rice
Fleet Captain, Power: Richard J. Chang
Fleet Captain, Sail: Graham Anderson
Staff Captain: Peter Z. Cahan
Trustees: Robert M. Alexander
Robert L. Anderson
Norman C. Blanchard
Joel H. Schroedel
Ralph H. Buseman
Miklos Endrody
John R. Allen
Robert W. Graham
John E. Rasmussen
Fleet Surgeon: Dr. Ralph Kamm
Judge Advocate: David Williams
Historian: Phil Luther
Committee Chairs
Advisory: Arden Steinhart
Binnacle Editor: William D. Chubb
Entertainment: Robert Walls
Finance: Benjamin E. Weeks
Grants in Aid: John L. Sylvester
House: Robert H. Gilmore
Junior Advisory: John P. Ford, III
Marine Traffic and Safety: Phil Duryee
Membership: Raymond Marty, M.D.
Mooring and Docking: Jack Austin
Murals: John Ford, Sr.
Norman C. Blanchard
Opening Day Admiral: Jim England
Vice Admiral: James W. Dupar
Admiralette: Claudia Rombauer
Outstation Acquisition: Irvin F. Matson
Eagle Harbor Outstation: Richard Haugan
Gig Harbor Outstation: Robert G. Bourgaize
Henry Island Outstation: Jack D. Minkler
Ovens Island Outstation: Richard Swan
Port Ludlow Outstation: Don Bjorkland
Port Madison Outstation: Donald H. Simpson
Permanent Planning: James G. McCurdy
Powerboat: Richard J. Chang
Press: Michele Shaw
Diane Benson
Sailboat: Graham Anderson
Bob Kaczor
Trophy: James W. Sylvester
Yearbook: Peggy and Walter Reid
Barnacle Bill: Jerry Caldwell
Bylaws Revision: Dave King
Women's Group President: La Rue Gove
USCG Flotilla 24 Commander: Hugh Blackwell
Junior Commodore: Linda Nelson

1981

Commodore: John N. Sylvester
Vice Commodore: Robert A. Berst
Rear Commodore: Robert W. Scarff
Secretary: Bill T. Stewart
Treasurer: David W. Rice
Fleet Captain, Power: Jerry Caldwell
Fleet Captain, Sail: Bob Kaczor
Staff Captain: Dick Chang
Trustees: Joel H. Schroedel
Ralph Buseman
Dick Chang
John R. Allen
Robert W. Graham
John E. Rasmussen
John N. Anderson

Eugene F. Clark
Donald H. Simpson
Fleet Surgeon: Dr. Eugene L. Kidd
Historian: Phil Luther
Judge Advocate: David Williams
Fleet Chaplain: William J. Sullivan, S.J.
Committee Chairs
Advisory: Phil Johnson
Binnacle Editor: Frank Kline
Entertainment: Sue and Robert Walls
Finance: Ben Weeks
Grants in Aid: William Chubb
Historical: Philip Johnson
House: Robert H. Gilmore
Junior Advisory: Brent Nichols
Marine Traffic and Safety: Robert W. Weber
Membership: Raymond Marty
Moorage and Docks: Jack Austin
Murals: Norm Blanchard
Opening Day Admiral: Edgar Rombauer
Vice Admiral: Jack Austin
Admiralette: Lou Bradley
Outstation Acquisition: Robert Anderson
Eagle Harbor Outstation: Richard Haugan
Gig Harbor Outstation: Barrie Arnett
Henry Island Outstation: James R. Tenneson
Ovens Island Outstation: Frank T. Rosenquist
Port Ludlow Outstation: Nicholas Schmitt, Jr.
Port Madison Outstation: Dr. William A. Freitag
Long Range Planning: Douglas Sherwood
Powerboat: Jerry Caldwell
Press: Joel Schroedel
Sailboat: G. Robert Kaczor
Trophy: Sally Laura
Yearbook: Peggy Reid
Barnacle Bill: Lon Davidson
Bylaws Revision: Anderson S. Joy
Pensions and Staff: John Rasmussen
Women's Group President: Diane Benson
USCG Flotilla 24 Commander: Howard E. Schroedel
Junior Commodore: Todd Hagan

1982

Commodore: Robert A. Berst
Vice Commodore: Robert W. Scarff
Rear Commodore: Donald H. Simpson
Secretary: Bill T. Stewart
Treasurer: David W. Rice
Fleet Captain, Power: Frank Kline
Fleet Captain, Sail: Evan Schwab
Staff Captain: Ralph Buseman
Trustees: John R. Allen
Robert W. Graham
John E. Rasmussen
John N. Anderson
Jack L. Cahill, M.D.
Brent Nichols
Dick Chang
Jim Erickson
Jeray Holmes
Fleet Physician: Ralph F. Kamm, M.D.
Historical: Dr. John C. Scott
Judge Advocate: David Williams
Fleet Chaplain: William J. Sullivan, S.J.
Committee Chairs
Active-Intermediate: Barbara Bradshaw
Advisory: John N. Sylvester
Binnacle Editor: Warren Ceely
Bylaws Revision: Anderson Joy
Entertainment: Carola and Ronald Kinsey
Finance: Douglas A. Kaiser
Grants in Aid: Bob Scarff
House: William L. Saunders
Junior Advisory: John P. Ford, III
Marine Traffic and Safety: Robert W. Weber
Membership: Ray Rairdon
Moorings and Docks: Herb Stevenson
Murals: Norm Blanchard
Opening Day Admiral: Joel Schroedel
Vice Admiral: Frank (Jimmy) James
Admiralette: Linda Blondin
Outstation Acquisition: Charles E. Erickson
Eagle Harbor Outstation: Larry Hills
Gig Harbor Outstation: Barrie Arnett
Henry Island Outstation: Jim R. Tenneson
Ovens Island Outstation: Frank Rosenquist
Port Ludlow Outstation: Robert L. Anderson
Port Madison Outstation: Dr. William A. Freitag
Pensions and Staff: Ken Clark
Permanent Planning: Douglas Sherwood
Powerboat: Frank Kline
Press: Barbara Hayes
Sailboat: Evan L. Schwab
Trophy: Sally Laura
Yearbook: Peggy Reid
USCG Flotilla 24 Commander: Herbert L. Stevenson
Women's Group President: Barbara Benton
Junior Commodore: Kellie Hayes

1983

Commodore: Robert W. Scarff
Vice Commodore: Donald H. Simpson
Rear Commodore: Ralph Buseman
Secretary: Robert B. Ovens
Treasurer: Louis H. Ford
Staff Captain: John E. Rasmussen
Trustees: John N. Anderson
Jack L. Cahill, M.D.
Brent Nichols
Dick Chang
Jim Erickson
Jeray Holmes
Jim Dupar
Pat Goodfellow
Doug Kaiser
Judge Advocate: David Williams
Fleet Captain, Power: Gil Middleton
Fleet Captain, Sail: Don Flynn
Fleet Physician: Dr. Ed Joneschild
Fleet Chaplain: Father William J. Sullivan, S.J.
Historical: Dr. John C. Scott
Committee Chairs
Active-Intermediate: William J. Wallace
Advisory: Robert A. Berst
Binnacle Editor: Ken Thurman
Bylaws Revision: Dave Williams
Entertainment: Bruce and Marlee McKibbin
Finance: David W. Rice
Grants in Aid: Don Simpson
House: Jack Johnston
Junior Advisory: Bob L. Cadranell
Marine Traffic and Safety: Phil Duryee
Membership: Randy Rairdon
Moorings and Docks: Herb Stevenson
Murals: Sally Laura
Opening Day Admiral: Warren Ceely
Vice Admiral: Charles Cravens
Admiralette: Betty Chang
Outstation Acquisition: Charles E. Erickson
Eagle Harbor Outstation: Larry Hills
Garden Bay Outstation: Norman Blanchard
Gig Harbor Outstation: Ken Schoenfeld
Henry Island Outstation: Ralph Kamm
Ovens Island Outstation: William C. Morse
Port Ludlow Outstation: Bob Anderson
Port Madison Outstation: Al Benz
Pensions and Staff: Ken Solid
Permanent Planning: Don Thompson
Powerboat: Dr. A. G. Middleton
Press: Diane Benson
Barbara Hayes
Sailboat: Don Flynn
Trophy: Barbara Bradshaw
Yearbook: Peggy and Wally Reid
USCG Flotilla 24 Commander: Howard E. Schroedel
Women's Group President: Kit Ford
Junior Commodore: Tom Kuhnle

1984

Commodore: Donald H. Simpson
Vice Commodore: Ralph Buseman
Rear Commodore: Jeray Holmes
Secretary: Robert B. Ovens
Treasurer: John Fedor
Staff Captain: Barrie Arnett
Trustees: Dick Chang
Jim Erickson
John P. Ford, III
David W. Rice
Jim Dupar
Pat Goodfellow
Doug Kaiser
Charles E. Erickson
Harry H. McGuane
Bill T. Stewart
Judge Advocate: John R. Allen
Fleet Captain, Power: Gil Middleton
Fleet Captain, Sail: Larry C. Hills
Fleet Physician: Dr. John W. Riley, III
Fleet Chaplain: Father William J. Sullivan, S.J.
Historical: Betty Stewart
Committee Chairs
Active-Intermediate: Peter Madsen
Don C. Oakland
Advisory: Robert W. Scarff
Binnacle Editors: Pam and Ken Thurman
Bylaws Revision: Dave Williams
Club Boats: Bill Bradshaw
Entertainment: Marlee McKibbin
Finance: Frank J. Kline
Foundation: Jeray A. Holmes
Grants in Aid: Ralph Buseman
House: Bruce McKibbin
Interclub: Dave Williams
Investment: John Fedor
Junior Advisory: Bob L. Cadranell
Marine Traffic and Safety: Phil Duryee
Membership: Jimmy James
Moorings and Docks: Burt Pearce
Murals: Sally Laura
Opening Day Admiral: Rod L. Proctor
Vice Admiral: William R. Saxon
Admiralette: Diane Hagan
Outstation Acquisition: Robert L. Landau
Eagle Harbor Outstation: Martin Crowder
Garden Bay Outstation: Norman Blanchard
Gig Harbor Outstation: Robert A. Berst
Henry Island Outstation: Ralph Kamm
Ovens Island Outstation: William C. Morse
Port Ludlow Outstation: Robert O. Sylvester
Port Madison Outstation: Al Benz
Poulsbo Outstation: Gary Horder
Pensions: Ken Solid
Permanent Planning: Eric P. Van
Powerboat: Dr. A. G. Middleton
Press: Stephen M. Koch
Sailboat: Larry C. Hills
Suma Regatta: Jeray A. Holmes
Trophy: Barbara Bradshaw
USCG Flotilla 24 Commander: Howard E. Schroedel
Junior Commodore: Charles C. Cadranell
Women's Group President: Diane Sweezey

1985

Commodore: Ralph Buseman
Vice Commodore: Jeray Holmes
Rear Commodore: Bill T. Stewart
Secretary: Robert B. Ovens
Treasurer: John Fedor
Staff Captain: Bruce McKibbon
Trustees: Jim Dupar
Pat Goodfellow
David W. Rice
Charles E. Erickson
Steve Koch
Harry H. McGuane
Bill Freitag

	Gil Middleton
	Bill Watkins
Judge Advocate:	Larry Salkield
Fleet Captain, Power:	Paul W. Sunich
Fleet Captain, Sail:	Robert A. Berst
Fleet Physician:	Dr. Merril P. Spencer
Fleet Chaplain:	Father William J. Sullivan, S.J.
Librarian:	Sally Laura
Protocol Officer:	Otto Noetzelman
Committee Chairs	
Active Intermediate:	Bill Wallace
Advisory:	Don Simpson
Binnacle Editors:	Marlene and David Foster
Bylaws Revision:	Larry Salkield
Club Boat:	Bill Bradshaw
	Frank Kline
Entertainment:	Gail and Brent Johnson
Finance:	Frank J. Kline
Foundation:	Bill Stewart
Grants in Aid:	Jeray A. Holmes
Historical:	George Heideman
House:	Bruce McKibbin
Interclub:	Dick Chang
	Dave Williams
Investment:	John Fedor
Junior Advisory:	Steve Leonard
Marine Traffic and Safety:	Phil Duryee
Membership:	G. Robert Kaczor
Moorings and Docks:	Burt Pearce
Murals:	John M. Bradley
Opening Day Admiral:	John Rasmussen
Vice Admiral:	Ken Thurman
Admiralette:	Diane Benson
Outstation Acquisition:	Barrie Arnett
Eagle Harbor Outstation:	Martin Crowder
Garden Bay Outstation:	James E. Clark
Gig Harbor Outstation:	Dick Gilbert
Henry Island Outstation:	Donald N. Kopp
Ovens Island Outstation:	Richard C. Swain
Port Ludlow Outstation:	Robert O. Sylvester
Port Madison Outstation:	Jim Erickson
Pensions:	Ken Solid
Permanent Planning:	Jack Austin
Powerboat:	Paul W. Sunich
Press:	Michele Shaw
Friends of Rowing:	Laura Boone
Sailboat:	Bob Berst
Sailboat Race:	Bill Bradshaw
Special People's Cruise:	F. E. Jimmy James
Trophy:	R. Bruce Peterson
USCG Flotilla 24 Commander:	Richard Chang
Yearbook:	Dorothy and Leroy McCormick
Junior Commodore:	Cyrina Thurman
Women's Group President:	Pat Saxon

1986

Commodore:	Jeray Holmes
Vice Commodore:	Bill T. Stewart
Rear Commodore:	Larry G. Salkield
Secretary:	Dave Williams
Treasurer:	John Fedor
Staff Captain:	Gerald T. Parks, Jr.
Trustees	Charles E. Erickson
	Steve Koch
	Harry H. McGuane
	Bill Freitag
	Gil Middleton
	Bill Watkins
	Frank Kline
	Bruce McKibbin
	Ben Weeks
Judge Advocate:	Larry Salkield
Fleet Captain, Power:	Paul W. Sunich
Fleet Captain, Sail:	John Lidral
Fleet Physician:	Dr. Merrill P. Spencer
Fleet Chaplain:	Father William J. Sullivan, S.J.
Librarian:	Sally Laura
Protocol Officer:	Otto Noetzelman
Committee Chairs	
Advisory:	Ralph Buseman
Binnacle Editors:	Molly and Bob Cadranell
Club Boats:	Bill Bradshaw
Entertainment:	Marilyn and Roger Priem
Finance:	Roger Anderson
Grants in Aid:	Bill Stewart
Historical:	Betty Stewart
	Katie Whitworth
House:	Gerald Parks, Jr.
Junior Advisory:	Donald Flynn
Marine Traffic and Safety:	Phil Duryee
Membership:	Theresa E. Dowell
Moorings and Docks:	John D. Quigley
Murals:	John M. Badley
Opening Day Admiral:	Ken Thurman
Vice Admiral:	Jerry Horrobin
Admiralette:	Sally Laura
Outstation Acquisition:	Mike Jared
Eagle Harbor Outstation:	Martin Crowder
Garden Bay Outstation:	James E. Clark
Gig Harbor Outstation:	Dick Gilbert
Henry Island Outstation:	Donald N. Kopp
Ovens Island Outstation:	Dale Dow
Port Ludlow Outstation:	Robert Simpson
Port Madison Outstation:	James P. Erickson
Pensions:	Robert A. Nathane
Permanent Planning:	Jack Austin
Powerboat:	Paul W. Sunich
Press:	Michele Shaw
Sailboat:	Jack Lidral
Sailboat Race:	Bill Bradshaw
Seattle Yacht Club Crew:	Laura Boon
Special People's Cruise:	F. E. Jimmy James
Trophy:	R. Bruce Peterson
USCG Flotilla 24 Commander:	Richard Chang
Yearbook:	Frances and William Morse
Junior Commodore:	Joey Ford
Women's Group President:	Pam Thurman

1987

Commodore:	Bill T. Stewart
Vice Commodore:	Larry G. Salkield
Rear Commodore:	William A. Freitag
Secretary:	Dave Williams
Treasurer:	Harold R. Ward
Staff Captain:	Gerald T. Parks, Jr.
Trustees	William C. Morse
	Gil Middleton
	Bill Watkins
	Frank Kline
	Bruce McKibbin
	Ben Weeks
	Richard O. Gilbert
	P. Gerry Maurer
	Robert O. Sylvester
Judge Advocate:	Theresa E. Dowell
Fleet Captain, Power:	Leroy C. McCormick
Fleet Captain, Sail:	Larry C. Hills
Fleet Physician:	Leland L. Burnett, M.D.
Fleet Chaplain:	Father William J. Sullivan, S.J.
Librarian:	Sally Laura
Protocol Officer:	George V. Fliflet
Committee Chairs	
Active Intermediate:	H. William Cramer
	Ryan R. Dunham
Advisory:	Jeray Holmes
Binnacle Editors:	Carol and Don Glocker
Club Boats:	William E. Bradshaw
Entertainment:	Marilyn and Roger Priem
Finance:	Roger L. Anderson
Grants in Aid:	G. Lawrence Salkield
Historical Centennial:	Norm Blanchard
	Don Whitworth
House:	Gerald T. Parks, Jr.
Junior Advisory:	Donald A. Flynn
Marine Traffic and Safety:	Phil Duryee
	Mark Johnson
Membership:	G. Robert Kaczor
Moorage Acquisition:	John E. Rasmussen
Moorage and Docks:	John D. Quigley
Opening Day Admiral:	Jerry Horrobin
Vice Admiral:	Jack Blondin
Admiralette:	Barbara Hayes
Outstation Acquisition:	Mike Jared
Outstation Council:	William A. Freitag
Eagle Harbor Outstation:	Martin Crowder
Garden Bay Outstation:	Robert L. Landau
Gig Harbor Outstation:	Robert A. Berst
Henry Island Outstation:	Paul W. Sunich
Ovens Island Outstation:	Dale Dow
Port Ludlow Outstation:	Robert W. Simpson, M.D.
Port Madison Outstation:	David B. Maples
Pensions:	Robert A. Nathane
Permanent Planning:	John R. Allen
Powerboat:	Leroy C. McCormick
Press:	David S. Robinson
Race:	William Bradshaw
Rowing:	Laura Boone
Sailboat:	Larry C. Hills
Trophy-Murals:	Sally Laura
Yearbook:	Donna and Foss Rodda
Junior Commodore:	Joey Ford
Women's Group President:	Gail Johnson

1988

Commodore:	G. Lawrence Salkield
Vice Commodore:	William A. Freitag
Rear Commodore:	Robert O. Sylvester
Secretary:	Theresa E. Dowell
Treasurer:	Harold R. Ward
Staff Captain:	Kenton M. Thurman
Trustees	Frank Kline
	Bruce McKibbin
	Gerald T. Parks, Jr.
	Richard O. Gilbert
	P. Gerry Maurer
	Craig R. Hopkins
	Larry C. Hills
	David Romano
	Paul W. Sunich
Judge Advocate:	David G. King
Fleet Captain, Power:	David B. Maples
Fleet Captain, Sail:	Michael B. Duffy
Fleet Physician:	Kenneth A. Briggs, M.D.
Fleet Chaplain:	Father William J. Sullivan, S.J.
Librarian:	Sally Laura
Protocol Officer:	George V. Fliflet
Committee Chairs	
Active Intermediate:	H. William Cramer
	M. Roberta Schmitz
Advisory:	Bill T. Stewart
Binnacle Editors:	Barbara Hayes
	Sally Laura
Club Boats:	Bill Bradshaw
Entertainment:	Marlene and David Foster
Finance:	Bert H. Weinrich
Grants in Aid:	Dr. William A. Freitag
Historical:	Norman C. Blanchard
	Don C. Whitworth
Interclub:	Don L. Santy
Junior Advisory:	Roger L. Anderson
Long Range Planning:	Robert A. Berst
Marine Traffic and Safety:	Phil Duryee
Membership:	Martin T. Crowder
Moorage and Docks:	Dr. Ralph H. Buseman
Opening Day Admiral:	John Q. Blondin
Vice Admiral:	Ronald (Buzz) Benson
Admiralette:	Diane Sweezey
Outstation Acquisition:	Charles E. Erickson
Outstation Council:	Robert O. Sylvester
Eagle Harbor Outstation:	Kenyon P. Kellogg
Garden Bay Outstation:	Robert L. Landau
Gig Harbor Outstation:	Eugene R. Johnson
Henry Island Outstation:	Herbert L. Stevenson
Ovens Island Outstation:	Wallace L. Ovens
	Gerald T. Parks, Jr.

Port Ludlow Outstation:	Donald H. Simpson
Port Madison Outstation:	Robert L. Anderson
Pensions:	Robert A. Nathane
Permanent Moorage Acquisition:	John E. Rasmussen
Powerboat:	David Maples
Press:	Molly and Harry McGuane
Race:	Bill Bradshaw
Rowing:	Larry Shelver Jack Austin
Sailboat:	Michael B. Duffy
Suma:	Larry C. Hills
Trophy:	Barbara L. Bradshaw
Yearbook:	Donna and Foss Rodda
Women's Group President:	Michele Shaw
Junior Commodore:	Andy Salkield

1989

Commodore:	William A. Freitag
Vice Commodore:	Robert O. Sylvester
Rear Commodore:	David Romano
Secretary:	Theresa E. Dowell
Treasurer:	Phillip L. Jordan
Staff Captain:	Kenton M. Thurman
Trustees	Richard O. Gilbert P. Gerry Maurer Craig R. Hopkins Larry C. Hills Paul W. Sunich William A. Bain Jack Q. Blondin Gerald E. Horrobin Herbert L. Stevenson
Judge Advocate:	David G. King
Fleet Captain, Power:	David B. Maples
Fleet Captain, Sail:	Michael B. Duffy
Fleet Physician:	Robert Camber, M.D.
Fleet Chaplain:	Meg Lewis
Librarian:	Sally Laura
Protocol Officer:	Hal Lewis
Committee Chairs	
Active Intermediate:	Mr. and Mrs. Charles A. Holland
Advisory:	Lawrence G. Salkield
Binnacle Editor:	Barbara Hayes Leslie Sally Laura
Building:	Roger Anderson
Bylaws:	David King
Club Boats:	Frank J. Kline
Entertainment:	Marlene and David Foster
Finance:	Bert H. Weinrich
Grants in Aid:	Robert Sylvester
Historical:	Bill T. Stewart
House:	Kenton M. Thurman
Interclub:	Don L. Santy
Investment:	William Watkins
Junior Advisory:	Leann and Stacey Wilson
Marine Traffic and Safety:	Phil Duryee Mark Johnson Robert Weber
Membership:	Gary R. Ritner John E. Rasmussen
Moorage Acquisition:	Pat Goodfellow
Moorage and Docks:	Dr. Ralph H. Buseman
Opening Day Admiral:	Ronald S. (Buzz) Benson
Vice Admiral:	Dwight Shaw
Admiralette:	Pam Thurman
Outstation Acquisition:	Charles E. Erickson
Outstation Council:	David Romano
Eagle Harbor Outstation:	Ken Kellogg
Garden Bay Outstation:	Norman C. Blanchard
Gig Harbor Outstation:	Eugene R. Johnson
Henry Island Outstation:	Kenneth S. Hammer
Ovens Island Outstation:	Wally Ovens
Port Ludlow Outstation:	Robert W. Simpson, M.D.
Port Madison Outstation:	C. Douglas Pratt
Pensions:	Frederic Lhamon
Permanent Planning:	Robert L. Anderson
Powerboat:	David B. Maples
Press:	Joel Schroedel
Race Committee:	Bobbie Schmitz
Rowing:	Laurence G. Shelver
Sailboat:	Michael B. Duffy
Special People's Cruise:	Carol Kessi
Trophy:	Barbara Bradshaw Dick Chang
Yearbook:	Leroy McCormick
Women's Group President:	Marlee McKibbin
Junior Commodore:	Molly Salkield

1990

Commodore:	Robert O. Sylvester
Vice Commodore:	David Romano
Rear Commodore:	P. Gerry Maurer
Secretary:	Anthony S. Laura
Treasurer:	Daniel C. Smith
Trustees	William A. Bain Larry C. Hills Paul W. Sunich Jack Q. Blondin Gerald E. Horrobin Herbert L. Stevenson Robert B. Ovens Robert W. Simpson, M.D. Kenton M. Thurman
Staff Captain:	Stephen M. Koch
Fleet Captain, Power:	A. Gilman Middleton, M.D.
Fleet Captain, Sail:	William (Stacey) Wilson
Judge Advocate:	Bert H. Weinrich
Quartermaster:	Martin T. Crowder
Librarian:	Richard J. Chang
Fleet Surgeon:	Robert Camber, M.D.
Committee Chairs	
Active Intermediate:	Charles Holland Myron Jared, III
Advisory:	William Freitag
Binnacle Editors:	Duse McLelan Michele Shaw
Building:	Robert Landau
Bylaws:	Bert Weinrich
Club Boats:	Frank Kline
Entertainment:	George Heideman Mr. and Mrs. John Van Duzor
Finance:	Leo Riley
Grants in Aid:	David Romano
Historical:	Bill Stewart
House:	Tammy Erickson David Foster
Interclub:	Harry McGuane
Investment:	William Watkins
Library Murals/Half Hull:	Richard Chang
Long Range Planning:	Bob Berst
Marine Environmental:	Lawrence Bailey
Marine Traffic and Safety:	Phil Duryee Mark Johnson Robert Weber
Membership:	Gary Ritner
Membership Activities:	Diane Sweezey
Moorage Acquisition:	Patrick Goodfellow
Moorage and Docks:	Donald Simpson
Opening Day Admiral:	Dwight Shaw
Vice Admiral:	Bruce McKibbin
Admiralette:	Molly Cadranell
Outstation Acquisition:	John Osberg
Outstation Council:	P. Gerry Maurer
Eagle Harbor Outstation:	Evan Schwab
Garden Bay Outstation:	Norman Blanchard
Gig Harbor Outstation:	Barrie Arnett
Henry Island Outstation:	Kenneth Hammer
Ovens Island Outstation:	Wallace Ovens Gerald Parks, Jr.
Port Ludlow Outstation:	David Williams
Port Madison Outstation:	Douglas Pratt
Pension Planning:	Frederic (Tad) Lhamon
Powerboat:	Gilman Middleton
Press:	Philip Luther
Race:	William Bradshaw
Rowing:	Brian Vickers
Sailboat:	Stacey Wilson
Special People's Cruise:	Carol Kessi
Suma:	John Lidral
Trophy:	Lawrence (Lon) Robinson
Yearbook:	Mr. and Mrs. David Maxwell
Junior Commodore:	Molly Salkield
Women's Group President:	Mary Fox

1991

Commodore:	David Romano
Vice Commodore:	P. Gerry Maurer
Rear Commodore:	John E. Rasmussen
Secretary:	A. Stan Laura
Treasurer:	Daniel C. Smith
Trustees	Jack Q. Blondin Gerald E. Horrobin Herbert L. Stevenson Robert B. Ovens Robert W. Simpson Kenton M. Thurman Roger L. Anderson Kenneth S. Hammer Richard H. Johnson
Staff Captain:	Paul W. Sunich
Fleet Captain, Power:	Murray Dorsey
Fleet Captain, Sail:	William F. Lenihan
Judge Advocate:	Martin T. Crowder
Quartermaster:	Frank N. Young, Jr.
Librarian:	Richard J. Chang
Committee Chairs	
Active Intermediate:	Myron S. Jared, III
Advisory:	Robert O. Sylvester
Binnacle Editors:	Duse McLean Michele Shaw
Building:	Robert L. Landau
Bylaws:	Martin T. Crowder
Club Boats:	Bonnie Sharpe
Eagle Harbor Outstation:	Evan L. Schwab
Entertainment:	George W. Heideman Donna and John Van Duzor
Finance:	Leo M. Riley
Garden Bay Outstation:	Van R. Caples
Gig Harbor Outstation:	Barrie Arnett
Grants in Aid:	P. Gerry Maurer
Henry Island Outstation:	James P. Erickson
Historical:	Bill T. Stewart
House:	Tammy Erickson David M. Foster
Interclub:	Harry H. McGuane
Investment:	Bennett A. Cozadd
Junior Advisory:	Leann and Stacey Wilson
Library Murals and Half Hull:	Richard J. Chang
Long Range Planning:	Ralph H. Buseman
Marine Environment:	Lawrence P. Bailey
Marine Traffic and Safety:	Phil Duryee
Membership:	C. Fred Roed
Membership Activities:	Diane Sweezey
Moorage and Boats:	Donald H. Simpson
Opening Day Admiral:	Bruce McKibbin
Vice Admiral:	William Freitag
Admiralette:	Audrey Salkield
Outstation Acquisition:	William C. Morse
Outstation Council:	John E. Rasmussen
Ovens Island Outstation:	Gerald T. Parks, Jr.
Pension Planning:	Gary J. Redman
Permanent Moorage Acquisition:	Patrick L. Goodfellow
Port Ludlow Outstation:	David L. Williams
Port Madison Outstation:	John Dugan
Powerboat:	Murray Dorsey
Press:	David S. Robinson
Race:	William E. Bradshaw
Rowing:	Brian N. Vickers
Sailboat:	William F. Lenihan
Special People's Cruise:	Carol C. Kessi
Trophy:	Lawrence W. (Lon) Robinson
Yearbook:	Jana Maxwell
Junior Commodore:	Ryland Halffman
Women's Group President:	Sally Laura

INDEX

Page numbers in *italics* refer to illustrations

C

D

E

F

G

H

L

M

N

T

U

V

W

X

Y

Z

Sidebar List